Criminal Law for the
Criminal Justice Professional

Second Edition

Criminal Law for the
Criminal Justice Professional

Norman M. Garland

Southwestern Law School

Mc Graw Hill **Higher Education**

Boston   Burr Ridge, IL   Dubuque, IA   New York   San Francisco   St. Louis
Bangkok   Bogotá   Caracas   Kuala Lumpur   Lisbon   London   Madrid   Mexico City
Milan   Montreal   New Delhi   Santiago   Seoul   Singapore   Sydney   Taipei   Toronto

The McGraw·Hill Companies

Higher Education

A Division of The McGraw-Hill Companies

Published by McGraw-Hill, an imprint of The McGraw-Hill Companies, Inc., 1221 Avenue of the Americas, New York, NY 10020. Copyright © 2009, 2003. All rights reserved. No part of this publication may be reproduced or distributed in any form or by any means, or stored in a database or retrieval system, without the prior written consent of The McGraw-Hill Companies, Inc., including, but not limited to, in any network or other electronic storage or transmission, or broadcast for distance learning.

This book is printed on acid-free paper.

3 4 5 6 7 8 9 0 DOC / DOC 0

ISBN: 978-0-07-340125-6
MHID: 0-07-340125-0

Vice President and Editor in Chief: *Michael Ryan*
Publisher: *Frank Mortimer*
Executive Editor: *Katie Stevens*
Editorial Coordinator: *Teresa Treacy*
Marketing Manager: *Leslie Oberhuber*
Developmental Editor: *Larry Goldberg*
Production Editor: *Catherine Morris*
Production Service: *Scratchgravel Publishing Services*
Manuscript Editor: *Margaret C. Tropp*
Design Manager: *Andrei Pasternak*
Cover Designer: *Andrei Pasternak*
Illustrator: *Gregory Draus, Scratchgravel Publishing Services*
Photo Research: *Sarah Evertson, Image Quest*
Production Supervisor: *Richard DeVitto*
Composition: *10/12 Adobe Caslon Pro by ICC Macmillan Inc.*
Printing: *PMS 3298, 45# New Era Matte Plus, R. R. Donnelley & Sons/Crawfordsville, IN*

Cover: Royalty-Free/Corbis

Credits: The credits section for this book begins on page 464 and is considered an extension of the copyright page.

Library of Congress Cataloging-in-Publication Data

Garland, Norman M.
    Criminal law for the criminal justice professional/Norman Garland.
—2nd ed.
    p. cm.
    Includes bibliographical references and index.
    ISBN-13: 978-0-07-340125-6 (alk. paper)
    ISBN-10: 0-07-340125-0 (alk. paper)
1. Criminal law—United States. I. Title.
    KF9219.85.G37 2008
    345.73—dc22

                                                    2008013221

The Internet addresses listed in the text were accurate at the time of publication. The inclusion of a Web site does not indicate an endorsement by the authors or McGraw-Hill, and McGraw-Hill does not guarantee the accuracy of the information presented at these sites.

www.mhhe.com

To my wife, Melissa Grossan,
whose help and support are immeasurable.
I could not have completed this book without her.

Brief Contents

Contents

PART II   The Elements of Crime

PART V   Crimes against the Community and Institutions

CHAPTER 12   *White-Collar Crimes 311*

Preface

Criminal Law for the Criminal Justice Professional, second edition, presents a complete basic introduction to the substance of those rules and laws that comprise the fabric of the criminal justice system in the United States. This text, like the first edition, describes the structure of the system, the theories underlying criminal responsibility, and the elements of specific crimes. The general principles that motivate the lawmakers have not changed since the development of Anglo-American criminal law, though legislative detail and focus have varied.

This new edition takes into account many of the shifts in emphasis of the lawmakers and courts in the development of American criminal law in the global political, economic, and social climate of the twenty-first century. Straightforward yet analytical, the text aims at delivering to students a timely overview of the state of American criminal law. The book is designed primarily for undergraduates enrolled in basic criminal law classes for Criminal Justice students.

⚖ Changes and Continuities in the Second Edition

The second edition of *Criminal Law for the Criminal Justice Professional* has undergone extensive revision. In response to reviewer feedback, I have not only updated all the definitions and references but also provided new examples of several important issues throughout the book. Some of the most important changes are as follows:

- Chapter 1, "Nature, Origins, Purposes, Structure, and Operation of the Criminal Justice System," combines Chapters 1 and 2 of the first edition, consolidating the introductory concepts into one overarching, easy-to-follow introduction to the American criminal justice system.

- Chapter 2, "Constitutional Limitations on the Criminal Law," provides a succinct overview of those principles that limit the legislatures and courts in defining criminal restrictions, with a survey of specific constitutional provisions and how they function.

- Chapters 3 through 6 present the basic principles of criminal responsibility, the elements of crimes, definitions of parties to crimes, explanation of incomplete crimes, and defenses to crimes. Basic criminal justice theory that has remained relevant over the decades is discussed in these chapters, with classic explanations and examples.

- A new chapter on punishment and sentencing (Chapter 7) concisely discusses the theories of punishment and the current state of the evolving American law of sentencing. In recent years, no other area of the law has changed so much, especially in the arena of sentencing guidelines and capital punishment.

- The remaining chapters present clear and concise definitions of specific crimes, relating the elements of each crime by subject area. The fundamentalist approach to cataloguing elements and updating where appropriate makes the coverage of the subjects complete yet user-friendly.

⚖ Features

A number of learning tools are included to make the text easier to teach and, for students, easier to learn, enlivening the material with practical, concrete examples and applications.

- Chapter Objectives that begin each chapter challenge, encourage, and alert students to the major concepts that follow. Next is a Chapter Outline of the major chapter headings, allowing students to preview at a glance the material to be covered.

- The Summary by Chapter Objectives concluding each chapter provides general answers to questions posed by the objectives, an invaluable tool for students who need summation and reinforcement of each chapter's main points.

- Key terms are highlighted in the margins, **boldfaced** in the text, listed at the end of the chapter, and defined in a comprehensive Glossary at the end of the book.

- Application Case boxes present brief descriptions of important cases pertinent to the text.

- On the Job boxes describe employment opportunities related to the subjects discussed in the chapters.

- Web Exploration boxes point to Web sites relevant to surrounding topics and contain questions that invite further study.

- Critical Thinking features—questions for students that ask them to reflect on important concepts and theories—conclude the main sections of each chapter.

- End-of-chapter Review Questions stimulate class discussion.

- Problem-Solving Exercises, Workplace Applications, and Ethics Exercises pertain to workplace issues, highlight major principles from the chapters, and enable students to begin applying what they've learned.

⚖ Supplements

Visit our book-specific Web site at www.mhhe.com/garland2e for robust student and instructor resources. Student study tools include online multiple-choice quizzes and Internet exercises. The password-protected instructor portion of the Web site includes the instructor's manual, test bank, lesson plans, and PowerPoint® presentations.

Acknowledgments

A number of people were of substantial help to me in the production of the new edition of this book. First are the research assistants from Southwestern Law School, without whom I could not have completed this work. They include Jessica Trotter and Alexandria Sawoya, both of the class of 2007, Lesley Braswell, class of 2009, and Lonnie McDowell, class of 2008. I would like to thank the dean, faculty, and board of trustees of Southwestern Law School. This text was written with the aid of a sabbatical research grant from the law school, and my research assistants were paid through the school's work-study program. I would also like to thank Richard M. Hough, Sr., University of West Florida, who provided student study tools, the Instructor's Manual, Lesson Plans, Test Bank, and PowerPoint® presentations for the book Web site. Finally, I would like to thank the reviewers of the second edition, who offered many helpful suggestions: Steven J. Dunker, Northeastern State University; Jennelle London Jóset, Bryant & Stratton College; Charles E. Reasons, Central Washington University; and Michael Whalen, Keiser College.

About the Author

Norman M. Garland is Professor of Law at Southwestern Law School in Los Angeles, where he teaches Evidence, Constitutional Criminal Procedure, Advanced Criminal Procedure, and Trial Advocacy. He received his B.S.B.A. from Northwestern University, his J.D. from Northwestern University School of Law, and his L.L.M. from Georgetown Law Center where he was an E. Barrett Prettyman Fellow in Trial Advocacy. Professor Garland is a member of the Illinois, District of Columbia, and California Bars. He has had ten years of trial experience as a criminal defense attorney, mainly in federal felony cases. In 1968 he joined the faculty of Northwestern University School of Law where he helped establish the Northwestern University Legal Clinic. He joined the faculty of Southwestern Law School in 1975 to help establish the Southwestern Conceptual Approach to Legal Education (SCALE). In the mid-1980s, he spent two summers as a Deputy District Attorney in Ventura County, California, where he gained experience as a prosecutor. He is coauthor of _Advanced Criminal Procedure in a Nutshell_ (2d ed., West 2006), _Criminal Evidence for the Law Enforcement Professional_ (5th ed., McGraw-Hill 2006), and _Exculpatory Evidence_ (3d ed., LexisNexis 2004). He has also authored a number of computer interactive lessons for law students available through the Center for Computer-Assisted Legal Instruction (CALI).

A Guided Tour

The second edition of *Criminal Law for the Criminal Justice Professional* presents a complete basic introduction to the substance of those rules and laws that comprise the fabric of the criminal justice system in the United States. This text, like the first edition, describes the structure of the system, the theories underlying criminal responsibility, and the elements of specific crimes.

⚖ Chapter Opener

Each chapter opens with a *photograph* that provides a visual connection to the chapter content and catches the student's attention. The *Chapter Objectives* challenge, encourage, and alert students to the major concepts that follow. The *Chapter Outline* allows students to preview at a glance the material to be covered.

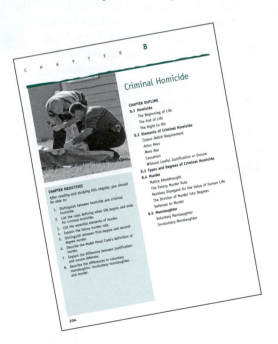

Box Features

[Reproduction of textbook page 192 showing "Federal Sentencing Guidelines" text and Application Case 7.2 "Blakely v. Washington / United States v. Booker"]

Application Case boxes present brief descriptions of important cases pertinent to the text.

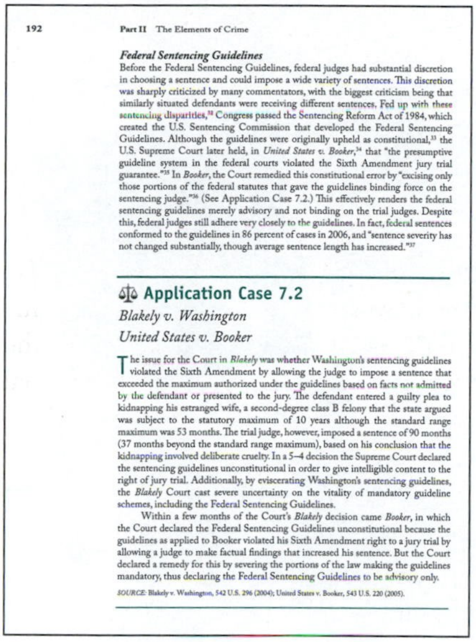

On the Job boxes describe employment opportunities related to chapter topics.

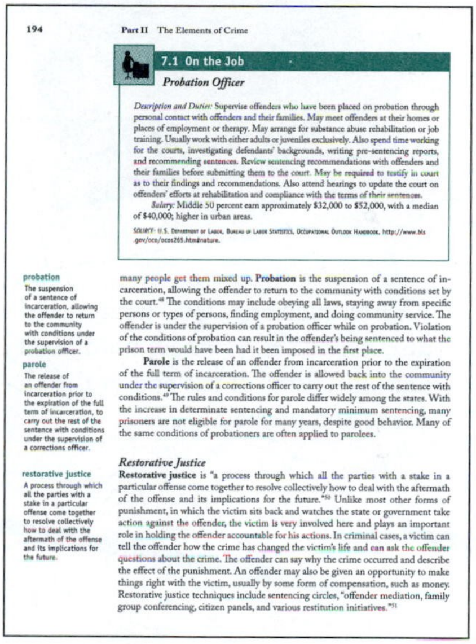

[Reproduction of textbook page 194 showing "7.1 On the Job — Probation Officer" box, and marginal glossary terms: probation, parole, restorative justice, with body text on probation, parole, and Restorative Justice]

Web Exploration boxes point to Web sites relevant to surrounding topics and invite further study.

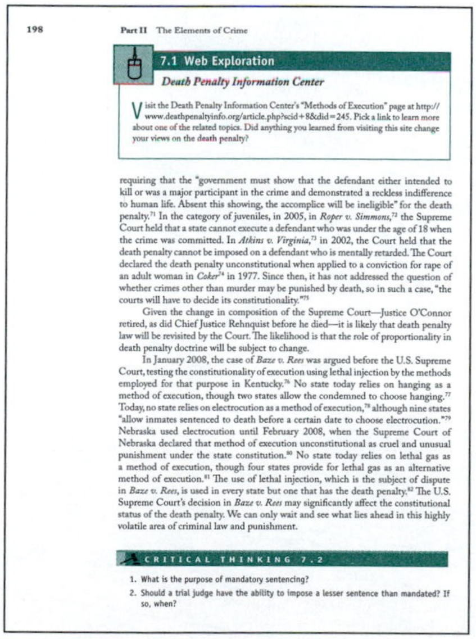

[Reproduction of textbook page 198 showing "7.1 Web Exploration — Death Penalty Information Center" box, body text on the death penalty, and "CRITICAL THINKING 7.2" questions]

⚖️ Visual and Textual Features

Photos bring the topics and concepts alive for the student.

Figures such as maps, statutes, and flowcharts amplify and clarify the concepts discussed. *Key terms* are **boldfaced** in the text, highlighted and defined in the margins, listed at the end of the chapter, and defined in a comprehensive Glossary at the end of the book.

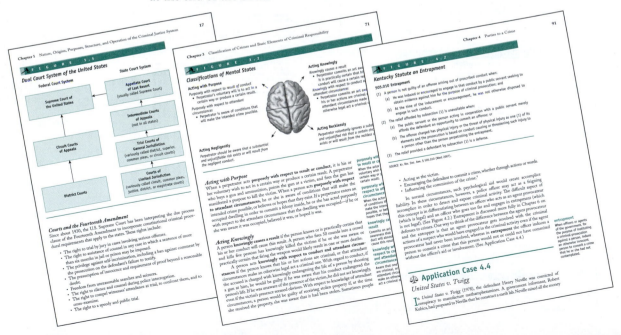

The *Critical Thinking* questions ask students to reflect on important concepts and theories after each main section in the chapters.

End-of-Chapter Review and Applications

The ***Summary by Chapter Objectives*** concludes each chapter and provides general answers to questions posed by the Chapter Objectives, an invaluable tool for students who need summation and reinforcement of each chapter's main points.

REVIEW AND APPLICATIONS

Summary by Chapter Objectives

1. **Explain the purpose of defining attempt as a crime.** Lawmakers created attempt crimes to prevent the commission of crimes before they take place. They also sought to protect the safety of the public by allowing police officers to stop the continuance of criminal activity.
2. **Explain the how the MPC test for the *actus reus* of attempt differs from all the other tests.** Under the MPC test to determine whether an attempt has occurred, the only requirement is to show that the suspect has done (or omitted to do) something that constitutes a substantial step in a course of conduct, which must be planned for the commission of the underlying crime. The sole inquiry is into whether the accused person's conduct strongly matches his or her criminal intent. Ambiguous factors, such as proximity or equivocality, are not considered.
3. **State the elements of an attempt.** A person is guilty of the crime of attempt if he or she intentionally commits the act constituting the *actus reus* (either the last act, proximity, or substantial step test), with the additional intent to commit the substantive crime or to cause the prohibited result that constitutes the underlying crime.
4. **Name the two principal defenses to attempt.** The two principal defenses to attempt are impossibility and abandonment (renunciation). Abandonment is not recognized in some jurisdictions; where it is recognized, a defendant's abandonment must fit within certain guidelines to be considered a valid defense.
5. **Explain when the crime of solicitation can be charged.** Solicitation is a crime only if the crime solicited has not been completed, attempted, or agreed to. This is because when any of these other three situations occur, the solicitor and solicited party become liable for other criminal acts instead.
   - If the person solicited agrees to commit a crime, then both the solicitor and the party solicited are criminally liable for conspiracy.
   - If the person solicited attempts to commit the crime, then both parties are criminally liable for attempt.
   - If the person solicited completes the crime, then both parties are criminally liable for the completed crime, the solicitor being responsible on a theory of accomplice liability.
6. **Define the crime of conspiracy.** Conspiracy is a partnership in crime; it is an agreement between two or more people to commit an unlawful act or acts, or to do a lawful act unlawfully.
7. **Define the *actus reus* requirement for conspiracy.** The *actus reus* requirement for conspiracy is the act of agreement. In addition, many jurisdictions require an overt act in furtherance of the conspiracy.

Key Terms highlighted and defined in the text and margins are listed with page numbers for easy reference.
Review Questions stimulate class discussion.

8. **Explain the *mens rea* requirement for conspiracy.** The mental state required for conspiracy has two facets: the intent to agree and the specific intent that the object of the agreement be achieved. In addition, both of these *mens rea* elements require that there be more than one person involved, because the crime contemplates agreement between two or more persons.

Key Terms

inchoate crimes (p. 113)
attempt (p. 115)
last act test (p. 117)
physical proximity test (p. 118)
dangerous proximity test (p. 118)
indispensable element test (p. 120)
unequivocality test (p. 121)
substantial step test (p. 121)
factual impossibility (p. 125)
legal impossibility (p. 126)
"hybrid" legal impossibility (p. 126)
genuine legal impossibility (p. 127)
abandonment (p. 128)
solicitation (incitement) (p. 131)

Review Questions

1. What is the six-stage process by which an actor commits a crime, and after what stage is a person liable for criminal punishment?
2. Explain the historical cases in which the crime of attempt was first recognized.
3. Your textbook names six of the various tests for the crime of attempt. How do they differ?
4. How does the MPC define the mental element of attempt, and how is this different from other definitions?
5. What are the similarities and differences between "hybrid" legal impossibility and pure legal impossibility?
6. What are some reasons why some jurisdictions recognize abandonment as a defense?
7. Why is solicitation designated as a crime, and what are some of the criticisms of this practice?
8. How does the treatment of conspiracy as a crime help law enforcement efforts?
9. What are all of the possible requirements to determine the *actus reus* of conspiracy?
10. How can the defenses of abandonment and impossibility apply to conspiracy?
11. What does the MPC allow in regard to defenses to conspiracy?

Problem-Solving Exercises

1. **Prostitution** Sandy and Luisa are bored housewives who are sick of their menial household responsibilities and their bratty kids. In desperate need of excitement, they decide to start a brothel and operate it as co-madams. For several weeks, they devise a plan of action, including soliciting customers, hiring female employees, creating a price list, and decorating various theme rooms in Sandy's house, which is to be used as the brothel. When they are ready to start business, a man tells Luisa he is interested and sets a time to come to the house

Problem-Solving Exercises, Workplace Applications, and ***Ethics Exercises*** highlight major principles from the chapters and enable students to begin applying what they've learned.

the next evening. When he arrives, he pays Sandy, chooses a girl, and then arrests everyone in the house. At this point, they realize that the man is an undercover vice detective. Answer the following questions:
   a. With what charges can Sandy and Luisa be charged? Explain your choices.
   b. With what charges, if any, could the other women be charged. Explain your choices.
   c. What do you think tipped off the detective to investigate their activities?
2. **Drug Trafficking** Fred and Raul are arrested for conspiracy to distribute cocaine by a police officer who was tipped off by an informant. Fred and Raul are charged with distributing, but due to a technical error in the warrant, the evidence is inadmissible and the case is dismissed. In response, the prosecutor charges them with conspiracy to distribute marijuana. As you interview Fred in the presence of his attorney, he begins to tell you that he has owed Raul $100,000 for the last two years as a result of a gambling loan. Fred believes that Raul will kill him unless he pays back the money somehow, but he has no way of repaying the loan. Raul told Fred that instead of being murdered, Fred could work for Raul for five years, assisting him in his narcotics distribution. Fred agreed. Answer the following questions:
   a. Was there a meeting of the minds?
   b. Was there an agreement to commit a criminal act?
   c. Will the conspiracy charge hold up when this evidence is presented?
3. **Attempted Murder** You are a police investigator. A distraught wife appears at the local police station and states that her husband has just informed her that he has been putting poison in her coffee for over a week. She also states that she was not feeling well and went to the doctor, who advised her that she had indigestion. Her husband confesses to you that he hates her, wants her dead, and has been putting a poisonous substance in her coffee for the past week. Upon investigation, you obtain the substance from the husband. The lab analyzes the substance and advises you that it is harmless.
   a. Do you trust that this is the substance that was used? What else will you do to determine this?
   b. If the substance was harmless and could not possibly poison the wife, with what crime(s), if any, will the husband be charged?

Workplace Applications

1. **Substantial Step Test** As a prosecutor, you are told that a man has been arrested for driving at high speed through a crowded residential neighborhood at 3:00 in the afternoon. He was driving 90 miles per hour in a 25-mile-per-hour zone when he struck and killed a child crossing the street on her way home from school. Answer the following questions:
   a. Can the driver be charged with murder? With any other charges? Explain your choices.
   b. What are some of the considerations for applying murder based on a substantial certainty?
   c. What defenses may the driver raise for his behavior? How will you respond?

2. **False Testimony** You are the prosecutor for a case in which the defendant is charged with the attempted murder and robbery of Mrs. Gray, a 78-year-old woman. In the middle of the trial, just before Mrs. Gray testifies, she tells you that she has a confession to make. She states that her original statement to the detective was slightly exaggerated. In this new statement, she tells you that the defendant attacked her in the parking lot and attempted to take her handbag, but was interrupted by someone walking by. Originally, Mrs. Gray told the detective who interviewed her that the defendant pointed a gun at her head and said, "If you don't give me your bag, I'll kill you." Now Mrs. Gray states that the defendant only grabbed her bag and said he would kill her but did not have a gun. Mrs. Gray explains to you that at the time of the attempted robbery, she was very upset and angry with the defendant; in her agitation, she embellished her story a little. Answer the following questions:
   a. As the prosecutor, do you continue the trial and advise Mrs. Gray she must stick with her original statement? Why or why not?
   b. Do you continue with the trial with Mrs. Gray's true story and hope that the jury convicts the defendant of attempted murder based solely on this statement? Why or why not?
   c. Do you drop the attempted murder charges and prosecute only the attempted robbery? Why or why not?
3. **Last Act Test** While on duty as a municipal police officer, you observe a female and two males sitting in a vehicle parked across the street from a bank. When you get closer to the vehicle, you observe the female holding a handgun. As you are in the process of arresting the female for possession of a firearm, you observe a bank employee drive up with equipment to fix a broken ATM machine. Upon further investigation, you learn two things from the bank employee: that the female is a former bank employee, and that someone had tampered with the machine, which guaranteed the arrival of a bank employee to fix it.
   a. Applying the last act test, is there sufficient evidence to charge the female and her two companions with attempted bank robbery?
   b. Would the result be different if you applied the dangerous proximity to success test?
   c. Was the fact that the robbery did not take place a matter of chance, or is it possible that the three individuals may have changed their minds just at the time the officer appeared?

Ethics Exercises

1. **Conspiracy to Commit Murder** Bill asks two friends to help him kill his wife. They agree, and the three of them work out a plan. A few days later, Bill gets cold feet; he tells the others that he wants nothing further to do with the plan and specifically asks them to abandon it. Later that evening, Bill comes to the police department and tells you about the plan. You plan your next day's schedule around conducting interviews of his friends as a means of investigating the matter further. Unfortunately, the night Bill comes to see you, Bill's friends carry out the original plan to kill his wife. When the friends are apprehended, they admit to killing Bill's

⚖️ A Dynamic Web Site

Visit our book-specific Web site at *www.mhhe.com/garland2e* for robust student and instructor resources. Student study tools include online multiple-choice quizzes and Internet exercises. The password-protected instructor portion of the Web site includes the instructor's manual, test bank, lesson plans, and PowerPoint® presentations.

Nature, Origins, Purposes, Structure, and Operation of the Criminal Justice System

CHAPTER OBJECTIVES

After reading and studying this chapter, you should be able to:

1. State a basic definition of law.
2. Explain what distinguishes the criminal law from other law.
3. Define the common law.
4. State the principle of legality.
5. Explain what the MPC is.
6. Describe the fundamental structure of the American criminal justice system.
7. Name the four basic police functions.
8. State what is required for a law enforcement officer to arrest a suspect.
9. State the purpose of a preliminary hearing.
10. Describe the two alternative methods for charging serious crimes.
11. List the three possible bases for a defendant's pretrial motion to dismiss.
12. State the four possible grounds for appeal of a criminal conviction.
13. State when a defendant is entitled to an attorney at trial.

1.1 The Nature and Origins of Law

The definition of the word *law* is multifaceted and ranges from simple to complex. For example:

- One dictionary definition of law is "a rule of conduct or procedure established by custom, agreement, or authority."[1]
- According to *Black's Law Dictionary,* law is "that which is laid down, ordained, or established."[2] In this very general sense, law could consist of a culture's moral code, the commandments of a religion, or the regulations enacted by a political body to govern its members.

law
The federal, state, or local enactments of legislative bodies; the known decisions of the courts of the federal and state governments; rules and regulations proclaimed by government bodies; and proclamations by executives of the federal, state, or local government.

In the United States today, most citizens understand the concept of **law** to consist of:

- The federal, state, or local enactments of legislative bodies.
- The known decisions of the courts of the federal and state governments.
- Rules and regulations proclaimed by administrative bodies.
- Proclamations by executives of the federal, state, or local government.

Lawmakers distinguish between two types of rules: (1) religious and moral values, and (2) rules created by government to protect individuals and promote social welfare. People recognize that some actions may be immoral even though they are not illegal. In addition, people generally believe that they should be able to live according to their religious principles, as long as their actions do not violate the law.

Citizens of the United States may share a common view of the legitimate sources of law, but may also disagree about what behaviors should be regulated by the government. For example, some people believe that abortion should be considered murder and thus should be prohibited by law; others hold that decisions about abortion should be made on personal religious or moral grounds, without governmental interference.

There is also disagreement on the role government should play in other matters of life and death, such as physician-assisted euthanasia, the use of reproductive technologies, and genetic screening. Other practices such as gambling and prostitution are considered immoral by some people, but morally acceptable by others. States differ in their approach to such practices: Gambling of all kinds is prohibited in some states, whereas others use lotteries as a way of raising revenues for public schools.

Many cultures do not make the distinction between secular (nonreligious) and religious law that is so central to American culture. For example, Islamic law, or Sha'ria, is derived from the sacred writings of the Koran. It provides the rules by which Muslim society is organized and governed, and the means for resolving conflicts between individuals and between individuals and the state. In the American colonies, witchcraft was an offense punishable by death under British law because of centuries-old church persecutions of people who were believed to practice beliefs other than Christianity. In Salem, Massachusetts, 20 persons (19 women and 1 man) were hanged as witches in 1692. The English statutes on witchcraft were not repealed until 1736, after thousands of women had been executed for the crime of practicing witchcraft.

Emergence of Written Law

From time immemorial, humankind has sought to minimize turmoil and chaos by the imposition of some set of rules by which to live. From the edicts of kings and conquerors to the U.S. Constitution, rules of conduct for society have been proclaimed and enforced.

Ancient Law

Although human societies have always had rules of conduct, the first known written laws are believed to be those found on clay tablets in Ur, one of the city-states of Sumeria. They were created about 5,000 years ago. A much more extensive set of laws was established by King Hammurabi, who ruled Babylonia from 1792 to 1750 BC. The *Code of Hammurabi* consisted of 282 laws that dealt with marriage, divorce, debt, wages, and the practice of slavery. It also defined criminal acts and penalties for committing them. The laws were carved on a black stone monument that was eight feet high.

English and American Common Law

Every ancient nation eventually developed formal legal codes, and the American legal code derives primarily from that of England. Before the Norman Conquest, the law in England was administered primarily according to Anglo-Saxon customs, with the church playing a major role. After William of Normandy conquered England in

The Origins of the Common Law Because the United States was originally an English colony, both countries share a common law heritage.

1066, he established the *eyre*—that is, a court with judges who traveled throughout the kingdom once every seven years to hear cases as representatives of the king. The decisions of these judges and of other members of the central judiciary created by the Normans to administer the law formed a large part of England's **common law**.

common law
Law created by judicial opinion. Historically, law from America's colonial and English past, which has set precedents that are still sometimes followed today.

In England after the Norman Conquest, crimes and civil wrongs were less clearly defined at first. There was no penal code or even a set of criminal taboos discernable from a body of judicial decisions. Common law offenses simply consisted of the use of force against others, violating the king's peace, which could result in both punishment and the imposition of monetary sanctions. Under common law, the use of violence was condemned, rather than the consequences of a violent act. In other words, the focus was on the violation of the king's peace, rather than on the harm done to the victim.

The common law developed from this foundation through judicial interpretation and elaboration of the concept of violence until crimes were recognized in such specific categories as homicide, robbery, arson, and assault. Eventually, especially from the 16th century on, enactments of Parliament added specific crimes to the array of common law offenses.[3]

Emergence of Modern Criminal Law

When the 13 colonies were established in America, they adopted England's common law. As the colonies developed and the United States was formed, the law of the United States developed separately from the English common law tradition. Eventually, **statutory law** replaced common law to meet citizens' needs. American statutory law was, and is, created through the state and federal legislatures. Today, the term *common law* refers to the body of law that is derived from judicial decisions rather than from legislative enactment. It can also refer to all of the laws that came from England and from colonial America.

statutory law
Law created through state and federal legislatures.

Today, virtually all criminal law is statutory law. This means that crimes are defined by the legislatures of the states and the federal government. The shift came because of the belief that crimes should be defined by elected legislative bodies that are more representative of the people rather than by the courts. You will learn about the two main types of law in the United States in the next section.

Civil Law versus Criminal Law

Today, the United States judicial system provides for criminal law violations, also called *crimes,* and civil law violations, also called *torts.*

Criminal Law

criminal law
Law that involves the violation of public rights and duties, creating a social harm.

Criminal law is different from other types of law, and from civil law in particular, because it involves a violation of public rights and duties, which create a *social harm.* Just as the common law considered a crime to be a violation of the king's peace, rather than a harm done to a victim, modern crimes are considered to be social harms that affect the entire community—and that, in turn, must be punished by the community. In other words, what distinguishes the criminal law from all other law is that the criminal law seeks to regulate acts that are contrary to the community interest of the social or governmental unit—federal, state, or local.[4]

Civil Law

Civil law deals with matters that are considered to be private concerns between individuals. It includes laws dealing with personal injury, contracts, and property, as well as administrative law. A violation of civil law is called a **tort**. When a tort is committed, civil law provides a remedy in the form of an action for damages. The same is true for violations of contractual obligations.

For legal purposes, the same act may be both an offense against the state, which is a crime, and an offense against an individual, which is a tort. If someone steals another person's property, the offender may be punished under criminal law by imprisonment and/or a monetary fine, and may be required to pay restitution to the victim. In addition, the victim can sue in civil court for monetary damages. The trials of O. J. Simpson in the 1990s illustrate the overlapping of civil and criminal law. In October 1995, Simpson was acquitted of the murders of Nicole Brown Simpson and Ronald Goldman. However, in February 1997, in a civil trial brought against Simpson by the family of Ronald Goldman, the jury awarded $8.5 million in damages.

civil law
Law that deals with matters considered to be private concerns between individuals.

tort
A civil violation; the civil law's equivalent of a crime.

CRITICAL THINKING 1.1

1. Why does the complexity of the definitions of law vary so much?

1.2 Criminal Law in the United States

The American and French revolutions stimulated a legislative movement in the area of criminal law. Of special concern was the severity of the criminal law: By 1800, more than 100 different kinds of offenses were punishable by death under English law.[5]

Much of the criminal law reform in England and the United States was influenced by the utilitarian legal philosopher Jeremy Bentham. Bentham reorganized the law of crimes according to the amount of social harm they caused, and most American states have adopted more or less coherent penal codes based on this approach. At least since the late 19th century, the criminal law has been expressed in a penal code in all but a few American jurisdictions.

Purpose of the Criminal Law

The underlying purpose of the criminal law is to prevent and control crime. The criminal justice system seeks to achieve this goal by sanctioning behavior that violates the criminal law. To say this, however, is only to begin the subject of inquiry. Other questions include:

- How do we know what conduct to sanction?
- Who, among those who may have engaged in the conduct, should be sanctioned?
- What sanction should be imposed?

The question of what conduct to sanction, also called the question of criminalization or decriminalization, has largely been answered with respect to what most people think of as crime—offenses such as murder, rape, assault, robbery, burglary, and traditional forms of theft. The modern focus of debate is on the question of criminalization in other areas, such as offenses designed to protect public morality, the economy, or the environment, or generally to promote public welfare.

The question of who among those who have engaged in the conduct should be sanctioned involves consideration of the basic elements of criminal culpability and criminal defenses. Generally, the criminal law seeks to sanction only those persons who intentionally violated the criminal law, under circumstances that did not involve excuse or justification. The question of what sanction to impose will be covered in a later section of this chapter, which will discuss punishment.

Substantive Law versus Procedural Law

Substantive criminal law consists of those laws, mostly statutory, that define what constitutes criminal conduct subject to prosecution by the state and set forth the punishment for such criminal acts. The substantive criminal law identifies the components required for liability, both mental and physical. Procedural criminal law dictates the methods and the means by which the state proceeds, through the police, public administrators, and the courts, to enforce rights or duties of the substantive law. For example, suppose a person is charged with robbery, which is defined as taking something from another person by force or fear. The possible punishment for robbery is imprisonment. The accused person has just been arraigned in court. The definition of robbery and the punishment that can result are substantive law; the arraignment is procedural law.

The Elements of a Crime

A more complete definition of a crime includes the specification of five elements. A crime has been committed when the following elements are present:

actus reus
A willful unlawful act.

mens rea
A guilty mind, or intent.

1. A willful unlawful act, the **actus reus**.
2. A guilty mind, the **mens rea**. The guilty mind element does not require intent to violate the law, but rather the intent to commit the act that the law prohibits.
3. A concurrence of act and intent.
4. The occurrence of harm to a person, property, or society.
5. A causal relationship between the criminal act and the harm.

Statutory Criminal Law

The development of the common law of crimes that began in 11th-century England continues to a smaller degree today, because some nonstatutory crimes are still recognized in some jurisdictions. Otherwise, the criminal law develops and is redefined by legislative enactment, often in response to societal pressures. For example, in response to a public outcry against rising crime, the U.S. Congress adopted the Violent Crime Control and Law Enforcement Act of 1994, which related to a range of problems from sexual offenses to drive-by shootings. Congress, through such enactments, refines and redefines the criminal law. Similarly, state legislatures regularly redefine the criminal law in each state.

F I G U R E   1 . 1

An Introductory Excerpt from the Violent Crime Control and Law Enforcement Act of 1994

U.S. Department of Justice Fact Sheet

The Violent Crime Control and Law Enforcement Act of 1994 represents the bipartisan product of six years of hard work. It is the largest crime bill in the history of the country and will provide for 100,000 new police officers, $9.7 billion in funding for prisons, and $6.1 billion in funding for prevention programs which were designed with significant input from experienced police officers. The Act also significantly expands the government's ability to deal with problems caused by criminal aliens.

The Crime Bill provides $2.6 billion in additional funding for the FBI, DEA, INS, United States Attorneys, and other Justice Department components, as well as the Federal courts and the Treasury Department.

SOURCE: http://www.ncjs.org/txtfiles/bills.txt.

All 50 states and the federal government have their own separate sets of criminal statutes. No state is bound by the criminal laws of another state, or by the laws of the federal government. For the most part, criminal law is a matter of state jurisdiction, although the reach of federal criminal law has expanded in recent times. Nonetheless, federal criminal law can apply only to those matters to which federal jurisdiction extends, such as national aspects of drug control or other crimes that involve interstate activities. (See Figure 1.1.)

The Principle of Legality

Another reason for the decline of judicially created criminal law definitions is the principle of **legality**, which is a core concept of the American system of criminal justice. Under this principle, no one can be punished for an act that was not defined as criminal before the person did the act.

The principle of legality is *nullum crimen sine lege, nulla poena sine crimen,* which means "no crime without law, no punishment without crime." Basically, this means "that conduct may not be treated as criminal unless it has been so defined by an authority having the institutional competence to do so before it [the conduct] has taken place."[6] This principle is deeply imbedded in the American system of justice. If a court declares conduct criminal that has not previously been defined as criminal, then the principle of legality is violated.

The principle of legality has three corollaries:

1. Criminal statutes should be understandable to reasonable law-abiding people.
2. Criminal statutes should be crafted so as not to delegate basic policy matters to police, judges, and juries for resolution on an ad hoc and subjective basis.
3. Judicial interpretation of ambiguous statutes should "be biased in favor of the accused."[7]

legality

The principle that no one can be punished for an act that was not defined as criminal before the person did the act.

Contemporary Applications of Common Law

Many states have abolished common law crimes, relying exclusively on statutory or code definitions. For example, Section 6 of the California Penal Code provides, "No act or omission . . . is criminal or punishable, except as prescribed or authorized by this Code."[8] But although modern criminal law is essentially statutory, the role of the courts continues. This is so because the criminal statutes often contain vague or general language that requires courts to interpret the statute's meaning when applied to a particular case.

A classic example is the statutory definition of burglary, which makes a "nighttime" burglary a more serious offense. The term *nighttime* was not defined in some statutes, requiring the courts to decide when a burglary would be considered to have occurred at night. You will read more about how modern laws have adapted to this issue in Chapter 9.

Even though the common law is but an antecedent to today's modern statutory criminal law in most jurisdictions, the common law definitions of crimes continue to play a role in understanding the criminal law. Some states have not abolished common law crimes and still expressly recognize common law offenses, although prosecution of such offenses in those jurisdictions is rare.[9]

Moreover, many states' criminal laws are but codifications of the common law crimes. Therefore, if there is a question of statutory meaning, the courts will look to the common law definitions to help understand the term in question. One example of this occurred when the California Supreme Court looked to the common law definition of human being to determine that a fetus could not be a murder victim (see Application Case 1.1).[10]

⚖️ Application Case 1.1

Keeler v. Superior Court

At one time the definition of murder in California, which had abolished the common law, was the unlawful killing of a human being with malice aforethought. In the case of *Keeler v. Superior Court* (1970), the defendant was charged with murder of a fetus that was stillborn as a result of the defendant's attack on the mother, his ex-wife. The defendant approached his ex-wife, said he heard she was pregnant, and, stating "I'm going to stomp it [the baby] out of you," shoved his knee into her abdomen and struck her.

The Supreme Court of California looked to the common law in concluding that a fetus born dead was not a "human being." As a result, the defendant's murder conviction was set aside. Soon after the *Keeler* decision, the California legislature redefined "human being" in the Code section defining murder to include a fetus.

SOURCE: Keeler v. Superior Court 470 P.2d 617 (Cal. 1970).

1.1 On the Job

Crime Prevention Officer

Description and Duties: Perform crime prevention tasks such as conducting and participating in general investigation of crimes, incidents, and cases. Can work on special units such as SWAT, Gang Prevention, DARE, GREAT, Narcotics, and Special Investigations.

   Salary: Salaries range from approximately $40,000 to almost $60,000.

   Other Information: Although all police officers are, to a certain extent, crime prevention officers, this position is generally held by an experienced police officer who has likely spent some years on patrol and now is more involved in the specific task of crime prevention.

The Model Penal Code

In 1923, the American Law Institute (ALI), an organization of lawyers, judges, and legal scholars, was founded for the purpose of clarifying and improving the law. One of the major factors leading to the establishment of the ALI was general dissatisfaction with the criminal law. (See Figure 1.2.) In 1931, a proposal for a model penal code was presented, but the Depression prevented funding the project. In 1950, a grant from the Rockefeller Foundation rekindled the model penal code project, which got under way in 1952. However, it was not until 1962, after 13 tentative drafts, that the American Law Institute published the Proposed Official Draft of the Model Penal Code.

   The **Model Penal Code (MPC)** is a comprehensive recodification of the principles of criminal responsibility. The drafters of the MPC relied upon existing sources of the criminal law, including codes, judicial opinions, and scholarly commentary. The ALI did not expect or intend that the MPC would be adopted in its entirety anywhere, or that it would result in a uniform national criminal law. The hope was that the MPC would generate a systematic reevaluation of the criminal law in the nation, and that hope has been fulfilled. An overwhelming majority of the states have adopted revised criminal codes as a result of the MPC. The MPC stands as a model for the reform of principles of American criminal responsibility.[11]

Model Penal Code (MPC)
A comprehensive recodification of the principles of American criminal responsibility.

The Growth of Federal Criminal Law

Prior to the Civil War, the power to define and punish crimes in the United States was exercised principally by the states. Since the Civil War, federal criminal law has expanded to overlap areas that previously were within the exclusive province of the states. Thus, there has been an increase in the overlap of federal and state criminal law authority.

   The U.S. Constitution restricts the power of the federal government, including its authority to define and prosecute crimes. The Constitution explicitly enumerates the federal crimes of treason, counterfeiting, crimes against the law of nations, and crimes committed on the high seas.[12] All other federal criminal jurisdiction emanates from the "necessary and proper" clause of article I, § 8 of the Constitution, which grants Congress the power to pass legislation necessary to implement any enumerated federal power.

F I G U R E   1 . 2

The American Law Institute

The American Law Institute was organized in 1923 following a study conducted by a group of prominent American judges, lawyers, and teachers known as "The Committee on the Establishment of a Permanent Organization for the Improvement of the Law." The Committee had reported that the two chief defects in American law, its uncertainty and its complexity, had produced a "general dissatisfaction with the administration of justice."

According to the Committee, part of the uncertainty of the law, as it then existed, was due to the lack of agreement among members of the profession on the fundamental principles of the common law. Other causes of uncertainty were reported as "lack of precision in the use of legal terms," "conflicting and badly drawn statutory provisions," "the great volume of recorded decisions," and "the number and nature of novel legal questions." The law's complexity, on the other hand, was attributed in significant part to its "lack of systematic development" and to its numerous variations within the different jurisdictions of the United States.

The Committee's recommendation that a lawyers' organization be formed to improve the law and its administration led to the creation of The American Law Institute. The Institute's charter stated its purpose to be "to promote the clarification and simplification of the law and its better adaptation to social needs, to secure the better administration of justice, and to encourage and carry on scholarly and scientific legal work." Its incorporators included Chief Justice and former President William Howard Taft, future Chief Justice Charles Evans Hughes, and former Secretary of State Elihu Root; Judges Benjamin N. Cardozo and Learned Hand were among its early leaders.

SOURCE: http://www.ali.org/ali/thisali.htm.

Since earliest times, the U.S. Supreme Court has upheld the exercise of this power. Especially since the Civil War, Congress has enacted criminal laws relating to a wide range of subjects, including civil rights, use of the mails, commerce, narcotics, extortion and robbery affecting interstate commerce, interstate travel to facilitate illegal activities associated with organized crime, organized crime itself, and racketeering.[13] Thus, the definition of federal crimes is an important aspect of the study of American criminal law.

C R I T I C A L   T H I N K I N G   1 . 2

1. Explain the historical significance of the common law.
2. Why is statutory law taking the place of common law in many situations?

1.3 Structure of the Criminal Justice System

The criminal justice system can be viewed from at least three perspectives: as a social system, as a body of legal rules, and as an administrative system.[14] Viewed as a social system, the criminal justice system encompasses all levels of society, from the legislature that enacts the penal code to the citizens whose acts are governed by those laws. This perspective on the criminal justice system is beyond the scope of this book. The criminal justice system as a body of legal rules will be the primary focus of subsequent chapters in this book.

The remainder of this chapter will analyze the criminal justice system as an administrative system. In this role, the criminal justice system is the official apparatus for enforcing the criminal law. It consists of law enforcement agencies, prosecution and defense attorneys, courts, and correctional institutions and agencies. Figure 1.3 provides an overview of the criminal justice system.

Law Enforcement

The main law enforcement agency in the United States is the police force. Police departments in cities, sheriff's departments in counties, state police, and state bureaus of investigation comprise the largest number of law enforcement officers in the country. In 1996, the national police/population ratio was 2.3 police officers per 1,000 citizens.[15] This statistic does not include the enormous number of private police (also known as private security) employed on private property such as in office buildings, apartment buildings, shopping malls, and private residential communities. The number of private police engaged in patrol is larger than the number of law enforcement officers engaged in the same activity.[16]

The four basic police functions are prevention, investigation, detection, and court preparation.

Prevention

Prevention is carried out by low-ranking officers assigned to cruise an area and watch for criminal activity. In the course of carrying out his or her duties, the police officer exercises substantial discretion in deciding whether to arrest a person suspected of criminal wrongdoing. It is impossible for police officers to arrest all the offenders they encounter. In addition to directly addressing crime, police departments spend a substantial amount of their time carrying out public services such as traffic control, crowd control, and emergency services.

Investigation

Investigation is performed by officers at all levels. Patrol officers often are the first to respond to the scene of a crime and are responsible for securing the area and sometimes gathering evidence. Detectives are usually then called in to perform the main investigation of the crime. Investigation may include crime scene investigation, speaking with witnesses, speaking with victims, taking photographs, and collecting evidence such as fingerprints or DNA to be sent to various labs. It may also entail showing victims photos of possible perpetrators, performing lineups, writing reports, and arresting suspects. For example, in murder cases, the Los Angeles Police Department puts together what they call a Murder Book, which includes all of the reports involved, a chronology, a witness list, information about the suspect(s), victim(s), and witness(es), photos, and lineup information. Police are often responsible for bringing a case to the district attorney's office to be filed.

◢ **F I G U R E   1 . 3**

Overview of the Criminal Justice System

Prosecution and Pretrial Procedures

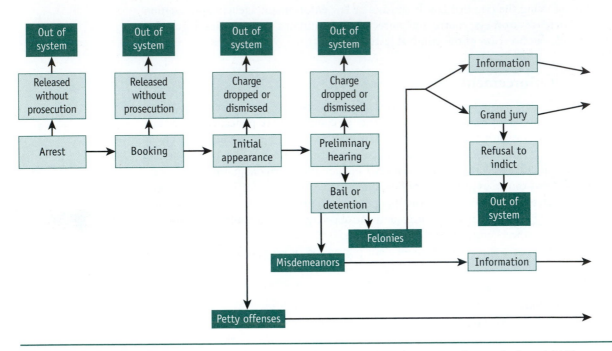

SOURCE: Based on Report of the President's Commission on Law Enforcement and the Administration of Justice: The Challenge of Crime in a Free Society 8 (1967).

Detection

Detection is usually performed by specialized squads consisting of older, more experienced, and higher-ranking officers. Activities associated with crime detection include organized police attempts to locate violators by such devices as setting up roadblocks to check for driving under the influence, monitoring activities in high-crime areas to observe drug trafficking, and using undercover agents to ferret out clandestine criminal activity. Another form of detection work, which has become the focus of popular television dramatic representation, is the use of forensic science in the solution of crimes as well as the preparation of such evidence for presentation at trial.

Court Preparation

The police officer's court preparation often begins with the gathering of evidence and the investigation. The officer then has to appear and testify at any and all hearings at which he or she is needed. Officers must prepare for court by reviewing the reports written during their investigation.

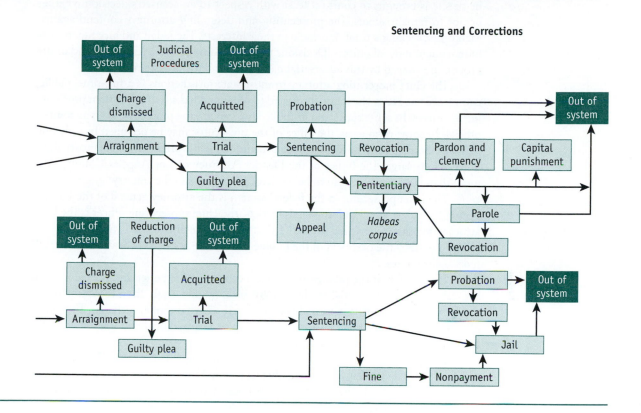

Sentencing and Corrections

Nationally, the Federal Bureau of Investigation (FBI) is charged with the responsibility of investigating federal law violations. Other federal law enforcement agencies include the Drug Enforcement Administration, the Bureau of Alcohol, Tobacco, and Firearms, the Customs Service, the Immigration and Naturalization Service, the United States Marshals Service, the Bureau of Postal Inspection, and the Secret Service.

All law enforcement agencies provide assistance to the prosecuting attorneys in presenting evidence in court to prosecute those arrested for criminal activities. Therefore, gathering evidence, maintaining the evidence collected, and preparing the evidence for presentation in a court of law are major functions of law enforcement agencies. For these purposes, most law enforcement agencies hire specially trained and educated personnel who are familiar with such specialized fields as ballistics, fingerprint analysis, blood stain analysis, and other areas of scientific methodology.

Prosecution and Defense

The American criminal justice system is an adversarial one. This means that the process by which guilt is determined is competitive, and the prosecution and defense are seen as adversaries, or rivals. In the American criminal justice system, the accused is presumed innocent until proven guilty, and the right to counsel attaches even before he or she is brought to court (at least with respect to an accused's decision whether or not to remain silent). The prosecuting and defending attorneys contend against each other, seeking a result favorable to their interests. The judge and jury function as independent judicial officers. Decisions from the point before arrest to the end of the process are shaped by this adversarial nature of the judicial system.

The chief prosecuting attorney in most state jurisdictions is a full-time, public, county official. He or she is usually elected to office and has a staff of assistant prosecuting attorneys. In some states and in the federal system, the prosecutor is an appointed official. In some rural areas, the office of the prosecutor may be occupied by only one person, who may work only part-time at the job. In many urban areas, the prosecutor's office is very large. The Office of the District Attorney of Los Angeles County, with more than 900 lawyers, is said to be the largest law office in the country.

The chief prosecutor in the federal system is the attorney general of the United States. In each of the 90-plus federal districts, the chief prosecuting officer is the U.S. attorney for that geographic district. The attorney general and the U.S. attorneys are all appointed by the president of the United States. The assistant U.S. attorneys are all federal employees.

It is the job of the prosecutor to take a case from the police and pursue it until the case terminates by trial verdict, guilty plea, or dismissal. The prosecutor must decide whether to pursue a formal charge and, if so, what crime to charge. The prosecutor is also responsible for conducting any plea negotiations, deciding whether to dismiss charges, and trying the case.

Beginning in the 1960s and as refined in recent years, the U.S. Constitution requires that a defendant who is actually incarcerated in jail or prison is entitled to an attorney whether or not he or she can afford one. Moreover, any suspect who is interrogated by the police is entitled to warnings about the right to remain silent and to have an attorney, whether or not the suspect can afford one, present during interrogation. Therefore, many states and the federal government find it necessary to provide defense counsel to many criminal suspects and defendants. This is accomplished either through the private bar (the local attorneys association) or a public defender system.

Defense counsel must zealously represent the criminal defendant from the point of interrogation through the trial process, demanding that the prosecution respect the defendant's rights, treat the defendant fairly, and meet the burden of proof beyond a reasonable doubt in the event the case goes to trial.

Courts

The United States has a dual judicial system consisting of the federal and state courts. Federal courts exist throughout the nation, and each state also has its own judicial system. All federal offenses are prosecuted in federal court, and all state offenses are prosecuted in state courts. The **jurisdiction** of a court is the scope of its power or authority to act with respect to any case before it. The judicial power of the federal courts, specified in Article II of the U.S. Constitution, "shall be vested in one Supreme Court, and in such inferior courts as the Congress may from time to time ordain and establish."

jurisdiction
The power or authority of a court to act with respect to any case before it.

1.2 On the Job

Public Defender

Description and Duties: Work with defendants, victims, witnesses, persons having an interest in criminal cases, and varying levels of other governmental organizations. Interact with persons of diverse backgrounds and educational levels. Effectively manage the public in emotional and occasionally hostile situations. Work flexibly with changing deadlines and priorities. Higher job levels require experience as an attorney in the practice of criminal law. Occasionally, experience in a civil or general practice law office can apply.

Salary: Salaries vary from approximately $35,000 to $95,000, depending on location and experience.

Other Information: This job is usually a valuable stepping stone for young attorneys seeking to gain experience, but some attorneys make it their career. State applicants are required to have active membership in their state's bar association and must provide a bar number when applying. Federal applicants should be in good standing with a state bar and become admitted to the federal court for which they are applying. Spanish language proficiency is highly desirable.

SOURCE: Orange County (California) Public Defender, http://www.oc.ca.gov/pd/emp.htm; Office of the State Public Defender, Colorado, http://www.state.co.us/defenders/employment.html.

The staff of the courts includes, in addition to the judge, courtroom clerks, judges' clerks, and bailiffs. Bailiffs are law enforcement personnel assigned to keep order in the courtroom, attend to juries, oversee prisoners who are in custody during their court appearances, and otherwise provide security in the courtroom. In many jurisdictions, the bailiff is a deputy sheriff; in the federal courts, the bailiffs are deputy U.S. marshals.

Federal Courts

The federal court system currently includes trial courts in each state and 13 federal courts of appeal, arranged by circuits. Twelve of these are numbered circuits and one is the federal circuit (see Figure 1.4). The federal courts have jurisdiction to consider cases charging defendants with violation of federal criminal laws.

State Courts

Each state also has its own court system. The structure of most state court systems is similar to that of the federal system: trial courts, intermediate appellate courts, and a supreme court. In most states, the trial courts are organized by county. Furthermore, in most states, the trial courts are divided into two levels, an inferior and a superior court. The inferior court, often called the municipal court or justice of the peace court, conducts preliminary hearings in felony cases and trials in cases involving misdemeanors or petty offenses. The superior court, sometimes called the circuit or district

The Federal Court Structure

United States Supreme Court

United States Courts of Appeals (12 Circuits)	United States Court of Appeals for the Federal Circuit	United States Court of Military Appeals

94 District Courts (includes 3 territorial courts for Guam, Virgin Islands, and Northern Mariana Islands)	United States Tax Court	United States Court of International Trade	United States Claims Court	United States Court of Veterans Appeals	Army, Navy, Marine Corps, Air Force, and Coast Guard Courts of Military Review

court, is a court of general jurisdiction and has jurisdiction over felony trials (see Figure 1.5).

Juvenile Courts

Each state also has a juvenile court system. Criminal offenders under a certain age, usually 18 or 16, are dealt with in juvenile courts by way of civil, rather than criminal, proceedings. If the offense is particularly serious, the juvenile may be treated as an adult, and the case will be heard in the criminal court. Many youthful offenders who commit offenses that would be crimes if committed by an adult are tried in the juvenile courts before specialized judges who seek to determine the youth's involvement and try to rehabilitate rather than punish the offender.

Juvenile court procedure was intended to be more informal than that of criminal courts. However, U.S. Supreme Court decisions since the 1960s have imposed due process restrictions on the juvenile courts that, although they have increased the rights of juvenile offenders, have also caused juvenile proceedings to become more formal and thus more like those in criminal courts.

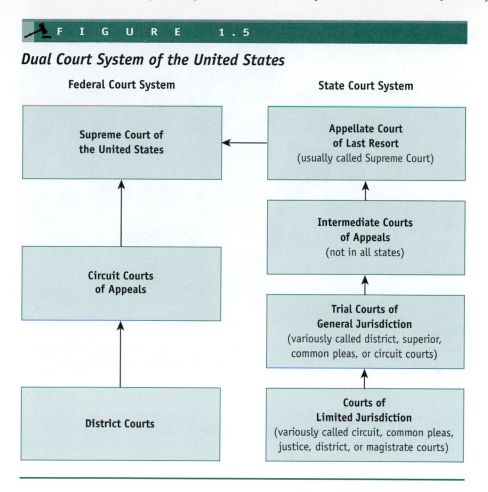

F I G U R E 1 . 5

Dual Court System of the United States

Federal Court System

State Court System

Supreme Court of the United States

Appellate Court of Last Resort
(usually called Supreme Court)

Intermediate Courts of Appeals
(not in all states)

Circuit Courts of Appeals

Trial Courts of General Jurisdiction
(variously called district, superior, common pleas, or circuit courts)

District Courts

Courts of Limited Jurisdiction
(variously called circuit, common pleas, justice, district, or magistrate courts)

Courts and the Fourteenth Amendment

Since about 1930, the U.S. Supreme Court has been interpreting the due process clause of the Fourteenth Amendment to incorporate constitutional criminal procedural requirements that apply to the states. These rights include:

- The right to trial by jury in cases involving serious offenses.
- The right to assistance of counsel in any case in which a sentence of more than six months in jail or prison may be imposed.
- The privilege against self-incrimination, including a ban against comment by the prosecution on the defendant's failure to testify.
- The presumption of innocence and requirement of proof beyond a reasonable doubt.
- Freedom from unreasonable searches and seizures.
- The right to silence and counsel during police interrogation.
- The right to compel witnesses' attendance at trial, to confront them, and to cross-examine.
- The right to a speedy and public trial.

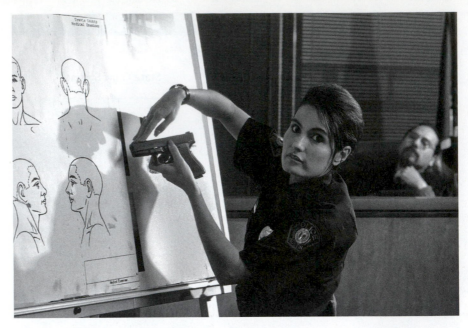

Testimony and Evidence Law enforcement officers frequently provide testimony for the prosecution. Anyone that gives testimony can be cross-examined by the opposing party.

- Freedom from double jeopardy.
- Freedom from cruel and unusual punishment.
- Freedom from racial and sexual discrimination in substantive and procedural criminal law.

Violation of these constitutional requirements can be the subject of both state appeals and federal *habeas corpus* claims by prisoners.

Corrections

The American correctional system is made up of correctional institutions, such as jails and prisons, and correctional agencies, such as probation and parole offices. In addition, the broad term *community corrections* includes drug rehabilitation centers, halfway houses, community corrections centers, community service programs, and many other services that are available to less serious criminals or those who have shown significant rehabilitation.

Jails are used to maintain custody of persons arrested pending prosecution and of those sentenced to short periods of confinement, usually up to but not more than one year. Most jails are operated by cities, counties, or both. Jails provide few services, since most inmates are there temporarily. Usually, there are separate jail facilities for women and for juveniles.

All states maintain state penal institutions (prisons), consisting of state penitentiaries and juvenile training facilities. Often the institutions are graded according to level of security, ranging from maximum to minimum security. The United

States has more than 1,000 state prison facilities, with a total population in all the country's jails and prisons of more than 1.3 million as of June 30, 2006.[17] Prison facilities are administered by a separate correctional agency of the state or federal government.

Two important features of the correctional system, which actually operate outside the walls of correctional institutions, are probation and parole.

Probation

Most court systems have a probation department attached to them. The probation department investigates defendants prior to sentencing and provides a pre-sentence probation report to the court. In addition, the probation department provides supervision over those persons placed on probation after conviction. Probation is the most frequent disposition for first-time offenders. Probationers are released back into the community and are required to stay out of trouble, avoid association with those involved in crime, attempt to find a job, avoid the use of alcohol and drugs, and report to a probation officer periodically. The probation service is designed to provide counseling, but because of the overwhelming caseload, probation officers usually are able to engage in only nominal supervision.

Parole

Parole supervision is similar to probation supervision, except that the parole service is an agency of the state correctional system rather than the court system. Violations of probation and parole lead to hearings that, in turn, lead to warning, incarceration, or reincarceration.

CRITICAL THINKING 1.3

1. Explain the differences between state and federal courts.
2. What roles do jails and prisons play in the criminal justice process? How do jails and prisons differ?

1.4 Operation of the Criminal Justice System

The organization of the United States government is based on the principle of **federalism**, which states that power resides in the states unless expressly granted to the federal government. For this reason, the criminal justice system operates in 51 arenas. The basic system, however, is similar in each jurisdiction. The fundamental structure of the criminal justice system consists of law enforcement agencies, prosecution and defense attorneys, courts, and correctional institutions and agencies.

Law enforcement agents learn about most criminal acts through reports of victims or witnesses. Police also learn about crimes while working on patrol, maintaining surveillance, or through undercover or other investigations. The overwhelming majority of reported crimes are not solved. Investigations of crimes against persons, particularly homicides, take priority; therefore, homicides are solved more often than other crimes.

federalism
The system of government of the United States whereby all power resides in the state governments unless specifically granted to the federal government.

Arrest

probable cause
Evidence that there is a fair probability that the suspect committed a crime; required for an arrest of a suspect by a law enforcement officer.

The criminal process most often begins with an arrest. An officer can arrest only if probable cause exists. **Probable cause** is evidence that there is a fair probability that the suspect committed a crime. An officer possessing probable cause may arrest the suspect without a warrant, unless the suspect is in his or her home. Alternatively, the officer can obtain a warrant from a court authorizing arrest of the suspect if there is a sufficient showing of probable cause. Arrests made by police on patrol are made without a warrant because of the need for a speedy response. Arrest with a warrant is likely to occur only when the arrest has resulted from investigation and there are no exigencies of a crime in progress or "hot pursuit."

Not all arrests result in prosecution. The decision whether or not to prosecute is made not by the police officer but by the prosecuting attorney and the courts. Often, a perpetrator will have committed a major crime, usually a felony, and several lesser misdemeanors. For example, a suspect may have committed rape, which is the charge that the officer and prosecutor most want to be sure results in a conviction. But the suspect may have also committed the crimes of criminal trespass, breaking and entering into a dwelling, burglary, assault and battery, or theft. The arresting officer should be sure to include in the police report all elements of all the possible crimes that the officer finds the suspect committed. The decision whether or not to charge the suspect with those crimes is up to the prosecutor, and the lesser crimes may be used as a bargaining chip by the prosecutor in plea negotiations.

Pretrial Procedures and Issues

After arrest and booking, and before the stage of the justice process at which the defendant may face a trial, the defendant must make several other court appearances. He or she will also most likely confer with his or her lawyer about plea bargaining, since approximately 90 percent of all felony cases are resolved in this manner. Plea bargaining, which you will learn more about shortly, is a process that helps expedite the justice system by enabling the courts to avoid a lengthy trial.

The key pretrial procedures and issues are bail, charging the crime, the preliminary hearing, the handling of misdemeanor charges, the use of an indictment or information for felony charges, arraignment and plea, plea bargaining, and (where applicable) dismissing the charges.

Bail

recognizance
A promise to appear in court.

bail
A deposit of cash, other property, or a bond, guaranteeing the accused will appear in court.

bond
A written promise to pay the bail sum, posted by a financially responsible person, usually a professional bondsman.

Most suspects are entitled to release after arrest and booking, either on the accused's own recognizance or on bail. **Recognizance** is a promise to appear in court. **Bail** is a deposit of cash, other property, or a bond, guaranteeing that the accused will appear in court. A **bond** is a written promise to pay the bail sum, posted by a financially responsible person, usually a professional bondsman. Bail is usually not very high, except in cases where it is shown that there is a risk that the accused will fail to appear for trial.

Charging the Crime

After arrest, the prosecutor will file a charge against the defendant if the prosecutor is satisfied that the evidence is sufficient to support the charge and that the case is worthy of prosecution.

Preliminary Hearing

After the prosecutor files the charge, a judge holds a **preliminary hearing** to determine whether probable cause exists. In some jurisdictions, the preliminary hearing is minimal, providing only a summary review of the sufficiency of the evidence. In other jurisdictions, the preliminary hearing is very extensive, amounting to a mini-trial.

At the preliminary hearing, an arresting officer has the first opportunity to present evidence against the defendant. Many times, the officer will not get to testify at a trial because the defendant decides to enter into a plea bargain after hearing all of the evidence presented at the preliminary hearing. Therefore, the law enforcement officer should view the preliminary hearing as an important step in achieving the best result in a criminal case.

preliminary hearing
A post-arrest, pretrial judicial proceeding at which the judge decides whether there is probable cause to prosecute the accused. In some jurisdictions, the preliminary hearing is minimal; in others, it is a mini-trial.

Misdemeanor Charges

If the prosecution establishes probable cause, the defendant is required to answer to the charge in the trial court. If the crime charged is a misdemeanor or petty offense, the defendant will respond to the complaint filed by the prosecutor and enter a plea of guilty or not guilty. If the plea is not guilty, the case will be assigned to a court for trial.

Felony Charges: Indictment and Information

When the crime charged is a felony, the procedure is more complex. The common law rule required that a felony be charged only by a grand jury indictment. A **grand jury** is a panel of persons chosen through strict court procedures to review criminal investigations and, in some instances, to conduct criminal investigations. Grand juries decide whether to charge crimes in the cases presented to them or investigated by them. When a grand jury charges a person with a crime, it does so by issuing an **indictment**.

In the federal system and in many states, felonies can still be prosecuted only by indictment of a grand jury (see Figure 1.6). In those jurisdictions, after the police investigate a crime, the prosecutor presents the case to the grand jury. The grand jury hears testimony and decides whether to indict the accused. When the defendant has been arrested on the street in the process of committing a crime, the case can be presented to the grand jury immediately after arrest. In those jurisdictions that do not follow the grand jury procedure, prosecutors file a formal felony charge called an **information**. The information is merely a written statement of the formal charge, signed by the prosecutor.

grand jury
A panel of persons chosen through strict court procedures to review criminal investigations and, in some instances, to conduct criminal investigations. Grand juries decide whether to charge crimes in the cases presented to them or investigated by them.

indictment
The paper issued by a grand jury that charges an accused with a felony.

information
The paper issued by a prosecutor that charges an accused of a felony.

Arraignment and Plea

After the formal charges have been filed against a defendant, either by indictment or information, the defendant appears in court at a proceeding called an arraignment or **arraignment and plea**. This is the defendant's appearance to respond formally to the charges. At this time, the defendant will enter a plea of guilty or not guilty. If the defendant pleads guilty, then the case will be set for sentencing. If the defendant pleads not guilty, the case will be set for trial.

arraignment and plea
The defendant's appearance to respond formally to the charges.

Plea Bargaining

Plea negotiations resolve a majority of all prosecutions filed.[18] Plea negotiations may result in a reduction of the original charge, which reduces the level of penalty that

F I G U R E   1 . 6

States That Use Grand Jury Indictment Only versus States That Use a Combination of Indictment and Information in Felony Cases

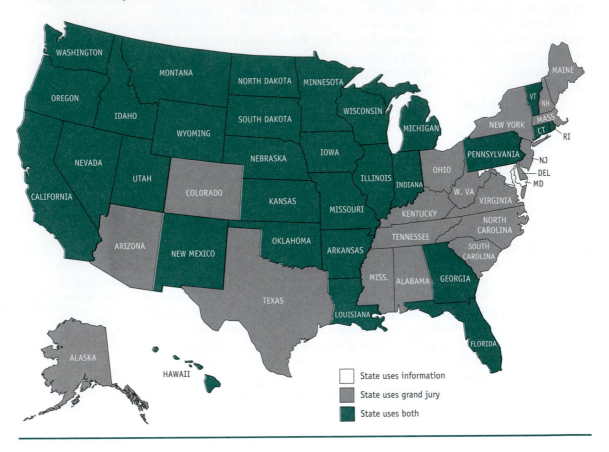

the judge may impose on the accused. Another result of plea negotiations is that the prosecution recommends a specific sentence to the court, usually involving a lesser punishment than otherwise would be the case. In return, the defense enters a plea of guilty, and the prosecution does not have to expend the time and expense involved in taking the case to trial.

Dismissing Charges

The defendant has a right to challenge the validity of the indictment or information by moving to dismiss the charges. There are only three bases for dismissal:

1. The crime charged is not a violation of the jurisdiction's law.
2. The facts asserted in the indictment or information, even if true, do not constitute the crime charged.
3. No reasonable jury could find the facts alleged on the basis of the evidence presented at the preliminary hearing.

In order to charge a crime, the prosecutor must allege facts as to each element of the crime as defined by law. (The definitions and elements of all major crimes are the focus of this book in Chapters 8 through 16.) The validity of a criminal charge is also determined by two other factors: the criminal statutes in effect in the jurisdiction, and federal and state constitutional law. In most jurisdictions, a valid criminal charge must allege that the defendant's acts violated some criminal statute. The federal constitutional provisions that relate to substantive criminal law issues include the due process clauses of the Fifth and Fourteenth Amendments and the cruel and unusual punishment clause of the Eighth Amendment. These issues are discussed in Chapter 2.

Trial of the Case

In the United States, an accused in a criminal case has a constitutional right to trial by jury for any crime for which the possible sentence is more than six months in jail or prison. The accused, however, can waive that right and have a trial before the judge alone. Before the trial commences, the judge will hear pretrial matters, including motions to exclude evidence.

In the case of a jury, the actual trial process begins with jury selection. The trial proceeds with an opening statement by the prosecution, telling the story of the case and describing the evidence that will be presented. The defense can make its opening next, or it can reserve its opening statement until after the prosecution has presented its case. The prosecution then presents its case, consisting of witnesses, physical evidence, and documents. The defense has the right to cross-examine each prosecution witness. At the conclusion of the prosecution's case, the defense will ask the judge to decide whether the prosecution's evidence is enough to go to the jury, by making a motion for judgment of acquittal. If the motion is granted, the case is over, and the defendant cannot be charged again with that crime.

If the defense's motion for judgment of acquittal is denied, the defendant may rest without presenting any evidence, because the prosecution has the burden of proving the defendant guilty beyond a reasonable doubt. However, in most cases, the defense will present some evidence. The defendant may or may not choose to testify, and neither the court nor the prosecution can make any comment on the defendant's failure to do so. The defense's witnesses are subject to cross-examination by the prosecution. After the defense has presented all of its witnesses, physical evidence, and documents, the prosecution can offer evidence to rebut the defense's case. After that, the defendant has a chance to introduce rebuttal evidence as well.

After the evidence for both the prosecution and defense has been completed—when each side has rested—both sides present closing arguments to the jury or, in a bench trial (a trial without a jury), to the judge. The judge then reads instructions on the law to the jury, after which the jury deliberates until it reaches a verdict.

In the event that the jury cannot reach a verdict on a charge, the judge will declare a mistrial and the prosecution may choose to retry the defendant. If the jury acquits the defendant, double jeopardy prohibits retrial or appeal by the prosecution. On the other hand, if the jury convicts, the accused can seek a new trial from the trial court or seek an appeal to an appellate court.

Post-Conviction Procedures and Issues

If a defendant is acquitted of the charges, he or she will be released from custody. Because of double jeopardy protections under the Fifth Amendment, the justice system cannot try the defendant twice for the same crime. Special exceptions to this exist when a defendant has violated different federal and state laws for the same crime, such as when a drug dealer violates state drug laws and federal organized crime laws simultaneously for the same crime. You will read more about this in Chapter 16.

If, however, a defendant is convicted, he or she must be sentenced. The defendant has the right to appeal the sentence, although more than 80 percent of appeals do not succeed. Other types of post-conviction relief include filing a writ of *habeas corpus*.

Sentencing

If the defendant is convicted, the judge will ordinarily order a pre-sentence (or probation) report that provides sufficient information on which to base a sentencing decision. Unless the charge carries a mandatory sentence, the judge will hold a sentencing hearing, entertaining arguments from the prosecution and defense. The judge will then sentence the defendant in accordance with the statutory range. When the prosecution seeks the death penalty, the sentencing hearing will be a second trial before a judge or jury, who will hear evidence of aggravating and mitigating factors. In some states, the jury can also impose a sentence other than the death penalty for serious offenses. See Chapter 7 for a more extensive discussion of sentencing.

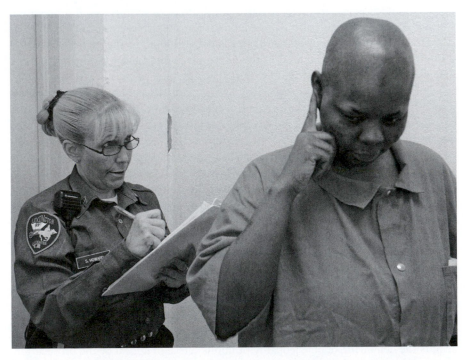

From Courtroom to Prison After a defendant receives a prison sentence, correctional authorities process her arrival and she becomes an inmate.

Appeal and Discretionary Review

The bases for appeal of a criminal conviction on substantive grounds are limited to four possibilities:

1. The charge on which the accused was convicted is not a crime, either because the legislature did not proscribe the conduct or because the proscription is unconstitutional.
2. The evidence was insufficient to support a finding of fact on all the elements of the crime beyond a reasonable doubt.
3. Not all of the necessary elements of the crime were alleged.
4. The jury was improperly instructed.

Other grounds for appeal, which do not relate to substantive criminal law issues, involve procedural and evidentiary errors alleged to have been committed by the trial court. In some jurisdictions, many claims to an appellate court are pursued by petition for *certiorari*, which allows the appellate court to decide, at its discretion, whether to hear the case.

An appeal from the state courts to the U.S. Supreme Court can only be pursued through a writ of *certiorari*, which is a written order from the U.S. Supreme Court to a lower court whose decision is being appealed to send the records of the case forward for review. The Supreme Court receives thousands of petitions each year, but it reviews only a handful of criminal cases, mainly those that will settle a question that has been answered differently by different appellate courts or that present a substantial policy question that the Court wishes to address.

Post-Conviction Relief

Habeas corpus, a common law remedy for illegal confinement, exists in modern American criminal procedure to test the validity of a person's incarceration. **Habeas corpus,** which literally means, "you have the body," is a legal action separate from the criminal case. It can be brought only by a prisoner who has exhausted all of the usual appellate remedies. A federal prisoner can seek *habeas corpus* relief in the proper federal district court; state prisoners may seek such relief in the proper state court.

Under federal law, a state prisoner may seek *habeas corpus* relief in federal court if the person alleges that the conviction violated his or her federal constitutional rights. As long as a defendant raises new grounds, he or she can file successive *habeas corpus* petitions. Just as with the original criminal conviction, these post-conviction petitions can be pursued from the trial court level all the way to the highest courts in the states and even to the U.S. Supreme Court. Only rarely, however, can a prisoner seek post-conviction relief based on an issue relating to a substantive criminal law claim (such as the definition, or elements, of a particular crime).

habeas corpus
Literally, "you have the body." A legal action separate from the criminal case, it can only be brought by a prisoner who has exhausted all the usual appellate remedies.

CRITICAL THINKING 1.4

1. What are the three bases for dismissing a trial?
2. Explain the various grounds on which convicted criminals appeal their convictions.

REVIEW AND APPLICATIONS

Summary by Chapter Objectives

1. **State a basic definition of law.** Law is a rule of conduct or procedure established by custom, agreement, or authority. Law, in its generic sense, is a body of rules of action or conduct prescribed by controlling authority and having binding legal force.

2. **Explain what distinguishes the criminal law from other law.** Criminal law seeks to regulate acts that are contrary to the community interest of the social or government unit—federal, state, or local. Therefore, a criminal act, though usually aimed at a personal victim, is perceived as involving a social harm and is prosecuted on behalf of the public.

3. **Define the common law.** The common law means law created by judicial opinion. The United States and England share a common heritage in the common law of England. When the 13 colonies were established in America, and when the United States gained independence, they adopted the common law of England.

4. **State the principle of legality.** A core concept of the American criminal justice system, legality holds that no one can be punished for an act that was not defined as criminal before the person did the act. If a court declares conduct criminal that has not previously been defined as criminal, then the principle of legality is violated.

5. **Explain what the MPC is.** The MPC (Model Penal Code) is a comprehensive recodification of the principles of criminal responsibility, drafted in reliance upon existing sources of the criminal law including codes, judicial opinions, and scholarly commentary. Though not adopted in any state, it has affected a reform of the criminal law in a majority of states, and it stands as a model for the reform of principles of American criminal responsibility.

6. **Describe the fundamental structure of the American criminal justice system.** The fundamental structure of the American criminal justice system consists of law enforcement agencies, prosecution and defense attorneys, courts, and correctional institutions and agencies. Moreover, the organization of American government is based on the principle of federalism, which holds that power resides in the states unless expressly granted to the federal government. For this reason, the criminal justice system operates in 51 arenas: the 50 state governments and the federal government (which includes the District of Columbia).

7. **Name the four basic police functions.** The four basic police functions are prevention, investigation, detection, and court preparation. The prevention function is carried out by low-ranking officers assigned to cruise an area

and watch for criminal activity. The investigation function is carried out at all levels and involves everything from gathering data at the crime scene to presenting suspects to victims at lineups. The detective function is usually performed by specialized squads consisting of older, more experienced, and higher-ranking officers. The court preparation function involves testifying at hearings and trial and presenting the evidence in an effort to convict the perpetrator.

8. **State what is required for a law enforcement officer to arrest a suspect.** In the case of felonies, a law enforcement officer must have probable cause to believe that a person has committed a crime before he or she may arrest the suspect. In the case of misdemeanors, an officer can only arrest for offenses committed in the officer's presence.

9. **State the purpose of a preliminary hearing.** The purpose of a preliminary hearing is for a judge to determine whether there is probable cause for the accused to answer to the crime charged. Since many cases do not go to trial because of plea bargaining, this is often the only chance that officers have to offer testimony and present evidence against the accused.

10. **Describe the two alternative methods for charging serious crimes.** Felonies are charged by either an indictment or an information. An indictment is issued by a grand jury, which is a panel of citizens that decides whether to charge crimes in the cases presented to them (or investigated by them). An information, which is a piece of paper on which the charge appears, is filed and signed by the prosecutor.

11. **List the three possible bases for a defendant's pretrial motion to dismiss.** The three possible bases for a defendant's pretrial motion to dismiss are:
    - The crime charged is not a violation of the jurisdiction's law.
    - The facts asserted in the indictment or information, even if true, do not constitute the crime charged.
    - No reasonable jury could find the facts alleged on the basis of the evidence given at the preliminary hearing.

12. **State the four possible grounds for appeal of a criminal conviction.** The four possible grounds for appeal of a criminal conviction are:
    - The charge on which the accused was convicted is not a crime, either because the legislature did not proscribe the conduct or because the proscription is unconstitutional.
    - The evidence was insufficient to support a finding of fact on all the elements of the crime beyond a reasonable doubt.
    - Not all of the necessary elements of the crime were alleged.
    - The jury was improperly instructed.

13. **State when a defendant is entitled to an attorney at trial.** A defendant who may be sentenced to more than six months in jail or prison is entitled to an attorney whether or not he or she can afford one. (Those who cannot afford an attorney will have one appointed by the court.)

Key Terms

law (p. 2)
common law (p. 4)
statutory law (p. 4)
criminal law (p. 4)
civil law (p. 5)
tort (p. 5)
actus reus (p. 6)
mens rea (p. 6)
legality (p. 7)
Model Penal Code (MPC) (p. 9)
jurisdiction (p. 14)

federalism (p. 19)
probable cause (p. 20)
recognizance (p. 20)
bail (p. 20)
bond (p. 20)
preliminary hearing (p. 21)
grand jury (p. 21)
indictment (p. 21)
information (p. 21)
arraignment and plea (p. 21)
habeas corpus (p. 25)

Review Questions

1. Name the various sources from which laws derive.
2. What is the difference between common law and statutory law?
3. What is the difference between criminal law and civil law?
4. What is the history of the common law?
5. How did Jeremy Bentham influence criminal law in England and the United States?
6. What is the Model Penal Code, and why was it created?
7. What document restricts federal law, and how?
8. Define *actus reus* and *mens rea*, and explain why they are needed for criminal charges.
9. Name some of the ways in which law enforcement agents learn about criminal acts.
10. Explain the difference between release upon recognizance and bail. What is a bond?
11. What is a grand jury, how does it work, and which jurisdictions use it?
12. What happens at an arraignment? What happens in response to a plea of guilty or not guilty?
13. What is the burden of proof in a criminal trial?
14. What are the basic elements of the criminal trial? Include the different motions and actions of the prosecution and defense.
15. Name and define the three main perspectives from which the criminal justice system can be viewed.
16. Name the different types of departments in which police work, and give some examples of federal agencies.
17. What are the duties of the prosecutor? Of defense counsel?
18. What is jurisdiction? What is the jurisdiction of federal courts?
19. Name three or four constitutional due process rights that apply to state prisoners.
20. What are the general duties of a probation department?

Problem-Solving Exercises

1. **Pretrial Detention** Immediately after being arrested and booked on drug charges or similar offenses, most white middle-class people are released from custody as soon as a family member arrives to post bail. But unemployed people from a lower socioeconomic class facing similar charges may be unable to post bail and may therefore remain in jail until their court appearance, which may be weeks or even months away. According to 1997 Bureau of Justice statistics, 378 state correctional facilities (27 percent of the total) were under court order to reduce population or improve conditions of confinement. Conditions in jails may include sleeping on the floor, long waits to call a family member or lawyer, and limited access to showers. In overcrowded jails, plumbing may fail, resulting in clogged toilets and flooding. Answer the following questions:
   a. Does being detained in such a setting prior to trial constitute punishment before trial?
   b. What issues are raised by the fact that the poor are more likely to experience pretrial confinement than are upper- and middle-class suspects?

2. **Protection against Cybercrime** You have heard that a new cybercrime has affected several other parts of the country but that prosecutors are unable to press charges because the crime has not been added to their statutes and there is no legal precedent (i.e., common law). You do not want your jurisdiction to have the same problem, and it is clear that this crime could easily happen here. Answer the following questions:
   a. How do you persuade legislators in your area to pass a law against this crime before it occurs?
   b. How do you persuade law enforcement to educate people about this crime when it is not yet a crime that they are legally required to enforce? What else can you do to help protect your jurisdiction?

3. **Sentencing Guidelines** You are a county judge and have been in your job for nearly a year. In that time, you have sentenced many drug offenders to the lengthy sentences that are within your options, and your community has strongly supported you. However, you are hearing from state prison authorities that their prisons are highly overcrowded, there are not enough funds to staff them properly, and nonviolent drug offenders are suffering negative consequences such as physical and sexual abuse from more hardened criminals. They strongly urge you to stop sentencing nonviolent drug offenders to any type of incarceration and to use treatment-based alternatives instead.
   a. Which option will you pick? Why?
   b. Will you suggest or implement any changes to sentencing guidelines or options so that more judges will pick treatment-based alternatives for drug offenders? Why or why not?

4. **Witness Treatment** A witness is called to court to testify against an individual charged with aggravated assault. The accused hit another man over the head with a cue stick in a barroom brawl, causing moderate injuries. The witness comes to court on his day off, waits all morning and part of the afternoon to testify, then at 4:00 p.m. is informed that he can leave because the prosecution

and defense have agreed that the defendant would plead guilty to a lesser included offense. Answer the following questions:

a. What has occurred here?

b. Did the attorneys have a legal obligation to inform the witness of what was going on? What about an ethical duty?

c. Should the witness be angry? Why or why not?

5. **Disclosure** You are a federal officer who has arrested a key participant in an undercover drug transaction. You let him transfer the drugs to you and gave him money in exchange; in other words, you caught the perpetrator red-handed. In preparing for the preliminary hearing, the prosecutor tells you not to mention the fact that you were tipped by an informant to go to the scene of the transaction. The prosecutor says that she wants to "spring" this information on the defense at trial.

a. Does the prosecutor have a legal right to do this? Why or why not?

b. What are the possible ramifications of such a move by the prosecutor?

c. Is such a move needed in this case? Why or why not?

d. What should you do? Why?

6. **Drug Possession** You are an appellate judge hearing the appeal of a convicted offender who was given a 25-year sentence for possession with intent to distribute cocaine and transporting a controlled substance. The cocaine was found in the car she was driving, which was registered in her name but shared with her two roommates; she insists that the drug was not hers and she had no idea that she was transporting it. On the other hand, police surveillance showed her visiting known drug dealers intermittently, and she had several bags in her car that would have been too large not to notice.

a. Does this defendant have a case? Why or why not?

b. Which factors influenced your decision, and what other factors would help you make this decision?

Workplace Applications

1. **Prison Budget** In 1995, for the first time in U.S. history, the total cost of state-issued bonds to finance prison construction surpassed the total for bonds to construct colleges. Compare the budgets for education and corrections in your county and state. Answer the following questions:

a. If you were a member of the stage legislature, what recommendations would you make concerning funding for these areas?

b. How would you set funding priorities for these budget items compared to others?

2. **Find Out about Law School** Contact a professor at your local law school (it might be at your college or university) and ask how a law student could focus his or her studies on criminal law.

a. What courses would the student need to take, and what kind of internship or part-time work would help provide useful job experience?

b. If one specializes in criminal law, what are some job options after passing the bar? After gaining a few years' full-time case experience?

3. **Revise a City Ordinance**   You are a judge hearing a case involving a city ordinance that forbids more than five women from living together in the same house. The ordinance is obviously outdated; it was passed during the time that your state was a territory and large numbers of women were imported for purposes of prostitution. The ordinance was thus meant to attack brothels, not law-abiding citizens sharing living quarters. The defendants in this case are six women who have been heavily involved in citywide police reform and have made some political enemies. The prosecutor is zealously trying to get them convicted, and has told you that he would like to see all of them in jail. You, however, feel that the ordinance needs to be struck from the books.

   a. How will you decide in this case? Why?

   b. Should you ever let political factors influence your decision? Why or why not?

4. **The Lesser of Two Evils**   You are a police officer, working late at night. You are alone in a squad car, patrolling a residential area that has been experiencing a rise in street crime. You observe a suspicious-looking group of three young men walking slowly down the street, carefully eyeing each house they pass and talking with each other as they eye the houses. You pull over before any of the youths notice you. At this time, a car speeds by, substantially exceeding the limit. Answer the following questions:

   a. Should you pursue the car or continue observing the youths? Why?

   b. Comparing the two possible dangers, which seems to pose a greater risk? Why?

   c. What can you do to ensure that the crime you choose *not* to prevent is handled in an appropriate manner?

5. **Trial by Jury**   You are a witness in a case that is on trial before a jury. The prosecution has called you, and you have testified and sat through cross-examination. As the case for the prosecution continues, you are permitted to sit in the courtroom and observe. Soon the prosecution announces that the state "rests its case." The defendant makes a motion for a directed verdict, which is denied. The defense then states that it "rests its case." Answer the following questions:

   a. What could happen next in this trial? Is this unusual?

   b. Do you believe the defense has provided an adequate defense? Why or why not?

   c. Could the defendant ever make the claim that his or her trial was mishandled because of the defense counsel's actions? Why or why not?

6. **Release and Bail**   You are a judge hearing the first appearance of a 17-year-old defendant who has been arrested for stealing a car and causing a serious accident that killed two people. Under the juvenile laws in your state, he will be tried as an adult. He has a history of drug abuse and violent crime, and his mother is mentally ill. Although he is upset about being arrested, he shows no apparent remorse for his crimes. His defense attorney, who is very persistent and well paid, is requesting that you allow his release upon recognizance. Your other options are to impose bail at whatever level you feel is appropriate or to deny bail altogether.

   a. Which option will you choose, and why?

   b. Which of the factors stated are considerations in your decision? Which are not?

Ethics Exercises

1. **Fireworks Ban** You are a county police officer patrolling the unincorporated areas of your county. While driving down a quiet road, you observe a stand selling fireworks to a long line of eager customers, who are loading their trunks with huge boxes of firecrackers, sparklers, roman candles, and even small (though legal) tubes of dynamite. It is June 29, and your county has passed an ordinance prohibiting the sale of fireworks as of July 1. Answer the following questions:
   a. Can you arrest the suspect? Why or why not? What can or should you do in response to this situation?
   b. If you return two days later and see any sales of fireworks, what can you do?

2. **Forensic Evidence** You are a prosecutor handling the case of a notorious child killer. It has taken investigators four years to build enough evidence to arrest him, and you are glad to see him off the streets. You have charged him with seven counts of murder and are asking for the death penalty. The public, which has been impatient to see this killer caught and punished, wants a quick resolution of the case. Shortly after the trial begins, however, a forensic scientist who works for your county tells you she has discovered a problem: It appears that the evidence from three of the cases indicates that a completely different offender was involved in these crimes—not the defendant, even as an accomplice. This could slow down the court process and possibly create a belief among the general public that the defendant is innocent of the other crimes as well.
   a. Do you charge the defendant with these crimes anyway? Why or why not?
   b. If the defendant is charged with these killings and the case is closed, what are the implications regarding arresting and charging the actual killer?

3. **Defense Attorney** You are a criminal defense attorney who typically defends low-income adults accused of drug offenses and other nonviolent crimes; your success rate is well known in your community. You receive a visit from the girlfriend of a man who is facing trial for a particularly brutal and heinous robbery-homicide. The victim was a seven-year-old child who was sexually assaulted and tortured before being murdered. The evidence against the accused is overwhelming, including a voluntary confession given to the arresting officer. It is clear that the confession was given without any prompting and that all procedures were followed. Nonetheless, the defendant has had a change of heart and is going to trial to zealously fight a conviction. The girlfriend offers you an enormous sum of money as a retainer, and makes it clear that you can name your price for defending this person. Answer the following questions:
   a. Would you defend this person? Why or why not?
   b. What if you were offered a sum that was the equivalent of five times your regular annual salary? Why or why not?
   c. What ethical issues could you face as the defense counsel for such a person?
   d. Is the case winnable? Why or why not? If it is not winnable, do you have anything to lose?

4. **Prosecution** You are a prosecutor closing a case against a man charged with murdering his wife. Although the defendant claims to be a recovered alcoholic, you have the option of bringing in character witnesses who can testify to his violent behavior while he drank. You believe that this evidence will guarantee a conviction.

You know that the defense will protest this evidence as irrelevant, but you also know that your personal friendship with the judge will cause him to allow it.

a. How does such evidence affect the jury's understanding that the defendant committed the crime "beyond a reasonable doubt"? Why?

b. Is it ethical to bring in such character evidence? Why or why not?

Notes

1. THE AMERICAN HERITAGE DICTIONARY OF THE ENGLISH LANGUAGE 993 (4th ed. 2006).
2. BLACK'S LAW DICTIONARY (8th ed. 2004).
3. Geoffrey C. Hazard, Jr., *Criminal Justice System: Overview, in* ENCYCLOPEDIA OF CRIME AND JUSTICE 450, 450 (Sanford H. Kadish ed., 1983).
4. *See* JOSHUA DRESSLER, UNDERSTANDING CRIMINAL LAW § 9.10[B], at 122 (4th ed. 2006).
5. Keeler v. Superior Court, 470 P.2d 617 (Cal. 1970).
6. JOSHUA DRESSLER, UNDERSTANDING CRIMINAL LAW § 5.01[C][2], at 45 n.26 (4th ed. 2006) (quoting Keeler v. Superior Court, 470 P.2d 617 (Cal. 1970)).
7. JOSHUA DRESSLER, UNDERSTANDING CRIMINAL LAW § 5.01[A], at 41–42 (4th ed. 2006).
8. CAL. PENAL CODE § 6 (West 1999).
9. *See* JOSHUA DRESSLER, UNDERSTANDING CRIMINAL LAW § 3.02[A], at 30–31 (4th ed. 2006).
10. 470 P.2d 617 (Cal. 1970).
11. *See* Charles McClain & Dan M. Kahan, *Criminal Law Reform: Historical Development in the United States, in* ENCYCLOPEDIA OF CRIME AND JUSTICE 422–24 (Joshua Dressler ed., 2d ed. 2002) (stating that 30 states had adopted revised criminal codes affected by the MPC by 1980 and another 9 had code revisions under way or completed and awaiting enactment); *see also* JOSHUA DRESSLER, UNDERSTANDING CRIMINAL LAW § 3.03, at 33 n.22 (4th ed. 2006) (citing Peter W. Low, *The Model Penal Code, the Common Law, and Mistakes of Fact: Recklessness, Negligence, or Strict Liability?* 19 RUTGERS L.J. 539, 539 (1988) (stating that the Model Penal Code stimulated adoption of revised penal codes in at least 37 states)).
12. *See* Sara Sun Beale, *Federal Criminal Jurisdiction, in* ENCYCLOPEDIA OF CRIME AND JUSTICE 694–98 (Joshua Dressler ed., 2d ed. 2002).
13. *Id.*
14. Kent Greenwalt, *Punishment, in* ENCYCLOPEDIA OF CRIME AND JUSTICE 1282–83 (Joshua Dressler ed., 2nd ed. 2002).
15. *See* Richard S. Frase, *Criminalization and Decriminalization, in* ENCYCLOPEDIA OF CRIME AND JUSTICE 347–48 (Joshua Dressler ed., 2nd ed. 2002).
16. *See* JOSHUA DRESSLER, UNDERSTANDING CRIMINAL LAW § 2.02, at 12–13 (4th ed. 2006).
17. BUREAU OF JUSTICE STATISTICS, BULLETIN: PRISON AND JAIL INMATES AT MIDYEAR 2006, http://www.ojp.usdoj.gov/bjs/pub/pdf/pjim06.pdf.
18. *See* Richard S. Frase & Robert R. Weidner, *Criminal Justice System, in* ENCYCLOPEDIA OF CRIME AND JUSTICE 371, 384–85 (Joshua Dressler ed., 2d ed. 2002).

Constitutional Limitations on the Criminal Law

CHAPTER OUTLINE

2.1 Criminal Law and the U.S. Constitution

The Question of Constitutionality

The Bill of Rights

2.2 Procedural Criminal Law

Due Process and Equal Protection

Search and Seizure

Bills of Attainder and *Ex Post Facto* Laws

Fair Notice and Vagueness

2.3 Substantive Criminal Law and Individual Due Process Rights

First Amendment Rights

Second Amendment Rights

Eighth Amendment Rights

The Right to Privacy

CHAPTER OBJECTIVES

After reading and studying this chapter, you should be able to:

1. Identify who determines whether a legislative enactment violates a constitutional prohibition.
2. List those areas of the Constitution that limit criminal law enactments.
3. Identify the one crime defined in the U.S. Constitution.
4. List the provisions of the Bill of Rights that limit the government's ability to prohibit and punish crimes.
5. State three categories of unprotected speech.
6. Name three areas of personal privacy protected by the U.S. Constitution as it affects crimes.

2.1 Criminal Law and the U.S. Constitution

American criminal law is mostly statutory, with courts interpreting the meaning of the penal codes when necessary. However, both the codes and the court decisions are limited by the U.S. Constitution. In this chapter, we examine the limitations imposed upon the criminal law by the Constitution.

Drafting, enacting, and enforcing criminal law involves action by government officials such as legislators, judges, police, and prosecutors. The content and the implementation of all criminal laws must be consistent with the federal Constitution and the constitution of the state in which the law is enacted and applied. Theoretically, neither the U.S. Congress nor state legislatures can enact laws that violate the Constitution; in reality, many laws are enacted that are later found to raise constitutional problems.

The Question of Constitutionality

Laws may be declared unconstitutional if they violate any of the following:

- Any dictate of the main body of the federal Constitution.
- Any federal constitutional amendments.
- Any provision of the constitution of the individual states.

Criminal statutes may be unconstitutional in either of two ways:

1. Because of their *content*, known as a violation "on its face."
2. Because of the way in which they are *enforced* by government officials, known as a violation "by application" or "as applied."

Any state or federal law that violates the Constitution is legally unenforceable and will be declared invalid. Any criminal conviction based on such a law will be reversed.

A state may provide protection for individuals within its borders that is greater than the protection provided by the U.S. Constitution. Situations involving greater state protection often arise with respect to criminal procedure law. For example:

- In the case of *United States v. Place* (1983), the U.S. Supreme Court ruled that dog sniffs are not searches and therefore need not be preceded by probable cause.[1] In 2005, the Supreme Court reaffirmed *Place* and held that "[a] dog sniff conducted during a concededly lawful traffic stop that reveals no information other than the location of a substance that no individual has any right to possess does not violate the Fourth Amendment."[2]
- In contrast, in the case of *Commonwealth v. Johnston*,[3] a Pennsylvania court declared that for the purpose of state prosecutions, dog sniffs are searches and can be conducted only if state or local police have probable cause to believe the person, place, or thing to be sniffed is connected to criminal action. Thus, in this case, the concept of a lawful search was defined more narrowly than in federal law.

Article III of the U.S. Constitution gives the power to determine the constitutionality and validity of a law. State courts determine the constitutionality of state laws and can also enforce federal constitutional principles in state cases. Federal courts decide the validity of state and federal laws that appear to violate the U.S. Constitution. In other words, the judiciary has the power to interpret, apply, or invalidate a law as it pertains to rights expressly created under the state or national constitution.

The U.S. Supreme Court has the final authority to interpret the federal Constitution. Cases reach the U.S. Supreme Court when at least four of the nine justices have elected to consider a certain case. In such instances, the Court grants a writ of *certiorari*, which is an order to the lower court to send the case forward for review.

The Bill of Rights

When the U.S. Constitution was first proposed, critics objected that it did not contain explicit protection of the rights of the people. On the basis of their experiences in England, critics of the Constitution were aware of ways that the government can abuse its authority. As a result, with issues of state sovereignty and individual liberty in mind, the first U.S. Congress adopted a set of 12 amendments to the Constitution defining the powers of the government and the rights of the people.

Bill of Rights

The first 10 amendments to the U.S. Constitution, especially those portions that guarantee fundamental individual rights vis-à-vis the government.

By 1791, the states had ratified 10 of these amendments, which became known as the **Bill of Rights**. The first eight amendments contain several guarantees of individual rights, including both procedural safeguards and a listing of specific individual liberties with which the government may not interfere without just cause. When originally adopted, the guarantees of the Bill of Rights protected the individual only against the federal government, not state government. The Supreme Court confirmed this in 1833,[4] and it remained that way until the 1960s.

With the enactment of the Fourteenth Amendment and subsequent decisions by the Supreme Court, the provisions of the Bill of Rights came to apply to the states as well. The only two exceptions are the Fifth Amendment's provision for prosecution of serious crimes only by indictment and the Eighth Amendment's ban on excessive bail.

> ◤ **CRITICAL THINKING 2.1**
>
> 1. How does the U.S. Constitution influence federal and state law?

2.2 Procedural Criminal Law

procedural criminal law

The rules governing how the criminal law is administered.

Procedural criminal law outlines the official mechanisms through which substantive criminal law is enforced. It sets forth the rules and laws to be followed from the investigative stage of a crime to the arrest, trial, and sentencing of the defendant.

The sources of procedural criminal law include Article I of the Constitution and the Fourth, Fifth, Sixth, and Fourteenth Amendments.

- The Fourth Amendment prohibits unreasonable searches and seizures.
- The Fifth Amendment provides due process protection, protects against double jeopardy and self-incrimination, and requires grand jury indictment in federal cases.

2.1 On the Job

Campus Police Officer

Description and Duties: Patrol campus to ensure safety and security of student population, which may involve hazardous and/or dangerous situations. Use tactful communication skills to interact effectively with a large and diverse constituency. Be physically capable of duty as a bicycle patrol officer. Demonstrate a strong customer service orientation, which includes presenting self in a professional manner.

Salary: Salaries range from approximately $25,000 to more than $40,000. Higher-range salaries often apply to those who have been promoted to sergeant or another supervisory role.

Other Information: Because many First Amendment issues—such as freedom of assembly, freedom of speech, and issues regarding locker searches—arise on campuses, campus police officers should have an understanding of constitutional rights. Like other police, campus police must be prepared to work overtime on short notice and to work regardless of weather conditions or other factors. In addition, they sometimes must work on holidays and at other nonstandard times.

SOURCE: Palomar College (California), http://www.palomar.edu; Arizona State University, http://www.asu.edu/hr/jobs.

- The Sixth Amendment establishes the right to counsel, the right to trial by an impartial jury, the right to a speedy and public trial, the right to confront opposing witnesses, the right to compel the attendance of witnesses favorable to the defendant, and the right to notice of the nature and cause of the accusation.
- The Fourteenth Amendment provides for due process and equal protection under the law.

Due Process and Equal Protection

As you can see, due process clauses appear in both the Fifth and Fourteenth Amendments to the U.S. Constitution. The Fifth Amendment states that no person shall be "deprived of life, liberty, or property, without due process of law." The Fourteenth Amendment provides that "no state shall deprive any person of life, liberty, or property, without due process or law. Over time, the courts have interpreted **due process** to encompass the multiple procedures and processes that must be followed before a person can be legally deprived of his or her life, liberty, or property.

The Fourteenth Amendment to the United States Constitution also provides that no state shall "deny to any person . . . the equal protection of the laws." A law that distinguishes between two classes of persons (e.g., men and women, wealthy and poor, minorities and nonminorities) is subject to attack if it does not provide **equal protection** to persons who should be treated equally with respect to the practice dealt with by the law.

For example, until the civil rights movement of the 1950s and 1960s, several states maintained laws that provided different rights for black and white residents under the "separate but equal doctrine" announced by the U.S. Supreme Court in the

due process
The multiple criminal justice procedures and processes that must be followed before a person can be legally deprived of his or her life, liberty, or property.

equal protection
The constitutional provision that all people should be treated equally with respect to the practice dealt with by the law.

1896 case *Plessy v. Ferguson*. Then, in *Loving v. Virginia* (1967), the Supreme Court struck down a Virginia statute that criminalized interracial marriage, relying on the equal protection clause. Similarly, in *Craig v. Boren* (1976), the Court declared invalid on equal protection grounds an Oklahoma law that prohibited the sale of beer to females under the age of 18 and males under the age of 21.[5]

Today, all laws that make a distinction between persons based on race, ethnicity, gender, religion, sexual orientation, or national origin are subject to constitutional scrutiny, even when they are designed to rectify past discrimination.

Search and Seizure

The Fourth Amendment to the U.S. Constitution prohibits "unreasonable searches and seizures" of "persons, houses, papers, and effects" and states that "no warrants shall issue, but upon probable cause." This amendment is often said to guarantee a right of privacy and is the major source of much of the procedural criminal law dealing with law enforcement activities in crime investigation. Constitutional restrictions on searches, seizures, and detention of persons suspected of and charged with violations of the criminal law are governed by principles stemming from this amendment.

Bills of Attainder and *Ex Post Facto* Laws

As we saw in the discussion of the principle of legality in Chapter 1, conduct cannot be punished retroactively. Consistent with this principle, the U.S. Constitution prohibits legislatures from enacting bills of attainder and *ex post facto* laws.

A **bill of attainder** is a legislative enactment that declares individuals or members of a group guilty of a crime and subject to punishment without trial. If an act imposes capital punishment on those supposed to be guilty of important crimes such as treason or felony, it is a bill of attainder. If it inflicts as lesser punishment, it is called a "bill of pains and penalties." Such laws are prohibited by Article I, Section 9 of the Constitution.

An *ex post facto* **law** is one that:

- Makes criminal an act done before passage of the law and punishes such action.
- Aggravates a crime, making it more serious than it had been when it was committed.
- Inflicts a greater punishment than the law imposed when the crime was committed or alters the legal rules of evidence, allowing evidence of guilt that is lesser or different from what the law required at the time the offense was committed (see Application Case 2.1).[6]

bill of attainder

A special legislative enactment that declares a person or group of persons guilty of a crime and subject to punishment without trial.

ex post facto law

A law that (1) makes criminal an act done before passage of the law against it, and punishes such action; (2) aggravates a crime, or makes it greater than it was when committed; or (3) inflicts a greater punishment than the law imposed or allows evidence of guilt that is less than what the law required at the time the offense was committed.

⚖️ Application Case 2.1

Carmell v. Texas

In *Carmell v. Texas* (1996), the court held that altering the rules of evidence in a trial for offenses that were committed before the effective date of the amendment was a violation of the prohibition against *ex post facto* laws. In 1996, the defendant was convicted of 15 counts of committing sexual offenses against his stepdaughter during a period from 1991 to 1995, when the victim was 12 to 16 years old. Under the Texas Criminal Code, a victim's testimony about a sexual offense could not support a conviction unless there was corroborating evidence or the victim informed another person of the offense within six months of the act. However, under a 1993 amendment to this law, the victim's testimony alone could support a conviction if the victim was under 14 at the time of the offense.

The defendant argued that the convictions for those offenses committed before the victim reached the age of 14 in July 1992 should be reversed, on the grounds that they were based solely on her testimony and there was no corroborating evidence. In agreement, the court was forced to hold that retroactive application of the 1993 amendment violated the federal constitutional prohibition against *ex post facto* laws.

SOURCE: Carmell v. Texas, 529 U.S. 513 (2000).

For example, although the courts have generally denied their claims, many previously convicted sex offenders argue that new state laws requiring them to register with the local police, who can then notify the community of their presence, amount to *ex post facto* punishment, because such requirements did not exist at the time that they pled or were found guilty. They also claim that such requirements continue to punish them even though they have already served their sentences. With few exceptions, the courts have rejected these claims, holding that the requirements of registration and community notification are not punishments but regulatory measures aimed at protecting the public.

Fair Notice and Vagueness

The due process clauses of the Fifth and Fourteenth Amendments require that the law provide **fair notice**. The right to "fair notice" means that the law must clearly define the precise conduct that is prohibited. Thus, statutes that are written ambiguously or in which the words are vague (subject to different interpretations by different people) also violate the constitutional requirement of due process (see Application Case 2.2).

fair notice

The due process requirement that people are entitled to know what they are forbidden to do so that they may shape their conduct accordingly.

2.1 Web Exploration

American Bar Association

Visit the American Bar Association's Web site at http://www.abanet.org, and explore "Legal Education" and "Public Resources." What services does the ABA provide for those who are not attorneys? What did you learn from visiting this site?

⚖️ Application Case 2.2

People v. Maness

In *People v. Maness* (2000), the Illinois Supreme Court affirmed a trial court's invalidation of a state statute. The defendant was charged with permitting the sexual abuse of a child, an offense created by the Wrongs to Children Act of 1992. The act provided that a parent or stepparent who "knowingly allows an act of criminal sexual abuse or criminal sexual assault on his or her minor child and fails to take reasonable steps to prevent its commission or future occurrences of such acts commits the offense of permitting the sexual abuse of a child."

The defendant's 13-year-old daughter was dating and having intercourse with a 17-year-old male. During the relationship, the defendant learned of the sexual conduct between her daughter and Owens; although she disapproved of it, she obtained birth control for her daughter and allowed Owens to spend the night at their home.

In a report from the Department of Children and Family Services, the defendant stated that she did not know what steps to take to prevent the sexual relationship her daughter was having with Owens. The defendant argued that the statute was unconstitutionally vague because it failed to define "reasonable steps" to prevent future acts of sexual abuse. The court agreed with the defendant, in that the statute is unconstitutionally vague if its terms are so indefinite that people of common intelligence must guess at its meaning. In addition, the court held that a statute must adequately define the offense in order to prevent its arbitrary and discriminatory enforcement, and it must provide explicit standards to regulate the discretion of governmental authorities.

SOURCE: People v. Maness, 732 N.E.2d 545 (Ill. 2000).

Under the due process clause of the Fourteenth Amendment, criminal statutes cannot be vague, ambiguous, or overly broad. Criminal statutes lacking clarity violate the fair notice requirement that people are entitled to know what they are forbidden to do so that they may shape their conduct accordingly. In addition, criminal statutes lacking in clarity are susceptible to enforcement in an arbitrary or discriminatory manner by the police, prosecutors, judges, and juries.[7]

An example of a statute found to be unconstitutionally vague and therefore invalid is a Jacksonville, Florida, city ordinance that prohibited various forms of vagrancy.[8] Other statues that have been found unconstitutionally vague include:

- One that punished a person who "publicly treats contemptuously the flag of the United States."
- An ordinance stating that "no person shall loiter . . . in or upon any street, park or public place, or in any public building," with no definition of the term "loiter."
- A harassment statute prohibiting conduct that "alarms or seriously annoys" another person.

All of the preceding statutes were also invalidated because they were overly broad, meaning that they could result in the punishment of individuals for engaging in conduct that is constitutionally protected. In short, as the Supreme Court held in the case of *Kolender v. Lawson*, "the void-for-vagueness doctrine requires that a penal statute define the criminal offense with sufficient definiteness that ordinary people can understand what conduct is prohibited and in a manner that does not encourage arbitrary and discriminatory enforcement.[9] In *Kolender*, Edward Lawson was detained or arrested on 15 occasions between March 1975 and January 1977 for violations of Cal. Penal Code § 647(e), which provided that "Every person who commits any of the following acts is guilty of disorderly conduct, a misdemeanor: . . . (e) Who loiters or wanders upon the streets or from place to place without apparent reason or business and who refuses to identify himself and to account for his presence when requested by any peace officer to do so, if the surrounding circumstances are such as to indicate to a reasonable man that the public safety demands such identification."

One police officer had apparently "stopped Lawson while walking on an otherwise vacant street because it was late at night, the area was isolated, and the area was located close to a high crime area." Another officer had "detained Lawson, who was walking at a late hour in a business area where some businesses were still open, and asked for identification because burglaries had been committed by unknown persons in the general area." Lawson was prosecuted twice and convicted once.

The U.S. Supreme Court held that "the statute was unconstitutionally vague by failing to clarify what was contemplated by the requirement that a suspect provide a 'credible and reliable' identification." The statute gave the police sole discretion to "determine whether the suspect has satisfied the statute and must be permitted to go on his way in the absence of probable cause to arrest." This violated the Fourth Amendment because while police may ask their questions in a way calculated to

Vagueness and Overbreadth in the Law Certain laws, such as those outlawing vagrancy, are overly vague and do not offer any specific guidelines for their enforcement. Therefore, they can be overly used or discriminatorily used.

obtain an answer, they may not force an answer from anyone, and the person must be allowed "to leave after a reasonably brief period of time unless the information they have acquired during the encounter has given them probable cause sufficient to justify an arrest." (See Application Case 2.3.)

⚖️ Application Case 2.3
City of Chicago v. Morales

In *City of Chicago v. Morales* (1999), in response to an increase in gang-related murders that also intimidated law-abiding citizens, Chicago enacted an ordinance that criminalized loitering. In sum, the Anti-Gang Loitering Ordinance stated that if "a police officer observes a person whom he reasonably believes to be a criminal street gang member loitering in any public place with one or more other persons, he shall order all such persons to disperse and remove themselves from the area. Any person who does not promptly obey such an order is in violation of this section."

Over a three-year period following enactment of the statute, 89,000 dispersal orders were given and 42,000 people were arrested. In *Morales*, each defendant was alleged to have been in the presence of a gang member, and each was arrested when he failed to disperse as directed by the police. The Court of Appeals held that the ordinance was unconstitutional because it violated freedom of association, congregation, and expression protected by the First Amendment.

In addition, the court held that the ordinance was unconstitutionally vague under the Illinois Constitution, which ensures the right to assemble in a peaceful manner. The court also stated that since the statute was intended to address the behavior of gang members but an innocent bystander could also be convicted, the statute failed to specify a standard of conduct and failed to provide minimal guidance to limit the discretion given to police officers to enforce the law.

SOURCE: City of Chicago v. Morales, 527 U.S. 41 (1999).

 CRITICAL THINKING 2.2

1. Why are *ex post facto* laws considered unconstitutional? Do you agree? Why or why not?

2. How do due process and equal protection protect people's rights?

2.3 Substantive Criminal Law and Individual Due Process Rights

substantive criminal law
The law defining acts that are criminal.

Substantive criminal law defines criminal conduct and prescribes the punishment to be imposed for such conduct. For example, the homicide section of a state's criminal code defines the elements of the offense of murder and states the punishment that can be imposed for the offense. Government power to define

---

F I G U R E   2 . 1

Liberties Granted by the Bill of Rights

First Amendment
Free speech
Free exercise of religion
Freedom of assembly

Second Amendment
Right to bear arms

Fourth Amendment
Freedom from unreasonable searches and
seizures

Fifth Amendment
Grand jury indictment in felony cases
No double jeopardy
No compelled self-incrimination

Sixth Amendment
Speedy and public trial
Impartial jury of the state and district where
crime occurred
Notice of nature and cause of accusation
Confront opposing witnesses
Compulsory process for obtaining favorable
witnesses
Right to counsel

Eighth Amendment
No excessive bail and fines
Prohibition of "cruel and unusual punishment"

---

criminal conduct is limited by certain individual liberties guaranteed in the Bill of Rights.

The individual liberties, or substantive rights, specifically enumerated and expressly guaranteed within the Bill of Rights (see Figure 2.1) include:

- Freedom of religion, speech, and assembly.
- The right to bring grievances against the government.
- The right to keep and bear arms.
- Protection against cruel and unusual punishment.

In addition, the right to personal privacy is derived from the right to be protected from unreasonable searches and seizures.

These rights affect the ability of both federal and state authorities to prohibit and punish individual conduct that falls within the protection of the Bill of Rights. This means that no state or federal agency can legally enact or enforce criminal statutes that unnecessarily inhibit the substantive rights identified in the amendments. Criminal statutes may run afoul of the specific dictates of the First or Second Amendment or the somewhat broader prohibitions in the Eighth Amendment, or they may interfere with the general exercise of liberty mentioned in both the Fifth and Fourteenth Amendments.

First Amendment Rights

The First Amendment provides that Congress shall make no law prohibiting the free exercise of religion or abridging the rights of free speech and peaceable assembly. Those guarantees of free exercise of religion, freedom of speech, and freedom of assembly are among the most protected rights. Freedom of religion and speech are sometimes grouped together as "freedom of expression."

Free Speech

In general, Americans can say what they like and are free to criticize the government without fear of punishment. However, the guarantee of free speech is not absolute. In order to protect the public, government can regulate certain kinds of speech. Such restrictions must be evaluated by the courts in light of the government's responsibility to meet the public's interest, as well as the individual's First Amendment guarantee of free speech.

clear and present danger test

A test to determine whether a defendant's words pose an immediate danger of bringing about substantive evils that Congress has the right (and duty) to prevent.

One of those limiting principles is the **clear and present danger test**. Justice Oliver Wendell Holmes expressed the test in memorable terms, in the 1919 case of *Schenck v. United States*:

> The most stringent protection of free speech would not protect a man in falsely shouting fire in a theater and causing a panic. It does not even protect a man from an injunction against uttering words that may have all the effect of force. The question in every case is whether the words used are used in such circumstances and are of such a nature as to create a clear and present danger that they will bring about the substantive evils that Congress has the right (and duty) to prevent. It is a question of proximity and degree. When a nation is at war many things that might be said in time of peace are such a hindrance to the war effort that their utterance will not be endured so long as men fight and . . . no Court could regard them as protected by any constitutional right.[10]

In the case from which the quote is taken, the defendant was convicted of interfering with the draft during wartime and of urging insubordination in the military. Justice Holmes's language suggests that the advocacy of unlawful conduct can be limited in order to protect public welfare. However, not every urging to violate the law satisfies the clear and present danger test, which was redefined by the Supreme Court to require advocacy of "imminent lawless action."[11] Given this redefinition, it is unlikely that the conduct and speech in the very case in which Justice Holmes announced the clear and present danger test would be considered criminal by the Supreme Court today.

Fighting words are another subcategory of unprotected speech that poses a clear and present danger. The Supreme Court has defined "fighting words" as "those which by their very utterance inflict injury or tend to incite an immediate breach of the peace."[12] Such speech threatens public peace or order by being so provocative that it is likely to induce a violent reaction.

Other areas of potentially unprotected speech include hate speech, profanity, libelous utterances, and obscenity. (Obscenity is discussed more fully in Chapter 13.) Questions relating to these types of speech present complex questions of balancing that yield no clear rule for determining how far the government may go to regulate such speech, if at all. For example, in *R.A.V. v. St. Paul*, the U.S. Supreme Court held unconstitutional a city ordinance banning the burning of a cross and the display of symbols such as swastikas.[13] Finally, with the advent of the Internet and other modern technologies, courts have been faced with new challenges to the First Amendment, and they have been evaluating statutes seeking to regulate the information transmitted in cyberspace. (See Application Case 2.4.)

⚖️ Application Case 2.4

Hatch v. Superior Court

In *Hatch v. Superior Court* (2000), the defendant was convicted pursuant to the California Penal Code for using the Internet to send harmful matter to a minor in an attempt to seduce her. In *Hatch*, Fox Television hired 20-year-old Jennifer Hersey to pose as a 13-year-old girl involved in Internet chats with persons interested in having sexual encounters with underaged girls.

The defendant made contact with Hersey, then engaged in a series of communications wherein she posed as girls named "Stacie" and "Lisa." He also sent Hersey pictures of nude girls and of young girls having sex with men. The defendant then attempted to arrange meetings for sexual encounters, and discussed via e-mail his plans to have sex with "Stacie" and "Lisa." Hersey agreed to meet the defendant at a hotel, and also forwarded her communication with the defendant to the police. The defendant was then convicted of attempting to seduce a minor by means of the Internet.

The defendant argued that the statute violated his First Amendment rights, but the Court of Appeals held that such communication did not enjoy First Amendment privileges. In addition, the statute was not seeking to prohibit forum communication (such as in chat rooms), but only adults seeking to seduce a child. Finally, the court stated that the statute is directed more toward an activity or conduct than toward communication.

SOURCE: Hatch v. Superior Court, 94 Cal. Rptr. 2d 453 (Cal. Ct. App. 2000).

The notion that the government has the power and obligation to provide for the common defense and promote the welfare of the general public by enacting laws is expressly written into the federal Constitution. Still, this concern for society as a whole must be addressed while also recognizing the rights of individuals. Under what has come to be known as the "police powers," federal, state, and local governments may enact laws and authorize enforcement activities that regulate the time, place, and manner in which an individual can exercise constitutionally protected rights, but these rights cannot be completely taken away or banned in the interest of the general public. They are balanced against the potential harm that might be caused to others in society.

Free Exercise of Religion

American courts will invalidate criminal statutes that are viewed as thinly veiled attempts to restrict the freedom of religion. For example:

- The U.S. Supreme Court struck down a state statute criminalizing door-to-door solicitation for religious purposes without prior approval from state officials, when the statute was used to prohibit Jehovah's Witnesses from their religious conduct.
- The Court also struck down an ordinance of the City of Hialeah, Florida, banning ritualistic animal sacrifice, which was aimed at a particular religion's practice.[14]

On the other hand, religious freedom claims have been rejected in upholding criminal convictions for:

- Polygamy.
- A Christian Scientist parent's withholding medical treatment for a child.
- The handling of poisonous snakes in religious ceremonies.
- The use of peyote as part of a religious practice.[15]

Clearly, not all claims based on the free exercise of religion will exempt a defendant from criminal liability. (See Chapter 14 for discussion of legislation on the use of peyote.)

Freedom of Assembly

The right of the people to assemble publicly is not absolute. Because public assembly may threaten public safety, peace, and order, the government has the right to impose reasonable restrictions on the time, place, and manner of assembly. In addition, specific statutes curtail the right to assemble under specific circumstances. For example, the Freedom of Access to Clinic Entrances Act (FACE), criminalizes "physical obstruction, intentionally . . . interfer[ing] with or attempt[ing] to . . . interfere with any person" who is or has been "obtaining or providing reproductive health services." In other words, although individuals can demonstrate in front of an abortion clinic, they cannot physically prevent individuals from going into the clinic.

Freedom of Assembly The First Amendment protects all Americans' rights to assemble peaceably to protest social or governmental wrongs.

State statutes that prohibit loitering also affect the right to assemble. Anti-loitering statutes have always been part of the United States criminal legal system. However, these laws are subject to scrutiny by the courts and may be unconstitutional if they are found to be vague. The statutes must also reasonably promote identifiable public interests in order to justify the interference with individual liberty.

Second Amendment Rights

The right to keep and bear arms provided in the Second Amendment is not absolute and has been the source of much litigation in recent years. While various organizations such as the National Rifle Association (NRA) contend that the right to bear arms is an individual one, the U.S. Supreme Court has held that this provision must be read in conjunction with the other, less-known clause of the Second Amendment, which requires a "well regulated militia." In 2008 the Supreme Court was considering a case that for the first time in U.S. history may decide the meaning of the right to bear arms.

Typical federal and state gun control statutes impose licensing requirements such as background checks and waiting periods; restrict carrying, concealing, and purchasing firearms; and prohibit firearm ownership by convicted felons. Under the Brady Bill, criminal offenses committed with a firearm carry more severe penalties than those committed without one.[16]

Eighth Amendment Rights

The Eighth Amendment to the U.S. Constitution prohibits the infliction of "cruel and unusual punishments." The Supreme Court has interpreted the Eighth Amendment requirement of **proportionality** to mean that the punishment inflicted for a criminal violation should not be grossly disproportionate to the crime committed. This proportionality requirement affects:

- The grading of offenses.
- The imposition of the death penalty.
- The assessment of the validity of terms of imprisonment.

proportionality

The constitutional principle that the punishment should fit the crime, expressed in the Eighth Amendment's cruel and unusual punishment clause.

Noncapital Cases

In the area of disproportionate sentences in noncapital cases, the Supreme Court's jurisprudence has not been a model of clarity. For example:

- In one case, a defendant with two previous convictions for theft was sentenced to life imprisonment for obtaining a check for $120.75 under false pretenses and cashing it. The Supreme Court upheld the defendant's sentence.
- In another case three years later, a defendant with seven prior felony convictions was sentenced to life imprisonment for a check-cashing violation. The Court held that this sentence was invalid.[17]

Why did this disparity occur? In the first case, the state had a liberal parole policy; in the second case, the defendant had been sentenced to life without the possibility of parole. The Court distinguished the two cases on those grounds.

Finally, in a third case, a defendant was sentenced to life imprisonment without the possibility of parole for a first-offense possession of 672 grams of cocaine.

The Supreme Court upheld the sentence, concluding that the sentence did not violate the Eighth Amendment.[18] The decision in all three cases was by a vote of 5–4. Because of this, proportionality is still an unresolved issue that can lead to controversial decisions.

Capital Cases

Whether the death penalty itself constitutes cruel and unusual punishment is another area of disagreement among Supreme Court justices, legislators, and citizens in general. The death penalty has been used since the early years of the nation—for example, in the Salem witch trials. The U.S. Supreme Court has placed limits on the circumstances under which the death penalty may be imposed under the Eighth Amendment.

- In *Coker v. Georgia* (1977),[19] the Court held that death was an excessive penalty for the rape of an adult woman.
- In *Edmund v. Florida* (1982),[20] the Court struck down the death penalty for unintentional killings.
- In *Thompson v. Oklahoma*,[21] the Court ruled that the death penalty cannot be imposed on a defendant who was less than 16 years old at the time of the offense.
- In 2002, in *Atkins v. Virginia*,[22] the Court held that execution of a mentally handicapped person categorically violated the Eighth Amendment.
- In 2005, in *Roper v. Simmons*,[23] the Court found that the execution of minors under the age of 18 constituted cruel and unusual punishment.

Furman v. Georgia

In the 1972 case of *Furman v. Georgia*,[24] the U.S. Supreme Court examined the imposition of the death penalty in three cases. Each of the three petitioners had been convicted in a state court and sentenced to death after a jury trial in which the jury had the discretion to determine whether to impose the death penalty. The Supreme Court analyzed in detail the constitutional issues raised by capital punishment.

In this landmark 5–4 decision, each of the nine justices wrote a separate opinion. The five justices in the majority believed that the death penalty was cruel and unusual because it was being implemented in a manner that discriminated against the poor and minorities. However, only three (Justices Brennan, Marshall, and Douglas) held that capital punishment was in itself cruel and unusual. The effect of this decision was an informal moratorium on the death penalty until the Court's five decisions in 1976,[25] reviewing the death penalty statutes enacted by a number of states in response to *Furman*. The Court approved three of the newly enacted statutes and there followed, in 1977, the execution by firing squad in Utah of Gary Gilmore.

In subsequent years, the Court issued a number of decisions that established the constitutionality of the death penalty under appropriate state and federal statutory provisions, and executions in the United States have continued to the present. Continuing concerns about the inequity in imposition of the death penalty and about the execution of innocent persons have fueled the national debate about the wisdom of the death penalty.[26]

2.2 Web Exploration

Constitutional Law at Findlaw.com

Visit Findlaw.com's section on constitutional law at http://supreme.lp.findlaw.com. Read the current articles on the front page, then write a half-page report explaining the breadth of issues you read about and how they are covered under constitutional law. Don't forget to include the amendments to which these issues pertain.

The Right to Privacy

Although the Constitution does not expressly mention a right of privacy, the U.S. Supreme Court has held that it is implied by the following constitutional provisions:

- The First Amendment right of free association.
- The Third Amendment dealing with the quartering of soldiers in private homes.
- The Fourth Amendment ban on unreasonable searches and seizures.

The right of privacy includes the right to be let alone, the right to be free from unwanted publicity, and the right to live without unwarranted interference. For example, the Court has recognized, within the concept of personal privacy, a person's right to decide "whether to bear or beget a child."[27] In various cases, the Court has held that government cannot interfere by statutory proscription with the availability of contraceptives and contraceptive devices for single or married persons.[28]

Abortion Rights

Another area of privacy relating to childbirth is the right of a woman to choose to terminate her pregnancy through abortion. In 1973, in *Roe v. Wade*,[29] the Supreme Court held that the right of privacy extended to protect a woman's right to abortion, and it invalidated the anti-abortion statute involved in that case. The Court reaffirmed this position on abortion in 1992, in the case of *Planned Parenthood v. Casey*,[30] but allowed the states to regulate and place restrictions on abortions so long as those regulations do not impose an undue burden on the woman's ability to make the abortion decision.

Consensual Sodomy

Interpersonal sexual conduct has also been recognized as an area protected by the right of privacy. For example, the Court has held that the right to privacy protects a right to engage in private consensual homosexual activity. In *Lawrence v. Texas*,[31] a state law made it a crime for two persons of the same sex to engage in certain intimate sexual conduct. The Court found that the law sought to control the lives of homosexual persons, the parties were consenting adults, the conduct was private, and the parties were entitled to privacy. The Court also noted that the reasoning and holding of its prior decision in *Bowers v. Hardwick*,[32] in which the Court refused to prevent a state from punishing homosexual acts committed by adults in private, had been rejected in other nations, and there was no showing that the governmental interest in the United States was more legitimate than the individual's privacy interest.

▲ C R I T I C A L   T H I N K I N G   2 . 3

1. Which Amendment of the Bill of Rights do you feel is most important to one's fundamental rights? Why?
2. Why is the right to privacy controversial in American society?

REVIEW AND APPLICATIONS

Summary by Chapter Objectives

1. **Identify who determines whether a legislative enactment violates a constitutional prohibition.** Both state and federal courts determine whether a legislative enactment violates a constitutional prohibition, but in different capacities. State courts can enforce both federal constitutional principles and state constitutional principles in state cases. Federal courts can enforce federal constitutional principles, which are principles relating to the U.S. Constitution.

2. **List those areas of the Constitution that limit criminal law enactments.** Constitutional subjects relating to the substantive criminal law include:
   - The principle of legality (which includes the prohibition of bills of attainder and *ex post facto* laws).
   - A number of rights specifically enumerated in the Bill of Rights, including freedom of religion, speech, and assembly, the right to keep and bear arms, due process, and the prohibition against cruel and unusual punishment.
   - The right of privacy, and equal protection of the law.

3. **Identify the one crime defined in the U.S. Constitution.** The only crime defined in the U.S. Constitution is treason.

4. **List those provisions of the Bill of Rights that limit the government's ability to prohibit and punish crimes.** The rights enumerated in the Bill of Rights that specifically limit the government's ability to prohibit and punish crimes are:
   - Freedom of religion, speech, and assembly, as protected by the First Amendment.
   - The right to keep and bear arms, as protected by the Second Amendment.
   - The Fifth Amendment's due process clause, as it relates to the vagueness or overreaching qualities of a criminal statute.
   - The Eighth Amendment's ban on cruel and unusual punishment, especially as it relates to the death penalty.

5. **State three categories of unprotected speech.** Three categories of unprotected speech are:
   - Speech that violates the clear and present danger test.
   - Speech advocating unlawful conduct.
   - Fighting words.

6. **Name three areas of personal privacy protected by the U.S. Constitution as it affects crimes.** Three areas of personal privacy that may be protected by the Constitution from statutory interference by the government are the availability of contraceptives and contraceptive devices for single or married persons, the right of a woman to chose to terminate her pregnancy through abortion, and private consensual sexual activity.

Key Terms

Bill of Rights (p. 36)
procedural criminal law (p. 36)
due process (p. 37)
equal protection (p. 37)
bill of attainder (p. 38)

ex post facto law (p. 38)
fair notice (p. 39)
substantive criminal law (p. 42)
clear and present danger test (p. 44)
proportionality (p. 47)

Review Questions

1. What is the difference between substantive and procedural criminal law?
2. Name at least five constitutional subjects relating to procedural criminal law.
3. Name the three possible definitions of an *ex post facto* law.
4. What are two possible problems that can arise from vague criminal statutes?
5. Define the due process clause of the Fourteenth Amendment, and explain its relevance to criminal law.
6. Name some examples of limitations on the First Amendment, as applied by the courts.
7. What are fighting words? How do these legally differ from hate speech or profanity?
8. What does the Eighth Amendment address, and how is this applied to criminal justice?
9. How does proportionality affect the grading of offenses?
10. Explain what "equal protection under the law" means and how it applies in criminal law.

Problem-Solving Exercises

1. **Juvenile Rights** You are a police officer working in the city. You see a group of youths on the corner of a busy intersection in the downtown area. They are standing around talking. You suspect they are involved in a drug transaction, because you recognize one of them as a member of a drug ring. What constitutional rights does the youth you recognize have that might prohibit you from taking any police action against him at this time?
2. **False Alarm** At a college football game, someone makes a loud noise like a banging gun and yells, "He has a gun!" In response, spectators in the immediate area panic and begin running for the exit. Six people are trampled, and two are seriously injured. During the investigation, campus police learn that nobody

had a gun; the panic was the result of two young men playing a practical joke. Answer the following questions:
   a. Which test would you apply to determine if this speech was protected by the First Amendment?
   b. What if someone either made the gunshot sound or only shouted, "He has a gun!" but it produced the same result? Would this be protected?
   c. What other factors would you consider as you write your report for this case? What, if anything, would you recommend to your prosecutor?
3. **Anti-Loitering Ordinance** Your city has passed an anti-loitering ordinance, and you are a prosecutor who must deal with the arrests that result from enforcement of this law. Recently, local police have started arresting teenagers who seem rather scruffy and aggressive, but who have no apparent drug or gang involvement. The defendants were loitering around a local strip mall that has had numerous drug activities but is also a popular hangout. Their arrests were legal under the current city ordinance.
   a. Is this ordinance constitutional or not? Why?
   b. How will you handle this case?

Workplace Applications

1. **Incitement to Riot** It is a hot night, and you are among a group of officers called into an inner-city neighborhood in response to a disturbance. When you arrive at the scene, you discover a group of angry citizens facing a line of officers who are struggling to hold them back. One very angry citizen is yelling above the crowd, urging the others to attack the police. Some of his comments are very violent and very specific, and he appears to be making the crowd even angrier. Answer the following questions:
   a. Is this man violating any laws? If so, what are they?
   b. Can you arrest this citizen without violating his constitutional rights? Why or why not?
   c. If he succeeds in inciting others to riot, do you think that there are any additional charges for which he may be liable? Why or why not?
2. **The Bill of Rights** Interview three or four friends (not in this class) and ask them to name 7 of the 10 Amendments in the Bill of Rights. Tally the results, then answer the following questions:
   a. Did they seem to have a fairly complete understanding of the Bill of Rights? Why or why not?
   b. Were you surprised by the results? Why or why not?
   c. What do your survey results say about the average American's understanding of the Bill of Rights? How can this affect people when they are unexpectedly caught up in the criminal justice system?
3. **Illegal Assembly** You are a judge hearing a case regarding an illegal assembly on a state university campus. The defendants, who are mainly students, state that they were denied a permit to protest for political reasons, and thus were deprived of their First Amendment rights to peaceful assembly; university officials, they claim, held back from issuing the permit so that they would have an excuse to

arrest them. You examine the relevant statutes and find that your state has a 1908 statute that requires student assemblies to have at least one "monitor or chaperone." In addition, the statute requires that the school approve all student activities.

a. Will you strike down this law, or apply it? Why?

b. If you apply it, in whose favor will you decide?

Ethics Exercises

1. **Ethnicity and the Law** You are a police investigator working in an ethnically diverse community. Over time, you confirm that young men from one ethnic group are most often involved in the criminal conduct that you investigate. You also notice that many of your colleagues make assumptions about the criminal behavior of all young men in that ethnic group. Answer the following questions:

   a. Is there anything improper in the way in which your colleagues take into account the ethnicity of a suspect when observing or investigating criminal activities? Why or why not?

   b. What can you do to make sure that your behavior is within constitutional limits?

   c. What can you do to influence or change your colleagues' behavior? What are some possible problems that may occur if they do not change?

   d. What other constitutional concerns might you have regarding this behavior?

2. **Domestic Violence** You are the mayor of a medium-sized city, which has an ordinance that requires arrest in domestic violence cases that "show evidence of physical injury." Unfortunately, the ordinance does not define physical injury. Most officers interpret this to mean any sign of physical injury, such as a black eye or bruised arm, but some officers choose to interpret it to mean only serious injuries such as fractures. As a result, some cases are ignored, and you have heard rumors that some victims are considering a civil lawsuit against the police department.

   a. What can be done to remedy this problem?

   b. What additional efforts should you make with the police and to the public?

Notes

1. United States v. Place, 462 U.S. 696 (1983).
2. Illinois v. Caballes, 543 U.S. 405, 410 (2005).
3. Commonwealth v. Johnston, 530 A.2d 74 (Pa. 1987).
4. Barron v. Baltimore, 32 U.S. (7 Pet.) 243 (1833).
5. Loving v. Virginia, 388 U.S. 1 (1967); Craig v. Boren, 429 U.S. 190 (1976); Plessey v. Ferguson, 163 U.S. 537 (1896).
6. See Calder v. Bull, 3 U.S. (3 Dall.) 386, 390 (1798), as quoted in JOSHUA DRESSLER, UNDERSTANDING CRIMINAL LAW § 50.1[C][1], at 30 n.3 (4th ed. 2006).
7. HERBERT L. PACKER, THE LIMITS OF THE CRIMINAL SANCTION 80 n.5 (1968); JOSHUA DRESSLER, UNDERSTANDING CRIMINAL LAW § 5.03, at 47 (4th ed. 2006).

8. Papachristou v. Jacksonville, 405 U.S. 156 (1972).
9. Kolender v. Lawson, 461 U.S. 352, 357 (1983).
10. Schenck v. United States, 249 U.S. 47, 51–52 (1919).
11. Brandenburg v. Ohio, 395 U.S. 444, 447 (1969).
12. Chaplinsky v. New Hampshire, 315 U.S. 568, 572 (1942).
13. R.A.V. v. St. Paul, 505 U.S. 377 (1992).
14. Cantwell v. Connecticut, 310 U.S. 296 (1940); Church of the Lukumi Babula Aye, Inc. v. City of Hialeah, 508 U.S. 520 (1993).
15. Reynolds v. United States, 98 U.S. (8 Otto) 145 (1878); Walker v. Superior Court, 763 P.2d 852 (Cal. 1988); Harden v. State, 216 S.W.2d 708 (Tenn. 1949); Employment Division v. Smith, 494 U.S. 872 (1990).
16. 18 U.S.C. § 924 (c)(a)(A) (2000).
17. Joshua Dressler, Understanding Criminal Law § 6.05[C], at 62–65 (4th ed. 2006) (citing Rummel v. Estelle, 445 U.S. 263 (1980); Solem v. Helm, 463 U.S. 277 (1983)).
18. Harmelin v. Michigan, 501 U.S. 957 (1991).
19. Coker v. Georgia, 433 U.S. 584 (1977).
20. Edmund v. Florida, 458 U.S. 782 (1982).
21. Thompson v. Oklahoma, 487 U.S. 815 (1988).
22. Atkins v. Virginia, 536 U.S. 304 (2002).
23. Roper v. Simmons, 543 U.S. 551 (2005).
24. Furman v. Georgia, 408 U.S. 238 (1972).
25. For a review of the post-Furman history of the death penalty, see Carol S. Steiker, *Capital Punishment: Legal Aspects,* in Encyclopedia of Crime and Justice 121–22 (Joshua Dressler ed., 2d ed. 2002).
26. For a review of the pros and cons of the debate, see Greta Proctor, *Reevaluating Capital Punishment: The Fallacy of a Foolproof System, the Focus on Reform, and the International Factor,* 42 Gonz. L. Rev. 211 (2007).
27. Eisenstadt v. Baird, 405 U.S. 438, 453 (1972).
28. *Id.;* Griswold v. Connecticut, 381 U.S. 479 (1965).
29. Roe v. Wade, 410 U.S. 113 (1973).
30. Planned Parenthood of Southeastern Pennsylvania v. Casey, 505 U.S. 833 (1992).
31. Lawrence v. Texas, 539 U.S. 558 (2003).
32. Bowers v. Hardwick, 478 U.S. 186 (1986).

Classification of Crimes and Basic Elements of Criminal Responsibility

CHAPTER OBJECTIVES

After reading and studying this chapter, you should be able to:

1. Differentiate criminal, tort, and moral responsibility.
2. Explain the difference between felonies, misdemeanors, and petty offenses.
3. Describe the requirement of a physical act (*actus reus*).
4. Understand the concept of a voluntary, willed act.
5. Explain the difference between thinking about committing an act and acting on the thought.
6. Describe the circumstances under which an omission constitutes an act for purposes of criminal responsibility.
7. Explain when words alone can constitute a criminal act.
8. State when possession can be a criminal act.
9. Understand and define the requirement of *mens rea* (guilty mind).
10. Distinguish between specific intent and general intent crimes.
11. Explain the doctrine of transferred intent.
12. Distinguish between the MPC's definitions of acting purposely and acting knowingly.
13. Understand the difference between acting recklessly and acting negligently under the MPC.
14. Distinguish cause-in-fact from the proximate cause of a crime.
15. Explain how a concurrence of events is needed for a crime to occur.

3.1 Classification of Crimes

The classification of specific conduct as criminal has significance for two reasons. First, only crimes can result in loss of liberty through incarceration; civil offenses, in contrast, may result in punitive damages but not incarceration. Also, in the United States, the U.S. Constitution and the constitutions of individual states require that special rights and protections be afforded to those accused of crimes. Relevant portions of the Bill of Rights, as we have seen, include the following:

- The Fifth Amendment's protection against self-incrimination and double jeopardy, and right to a grand jury indictment.
- The Sixth Amendment's rights to a speedy and public trial, trial by jury, confrontation and cross-examination of witnesses, and counsel.
- The Eighth Amendment's protection against excessive bail, excessive fines, and cruel and unusual punishment.
- The Fourteenth Amendment's right to due process of law, which means that the federal government must grant all of the aforementioned rights to every defendant, and state governments must grant most of them.

In short, criminal defendants have many more protections than do those accused of civil or moral wrongs, because criminal defendants have considerably more to lose through criminal punishment. For the same reason, the burden of proof in a criminal trial is guilt "beyond a reasonable doubt," but in civil trials is only a "preponderance [50% plus a feather] of the evidence." For moral wrongs that are neither criminal nor civil offenses, no burden of proof is necessary because such wrongs are not heard or tried in the American court system.

Criminal, Civil, and Moral Responsibility

In order to understand the complexities of criminal law, it is not only important to distinguish different classifications under the criminal law. It is also important to distinguish among crimes, civil offenses, and moral wrongs.

Crimes

Most people informally define a crime as an act that is deeply wrong, that is worthy of strong community disapproval, and that calls for a punitive sanction. In everyday conversation, people may refer to certain legal conduct as criminal, as in "It's a crime that he got away with charging that much."

Formal definitions of crime, in contrast, are stated in the criminal law of federal, state, or local legal systems. A **crime** is any act or omission that is forbidden by law (or penal code) as a violation of the public interest. Although the actual victim of a crime is often a person, legally the victim is the community. By definition, therefore, a crime involves social harm and requires vindication through a public process. It is prosecuted by government attorneys who represent the community as a whole, not the individual or individuals who have been victimized by the specific offense. A victim may initiate the investigation that leads to prosecution by going to the police, and may aid the prosecution by testifying at the criminal trial, but does not actually prosecute a perpetrator for a criminal act. Thus, criminal cases have names such as

crime
An act or omission that the law makes punishable, generally by fine, penalty, forfeiture, or confinement.

State v. Jones or *U.S. v. Smith*, showing that the defendant is accused of violating the laws of an entire society and must answer in turn to that society.

American criminal law has developed from English common law, which recognized the importance of holding individuals accountable for immoral actions that deserve punishment. What is considered immoral and deserving of punishment, however, can vary considerably depending on the time and culture. Consider that acts such as breaking the Sabbath, smoking (for women), and interracial marriage were once illegal in some American jurisdictions. Therefore, definitions of "immoral" and "deserving of punishment" are extremely flexible, depending on who defines them and when.

An important aspect of crime is punishment. Whereas a person who commits a civil wrong may have to pay damages or perform some specific act to compensate for the wrong, a person convicted of a crime is punished. *Punishment* can take many forms, all of which carry one essential characteristic that distinguishes criminal from civil wrongdoing in Anglo-American law: the condemnation and stigma that accompanies conviction of a crime. For example, even if a punishment is only a fine, such a fine serves a different purpose than an award of damages in a civil case. The criminal punishment (or *sanction*) of a fine expresses social disapproval; it is not a method of compensating an individual. Such differences in the nature and aims of civil judgments and criminal sanctions help to explain why they are handled though separate court systems. (For a more thorough discussion of punishment and sentencing, see Chapter 7.)

Civil Wrongs

A civil wrong can be classified as a **tort**—a wrongful act that results in injury and leaves the injured party entitled to compensation—or a breach of contract or trust. Although criminal and civil law both involve holding individuals accountable for actions that the law deems inappropriate, there are two significant differences between criminal liability and civil liability.

First, a crime is committed against the community at large, whereas a tort is a wrong against specific individuals only. Therefore, the pursuit of a tort remedy (as through a lawsuit) involves not government action against individual defendants, but the action of one or more private citizens against another individual or individuals who have violated civil law. For example, a lawsuit often involves one person seeking monetary damages from another. A class action lawsuit involves several people taking legal action against a person or corporation that has wronged them.

Second, the consequences of tort liability are less than the consequences of criminal liability. A party in a civil suit does not face the possibility of punishment, such as loss of liberty or life. Although many people would consider punitive damages a form of punishment, it is not considered equivalent to incarceration and does not carry the stigma of conviction.

A single act may constitute both a crime and a tort and thus may be punishable under both criminal and civil law. Suppose that a drunk driver kills a pedestrian. The driver can be prosecuted for vehicular homicide and sued in civil court for medical costs, funeral costs, and punitive damages. In cases such as this, the same action (hitting a pedestrian while driving drunk) is tried in different courts for somewhat different reasons and aims. The criminal prosecution is to punish the driver for the harm caused to society, and the civil prosecution is to compensate the individual's family for the expenses and suffering they have incurred by the death of their relative.

tort
A wrongful act that results in injury and leaves the injured party entitled to compensation.

Moral Wrongs

If one commits an act that is morally bad, it may lead to both civil and criminal proceedings. For example, a murder can lead to criminal sanctions, civil action for wrongful death, and moral condemnation from others. However, not all morally wrongful conduct is classified as criminally or even civilly wrong. Because a foundation of American philosophy is individual freedom, the criminal law prohibits only extreme conduct, not all morally reprehensible conduct. Returning to the example of murder, this qualifies as extreme conduct and is considered criminal in every jurisdiction. On the other hand, standing by and watching while another person commits a robbery without offering assistance when one could easily do so may be considered morally reprehensible by some people, but is not extreme enough to require a civil or criminal remedy.

Furthermore, the criminal law does not seek to punish thoughts or moral character, only conduct such as actions and specific omissions that cause social harm. For example, thinking about a criminal act or writing stories about imagined criminal acts is not a crime. Possessing questionable moral character is not a crime, as long as it does not lead to criminal conduct. In contrast, committing an illegal act or an illegal omission (such as neglecting to take care of a sick child, which leads to that child's death) is a crime.

Felonies, Misdemeanors, and Petty Offenses

Perhaps the most common way to classify crimes is according to their punishment. Crimes can be broken into three major categories: felonies, misdemeanors, and petty offenses (see Figure 3.1).

F I G U R E   3 . 1

Felonies, Misdemeanors, and Petty Offenses

Felonies

- Serious crime
- Punishable by more than a year of imprisonment or death
- Sentences usually served in prison

Examples: homicide, rape, robbery, possession or distribution of illegal narcotics, arson

Misdemeanors

- Less serious than felonies
- Punishable by fines, penalties, or incarceration of less than one year
- Sentences usually served in local or county jail or alternative programs

Examples: shoplifting, disorderly conduct

Petty Offenses

- Insignificant crime involving minor misconduct
- Punishable by fines and community service

Examples: traffic violations and other infractions

Felonies

At common law, felonies were the most serious class of criminal offense and were uniformly punishable by death. All other offenses were considered misdemeanors and thus were not punishable by death. The modern definition of a **felony** is any serious crime that is punishable by more than a year of imprisonment or by death. Felonies include, but are not limited to, various degrees of homicide, rape, robbery, possession or distribution of illegal narcotics, and arson. It is important to understand that a crime does not have to be violent or even be perpetrated against a specific individual victim to constitute a felony. For example, *white-collar crime*, a term that covers several types of felonies relating to dishonesty in commercial matters, is generally nonviolent. Both federal and state legislatures have enacted laws that criminalize other nonviolent acts as well, such as drug crimes.

     The majority of modern jurisdictions divide felonies into various categories or degrees, in order to treat some offenses as more serious than others. This can be seen in homicide cases, where a person may be charged with first-degree murder, second-degree murder, voluntary manslaughter, or involuntary manslaughter in jurisdictions that make these distinctions. One reason for these distinctions is the level of punishment: First-degree murder can be punishable by death, while other levels of homicide usually are not.

felony
A serious crime that is usually punishable by imprisonment for more than one year or by death.

Misdemeanors

The common law classified all crimes that were not felonies as misdemeanors. Similarly, modern law defines a **misdemeanor** as a crime that is less serious than a felony and is usually punishable by fines, penalties, or incarceration of less than one year. Examples of misdemeanors include shoplifting and disorderly conduct. A person who is convicted of a misdemeanor and incarcerated usually serves his or her sentence in a local or county jail. In contrast, a convicted felon serves his or her sentence in a state penitentiary, and the term will exceed one year. Misdemeanor punishment may also include forms of incarceration other than jail, such as boot camps and in-patient drug treatment programs.

     In modern law, the line between felonies and misdemeanors can be quite unclear. In fact, many jurisdictions have enacted laws that allow certain offenses to be prosecuted as either felonies or misdemeanors (wobblers), depending on the circumstances. Some factors that a prosecutor may consider in deciding whether to charge an offense as a felony or a misdemeanor include:

misdemeanor
A crime that is less serious then a felony and is usually punishable by fine, penalty, forfeiture, or confinement in a jail for less than one year.

- Prior offenses.
- Seriousness of the offense.
- Number of victims.
- Age of the perpetrator.

In plea bargaining, a defense attorney will often attempt to reduce a felony to a misdemeanor when this option exists.

Petty Offenses

A **petty offense** is any insignificant crime involving very minor misconduct. Petty offenses often consist of violations that protect the public welfare. In fact, they are

petty offense
A minor or insignificant crime, also known as a violation or infraction.

Petty Offenses Most of us have committed petty offenses, such as jaywalking or speeding.

usually called violations or infractions rather than crimes; a common example of a petty offense is a traffic violation. Petty offenses are usually not punishable by incarceration, but by monetary fines or community service requirements. The stigma attached to a conviction for a petty offense is usually minimal; one possible exception occurs when a person commits enough traffic violations to have his or her license suspended or revoked.

Although petty offenses may be technically offenses classified under criminal codes, the MPC classifies them as noncriminal. It limits the sentence for a petty offense to a fine, fine and forfeiture, or other civil penalty such as the cancellation or suspension of a license. Many citizens have experienced petty offense convictions, such as for speeding or jaywalking. The position of the MPC and the states that follow this approach is that penal sanctions are justified only for conduct warranting the moral condemnation implicit in the concept of a crime. Note that constitutional protections that are accorded persons charged with crimes often do not apply to those facing noncriminal charges.

CRITICAL THINKING 3.1

1. Give one example each of a felony, a misdemeanor, and a petty offense. In what important ways do these offenses differ?

3.2 Basic Elements of Criminal Culpability

You have just learned about the broad categories of liability and criminal liability as defined by modern law. However, before looking at the specific elements of any specific offense, you must first understand the basic requirements of criminal culpability—that is, the actions and state of mind required in order to hold an individual criminally responsible.

Under the general principles of American criminal law and its predecessor, English common law, criminal liability requires a concurrence, or unity, of two general criteria: an act or physical element, known as the *actus reus*; and a certain mental state or intent, known as the *mens rea*. In addition, under the general principles of criminal responsibility developed from the common law tradition, the physical act must be voluntary and cause social harm. Criminal responsibility or liability, therefore, has five elements:

1. The *actus reus*.
2. The *mens rea*.
3. A unity of *actus reus* and *mens rea*.
4. Causation.
5. Resulting social harm.

Unless a person who fulfills these five elements is justified or excused, he or she can be punished under the criminal law.

The next two sections will discuss the first two elements, the *actus reus* and the *mens rea*.

<hr>

CRITICAL THINKING 3.2

1. Explain why these five elements of criminal responsibility are required.

3.3 The Physical Act: *Actus Reus*

The *actus reus* is the physical action that a person must take in order to be responsible for a criminal offense. As will be discussed later, it is also possible for one to commit a crime by an omission rather than by an affirmative act; that is, a failure to do something may constitute the necessary *actus reus*. In this context, one may look at the *actus reus* element as any act or omission containing the ingredients of causation and social harm. Suppose that Rick shoots Allan in the leg, causing Allan serious injury. Rick committed the voluntary act of shooting Allan, which caused the social harm of Allan's serious injury. Now suppose that Amber neglects to file or pay income tax for five years. Amber's voluntary failure to perform the legally required act of filing and paying taxes causes the social harm of unpaid taxes.

In order to be responsible for a particular crime, a person must in some way perform the act legally required for that crime. For example, the *actus reus* required for burglary is that the defendant must break and enter into a roofed structure or into a vehicle. Many specific actions could potentially constitute this *actus reus*, such as pulling the trigger to shoot through a closed door or smashing a window to break into a car.

As you will read later in this section, the *actus reus* is different from a hope, a desire, or a wish. A person may wish to commit a crime and may think about that crime often, but until he or she actually carries out that action, the crime has not been committed, and the person cannot be held responsible.

Voluntary Action

The *actus reus* usually consists of a voluntary action. That is, except for a few limited circumstances, people are not responsible for actions over which they have no control. A good example would be a person who suffers from epilepsy and experiences uncontrolled seizures. If that person were at a grocery store shopping, had a seizure, and as a result caused property damage, she probably would not be criminally responsible. On the other hand, if that same person were not allowed to drive a car because of an epileptic condition but went out and did so anyway, she would be responsible for injuries or damage caused if she had a seizure and lost control of the car. (See Application Case 3.1.)

⚖️ Application Case 3.1

People v. Decina

In the 1956 New York case of *People v. Decina*, the defendant, who suffered from epilepsy, killed four children when his car went out of control during a seizure. The defendant was convicted of criminal negligence because he knew that he was highly susceptible to seizures and failed to take proper precautions. Although the ultimate act that caused the deaths was involuntary, the act of driving a car under these circumstances constituted the necessary *actus reus*.

SOURCE: People v. Decina, 138 N.E.2d 799 (N.Y. 1956).

For an act to be voluntary, the defendant must possess sufficient free will to exercise choice and be responsible for his conduct. Even if a person who has acted voluntarily later regrets the act, he is still held responsible. This requirement is consistent with the fundamental principle of individuality on which the Anglo-American legal system is based. For example, a person who is forced at gunpoint to steal a car will probably not have the same level of criminal responsibility as a person who single-handedly and voluntarily breaks into a car. Likewise, conditions such as mental infirmity or extreme youth can also diminish a person's criminal responsibility.

Thoughts versus Acts

To fully understand *actus reus*, it is important to understand the difference between voluntary actions and mere thoughts. You cannot be punished for thinking about committing a crime. Only if you act on those thoughts and perform the physical actions connected to your thoughts do you become criminally liable. No doubt you can think of times when you were angry at someone and wished that something bad would happen to that person. However, even if something bad did happen, you would not be criminally responsible unless you had acted to cause the harm.

Omissions as Acts

An *actus reus* usually involves a physical act. In certain circumstances, however, a person may be guilty of a crime by *failing to act*. In this sense, **omissions** are legally viewed as actions that can lead to criminal liability, usually in one of two situations. The first situation occurs where the definition of a crime specifically designates an omission as punishable. Examples include failure to register for the draft or failure to file an income tax return. The second situation occurs when a person has an affirmative duty to act in some way but fails to do so, and such failure causes a criminal result.

omissions
Narrowly defined circumstances in which a failure to act is viewed as a criminal act.

An example of this second situation is child neglect. Almost every jurisdiction has laws that require parents and legal guardians to take care of children in a way that will not injure them or threaten their well-being. By failing to protect a child, a parent or guardian may be criminally liable without having engaged in any physical acts, such as battering the child. If, for example, a parent stopped feeding a child and that child died from starvation, the parent would be criminally liable. The omission of necessary care for a child would constitute the *actus reus* of the crime.

A legal duty to act can arise from a relationship, such as those between a parent and a child or between a doctor and a patient. It can also be imposed by law, such as the requirement that a driver must stop and help if he or she is involved in an automobile accident. It can also arise from a contractual relationship, such as that imposed upon a lifeguard or nurse. However, absent a relationship that is not defined as these are, a person usually does not have a duty to provide assistance in all situations. Even though most people would feel obligated to act if someone's life were in danger, numerous judicial decisions have held that there was no criminal liability when a person stood by and did nothing to help someone else in jeopardy. (See Application Cases 3.2, 3.3, and 3.4.)

⚖️ Application Case 3.2

Jones v. United States

The case of *Jones v. United States* (1962) states the basic principles upon which criminal responsibility for omission to act may rest. In this case, the accused was found guilty of involuntary manslaughter in the death of 10-month-old Anthony Lee Green, the illegitimate child of Shirley Green. The baby died from a lack of care while staying with the defendant, a family friend of Ms. Green, who lived in the same house. There was conflicting evidence on the question of whether the defendant was paid for taking care of the baby, but there was no conflict on the evidence that the defendant had ample means to provide food and medical care, but did not do so. The trial court had refused to instruct the jury that it had to find beyond a reasonable doubt as an element of the crime that the defendant was under a legal duty to supply food and necessities to the child.

The U.S. Court of Appeals for the District of Columbia Circuit reversed the conviction because of the trial court's failure to give this instruction. In doing so, the court stated:

> There are at least four situations in which the failure to act may constitute breach of a legal duty. One can be held criminally liable: first, where a statute imposes a duty to care for another; second, where one stands in a certain status relationship to another; third, where one has assumed a contractual duty to care for another; and fourth, where one has voluntarily assumed the care of another and so secluded the helpless person as to prevent others from rendering aid.

SOURCE: Jones v. United States, 308 F.2d 307 (D.C. Cir. 1962).

⚖ Application Case 3.3

People v. Beardsley

The court that decided the *Jones* case relied on another case, *People v. Beardsley* (1907), which is instructive of the law's view of the duty requirement before criminal liability will be imposed for an omission. In that case, Beardsley spent a weekend at his home with a female friend, Blanche Burns, while his wife was away. Ms. Burns took a fatal dose of morphine, and Beardsley failed to call a physician to help her. She died, and Beardsley was charged with and convicted of manslaughter. The Supreme Court of Michigan reversed the conviction on the ground that Beardsley had no legal duty to help Ms. Burns, even though he may have had a moral duty to help her.

SOURCE: People v. Beardsley, 113 N.W. 1128 (Mich. 1907).

⚖ Application Case 3.4

Barber v. Superior Court

In *Barber v. Superior Court*, the California Court of Appeals held that doctors who turned off the life support equipment sustaining the life of Clarence Herbert, who was in a coma, did not commit an unlawful act for which they could be charged with homicide. The doctors were acting with the permission of Mr. Herbert's family. In resolving the legal question, the court concluded that, even though physicians have a relationship from which a legal duty to act may result, the doctors' omission to act in this case did not constitute an unlawful failure to perform a legal duty.

SOURCE: Barber v. Superior Court, 195 Cal. Rptr. 484 (Cal. Ct. App. 1983).

The 1964 murder of Kitty Genovese is a notorious example of a failure to act that did not lead to criminal liability. Genovese was brutally attacked late one night outside her Queens, New York, home. She cried out for help for half an hour before being stabbed to death. A reported 38 neighbors heard her screams and witnessed the attack, yet did nothing to help her. It was not simply that they refused to go outside and try to stop the assailant; they did not even call the police from the comfort of their homes. While the unwillingness of Genovese's neighbors to act is morally reprehensible, they were not prosecuted for their failure to act because they were under no legal duty to do so.

Another notorious case involving the question of the failure to act was the heinous killing of seven-year-old Sherrice Iverson by Jeremy Strohmeyer. Strohmeyer's friend David Cash watched the assailant haul the victim into a bathroom stall, begin to assault her, and threaten to kill her. Cash just turned away as she fought for her life. Strohmeyer pled guilty to murder and, in exchange for his plea, was sentenced to life imprisonment without the possibility of parole. Cash, who could have tried to stop the killing, went off to college and was never charged with any crime.

The law's failure to hold Cash responsible, or the neighbors who did not come to the aid of Kitty Genovese, raises difficult moral questions and leaves many Americans dissatisfied with this aspect of the American legal system. Many jurisdictions have been reluctant to impose criminal liability in the absence of a legal duty, and lawmakers have been reluctant to enact statutes that create liability in such circumstances. In contrast, an Israeli court convicted Margalit Harshefi, a friend of the assassin of Prime Minister Rabin, under a law that holds a person criminally liable for having knowledge or full awareness of the possibility that another person is about to commit a felony. This law, which exists in Israel as a remnant of colonialism, has been rarely used and is generally unpopular. Nonetheless, after Rabin's assassination, there was no public objection to using the law against Ms. Harshefi.[1]

Words as Acts

In most cases, as has been discussed, the *actus reus* requirement for criminal liability is satisfied by overt, willed physical acts. In other cases, it is met by specific omissions. In still other cases, under certain circumstances, mere words can constitute the *actus reus*. Such words are so offensive that they can constitute a threat or cause further physical actions that society views as a social harm.

Where and how a person makes a statement has a lot to do with whether the statement could be considered a criminal act. Often, context alone can determine whether a statement counts as an *actus reus*. For example, falsely yelling "Fire!" in a crowded theater can be criminally prosecuted. The effect of yelling that word in that context would be to cause such a panic among the crowd that the word itself meets the *actus reus* requirement. Another example is certain types of threats. Because of the high social value in preventing harm to the president, making a threat to harm the president of the United States is a criminal act. Even if a person has no intention of carrying out the threat, the words alone are enough to trigger the *actus reus* requirement.

Defining words as criminal acts can create conflict with the First Amendment, which guarantees freedom of speech. Free speech advocates argue that prosecuting people for self-expression directly violates the First Amendment. Those who defend the concept of criminal speech argue that words that have a very good possibility of causing physical harm should be illegal. Ideally, the law should balance the interests of people wishing to protect their right to free speech and people who may be harmed by another's words.

Possession as an Act

possessory offenses

Criminal offenses in which the law defines possession as an act.

Virtually all jurisdictions have statutes for **possessory offenses**, which criminalize the possession of certain items or substances. A person can be guilty of such crimes without any further act than possession of the prohibited article. For example, possession of illegal drugs and possession of criminal instruments such as burglar's tools both constitute criminal acts. Actual possession is usually required. For example, a houseguest at a dwelling where illegal narcotics are found would not be in actual possession of the drugs, and thus would not be guilty of the crime of possession.

To prove a possessory offense, the prosecutor must prove that the accused person knowingly possessed the illegal item. The MPC states that possession is a criminal act if the possessor either knowingly obtained the object possessed, or knew he or she was in control of it for a sufficient period to have been able to terminate possession.[2]

Possessory offenses are limited to circumstances in which it is likely that an individual will use what he or she possesses to commit a crime. Their purpose is to deter future criminal activity; holding someone criminally liable for possessing the tools to commit a crime is intended to minimize future social harm. Thus, a locksmith who possesses tools that burglars also use would not be criminally liable, because it would be clear that the locksmith plans to use the tools for a legitimate purpose.

CRITICAL THINKING 3.3

1. How can omissions be legally treated as the *actus reus*?
2. How can words be legally treated as the *actus reus*?

3.4 The Mental State: *Mens Rea*

Actus reus makes up only one part of the criminal culpability requirement. Only in rare circumstances can someone be convicted of a crime without both the physical act *and* the guilty mind. (Statutory rape, for example, is a strict liability crime in which only the physical act needs to be proved to obtain a conviction.) The guilty mind is known as *mens rea*; it is also called *intent* or *culpability*. You will read about *mens rea* several times throughout this book.

Broadly speaking, *mens rea* is the mental state that a person has at the time that he or she performs the acts that constitute the commission of a crime. For example, if the accused stabbed the victim with desire to cause the victim's death, then the accused had the *mens rea* of "specific intent to kill," which is one variety of *mens rea* that makes a person criminally liable for murder. You will learn more about different types of intent later in this section.

Motive, a term sometimes used to mean intent, is actually slightly different from *mens rea*. **Motive** usually means the emotion prompting a person to act. For instance, the motive for a man's killing his wife's lover would be jealousy. In this sense, motive is not a form of *mens rea* and is not an element of required proof for criminal culpability. In other words, the criminal actor is not liable for the jealousy that motivated him to commit the killing (although he may be liable for the killing in other ways). Nonetheless, motive is often important as a matter of proof because it may help to identify the perpetrator of a crime or explain *why* a suspect may have acted in a particular way.

As you will learn, *mens rea* may be satisfied in different ways for different crimes, or even for the same crime. The *mens rea* requirement for murder in many jurisdictions is *malice aforethought*, a form of *mens rea* that can exist in four different mental states:

1. A specific intent to kill.
2. An intent to inflict serious bodily injury.
3. A wanton disregard for human life.
4. The commission of a dangerous felony.[3]

For voluntary manslaughter, many jurisdictions require the *mens rea* of intent to kill, but in the sudden heat of passion. Involuntary manslaughter requires only the *mens rea* of negligence or the commission of an unlawful act not amounting to a felony. Although a variety of mental states may satisfy the requirement of *mens rea*, some form of *mens rea* will be required. Thus, it is essential for prosecutors to understand what mental state is required for criminal culpability with respect to any particular crime.

motive
The emotion that prompts a person to act. It is not an element of a crime that is required to prove criminal liability, but it is often shown in order to identify the perpetrator of a crime or explain his or her reason for acting.

Specific Intent and General Intent

Specific intent and general intent have been used in Anglo-American law for centuries, but have been confusing to many lawmakers and judges. **Specific intent** can be any one of the following:

- The intention to do an act for the purpose of doing some additional future act.
- The intention to do an act to achieve some further consequences beyond the conduct or result that constitutes the *actus reus* of the offense.
- The intention to do an act with the awareness of a statutory attendant circumstance.[4]

A crime that does not require any of these states of mind is a general intent crime. **General intent** is the intent only to do the *actus reus* of the crime.

For example, common law burglary is a specific intent crime. It requires that a person break and enter the dwelling of another at night, not merely knowingly or on purpose, but with the further purpose of committing a felony inside the dwelling. The *actus reus* of common law burglary, therefore, is the breaking and entering of a particular dwelling. If the perpetrator plans the future act of committing a felony, then the requirement of *mens rea* is also satisfied. The crime is complete upon the

specific intent
The intention to commit an act for the purpose of doing some additional future act, to achieve some further consequences, or with the awareness of a statutory attendant circumstance.

general intent
The intent only to do the *actus reus* of the crime, without any of the elements of specific intent.

entry, and the accused can be convicted of burglary, even if he or she does not actually commit a felony inside. (See Application Case 3.5.)

⚖️ Application Case 3.5

United States v. Melton

In *United States v. Melton*, Ms. Vessels was awakened by the sounds of a loud noise. She went downstairs to investigate and found several pieces of plywood that had been stacked against a door that opened inward from an unheated sunroom. She went next door to a neighbor's house and called the police. When the police arrived, they found the door to the sunroom partially open and discovered the defendant lying on the floor. He was charged with and convicted of first-degree burglary, which requires the unlawful breaking and entering into the dwelling of another with intent to commit a criminal offense—in this case, larceny.

The court reversed the defendant's conviction on the basis that there was insufficient evidence to sustain a conviction for burglary. The court reasoned that intent was the element that separates unlawful entry, or trespassing, from burglary. Unlike trespassing, burglary requires intent to commit a crime once unlawful entry is accomplished. What was lacking in this case was circumstantial evidence that showed a purpose other than unlawful entry. Such circumstantial evidence includes flight upon discovery, carrying or trying to conceal stolen goods, or an assault upon a resident. Since the defendant did not attempt to escape or resist arrest, even though there was an open window nearby, and since no stolen goods, weapons, or burglary tools were recovered from him, there was insufficient proof that the defendant was on the premises to commit larceny.

SOURCE: United States v. Melton, 491 F.2d 45 (D.C. Cir. 1973).

Other examples of specific intent crimes are assault with intent to kill, larceny, and receiving stolen property with the knowledge that it is stolen. Each of these crimes consists of an *actus reus* that involves intentional acts, but each also requires either an additional purpose or knowledge of an attendant circumstance.

- Assault with intent to kill requires that a person commit a battery, which is the intentional application of unlawful force upon another, with the specific further purpose of killing that person.
- Larceny is the trespassory taking and carrying away of the personal property of another with the further specific purpose of permanently depriving the other person of that property.
- A person is guilty of receiving stolen property with knowledge that it is stolen only if the accused has knowledge that the property was stolen.

In contrast are the general intent crimes. A perpetrator who breaks and enters a dwelling is guilty of the general intent crime of trespass even if he or she had no additional intent to commit a felony inside. The general intent crimes of bigamy and statutory rape provide further examples. The crime of bigamy is committed when a married person remarries while having a spouse living; since it does not require that the perpetrator specifically know that his or her spouse is living, it is a general intent crime. In most jurisdictions, statutory rape requires sexual intercourse with a child who is underage, but the perpetrator does not have to be shown to have specific knowledge that the girl or boy was underage.

Transferred Intent

Transferred intent holds a person criminally liable even when the consequence of his or her action is not what the actor actually intended. If a person intends to harm one person but mistakenly injures or kills another, the required criminal element of intent transfers to the harm committed against the unintended victim. If a perpetrator fires a gun out of his car window with the intent of killing a rival gang member, but the bullet misses the gang member and kills a three-year-old girl, he is guilty under the doctrine of transferred intent. Even though the perpetrator had no intention of shooting the child, his intent to kill the gang member transfers to her. As a result, he will be found to have had the same *mens rea* as if he intended to kill the child.

Transferred intent is sometimes called a "legal fiction" because a prosecutor cannot definitely prove that the actor had the intent necessary to punish him for the injury to the innocent bystander. The transferred intent doctrine exists to ensure that a person is punished for his criminal culpability, even though the intended harm was accidentally directed at the wrong person. In other words, if a perpetrator is a lousy shot or burgles the wrong address, that should not make him free from guilt. (See Application Case 3.6.)

transferred intent
A doctrine that holds a person criminally liable even when the consequence of his or her action is not what the actor actually intended.

⚖ Application Case 3.6

People v. Scott

In *People v. Scott* (1996), the defendants were convicted of murder in the second degree for the killing of an innocent bystander and of attempted murder of the intended victims. As a result of a family vendetta, the defendants tried to kill Calvin Hughes, the ex-boyfriend of their mother, Elaine Scott. Following a physical altercation with Scott, Hughes returned to their apartment with a friend to remove his personal belongings. Scott refused to let him in, but Hughes forced his way in and removed his belongings. Scott threatened to page the defendants, who were her sons.

Hughes and his friend then went to a local park. They parked next to Nathan Kelly, whose teenage son Jack Gibson was parked nearby. As Hughes stood beside Kelly's car, talking to him through the open window, three cars entered the park. The first vehicle contained the defendants, who sprayed the area with bullets. Hughes ran for cover behind the front bumper of Kelly's car, then sprinted toward the park and was immediately followed by a hail of gunfire. One bullet hit the heel of his shoe, and the shooting did not stop until Hughes took cover behind the gym. During the shooting, both Kelly's and Gibson's car were riddled with bullets. Kelly was shot in the leg and buttocks, and his son Jack Gibson was shot in the head and killed.

Following their conviction for one count of murder in the second degree and two counts of attempted murder, the defendants argued that the jury should not have been instructed to apply the doctrine of transferred intent to the unintended victim because they were also charged with the attempted murder of an intended victim. The court rejected the appeal and affirmed the convictions, holding that intent is not capable of being "used up" once it is used to convict a defendant of the crime that he or she intended to commit. Hence, the prosecutor successfully used the doctrine of transferred intent to convict for both the intended and unintended crimes.

SOURCE: People v. Scott, 927 P.2d 288 (1996).

strict liability
When a person can be convicted of a crime without having any requisite mental state or intention to commit the crime.

Strict Liability

Strict liability means that a person can be convicted of a crime without having any requisite mental state or intention to commit the crime. The most common examples are those involving mistake as to the age of a victim or, in the case of liquor sales, of the purchaser. For example, the offense of statutory rape requires only proof of the physical act of sex with a minor in order to secure a conviction. The imposition of strict criminal liability is rare in Anglo-American law, and the MPC "expressly rejects the general notion of strict criminal liability."[5]

Transferred Intent
Under the doctrine of transferred intent, if this robber intended to kill a teller but instead shoots and kills an innocent bystander, he is equally liable for murder.

Model Penal Code Classifications of Mental States

The MPC, which has greatly influenced modern American criminal law, designates four kinds of *mens rea* by which a person can be found criminally liable. The MPC provides that "a person is not guilty of an offense unless he acted purposely, knowingly, recklessly or negligently, as the law may require, with respect to each material element of the offense."[6] This makes a person criminally liable only if he or she possesses one of these specific states of mind, but not for mere immorality. This provision is an attempt to simplify the concept of *mens rea* by doing away with specific intent, general intent, and other older terms.

Under the MPC, to be held criminally liable, a person must act with one of four types of mental states, described in the following paragraphs and summarized in Figure 3.2. The first two are broken in two subcategories each.

Classifications of Mental States

Acting with Purpose

Purposely with respect to result of conduct
- Perpetrator's voluntary will is to act in a certain way or produce a certain result.

Purposely with respect to attendant circumstances
- Perpetrator is aware of conditions that will make the intended crime possible.

Acting Knowingly

Knowingly causes a result
- Perpetrator commits an act aware that it is practically certain that his or her conduct will cause a certain result.

Knowingly with respect to conduct and attendant circumstances
- Perpetrator commits an act aware that his or her actions are criminal or that attendant circumstances made an otherwise legal act a criminal one.

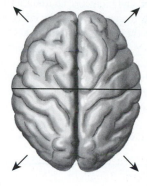

Acting Negligently

Perpetrator should be aware that a substantial and unjustifiable risk exists or will result from the negligent conduct.

Acting Recklessly

Perpetrator voluntarily ignores a substantial and unjustified risk that a certain circumstance exists or will result from the reckless conduct.

Acting with Purpose

When a perpetrator acts **purposely with respect to result or conduct**, it is his or her voluntary wish to act in a certain way or produce a certain result. A perpetrator who buys a gun and ammunition, points the gun at a victim, and fires the gun has manifested a purpose to kill the victim. When a person acts **purposely with respect to attendant circumstances**, he or she is aware of conditions that will make the intended crime possible, or believes or hopes that they exist. If a perpetrator enters an occupied dwelling in order to commit a felony inside, he or she has acted purposely with respect to the attendant circumstance that the dwelling was occupied—if he or she was aware it was occupied, believed it was, or hoped it was.

Acting Knowingly

A person **knowingly causes a result** if the person knows or is practically certain that his or her conduct will cause this result. A person who fires 50 rounds into a crowd and kills five persons has knowingly killed the victims if he or she was aware or practically certain that firing the weapon would likely result in one or more deaths.

A person acts **knowingly with respect to conduct and attendant circumstances** if the person knows that his or her actions are criminal, or that attendant circumstances make an otherwise legal act a criminal one. With regard to conduct, if the accused is charged with knowingly endangering the life of a person by shooting a gun at him, he would be guilty if he was aware that his conduct endangered the person's life. If he was unaware of the presence of the victim, he did not act knowingly, even if the victim's presence seemed obvious. With respect to knowledge of attendant circumstances, a person would be guilty of receiving stolen property if, at the time she received the property, she was aware that it had been stolen. Sometimes people

purposely with respect to result or conduct

When the actor has a voluntary wish to act in a certain way or produce a certain result.

purposely with respect to attendant circumstances

When the actor is aware of conditions that will make the intended crime possible, or believes or hopes that they exist.

knowingly causes a result

Commits an act in the awareness that one's conduct will almost certainly cause this result.

knowingly with respect to conduct and attendant circumstances

Aware that one's actions are criminal, or that attendant circumstances make an otherwise legal act a criminal one.

3.1 On the Job

Jury Coordinator

Description and Duties: Responsible for the management and processing of jurors for superior, district, and municipal courts. Ensures that courts are supplied with adequate jurors in a timely manner. Uses strong interpersonal skills in working with jurors, either in person or on the phone, to ensure that their needs and the needs of the courts are met. Coordinates the handling of juror excuse requests. Conducts juror orientation classes in any of three trial court locations, as often as four times per week.

   Salary: Salaries range from approximately $25,000 to $40,000.

   Other Information: Jury coordinators generally provide jurors with miscellaneous information, such as dress codes, a list of local restaurants for lunch break, and parking information.

SOURCE: http://www.co.pinellas.fl.us/persnl/pay&clas/specs/18784.htm.

---

engage in "willful blindness," not asking questions in highly suspicious circumstances and then claiming a lack of knowledge and hence a lack of *mens rea*. To avoid such manipulation, the MPC provides that knowledge is established if a person knows that there is a high probability of such an attendant circumstance.

Acting Recklessly

recklessly
Acting in a manner that voluntarily ignores a substantial and unjustified risk that a certain circumstance exists or will result from one's actions.

The MPC states that a person acts **recklessly** if the person voluntarily ignores a substantial and unjustified risk that a certain circumstance exists or will result from his actions. A risk is considered substantial and unjustified if a reasonable law-abiding citizen considers it a clear deviation from how a reasonable person would behave. Since this standard is rather vague, juries are required to look at the defendant's perspective when determining whether his actions created a substantial and unjustified risk. Particular characteristics of the defendant may be taken into account when determining whether he acted recklessly. For example, physical traits such as blindness may compel a person to act differently than someone with sight, and a jury can be instructed to take that into account.

Acting Negligently

negligently
Acting in a manner that ignores a substantial and unjustified risk of which one should have been aware.

Under the MPC, a person acts **negligently** if the person should be aware that a substantial and unjustified risk exists or will result from the negligent conduct. As with recklessness, the risk involved for negligence must be substantial and unjustified. The difference between negligence and recklessness is that the reckless person consciously disregards the risk, whereas a negligent person does so unknowingly. It could be said, however, that the negligent person should have known that her actions would create the risk. A jury determines whether someone is negligent by deciding whether the risk taken would have been taken by a reasonable person in the same situation. If the risk would not have been taken, the person is found to be negligent. As in determining recklessness, a jury is required to look at the perspective of the accused individual to decide whether she should have known that her actions created a substantial and unjustified risk.

CRITICAL THINKING 3.4

1. Explain the doctrine of transferred intent. Though a "legal fiction," is this doctrine valid? Why or why not?

2. How do purpose and knowledge differ in regard to criminal liability?

3. Discuss intent when undercover agents act as decoys to trap Internet stalkers and child molesters.

3.5 Causation and Concurrence

Although causation is an ingredient of the *actus reus* requirement for all criminal culpability, it is only an issue in the case of *result crimes*—crimes that cause a specific result. The best example of a result crime is homicide, in which the defendant's conduct results in the death of another human being. Inchoate offenses and possessory offenses are not result crimes.

There are two steps in determining whether an act caused a specific result:

1. The accused person's act must be the *cause-in-fact* of the result.
2. If it was, then the accused person's actions must also be the *proximate cause* of the result.

If both conditions are satisfied, the accused can be said to have caused the result.

Cause-in-Fact and But-For Tests

To determine whether the defendant's actions were the **cause-in-fact** of the result, courts apply the **but-for test**. This test asks, "But for the defendant's conduct, would the social harm have occurred when it did?" In other words, would the result have occurred if the defendant had not acted?

Suppose that a defendant shoots a victim, causing only minor injuries. During surgery for these injuries, a doctor acts negligently and causes the victim's death. The defendant's act of shooting the victim is still the cause-in-fact of the death because "but for" the shooting, the victim would never have required surgery in the first place. With one limited exception, the prosecution must prove beyond a reasonable doubt that the accused was the but-for cause of the social harm in order to hold the accused criminally responsible. The single exception is the situation in which two independent causes operate simultaneously, either of which could have caused the result. This could occur, for example, if two people independently shot a victim at exactly the same time. In this case, both can be viewed as the cause-in-fact.[7]

Proximate and Intervening Causes

If the defendant's actions were the cause-in-fact of the social harm, the next step is to determine whether the action was the proximate cause of the result. **Proximate cause** is that cause, from among all of the causes-in-fact that may exist, that is the *legally defined* cause of the social harm. Often, there is no question about proximate cause

cause-in-fact
The cause of the social harm in a criminal act, as determined by the but-for test.

but-for test
The test that asks whether the result would have occurred if the defendant had not acted.

proximate cause
That cause, from among all of the causes-in-fact that may exist, that is the legal cause of the social harm.

because the accused person's conduct is the direct cause of social harm. For example, if the accused shoots a victim who dies at the scene of the shooting, there is no other possible cause of the social harm of death. In such a case, where the defendant's act is the direct cause, no other possible proximate causes need to be considered.

Sometimes, though, a case involves various types of intervening causes. An **intervening cause** is a cause other than the defendant's conduct that contributes to the social harm. For example, if a defendant recklessly hits a child with his car and then another driver runs over the child, this second action is an intervening cause. One way to deal with intervening causes is to ask, "Under what circumstances does the intervening conduct of a third party, the victim, or a natural force make it no longer seem fair to say that the social harm was caused by the defendant's conduct?"[8] Generally, when an intervening cause relieves the accused of criminal responsibility, it is because the law has described the intervening event as a more important cause of the harm.

When there are competing causes that could qualify as the proximate cause, a court or jury must select one. Usually, proximate cause will be decided by distinguishing between dependent and independent intervening causes. *Dependent intervening causes* are intervening causes that are either largely foreseeable or related to the defendant's conduct, so their existence still makes the defendant liable for the resulting social harm. Returning to the earlier example of the shooting victim, if the accused shoots a victim who is then taken to a hospital and receives poor medical treatment, the accused's conduct will still be the proximate cause of the victim's death because the shooting is still the proximate cause of the social harm.

An *independent intervening cause* is one that is deemed separate enough from the defendant's actions that it would be unfair to hold him or her responsible for its results. If this same shooting victim were taken to the hospital and, while recovering there from the nonfatal wound, was poisoned by another person, the conduct of the accused who shot him would not be the proximate cause of the victim's death.[9]

Concurrence of Elements

In addition to the two elements of *actus reus* and *mens rea*, a crime also requires the concurrence of these two elements. This **concurrence of elements** requirement means that a person cannot be convicted of a crime unless the prosecution proves beyond a reasonable doubt that the accused performed a voluntary act *accompanied by* the required mental state that actually and proximately caused the prohibited social harm. This requirement of concurrence has two components:

1. The *mens rea* must have been present at the same moment in time that the accused did the act (or omission) that caused the social harm.
2. The concurrence must be motivational.

The first requirement of concurrence, known as the *temporal requirement*, simply means that the accused must have had the required *mens rea* at the same time that he or she did the voluntary act or omission. The fact that the defendant had the requisite *mens rea* at some other point in time does not satisfy the concurrence requirement. For example, it is not enough that the defendant had the intent to kill the victim but did not act upon it, then later accidentally kills the victim.

intervening cause
A cause other than the defendant's conduct that contributes to the social harm.

concurrence of elements
Requirement for criminal liability that the accused performed a voluntary act *accompanied by* the required mental state that actually and proximately caused the prohibited social harm.

The second requirement of concurrence, known as the *motivational requirement*, means that the motivation to commit a specific crime must be present. If, for example, a defendant plans to kill someone and picks up a gun he believes to be unloaded to test the trigger, but then accidentally shoots the victim when he unexpectedly walks into the line of fire, the motivational requirement is not present. In this example, the temporal requirement was met because the intent to cause death was present, but the motivational concurrence was not present because the actuating force behind pulling the trigger was the desire to test the gun.

CRITICAL THINKING 3.5

1. Explain how causation is tested.

2. What concurrence of elements is necessary to constitute a crime?

REVIEW AND APPLICATIONS

Summary by Chapter Objectives

1. **Differentiate criminal, tort, and moral responsibility.** Criminal responsibility leads to the imposition of punishment, including the possibility of incarceration. Tort responsibility leads to monetary loss only, does not involve the stigma of being labeled a criminal, and involves a lawsuit by one party against another, not an action in the name of the public. Moral responsibility carries no legal consequences.

2. **Explain the difference between felonies, misdemeanors, and petty offenses.** A felony is punishable by imprisonment for more than a year or by death. A misdemeanor is a crime usually less serious then a felony and is usually punishable by fine, penalty, forfeiture, or confinement in a place other than prison. A petty offense is a minor or insignificant crime.

3. **Describe the requirement of a physical act (*actus reus*).** The *actus reus* is the requirement for criminal culpability that consists of a willed, voluntary act that causes proscribed social harm.

4. **Understand the concept of a voluntary, willed act.** A voluntary, willed act occurs when a person does something as a matter of choice, as opposed to involuntary conduct such as a twitch or an epileptic seizure.

5. **Explain the difference between thinking about committing an act and acting on the thought.** The law imposes no criminal punishment for merely thinking about committing an act, as opposed to acting on the thought.

6. **Describe the circumstances under which an omission constitutes an act for purposes of criminal responsibility.** Omissions constitute criminal acts in two situations. The first is when the law requires an act and a person omits doing the act, such as failing to file an income tax return. The second is when

a person has an affirmative duty to act in some way, the person fails to act, and the failure causes a criminal result. An example of this would be child neglect.

7. **Explain when words alone can constitute a criminal act.** Words can constitute a criminal act when the words themselves constitute a threat that society views as a social harm that may lead to actual physical acts.

8. **State when possession can be a criminal act.** Actual possession of a prohibited object can constitute a criminal act, such as possession of illegal drugs.

9. **Understand and define the requirement of *mens rea* (guilty mind).** To be criminally culpable, a person must perform a proscribed act with the accompanying mental state required for the crime, such as intent.

10. **Distinguish between specific intent and general intent crimes.** General intent usually means that the person intended to do the act that constitutes the *actus reus* of the crime. Specific intent usually means that the person intended to do an act for the purpose of doing some additional future act, to achieve some further consequences beyond the conduct or result that constitutes the *actus reus*, or with awareness of a statutory attendant circumstance.

11. **Explain the doctrine of transferred intent.** The doctrine of transferred intent is the legal fiction that holds a person criminally liable even when the consequence of his or her action is not what the person actually intended. If a person intends to harm one person but, by mistake, unintentionally harms another, the doctrine of transferred intent carries over to the harm committed against the unintended victim.

12. **Distinguish between the MPC's definitions of acting purposely and acting knowingly.** A person acts purposely with respect to a result if it is his or her conscious objective to produce a certain result. A person acts purposely with respect to an attendant circumstance if he or she is aware of conditions that will make the intended crime possible, or believes or hopes that they exist. A person acts knowingly with respect to a result if the person is aware that it is practically certain that his or her conduct will cause this result. A person acts knowingly with respect to conduct and attendant circumstances if the person is aware that his or her conduct is criminal or that attendant circumstances make an otherwise legal act a criminal one.

13. **Understand the difference between acting recklessly and acting negligently under the MPC.** A person acts recklessly with respect to a material element if the person consciously disregards a substantial and unjustified risk that the material element exists or will result from his or her conduct. A person acts negligently with respect to a material element if the person ignores a substantial and unjustified risk of which he or she should have been aware that the material element exists or will result from his or her conduct.

14. **Distinguish cause-in-fact from the proximate cause of a crime.** The cause-in-fact is that cause of the social harm in a criminal act that is determined by the but-for test. Proximate cause is that cause, from among all of the causes-in-fact that may exist, which is the legal cause of the social harm.

15. **Explain how a concurrence of events is needed for a crime to occur.** A crime requires a concurrence of the two elements of *actus reus* and *mens rea*. In other words, a prosecutor must prove that a defendant performed a voluntary act accompanied by the required mental state that caused the social harm in order to convict. This requirement has two elements:

- The *mens rea* must have been present at the same moment in time that the accused did the act (or omission) that caused the social harm.
- The concurrence must be motivational as well.

Key Terms

crime (p. 56)
tort (p. 57)
felony (p. 59)
misdemeanor (p. 59)
petty offense (p. 59)
omissions (p. 63)
possessory offenses (p. 66)
motive (p. 67)
specific intent (p. 67)
general intent (p. 67)
transferred intent (p. 69)
strict liability (p. 70)
purposely with respect to result or
     conduct (p. 71)

purposely with respect to attendant
     circumstance (p. 71)
knowingly causes a result (p. 71)
knowingly with respect to conduct and
     attendant circumstances (p. 71)
recklessly (p. 72)
negligently (p. 72)
cause-in-fact (p. 73)
but-for test (p. 73)
proximate cause (p. 73)
intervening cause (p. 74)
concurrence of elements (p. 74)

Review Questions

1. How can some actions be torts and crimes at the same time, and what is the essential difference between torts and crimes?
2. What is a voluntary, willed act?
3. What is the difference between thinking about committing an act and acting on the thought?
4. How do *actus reus* and *mens rea* work together to create a criminal act?
5. Why must an act be voluntary to be a crime, and how does this work in situations where a person commits a voluntary act with involuntary consequences (such as drunk driving)?
6. When does an omission constitute an act for purposes of criminal responsibility?
7. When do words alone constitute a criminal act?
8. Explain the difference between motive and intent.
9. Explain the doctrine of transferred intent.
10. What is the difference between the MPC's definitions of acting purposely and acting knowingly?
11. According to the MPC, when does a person act recklessly? Negligently?

Problem-Solving Exercises

1. **Hazardous Waste** Assume that negligent handling of hazardous waste is a strict liability crime and carries a penalty of up to a year in jail. Rollie Davis bought a manufacturing company, but had no intention of being involved in the operation of the business; he lives in a different part of the county and lets the business's long-time managers handle the day-to-day operations. A year later, authorities discover that Davis's company has been illegally dumping hazardous waste for the past 10 years, well before he bought the company. Can Davis be held criminally liable for the company's past conduct of illegal handling of hazardous waste? Why or why not? What about for the last year of dumping? Why or why not?

2. **Battery** Brittany and Josh were girlfriend and boyfriend for the last three years of high school. At the end of Josh's senior year, they had an amicable breakup, then both went off to college in different parts of the country. In the fall of their first year of college, both of them went to a high school reunion. They had not seen each other or spoken for almost six months. When Josh saw Brittany, he excitedly ran up to her, grabbed her, and kissed her in front of several of his friends. Brittany tried to push him away, but he did not let her go until after her third attempt to break free. She was not injured, but she was very angry and reported the incident to the police. You are the officer who receives the report. You consider the possibility that Josh may be guilty of committing a battery, which is defined as the intentional application of unlawful force upon another. Josh claims he did not intend to commit a crime. Did Josh's conduct constitute the *actus reus* and *mens rea* of the offense of battery? Why or why not? Should he be charged with the crime? Why or why not?

Workplace Applications

1. **Deciding on Charges** You are a police officer writing up the paperwork for someone whom you caught in the act of attempting a burglary. He is armed with an unloaded handgun, but seems remorseful and is embarrassed for his family. This is his first offense. You have the option of charging him with attempted burglary as a misdemeanor, attempted burglary as a felony, or aggravated attempted burglary because he possessed a weapon—although he told you that he wasn't planning to use it, and you believe him because he appears naïve. In your jurisdiction, a felony charge carries a minimum of three years' imprisonment.
   a. How will you charge this suspect, and why?
   b. How would you charge him if he seemed aggressive and unremorseful? If this was not his first offense? Why?

2. **Deciding on Defense** You are a defense attorney whose client is charged with robbery. Your client states that she had formerly planned to rob the victim, her stepaunt, but was not thinking of it when she went to visit her on the day of the crime. That day, she visited to have lunch, they began to fight, and the fight

ended when the defendant physically intimidated her stepaunt and stole her jewelry, which was later recovered.

a. Is the element of *actus reus* present?

b. If the jewelry was recovered, is causation still a factor? Why or why not?

Ethics Exercises

1. **Child Neglect** You are a prosecutor negotiating a plea bargain for a woman who is accused of child neglect. It is her third offense of child neglect, and this time the child nearly starved to death. You have the option of accepting a plea bargain that would give her five years' probation and allow her to continue to raise her child. If you decline the plea bargain, she faces a minimum of three years' imprisonment; the child will be taken into state care, and possibly placed in a foster home. The child, who is eight, does not want to be separated from his mother. The mother, who has an IQ of 81, seems remorseful that the child has been harmed and does not fully understand the charges against her.

a. Which choice will you make? What else can you do?

b. Does the mother appear to possess the required *mens rea?* Does this matter regarding her sentence? Regarding the child's welfare?

Notes

1. The account of this case comes from an e-mail message distributed to the Crimprof Listserv, October 14, 1998, by Dr. Ron Shapira, Professor of Law, Tel Aviv University.
2. MODEL PENAL CODE § 2.01(4) (1985).
3. CAL. PENAL CODE § 188 (West 1999).
4. JOSHUA DRESSLER, UNDERSTANDING CRIMINAL LAW § 10.06 at 147 n.115 (4th ed. 2006) (citing People v. Hood, 462 P.2d 370, 378 (Cal. 1969); Dorador v. State, 573 P.2d 839, 843 (Wyo. 1978)).
5. MODEL PENAL CODE § 2.05 (1985). See Richard G. Singer, *Strict Liability, in* ENCYCLOPEDIA OF CRIME AND JUSTICE 1541–46 (Joshua Dressler ed., 2d ed. 2002).
6. MODEL PENAL CODE § 2.02(1) (1985).
7. WAYNE R. LaFAVE, CRIMINAL LAW § 6.4(b), at 334 (4th ed. 2003).
8. JOSHUA DRESSLER, UNDERSTANDING CRIMINAL LAW § 14.03 [B] at 202 (4th ed. 2006) (citing and quoting State v. Malone, 819 P.2d 34, 37 (Alaska Ct. App. 1991)).
9. WAYNE R. LaFAVE, CRIMINAL LAW § 6.4(b), at 334–35 (4th ed. 2003).

Parties to a Crime

CHAPTER OBJECTIVES

After reading and studying this chapter, you should be able to:

1. Learn how an accomplice can aid and abet in a criminal activity.
2. Understand the difference between an accessory and a principal.
3. Know the difference between an affirmative act and an act of omission.
4. Explain how causation affects accomplice liability.
5. Understand the *mens rea* of accomplice liability.
6. Describe the natural and probable consequences doctrine.
7. Learn how justifications and excuses affect accomplice liability.
8. Explain the difference between accessorial and conspiratorial liability.

4.1 The Role of the Accomplice

In the criminal law, people other than the principal criminal actor can be held accountable for criminal conduct. An **accomplice** is someone who knowingly and willingly associates with others in the commission of a criminal offense, and who intentionally assists another person in the commission of a crime. Accomplices are said to **aid and abet** another in the commission of a crime when they assist or facilitate that person in accomplishing the crime. Other ways in which a person can act as an accomplice are by encouraging, soliciting, or advising. In other words, a person can be an accomplice to a crime through many actions that help or promote the crime's commission, including:

- Offering words of encouragement.
- Providing a weapon to be used during the offense.
- Being a lookout during the criminal act.
- Driving the getaway car.

As you can see, a person can be an accomplice to a criminal act committed by another without being present when the crime was committed. There are different degrees of accomplice liability.

Accomplices are held criminally responsible for their actions. In essence, one who is an accomplice can be held liable for an underlying criminal act without actually committing that underlying criminal act. **Accomplice liability** is thus the accountability of one individual for the criminal act or acts of another. Accomplice liability, also referred to as *complicity*, does not constitute an independent criminal offense. Rather, it exists only when a person is held liable *as a result* of a criminal offense committed by another. Accomplice liability ensures that a person who is affiliated with criminal activity does not go unpunished.

The criminal law holds an accomplice accountable to the same extent as a principal actor. This accountability is justified because an accomplice:

- Intentionally participates in the criminal goal.
- Voluntarily identifies with the primary actor.
- Willingly consents to the same liability.

Moreover, the theory of moral culpability holds a person who is intimately connected with a crime responsible for the criminal act, even if he or she did not physically participate in its commission.

Common Law Distinctions

The common law rule separated accomplice liability into four categories. The first two categories center on the roles of the **principal**, who is present at the crime and participates in it in some way, or who uses an innocent agent (such as an insane person or a child) to commit the crime. (The role of the innocent agent or instrumentality will be discussed later in this chapter.) The second two categories turn on the roles of the **accessory**, who aids in the commission of a crime without being present when the crime is committed. For example, an accessory would be one who furnishes the principal actor with the gun and masks to be used in a robbery, or plans the details of how to commit the crime.

accomplice
Someone who knowingly and willingly associates in the commision of a criminal offense, and who intentionally assists another in the commission of a crime.

aid and abet
To assist or faciliate a person in accomplishing a crime.

accomplice liability
The accountablity of one individual for the criminal act or acts of another.

principal
One who is present at and participates in the crime charged or who procures an innocent agent to commit the crime.

accessory
One who aids in the commission of a crime without being present when the crime is committed.

Principal in the First Degree

principal in the first degree
Usually the primary actor or perpetrator of the crime.

A **principal in the first degree** is usually the primary actor or perpetrator of the crime. A person is a principal in the first degree if he or she physically commits the criminal act or commits the offense by use of an innocent instrumentality. For example, one who robs the clerk at a convenience store is a principal in the first degree.

Principal in the Second Degree

principal in the second degree
One who intentionally assists in the commission of a crime in his or her presence; such presence may be actual or constructive.

A **principal in the second degree** is one who intentionally assists in the commission of a crime in his or her presence. This presence may be actual or constructive. Actual presence means physical presence at the scene of the crime. **Constructive presence** is satisfied if the individual is within the vicinity of the crime and is able to assist the primary actor if necessary. For example, one who waits in the getaway car or who acts as a lookout is constructively present at the scene of the crime and would be a principal in the second degree.

constructive presence
When an individual is within the vicinity of the crime and is able to assist the primary actor if necessary.

Accessory before the Fact

accessory before the fact
One who intentionally counsels, solicits, or commands another in the commission of a crime.

An **accessory before the fact** is a person who intentionally counsels, solicits, or commands another in committing a criminal act. A person who "cases" a bank to determine where the vaults are and provides the layout of the bank, but does not physically participate in the robbery, is an accessory before the fact. The major difference between a principal in the second degree and an accessory before the fact is that the latter is not present *during* the commission of the crime.

Accessory after the Fact

accessory after the fact
One who intentionally aids another whom he or she knows has committed a felony, in order for the person assisted to avoid criminal prosecution and punishment.

An **accessory after the fact** is a person who intentionally aids another whom he or she knows has committed a felony, in order to help that person avoid criminal prosecution and punishment. An accessory after the fact might provide the principal or accomplices with a place to hide, a plane ticket to leave the jurisdiction in which the crime was committed, or a car in which to escape.

Historically, the distinction between principals and accessories regarding accomplice liability has been of great importance. At one time, all felons were subject to the death sentence, and judges did not possess the discretion that today's law provides. Because accomplice liability did not originally distinguish between principals and accessories, accomplices faced prosecution and punishment for the same criminal offense as the principal actor. This created the concern that the punishment did not always fit the crime—which, in the case of accomplices, is often determined by the individual's degree of culpability.

In response, the common law created a separate category of parties—aiders and abettors—that allowed judges to distinguish among different types of felons and thus punish accessories less severely than principals. In time, judges gradually acquired more authority in sentencing discretion; as a result, the distinction between principals and accessories became less crucial.

Modern Parties to a Crime

As you have learned, the Model Penal Code (MPC) functions as a model for the reform of principles of American criminal responsibility; the result of its initial

FIGURE 4.1

California Statute on the Definition of an Accomplice

30. CLASSIFICATION OF PARTIES TO CRIME. The parties to crimes are classified as:

1. Principals; and,

2. Accessories.

31. WHO ARE PRINCIPALS. All persons concerned in the commission of a crime, whether it be felony or misdemeanor, and whether they directly commit the act constituting the offense, or aid and abet in its commission, or, not being present, have advised and encouraged its commission, and all persons counseling, advising, or encouraging children under the age of fourteen years, or persons who are mentally incapacitated, to commit any crime, or who, by fraud, contrivance, or force, occasion the drunkenness of another for the purpose of causing him to commit any crime, or who, by threats, menaces, command, or coercion, compel another to commit any crime, are principals in any crime so committed. It is the intent of the Legislature, in enacting this act, not to adversely affect decisional case law that has previously interpreted, or used, the terms "idiot," "imbecility," or "lunatic," or any variation thereof.

32. ACCESSORIES DEFINED. Every person who, after a felony has been committed, harbors, conceals or aids a principal in such felony, with the intent that said principal may avoid or escape from arrest, trial, conviction or punishment, having knowledge that said principal has committed such felony or has been charged with such felony or convicted thereof, is an accessory to such felony.

33. ACCESSORIES: PUNISHMENT. Except in cases where a different punishment is prescribed, an accessory is punishable by a fine not exceeding five thousand dollars ($5,000), or by imprisonment in the state prison, or in a county jail not exceeding one year, or by both such fine and imprisonment.

SOURCE: CAL. PENAL CODE §§ 30–33 (West 2007).

publication in 1962 is that an overwhelming majority of the states have revised their criminal codes. Even before the development of the MPC, however, many state legislatures had eliminated the distinction between principals and accessories, which the MPC recommends.

The California Penal Code offers a typical example. It defines principals in the commission of a crime as anyone "concerned in the commission of a crime," whether directly or not, and whether as aiders, abettors, or accessories before the fact. It adds that "[t]he distinction between an accessory before the fact and a principal, and between principals in the first and second degree is abrogated," which means that such former distinctions were put aside and ended.[1]

In other words, principals, aiders, abettors, and accessories are all prosecuted as principals under modern law. The sole exception is an accessory after the fact: one who assists after the crime has been committed. Most modern state statutes, including California's (see Figure 4.1), classify an accessory after the fact as a separate crime and treat it as a less serious offense, carrying a lighter punishment.

CRITICAL THINKING 4.1

1. What is the difference between a principal in the first degree and a principal in the second degree?

2. What is constructive presence? How is someone who is constructively present at a crime scene charged?

4.2 *Actus Reus* of Accomplice Liability

Accomplice liability may appear to be lacking in one of the law's basic prerequisites for criminally liability, which is the requirement of the *actus reus*, or act of the crime. After all, if the accomplice did not actually commit the crime, how is he or she liable? The law responds to this by requiring, for accomplice liability, some act or conduct that *contributes* to the commission of a crime. This contribution may arise either through some affirmative act or by an omission.

Affirmative Acts

An *affirmative act* may be either physical assistance or psychological influence. Physical assistance in the commission of a crime is the clearest form of accomplice liability. This includes casing the scene of the crime, masterminding the crime, providing a weapon to use during the crime, preventing help from reaching an intended victim, or driving a getaway car. A person may also be an accomplice by exerting psychological influence in the form of words of encouragement, assurance by being present at the scene of a crime and being ready to offer assistance if necessary, or provoking someone to commit a crime. A person who "blends in" with a crime scene by not physically assisting with the commission of a crime is still an accomplice if there is a prior understanding that his or her presence indicates a willingness to assist if necessary. Accomplice liability can also result if the situation fits the criteria for conspiracy. This will be discussed in greater detail later in this chapter.

If a person aids another in the commission of a crime, there is no requirement of a certain level of aid. Any kind of aid, no matter how trivial, made toward the commission of an offense establishes accomplice liability. Even psychological support can be enough to establish accomplice liability if it aids or facilitates the commission of the crime. For example, Ted, who had aided Bob in a previous bank robbery, discovers that Bob is plotting to rob a bank. Since Ted does not want to get Bob in trouble, he assures Bob that he will not inform the police of his illegal plan. Ted is liable as an accomplice because he provided psychological reassurance to Bob and, by so doing, facilitated the commission of the crime. As another example, suppose that someone feeds a hearty meal to a perpetrator in order to give him the strength and stamina needed to complete the crime. Although the act of preparing a meal seems insignificant, the person who prepared it is an accomplice if he or she acts with the intent that the perpetrator commit the crime and succeed.

Acts of Omission

Failure to act to prevent another from committing a crime—known as an *omission*—can be a basis for complicity if the person has a legal duty to act or intervene. An accomplice must still act with the required *mens rea*; in other words, an omission must be accompanied with the *intent* to facilitate the actor in accomplishing the crime. For example, a police officer who fails to prevent a crime or stop a crime in progress is liable for the substantive crime on the basis of accomplice liability, because a law enforcement officer has a legal duty to act in such a situation.

Another common example, and one that can present legal obstacles, is a parent's failure to intervene to prevent a crime against his or her child. (See Application Case 4.1.) Although such an act of omission satisfies the *actus reus* of accomplice liability, the requisite *mens rea* (or required mental state) may appear to be lacking, especially if the accomplice is another parent and is a nonabuser. A North Carolina court made an attempt to resolve this *mens rea* issue in the case of *State v. Walden* (1982). The court held that "the failure of a parent who is present to take all steps reasonably possible to protect the parent's child from an attack by another person constitutes an act of omission by the parent showing the parent's consent and contribution to the crime being committed." It suggested that the parent's "consent," regardless of the reason why it is given, satisfies the mental state of the criminal act, thus establishing accomplice liability. However, in order for the nonabusing parent to be prosecuted as a primary actor, the omission must also be "an actual and proximate cause of the result."[2]

⚖️ Application Case 4.1

People v. Stanciel

In the Illinois case *People v. Stanciel* (1992), Violetta Burgos was charged as an accomplice to murder when her boyfriend Elijah Stanciel beat her three-year-old daughter, Eleticia Asbury, to death. Burgos had violated a court order to keep Stanciel away from her child. Instead, she allowed Stanciel to discipline the child, which led to the child's death. An autopsy revealed approximately 130 bodily injuries and evidence of sexual abuse. Although Burgos did not aid or participate in the beating, the court found her liable as an accomplice for failing to prevent the beating and for not protecting her child in a situation in which she had a legal duty to act.

SOURCE: People v. Stanciel, 606 N.E.2d 1201 (Ill. 1992).

The MPC has stricter requirements regarding liability. It requires a person to act with the *purpose* of promoting or facilitating a crime in order to be held liable as an accomplice by an act of omission. Under the MPC, the outcome of the *Stanciel* case (Application Case 4.1) would be different if the prosecution could not prove that the mother shared the same purpose as the actual perpetrator of the crime, her

4.1 Web Exploration

Criminal Law Online: Child Abuse

The problem of child abuse and the culpability of parents, including parents who expose their children to adults who abuse and sometimes kill them, is discussed at the Web site of the National Clearinghouse for Child Abuse and Neglect Information at http://www.childwelfare.gov. Explore this site and determine how child abuse laws and American society's awareness of child abuse are changing—and still need to change.

boyfriend. According to the MPC guidelines, in order to establish accomplice liability when someone fails to act when a legal duty is owed, mere knowledge of a criminal act and failure to prevent or stop the crime is not enough. Purpose or intent to achieve the underlying crime is necessary for prosecution. The legal differences between knowledge and purpose will be discussed later in this chapter.

Accountability

Under the MPC, accomplice liability rests on accountability: "A person is guilty of an offense if it is committed by his own conduct, by the conduct of another person for which he is legally accountable, or both." The MPC provides that a person is an accomplice if he or she:

- Solicits another to commit a crime.
- "Aids or agrees or attempts to aid such other person in planning or committing" a crime.
- Has a legal duty to prevent the commission of a crime, but "fails to make proper effort to do so."[3]

Accomplice liability may appear to lack another of the law's basic prerequisites for criminal liability: the causation of harm or injury. Although causation is a necessary element of a criminal offense, the assistance given does not have to cause the intended result for an accomplice to be liable. Even though the same result might have occurred without the assistance rendered by the accomplice, liability is established if the assistance can be shown to facilitate the crime in any way.

The lack of a causation requirement makes sense because the liability of an accomplice is derived from the criminal act of the principal actor. An important principle to remember regarding accomplice liability is that an accomplice, "by [his or] her actions and state of mind, has chosen to adopt [the primary actor's] criminal act as [his or] her own."[4] Therefore, the prosecution only needs to prove that a criminal act was committed and that the person being charged as an accomplice somehow assisted in the commission of the crime.

Sometimes assistance is not accepted, not needed, or does not help the perpetrator in committing the crime. This is known as *ineffectual assistance*. For example, suppose that a would-be accomplice provides a gun that is not used, or that

Actions and Accomplice Liability By committing affirmative acts such as aiding or abetting a crime, accomplices make themselves criminally liable.

malfunctions and cannot be used, during the crime. At common law, if assistance in a criminal activity was ineffective, the person who rendered the ineffective aid was not considered an accomplice. What this means today is that in order for one to be liable as an accomplice, one's conduct must in fact assist or facilitate the crime, and not merely attempt to do so.

A person's unpremeditated presence at a crime scene in order to provide assistance does not establish liability if that person is never called upon for assistance. Suppose that Leah walks into a liquor store as her friend Freddie is robbing it, but Leah did not know that Freddie was planning to rob the store and does not assist him in any way. Leah is not liable as an accomplice, even though it could be proven that she would have helped her friend if he asked her. On the other hand, when one's presence at a crime scene is coupled with a previous conspiracy or agreement to be present and to provide assistance if necessary, even though assistance is never needed or called upon, liability can be based on either accomplice liability or conspiracy principles. Thus, if Leah arrived at the liquor store just pretending to be a customer, but actually had agreed in advance to work as a lookout for Freddie, she would be considered an accomplice.

CRITICAL THINKING 4.2

1. Under the MPC, what are the three factors that, individually or together, determine if a person is an accomplice?

4.3 *Mens Rea* of Accomplice Liability

The act of aiding or assisting must be accompanied by the requisite *mens rea*, also known as intent or mental state, in order to establish accomplice liability. A person is an accomplice only if he or she:

- Aids or assists another in the commission of a crime.
- Possesses the intent to support or encourage the commission of the crime.
- Intends that the primary party commit the underlying offense.

In the U.S. Supreme Court case *Hicks v. United States* (1893), John Hicks and Stand Rowe, who were both Native Americans, were jointly indicted for the murder of one Andrew J. Colvard. Colvard, who was not a Native American, was married to a Cherokee woman and was friendly with both of the defendants.

One day, Colvard and Hicks were riding their horses when Rowe approached them. Rowe raised his rifle toward Colvard twice, and then lowered it. At that point, Hicks allegedly told Colvard to take off his hat and die like a man. When Colvard removed his hat, Rowe raised his rifle for a third time and fatally shot Colvard. Originally, Hicks was convicted as an accomplice, but the U.S. Supreme Court reversed Hicks's conviction. The Court held that absent proof of a "previous conspiracy" between Rowe and Hicks, there was no evidence that Hicks shared Rowe's intent to kill Colvard. Hicks's statement to Colvard about taking off his hat was ambiguous, and could not be clearly interpreted as encouraging Rowe to kill Colvard. In addition, Hicks also testified that he feared Rowe and left a few minutes after the shooting. With no evidence that Hicks had intended to encourage Rowe, Hicks could not be held to be an aider and abettor in Rowe's killing of Colvard. Although Rowe was convicted of murder, Hicks's conviction was reversed, and the case was remanded for a new trial.[5]

Purpose and Knowledge

The MPC is strict in its requirements for defining intent, and it clearly distinguishes between purpose and knowledge for accomplice liability. This distinction is necessary because the line between purpose and knowledge often seems to blur.

The most common example illustrating the thin line between the two concepts is when a person provides someone else with a critical item to be used in the commission of a crime. *Purpose*, which is the mental state of intent, makes one liable as an accomplice. Some examples of purpose are:

- A storeowner sells a gun or explosive to an individual whom he knows intends to use it in a criminal manner.
- A pharmacist sells prescription drugs to someone that she knows will illegally resell them to minors.
- A person provides an answering service for a prostitution ring.

All of these people are criminally liable for having provided a means for the criminal to achieve the criminal act. There may be an economic motive to provide these means, and proof of a continuous economic stake in an illegal operation can establish the requisite *mens rea*; however, this is not necessary. All that is necessary is the required purpose to advance the commission of the criminal offense.

Without the required mental state of purpose to advance the commission of a criminal offense, mere *knowledge* that one's act *may* facilitate a crime does not necessarily establish accomplice liability. (See Application Case 4.2.) For instance, the fact that a person sells a gun to someone who may use it for a criminal purpose does not make the gun seller an accessory to any crimes committed by the buyer. If such were the case, all gun sellers would be held liable for crimes committed with the weapons they have sold. On the other hand, if someone sells a gun to someone who the seller knows intends to use it in a criminal manner, that seller is liable as an accessory.

⚖️ Application Case 4.2

State v. Gladstone

The legal difference between purpose and knowledge is illustrated in *State v. Gladstone* (1980), in which an undercover police officer approached the defendant seeking to buy marijuana. The defendant told the officer that he did not have any marijuana to sell, but directed him to another person, Kent, who the defendant said could provide the officer with the marijuana. The defendant had never communicated with Kent, nor did he have a business association with him. The court concluded that since the defendant had no interest in the sale (because he would not benefit from it in any way), he was not liable as an accomplice.

SOURCE: State v. Gladstone, 474 P.2d 274 (Wash. 1980).

Some lawmakers believe that mere knowledge can make a person liable to a lesser degree. To address this concern, a few jurisdictions address the distinction between purpose and knowledge by making mere knowledge a crime with a lesser penalty than the penalty for one who aids with specific purpose. This crime is called **criminal facilitation**. For example, New York State has added criminal facilitation to its penal code. The statute provides that a person is guilty of this crime when "believing it probable that he is rendering aid . . . to a person who intends to commit a crime, he engages in conduct which provides such person with means or opportunity for the commission thereof and which in fact aids such person to commit a felony."[6]

In *United States v. Fountain* (1985), a federal court of appeals held that when the offense is serious, mere knowledge of a principal's purpose is enough to establish accomplice liability. If someone furnishes a gun knowing that it will be used for a murder, or sells explosives knowing that they will be used in a terrorist attack, that person is liable. In *Fountain*, prison inmate Randy Gometz was found guilty of aiding and abetting fellow inmate Scott A. Fountain to murder a corrections officer. Immediately before the attack, Fountain was being led down a hallway in handcuffs. He then thrust his manacled hands through the bars of Gometz's cell as he went by. Gometz immediately pulled up his shirt to reveal a knife in his waistband. Fountain got his hands free, seized the knife, and fatally stabbed the guard with it. In upholding Gometz's conviction, the court held that it was not necessary for the prosecution to prove that it was Gometz's purpose that Fountain should kill the officer. By providing

criminal facilitation
When an individual knowingly aids another, but does not truly have a separate intent to aid in the commission of the underlying offense.

Fountain with a contraband weapon, Gometz's knowledge was enough. Both Gometz and Fountain received sentences of 50 to 150 years' imprisonment.[7]

Agents Provocateur and Entrapment

In rare cases, primary actors think that they are receiving assistance from someone who actually wishes to set them up. Such an accomplice is known as an **agent provocateur** or *feigning accomplice*. An agent provocateur intends for the principal to fail in his or her illegal venture. Because of the causation factor, such an individual is not an accomplice: The individual has the requisite intent to assist, but does not have the additional intent that the underlying crime be completed successfully. This situation is similar to the one in which someone provides ineffectual assistance, except that here the lack of helpful assistance is deliberate, and the agent provocateur's actions may extend to helping police apprehend the principal. (See Application Case 4.3.)

agent provocateur
Someone who intends for the principal to fail in his or her illegal venture and, because of this lack of causation, is not an accomplice.

⚖ Application Case 4.3

Wilson v. People

A classic case of an agent provocateur is *Wilson v. People* (1939). Wilson and Pierce were drinking together one night, and Wilson accused Pierce of stealing his watch. After the argument appeared to die out, the pair agreed to burglarize a drugstore. Wilson boosted Pierce through a transom into the store, then telephoned the police while Pierce was inside the store. Wilson returned to the drugstore and the police arrived. After the police discovered that Pierce had escaped, Wilson directed them to Pierce's hotel room. After Pierce's arrest, Wilson told the police that he had been involved in the burglary for the purpose of getting even with Pierce for taking his watch, which he hoped to recover (but never did).

Wilson was convicted of the burglary, but the Colorado Supreme Court reversed his conviction on appeal. The court reasoned that Wilson's actions were similar to those of a detective who enters into criminal activity in order to expose it. This reasoning is questionable, because Wilson specifically planned the crime to set up Pierce, and he did aid Pierce in illegally breaking in and entering the drugstore. However, by calling the police, he demonstrated that he did not have the requisite intent to permanently deprive the drugstore of its property and therefore was not guilty of burglary.

SOURCE: Wilson v. People, 87 P.2d 5 (Colo. 1939).

The concept of the agent provocateur is especially important in police undercover activities, "when a police officer . . . joins a criminal endeavor as an 'accomplice' and feigns a criminal intent in order to obtain incriminating evidence against the primary party or in order to ensnare the other in criminal activity."[8] Sometimes, police officers have to use encouragement of some kind in order to detect criminal activity that occurs between private people. Encouragement by the police can take several forms, including:

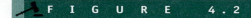

FIGURE 4.2

Kentucky Statute on Entrapment

505.010 Entrapment

(1) A person is not guilty of an offense arising out of proscribed conduct when:

    (a) He was induced or encouraged to engage in that conduct by a public servant seeking to obtain evidence against him for the purpose of criminal prosecution; and

    (b) At the time of the inducement or encouragement, he was not otherwise disposed to engage in such conduct.

(2) The relief afforded by subsection (1) is unavailable when:

    (a) The public servant or the person acting in cooperation with a public servant merely affords the defendant an opportunity to commit an offense; or

    (b) The offense charged has physical injury or the threat of physical injury as one (1) of its elements and the prosecution is based on conduct causing or threatening such injury to a person other than the person perpetrating the entrapment.

(3) The relief provided a defendant by subsection (1) is a defense.

SOURCE: Ky. Rev. Stat. Ann. § 505.010 (West 2007).

- Acting as the victim.
- Encouraging the defendant to commit a crime, whether through actions or words.
- Influencing the commission of the crime.[9]

In normal circumstances, such psychological aid would create accomplice liability. In these circumstances, however, a police officer may act as a feigning accomplice in order to detect and expose criminal activity. The difficult aspect of this concept is in differentiating between an officer who acts as an agent provocateur (which is legal) and an officer who goes too far and engages in entrapment (which is not legal). (See Figure 4.2.) Entrapment is discussed more fully in Chapter 6 on defenses to crimes. One way to think of the difference between the agent provocateur and the entrapper is that an agent provocateur gets involved with the criminal actions of a suspect who would have engaged in the criminal activity even if the agent provocateur had never been involved, whereas in **entrapment** the officer induces a person to commit a crime that this person would not or could not have committed without the officer's aid or involvement. (See Application Case 4.4.)

entrapment
When officers or agents of the government, for the purpose of instituting a criminal prosecution against a person, induce an otherwise innocent person to commit a crime that he or she had not contemplated.

⚖️ Application Case 4.4

United States v. Twigg

In *United States v. Twigg* (1978), the defendant Henry Neville was convicted of conspiracy to manufacture methamphetamines. A government informant, Robert Kubica, had proposed to Neville that he construct a meth lab. Neville raised all the money for the operation and handled the distribution of the drugs. The informant supplied the equipment, raw materials, and lab site and worked completely alone in the lab when making the drugs; in fact, he was the only one who knew how to make the drugs.

Because Neville could not demonstrate that he was not predisposed to join Kubica in the criminal enterprise, the trial court concluded that there was no basis for an entrapment defense. However, the appeals court reversed Neville's conviction. As the court put it, "although proof of predisposition to commit the crime will bar application of the entrapment defense, fundamental fairness will not permit any defendant to be convicted of a crime in which police conduct was 'outrageous.'"

The court found that the police conduct was sufficiently outrageous to prevent prosecution on due process grounds, given that the circumstances in this case:

- At the behest of the Drug Enforcement Agency (DEA), Kubica, a convicted felon seeking to reduce the severity of his sentence, contacted Neville and suggested the establishment of a speed laboratory.
- The government gratuitously supplied about 20 percent of the glassware and the indispensible ingredient, phenyl-2-propanone.
- The DEA made arrangements with chemical supply houses to facilitate purchase of the rest of the materials.
- Kubica, operating under the business name Chem Kleen supplied by the DEA, actually purchased all of the supplies with the exception of a separatory funnel.
- When problems were encountered in locating an adequate production site, the government found the solution by providing an isolated farmhouse well-suited for the location of an illegally operated laboratory.
- At all times during the production process, Kubica was completely in charge and furnished all of the laboratory expertise.
- The only evidence that Neville was predisposed to commit the crime was his receptivity to Kubica's proposal to engage in the venture and the testimony of Kubica that he had worked with Neville in a similar laboratory four years earlier.

SOURCE: United States v. Twigg, 588 F.2d 373 (3d Cir. 1978).

Ignorance of the law is generally not accepted as an excuse for accomplice liability. If a person encourages or aids another person in committing a crime, the aider is guilty as an accomplice even if he or she did not know the act was criminal. But what if the aider is merely reckless or negligent regarding the circumstances that make the underlying act criminal? For example, Mark encourages his friend Rick to have sexual relations with a female who they do not know is underage. If the crime of statutory rape only requires that Rick, the primary actor, be negligent as to the age of the victim, can Mark be held liable as an accomplice based on negligence, or must he have known for certain that the victim was underage?[10]

In the absence of a statute that covers cases such as these, the aider could be held liable if he or she has a state of mind with respect to the attendant circumstances sufficient to be convicted as a principal. In other words, if Mark was negligent about the age of the victim, he could have liability as an accomplice. In such a case, it may appear that intent is lacking; however, if intent exists in relation to the general act, ignorance that the act is criminal (in this case, ignorance of the girl's age) should not allow an individual to escape liability as an accomplice.

> ### CRITICAL THINKING 4.3
>
> 1. What is the difference between purpose and knowledge?
> 2. Define an agent provocateur, and explain how an agent provocateur differs from one who commits entrapment.

4.4 Extent of Accomplice Liability

Because accomplice liability requires a specific intent relating to the accomplishment of a target crime, and because it allows liability to extend to one person for the criminal acts of another, the *extent* of liability attributed to an accomplice is an important factor. As stated above, most states hold an accomplice liable only for the crime or crimes of the principal actor that the accomplice intended to aid or encourage. However, some jurisdictions hold accomplices to a greater responsibility and apply the **natural and probable consequences doctrine**. This doctrine holds an accomplice liable "not only of the offense he intended to facilitate or encourage, but also of any reasonably foreseeable offense committed by the person he aids and abets." Liability not only extends to the actual crime contemplated by the accomplice, but may also reach beyond the crime planned or intended.[11] The reasoning of the natural and probable consequences doctrine is based on the belief that aiders and abettors should be held "responsible for the criminal harms they have naturally, probably and foreseeably put in motion."[12] (See Application Case 4.5.)

natural and probable consequences doctrine
A doctrine that holds an accomplice liable not only for the offense he or she intended to facilitate or encourage, but also for any natural and foreseeable additional offenses committed by the principal to whom he or she is an accomplice.

⚖️ Application Case 4.5

People v. Luparello

In *People v. Luparello* (1987), the defendant Thomas Luparello's ex-girlfriend Terri Cosak had left him to marry someone else, and he wanted to know her whereabouts "at any cost." A few of Luparello's friends visited Mark Martin, a friend of Terri Cosak's husband, to find out where she was. Because Martin failed to provide the information they wanted, Luparello's friends returned the next day, and one of them shot and killed Martin. Although Luparello was not present at the murder and did not intend for Martin to be killed, he was charged with (and convicted of) the murder and conspiracy along with one of his friends. The court held that Luparello was responsible for the actions he set in motion and for all reasonably foreseeable crimes committed. This case illustrates the principle that liability can extend beyond the crime planned or intended.

SOURCE: People v. Luparello, 231 Cal. Rptr. 832 (Cal. Ct. App. 1987).

Natural and Foreseeable Consequences

In applying the natural and probable consequences doctrine, there may be some difficulty in defining what exactly is natural and foreseeable. Generally, any additional criminal act that is necessary to accomplish the criminal goal will be considered a natural and foreseeable consequence. This legal question is initially decided by the judge, and once he or she concludes that the defendant can be held legally accountable, the question goes to the jury.

An accomplice will not usually be held liable for an act that is not in furtherance of the target crime, or for an act motivated by a separate and independent intent from that of the ultimate criminal goal. For example, a person who aids another in a bank robbery will be liable as an accomplice for the robbery. This accomplice will also be liable for any kidnapping of patrons, security guards, or employees, as well as for any resulting injuries or deaths in furtherance of the robbery. The accomplice will not be held liable for crimes committed during the robbery that are not in furtherance of that crime or of any other to which the accomplice has not agreed.

Suppose that David, the primary actor, is committing a bank robbery with two accomplices when he sees his wife in the bank with her lover. In a rage, he shoots and kills his wife. As the primary actor, he will be charged with both the robbery and the killing of his wife. Because the killing was independent of the robbery, personally motivated, and in no way related to the goal of furthering the robbery, his two accomplices will probably not be held liable for her murder. On the other hand, suppose that David kills his wife because she is jeopardizing the success of the robbery; for example, she could be trying to prevent the robbery by calling the police on her cell phone. In this case, David's two accomplices will be liable for the murder because the act was done in furtherance of the criminal goal, and thus was a natural and foreseeable consequence.

The MPC does not follow the natural and probable consequences doctrine; it does not extend accomplice liability to crimes that were not agreed to, or to crimes the accomplice did not aid or intend. Under the MPC, an accomplice is not liable for crimes that follow as a natural extension of the target crime and are necessary to the success of the intended crime to which the accomplice is an aider and abettor. In the bank robbery example, the two accomplices would be liable only for the robbery and not for the individual acts of David during the course of the robbery.

Negligent Acts

Liability as an accomplice can also extend to negligent and reckless conduct on the part of the primary actor that results in a criminal offense. Since a person who commits a crime of negligence or recklessness automatically lacks specific intent, it seems logical that one could not be an accomplice to a crime involving negligence or recklessness. Accomplice liability is, after all, founded upon the theory that the accomplice *wants* the primary party to commit the crime. One who acts negligently or recklessly does not intend the consequences; therefore, one who aids a negligent or reckless actor cannot know that the criminal result will be achieved.

Some jurisdictions refuse to extend accomplice liability to those who encourage negligent or reckless behavior because there is no intent for the criminal outcome. Under the MPC, an accomplice is judged by the same *mens rea* as would be required for the conviction of the perpetrator of the offense; a core requirement of accomplice liability under the MPC is acting with purpose to commit a *specific* crime. On the other hand, a majority of jurisdictions do allow prosecution of an accomplice for aiding a negligent or reckless act. Most of these jurisdictions require that the accomplice have intent to aid or encourage the general behavior that negligently or recklessly caused harm, but do not require intent that the principal commit the specific crime.

A clear example of this occurred in *State v. McVay* (1926), in which the defendant Kelley ordered the captain and engineer of a steamer carrying several hundred passengers to fire the boiler of the vessel although he knew that it was dangerous to do so. The boiler burst and several people died as a result. Kelley was charged as an accessory before the fact of the captain's and engineer's felonious manslaughter. Kelley claimed that since the principals' crime was unintentional, it would be contradictory to hold him as an accessory. The Supreme Court of Rhode Island disagreed, stating that since it was possible for Kelley to "intentionally direct and counsel the grossly negligent" acts of the principals, he could be culpable. The court further stated, "There is no inherent reason why, prior to the commission of such a crime, one may not aid, abet, counsel, command, or procure the doing of the unlawful act or of the lawful act in a negligent manner."[13]

A classic case of accomplice liability for a crime committed by negligent conduct is one involving two or more persons who are drag racing, where each encourages the other to participate in reckless conduct. Liability as an accessory is established in such a case because the negligent conduct is deliberate, even though any criminal results (other than reckless driving) are not intended. At least one court has found a drag racer guilty on an accomplice theory based on this reasoning.[14] (See also Application Case 4.6.)

⚖️ Application Case 4.6

Riley v. State

In *Riley v. State* (2002), the defendant Richard L. Riley and another man, Edward F. Portalla, opened fire on a crowd of young people having a bonfire. Two of the young people were seriously injured. The problem facing the state in proving its case was that the bullet from one of the victims was never recovered, and the bullet from the second victim was so badly deformed that it could not be matched to either Riley's or Portalla's gun. The jury ended up finding Riley guilty of assault charges as an accomplice in the wounding of the two victims.

The conviction was upheld because the court reasoned that the requirement that Riley intended to promote the offense could be found from his facilitating the conduct that was the *actus reus* of the offense. Thus, Riley could have been convicted for simply firing his gun into the crowd of young people, even if he did not intend to injure anyone.

SOURCE: Riley v. State, 60 P.3d 204 (Alaska Ct. App. 2002).

CRITICAL THINKING 4.4

1. For what does the natural and probable consequences doctrine hold an accomplice liable?

2. What is a natural and foreseeable consequence?

4.5 Relationship between the Principal Actor and the Accomplice

This section will discuss three complex situations that affect the actor/accomplice relationship. The first is the primary actor's use of an innocent agent or instrumentality, in which case the primary actor is considered to be a principal (and not an accomplice) because the innocent agent could not form intent. The second is accomplice liability when the principal is a feigning primary party, which means that the principal is not culpable for his or her involvement in the crime. The third issue is accomplice liability when the principal actor is acquitted; contrary to popular belief, accomplices can still be liable for a crime even when the principal actor is acquitted for individual reasons.

Innocent Agent or Instrumentality

innocent agent or instrumentality

An object, animal, or person who cannot be culpable under the law, such as an insane person or a child, that is used by a principal to commit a crime.

An **innocent agent or instrumentality** is a person, animal, or inanimate object that cannot be culpable under the law because of an inability to form intent, but that is used by a principal to commit a crime. When the innocent agent is a person, that person physically commits the criminal act but does not act with criminal intent because he or she was coerced, forced, or tricked into committing the act.

An innocent agent can be a nonresponsible person, such as an insane person or a child, or even a normally functioning adult who simply does not know that he or she is participating in a crime. For example, if a messenger takes a package from a customer and delivers it, the messenger is an innocent agent if he or she was unaware that the package contains an illegal substance such as drugs. The messenger, lacking guilty knowledge, was tricked into carrying the package and does not have the mental state required to be guilty of the crime. Instead, the sender of the package will be treated as the principal actor.

A person used as an innocent agent who has any of the following excuses will not be held liable for a criminal offense:

- Insanity.
- Infancy, or being younger than the minimum age at which one is considered able to form intent. At common law and under many current laws, children under the age of seven are considered unable to form intent. Under today's juvenile laws, children under the age of 16–18 (the age varies depending on the state) are considered unable to form the same intent as adults, but can be prosecuted through the juvenile justice system.
- Duress. To commit an act "under duress" is to commit it against one's will.

As mentioned earlier, an innocent, nonhuman object or instrumentality (such as an animal or a mechanical object) may also be used to commit a crime. Such objects cannot formulate the mental state required to commit the crime. Thus, if a person trains a dog or programs a robot to place an explosive device in a building, that person will be treated as if he or she physically placed the explosive.

A person who uses an innocent agent to commit a crime is considered a principal, not an accomplice, because the innocent agent is not liable for the crime. Current law treats an individual who uses an innocent agent to commit a crime with the same level of culpability as if the user had physically committed the crime himself or herself. Thus, a person who manipulates and takes advantage of an unsuspecting individual, using that innocent agent to achieve a criminal goal, will be prosecuted as if he or she actually committed the crime.

The MPC explicitly states what is required for a person to be prosecuted as a principal when the crime is committed by an innocent agent:

- A person who "causes an innocent or irresponsible person to engage in [criminal] conduct" is liable for that conduct or act.[15]
- The accused must cause the agent to commit the criminal act. In other words, the innocent agent must be manipulated, forced, or coerced to commit the act, and it must be proven that the agent would not have committed the offense otherwise.
- The defendant must act with the intent to commit the crime. For example, the messenger who unknowingly delivers a package full of cocaine is not liable for the drug offense; the customer who sent the package is.

The concept of intent, and of being an innocent instrumentality, can go both ways. If that same messenger knowingly plants an explosive in the same package, and it results in injury or death to the recipient, the sender of the package will not be liable for this act because he or she only intended to deliver drugs, not to cause physical harm or death by an explosive.

Sometimes the doctrine of innocent instrumentality is difficult to apply, even when it is clear that the accused possessed the intent to accomplish the criminal goal and that the innocent agent is not culpable. The doctrine runs into technical problems in two cases:

1. When a statute only applies to a certain class of people by definition. This arises when a statute defines a particular group of persons who can be liable for a crime. A person who intended the crime but who is not a member of the specified class cannot be held liable as an accomplice when he or she uses an innocent agent from this specific group to commit the crime. This does not apply only to the underaged or mentally infirm. For example, if a statute prohibits any officer or employee of a bank from entering false records of transactions, then a person who is not an officer or employee cannot commit the offense. If a person who is not an officer or employee dupes an innocent employee or officer into entering a false record, "the absence of a guilty principal precludes accomplice liability."

2. When the crime can only be performed by the person himself or herself and not through an agent. Such a crime is called a **nonproxyable offense**. Problems that arise with these offenses derive from the nature of the prohibited action. For example, a sober defendant may cause a disorderly

nonproxyable offense
A crime that can only be committed through the actor's own conduct and cannot be committed by an agent.

drunk to appear in a public place by physically placing the drunk in public. However, it could not be said that the sober person has, through the instrumentality of the drunk person, himself or herself committed the crime of being drunk and disorderly in public.[16]

Federal prosecutors have found ways around the statute and class problems in innocent actor cases. Usually, they will find a loophole and interpret the federal aiding and abetting statute to include these unusual cases. Also, some courts interpret accomplice liability to apply to those perpetrators who cause another to commit the criminal act even though a statute may not include the accomplice as a member capable of committing the crime (see Application Case 4.7).[17] Usually, though, many jurisdictions will not allow convictions for nonproxyable crimes.

⚖ Application Case 4.7
United States v. Walser

One example of a nonproxyable action is perjury, which can only be committed by the person who testifies falsely under oath. A federal appellate court, however, affirmed a defendant's perjury conviction even though she did not personally give false testimony under oath. In *United States v. Walser* (1993), the defendant Viginia Walser was charged with defrauding an insurance company. She called an insurance specialist to testify about two documents that supported her claim of innocence and was acquitted of the fraud charges in part because of the specialist's testimony. Walser, however, had falsified one of the documents to which the specialist had testified, causing him to give false testimony under oath.

SOURCE: United States v. Walser, 3 F.3d 380 (11th Cir. 1993).

The application of the innocent agent doctrine varies from jurisdiction to jurisdiction; good examples of these variations can be seen in the way that rape cases are handled. In *Dusenberry v. Virginia* (1980), a Virginia court refused to uphold a conviction of rape against an armed guard who coerced a teenage couple to have sex while he watched, threatening to tell their parents if they did not comply. The court held that the theory of innocent agency did not apply because an element of rape was not met (penetration of the female organ by the defendant).[18] However, in *People v. Hernandez* (1971), a California court upheld a conviction of rape against a woman, as a principal actor, who compelled her husband to have sexual intercourse with an unwilling woman. Although the act of rape is generally considered nonproxyable, the court applied the doctrine of innocent agency.[19]

When a crime has been committed through an innocent instrumentality, the courts aim to punish the perpetrator who possesses the intent to accomplish the crime. The principal who induces an innocent agent to commit a crime on his or her behalf is, to many, the most morally reprehensible of all perpetrators. This is why many courts apply a liberal and somewhat flexible interpretation of this doctrine: "If a defendant may fairly be held liable when he aids or encourages a *guilty* principal to commit the crime (even where the defendant is not within the defined class or where the criminal action is nonproxyable)," wrote one commentator, "there are no moral or policy reasons why he should not be similarly treated if he causes the prohibited actions of an *unwitting* primary actor."[20]

Feigning Primary Party

The *feigning primary party* is the converse of the agent provocateur, also known as a feigning accomplice. In this situation, the principal pretends to have the required intent to be culpable of a crime, but does not actually possess this intent. In the case of undercover police work, a feigning primary party can set up willing accomplices for arrest by pretending to commit any type of crime. Since the accomplice's liability derives from the acts of the principal, and the principal is not sincere in his or her intent, the question is: How can the accomplice be criminally liable if the principal is not?

The answer usually lies in the specific actions of each party (see Application Case 4.8). For example, if an accomplice carries through with every element necessary to be culpable of a crime, he or she may be convicted regardless of whether the primary party has the requisite mental state. "Where each of the overt acts going to make up the crime charged is personally done by the defendant, and with criminal intent," stated one judge, "his guilt is complete, no matter what motives may prompt or what acts be done by the party who is with him, and apparently assisting him."[21] On the other hand, if a feigning party such as an undercover police officer or a private person carries out some act that is essential to the commission of a crime, and the accomplice is not involved in that aspect, the feigning party's actions cannot be imputed to the accomplice, and the accomplice cannot be guilty of the crime. As you recall from earlier, any attempt to prosecute accomplices in cases such as this would not succeed because entrapment has taken place.

⚖ Application Case 4.8

Vaden v. State

In *Vaden v. State* (1989), Department of Fish and Wildlife officers in Alaska received information that Vaden, a local guide, was facilitating illegal hunting practices by his customers. An undercover officer posed as a hunter and hired Vaden as a guide. Vaden then navigated a small airplane so that the undercover officer could illegally shoot and kill four foxes. Even though the officer was not criminally liable, Vaden was convicted as an accomplice. On appeal, Vaden argued that he could not be guilty as an accomplice because the officer's actions were justified under a "public authority jusification." The Supreme Court of Alaska disagreed with him, reasoning that the justification that excused the officer from criminal liability was individual; it could not vicariously apply to Vaden. Although the officer carried out the actual shooting, Vaden's actions in guiding the officer to do so were enough for him to be convicted.

SOURCE: Vaden v. State, 768 P.2d 1102 (Alaska 1989).

Entrapment When a police officer or someone acting on behalf of the police (such as an informant) induces someone to commit a crime that he or she would not have otherwise committed.

Indeed, an accomplice will likely raise the defense of entrapment when charged with an offense that was perpetrated by a feigning principal party. In cases involving a feigning primary party, the individual steps each person took in committing the crime will be critical in determining whether an accomplice is criminally culpable. Additionally, the entrapment defense is available only when the conduct in question is that of a law enforcement officer or an agent of a law enforcement officer, such as an informant. If a private person working solely for his or her own motives induces someone to commit a criminal act, the accused will not be able to raise a successful entrapment defense.

To help determine if entrapment has occurred, many jurisdictions have adopted the *Sherman-Sorrells* test. Under this test, the first inquiry determines whether the offense was induced by a government agent. The second inquiry determines whether the defendant was predisposed to commit the offense. The court looks at whether the defendant was ready and willing to commit the crime at any time prior to or after being encouraged by the officer or agent. Thus, the court looks at the defendant's willingness to commit the crime rather than the officer's wrongdoing. If a defendant raises the entrapment defense in a jurisdiction that follows the *Sherman-Sorrells* test, evidence that normally would not be admitted in a trial will be allowed. For example, the prosecutor can introduce the defendant's criminal history and reputation to demonstrate the required propensity to commit the act.

Other jurisdictions use a different approach, the objective test of the MPC, to determine whether an entrapment defense is valid. The objective test focuses on the officer's actions, asking whether that officer or agent "employ[ed] methods of persuasion or inducement which create a substantial risk that such an offense will be committed by persons other than those who are ready to commit it."[22] The reason for using the objective test is to deter police from engaging in wrongdoing by encouraging defendants to commit crimes that they would not otherwise have committed.

When the Principal Actor Is Acquitted

At common law, an accomplice could not be convicted of a crime unless the primary actor was also convicted. Because accomplice liability is derivative, it made logical sense that the accomplice's liability depended on the conviction of the person whom he or she aided. Sometimes, though, the primary party escaped liability and punishment when evidence against the principal was insufficient, when a technicality prevented prosecution, or when the primary actor used an excuse that justified his or her conduct. Eventually, this old common law rule was ended. In its place, various jurisdictions created statutes enabling prosecution of individuals for aiding and abetting another in the commission of a crime as long as the prosecutor could prove that a crime was actually committed. In jurisdictions following this rule, an accomplice may be liable even when the principal is not identified or when a principal is acquitted.[23]

Still, if the court finds that the principal did not commit a wrongful act, the accomplice will usually escape liability. If the criminal conduct of the primary actor is justified, the implication is that no wrongful act was committed, and therefore there is no criminal liability. In addition, although justification of a criminal act is often personal, some courts will allow a defense of justification to be raised by an accomplice as well as by a principal. For example, Stephanie and Julie get into a fight at a bar. Stephanie is heavily intoxicated and threatens Julie's life with a pocket knife. Fearing for Julie's safety, Julie's boyfriend Chris throws her his pocket knife to defend herself against the unlawful attack. In the course of the fight, Julie stabs and kills Stephanie in self-defense. Julie's action is justified based on a claim of self-defense, and therefore Chris will also likely avoid liability as an accomplice.

Sometimes, the principal has a legal excuse that allows him or her to avoid liability by virtue of a condition that the accomplice lacks. A principal who commits a criminal offense may avoid culpability if he or she is entitled to a legal defense that proves a lack of capacity, but someone who acts as an accomplice to the same criminal act does not escape liability if he or she is not personally entitled to such an excuse. In this situation, although the principal avoids punishment because of incapacity, he or she is still regarded as guilty of a crime. It is important to remember that the accomplice derives liability from the principal's *guilt* rather than from legal liability. Other personal defenses that enable the principal to escape liability while imposing criminal liability on the accomplice include duress, insanity, infancy, and involuntary intoxication. In some of these situations, the theory of an innocent agent could apply instead, thus turning the accomplice into the principal actor.

An acquittal of the principal because of an excuse defense does not morally excuse a criminal action, nor does it amount to a proclamation that the act is not wrongful. An excuse allows the principal to escape liability because:

- The law protects anyone who is part of a certain class from being prosecuted.
- The principal is not responsible for the conduct because he or she did not possess the requisite *mens rea*.
- The law provides a defense of some other excusing condition.

In summary, a person who intentionally assists in a crime and intends that the crime be completed, even when the principal is excused, is culpable and faces liability as an accomplice. (See Application Case 4.9.)

4.1 On the Job

Undercover Police Investigator

Description and Duties: To investigate and regulate all vice, liquor, tobacco, gambling, and other vice-related criminal activities. To obtain physical evidence that others are committing crimes and obtain arrest warrants. To make large numbers of arrests by maximizing contacts in a crime ring, or by convincing a number of contacts to become informants. Undercover work can also include surveillance, eavesdropping, and espionage.

   Salary: For undercover work in police departments, salaries can range from approximately $35,000 to $60,000, depending on the jurisdiction. Since undercover police are experienced, their salaries are somewhat higher than that of a rookie officer. Private undercover investigator salaries range more widely, but an average estimate is $30,000 to 40,000.

   Other Information: Undercover officers are experienced police officers who have generally served in their departments in other capacities (such as patrol) before going undercover. Ethical issues in undercover work include entrapment, corruption, and the ethical management of informants.

SOURCE: Police Undercover Work, http://faculty.ncwc.edu/toconnor/205/205lect08a.htm.

⚖ Application Case 4.9

People v. Eberhardt

In *People v. Eberhardt* (1985), a husband and wife violated the California Fish and Game Code, which prohibited salmon net fishing and the sale of salmon harvested from California waters. The defendant's wife was Native American, and because of federal laws that protect Native Americans' extended rights to hunt and fish, she was immune from prosecution by the state. Her husband, however, was not Native American and therefore was not granted this immunity. Although the wife as the principal actor could not be convicted, her husband—who was the accessory and who was found guilty of assisting the crime—was prosecuted and convicted.

SOURCE: People v. Eberhardt, 215 Cal. Rptr. 161 (Cal. Ct. App. 1985).

⚖ CRITICAL THINKING 4.5

1. What is a feigning primary party?

2. Why have the laws changed for convicting accomplices in cases in which, for whatever reason, the principal is acquitted?

4.6   Issues in Accomplice Liability

At common law, an accessory could not be convicted of a greater criminal offense than the offense for which the principal was convicted. The sole exception was for criminal homicide; in these cases, depending on the circumstances, the accomplice could be convicted of a higher degree of homicide than the principal.[24] Today, there is no obstacle that prevents conviction of an accomplice for a more serious crime than that committed by the principal. At first glance, the common law rule seems appropriate due to the derivative nature of accomplice liability. However, when individuals act in concert to achieve a common criminal goal, the courts look to the *actus reus* of the principal and the separate mental state of each participant to assess individual culpability.

For example, a husband who discovers his wife is having an affair might, in a heat of passion and rage, solicit a hitman to kill his wife. In this case, the husband, as an accomplice, could be found guilty of manslaughter while the hitman, the principal, would be guilty of first-degree murder.[25] The reverse can also be true. Suppose that a spiteful friend purposefully and incorrectly informs a husband that his wife is having an affair with another man. This causes the husband to beat his wife to death in a drunken rage. The husband will be charged with manslaughter. In contrast, if the spiteful friend intentionally set out to have the husband kill his wife by inciting and provoking him, the friend—as an accomplice—could be charged with first-degree murder.[26] In the scenarios above, the crime of murder is viewed as one act, and the degree of culpability of the primary and secondary parties is assessed by the accomplice's and primary actor's individual mental states.

Limitations of and Defenses to Complicity: Abandonment

A person who aids and abets another in the commission of a crime might have a change of heart and wish to get out of the agreement to commit the planned offense. In order to end liability as an accomplice, the aider and abettor must abandon the agreement. However, it is not enough to silently renounce the criminal plot and relinquish responsibility. The accomplice must effectively inform the principal of his or her intent to withdraw support and communicate the lack of a shared common intent that the crime be committed. Additionally, the accomplice must attempt to make ineffectual any aid given to the principal that facilitates commission of the offense. Thus, if the accomplice provided a critical instrument such as a weapon, he or she must attempt to reclaim possession or render it useless. If police have been notified, and if they think that the accomplice has already gone too far in the activity to avoid prosecution, this would be an appropriate time to contact the prosecutor, inform him or her of the situation, and try to facilitate a plea bargain agreement to allow the officer to go forward in pursuing the other actors.

The MPC stipulates that termination of complicity must be made prior to commission of the crime. The Code additionally requires that the accomplice either "wholly deprive [the aid] of effectiveness in the commission of the offense; or give timely warning to the law enforcement authorities or otherwise make proper effort to prevent the commission of the offense."[27]

Accomplice Liability versus Conspiracy: The *Pinkerton* Doctrine

conspiracy

A partnership in crime, defined as an agreement between two or more people to achieve a criminal purpose or to achieve a lawful purpose using unlawful means. Also called a common criminal enterprise.

A **conspiracy** is a partnership in crime, defined as an agreement between two or more people to achieve a criminal purpose or to achieve a lawful purpose using unlawful means. It is also called a common criminal enterprise. A conspiracy can exist with a single criminal act as its goal. However, it is quite common for a conspiracy to involve an ongoing, organized criminal activity, such as illegal gambling, distribution of drugs, or a series of robberies. Because conspiracy is continuous and open-ended, several crimes may be committed during the course of the activity in order to achieve the criminal goal.

Criminal liability based on a conspiracy theory differs from accomplice liability in that to be guilty of conspiracy, the perpetrator must actually agree to the ongoing criminal enterprise, not just to single crimes. In turn, conspiracy liability can impose broader criminal responsiblity on those involved in a criminal plot. A co-conspirator is liable for the acts of his or her partners in crime for any criminal conduct engaged in by any one of them that is perpetrated during the course of and in furtherance of the conspiracy. In addition, conspiracy is itself a separate criminal offense. This extended conspiratorial liability is based on **agency theory**, which holds that all conspirators act as the agents of (or represent) the other conspirators involved in the criminal scheme and are liable for all criminal acts committed by any of their co-conspirators.

agency theory

The theory that all conspirators act as the agents of (and represent) their co-conspirators in a criminal scheme and are liable for all criminal acts commited by any of their co-conspirators.

One may be guilty of conspiracy even though one did nothing more than *agree* to the criminal enterprise, even if the underlying goal of the conspiracy is not accomplished, or sometimes even if the underlying criminal goal has not been attempted. In short, all that is necessary for conspiracy is an agreement and any overt act in pursuance of the conspiracy by any of its members. The conspiracy may involve several conspirators who are personally unknown to one another and are associated only through the principal. Still, someone who agrees to the conspiracy will be liable for the criminal acts of any co-conspirator even if he or she does not know that a crime was committed, does not agree to that particular crime, or does not know the other participants in the conspiracy.

Accomplice liability can derive from encouragement, assistance, or sometimes mere knowledge. In most situations, an accomplice will also be a co-conspirator with the primary actor, but one can be a conspirator without being an accomplice. Again, conspiratorial liability may impose liability for any and every criminal act committed by a co-conspirator in furtherance of the common criminal scheme. This theory of liability is derived from principles of conspiracy, not accessory, liability.

Pinkerton doctrine

The doctrine that holds a person associated with a conspiracy responsible for any criminal act commited by a co-conspirator if the act is within the scope of the conspiracy and is a forseeable result of the criminal scheme.

Under one doctrine of extended conspiracy liability, a conspirator is liable for *any* act, planned or unplanned, committed by a co-conspirator that is a forseeable consequence of the unlawful agreement. The **Pinkerton doctrine**, named after *Pinkerton v. United States* (1946; see Application Case 4.10), holds a person associated with a conspiracy culpable for any criminal act committed by a co-conspirator if the act is within the scope of the conspiracy and is a foreseeable result of the criminal scheme. Under this doctrine, when the principal actor and the conspirator have agreed to violate certain laws and the principal then commits the crimes, even if the conspirator is incarcerated in prison at the time (for reasons having nothing to do with the conspiracy), the conspirator is still liable for the principal's criminal act. The theory of prosecution is not based on a claim that the conspirator assisted the perpetrator in the planning or commission of the offenses; rather, the conspirator's liability is based on his prior agreement, as a conspirator, to the perpetrator's criminal activity.

⚖️ Application Case 4.10

Pinkerton v. United States

In *Pinkerton v. United States* (1946), brothers Daniel and Walter Pinkerton were charged with violations of the Internal Revenue Code, including 10 substantive offenses and one count of conspiracy. There was no evidence that Daniel directly participated in the substantive offenses because he was in the penitentiary when they occurred. There was sufficient evidence to prove that Walter committed the substantive offenses. Since the conspiracy between the two brothers was continuous and had never ended, Daniel could be (and was) charged with any act committed by his co-conspirator Walter in furtherance of the conspiracy.

SOURCE: Pinkerton v. United States, 328 U.S. 640 (1946).

Under *Pinkerton*, a conspirator may be liable for a crime he or she did not assist in, intend to commit, or wish to occur. For example, those involved in a common agreement to commit a series of bank robberies will be liable for grand theft of an automobile if a co-conspirator steals a car for a getaway during one of the robberies. Even when a person only aids the conspiracy by casing the bank, that conspirator is liable for any crimes committed in furtherance of the common scheme, even those the conspirator was not present for, did not agree to, or were unknown to him or her.

The MPC rejects the extended liability imposed by the *Pinkerton* doctrine, and requires an accomplice or conspirator to have an intent or purpose that the crime be committed. It does not allow liability for any and all crimes that extend from the agreed crime if an accomplice or conspirator did not participate in, aid, or encourage those additional crimes. Most state jurisidictions agree, and they require more then membership for someone to be guilty of conspiracy. Nonetheless, the *Pinkerton* doctrine has been adopted in the federal penal system, where many defendants have been convicted of conspiracy for large-scale drug operations that fall under federal jurisdiction. Even though these defendants are not tried for the substantive offense (because prosecutors do not have enough evidence to convict on specific offenses), prosecutors can prove conspiracy under *Pinkerton*. Since criminal conspiracy is an important target of federal law enforcement, this approach can be seen as practical and appropriate.

How Far Should Accomplice Liability Reach?

As you have learned in this chapter, criminal liability can be extended to include individuals who play only seemingly minor roles in criminal conduct. This seems

4.2 Web Exploration

Criminal Law Online: Industry Liability

To better understand industry liability, examine the theories that plaintiffs are offering in support of their lawsuits against cigarette, pharmaceutical, and firearms manufacturers. One such organization is the Brady Campaign to Prevent Gun Violence, Located at http://www.handguncontrol.org. Explore this site, then answer the question: Should accomplice liability be imposed on a company that sells a dangerous product, if it can be proven that it is likely that the product will be used to injure or kill someone?

particularly true in the case of conspiracy, yet criminal conspiracies can have extremely dangerous and far-reaching consequences. Criminal liability for the actions of another raises important public policy questions that legislators and courts must face. If an individual can be liable for assisting in some small way in criminal conduct, what type of liability should be imposed on a conspiracy—or on an industry, such as those that sell prescription drugs or firearms? This has been a particularly controversial area that will continue to challenge lawmakers in the years to come.

 CRITICAL THINKING 4.6

1. What must a person do to legally abandon an agreement to commit a crime and end his or her liability as an accomplice?

2. What is agency theory, and how does it relate to the *Pinkerton* doctrine?

REVIEW AND APPLICATIONS

Summary by Chapter Objectives

1. **Learn how an accomplice can aid and abet in a criminal activity.** An accomplice can aid and abet another in the commission of a crime in a variety of ways:
   • Offering words of encouragement.
   • Providing a weapon to be used during the offense.
   • Being a lookout during the criminal act.
   • Driving the getaway car.

2. **Understand the difference between an accessory and a principal.** Under common law, all felons were subject to death. As the law changed, it developed accessory liability to allow gradation in the sentencing of felons and to permit judges to punish accessories less severely than principals. Today, a principal is someone who is present at the crime and participates in it in some way, or who

uses an innocent agent (such as an insane person or a child) to commit the crime; an accessory is someone who aids in the commission of a crime without being present when the crime is committed.

3. **Know the difference between an affirmative act and an act of omission.** An affirmative act is any overt physical assistance, such as:
   • Casing the scene of the crime.
   • Masterminding the crime.
   • Providing information on the person or place to be attacked.
   • Preventing help from reaching an intended victim.
   An act of omission is the failure to act to prevent another from committing a crime when the person has a legal duty to act or intervene. A common example is in child abuse cases, when one parent fails to report the abusive behavior of the other.

4. **Explain how causation affects accomplice liability.** Causation is satisfied if the assistance faciliates the crime because an accomplice, by his or her actions (*actus reus*) and state of mind (*mens rea*), has chosen to adopt and share responsibility for the principal's criminal act.

5. **Understand the *mens rea* of accomplice liability.** To be liable as an accomplice, one must act with the requisite *mens rea*, also known as intent or mental state. A person is an accomplice only if he or she:
   • Aids or assists another in the commission of a crime.
   • Possesses the intent to support or encourage the commission of the crime.
   • Intends that the primary party commit the underlying offense.

6. **Describe the natural and probable consequences doctrine.** The natural and probable consequences doctrine holds an accomplice liable not only for the offense he intended to facilitate or encourage, but also for any natural and foreseeable offense committed by the person he aids and abets. Therefore, an accomplice to a bank robbery is liable for any kidnappings or murders that result during the commission of the robbery, even if all of these additional crimes were committed by the principal.

7. **Learn how justifications and excuses affect accomplice liability.** When a primary party escapes liability because of membership in a certain class (such as the underaged or mentally infirm), a technicality, or a privilege, the accomplice will still be held accountable if the accomplice cannot also provide a personal excuse that releases him or her from liability. This is because the principal, although not punished, is still considered guilty and has escaped punishment for a personal reason that cannot be transferred to someone else. In other situations, however, when a principal is not held culpable, the accomplice is also relieved of criminal liability. One example is in cases of self-defense, when a defendant helps another person defend himself or herself against an illegal attack.

8. **Explain the difference between accessorial and conspiratorial liability.** Accessorial liability holds that accomplices are criminally responsible for their actions. One who is an accomplice can be held liable for an underlying criminal act, even though he or she did not commit that underlying criminal

act. Conspiratorial liability requires the additional intent to agree to an ongoing criminal enterprise, in which several crimes may be committed to achieve a particular lawful or unlawful goal. Conspiratorial liability extends farther than accessorial liability because a member of a conspiracy can be liable for crimes committed by co-conspirators that the member did not participate in, agree to, or sometimes even know about.

Key Terms

accomplice (p. 81)
aid and abet (p. 81)
accomplice liability (p. 81)
principal (p. 81)
accessory (p. 81)
principal in the first degree (p. 82)
principal in the second degree (p. 82)
constructive presence (p. 82)
accessory before the fact (p. 82)
accessory after the fact (p. 82)
criminal facilitation (p. 89)

agent provocateur (p. 90)
entrapment (p. 91)
natural and probable consequences
     doctrine (p. 93)
innocent agent or instrumentality
     (p. 96)
nonproxyable offense (p. 97)
conspiracy (p. 104)
agency theory (p. 104)
Pinkerton doctrine (p. 104)

Review Questions

1. What are the two categories of accessories and principals?
2. How are accessories after the fact treated differently than principals under modern law?
3. How significant must one's actions be for one to be culpable as an accomplice?
4. What is the difference between an agent provocateur and one who commits entrapment?
5. What is the nonproxyable offense theory or doctrine of innocent agency?
6. Can an accomplice still be convicted even when a principal is acquitted? Why or why not?
7. What is the difference between a feigning accomplice (agent provocateur) and a feigning primary party?
8. How can an accomplice abandon an agreement to aid a crime?
9. What is conspiracy?
10. What are agency theory and the *Pinkerton* doctrine?

Problem-Solving Exercises

1. **Accomplice or Not?** Ron has been selling cocaine and marijuana out of his apartment for several years. He is a notorious and ruthless drug dealer whom the local authorities have been watching for several years. Marisol is Ron's live-in girlfriend. Although she does not directly sell drugs, at times she packages the drugs when Ron is selling large quantities, takes messages for Ron, and instructs

buyers when to come by. Ron's operation ends when police execute a search warrant and discover large quantities of cocaine. They charge Marisol as an accessory after Ron informs them that she has been helping him by packaging the drugs and assisting buyers. Answer the following questions:

a. Can Marisol be convicted as an accomplice? Why or why not?

b. Does it matter if Marisol was never in the house when the actual drug sales took place?

2. **An Abandoned Crime?** Paul is angry at his longtime friend Tim for abandoning a criminal plan at the last minute. A few days before the day on which they planned to rob a liquor store, Tim showed up at Paul's house. He stated clearly in front of Paul and Paul's girlfriend that he did not want to take part in the robbery, then retrieved some notes he had left with Paul about the liquor store's hours and employees. Paul committed the robbery anyway, using an unregistered gun that Tim had given him several years ago. When questioned by police, he named Tim as an accomplice, stating that Tim had given him the weapon he used to commit the robbery. Answer the following questions:

a. Is Tim an accomplice? Why or why not?

b. How does Tim's intent affect his liability as an accomplice?

c. Could Tim be charged with anything in this case? Why or why not?

3. **Guilty of Child Abuse?** You are a police officer and have taken into custody a married couple accused of child abuse. The mother physically abused the child while the father, who is a cocaine addict, sat in the other room and watched television. The father stated that he knew the abuse was going on and could hear his child crying, but was afraid to get involved because his wife is violent.

a. Is the husband guilty of any crime? Why or why not?

b. Is his excuse for not stopping the abuse adequate? Why or why not?

Workplace Applications

1. **Accomplice Liability** You are a police officer and are the first to arrive at the scene of a bank robbery in progress. You are able to catch and arrest the robbers. Once they are in custody and you begin interviewing witnesses for additional information, you discover that the teller who received the holdup note personally knows two of the robbers. She informs you that several weeks ago she was at a party where one of the robbers questioned her about her job, asking how many security guards there were, where the cameras were placed, and who knew the vault combination. The teller admits that she naively discussed these facts, but says she did not intend to faciliate a robbery. According to her, her intention was only to brag about her important position at the bank. Consider the facts, then write a statement for the prosecutor recommending whether to charge her as an accomplice.

2. **Defining an Accomplice** Contact your local prosecutor's office and ask someone if your jurisdiction holds people responsible as accomplices when they possess knowledge, but not purpose, that a crime will be committed. Ask them the following questions, or use these questions as a basis for your interview:

    a. Why did they make this choice, and what caused it?

    b. How well is it working?

    c. Do they see any need for modifications in the future?

    Note: You might also ask them the same basic questions about whether they apply the *Pinkerton* doctrine.

3. **Principal in the Second Degree** You are a witness to the robbery of a school bookstore. While you were in line, the defendant came into the store and said "Hi, Recia" to your cashier. During the robbery, the store manager frantically signaled Recia to press an alarm button under her cash register, but she did not do so. She later stated that she knew the defendant but was not friends with him and had no knowledge of the robbery.

    a. In your opinion, is Recia an accomplice? Why or why not?

    b. What other information do you need to help you decide whether to press charges?

Ethics Exercises

1. **Aiding and Abetting** Your nephew, who lives down the street with his mother, is accused of burglarizing serveral homes in the neighborhood. You know that he was severely abused by his father during his early childhood and that his mother has struggled to bring him up on her own. Therefore, you know him well and feel sorry for him; you also feel that he can be rehabilitated. Your sister, who is his mother, calls you and asks you to lie to police that he visited your home last Wednesday night. If you don't, she tells you, he will be tried as an adult and face a felony sentence.

    a. What will you tell your sister, and what will you do?

    b. Is your sister aiding and abetting her son? Why or why not?

Notes

1. CAL. PENAL CODE § 971 (1997).
2. JOSHUA DRESSLER, UNDERSTANDING CRIMINAL LAW § 30.04[A][4], at 508, n.57 (4th ed. 2006) (citing State v. Walden, 293 S.E.2d 780, 786–87 (N.C. 1982)).
3. MODEL PENAL CODE § 2.06(1) (1985); MODEL PENAL CODE § 2.06(2)(a)–(c) (1985); MODEL PENAL CODE §2.06(3)(a)(ii) (1980).
4. JOSHUA DRESSLER, UNDERSTANDING CRIMINAL LAW § 30.02[A][2], at 498 (4th ed. 2006).
5. Hicks v. United States, 150 U.S. 442 (1893).
6. N.Y. PENAL LAW § 115 (McKinney 2004); *see also* SANFORD H. KADISH & STEPHEN J. SCHULHOFER, CRIMINAL LAW AND ITS PROCESSES: CASES AND MATERIALS 614 n.2 (7th ed. 2001) (noting that Arizona, Kentucky, and North Dakota have followed New York in enacting a law defining criminal facilitation as a crime).
7. United States v. Fountain, 768 F.2d 790 (7th Cir. 1985).

8. Joshua Dressler, Understanding Criminal Law § 30.05[B][1], at 512 (4th ed. 2006).

9. L. Tiffany, D. McIntyre & D. Rotenberg, Detections of Crime 210 (1967), *as cited in* Wayne R. LaFave, Criminal Law § 9.8 n.1 (4th ed. 2003).

10. This hypothetical appears in Sanford H. Kadish & Stephen J. Schulhofer, Criminal Law and Its Processes: Cases and Materials 622–23 (7th ed. 2001) and in Joshua Dressler, Understanding Criminal Law § 30.05[B][4], at 516 (4th ed. 2006).

11. People v. Luparello, 231 Cal. Rptr. 832 (Cal. Ct. App. 1987) (quoting People v. Croy, 710 P.2d 392 (Cal. 1985)).

12. People v. Prettyman, 926 P.2d 1013, 1019 (Cal. 1996) (quoting People v. Luparello, 231 Cal. Rptr. 832 (Cal. Ct. App. 1987)).

13. State v. McVay, 132 A. 436 (R.I. 1926).

14. People v. Abbott, 445 N.Y.S.2d 344 (N.Y. App. Div. 1981).

15. Model Penal Code § 2.06(2)(a) (1985).

16. Sanford H. Kadish & Stephen J. Schulhofer, Criminal Law and Its Processes: Cases and Materials 641 (7th ed. 2001) (quoting Sanford H. Kadish, Blame and Punishment: Essays in the Criminal Law 171–72 (1987)).

17. In addition to Walser, *see* United States v. Ruffin, 613 F.2d 408 (2d Cir. 1979).

18. Dusenbury v. Commonwealth, 263 S.E.2d 392, 394 (Va. 1980).

19. People v. Hernandez, 96 Cal. Rptr. 71, 74 (Cal. Ct. App. 1971).

20. Sanford H. Kadish, Blame and Punishment: Essays in the Criminal Law 173 (1987).

21. State v. Hayes, 16 S.W. 514, 515 (Mo. 1891) (quoting State v. Jansen, 22 Kan. 498 (Kan. 1879)).

22. Model Penal Code § 2.13 (1985).

23. Sanford H. Kadish, *Complicity, Cause and Blame: A Study in the Interpretation of Doctrine*, 73 Calif. L. Rev. 323, 340 (1985) (citing Standefer v. United States, 447 U.S. 10 (1980)).

24. Joshua Dressler, Understanding Criminal Law § 30.03[B][6], at 506 (4th ed. 2006).

25. Sanford H. Kadish & Stephen J. Schulhofer, Criminal Law and Its Processes: Cases and Materials 681 (7th ed. 2001) (citing Moore v. Lowe, 180 S.E. 1 (Va. 1935)).

26. Sanford H. Kadish, Blame and Punishment: Essays in the Criminal Law 182–83 (1987).

27. Model Penal Code § 2.06(6)(c)(I)(ii) (1985).

Incomplete Crimes

CHAPTER OUTLINE

CHAPTER OBJECTIVES

After reading and studying this chapter, you should be able to:

1. Explain the purpose of defining attempt as a crime.
2. Explain how the Model Penal Code test for the *actus reus* of attempt differs from all the other tests.
3. State the elements of an attempt.
4. Name the two principal defenses to attempt.
5. Explain when the crime of solicitation can be charged.
6. Define the crime of conspiracy.
7. Define the *actus reus* requirement for conspiracy.
8. Explain the *mens rea* requirement for conspiracy.

5.1   Attempted Crimes

This chapter discusses **inchoate crimes**, which are criminal acts that are detected and punished before the ultimate or intended crime actually occurs. The most common inchoate crimes are attempt, conspiracy, and solicitation. The word *inchoate* means imperfect or partial. Thus, an inchoate crime is defined by the fact that it was not completed, although it was intended to be.

For instance, an accused may intend to commit a crime but be unable to complete it because he or she is unexpectedly interrupted. Such an incomplete criminal scheme or plan is still punishable as a crime that is separate from the intended harm. In other words, the law punishes agreements to engage in criminal conduct, soliciting such conduct, and taking a substantial step toward engaging in such conduct. The focus is on anticipatory, preparatory, or unsuccessful conduct.

It should be noted that the three most common inchoate crimes—attempt, conspiracy, and solicitation—are not crimes in and of themselves. They are criminal only when they occur in conjunction with other crimes or are defined by reference to other crimes, such as murder, robbery, and battery. For example, when attempt is combined with the target offense of murder, it becomes the crime of *attempted murder*, or when two or more persons agree to commit a murder, that becomes *conspiracy to commit murder*.

Lawmakers enact statutes that punish individuals for incomplete crimes in order to avoid the social harm that will result if the crime is actually carried out. Because society has an interest in preventing harm, such crimes are defined with a view toward punishing an individual before certain harms are completed. It would be unduly burdensome to require society to wait until someone is harmed before dispensing punishment for the intended act. In addition, failing to punish attempts would greatly hamper the ability of the police to prevent or intervene in the commission of a substantive crime. Therefore, the purpose of these crimes is to deter a greater harm than that resulting from the incomplete crime.

On the other hand, if unsuccessful attempts are criminalized too easily, innocent people might be punished. For instance, there is a risk that an individual's intention may have been misinterpreted as criminal or that the individual would have ultimately abandoned the plan. Premature punishment would result in punishing an individual for little more than an evil thought. The mere intent to commit a crime is not sufficient for attempt; the intent must be accompanied by some conduct on the part of the accused.

Several other crimes also have a large pre-action (inchoate) aspect:

- Larceny.
- Forgery.
- Kidnapping.
- Arson.
- Burglary.
- Possession of burglary tools.
- Stalking.
- Drunk driving.

As an example, the crime of drunk driving is preventive in nature because the law seeks to prevent accidents that would cause personal injury and property damage.

inchoate crime
A criminal act that is detected and punished before the ultimate or intended crime actually occurs. The principal modern inchoate crimes are attempt, conspiracy, and solicitation.

5.1 Web Exploration

Inchoate Crimes and Modern Technology

You can learn more about new types of inchoate crimes by visiting http://www.apsu .edu/oconnort/3010/3010lect03a.htm. What are the elements of stalking? What acts are punishable as cybercrimes?

Inchoate crimes also have *actus reus* and *mens rea* requirements, which will be discussed later in this chapter. Defenses to inchoate crimes, such as legal impossibility and renunciation, will also be discussed later.

The Six Stages of Committing a Crime

In order to better understand the concept behind the law's treatment of the inchoate crimes of attempt, conspiracy, and solicitation, you need to understand the process by which a person intentionally commits a crime. It is a six-stage process in which the actor:

1. Conceives the idea of committing the crime.
2. Evaluates the idea, considering whether or not to proceed.
3. Forms the intention to go forward.
4. Prepares to commit the crime—for example, by obtaining a gun.
5. Commences commission of the offense.
6. Completes the action, achieving the goal.[1]

Only after the fourth stage is a person liable for criminal punishment under Anglo-American law.

Both a *mens rea* and an *actus reus* are necessary for criminal liability. As will be shown, the legal definitions of inchoate crimes such as attempt, conspiracy, and solicitation require that the perpetrator advance past the third stage described above.

Historical Development

The crime of attempt has caused confusion and controversy for centuries. Although almost all modern jurisdictions criminalize attempt, it was not recognized as a crime before the late 1700s. Before that time, the *mens rea* requirement for attempt was that the accused must have manifested his or her intent "by some open deed tending to the execution of his intent. So as if a man had compassed the death of another, and had uttered the same by words or writing, yet he should not have died for it, for there wanted an overt deed tending to the execution of his compassing."[2] Convictions for attempt were rare before the late 1700s. As long as a perpetrator did not actually carry out the offense, he or she was usually off the hook unless the crime was particularly heinous.

The crimes of attempt and solicitation were developed through case law, as the following two landmark cases illustrate.

Rex v. Scofield

In 1784, the English court in *Rex v. Scofield* first recognized the crime of attempt. In that case, the defendant was charged with placing a lighted candle and combustible material in a rented house with the intent to set it on fire. Although there was no allegation or proof that the house was burned, the court held that the defendant turned an otherwise innocent act into a criminal one. In addition, the court found that the completion of a criminal act was not necessary to constitute criminality.[3]

Rex v. Higgins

In 1801, the idea that attempt was itself a crime was recognized in the case of *Rex v. Higgins*. In that case, in which the accused solicited a servant to steal his master's property, a British court upheld an indictment charging an unsuccessful attempt to steal. After *Higgins*, the common law adopted the widespread principle that an attempt to commit either a felony or a misdemeanor was itself an indictable crime, usually a misdemeanor. The common law treated all attempts as misdemeanors, even an attempt to commit a felony.[4]

Today, according to the MPC, a person is guilty of **attempt** to commit a crime if, acting with the kind of culpability otherwise required for commission of the crime, he or she:

attempt
When a person, with the intent to commit an offense, performs any act that constitutes a substantial step toward the commission of that offense.

- Purposely engages in conduct that would constitute the crime if the attendant circumstances were as he or she believes them to be.
- When causing a particular result is an element of the crime, does or omits to do anything with the purpose of causing or with the belief that it will cause such result without further conduct on his or her part.
- Purposely does or omits to do anything that, under the circumstances as he or she believes them to be, is an act or omission constituting a substantial step in a course of conduct planned to culminate in commission of the crime.

Under modern law, an attempt to commit a substantive crime is usually classified as a lesser crime than the target or object offense. An attempt to commit a felony is usually treated as a felony but is punishable to a lesser degree than the underlying substantive offense. An attempt to commit a capital crime or a crime punishable by life imprisonment, for example, is usually punishable by a specific number of years of imprisonment.

Mens Rea of Attempt

The crime of attempt requires the specific *mens rea*, or intent, to commit an act that, if carried out, would have resulted in a completed substantive crime. It is not enough that the defendant intended to commit some other innocent or even criminal act. For example, if the actor lit a match with the intent to set fire to a building, the actor would be guilty of attempted arson. However, if the actor intended only to light a cigarette, then he would not be guilty of attempted arson even though he intentionally lit the match, because he lacked the specific intent to burn a building. In short, attempt is a specific intent crime, even if the underlying substantive offense is a general intent crime.

The Crime of Attempt When all of the elements of a crime are in place and a person is near completing a criminal act, but does not succeed, he or she is still liable for the crime of attempt.

For crimes that are defined by prohibiting a certain result, the defendant must have had the intent to cause that result. For example, if a person randomly shot a gun in the air on New Year's Eve, almost hitting an innocent victim, but did not have the specific intent to kill someone, he or she would not be guilty of attempted murder. The specific intent requirement for attempt crimes makes sense, because the concept of attempt encompasses the idea that a person is trying to do something specific. Without that specific goal, the actor could not be said to have tried to cause the result. A good example of an attempt statute is the Wisconsin law that requires "that the actor have intent to perform acts and attain a result which, if accomplished, would constitute such crime."[5]

Mens Rea and the MPC

The MPC takes a slightly different approach to the mental element of attempt. Section 5.01(1) provides that a person is guilty of attempt if it was his or her purpose to engage in the conduct or to cause the result that would constitute the substantive offense, with two exceptions:

1. A person may be guilty of attempt to cause a criminal result if he or she believes that the result will occur, even if it is not the actor's conscious object to cause the result.
2. In holding a person culpable for attempt when he or she acts "with the kind of culpability otherwise required for the commission of the crime," the Code does not require that the *mens rea* of "purpose" or "belief" apply to the attendant circumstances.

For such attendant circumstance elements to be present, the actor can be guilty of attempt without specific intent to cause the result if the underlying crime could be committed by less than purposeful achievement of the result. For example, a perpetrator could be found guilty of attempted statutory rape if there was proof that he was reckless with respect to learning the girl's age.

Here is Section 5.01(1) of the MPC, in its entirety:

(1) Definition of Attempt. A person is guilty of an attempt to commit a crime if, acting with the kind of culpability otherwise required for commission of the crime, he:
   (a) purposely engages in conduct that would constitute the crime if the attendant circumstances were as he believes them to be; or
   (b) when causing a particular result is an element of the crime, does or omits to do anything with the purpose of causing or with the belief that it will cause such result without further conduct on his part; or
   (c) purposely does or omits to do anything that, under the circumstances as he believes them to be, is an act or omission constituting a substantial step in a course of conduct planned to culminate in his commission of the crime.

Under the reasoning of the Model Penal Code, the intent requirement can be met even though a defendant may not have desired or wanted a particular result, *if* it can be shown that the defendant acted with a substantial certainty that a certain result would occur. For instance, a defendant who detonates a bomb, intending to destroy a building, with knowledge that the people inside will almost certainly be killed, can be convicted of attempted murder. This is because the defendant knew with substantial certainty that a certain result would occur, that people would be killed. He or she can be convicted of attempted murder even if the ultimate intent was only to destroy the building.

Actus Reus of Attempt

The conduct element, known as the *actus reus*, is essential to the crime of attempt. It is generally accepted that a defendant cannot be held liable for an attempt unless the defendant has committed some act to further his or her plan to commit the substantive offense. This is because one of the basic principles of Anglo-American criminal law is that the law does not punish people for their thoughts or, in general, for their speech.

One of the biggest problems in imposing criminal responsibility for an attempt is determining *when* a suspect has crossed the line from mere preparation or planning. Only prohibited criminal conduct justifies prosecution for the crime of attempt. (See the discussion of First Amendment rights in Chapter 2.) Therefore, a prosecutor must prove that the accused took enough steps to show that he or she would have carried out the substantive crime had the plans not been interrupted.

The law has created several tests to help measure when a person is actually guilty of the crime of attempt.

The Last Act Test

Under the **last act test**, established in England in the case of *Regina v. Eagleton* (see Application Case 5.1), an attempt occurs when a person has performed all of the acts that he or she believed were necessary to carry out the action that would constitute the underlying offense.

last act test
A test that determines that an attempt has occurred when a person has performed all of the acts that he or she believed were necessary to commit the underlying offense.

⚖️ Application Case 5.1

Regina v. Eagleton

In this English case, a welfare office hired the defendant to provide bread to the poor. The process required the defendant to provide loaves of bread to poor people; in turn, each poor person would provide him with a ticket that he later turned in to the welfare office. Following submission of the ticket to the office, the defendant would receive credit for a payment to be made by the welfare office at a later date. The defendant delivered underweight loaves but received tickets for the credit he should have received for loaves of full weight, then turned in these tickets. He was charged with the attempt to obtain money by false pretenses from the welfare office. The defendant argued that because he had not yet received any money, he was not guilty. However, the court held that the defendant was still liable for attempting to obtain the money by false pretenses based on the fact that no other acts were required to complete the crime. Turning in the ticket was the last act toward obtaining the money and was therefore sufficient for attempt liability.

SOURCE: Regina v. Eagleton, 6 Cox Crim. Cas. 559, 571 (1855), *as cited in* Joshua Dressler, Understanding Criminal Law, § 27.06[B][2] at 425 n.98 (4th ed. 2006).

According to the last act test, an attempted murder would not occur until the trigger had been pulled and an attempted arson would not occur until the fire had been set. This test is no longer utilized because most lawmakers believe that a person does not have to take the very last step to be criminally culpable. Opponents of the last act test point out that it defeats the policy of making attempt a separate crime, because such a test prohibits arrest of a suspect until it is too late to prevent the harm.

The Physical Proximity Test

physical proximity test
A test that determines that an attempt has occurred when the perpetrator's conduct, though not having advanced so far as the last act, approaches sufficiently near to the completed crime as to be a substantial step toward commission of the offense.

Some courts follow the **physical proximity test**. Under this test, the perpetrator need not have advanced so far as the last act, but the conduct must be "proximate" to, or very near, the completed crime. The accused's conduct must reflect either a first or later step in physically carrying out a crime *after* planning that crime. Under this approach, an attempt has not been committed unless the accused has the immediate power to actually carry through with the crime at the time the police intervene. For example, under the physical proximity test, a person would not be convicted of attempted bank robbery unless the person was approaching the bank, was armed, and was carrying a holdup note.

The Dangerous Proximity Test

dangerous proximity test
A test that determines that an attempt has occurred when the perpetrator's conduct is in dangerous proximity to success, or when an act is so near to the result that the danger of its success is very great.

The **dangerous proximity test** incorporates the physical proximity test but is somewhat more flexible. Under this test, a person is guilty of attempt when his or her conduct is in "dangerous proximity" to succeeding at the crime. There is no clear point when a defendant has met this test's requirements, but factors used are closeness of the danger, significance of the harm, and the level of apprehension felt by a potential victim. In some cases, preparation may not be sufficient to sustain an attempt when there are circumstances outside the perpetrator's control that prevents completion of the crime. In others, certain preparation may be enough, depending on the degree and closeness of the preparation to completion of the act. Thus, dangerous proximity is evaluated on a case-by-case basis.

Courts have applied this test in a variety of different situations, with different results. In the *Rizzo* decision (see Application Case 5.2) and also in *United States v. Harper* (1994), the court held that making an appointment with a potential victim does not constitute an attempt and is not a sufficient commitment to an intended crime even if it made a later attempt possible. Compare this to the California case *People v. Vizcarra* (see Application Case 5.3). Also, compare it to *People v. Parrish*, in which the defendant was convicted of attempted murder for going to the home of his wife with a loaded gun and listening outside to be sure she was alone.[6]

⚖ Application Case 5.2

People v. Rizzo

In *People v. Rizzo*, the court adopted the dangerous proximity test, which led to the reversal of the defendant's conviction for attempted robbery. The defendant and three other armed men planned to rob an individual while he was carrying his company's payroll from the bank. The defendant and the other men drove around looking for a man who they believed would be withdrawing a large amount of money from a bank. They first went to the bank and entered various buildings, looking for the victim. They failed to find him or any other payroll messenger, but as they were searching, the police became suspicious and arrested them.

The court found that the defendants were not dangerously close to success because they had never located the victim. Therefore, they were not guilty of attempted robbery. The court ruled that the defendants could not be found guilty of attempted robbery prior to locating the victim. Neither could they be found guilty of attempted burglary if they were in the process of searching for the building where the victim was located. It was at least necessary to locate the victim to be guilty of attempted robbery.

SOURCE: People v. Rizzo, 158 N.E. 888 (N.Y. 1927).

⚖ Application Case 5.3

People v. Vizcarra

In *People v. Vizcarra*, the defendant was observed standing in front of a liquor store at night, wearing a poncho, and carrying a rifle. He was standing on a walkway approximately four feet wide. When a customer came by on the walkway, the defendant turned away so that his nose was right up against the block wall. The customer observed the defendant's strange behavior and the butt of the rifle protruding from his poncho. The defendant then returned to the car that was parked across the street and drove past the liquor store.

In upholding the defendant's attempted robbery conviction, the court held that approaching the liquor store with the rifle and attempting to hide on the walkway when observed by a customer was a sufficient direct act toward accomplishment of the robbery. The court reasoned that the proximate act need not be the final act necessary to complete the crime. It is sufficient that the overt acts (acts in preparation) reach far enough toward accomplishment of the offense to amount to a beginning of the substantive act.

SOURCE: People v. Vizcarra, 168 Cal. Rptr. 257 (Cal. Ct. App. 1980).

The Indispensable Element Test

indispensable element test

A test that determines that no attempt has occurred when a suspect has not yet gained control over an indispensable instrumentality of the criminal plan.

Yet another aspect of proximity utilized in evaluating an attempt is the **indispensable element test**. Under this test, a suspect who has not yet gained control over an indispensable instrumentality of the criminal plan cannot be guilty of attempt. For example, a person planning a killing by shooting who has not obtained a gun, or a person planning arson who has not yet acquired the incendiary material necessary to start the fire, could not be held for attempted murder or arson under this test.

This test does not look into the actor's mental state or intent but, rather, focuses on whether he or she possesses the necessary instruments to carry out the offense. (See Application Case 5.4.) At times, the objectivity of this test could be unfair, for a defendant who may have had a change of heart or held the instrument for a different purpose could still be criminally culpable. On the other hand, when acts are dependent on other parties, the defendant may escape liability.

⚖️ Application Case 5.4

People v. Orndorff

In *People v. Orndorff*, the defendant was a professional con man engaged in a plan to steal money from the victim. The plan required the victim to go to a bank and withdraw her money, which the defendant planned to switch with counterfeit money. However, the defendant drove away while the victim was in the bank. He was later arrested and charged with attempted grand theft. The court held that the defendant did not go far enough to be liable for attempt, because the scheme required the victim to withdraw the money from the bank and give it to the defendant. It could not have succeeded without this step; hence, the act did not go beyond mere preparation.

SOURCE: People v. Orndorff, 67 Cal. Rptr. 824 (Cal. App. 1968).

The Unequivocality Test

The **unequivocality test** does not look at how close the defendant came to succeeding, but at whether the defendant's conduct was indicative of his or her criminal intent. Under this test, an attempt occurs when a person's conduct in itself unambiguously manifests his or her criminal intent. Thus, the defendant's conduct must clearly indicate a criminal intent and not a possible innocent one.

The leading case supporting this test is *King v. Barker* (1924), which stated that buying a box of matches to burn a haystack was too ambiguous to justify conviction for attempted arson, but that taking matches to a haystack and lighting one there is an unambiguous act.[7] This conclusion has been criticized, though, because even in the haystack example, the person who struck a match near the haystack might have intended only to light a pipe.

unequivocality test
A test that determines that an attempt has occurred when a person's conduct, standing alone, unambiguously manifests his or her criminal intent.

The Substantial Step Test

The MPC adopts an entirely different test for the *actus reus* of attempt—the **substantial step test**. This test requires that the suspect must have done or omitted to do something that constitutes a "substantial step" toward committing the substantive offense. In addition, conduct falling within the realm of a substantial step requires strong corroboration of the actor's criminal intent.

It may be easiest to convict a person for attempt under this test because a prosecutor only has to show that the defendant took a substantial step. For example, a person who purchases flammable materials and soaks rags in them can be convicted of attempted arson without doing anything else, because the purchase, coupled with the act of soaking the rags, may be deemed a substantial step toward arson. Under this test, close proximity is not required, and attempt liability may attach even if the actor does not get far along in consummating the crime.

The MPC provides several examples of conduct that would be considered a substantial step toward the commission of a crime:

substantial step test
The MPC's test to determine whether the *actus reus* of attempt has occurred, which requires that the suspect must have done or omitted to do something that constitutes "a substantial step" in the commission of the substantive offense.

- Lying in wait, searching for or following the contemplated victim of the crime.
- Enticing or seeking to entice the contemplated victim of the crime to go to the place contemplated for its commission.
- Reconnoitering the place contemplated for the commission of the crime.
- Unlawful entry of a structure, vehicle or enclosure in which it is contemplated that the crime will be committed.
- Possession of materials to be employed in the commission of the crime, that are specially designed for such unlawful use or that can serve no lawful purpose of the actor under the circumstances.
- Possession, collection or fabrication of materials to be employed in the commission of the crime, at or near the place contemplated for its commission, if such possession, collection or fabrication serves no lawful purpose of the actor under the circumstances.
- Soliciting an innocent agent to engage in conduct constituting an element of the crime.[8]

For a summary of the various tests for attempt liability, see Figure 5.1.

F I G U R E   5 . 1

A Comparison of the Various Tests for Attempt Liability

The Last Act Test
- Perpetrator has performed all of the acts that he or she believed necessary to commit the intended offense.

The Physical Proximity Test
- Perpetrator must be very close to completing all of the acts necessary to commit the intended offense.

The Dangerous Proximity Test
- Perpetrator is guilty of attempt when his or her actions are in dangerous proximity to success or when an act is so near the result that the danger of its success is very great.

The Indispensable Element Test
- Perpetrator is innocent until he or she gains control over an indispensable instrumentality of the criminal plan.

The Unequivocality Test
- Perpetrator's conduct, regardless of other factors, unambiguously manifests his or her criminal intent.

The Substantial Step Test
- Perpetrator must have done something or omitted to do something that constitutes a "substantial step" toward the commission of the substantive offense.

Courts in various jurisdictions determine the *actus reus* of attempt based on the circumstances and utilizing one of the tests discussed above. Ultimately, it must be determined whether the actor went beyond mere preparation and can be held culpable for attempt. In some jurisdictions, the courts hold that the *actus reus* has been met if the actions of the defendant in preparing to commit a crime pose serious danger to the public that would warrant involvement of the police. Depending on which test a particular jurisdiction adopts, a person can be guilty of attempt if the person has the intent to commit the substantive crime and takes steps that a jury would find sufficient to indicate that he or she was in the process of committing the act.

Handling Multiple Counts of Attempt

Multiple counts of attempt can arise from a single act that goes beyond mere preparation. The issue in this type of case is whether the particular act was sufficient to prove beyond a reasonable doubt that the accused had multiple purposes (intents) accompanying the single act. In other words, the act must be sufficient to support an attempt to commit each substantive offense. A simple case of a single act producing multiple counts of attempt would be a person's firing a gun at two or more persons or in some other way attempting to injure multiple persons with a single act. In such a case, the defendant would be charged with the attempted murder of each victim. However, a more difficult application occurs when a single act by the defendant is taken to show the intent to commit several different substantive offenses.

Other Elements and Issues

Usually, attempt has been committed if an individual has the requisite intent to carry out the underlying offense but, for whatever reason, falls short of doing so. There are a number of reasons why a person may be stopped prior to completing the underlying crime and therefore be guilty only of attempt.

For example, Bob devises a plan to rob the First Bank of Westmoreland. He has observed the bank for several weeks and picks a time when the guard is out to lunch and there are few customers. He writes a holdup note with a threat of harm, demanding all of the cashier's money. He purchases a semiautomatic machine gun, ski mask, and gloves. Bob arrives at the bank at the designated time, with the ski mask on, the holdup note in his pocket, and the gun in his hand.

As he is walking into the bank, an armed off-duty police officer notices Bob, becomes suspicious, and stops him before he enters the bank. At this point, Bob can be arrested for attempted robbery because, but for the officer being there, he would have carried out the actual offense. At trial, Bob may argue that he was planning on abandoning the crime and not going through with it; however, his abandonment argument would probably not be believed, because he was so close to carrying out the crime, and he would likely be convicted.

As in the case of Bob, a crime may never get beyond the level of attempt because the police may stop it before it happens. Other possible reasons are that a defendant's plan to commit a crime does not work out, or a defendant gets concerned that the police are about to intercept his actions and stops out of fear of being caught.

Whatever the reason, attempt is a very common charge that is used to punish individuals who were going to commit an underlying crime, even if they didn't actually do so. The purpose of the law's defining attempt as a crime is to prevent the commission of crimes before they take place and to protect the safety of the public by allowing police officers to stop the continuance of criminal activity. Defining attempt as a crime makes sense, because a person who has taken a substantial step toward the commission of a substantive offense with the intent to do so deserves punishment. (See Application Case 5.5.)

⚖️ Application Case 5.5

People v. Kraft

In *People v. Kraft*, the defendant forced the victim's car off of the road when the victim attempted to pass him. The victim later noticed the defendant's vehicle and pulled up next to it to say something to the defendant. Before the victim had a chance to speak, the defendant pulled out a gun and fired several shots, some going above the car and one hitting the back of it. The victim then notified police of the incident, and, as a police officer approached the defendant's car, he pointed a gun at the officer and shot at him.

At trial, the defendant testified that when the victim approached his car he was scared and was only trying to scare the victim away. He stated that when he shot at the officer, he was in shock and only wanted to kill himself. The trial court instructed the jury that the defendant could be found guilty of attempted murder if he did "any act which constitutes a substantial step toward the commission of the offense of murder" with the *mens rea* to commit murder. The trial court further instructed the jury that the *mens rea* for murder included doing acts that create "a strong probability of death." The appellate court held that the jury instructions given were wrong for the charge of attempt and that "[t]he offense of attempted murder requires the mental state of specific intent to commit murder, to kill someone." On this basis, the appellate court overturned the defendant's conviction.

SOURCE: People v. Kraft, 478 N.E.2d 1154 (Ill. App. Ct. 1985).

CRITICAL THINKING 5.1

1. Why are inchoate crimes considered criminal behavior?
2. In your own words, how does the MPC define attempt?
3. Why must the *actus reus* be accompanied by the *mens rea*?

5.2 Defenses to Attempt

A defendant may have done everything in his or her power to accomplish a specific result, but due to uncontrollable circumstances could not commit the substantive crime. Two examples of this are:

- A would-be pickpocket reaches into the pocket of another to remove money without that person's knowledge, but the defendant discovers that the pocket is empty. Was his reaching a case of attempted theft?
- A man smokes what he believes to be marijuana, but is in fact a garden weed. Can he be convicted of attempted possession of marijuana?

These defendants may claim that they cannot be convicted of attempt crimes because the money and the marijuana were not present, so they could not have committed the crimes intended. This type of defense is called the impossibility defense, which you will learn about in the following section.

Impossibility

Under what circumstances can a defendant successfully claim impossibility as a defense? The question is whether the law should punish a person who has attempted to do what was not possible under the existing circumstances. The impossibility defense has different components, including factual and legal impossibility. This discussion will explore circumstances under which impossibility can be a defense to the crime of attempt.

At common law, the traditional answer to the impossibility question turned upon the distinction between legal impossibility, on the one hand, and factual impossibility, on the other. Legal impossibility could be a defense; factual impossibility could not. The problem, however, is that courts have great difficulty distinguishing between legal and factual impossibility.

Factual Impossibility

Factual impossibility is a defense used when a person's intended end result constitutes a crime, but the actor does not complete the act that would have been a crime because an attendant circumstance is unknown to him or her or is beyond his or her control. In factual impossibility cases, the defendant is mistaken regarding some fact that is critical to the success of the crime. A person who attempts to detonate a bomb containing no explosive material and an impotent man who tries to rape a woman are two examples of factual impossibility.

Under both common law and modern law, factual impossibility is not a defense that would bar conviction for attempt. In such cases, the actor had the mental state necessary to be guilty of the crime and by committing the acts has proven his or her dangerousness. The accused in each of these cases, therefore, is deserving of criminal punishment, and there is no policy reason for the law to treat the person otherwise. Therefore, the physical impossibility of accomplishing the crime will not prevent conviction. (See Application Case 5.6.)

factual impossibility

When a person's intended end constitutes a crime, but the person fails to consummate the offense because of an attendant circumstance that is unknown or beyond his or her control, making commission of the crime impossible.

⚖️ Application Case 5.6

United States v. Thomas

In *United States v. Thomas*, three enlisted Navy men met a woman at a bar. While she was dancing with one of the defendants, she collapsed in his arms. Believing that she was drunk and had merely passed out, they placed her in the back seat of their car and drove home. One of the defendants suggested having sexual intercourse with her, since she appeared drunk and would not remember what happened. The three of them proceeded to have sexual intercourse with her. It was later discovered that she had not fainted, but had died of a heart attack (acute interstitial myocarditis); in this type of death, rigor mortis may not set in for hours. As a result, the defendants were not aware that she was dead.

While it was generally undisputed that the time of death was probably when she collapsed on the dance floor, the defendants were nevertheless tried and convicted of attempted rape and conspiracy to commit rape. The defendants argued that it was legally impossible to rape a corpse, and hence they could not be guilty of attempted rape. An appeal court affirmed the conviction, following the Model Penal Code's position on crime of attempt. The court reasoned that various legal authorities had addressed the difficult issues surrounding the crime of attempt, and that prior cases had established that physical impossibility is never a defense.

SOURCE: United States v. Thomas, 32 C.M.R. 278 (1962).

In some cases, the sheer impossibility of committing certain crimes may establish that the defendant lacked the requisite mental state to be criminally culpable. To address this, some jurisdictions look to the defendant's *mens rea* in determining whether factual impossibility would justify an acquittal. For example, if a person "attempted to murder" someone by swatting them over the head with a fly swatter, the defense would likely be able to prove that the defendant did not have the *mens rea* to murder, because it is impossible to kill someone in this manner.

Legal Impossibility

legal impossibility

When the intended acts, even if completed, would not amount to a crime. Legal impossibility is a common law defense to the crime of attempt.

Legal impossibility exists when the intended acts, even if completed, would not have amounted to a crime. For instance, if a defendant bribes a person because she wrongly believes that individual to be a juror, the defendant could not be convicted of attempting to bribe a juror. The classification of legal impossibility has been criticized because in most instances the case could just as easily be classified as one of factual impossibility.

"Hybrid" Legal Impossibility

"hybrid" legal impossibility

An ambiguous case in which impossibility could be considered either legal or factual, as distinguished from cases of true legal impossibility.

Some cases demonstrate that the distinction between legal and factual impossibility fails, because the reasons for punishing unsuccessful attempts apply equally to acts in both categories. One commentator calls these cases **"hybrid" legal impossibility**. Attempts to pick an empty pocket or to shoot a dead body believed to be alive have been treated as factual impossibility that resulted in liability for attempt, but these are equally capable of being classed as legal impossibility, which could possibly result in no liability. For an example of another case that could have been defended either way, see Application Case 5.7.

⚖️ Application Case 5.7

United States v. Berrigan

A classic example of legal impossibility is the case of *United States v. Berrigan*. In this case, federal prisoner Father Daniel Berrigan was charged with the federal offense of attempting to smuggle letters out of prison without the knowledge of the warden. The warden discovered the plot, although Berrigan was unaware of the warden's discovery.

The defendant was convicted of attempting to smuggle the letters, but the Court of Appeals treated the case as one of legal impossibility, reversing the defendant's conviction for attempt. In addition, the Court of Appeals acknowledged the varying views and opinions on the law of attempt and outlined the following criteria for legal impossibility:

where,

1. the motive, desire and expectation is to perform an act in violation of the law;
2. there is intention to perform a physical act;

3. there is a performance of the intended physical act; and

4. the consequence resulting from the intended act does not amount to a crime.

The court held it was a legal impossibility to smuggle the letters, because the warden was aware of their existence. Incidentally, this case, like many others dealing with legal impossibility, could just as easily have been treated as one of factual impossibility.

SOURCE: United States v. Berrigan, 482 F.2d 171, 188–89 (3rd Cir. 1973).

The true question is whether the suspect acted with the intent to commit the offense. If so, then the perpetrator's conduct would constitute the crime if the circumstances had been as he or she believed them to be. Such an actor would have demonstrated culpability and dangerousness to the same degree as a perpetrator who successfully completed the crime, and therefore should be charged with attempt. A similar approach is taken by most modern statutes and by the MPC. In fact, with the exception of true legal impossibility, the MPC favors abolishing the defense of impossibility in all situations. True legal impossibility is described in the next section.

Genuine Legal Impossibility

Genuine legal impossibility, or pure legal impossibility, exists when the law does not define as criminal the goal the defendant sought to achieve. In such cases, the defense of impossibility is valid under any view. The defendant cannot be convicted because, by definition, the result, if achieved, would not be a crime. Genuine legal impossibility, therefore, is really just an application of the principle of legality (discussed in Chapter 1). Few cases justify the application of the principle of pure legal impossibility. If the defendant commits an act that he or she believes to be a crime and no such offense exists, there is no liability for attempt. (See Application Case 5.8.)

genuine legal impossibility
Where the law does not define as criminal the goal the defendant sought to achieve. This is a valid defense to the crime of attempt.

⚖️ Application Case 5.8

Wilson v. State

An example of genuine legal impossibility is the case of *Wilson v. State* (1905), in which the defendant was prosecuted for forgery. He had altered a check made out to him for "$2.50" to read "$12.50," by adding the number "1." However, the defendant did not alter the words "two dollars and fifty cents." Pursuant to the banking rules, when there is a conflict between figures and words on a check, only the words are legally operative. The trial judge instructed the jury that they could not convict him of forgery, but that they could convict him of attempted forgery. The jury did so.

The Supreme Court of Mississippi reversed the defendant's conviction on the basis that what he did was not a crime because he did not alter the words on the check. Therefore, the defendant's act did not amount to attempted forgery as a matter of law.

SOURCE: Wilson v. State, 38 So. 46 (Miss. 1905).

Abandonment

What if a defendant has the required mental state and has taken the necessary steps toward commission of the act, but then changes his or her mind? Should the defendant still be guilty of an attempt to commit a crime? **Abandonment**, also called *renunciation* by the MPC, is an affirmative defense to the crime of attempt. It is used when the defendant claims to have freely and voluntarily abandoned a crime before it is completed. An accused may argue that he or she abandoned the criminal enterprise, did not intend to actually commit the crime, and therefore cannot be charged with nor found guilty of attempt.

abandonment

An affirmative defense to the crime of attempt that exists only if the defendant voluntarily and completely renounces his or her criminal purpose.

The MPC provides for this defense if the actor abandons his or her effort or otherwise prevents the commission of the crime, "under circumstances manifesting a complete and voluntary renunciation of his [or her] criminal purpose." If a person truly abandons his or her purpose of committing a crime "it would be only just to interpret his [or her] previous intention where possible as only half-formed or provisional, and hold it to be insufficient *mens rea*."

Controversy over the Abandonment Defense

Should abandonment be a defense? If considered a defense, under what circumstances should a defendant escape criminal liability? On the one hand, it is easy for a perpetrator, once detected, to claim that he or she did not mean to complete the job. For this reason, the common law did not consider abandonment a valid defense to attempt. On the other hand, an actor who truly has voluntarily terminated the criminal enterprise arguably should not be held criminally liable. As a result, some jurisdictions recognize a defense in such circumstances.

Abandonment is a valid defense only when the defendant has had a change of heart on his or her own because of a sincere belief that furtherance of the act is wrong, and not because he or she was unable to carry out the attempt because of some logistical or technical reason

Valid Abandonment To establish a valid defense, one must verbally renounce one's interest in committing a crime to all parties, retrieve any materials provided to help in the commission of the crime, and sometimes even report the plans to authorities.

or because law enforcement intervened. Nor is abandonment a defense when the defendant ceases his or her action out of fear that the police are closing in, or if he or she postpones the project until a better time arises to carry out the crime.

Abandonment and the Common Law

At common law, abandonment was not a defense. Jurisdictions that recognize abandonment as a defense to the crime of attempt do so for various reasons, such as:

- The defense may deter an actor from continuing the plan to commit a crime.
- By abandoning plans to commit a crime, a person has demonstrated that he or she does not threaten the safety of the public in the same way as someone who continues plans to carry out a crime.

On the other hand, one argument against the defense is that it allows an actor to undo criminal plans by renunciation and avoid punishment, a possibility that may encourage persons to take preliminary steps toward a crime. Some of the questions raised by this defense are:

- Should a defendant who sincerely abandons his or her plan escape liability?
- Is the timing of the abandonment relevant?
- If a thief who returns the stolen property is still guilty of larceny, should a defendant who has committed the offense of attempt (overt act beyond mere preparation), but later decides to abandon, be treated the same as the thief who returns the stolen property? Is the rationale for punishment the same in both in circumstances?

Clearly, abandonment is a complex issue, and the above questions will help juries and judges to determine the best approach in each different case. (See Application Case 5.9.)

⚖ Application Case 5.9

People v. Kimball

The defendant in *People v. Kimball* was charged with and convicted of attempted armed robbery. The factual allegations surrounding the events in issue were not in dispute, but the Court of Appeals determined that what was in dispute was whether the actions amounted to a criminal offense or merely a bad joke.

On the day in question, the defendant went to the home of a friend, where he consumed a large amount of vodka mixed with orange juice. He also took medication for insect stings he had received the previous day. The defendant and his friend then went to a store. The defendant went inside and, according to the store clerk, began talking and whistling to the guard dog, a Doberman pinscher. The clerk stated that she gave the defendant a dirty look because she did not want him playing with the dog. The defendant then approached the cash register and demanded money. She said she thought he was joking and told him so, until the defendant demanded money again. The clerk stated that when she began separating the checks from the 20-dollar bills, the defendant stated to her, "I won't do it to you; you're good-looking, and I won't do it to you this time, but if you're here next time, it won't matter."

At trial, the defendant argued that he was not guilty because he voluntarily abandoned his criminal enterprise before completing the offense attempted. Pursuant to the Michigan statute, a person who abandons a criminal scheme voluntarily, rather than through the intervention of outside forces, has not committed an attempt. The trial court rejected the defendant's arguments for an abandonment defense, holding that an attempt may still be shown even if the defendant fails to consummate the offense due to mere lack of perseverance.

The appellate court noted that the trial court should have considered the affirmative defense of abandonment. Abandonment requires the defendant to establish by a preponderance of the evidence that he voluntarily and completely abandoned his criminal purpose. The abandonment is not voluntary only if the defendant fails to complete the attempted crime because of unanticipated difficulties, unexpected resistance or circumstances that increase the probability of detention or apprehension, or a decision to postpone until another time. The appellate court reversed the defendant's conviction, then remanded the case for consideration of an affirmative defense of abandonment and to determine whether the abandonment was voluntary or involuntary.

SOURCE: People v. Kimball, 311 N.W.2d 343 (Mich. Ct. App. 1981).

For a summary of the various defenses to attempt liability, see Figure 5.2.

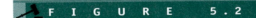

F I G U R E   5 . 2

Defenses to Attempt Liability

Factual Impossibility

- A person intends to commit a crime but is unaware of an attendant circumstance beyond his or her control.

Legal Impossibility

- A person attempts to commit an act that would not amount to a crime if completed.

"Hybrid" Legal Impossibility

- An ambiguous case, in which impossibility could be considered legal or factual, as distinguished from cases of true legal impossibility.

Genuine Legal Impossibility

- The goal that the actor intended to achieve is not defined as criminal by law.

Abandonment

- An actor voluntarily renounces his or her criminal purpose.

1. In your own words, what are the differences between factual and legal impossibility? Give an example of each.

2. What elements are generally required for a successful abandonment defense?

5.3 Solicitation

The crime of **solicitation**, also known as **incitement**, is the act of seeking to persuade someone else to commit a crime with the intent that the crime be committed. It is designated a crime because a deliberate inducement of another to commit a crime is sufficiently dangerous behavior to call for the imposition of criminal penalties. A person is guilty of solicitation when he or she advises, commands, counsels, encourages, entreats, hires, importunes, incites, instigates, invites, procures, requests, stimulates, or urges another to commit any felony, or any misdemeanor relating to obstruction of justice or a breach of the peace.

Solicitation exists only if the crime solicited has not been completed, attempted, or agreed to. If the person solicited agrees to commit a crime, then both the solicitor and the party solicited are criminally liable for conspiracy. If the person solicited attempts to commit the crime, then both parties are criminally liable for attempt. If the person solicited completes the crime, then both parties are criminally liable for the completed crime, the solicitor being responsible on a theory of accomplice liability. A common example of solicitation is a person hiring a "hit man" to kill another person. Under the MPC, a person does not have to directly communicate his or her request to solicit as long as the conduct effects such communication.

The common law crime of solicitation, a misdemeanor, was first recognized in 1801, in the case of *Rex v. Higgins*. In that case, the court held that the solicitation of a servant to steal his master's goods was an offense even though the servant ignored the suggestion.[9] This case demonstrates that solicitation occurs when one requests or encourages another to engage in a criminal act, whether or not the person agrees to do so. Solicitation was a specific intent crime at common law, and is still one under current statutes that consider it a crime.

Solicitation has been criticized for various reasons:

- Because the crime requires an independent individual capable of forming his or her own moral judgments to act on behalf of the solicitor, it is always possible that the individual will refuse.
- It has also been argued that the solicitor personally manifests reluctance to commit the crime, and thus is not "a significant menace."
- As with inchoate crimes in general, the ultimate criticism of solicitation is that an unsuccessful solicitation is so far removed from any actual societal harm that its punishment comes close to punishing evil thoughts or intentions alone, thus raising First Amendment issues.

solicitation (incitement)

The act of seeking to persuade someone else to commit a crime with the intent that the crime be committed.

Mens Rea of Solicitation

Common law solicitation is a specific intent crime. A person can be convicted only if he or she requests, encourages, or commands another to commit a crime, with the specific intent that the other person successfully complete the solicited crime. All modern jurisdictions similarly require that the solicitor have a mental state of desiring that the crime be carried out. Expressing a vague desire that an act be committed or hoping that someone else will decide on his or her own to commit a crime is usually not enough to prove the requisite mental state for this specific intent offense. When the specific intent exists at the same time as the solicitor's communication, the crime is complete. Therefore, even if the completion of the intended underlying crime is impossible, the actor is criminally liable for solicitation.

Intent by the solicitor can be established a number of ways. Usually, the mere speaking of words demonstrates the intent necessary to be culpable. Expressing the intent in writing is another way to prove the requisite intent. For example, if a man in jail writes to his friend and asks him to kill the person who is going to testify against him in his upcoming robbery trial, the letter will be enough to prove the inmate's criminal intent to solicit for murder.

Actus Reus of Solicitation

The physical act of solicitation occurs when the solicitor takes any action, whether verbal or otherwise, to urge another to commit a crime. Speaking or writing the words of solicitation is an act, and when that act is done with the intent that the person solicited commit the underlying crime, the crime of solicitation is complete.

If the solicitor attempts to solicit someone but fails because an intermediary did not reach the person or a letter was never received, most jurisdictions still consider the solicitation complete. Some juries would consider it to be only attempted solicitation. In *State v. Cotton*, however, a defendant in jail wrote to his wife soliciting certain criminal activities. There was no evidence that the wife received the letter, and the court held that the defendant could not be convicted of solicitation.[10]

Defenses to Solicitation

Although apparently not a defense at common law and currently not a defense in some jurisdictions, abandonment is a defense under modern penal codes. The MPC, in Section 5.02(3), provides that "renunciation of criminal purpose" is a defense to solicitation when two actions occur:

1. The solicitor "completely and voluntarily renounces his criminal intent."
2. The solicitor "either persuades the solicited party not to commit the offense or otherwise prevents him from committing the crime."

Suppose that David hires a hit man to kill his wife and pays him half of the money to carry out the murder. Then he realizes that he still loves his wife and does not want her to die. He calls the hit man and tells him about his change of heart, saying that he can keep the money already received, but that he will not be sending any more money and that he wants all plans to carry out the crime to stop.

If the hit man agrees at that point, then most likely David will not be charged with solicitation even if the police find out. However, if the hit man refuses to stop the plans as a form of blackmail to get the rest of the money, David can be charged with solicitation unless he goes to the police and informs them of everything. By doing so, he would be able to prevent the commission of the crime, which would be a valid defense.

CRITICAL THINKING 5.3

1. Why is solicitation considered a crime?
2. Briefly, what are the *actus reus* and *mens rea* required for a solicitation conviction?

5.4 Conspiracy

A *conspiracy*, as we saw in Chapter 4, is an agreement between two or more people to commit an unlawful act or acts or to do a lawful act unlawfully. It is also called a *partnership in crime*. The gist of this offense is the agreement. To ensure that the law does not punish a person for his or her thoughts or intentions alone, most modern jurisdictions require that one of the parties to the conspiracy engage in an overt act. Conspirators can also become "accessories" once the planned crime is committed.

For example, if Dick and Dan discuss a plan to rob a bank and reach an agreement to do so, and Dick then buys a gun and mask to be used in the robbery, both Dick and Dan are criminally liable for the crime of conspiracy to rob a bank. Furthermore, if the two of them carry out the robbery, each can be prosecuted and convicted for both robbery and conspiracy to commit robbery.

Conspiracy has been the subject of longstanding criticism by legal scholars. Many people have called for reformation or abolition of the crime on the grounds that the law is vague and requires that a defendant do very little in order to be convicted of the crime. Conspiracy punishes people who come together and have a "meeting of the minds" with the purpose of formulating a criminal plan. The crime focuses primarily on the *mens rea* of the defendants, rather than the *actus reus*. The accused need not be charged with a substantive offense to be convicted of conspiracy. In fact, federal law imposes stiff penalties for conspiring to commit a number of offenses, and the punishment for conspiracy in some instances is greater than for the corresponding substantive offenses if committed absent the element of conspiracy.

On the other hand, the crime of conspiracy is said to exist as a necessary and important aid to law enforcement. Most criminal enterprises that involve more than one person are carried out in secret. Such secret enterprises threaten society and are extremely difficult to detect. Even if detected, proof of the conduct that constitutes the underlying crimes is extremely difficult. The dangerousness of crimes planned by groups justifies the law's definition of the agreement stage as constituting the crime of conspiracy, even though the agreement has not ripened into the completed criminal plan. As the Supreme Court has stated, "The strength, opportunities and resources of many [are] obviously more dangerous and more difficult to police than the efforts of a lone wrongdoer."[11]

5.1 On the Job

FBI Special Agent

Description and Duties: Investigate "organized crime, white-collar crime, public corruption, financial crime, fraud against the government, bribery, copyright matters, civil rights violations, bank robbery, extortion, kidnapping, air piracy, terrorism, foreign counterintelligence, interstate criminal activity, fugitive and drug-trafficking matters, and other violations of federal statutes." Work with other law enforcement agencies at the federal, state, or local level to investigate crime. Wear or have immediate access to a firearm at all times when on duty, and be prepared to use deadly force when needed.

Salary: Salaries are based on government salary scales, which change often. Most special agents start at the GS-10 level and can advance to GS-13, which is between $43,824 and $89,217 a year.

Other Information: The application process is lengthy and requires a variety of tests and security checks. Applicants who are fluent in a foreign language, or who have a degree in law or accounting, can enter with a four-year degree. Others must have an advanced degree or work experience.

SOURCE: FBI Web site, http://www.fbijobs.gov.

Modern penal law universally recognizes conspiracy, and it is more severely punished today than it was under the common law rule. In Section 5.03(1), the MPC provides that someone is guilty of conspiracy

> if with the purpose of promoting or facilitating its commission he: agrees with such other person or persons that they or one or more of them will engage in conduct that constitutes such crime or an attempt or solicitation to commit such crime; or agrees to aid such other person or persons in the planning or commission of such crime or of an attempt or solicitation to commit such crime.

Mens Rea of Conspiracy

The mental state required for conspiracy is two-tiered; the parties must have both the intent to agree and the specific intent that the object of the agreement be achieved. Both *mens rea* elements require that there be more than one person involved. The act of agreement is virtually indistinguishable from the first *mens rea* requirement. Therefore, proof of the *actus reus*, the existence of the agreement, will satisfy the first *mens rea* element as well. The specific intent requirement is in addition to the intent to agree. However, the question arises whether a showing of knowledge can satisfy this element, or whether the element requires proof of the actor's purpose to achieve the result.

The following three examples help illustrate the point of whether a supplier should be held criminally liable for conspiracy when that supplier furnishes goods or services to another person or group knowing that the goods or services will be used for illegal purposes:

- A woman goes to a gun dealer to buy a gun to kill her husband; the dealer knows the wife's plan but nonetheless sells her the gun.
- The defendant, a drug wholesaler, sells legal drugs to a person who he knows will use them for unlawful purposes.

5.2 Web Exploration

Conspiracies

Details regarding major multiple-party conspiracies can be found by visiting http://www
.fbi.gov/hq/cid/orgcrime/casestudies.htm. What offenses are most typical of large-scale
conspiracies, and why?

- The operator of a telephone answering service provides telephone messaging
  services for known prostitutes.[12]

The courts are divided on the issue of whether knowledge alone is enough, but
they are consistent in concluding that if purpose is required it may "often" be inferred
from the accused's knowledge of the recipient's plans. Under the MPC, a person cannot be guilty of conspiracy "unless the conspiratorial agreement was made with the
purpose of promoting or facilitating the commission of the substantive offense."[13]

Actus Reus of Conspiracy

The *actus reus* of conspiracy is the act of reaching an agreement. Such an act constitutes a person's advancement of the intent to further the criminal purpose, and it is
that advancement that justifies the law's intervention. An agreement can, of course,
be proven by direct evidence, by either spoken or written words. However, most people do not form illegal agreements openly, and sometimes all participants may not
know the identity of all conspirators. Therefore, proof of the existence of conspiracy
can only be inferred from proof of conduct of the defendants, often in the form of
proof of their cooperation. In other words, proof of conduct of one or more of the
alleged co-conspirators often forms the basis of the prosecution's case in a conspiracy
prosecution. But the gist of the crime is still agreement, and the prosecution has the
burden of convincing the jury not only that the alleged co-conspirators acted toward
the accomplishment of the conspiracy's goal, but also that they actually agreed to try
to achieve the goal. (See Application Case 5.10.)

⚖ Application Case 5.10

United States v. Alvarez

In *United States v. Alvarez*, the defendant was convicted of conspiracy to import
marijuana. Others had arranged for the shipment of marijuana to be made to
supposed buyers, who were actually undercover agents. One of the persons who had
arranged the shipment, in the presence of the defendant, told an undercover agent that
the defendant would unload the shipment when it arrived in the United States. When
the undercover agent asked the defendant if that were true, the defendant nodded.

The court of appeals reversed the defendant's conspiracy conviction, holding
that the evidence, though sufficient to show defendant's knowledge that something

illegal was transpiring, was not sufficient to show his knowledge of an agreement or his having joined in it.

SOURCE: United States v. Alvarez, 610 F.2d 1250 (5th Cir. 1980), *as cited in* James A. Burke & Sanford H. Kadish, *Conspiracy, in* 1 ENCYCLOPEDIA OF CRIME AND JUSTICE 231, 233 (S.H. Kadish ed., 1983).

Although the common law and some modern jurisdictions require for the *actus reus* of conspiracy only that two or more persons agree to engage in criminal conduct, most jurisdictions require that the prosecutor prove, in addition to the agreement, that some overt act was committed in furtherance of the conspiracy. The purpose of the requirement of an overt act is to prove that the conspiracy is actually alive and at work. This requirement does not pose a substantial hurdle in most prosecutions, however, because almost any act is applicable. Thus, as noted before, the purchase of a mask by a conspirator to a bank robbery would constitute a sufficient overt act to satisfy the requirement. (See Figure 5.3.)

F I G U R E   5 . 3

Alaska's Statute on Conspiracy

AS 11.31.120.   Conspiracy

(a) An offender commits the crime of conspiracy if, with the intent to promote or facilitate a serious felony offense, the offender agrees with one or more persons to engage in or cause the performance of that activity and the offender or one of the persons does an overt act in furtherance of the conspiracy.

(b) If an offender commits the crime of conspiracy and knows that a person with whom the offender conspires to commit a serious felony offense has conspired or will conspire with another person or persons to commit the same serious felony offense, the offender is guilty of conspiring with that other person or persons to commit that crime whether or not the offender knows their identities.

(c) In a prosecution under this section, it is not a defense that a person with whom the defendant conspires could not be guilty of the crime that is the object of the conspiracy because of

(1) lack of criminal responsibility or other legal incapacity or exemption;

(2) belonging to a class of persons who by definition are legally incapable in an individual capacity of committing the crime that is the object of the conspiracy;

(3) unawareness of the criminal nature of the conduct in question or of the criminal purpose of the defendant; or

(4) any other factor precluding the culpable mental state required for the commission of the crime.

(d) If the offense that the conspiracy is intended to promote or facilitate is actually committed, a defendant may not be convicted of conspiring to commit that offense with another person for whose conduct the defendant is not legally accountable under AS 11.16.120(b).

(e) In a prosecution under this section, it is an affirmative defense that the defendant, under circumstances manifesting a voluntary and complete renunciation of the defendant's criminal intent, either (1) gave timely warning to law enforcement authorities; or (2) otherwise made proper effort that prevented the commission of the crime that was the object of the conspiracy. Renunciation by one conspirator does not affect the liability of another conspirator who does not join in the renunciation.

(f) Notwithstanding AS 22.10.030, venue in actions in which the crime of conspiracy is alleged to have been committed may not be based solely on the location of overt acts done in furtherance of the conspiracy.

SOURCE: ALASKA STAT. § 11.31.120 (2006).

Defenses to Conspiracy

Impossibility, such a thorny problem in the area of attempt law, is dealt with more simply in the realm of conspiracy law. Most courts hold that impossibility of any kind is not a defense to a charge of conspiracy, though a few decisions exist that hold impossibility is a defense. The MPC does not recognize impossibility as a defense to conspiracy charges.

The crime of conspiracy is complete in some jurisdictions at the moment the agreement is reached, and in other jurisdictions upon commission of an overt act in furtherance of the conspiracy. Once the offense is complete, abandonment or withdrawal from the conspiracy cannot be a defense. However, abandonment or withdrawal has the effect of terminating the abandoning conspirator's liability for subsequent acts by other conspirators in furtherance of the conspiracy, and of starting the statute of limitations to run.

Where abandonment is provable, either to limit liability or to show that the statute of limitations has run, courts have imposed strict requirements of proof of abandonment. Almost all jurisdictions have applied the same test in determining whether a participant in a conspiracy has withdrawn early enough not to be convicted. Courts look for an affirmative act that will prove that abandonment was timely and effective. "Effective" can be defined as an effort that would make a reasonable person understand that the conspirator is withdrawing. In addition, the conspirator who is withdrawing must give notice to everyone involved in order for it to be a valid withdrawal.

Some jurisdictions go even further and recognize withdrawal only if the defendant not only abandons the planned crime, but also talks his or her co-conspirators out of committing the act. The MPC provides "that withdrawal by an individual occurs only if and when he advises those with whom he conspired of his abandonment or he informs law enforcement authorities of the existence of the conspiracy and of his participation therein." The MPC does allow withdrawal to be an affirmative defense to conspiracy but requires that the defendant "thwarted the success of the conspiracy, under circumstances manifesting a complete and voluntary renunciation of his criminal purpose."[14] In other words, a defendant may validly assert withdrawal as a defense if he or she was able to stop the other co-conspirators from continuing plans to commit a crime. Some jurisdictions that follow the MPC's approach provide that withdrawal is a valid defense if a conspirator notifies police of the criminal activity as a way to end the activity.

CRITICAL THINKING 5.4

1. How does this text's definition of conspiracy differ from your original conception of the crime? Why do you think that there is a frequent misunderstanding of it?

2. What factors help justify making conspiracy a crime?

REVIEW AND APPLICATIONS

Summary by Chapter Objectives

1. **Explain the purpose of defining attempt as a crime.** Lawmakers created attempt crimes to prevent the commission of crimes before they take place. They also sought to protect the safety of the public by allowing police officers to stop the continuance of criminal activity.

2. **Explain the how the MPC test for the *actus reus* of attempt differs from all the other tests.** Under the MPC test to determine whether an attempt has occurred, the only requirement is to show that the suspect has done (or omitted to do) something that constitutes a substantial step in a course of conduct, which must be planned for the commission of the underlying crime. The sole inquiry is into whether the accused person's conduct strongly matches his or her criminal intent. Ambiguous factors, such as proximity or equivocality, are not considered.

3. **State the elements of an attempt.** A person is guilty of the crime of attempt if he or she intentionally commits the act constituting the *actus reus* (either the last act, proximity, or substantial step test), with the additional intent to commit the substantive crime or to cause the prohibited result that constitutes the underlying crime.

4. **Name the two principal defenses to attempt.** The two principal defenses to attempt are impossibility and abandonment (renunciation). Abandonment is not recognized in some jurisdictions; where it is recognized, a defendant's abandonment must fit within certain guidelines to be considered a valid defense.

5. **Explain when the crime of solicitation can be charged.** Solicitation is a crime only if the crime solicited has not been completed, attempted, or agreed to. This is because when any of these other three situations occur, the solicitor and solicited party become liable for other criminal acts instead.
   - If the person solicited agrees to commit a crime, then both the solicitor and the party solicited are criminally liable for conspiracy.
   - If the person solicited attempts to commit the crime, then both parties are criminally liable for attempt.
   - If the person solicited completes the crime, then both parties are criminally liable for the completed crime, the solicitor being responsible on a theory of accomplice liability.

6. **Define the crime of conspiracy.** Conspiracy is a partnership in crime; it is an agreement between two or more people to commit an unlawful act or acts, or to do a lawful act unlawfully.

7. **Define the *actus reus* requirement for conspiracy.** The *actus reus* requirement for conspiracy is the act of agreement. In addition, many jurisdictions require an overt act in furtherance of the conspiracy.

8. **Explain the *mens rea* requirement for conspiracy.** The mental state required for conspiracy has two facets: the intent to agree and the specific intent that the object of the agreement be achieved. In addition, both of these *mens rea* elements require that there be more than one person involved, because the crime contemplates agreement between two or more persons.

Key Terms

inchoate crimes (p. 113)
attempt (p. 115)
last act test (p. 117)
physical proximity test (p. 118)
dangerous proximity test (p. 118)
indispensable element test (p. 120)
unequivocality test (p. 121)

substantial step test (p. 121)
factual impossibility (p. 125)
legal impossibility (p. 126)
"hybrid" legal impossibility (p. 126)
genuine legal impossibility (p. 127)
abandonment (p. 128)
solicitation (incitement) (p. 131)

Review Questions

1. What is the six-stage process by which an actor commits a crime, and after what stage is a person liable for criminal punishment?
2. Explain the historical cases in which the crime of attempt was first recognized.
3. Your textbook names six of the various tests for the crime of attempt. How do they differ?
4. How does the MPC define the mental element of attempt, and how is this different from other definitions?
5. What are the similarities and differences between "hybrid" legal impossibility and pure legal impossibility?
6. What are some reasons why some jurisdictions recognize abandonment as a defense?
7. Why is solicitation designated as a crime, and what are some of the criticisms of this practice?
8. How does the treatment of conspiracy as a crime help law enforcement efforts?
9. What are all of the possible requirements to determine the *actus reus* of conspiracy?
10. How can the defenses of abandonment and impossibility apply to conspiracy?
11. What does the MPC allow in regard to defenses to conspiracy?

Problem-Solving Exercises

1. **Prostitution** Sandy and Luisa are bored housewives who are sick of their menial household responsibilities and their bratty kids. In desperate need of excitement, they decide to start a brothel and operate it as co-madams. For several weeks, they devise a plan of action, including soliciting customers, hiring female employees, creating a price list, and decorating various theme rooms in Sandy's house, which is to be used as the brothel. When they are ready to start business, a man tells Luisa he is interested and sets a time to come to the house

the next evening. When he arrives, he pays Sandy, chooses a girl, and then arrests everyone in the house. At this point, they realize that the man is an undercover vice detective. Answer the following questions:

a. With what charges can Sandy and Luisa be charged? Explain your choices.

b. With what charges, if any, could the other women be charged. Explain your choices.

c. What do you think tipped off the detective to investigate their activities?

2. **Drug Trafficking** Fred and Raul are arrested for conspiracy to distribute cocaine by a police officer who was tipped off by an informant. Fred and Raul are charged with distributing, but due to a technical error in the warrant, the evidence is inadmissible and the case is dismissed. In response, the prosecutor charges them with conspiracy to distribute marijuana. As you interview Fred in the presence of his attorney, he begins to tell you that he has owed Raul $100,000 for the last two years as a result of a gambling loan. Fred believes that Raul will kill him unless he pays back the money somehow, but he has no way of repaying the loan. Raul told Fred that instead of being murdered, Fred could work for Raul for five years, assisting him in his narcotics distribution. Fred agreed. Answer the following questions:

a. Was there a meeting of the minds?

b. Was there an agreement to commit a criminal act?

c. Will the conspiracy charge hold up when this evidence is presented?

3. **Attempted Murder** You are a police investigator. A distraught wife appears at the local police station and states that her husband has just informed her that he has been putting poison in her coffee for over a week. She also states that she was not feeling well and went to the doctor, who advised her that she had indigestion. Her husband confesses to you that he hates her, wants her dead, and has been putting a poisonous substance in her coffee for the past week. Upon investigation, you obtain the substance from the husband. The lab analyzes the substance and advises you that it is harmless.

a. Do you trust that this is the substance that was used? What else will you do to determine this?

b. If the substance was harmless and could not possibly poison the wife, with what crime(s), if any, will the husband be charged?

Workplace Applications

1. **Substantial Step Test** As a prosecutor, you are told that a man has been arrested for driving at high speed through a crowded residential neighborhood at 3:00 in the afternoon. He was driving 90 miles per hour in a 25-mile-per-hour zone when he struck and killed a child crossing the street on her way home from school. Answer the following questions:

a. Can the driver be charged with murder? With any other charges? Explain your choices.

b. What are some of the considerations for applying murder based on a substantial certainty?

c. What defenses may the driver raise for his behavior? How will you respond?

2. **False Testimony** You are the prosecutor for a case in which the defendant is charged with the attempted murder and robbery of Mrs. Gray, a 78-year-old woman. In the middle of the trial, just before Mrs. Gray testifies, she tells you that she has a confession to make. She states that her original statement to the detective was slightly exaggerated. In this new statement, she tells you that the defendant attacked her in the parking lot and attempted to take her handbag, but was interrupted by someone walking by. Originally, Mrs. Gray told the detective who interviewed her that the defendant pointed a gun at her head and said, "If you don't give me your bag, I'll kill you." Now Mrs. Gray states that the defendant only grabbed her bag and said he would kill her but did not have a gun. Mrs. Gray explains to you that at the time of the attempted robbery, she was very upset and angry with the defendant; in her agitation, she embellished her story a little. Answer the following questions:

   a. As the prosecutor, do you continue the trial and advise Mrs. Gray she must stick with her original statement? Why or why not?

   b. Do you continue with the trial with Mrs. Gray's true story and hope that the jury convicts the defendant of attempted murder based solely on this statement? Why or why not?

   c. Do you drop the attempted murder charges and prosecute only the attempted robbery? Why or why not?

3. **Last Act Test** While on duty as a municipal police officer, you observe a female and two males sitting in a vehicle parked across the street from a bank. When you get closer to the vehicle, you observe the female holding a handgun. As you are in the process of arresting the female for possession of a firearm, you observe a bank employee drive up with equipment to fix a broken ATM machine. Upon further investigation, you learn two things from the bank employee: that the female is a former bank employee, and that someone had tampered with the machine, which guaranteed the arrival of a bank employee to fix it.

   a. Applying the last act test, is there sufficient evidence to charge the female and her two companions with attempted bank robbery?

   b. Would the result be different if you applied the dangerous proximity to success test?

   c. Was the fact that the robbery did not take place a matter of chance, or is it possible that the three individuals may have changed their minds just at the time the officer appeared?

Ethics Exercises

1. **Conspiracy to Commit Murder** Bill asks two friends to help him kill his wife. They agree, and the three of them work out a plan. A few days later, Bill gets cold feet; he tells the others that he wants nothing further to do with the plan and specifically asks them to abandon it. Later that evening, Bill comes to the police department and tells you about the plan. You plan your next day's schedule around conducting interviews of his friends as a means of investigating the matter further. Unfortunately, the night Bill comes to see you, Bill's friends carry out the original plan to kill his wife. When the friends are apprehended, they admit to killing Bill's

wife but insist that Bill "planned the whole thing." The prosecutor is preparing to indict all three for conspiracy and first-degree murder.

   a. Should you tell the prosecutor about your meeting with Bill? Why or why not?

   b. What, if anything, should Bill be charged with?

   c. Does Bill have any legal liability in this case? Why or why not? What about his friends? Why or why not?

2. **Charge for an Incomplete Crime** Bob decides to rob the neighborhood store because he desperately needs money to pay his rent. He points the gun at the cashier and demands the large bills. The cashier tells Bob that he needs to reconsider his actions and that he could go to jail for a long time. She tells him that she will not call the police if he simply leaves the store. Bob decides that she is right, that he might get caught and go to jail. He immediately leaves the store, but is arrested while walking to his car.

   a. Has Bob committed attempted robbery?

   b. Did Bob abandon his plan? Was the abandonment voluntary or involuntary?

Notes

1. MODEL PENAL CODE, "Introduction to Article 5 (Inchoate Crimes)" (1985).

2. JOSHUA DRESSLER, UNDERSTANDING CRIMINAL LAW § 27.02[B] at 406 n.9 (4th ed. 2006) (citing Dabrey v. State, 858 A.2d 1084, 1089 (Md. Ct. Spec. App. 2004); *see also* MODEL PENAL CODE, "Introduction to Article 5 (Inchoate Crimes)" (1985).

3. *See* WAYNE R. LaFAVE, CRIMINAL LAW § 11.2(a) n.15 (4th ed. 2003) (citing Rex v. Scofield, Cald. 397 (1784)).

4. Rex v. Higgins, 102 Eng. Rep. 269 (K.B. 1801), *as cited in* Ira P. Robbins & Dan M. Kahan, *Solicitation, in* ENCYCLOPEDIA OF CRIME AND JUSTICE 1491–92 (Joshua Dressler ed., 2d ed. 2002).

5. Wis. Stat. Ann. § 939.32(3) (West 2005).

6. People v. Parrish, 87 Cal.App. 2d 853 (Cal. Ct. App. 1948).

7. King v. Barker, [1924] N.Z.L.R. 865.

8. MODEL PENAL CODE § 5.01(a)–(c) (1985).

9. Rex v. Higgins, 102 Eng. Rep. 269 (K.B. 1801), *as cited in* Ira P. Robbins & Dan M. Kahan, *Solicitation, in* ENCYCLOPEDIA OF CRIME AND JUSTICE 1491–92 (Joshua Dressler ed., 2d ed. 2002).

10. State v. Cotton, 790 P.2d 1050 (N.M. Ct. App. 1990).

11. Krulewitch v. United States, 336 U.S. 440, 448–49 (1949).

12. JOSHUA DRESSLER, UNDERSTANDING CRIMINAL LAW § 29.05[B] at 470 (4th ed. 2006) (citing United States v. Falcone, 109 F.2d 579 (2d Cir. 1940); Direct Sales Co. v. United States, 319 U.S. 703 (1943); People v. Lauria, 59 Cal. Rptr. 628 (Cal. Ct. App. 1967)).

13. MODEL PENAL CODE § 5.02 cmt. 1 (1985), citing State v. Davis, 6 S.W.2d 609, 615 (Mo. 1928) (concurring opinion).

14. MODEL PENAL CODE § 5.03(7)(c) and § 5.03(6) (1985).

Defenses to Crimes

CHAPTER OBJECTIVES

After reading and studying this chapter, you should be able to:

1. List the three elements of self-defense.
2. Describe when deadly force may be used in self-defense.
3. Name two situations in which a first aggressor can claim self-defense.
4. Describe the circumstances in which a person can use force to defend property.
5. Explain when a police officer may use deadly force in effecting an arrest or preventing escape.
6. List five tests for determining insanity.

6.1 Types of Defenses

Once a defendant has been charged with a criminal offense, the prosecutor has the burden of producing evidence and proving beyond a reasonable doubt the existence of the five elements of criminal culpability:

1. *Actus reus*, the defendant's voluntary act (or omission when there was a duty to act).
2. The requisite *mens rea*.
3. A unity of *actus reus* and *mens rea*.
4. An actual and proximate causal connection between the *actus reus* and the social harm.
5. The social harm resulting from the offense.

Even if the prosecutor introduces evidence to prove all five elements, the defendant can and may raise a defense to the charge, which can lead to an acquittal. **Defense** "is commonly used, at least in a casual sense, to mean any set of identifiable conditions or circumstances which may prevent a conviction for an offense."[1] A defense may consist either of a failure of proof by the prosecution or of a statement by the defense of a reason why the prosecutor has no valid case against the defendant.

defense

Either a failure of proof by the prosecution, or a defendant's statement of a reason why the prosecutor has no valid case against him or her.

Failures of Proof versus True Defenses

Failure of proof occurs when the prosecution fails to prove the cause of action in its entire scope and meaning. The defendant may succeed in presenting a failure of proof defense in one of two ways. The defendant may "rest" after the prosecution's case-in-chief, make a motion for judgment of acquittal, and successfully argue that the prosecution has failed to introduce evidence on each element sufficient to sustain a jury finding of guilt beyond a reasonable doubt. More commonly, the defendant will introduce evidence to show that the prosecution's case does not provide sufficient basis for conviction. In a homicide prosecution, for example, the defendant might claim that he mistakenly believed the object at which he fired his gun was a tree stump rather than a human being; this would be a mistake of fact. Or the defendant might claim that he was not at the scene when the crime was committed and therefore was misidentified as the offender. These would be the defenses of mistaken identity and of alibi.[2]

Contrasted with such failure of proof defenses are true defenses, also referred to as *affirmative defenses*. A **true defense**, if proved, results in the acquittal of a defendant, even though the prosecutor has proved the defendant's guilt beyond a reasonable doubt.

failure of proof

A defense in which either the defense counsel makes a motion for judgment of acquittal or the defendant introduces evidence that shows that the prosecution's case is lacking.

true defense

A defense that, if proved, results in the acquittal of a defendant, even though the prosecutor has proved the defendant's guilt beyond a reasonable doubt.

Burden of Proof

As noted in previous chapters, the prosecution bears the burden in all criminal cases of proving the defendant's guilt, and the standard of proof required is beyond a reasonable doubt. This standard is both a customary and a constitutional requirement since the 1970 Supreme Court decision in *In re Winship*.[3] This **burden of proof** requires that the prosecution both provide factual evidence of the defendant's guilt and persuade the jury that the evidence presented establishes the defendant's guilt

burden of proof

The onus of producing evidence and also of persuading the jury with the required level of proof, which in a criminal case is "beyond a reasonable doubt."

beyond a reasonable doubt. This means that the jury need not be absolutely certain of the defendant's guilt; absent a successful legal defense, reasonable certainty is sufficient to convict.

If the defense asserted falls into the "failure of proof" category, not only must the prosecution introduce its own evidence of the defendant's guilt, it must also disprove the defendant's failure of proof claim beyond a reasonable doubt. For example, if the defendant claims that he or she has an alibi and that the charges are based on mistaken identity, the prosecution must disprove both these claims beyond a reasonable doubt.

With respect to a true defense, criminal statutes sometimes require that the defendant (via his or her attorney) introduce evidence of the claimed defense and bear the burden of persuading the jury of the facts establishing the defense by a preponderance of the evidence (the same level of proof required in civil cases; see Chapter 1). Once the defendant has met that burden, it is the responsibility of the prosecutor to disprove the defense, beyond a reasonable doubt.

This shifting burden of proof has raised constitutional concerns in some cases (see *Mullaney v. Wilbur*[4]), but it is generally recognized as the primary means of establishing an affirmative defense (see *Patterson v. New York*[5]). An **affirmative defense** is one in which the defendant admits to the existence of all of the necessary legal elements for criminal liability but offers one or more legally recognized reasons (a true defense or defenses) why he or she should nonetheless be acquitted.

For example, in *Mullaney v. Wilbur*, the defendant was charged with murder under the laws of the state of Maine. The Maine statute defined murder as unlawful and intentional homicide. The defendant raised a "heat of passion or sudden provocation" defense, an excuse defense that, if successful, would mitigate the crime from murder to manslaughter. The U.S. Supreme Court ruled that once the defendant had introduced the heat of passion defense, the prosecution bore the burden of establishing that the defense did not exist. In contrast, in *Patterson v. New York*, Patterson was charged with murder under New York law, which defined the crime simply as a killing caused by the accused where the accused intended the result, rather than as a killing both intentional and unlawful. Patterson raised the affirmative defense of extreme emotional disturbance, which would have mitigated the crime from murder to manslaughter. In this case, the Supreme Court held that the defense had the burden of proving the existence of the defense. In contrast to the Maine statutory definitions in *Mullaney*, the New York law placed the burden of production and persuasion, with respect to the affirmative defense, on the defendant. The U.S. Supreme Court held that this was constitutionally permissible and consistent with the *Mullaney* decision.

> **affirmative defense**
> A defense in which the defendant admits to the existence of all of the necessary legal elements for criminal liability, but offers one or more legally recognized reasons why he or she should nonetheless be acquitted.

Mitigating versus Complete Defenses

Another way to classify defenses is as either mitigating or complete. A mitigating defense reduces the level of offense for which the defendant may legally be convicted—for example, from murder to manslaughter (this is covered in greater detail in Chapter 8). A complete defense, if successfully established by the defense and not disproved by the prosecution, results in an acquittal of any wrongdoing.

The bulk of this chapter consists of a discussion of complete or true defenses, but an example of a defendant's attempt to use a mitigating defense is *Patterson v. New York*. In the *Patterson* case noted above, although the defendant admitted to intentionally killing the victim, he sought to have the charge of second-degree murder reduced to manslaughter by raising the defense of extreme emotional disturbance. The jury rejected this defense and found the defendant guilty of murder as charged. The evidence of provocation presented by the defendant was not sufficient to convince the jury that he was guilty only of the lesser crime.

Justification versus Excuse as the Basis of a Defense

The two most important categories of true defenses are justification and excuse. In early English legal history, there could be significant differences between the legal results of defenses based on justification versus defenses based on excuse. Today, however, justified and excused actors are treated the same by the criminal justice system. Criminal defendants who successfully assert either type of defense are acquitted of the offense and are not punished for their conduct. However, there is a difference between the two defenses in terms of the underlying theory of why their successful assertion should result in an actor's going unpunished. A defense based on **justification** renders lawful conduct that would otherwise constitute a violation of the criminal law. In other words, a successful justification defense exempts the actor from criminal sanctions.

> **justification**
> A defense that, because of the circumstances, renders criminal conduct lawful and therefore exempts the actor from criminal sanctions.

For example, if a person were to kill another who was an aggressor (i.e., the one who first displayed hostile force), and the killing was a necessary and reasonable response to prevent the aggressor from inflicting death or serious injury on the accused, killing the aggressor would be justifiable self-defense and therefore lawful. "Those who act in self-defense exercise a privilege and act in conformity with the law."[6] Even the early common law recognized justifiable homicide—based largely on a theory of necessity—such as a law enforcement officer who kills in the line of duty, an executioner carrying out a death sentence imposed by law, or a person who kills in order to prevent any "forcible and atrocious crime."[7]

> **excuse**
> A defense in which the criminal actor has committed an unjustified crime, but there is a reason for not holding him or her personally accountable for it.

A defense is based on **excuse** when the actor has violated a criminal statue but there is a reason for not holding him or her personally accountable. An excuse defense thus frees the accused from criminal responsibility for his or her actions. For example, a person who kills another but who, because of psychological incapacity (mental illness/insanity), either does not realize that what he is doing is wrong or cannot prevent himself from doing so, cannot be blamed for his violation of the law.

Although the common law distinction between excuse and justification defenses differed to some degree from the distinction today, with few exceptions, the contemporary impact of successfully establishing either category of offense is that the actor is not punished.

A few commentators have suggested that it is worthwhile to distinguish between justified and excused conduct in the criminal law for at least four reasons: for moral guidance, and to determine criminal responsibility with respect to questions of retroactivity, accomplice liability, and third-party conduct.[8] As for moral guidance, "people should take justifiable, rather than wrongful-but-excusable paths" whenever possible.[9] With respect to determining responsibility when there are questions of retroactivity, accomplice liability, and third-party conduct, an actor's liability might exist if the defense were based on excuse, but not liable if the defense were based on justification.[10]

> **CRITICAL THINKING 6.1**
>
> 1. In your own words, distinguish between failure of proof and a true defense.
>
> 2. Explain the differences between mitigating and complete defenses.

6.2 Defenses Based on Justification

There are five major types of defenses based on justification:

1. Self-defense.
2. Defense of others.
3. Defense of property or habitation.
4. Crime prevention and law enforcement.
5. Necessity.

In specific situations, consent may also function as a defense. The following sections will discuss all of these defenses in greater detail.

Self-Defense

Self-defense is the justified use of reasonable force by one who is not an aggressor, when the actor-defendant reasonably believed it was necessary to defend against what the defendant reasonably perceived to be an unlawful and imminent attack upon the defendant's person. Self-defense is probably the most common of the affirmative defenses, certainly of the justification defenses. Under the early common law rule, it was not a complete defense; an accused who killed in self-defense would be convicted but pardoned by the king. By about 1535, the defense became a defense to conviction itself.[11] Self-defense is universally recognized in American criminal law—every jurisdiction now recognizes self-defense as a justification for committing a crime and even permits the use of deadly force if the defendant is able to prove the elements of the defense.

Usually, a defendant must prove three elements in order to be acquitted of a crime because of self-defense:

1. The necessity of using force (including the use of deadly force only to prevent imminent and unlawful use of deadly force by the aggressor).
2. The proportionality of the force to the threat (i.e., the level of force used in self-defense cannot be excessive in light of the level of force threatened).
3. The reasonableness of the belief that force was necessary.

An **aggressor** is one who first employs hostile force, by either threatening or striking another in such a way that it justifies a similar response. With respect to the necessity of force, the defendant must show that he or she honestly and reasonably believed that there was no reasonable alternative to the use of force against an aggressor for self-protection. For example, if the defendant were threatened with a physical attack by an aggressor who was so ill or otherwise incapacitated that he or she could not carry out the threat, the defendant would be unable to show necessity for the use of force. With respect to the requirement of proportionality, the level of force

self-defense
The justified use of reasonable force by one who is not an aggressor, when the actor reasonably believed it was necessary to defend against what he or she reasonably perceived to be an unlawful and imminent physical attack.

aggressor
One who first employs hostile force, either by threatening or striking another, which justifies like response.

used by an actor pleading self-defense must be warranted by the harm threatened by the aggressor. For example, use of deadly force to repel an attack by someone using a peashooter would not be justified.

Finally, both the necessity and proportionality requirements are subject to a reasonableness standard. A person may succeed in a self-defense claim only if he or she had an honest belief that the use of force was necessary and, in addition, there were reasonable grounds for that belief. A defendant who has an honest but unreasonable belief that he or she was required to use force or that a certain level of force was necessary for self-protection usually will not be able to use this defense and will be criminally culpable for his or her actions (see Application Case 6.1). A few states allow an unreasonably mistaken defendant to assert an "imperfect" self-defense claim, in which case a murder offense can be mitigated to manslaughter.

⚖️ Application Case 6.1

People v. Goetz

People v. Goetz (1984) involved a notorious subway shooting in New York. Bernard Goetz, a previous mugging victim, shot four youths and claimed that he feared imminent attack. Allegedly, one of the youths approached Goetz and demanded that he hand over $5.00, but there was no evidence that any of the youths had weapons or threatened physical violence against Goetz. When the money demand was made, Goetz pulled out a handgun and fired four shots. He struck three of the youths, one of whom suffered permanent injuries. He then looked around and fired an additional shot at the youth who had demanded the $5.00.

When Goetz was arrested, he stated that he carried a weapon because he had been mugged on several occasions and that, based on these incidents, he was fearful of being maimed by the youths although he knew they had no weapons. He admitted that his intention in shooting was to kill the youths and to make them suffer as much as possible. In fact, he fired the additional round at the instigator, Darryl Cabey, when it appeared that he had not hurt him with the first shots. Goetz was convicted of carrying an unlicensed, concealed weapon but acquitted of attempted murder.

A number of legal commentators expressed dissatisfaction with the verdict because they felt that the verdict was not based on the evidence presented. They thought that the evidence clearly showed that Goetz overstepped the bounds of self-defense. These critics thought the verdict resulted because the jury, like the general New York public, was tired of living with uncontrollable urban violence.

In 1996, the instigating youth, Darryl Cabey, who suffered paralysis and brain damage, sued Goetz for damages for reckless and deliberate infliction of emotional distress. The jury awarded Cabey millions of dollars in damages, both compensatory and punitive, making a poignant statement of disapproval of the use of excessive force by Goetz in this case.

SOURCE: People v. Goetz, 497 N.E.2d 41 (N.Y. 1986).

Most frequently, self-defense is asserted in a homicide case, thus raising the question of when the use of deadly force is justified. As noted above, usually a nonaggressor (the person who does not initiate the situation in which the use of force becomes necessary) may use deadly force if he or she reasonably believes that such force is necessary to protect against imminent use of unlawful deadly force by the aggressor. **Deadly force** is defined as "force likely or intended to cause death or great bodily harm."

For example, John is dancing in a bar with a girl he just met. The girl's boyfriend, Dave, walks in and approaches the dancing couple. Dave becomes hostile and punches John. John initially responds by punching Dave back, and a fight ensues. John would not be justified in pulling out a gun and shooting Dave in the head. John would have a difficult time convincing a jury that it was necessary to shoot and kill Dave in order to protect himself from death or grievous bodily injury. On the other hand, suppose John has heard that Dave is a gun-carrying hothead who has previously shot another person. In this case, John has a good chance of escaping criminal culpability by raising the claim of self-defense, because it may have been reasonable for him to use deadly force against Dave in the circumstances.

Valid Self-Defense Claims A person is justified in a self-defense claim when he or she has reason to fear physical harm from the aggressor.

deadly force
Force likely or intended to cause death or great bodily harm.

In most jurisdictions, a person who initiates the aggressive behavior—the first or initial aggressor—may not raise the self-defense claim in order to escape criminal culpability. However, there are two situations in which an aggressor may legitimately argue self-defense:

1. When a nondeadly aggressor is met with deadly force. For example, suppose a first aggressor initiates a dispute by calling someone a name or pushing someone lightly, and that person retaliates by pulling out a weapon that could kill the first aggressor. The first aggressor may then be justified in taking defensive action, because his or her conduct was not reasonably calculated to produce a fatal or seriously harmful response.

2. An aggressor may completely withdraw from any continued conflict with the other person. To effectively withdraw, the aggressor must take reasonable steps to notify the other person of his or her intention to withdraw from

the conflict situation after the initial aggressive act.[12] If the other person continues to threaten harm to the initial aggressor, the initial aggressor is "purge[d] . . . of that status and regain[s] the right of self-defense."[13] However, deadly force can be used only if the initial nonaggressor is threatening fairly immediate harm of a serious physically harmful nature or death.

In order to succeed in a claim of self-defense, a person must show why it was necessary to use force for self-protection. In many circumstances, there may be an alternative to using force, such as avoiding the threatened harm by escaping or retreating. Almost all jurisdictions allow for self-defense in cases of nondeadly force, even if a person could have safely retreated.

In deadly force cases, some jurisdictions have adopted the no-retreat rule, which states that a nonaggressor is permitted to use deadly force when faced with deadly force, even if he or she has the opportunity to escape to complete safety. Under common law, this rule is typically limited to situations in which individuals are attacked in their own home. Modern case law has extended this no-retreat rule to cover situations in which an individual is attacked within his or her workplace or office. However, some states require a person threatened by deadly force to retreat if he or she is aware that retreat is possible and safe. (See Figure 6.1.)

The common law rule, case law, and statutes concerning self-defense require that the defendant reasonably believe that his or her adversary's unlawful violence, especially deadly force, is imminent—that is, almost immediately forthcoming, or about to happen at once. The imminence requirement is also closely related to the reasonable belief requirement, imposing an objective standard on the defendant. Both of these principles have been severely tested in recent years.

◢ F I G U R E   6 . 1

Alaska Statute Regarding Use of Deadly Force

AS 11.81.335.   Justification: Use of Deadly Force in Defense of Self.

(a) Except as provided in (b) of this section, a person may use deadly force upon another person when and to the extent:

    (1) the use of nondeadly force is justified under AS 11.81.330; and

    (2) the person reasonably believes the use of deadly force is necessary for self-defense against death, serious physical injury, kidnapping, sexual assault in the first degree, sexual assault in the second degree, or robbery in any degree.

(b) A person may not use deadly force under this section if the person knows that, with complete personal safety and with complete safety as to others, the person can avoid the necessity of using deadly force by retreating, except there is no duty to retreat if the person is:

    (1) on premises which the person owns or leases and the person is not the initial aggressor; or

    (2) a peace officer acting within the scope and authority of the officer's employment or a person assisting a peace officer under AS 11.81.380.

SOURCE: http://touchngo.com/lglcntr/akstats/Statutes/title11/Chapter81/Section335.htm.

Another area in which imminence of the aggressor's attack and the reasonableness of the defendant's claimed perception of it arise is that of battered person syndrome, most commonly arising in the case of battered women. In recent years, self-defense claims have been made by persons who have killed an abuser after being subjected to a pattern of abuse over a period of months or years. Women who have been abused by their husbands or lovers have sought to assert the defense and to introduce evidence of "battered woman syndrome." Courts generally allow evidence of the history of the man's abuse to support the woman's claim of self-defense.

Legal controversy surrounds how this evidence should be used. If the woman kills the man in the midst of a battering incident, then traditional principles of imminence and reasonableness apply with little difficulty. However, if the woman kills her batterer at a time when abuse is not actually taking place, the traditional imminence and reasonableness requirements may not be satisfied. An expert witness may present evidence of battered woman syndrome and of the battering behavior to explain a woman's belief that the threat of deadly harm is imminent. (See Application Case 6.2.) Such evidence may be presented as a justification for killing the batterer, even while he is sleeping.

⚖ Application Case 6.2

State v. Kelly

In *State v. Kelly* (1984), Gladys Kelly stabbed her husband to death with a pair of scissors, arguing that she did so in self-defense. Kelly's defense was that her husband had repeatedly and brutally beaten her over a seven-year period, and that he had threatened to kill her if she ever tried to leave him. On the day of the killing, Mr. Kelly became enraged and began beating his wife on a public street in front of a crowd of people. Some of the observers broke up the altercation, and the two were separated for a short time. Mrs. Kelly testified that later that day, Mr. Kelly began running toward her with his hands raised. Unsure of whether he had a weapon, she took the scissors out of her purse and began stabbing him.

Ms. Kelly called an expert witness to testify about battered woman syndrome. Although the lower court denied this evidence, the Supreme Court of New Jersey reversed the decision and allowed the evidence to be introduced. In brief, battered woman syndrome exists when someone is repeatedly subjected to physical brutality by her (or his) domestic partner and does not feel that she can leave the relationship out of fear that the domestic partner will kill her. As a result, this continued abuse creates the perception in the battered person that she must use physical force as protection or be killed. (You will read more about battered woman syndrome in Chapter 9.) In the *Kelly* case, the expert was called to show the reasonableness of Mrs. Kelly's perception—that she believed she was in imminent danger of death or serious injury.

SOURCE: State v. Kelly, 478 A.2d 364 (N.J. 1984).

Taking evidence of a battering syndrome into account requires a "subjectification" of the reasonableness test, an objective standard that all persons are expected to meet. Most courts are unwilling to change the universal notion of reasonableness into one that recognizes and accepts individual circumstances, temperaments, or peculiarities. Courts are divided on whether self-defense may be claimed when, reasonably or not, the woman believed that the threat of deadly harm was imminent.[14] In cases where the defendant has hired another to kill the claimed abuser, courts have not allowed the defense.[15]

Historically, the self-defense justification seems to have applied to two people of approximately equal fighting ability. Advocates for battered women have argued that their situations do not fit this model. Such women may have few options (e.g., no money, no car), and they may fear for their lives, knowing that they cannot win a physical fight with their stronger male partners. In fact, many battered women who leave are hunted down and killed by their abusers. On the other hand, some battered women do get away, often with the help of the staff at shelters for battered women.

The abuse defense may extend to other scenarios as well and cover many types of abuse, including physical abuse, sexual abuse, and psychological abuse. In addition to battered woman syndrome, other types include rape trauma syndrome, child abuse accommodation syndrome, and parent abuse syndrome. One of the most famous cases in which the defendants used the abuse defense unsuccessfully was that of the Menendez brothers. In 1996, both of the Menendez brothers were found guilty of murdering their parents, despite their claims of being victims of sexual abuse at the hands of their parents.[16]

Another form of abuse defense is urban survival syndrome, in which a defendant may argue that because he was trying to survive within a turbulent violent urban area, he should not be held criminally liable for crimes. The idea is that people who live in fear will eventually snap. This defense is similar to self-defense, but it is not medically recognized. Black rage defense is a political defense in which defense lawyers will argue that "their clients' crimes were in part a product of societal racism." It explores the relationship between a person's environment and crime. No jurisdiction has recognized racial discrimination as a defense, but lawyers are free to argue racism "in defense of charges or in mitigation of the penalties."[17]

Defense of Others

Universally, the law recognizes a defense based on protection of another person from attack. The defense likely grew out of the right of persons to defend their property. It was extended to include the right to protect spouse, children, and servants, in whom the law recognized a property interest similar to that in personal property. However, as the defense developed, the persons who could be defended expanded to include others in the household and beyond—eventually even including strangers. Thus, in most jurisdictions, a person is justified in using reasonable force to defend someone else when that person reasonably believes that the other person is in imminent danger of bodily harm from an unlawful aggressor and that using force is necessary to avoid the harm.

Although the right to prevent harm to another is universally recognized as a defense, there are two problem areas. The first problem is determining the category of persons who can be assisted; the second is identifying situations in which the person defended had a legal right to act in self-defense. The early common law rule allowed force to be used to defend others only when they stood in a special relationship to their protector, such as that of spouse, child, parent, employer, or employee. Though a number of states retained this restriction, those states also adopted legal provisions allowing the use of force to prevent the commission of a crime. In effect, then, even strangers can be protected against criminal attack. However, some states still have laws that are intended to limit the use of force in defense of others to defending persons who are in a certain relationship to the defender.[18] (See Figure 6.2.)

The second problem concerning the applicability of the defense arises in situations such as the following. Al attacks Bill, and Bill uses force in self-defense. Dave, a stranger to both Al and Bill, comes upon the scene and, believing that Bill is attacking Al, uses force upon Bill to protect Al. From the point of view of

FIGURE 6.2

Defense of Others Laws by State

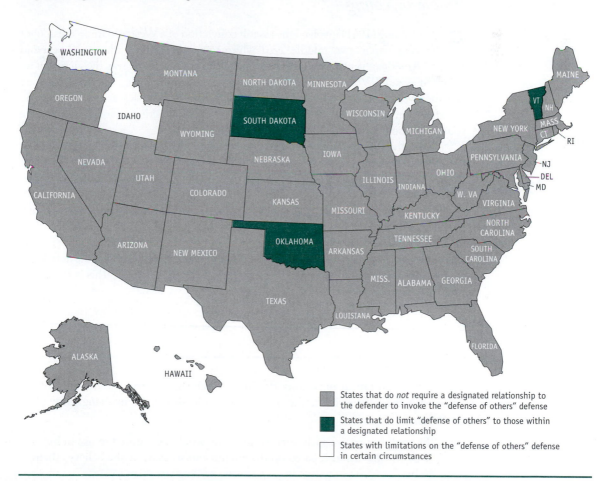

States that do *not* require a designated relationship to the defender to invoke the "defense of others" defense

States that do limit "defense of others" to those within a designated relationship

States with limitations on the "defense of others" defense in certain circumstances justification, Dave's reasonable belief that Al is under attack from Bill justifies Dave's use of reasonable force to protect Al. However, since Bill was not engaged in criminal conduct (he was acting in justifiable self-defense), some courts would hold that Dave could not assert the defense of others in acting to protect Al.

If the defense were limited to the defense of loved ones (or others close to the actor), then the actor would be more likely to know whether the situation of the person defended justified intervention. In other words, to minimize the possibility of error, we should act at our peril when we attempt to protect a stranger. Some states retain this act-at-peril rule, but, under the influence of the MPC, most states have adopted a reasonable appearance rule. Under the latter rule, the actor can claim the defense as long as he or she uses force based on what reasonably appears necessary. (See Application Case 6.3.)

⚖ Application Case 6.3

People v. Young

People v. Young (1961) involved the assault conviction of a Western Union messenger who came upon two middle-aged white men struggling with an 18-year-old African American youth. The defendant believed that the youth was the victim of an unlawful assault. When he intervened, his leg locked with the leg of one of the men and the two fell. The weight of the fall broke the other man's leg at the kneecap. As it turned out, the two men were plainclothes detectives making a lawful arrest of the youth for disorderly conduct.

Initially, a lower appellate court reversed the conviction, based on the fact that the defendant had acted reasonably when he intervened. The New York Court of Appeals reversed that reversal, upholding the conviction and holding that one who goes to the aid of a third person does so at his own peril. According to this court, the "right of a person to defend another ordinarily should not be greater than such person's right to defend himself."

Ultimately, the New York legislature chose not to follow the act-at-peril rule and enacted a statute that allows for the justification defense of others if the defendant reasonably believed force was necessary to defend the third person. This is the law in most jurisdictions today.

SOURCE: People v. Young, 210 N.Y.S.2d 358 (N.Y. App. Div. 1961), *rev'd*, 183 N.E.2d 319 (N.Y. 1962); *see* People v. Melendez, 588 N.Y.S.2d 718 (N.Y. Sup. Ct. 1992) (referring to N.Y. PENAL LAW § 35.15(1)(b), added in 1968).

Subject to retreat provisions, the MPC establishes three conditions that must be met for the defense of another to be asserted in situations involving third-party protection:

1.   The actor must use such force as he or she would be entitled to use in his or her own self-defense, based on the circumstances as he or she believes them to be.

6.1 Web Exploration

Good Samaritan Laws

You can learn more about Good Samaritan laws by visiting http://medi-smart/gslaw.htm. What steps should be taken in case of an emergency? Are you protected from being sued if you are found to be responsible for any injuries incurred by the victim?

2. Under the circumstances as the actor believes them to be, the third person must be legally justified in using such protective force.
3. The actor must believe that his or her action is necessary for the protection of the third person.

Focusing on the second condition, for example, if the person protected were resisting arrest by a known police officer, or if he or she were using excessive force in making an arrest, the person protected would have no defense. If the third-party actor knew those circumstances, he or she would have no defense either.

With respect to retreat, the MPC adapts the requirements for self-defense to apply to the defense of others. The actor need not retreat before using force to protect a third person unless he or she knows that doing so is possible while still assuring the complete safety of that person. For example, if a child is attacked, the actor must, if possible, pick up the child and retreat with the child, rather than use fatal force in the child's defense. The actor must attempt to secure the retreat of the person needing protection in those situations where retreat would be required under the rules of self-defense.

Defense of Property and Habitation

A person is justified in the use of force to protect his or her property from encroachment. However, unless the threat is against habitation (a person's residence), the actor is not justified in the use of deadly force. In short, the law generally values life over property. A person may use force to prevent another from dispossessing him or her of real or personal property or to regain possession of property immediately after dispossession. However, the actor can never use deadly force solely to protect property. Nonetheless, the notion that "every Englishman's home was his last retreat from a hostile world" was at the root of the common law rule that deadly force could be used in "defense of the home that sheltered life."[19] Thus, when there is a threat of unlawful entry into a home, the dweller inside may, under some circumstances, use deadly force to defend his or her dwelling.

The earliest common law rule on the use of deadly force to defend one's home was that, under the category of crime prevention, a homicide to prevent breaking into a house at night was justifiable. The rule subsequently evolved to allow a dweller to use deadly force if he or she reasonably believes it necessary to do so to prevent an imminent, unlawful entry of his or her dwelling. This is sometimes referred to as the *castle rule*. Some jurisdictions have taken a narrower approach to the defense of

---

FIGURE 6.3

Utah Statute on the Use of Force in Defense of Habitation

76-2-405.   Force in defense of habitation.

(1)   A person is justified in using force against another when and to the extent that he reasonably believes that the force is necessary to prevent or terminate the other's unlawful entry into or attack upon his habitation; however, he is justified in the use of force which is intended or likely to cause death or serious bodily injury only if:

   (a)   the entry is made or attempted in a violent and tumultuous manner, surreptitiously, or by stealth, and he reasonably believes that the entry is attempted or made for the purpose of assaulting or offering personal violence to any person, dwelling, or being in the habitation and he reasonably believes that the force is necessary to prevent the assault or offer of personal violence; or

   (b)   he reasonably believes that the entry is made or attempted for the purpose of committing a felony in the habitation and that the force is necessary to prevent the commission of the felony.

(2)   The person using force or deadly force in defense of habitation is presumed for the purpose of both civil and criminal cases to have acted reasonably and had a reasonable fear of imminent peril of death or serious bodily injury if the entry or attempted entry is unlawful and is made or attempted by use of force, or in a violent and tumultuous manner, or surreptitiously or by stealth, or for the purpose of committing a felony.

SOURCE: http://le.utah.gov/~code/TITLE76/htm/76_02025.htm.

---

habitation, allowing the use of deadly force only when the actor believes that the intruder intends to injure the actor or another occupant, and deadly force is necessary to repel the intruder. (See Figure 6.3.)

Other jurisdictions have imposed an even narrower rule, requiring that:

- The actor reasonably believes that the intruder intends to commit a forcible felony in the dwelling or to kill or seriously injure an occupant.
- Deadly force is necessary to repel the intrusion.

The MPC limits the use of deadly force to instances in which there is a substantial risk to the person.

In contrast to the defense of habitation, a person may use reasonable, but not deadly, force in the defense of property from trespass or theft when the actor reasonably believes that the property is in immediate danger of unlawful interference and that force is necessary to prevent the interference. Only if the interference with the property is accompanied by a threat of deadly force would the actor be justified in defending with deadly force. But in this case, the use of such deadly force would really be based upon self-defense, as described in an earlier section of this chapter.

The amount of force used in protecting the property must be proportional to what is needed to protect the property. If the property can be protected without resorting to physical force, the owner must do so. Most jurisdictions require an owner to ask the perpetrator to refrain from taking the property before resorting to physical force, unless it is clear from the circumstances that a request to desist would be useless or would put the owner in a more dangerous situation. As a policy consideration, the protection of property is not thought to be as important as the protection of a human life; therefore, the law requires that steps be taken to avoid any physical harm to persons when protecting one's property.

The MPC provides that an individual can use nondeadly force to protect his or her property if three conditions are met:

1. The other person's interference with the property must be unlawful.
2. The property owner must have possession of the property in question or must be acting on behalf of someone who is in possession of the property.
3. Force must be immediately necessary to protect the property, or the actor must believe that the person against whom he uses force has no rightful claim to the property and, in the case of land, the circumstances must be such that it would be an exceptional hardship to postpone the entry or reentry until a court order is obtained.

A property owner is forbidden to use any mechanical device, such as a spring gun, that would cause disproportional harm, such as a severe injury or death, to protect his or her property from trespass or theft.[20] Use of a device that killed someone for trespassing would be justified only if the person who employed the device would have been justified in killing the trespasser had he been present to physically carry out the act himself.

Under the MPC, however, the use of devices that kill is not justifiable under any circumstances.[21] (See Application Case 6.4.) Mechanical devices such as warning alarms or electric fences may be used if they are reasonable and give adequate warning to the intruder that they exist. The MPC requires three things in order to maintain nondeadly mechanical devices:

1. The device must not be designed to cause or create a substantial risk of death or serious injury.
2. Use of the device must be reasonable under the circumstances.
3. The device must be one that is customarily used for the purpose of protection, and reasonable care must be taken to make probable intruders aware that the device is being used.

⚖️ Application Case 6.4

People v. Caballos

In *People v. Caballos*, the defendant was convicted of assault with a deadly weapon for rigging a loaded .22 caliber pistol to go off when the door of his dwelling opened. The defendant had been robbed of expensive equipment on previous occasions and rigged the gun as a way of catching any future perpetrators. Two teenage boys, who had been the perpetrators in the previous break-in, tried to break in again. One of them was shot in the face.

The defendant argued that he should not have been convicted because had he been physically present he would have been justified in shooting the two boys. The court disagreed, stating that "where the character and manner of the burglary do not reasonably create a fear of great bodily harm, there is no cause for exaction of human life . . . or for the use of deadly force. The character . . . of the burglary could not reasonably create such a fear unless the burglary threatened, or was reasonably believed to threaten, death or serious bodily harm."

The court reached this decision partly because it believed that to allow people to employ deadly mechanical devices in the defense of property would imperil the lives of children, as well as firefighters, police officers, and others acting within the scope of their employment. The court also stated that even when one is home when intruders enter, the dweller might resort to other options besides using deadly force or inflicting serious injury.

SOURCE: People v. Caballos, 526 P.2d 241 (Cal. 1974).

Defenses Related to Crime Prevention and Law Enforcement

There is some overlap among justifications in the areas of defense of others and crime prevention or law enforcement. Although private citizens and private security agencies can act in a law enforcement capacity, their powers to do so are not as broad as those of sworn police officers. The rules for private citizens have been covered in the section on defense of others. A few additional points will be made here. However, the primary purpose of this section is to discuss the justification defense as it applies to sworn police officers in the exercise of their duties.

A category of defense that may be labeled "law enforcement" authorizes the use of force by law enforcement officers in various circumstances. Law enforcement officers are allowed to use nondeadly force:

- To stop and arrest someone who is committing or who has committed a crime.
- To prevent an escape from custody by someone subject to arrest or who has been arrested.
- To prevent the commission of a crime.
- To suppress riots and disorders.[22]

Because of the nature of their jobs, police officers are at times compelled to use lawful force in order to prevent criminals from causing further harm to society. A police officer must always act reasonably when using force and must not deprive suspects of important constitutional rights. For example, a police officer who wrongfully arrests an individual for a crime the arrested person did not commit and then physically restrains the person when he or she attempts to flee might be charged with false imprisonment or some other offense. Therefore, it is very important for a police officer and anyone acting as a law enforcement agent to understand when it is appropriate to use force on a person and what degree of force is considered reasonable.

Private citizens can make arrests under the common law rule. Such a citizen's arrest can be made for a felony or for a misdemeanor involving a breach of the peace, if the crime actually occurred and the citizen reasonably believes the suspect committed the offense. A citizen's arrest for other misdemeanors in the citizen's presence is also authorized.

A police officer making a lawful arrest may be met with resistance and may reasonably believe that using force is the only way to stop a suspect from physically harming the police officer or some other innocent person. A law enforcement officer or private citizen authorized to arrest may use nondeadly force in making an arrest when it is necessary to prevent the commission of a crime, to prevent the escape of an arrestee, or to complete an arrest.[23] When a person who has been arrested flees, an officer may use the degree of force necessary to make the arrest. This does not mean that an officer can always use deadly force in such cases; the requirements governing the use of deadly force are much more rigorous.

As Blackstone noted, early common law permitted the use of deadly force "where a man by the commandment of the law is bound to arrest another for any capital offense or to disperse a riot, and resistance is made to his authority: it is here justifiable and even necessary to beat, to wound, or perhaps to kill the offenders, rather than permit the murderer to escape or the riot to continue."[24] The common law rule permitted a law enforcement officer to use deadly force to effect an arrest or even a detention. The common law rule was subsequently modified to reduce the circumstances in which deadly force can be used.

Under the modified common law rule, a law enforcement officer is justified in using deadly force upon another if the officer reasonably believes that the suspect committed a felony and that such force is necessary (that is, the legal objective of arrest cannot be achieved without such action, or, without such force, the suspect will escape). Beginning in the late nineteenth century, some states modified this rule to allow the use of deadly force to effect an arrest for a forcible or atrocious felony.[25] The use of deadly force by a law enforcement officer is also subject to constitutional limitations, which will be discussed below.

Use of deadly force by a private citizen is more restricted than for police officers, in part to prevent vigilantism. Although the law is not uniform throughout the states, private citizens may use deadly force in effecting a felony arrest only when the offense is a forcible felony, the arresting citizen gives notice of the intent to make an arrest, and the citizen correctly believes that the person committed the felony. However, constitutional limitations that apply to law enforcement officers, such as probable cause and warrants, do not apply to private citizens.

The MPC's provisions with respect to the use of deadly force are much narrower than the common law rule. An officer or private citizen may not use deadly force to prevent the commission of a crime unless he or she believes:

- That there is a substantial risk that the suspect will cause death or serious bodily injury to another person unless prevented from doing so.
- That the use of deadly force presents no substantial risk to bystanders.[26]

A private citizen acting on his or her own cannot use deadly force to effect an arrest or prevent an escape. A law enforcement officer or a citizen assisting someone believed to be a police officer may use deadly force to make an arrest or prevent an escape only under the following conditions:

- When the arrest is for a felony.
- When the actor believes force is necessary.
- When the actor makes known to the suspect the purpose of the arrest.

- When the actor believes that the use of deadly force creates no substantial risk of harm to innocent bystanders.
- When the actor believes either that the crime for which the arrest is made involved the use or threatened use of deadly force, or that there is a substantial risk that the suspect will kill or seriously injure someone if the arrest is delayed or the suspect escapes.

For a detailed discussion of the constitutional limits of the use of deadly force by law enforcement, see Application Case 6.5.

⚖️ Application Case 6.5

Tennessee v. Garner

The final limitation on the use of deadly force by a law enforcement officer in effecting an arrest is the constitutional limitation imposed by the U.S. Supreme Court in its decision in *Tennessee v. Garner.* In that case, police officers responded to a call at night that there was a prowler inside a home. One of the investigating officers saw someone running in the backyard of the house that was being burglarized. The suspect was a 15-year-old boy who ran to a six-foot chain-link fence in the back of the yard. The officer shone his flashlight on the boy and did not see a weapon. In fact, the officer stated that he was "reasonably sure" that the boy did not have a weapon. The boy began climbing the fence, and as he did so, the officer yelled "Police, halt!" When the boy did not stop, the officer shot him in the back of the head, killing him.

Under Tennessee law, the officer's actions were justified because he was permitted to use deadly force to arrest a suspect for any felony. However, the suspect's father brought a federal action seeking damages for violations of the boy's constitutional rights. In this case, the Supreme Court held that an officer using deadly force violates a suspect's Fourth Amendment right to be free from unreasonable search and seizure unless the officer has probable cause to believe "that the suspect poses a significant threat of death or serious physical injury to the officer or others, and such force is necessary to make the arrest or prevent escape. In regard to the necessity element, a warning, if feasible, must be given to the suspect before deadly force is employed."

The Court held that an arrest constitutes a "seizure" that is unreasonable when deadly force is disproportionate to a suspect's actions. Furthermore, the Court said that "[w]here the suspect poses no immediate threat to the officer and no threat to others, the harm resulting from failing to apprehend [the nonviolent felon] does not justify the use of deadly force." The gist of the Court's decision is summed up in this statement: "It is not better that all felony suspects die than that they escape."

SOURCE: Tennessee v. Garner, 471 U.S. 1 (1985).

6.2 Web Exploration

Use of Force by Law Enforcement

You can learn how often law enforcement personnel use force in the line of duty by visiting the National Criminal Justice Reference Service Web site at http://virlib .ncjrs.org/LawEnforcement.asp. As part of the Violent Crime Control and Law Enforcement Act of 1994, the National Institute of Justice and the Bureau of Statistics have combined efforts to collect data and research police-citizen contact. Is the use of force in police-citizen contacts rare or prevalent? Is it usually accompanied by provocative behavior on the part of suspects?

Necessity (Choice of Evils)

Sometimes a person is faced with a choice between two courses of action, both of which will cause harm. If the actor chooses the lesser of the evils, he or she can claim the defense of **necessity**. The defense of necessity, therefore, is also known as the choice of evils, or the choice of lesser evils. It is a justification-based defense, in that if it applies, the actor is not held criminally liable at all. It overlaps with other defenses; for example, self-defense is grounded in part on the necessity of using force to prevent harm to oneself. Blackstone listed self-defense as one of the situations in which the actor cannot be convicted of a crime due to necessity: "in such a case [where an actor kills an assailant] he is permitted to kill the assailant; for there the law of nature, and self-defense [its] primary [canon], have made him his own protector."[27]

When, under the pressure of circumstances, a person commits what would otherwise be a crime, he or she is considered legally justified in acting if his or her actions were a necessity designed to prevent some greater harm. Necessity as a defense can be successful in producing an acquittal as long as the harm produced is less than the harm that would have occurred without the action.[28] The defense has been recognized in a variety of situations.

With respect to necessity as a defense to a charge of homicide, the law has not been so clear. The MPC "choice of evils" defense[29] has influenced many American states to adopt statutes recognizing the defense. Nearly half have done so (see Figure 6.4). But in other jurisdictions, the common law definition of the defense still prevails. According to common law, a person is justified in violating a criminal law if the following six elements are present:

1. The actor must be faced with a clear and imminent danger.
2. The actor must expect, as a reasonable person, that his or her action will be effective in abating the danger sought to be avoided.
3. The actor may not successfully claim the defense if there is an effective legal alternative available.
4. The harm caused must be less than the harm avoided.
5. The legislature in the state must not have decided the balancing of the choice and legislated against it. For example, if the legislature considered approving marijuana use for medical reasons and rejected the choice, a person cannot

necessity
A defense in which a person, faced with a choice between two courses of action, chooses the lesser of evils, as long as the harm produced is less than the harm that would have occurred without the action.

FIGURE 6.4

States That Define the Necessity Defense and Those That Do Not

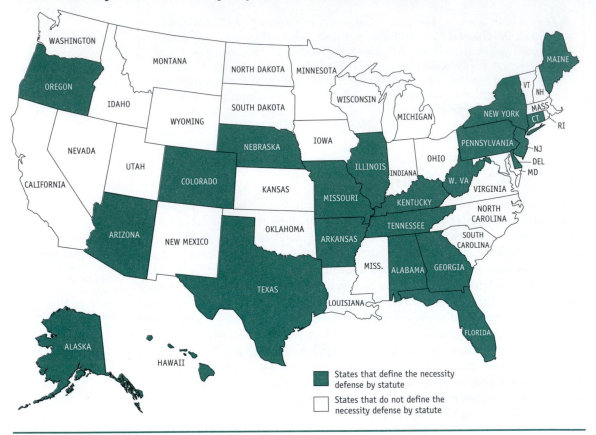

States that define the necessity defense by statute

States that do not define the necessity defense by statute

claim that choosing to use marijuana for this purpose was a lesser evil than not treating the condition for which it was used. If the legislature has defined the circumstances under which abortion is legal, the actor cannot claim that necessity justified an abortion under circumstances not authorized by law.

6. The actor must not have wrongfully placed himself or herself in the situation that requires the choice of evils.

In addition to these elements, the defense may also be subject to three limitations:

1. Some states limit the defense to situations created by natural forces.
2. The defense may not apply in homicide cases.
3. A person may not act merely to protect his or her reputation or economic interests.[30]

As noted above, the MPC's choice of evils defense broadened the common law rule. First, with respect to defense in a homicide case, the examples given in the comments accompanying the MPC are illuminating. First, the comment recognizes the sanctity of human life but then notes that conduct resulting in the taking of life may promote the very value that the law against homicide seeks to protect. The comment then presents two examples to illustrate this possibility:

1. An actor who makes a breach in a dike, knowing that doing so will flood a nearby farm, but that this is the only course available to save an entire town. If charged with homicide, the accused could rightly point to the net saving of innocent lives and "the numerical preponderance in the lives saved compared to those sacrificed surely should establish legal justification for the act."

2. A mountain climber, "roped to a companion who has fallen over a precipice, who holds on as long as possible, but eventually cuts the rope." According to the comment, the actor "must certainly be granted the defense that he accelerated one death slightly but avoided the only alternative, the certain death of both."[31]

It should be noted that the MPC defense still would not apply to the situation in which the actor kills one person to save another, or where a person acts to save himself at the expense of another. These are choices of equal, not lesser, evils, and the defense of necessity would not be available under the common law or the MPC in those situations. (See Application Cases 6.6 and 6.7.)

⚖️ Application Case 6.6

Regina v. Dudley and Stephens

In the English case *Regina v. Dudley and Stephens* (1884), three seamen and a 17-year-old boy were stranded in the open sea for 20 days after their ship sank. They were without food for the last nine days and without water the last seven days. The boy was seriously ill, and all were very weak. Two of the men killed the boy in order to eat his flesh and drink his blood for survival. Four days later they were saved, and the two men were charged with the boy's murder.

The men raised the defense of necessity, arguing that had they not killed the victim, all of them would have died. The court rejected their claim, holding that they were not justified in taking another's life to save their own unless acting in self-defense against the other person. The defendants were convicted of murder, but their sentences were commuted to six months' imprisonment.

SOURCE: Regina v. Dudley and Stephens, L.R. 14 Q.B.D. 273 (1884).

⚖️ Application Case 6.7

United States v. Holmes

In *United States v. Holmes* (1842), nine seamen and 32 passengers were in an overloaded lifeboat after a shipwreck. A storm threatened to sink the lifeboat, and, in order to lighten the boat to ride out the storm, the crew members, including the defendant, threw 14 male passengers overboard. The passengers, as expected, died. The lightened boat survived the storm, and the defendant was charged with and convicted of manslaughter, a conviction that was upheld on appeal. The trial court instructed the jury that the crew not necessary to man the boat should have been sacrificed before the passengers and that between those in an equal situation, those to be sacrificed should have been determined by lot.

SOURCE: United States v. Holmes, 26 F. Cas. 360 (No. 15,383) (E.D. Pa. 1842).

Necessity is related to the defense of duress. The major difference is that duress involves coercive threats from human beings rather than from physical or natural circumstances. Duress is considered primarily an excuse rather than a justification defense and is discussed in the following section on excuse-based defenses.

Finally, with respect to the defense of necessity, it is worthwhile to mention its use in cases involving political protests. From time to time, a person charged with violating some law as a matter of civil disobedience, or protest, raises the claim of necessity as a defense. For example, during the Vietnam War, protests against the draft system involved illegal acts against the government and led to prosecutions. More recently, protesters of U.S. policies in Nicaragua and El Salvador have raised the defense. Most appellate courts have "consistently" rejected it.[32]

Consent

consent

A defense, in certain circumstances, in which the victim agrees to the actor's conduct. The consent negates an element of the offense or precludes infliction of the harm to be prevented by the law defining the offense.

Consent is normally not a defense in criminal cases. However, in some circumstances when the victim agrees to the actor's conduct, the defense of **consent** may be raised when it negates an element of the offense or prevents the harm addressed by the law defining the offense. In this sense, it is more appropriately classed as a defense that negates an element of the offense, rather than a true defense. The reason that consent is rarely accepted as a defense is that crimes are viewed as perpetrated against society as a whole and not just against the individual victim. Consent is not a defense even if the victim contributes to the negligence or somehow aids the defendant in the commission of the crime. However, certain crimes do make lack of consent an element of the crime, explicitly or implicitly, and in those situations, a defendant can assert consent as a complete defense. Hence, it is appropriate to discuss the defense under the heading of a justification defense.

For example, a defendant may be convicted of rape only if the sexual act against the victim was nonconsensual. The prosecutor normally must prove the victim's lack of consent to the sexual act as an essential element of the crime. If the defendant can show that he knew the victim and that, in fact, the sexual relationship with the victim was consensual, he will be acquitted. The defendant must still show that the victim consented to the particular sexual act in question.

Consent is normally not a valid defense in statutory rape cases, where the defendant is charged with having sexual relations with a minor. This is a result of strict liability laws. Even if the minor expressed a willingness to engage in sex, the law does not accept this as actual consent because the minor is deemed incapable of making a valid choice.

The MPC provides that consent is a defense "if such consent negatives an element of the offense or precludes the infliction of the harm or evil sought to be prevented by the law defining such an offense."[33] The Code also provides that consent is not effective if the victim is legally incompetent to authorize consent, consent is given by a person who is unable to make a reasonable judgment, consent is given by someone "whose improvident consent is sought to be prevented by the law defining the offense," or the consent is induced "by force, duress or deception of a kind sought to be prevented by the law defining the offense."

Some sports involve combat or conflict, are inherently dangerous, or involve aggressive or violent behavior. Participants in such sports impliedly consent to the conflict and reasonably foreseeable effects, even though they often get injured, sometimes severely, while playing these sports. A defendant will want to argue an assumption of risk defense, if available in the jurisdiction, claiming that the plaintiff, by participating in an inherently dangerous activity, assumed the risk involved with that activity and consented to foreseeable injuries (or death). Nonetheless, if the defendant exceeded the scope of expected or foreseeable violence, the defense can fail.[34]

▲ CRITICAL THINKING 6.2

1. How can self-defense be used as a complete defense? As a mitigating defense?

2. What are the two problem areas that arise from a defense based on protection of another person?

6.3 Defenses Based on Excuse

As previously stated, an excuse defense is one establishing that even though an actor's conduct was criminal, he or she is not legally culpable. Whereas justification defenses tend to focus on the act, excuse defenses focus on the actor. An actor is able to offer a valid excuse for his or her behavior, and society chooses not to punish the actor for the conduct. The major legal excuses are:

- Age/infancy of the actor.
- Duress.
- Intoxication.
- Insanity.
- Diminished capacity.

Other excuses include mistake, entrapment, and various specialized defenses.

Age/Infancy

Under the common law, children under the age of 7 were considered conclusively incapable of realistically forming the "evil" state of mind necessary for legal (and moral) culpability. With respect to persons between the ages of 7 and 14, a prosecutor could introduce evidence that although the defendant was young, he or she was mature enough to recognize the difference between right and wrong and the consequences of his or her voluntary actions. Any person age 14 or older was considered criminally responsible. Today, by statute, most jurisdictions have written some variation of this age scheme into their criminal code. Based on an approximate 20-year upswing in the number of crimes committed by juveniles, the current trend in criminal law is to reduce rather than increase the age at which children can be held criminally responsible. In New York, for example, juveniles as young as age 13 can be tried as adults if they commit a serious felony offense. However, for youth below the common law or statutory age of criminal responsibility, age is a complete defense to the charge, regardless of the harm caused by their conduct.

Duress

A person who commits an unlawful act because of a threat of imminent death or serious bodily injury to self or to another is entitled to assert the common law defense of **duress**, or coercion, unless the actor intentionally kills an innocent third person. This statement of the defense is generally accurate, but it requires some refinement and explanation to be complete. The modern statutory versions of the defense are generally the same as the common law rule, although both the harm threatened and the crimes committed have been broadened by the MPC and many state enactments. Duress is a form of choice of evils and, in that respect, is similar to the defense of necessity. As the U.S. Supreme Court said in 1980, "Modern cases have tended to blur the distinction between duress and necessity."[35]

The simple distinction that necessity is a choice of evils created by natural threats or physical circumstances, whereas duress is a choice of evils created by human threats, is not the only distinction. For example, if Tom threatened to cut off Don's arm unless Don cut off Vince's arm, the harms are of equal severity, but Don could assert the defense of duress (but not necessity) if he complied with Tom's demand.[36]

The reason for the defense of duress has been explained as a circumstance in which the "will of the accused is . . . 'neutralized' or 'destroyed' so that the behavior is no longer the voluntary act of the accused."[37] According to this view, the defense is one that negates the mental state required as an essential element of the crime charged. However, this rationale is generally rejected, and duress is more likely to be viewed as reducing the range of choice of the accused. In other words, a person acting under duress does act voluntarily, even if the act is contrary to his or her own true wishes.

Although jurisdictions vary in the requirements for the defense, a person will usually be acquitted of any offense (except intentional killing) based on the defense of duress, if the following circumstances exist:

- Another person must threaten to seriously injure or kill the actor or a third person (especially a close relative) unless the actor commits the crime.
- The actor must reasonably believe that the threat is real.
- The threat must be immediate or imminent at the time the actor commits the crime.
- There must be no reasonable means of escape from or avoidance of the threat other than for the actor to commit the crime.
- The actor must not be at fault in exposing himself or herself to the threat.

duress
A defense that arises when a person commits an unlawful act because of a threat of imminent death or serious bodily injury to himself or another, unless the actor intentionally kills an innocent third person.

Some jurisdictions that do not recognize duress as a complete defense for intentional killing will allow it to reduce the crime from murder to manslaughter.

The MPC has broadened the defense in a number of ways. The defense can be asserted if "a person of reasonable firmness in his [or her] situation would have been unable to resist" the threat.[38] Thus, the MPC eliminates the requirements that the threat involve deadly force (the use of force need only be unlawful) and that the threat be imminent. It does not bar the defense in the case of certain offenses (including intentional homicide) and does not place restrictions on the category of imperiled persons (e.g., that the threat be to harm a member of the actor's family). Since the MPC requires that the threat be one of "unlawful force," duress is an affirmative defense only to threats made by persons, not to threats arising from natural sources. The MPC continues the common law restriction of the defense to threats to the actor or another person; threats to property or reputation cannot be the basis for the defense.

There are some other noteworthy situations that would lead to a valid assertion of the duress defense under the MPC but not at common law:

- A person who is "brainwashed" or "coerced" over time into committing an illegal act by responding to earlier threats that have rendered the actor submissive. The MPC would allow the defense of duress in such a situation; because of the immediacy and imminence requirements of the common law rule, the defense would not be available under the latter.
- An escape from prison to avoid an intolerable condition or circumstance. The drafters of the MPC give an example of a prisoner, threatened with a homosexual assault, who escapes from prison to avoid the assault. The drafters note that this is a situation in which the accused could assert both the necessity defense and the duress defense, even though the crime committed by the coerced actor is different from the one that the person making the threats demanded. (See Application Case 6.8.)

⚖️ Application Case 6.8

People v. Unger

In *People v. Unger* (1975), the defendant was charged with escape after he walked away from a minimum-security prison farm. He claimed that he left the camp after having been sexually assaulted by a group of inmates, then receiving a threatening telephone call saying that he would be killed because the caller had heard that he planned to go to the authorities about the incident.

When Unger was apprehended, he claimed that he was in fear of his life if he remained at the prison farm. His conviction for escape was reversed when the appellate court held that is was legal error for the trial court judge to instruct the jury that the reason given for the escape was immaterial and not to be considered as justifying *or* excusing the escape.

SOURCE: People v. Unger, 338 N.E.2d 442 (Ill. Ct. App. 1975).

The last situation in which the MPC might allow assertion of the duress defense arises when a battered woman "commits a crime at the 'suggestion' of her abusive partner." Though it may be argued that such a person could possibly raise the defense under the modern statutes in some states, the defense is more likely available under the MPC version of the duress defense. However, the MPC does specify in section 2.09(3) that "It is not a defense that a woman acted on the command of her husband, unless she acted under such coercion as would establish a defense under this Section." At common law, there was a legal presumption that a woman acting in the presence of her husband is coerced by him. The MPC abolishes that rule, placing wives and husbands on a par with any other pairs claiming that their actions were coerced or coercive.

As noted earlier, some jurisdictions consider duress to be a justification defense, others consider it as both a justification and an excuse defense, and some jurisdictions choose not to differentiate between excuse and justification when duress is raised. Those who regard duress as a justification defense argue that one will always commit the lesser of two evils in avoiding a greater harm. Those who regard duress as an excuse defense argue that the actor should not be punished because he or she had no choice but to act—having no freedom of choice because of the limitations created by circumstances. The requirements of the duress defense are the same regardless of whether a jurisdiction defines it as an excuse or as a justification. (See Application Case 6.9.)

⚖️ Application Case 6.9

State v. Toscano

In *State v. Toscano* (1977), the defendant, a chiropractor, was convicted at trial of conspiring to obtain money by false pretenses. The defendant claimed that he had aided in the preparation of false insurance claims as a result of threats against him by the ringleader of a criminal conspiracy, to whom Toscano owed gambling debts. The ringleader said to Toscano, after he initially refused to aid in the conspiracy, "Remember, you just moved into a place that has a very dark entrance and you live there with your wife. . . . You and your wife are going to jump at shadows when you leave that dark entrance." The defendant argued that he was forced to prepare the claims in order to protect himself and his wife. As the threats continued, the defendant moved to a new residence and changed his telephone number to an unlisted number.

The trial court instructed the jury that duress was not an available defense for Toscano because the harm threatened was not "imminent, present, and pending." At the time this case came before the New Jersey Supreme Court, there was no statute on duress, but the MPC had been adopted. The court, adopting a revision to the common law rule, reversed the conviction and held that "duress shall be a defense to a crime other than murder if the defendant engaged in conduct because he was coerced to do so by the use of, or threat to use, unlawful force against his person or the person of another, which a person of reasonable firmness in his situation would have been unable to resist." Thereafter, the New Jersey legislature adopted a duress statute patterned after the MPC.

SOURCE: State v. Toscano, 378 A.2d 755 (N.J. 1977).

Intoxication

Although "it is a maxim of the common law that 'intoxication is no excuse,' . . . [s]ince the mid-nineteenth century . . . courts have developed doctrine that . . . allows intoxication to serve as a partial defense." The MPC defines intoxication as "a disturbance of mental or physical capacities resulting from the introduction of substances into the body."[39] Although **intoxication** most commonly results from the ingestion of alcohol, any substance that causes a distortion of the senses and judgment can cause intoxication. A person accused of a crime can claim that, due to intoxication, he or she should not be held to blame for the crime. Intoxication as a defense can take the form of a failure of proof claim. That is, it can be used to show that an element of the crime, such as *mens rea*, was lacking, or that the act was not voluntary (because the accused was unconscious).

Alternatively, the claim of intoxication might be closer to a claim of insanity, either temporary or long-term, based on the effects of the intoxicant. Voluntary intoxication is rarely a basis for a defendant's acquittal of criminal charges, under the common law rule, modern statutes, or the MPC. Involuntary intoxication, far less common, may negate an element of the offense or may even constitute an affirmative defense.

Voluntary intoxication is a person's willful act of introducing substances into the body that a person knows or should know are likely to have intoxicating effects. Intoxication usually arises as a defense when the defendant voluntarily drank alcohol or took drugs. As long as the defendant is the one responsible for getting intoxicated, he or she has acted voluntarily. Intoxication can be considered voluntary even if the defendant is physically addicted to drugs or alcohol.

Usually, a defendant may not raise the intoxication defense when he or she voluntarily became intoxicated. There are, however, a few circumstances in which a person may be acquitted: first, if the defendant did not have the specific state of mind that is required to be criminally culpable for that crime; second, if long-term intoxication caused permanent brain damage that rendered the defendant incapacitated during the criminal act.

Voluntary intoxication is never a defense to a general intent crime. As long as the actor voluntarily ingested the drugs or alcohol, the law treats this act as the *mens rea* required for general intent crimes. Usually voluntary intoxication constitutes recklessness for *mens rea* purposes, because the law assumes that a person who voluntarily intoxicates himself or herself knows of the risk associated with doing so.

The defense is valid for specific intent crimes. If a person, at the time the crime was committed, was incapable of forming the specific intent to commit the act, he or she will be acquitted of the crime. The defendant may introduce evidence, such as a blood test that produces a positive result for drugs or alcohol, to prove that he or she was so intoxicated at the time of the offense that he or she could not have had the specific intent to act.

Usually a defendant must be severely intoxicated for this to be a valid excuse. If the legislature has designated a particular state of mind as a material element of the crime, evidence of intoxication to the point of being unable to form the required intent will be a valid defense. In murder cases, a defendant can usually introduce evidence of intoxication to show that he or she was incapable of forming the premeditated intent required for a conviction of first-degree murder. The crime may be reduced to second-degree murder or manslaughter.

intoxication
A disturbance of mental or physical capacities resulting from the introduction of any substance into the body.

voluntary intoxication
A person's self-willed act to introduce substances into the body that the person knows or should know are likely to have intoxicating effects.

involuntary intoxication

Intoxication that occurs when the actor does not consume drugs or alcohol voluntarily or if the actor is not to blame for becoming intoxicated because, for example, he or she has an unanticipated reaction to drugs or alcohol.

Involuntary intoxication occurs when the actor does not consume drugs or alcohol voluntarily or when the actor is not to blame for becoming intoxicated because, for example, he or she has an unanticipated reaction to drugs or alcohol. Four different kinds of involuntary intoxication have been recognized:

1. Coerced intoxication, which is intoxication that is involuntarily induced by duress or coercion.
2. Pathological intoxication, which is grossly excessive intoxication given the amount of the intoxicant, to which the actor does not know he or she is susceptible. [40]
3. Intoxication by innocent mistake, which occurs where the actor is mistaken about the character of the substance taken, as when another person tricks him or her into taking the substance.
4. Unexpected intoxication, which results from the ingestion of a medically prescribed drug.[41]

If a person can show one of the four types of involuntary intoxication, he or she is usually entitled to an acquittal for both specific intent and general intent offenses. Furthermore, one who suffers from a temporary involuntary intoxication-induced mental condition that satisfies the jurisdiction's definition of insanity is excused for his or her criminal conduct.

The MPC distinguishes three types of intoxication: self-induced, pathological, and involuntary (not self-induced).[42] Under the MPC, any form of intoxication can operate as a defense if it negates an element of the offense. Also, both pathological and involuntary intoxication are affirmative defenses if the intoxication caused the actor to suffer from a mental condition comparable to that which constitutes insanity under the MPC.

Insanity

insanity

A defense in which the law recognizes that the accused was suffering from mental disease when the crime occurred, and thus may be relieved of criminal responsibility.

Beginning with English common law and continuing to the present, the law has recognized that a person accused of a crime who was suffering from mental disease when the crime occurred may be relieved of criminal responsibility by asserting the defense of **insanity**.[43] Although the defense of insanity receives a lot of coverage in the media, it is rarely asserted, probably because even if successfully asserted, it does not lead to freedom of the accused. Instead, a defendant who is found not guilty by reason of insanity will be committed to a mental hospital for a determination of whether he or she should be institutionalized until such time as he or she is no longer dangerous.

Because of this indeterminate nature of a "sentence" resulting from an insanity plea, a defendant is more likely to seek alternatives other than insanity as a defense, even where it can be asserted. For instance, the defendant may seek a plea bargain according to which he or she receives a reduced sentence because of the claimed mental problem. Or, in some states, the defendant may argue for a finding of "diminished capacity" or "partial responsibility."

incompetency

An accused person's inability to rationally consult with an attorney or to understand the nature of the proceedings against him or her.

Another factor limits the actual use of the insanity defense. If a person is suffering from a mental defect and is accused of committing a crime, that person must be mentally competent to stand trial. **Incompetency** is a person's inability to consult rationally with an attorney or to understand the nature of the proceedings against

6.1 On the Job

Clinical Social Worker

Description and Duties: Determine client needs for basic social services for children and adults. Perform social services requiring a high level of expertise and application of advanced techniques related to the provision of protective services for children and adults. Interview clients. Periodically reassess client needs and refer clients to community resources or other agency personnel.

Salary: Salaries range from approximately $25,000 to $45,000, depending on location and experience.

Other Information: Social worker positions tend to require a strong education. Many positions require a master's degree in social work or an equivalent, or completion of all requirements for a Marriage, Family and Child Counseling (MFCC) state registration number.

him or her. The issue of competency can be raised by the prosecution or the court, as well as by the accused. When the question of competency is raised, the trial court will decide the issue on the basis of a psychiatric examination. If an accused is found incompetent to stand trial, the person will be committed to a mental hospital until, if ever, he or she regains the mental health to stand trial. If that time comes, the defendant still may opt for the more certain alternatives of ordinary criminal conviction rather than asserting an insanity defense.

If the insanity defense is raised, a jury is usually responsible for determining whether a defendant should be acquitted. In most jurisdictions, a jury may give one of three verdicts: guilty, not guilty, or not guilty by reason of insanity. In some jurisdictions, however, a court will bifurcate a criminal trial when the insanity defense is raised. A **bifurcated trial** is a division of the criminal trial into two parts. First, a jury decides whether the defendant is guilty or not guilty. If the verdict is not guilty, the person is acquitted and the proceedings end. If the defendant is found guilty but asserts the insanity defense, the fact finder (whether that be a judge or jury) will hold a separate trial after the verdict to determine whether to enter an additional verdict of not guilty by reason of insanity. In the second trial, the evidence introduced, principally expert psychiatric testimony, will relate solely to the issue of the defendant's mental health. (A bifurcated trial is also used to determine the penalty that will be imposed when a defendant is convicted of a crime for which the death sentence can be imposed.)

bifurcated trial
The division of a criminal trial into two parts, the first part leading to a verdict of guilty or not guilty, and the second relating to another issue, such as the sanity of the accused (or the penalty phase of a death penalty case).

Since insanity is an affirmative defense, the prosecution need not disprove the defense until the accused introduces evidence of it. Until the 1980s, most American jurisdictions followed this procedure. It is constitutional for the legislature to require the defendant to bear the burden of persuasion on the defense of insanity, and currently most jurisdictions require the defendant to prove by a preponderance of evidence that he or she was insane at the time of the offense. A preponderance of evidence is not as high a burden as beyond a reasonable doubt. In the federal system, however, a defendant asserting the defense of insanity must prove by clear and convincing evidence that he or she was insane at the time of the offense. This is a higher burden than a preponderance of evidence.

The Controversial Insanity Defense   The acquittal of John Hinckley, who attempted to assassinate President Ronald Reagan in 1981, was due to his successful use of the insanity defense. Many believed that this defense should not have been allowed and that the verdict was incorrect.

Four legal tests, or rules, have been adopted by jurisdictions in the United States to determine the sanity of an accused:

1. The M'Naghten (right-wrong) test.
2. The irresistible impulse test.
3. The MPC (American Law Institute) test.
4. The federal test.

A fifth test, the product test, was based on the *Durham* case and applied only in the District of Columbia, but it is no longer used. Depending on the jurisdiction, the defendant must meet one of these tests in order to be found not guilty by reason of insanity.

The **M'Naghten test**, also known as the right-wrong test, comes from the 1843 English House of Lords case in which Daniel M'Naghten shot and killed the secretary of a high-ranking government official, believing that the official was heading a conspiracy to kill him. M'Naghten claimed insanity because he was delusional. A jury agreed and found him not guilty. The verdict created controversy in England, and, as a result, the House of Lords debated the issue of insanity. The majority concluded that a defendant could be found not guilty by reason of insanity only if his mental disorder made him unable to understand the nature of the act or the fact that it was wrong. The M'Naghten test tells the jury simply:

M'Naghten test

The rule used to establish an insanity defense. Under this rule, it must be clearly proved that, at the time of the offense, the accused was laboring under such a mental illness as not to know the nature and quality of what he or she was doing or, if he or she did know it, did not know that it was wrong.

that every man is to be presumed to be sane, and . . . that to establish a defense on the ground of insanity, it must be clearly proved that, at the time of the committing of the act, the party accused was laboring under such a defect of reason, from disease of the mind, as not to know the nature and quality of the act he was doing; or if he did know it, that he did not know he was doing what was wrong.[44]

The right-wrong test is used by a majority of jurisdictions in the United States. Many different mental disorders could fall within the definition of this test, but the defendant must always show that a disease of the mind caused his or her actions. There is no clear definition as to what a disease of the mind is; however, some examples are psychosis, neurosis, and brain disorder.

When a person does not know the nature of the act he or she is committing under the M'Naghten test, many legal scholars interpret this to mean that the defendant does not know the difference between right and wrong. In other words, the actor does not understand the consequences of the act that he or she is committing. For example, if a person starts a fire in a home without understanding that this act will burn the house down and instead believes that the fire will ward off evil spirits, the actor may be found not guilty by reason of insanity. Because this person does not understand the consequences of his or her action, the person will not realize the action is wrong.

Sometimes, however, a person understands the nature of the act but still does not understand that it is wrong. For example, a delusional person may kill someone whom he or she mistakenly believes is going to kill him or her. The killer understands that he or she is killing someone but thinks that this action is justified. The delusional actor does not know that, at the time of the murder, he or she was acting wrongly. Under this test, the actor could be found not guilty by reason of insanity under the M'Naghten rule. (See Application Case 6.10.)

⚖️ Application Case 6.10

State v. Cameron

In *State v. Cameron,* the defendant stabbed his stepmother to death, leaving the knife in her heart. The defendant left the scene without making any attempt to hide the body or any evidence. He was later picked up hitchhiking, wearing women's clothing and only one shoe. He confessed to the killing and claimed that he did it because his stepmother was an evil woman. A psychologist testified that the defendant had a delusional belief at the time of the killing that his stepmother was an agent of Satan. The defendant testified that he believed he was killing an agent of Satan at the direction of God and that at the time he believed that he was the Messiah.

The trial court gave a jury instruction stating that if the defendant knew that his actions were against the law of man, he was not insane. The Supreme Court of Washington agreed, holding that a person will not be found insane if he knew that the act was prohibited by the law of man. The court, however, held in this case that the defendant suffered from a mental disease and that because of it, it was impossible for the defendant to realize that his actions were wrong. The court therefore reversed the trial court's decision, finding that the jury instructions were incorrect.

SOURCE: State v. Cameron, 674 P.2d 650 (Wash. 1983).

The M'Naghten test of insanity is still followed in a number of American states. In some of those states, an additional test has also been adopted—the irresistible impulse, or control, test. This **irresistible impulse test**[45] requires a verdict of not guilty by reason of insanity if the fact-finder concludes that the accused had a mental disease that kept him or her from controlling his or her conduct. Under this test, generally, a defendant is insane if, at the time of the offense, he or she acted as a result of an uncontrollable impulse, lost the power to choose between right and wrong and

irresistible impulse test

A test for insanity that permits a verdict of not guilty by reason of insanity if the fact-finder concludes that the accused had a mental disease that kept him or her from controlling his or her conduct.

to avoid doing the act in question, or did not have the will necessary to control his or her actions. Under the irresistible impulse test, the focus is on the defendant's ability to control his or her actions, not on his or her understanding of the criminal act. By losing control, the defendant is said to have lost his or her ability to act voluntarily and is therefore excused from criminal punishment.

MPC test

A test for insanity that provides that a person is not responsible for criminal conduct if he or she is found to lack substantial capacity to appreciate the criminality of the conduct or to conform his or her conduct to the requirements of the law.

Under the **MPC test**,[46] a person is not responsible for criminal conduct if he or she lacked substantial capacity to appreciate the criminality or wrongfulness of the conduct or to conform his or her conduct to the requirements of the law. The MPC test is a modified version of the M'Naghten and irresistible impulse tests, containing the second, cognitive prong of the M'Naghten test and the volitional aspects of the irresistible impulse test. The test differs from the M'Naghten test in that it uses the term "appreciate" rather than "know," and, unlike the irresistible impulse test, does not use the word "impulse" at all. Both prongs of the test are modified by the words "lacks substantial capacity," thus allowing an accused person to use the insanity defense with a showing of less than total incapacity.

federal test

The federal statutory definition of insanity, which provides that a person is excused by reason of insanity if he or she proves by clear and convincing evidence that at the time of the offense, as a result of a severe mental disease or defect, he or she was unable to appreciate the nature and quality of his or her act, or the wrongfulness of his or her conduct.

The **federal test** is the result of a statutory enactment in 1984 when Congress defined insanity.[47] The statute provides that a person is excused by reason of insanity if he or she proves by clear and convincing evidence that at the time of the offense, as a result of a severe mental disease or defect, he or she was unable to appreciate the nature and quality of his or her act, or the wrongfulness of his or her conduct. This law, unlike previous rules, requires that the accused show that he or she suffered from a "severe" mental disorder. Like the M'Naghten test, but unlike the MPC test, this law requires total cognitive incapacity. Finally, like the MPC test, the federal test uses the word "appreciate" rather than "know," making the test broader than the M'Naghten test in this respect.

Finally, the short-lived Durham test[48] stated that a person is excused by reason of insanity if the actor's unlawful act was the product of a mental disease or defect. Under this test, the fact-finder merely determines whether the defendant suffered from a mental disease or defect and, if so, whether the criminal conduct would have occurred but for the condition. The test was adopted only by the District of Columbia and was abandoned there in 1972.

There has been much criticism of the insanity defense, especially in high-profile cases where the public has witnessed the effect of the defense (see Application Case 6.11). As a result, some states have abolished the defense completely, while others have reformed their laws to make it more difficult to avoid criminal punishment.

⚖ Application Case 6.11

United States v. John Hinckley, Jr.

On March 30, 1981, John Hinckley, Jr., attempted to kill President Ronald Reagan at the Washington Hilton hotel. Although he failed to assassinate the president, he did wound Reagan, along with a police officer, a Secret Service agent, and Press Secretary James Brady.

During the trial, it was revealed that Hinckley had been stalking Reagan and, before him, President Jimmy Carter. Hinckley's obsession with the film *Taxi Driver* and one of its stars, Jodie Foster, was also brought to light as his defense team tried to prove that he was insane at the time of the shooting. Expert witnesses for both the prosecution and the defense stated that Hinckley suffered from "narcissistic personality disorder."

The prosecution attempted to show that Hinckley was sane and had pre-meditated the assassination attempt. He had purchased bullets and guns ahead of time. A short while before the incident, he wrote a letter to Jodie Foster saying that he was about to kill Reagan.

In the end, the jury returned a verdict of not guilty by reason of insanity. Hinckley was committed to St. Elizabeth's Mental Hospital in Washington, D.C. The public outrage over the verdict caused changes across the country. In the three years after his acquittal, Congress and half of the states made it more difficult to use the insanity defense. Twelve states created a new verdict of guilty but mentally ill, and Utah did away with the defense altogether.

SOURCE: http://www.law.umkc.edu/faculty/projects/ftrials/hinckley/hinckleytrial.html; http://www.pbs.org/wgbh/amex/reagan/peopleevents/pande02.html.

For example, 12 states have reformed their law to include a guilty but mentally ill verdict. A defendant who is found guilty but mentally ill will still be sentenced to prison but will receive psychiatric care while there. For those who oppose the insanity defense because people are not punished for their actions, the guilty but mentally ill verdict provides a way to punish people while still offering mental health treatment.

Diminished Capacity

Accused persons who, at the time of the act charged, were suffering from a mental condition insufficient to support a successful insanity defense under the test applicable in the jurisdiction might nonetheless be able to introduce evidence of their mental condition on the question of whether they had the mental state required for conviction of the crime charged. The so-called **diminished capacity** defense, or partial responsibility defense, may be available in such a circumstance.

Diminished capacity is a misleading and potentially confusing term. It can be used to describe two circumstances in which a mental condition short of insanity will exonerate the accused or lessen the crime for which he or she is convicted. The first circumstance is a failure of proof defense, in which the accused raises the condition to negate an element of the crime—a *mens rea* use of the defense. The second circumstance is a true partial defense, whereby the crime of murder can be mitigated to manslaughter.

The MPC and a few states allow the defendant to introduce evidence of mental illness when it is relevant to prove that the defendant lacked a mental state that is an element of the charged offense. For example, a childlike, retarded defendant facing a burglary charge could introduce evidence that his condition did not allow him to form the requisite *mens rea* to commit a felony after he entered the building where the act took place.

Other jurisdictions limit the introduction of mental illness evidence to murder cases. In these jurisdictions, a defendant can introduce evidence that would either

diminished capacity
A term used to describe two circumstances in which a mental condition short of insanity will lead to an acquittal or lessened charges: (1) where the accused raises the condition as a failure of proof defense, and (2) a true partial defense, whereby the crime of murder can be mitigated to manslaughter.

reduce murder charges to a lesser offense or lead to acquittal. Many jurisdictions allow a defendant to introduce mental illness evidence that will negate the specific intent for specific intent crimes. A defendant using a mental condition to negate specific intent usually will not escape criminal punishment completely, because there is usually a lesser charge involving general intent for which he or she can be convicted.

The diminished capacity doctrine used as a true partial responsibility defense is recognized in the MPC and in only a few states, and it is limited to use as a basis for mitigating the offense from murder to manslaughter. The California Supreme Court adopted a partial responsibility defense by redefining *mens rea*. However, the defense was abolished by the state legislature and the electorate in the 1980s.[49] The MPC adopted this defense in its provision that mitigates murder to manslaughter due to "extreme mental or emotional disturbance for which there is a reasonable explanation or excuse."[50]

Another example of a diminished capacity defense stems from a defendant's claim that some biological factor excuses him or her from criminal liability. Arguably the most famous biological defense is the "Twinkie defense" from the trial of Dan White, who assassinated San Francisco Mayor George Moscone and Supervisor Harvey Milk on November 27, 1978. During the trial, the defense presented testimony that White was depressed, he had quit his job, his personal life was a mess, and he had been consuming a lot of Twinkies and Coca-Cola. White was acquitted of murder but convicted of manslaughter. Public outrage over this verdict resulted in abolition of the diminished capacity defense in California by voters in a public referendum. The "Twinkie defense" and the public referendum are discussed in detail in the case of *Massachusetts Mut. Life Ins. Co. v. Woodall.*[51]

Mistake

Under mistake as an excuse negating moral culpability, the defendant acts without an "evil" state of mind because of his or her erroneous belief as to either the facts or the law applicable in a particular situation. (See the earlier example of the person who believes he is shooting at a tree stump when in fact he is shooting at a person). While it is true that "ignorance of the law is not an excuse," in limited circumstances people may avail themselves of a "mistake of law" defense and avoid criminal responsibility. An example would be when the law is written so imprecisely that a reasonable person cannot be certain whether his or her conduct falls within or outside of that defined in the statute, and thus may make an inaccurate interpretation that his or her conduct is not prohibited. (See Application Case 6.12.)

⚖️ **Application Case 6.12**

People v. Evans

In *People v. Evans*, the 37-year-old defendant approached a female college student who was departing from a plane at a New York airport. The woman was from a small town and was fairly naïve. The defendant told the woman that he was a prominent psychologist doing a study for a magazine in which he observed the reactions of men and women in singles bars. He convinced the woman to ride with him into the city and took her to a bar where he was supposedly observing her interaction.

He then convinced the woman to come up to his apartment, which he pretended was one of his five offices. The defendant approached the woman in his apartment and, when she resisted his advances, informed her that she had failed the test and that, in fact, his advances were part of his research. He then proceeded to intimidate her by explaining that she was in a stranger's apartment and could easily be killed or raped.

The woman testified that at this point she became frightened of the man and therefore engaged in sexual activity that lasted throughout the evening. She left the next morning. The defendant, who was prosecuted for rape, argued that he did not force her to do anything and therefore was not guilty of the crime.

The court found that the defendant's statements regarding his intimidation of the victim were ambiguous and could not be construed beyond a reasonable doubt as constituting force by threats. The court held that the defendant was therefore not guilty of rape, but did note that the defendant's actions were morally reprehensible and predatory.

SOURCE: People v. Evans, 379 N.Y.S.2d 912 (N.Y. Sup. Ct. 1975).

Entrapment

The defense of entrapment may be complicated in its variations from state to state, but the general idea is that the defendant is tricked or otherwise induced by law enforcement agents to commit an illegal act that he or she would not otherwise have committed. For example, in a couple of cases involving sentencing enhancement entrapment, federal agents insisted that the defendant "cook up" the powdered cocaine the agents were buying into crack cocaine, in order to charge the defendant with a more serious offense.[52]

Specialized Defenses

There are some specialized defenses that apply only to certain crimes—for example, the defense of legal impossibility (a defense to attempt) and abandonment (a defense, in some states, to attempt and conspiracy; see Chapter 5). Other so-called extrinsic defenses are those that are not related to the nature of the crime or the defendant but are based on public policy concerns. These defenses include the statute of limitations (a time period beyond which prosecution for certain types of offenses cannot be pursued), diplomatic immunity (which shields certain government agents or foreign officials/dignitaries from prosecution for crimes), and the defendant's incompetence to stand trial (discussed earlier in this chapter).

CRITICAL THINKING 6.3

1. Explain the differences between insanity and diminished capacity.
2. Explain the elements that must be in place for entrapment to occur.

REVIEW AND APPLICATIONS

Summary by Chapter Objectives

1. **List the three elements of self-defense.** The three elements of self-defense are:
   - The necessity to use force, including the use of deadly force, only "to prevent imminent and unlawful use of deadly force by the aggressor."
   - The proportionality of the force to the threat.
   - The reasonableness of the belief that force was necessary.

2. **Describe when deadly force may be used in self-defense.** A nonaggressor may use deadly force if he or she reasonably believes that such force is necessary to protect against imminent use of unlawful deadly force by the aggressor.

3. **Name two situations in which a first aggressor can claim self-defense.** The first is where a nondeadly aggressor is met with deadly force. The second is where an aggressor completely withdraws from any continued conflict with the other person by taking reasonable steps to notify the other person of his or her intentions, but the other person continues to instigate harm.

4. **Describe the circumstances in which a person can use force to defend property.** In the defense of property from trespass or theft, the actor may use reasonable, but not deadly, force when he or she reasonably believes (1) that his or her property is in immediate danger of such an unlawful interference and (2) that the use of such force is necessary to avoid that danger.

5. **Explain when a police officer may use deadly force in effecting an arrest or preventing escape.** A police officer can use deadly force only if the officer has probable cause to believe that the suspect poses a significant threat of death or serious physical injury to the officer or others, and that such force is necessary to make the arrest or prevent escape. If feasible, a warning must be given to the suspect before deadly force is employed.

6. **List five tests for determining insanity.** The five tests for determining insanity are:
   - The M'Naghten (right-wrong) test.
   - The irresistible impulse test.
   - The MPC test.
   - The federal test.
   - The product test based on the *Durham* case.

Key Terms

defense (p. 144)

failure of proof (p. 144)

true defense (p. 144)

burden of proof (p. 144)

affirmative defense (p. 145)

justification (p. 146)

excuse (p. 146)

self-defense (p. 147)

aggressor (p. 147)
deadly force (p. 149)
necessity (p. 161)
consent (p. 164)
duress (p. 166)
intoxication (p. 169)
voluntary intoxication (p. 169)
involuntary intoxication (p. 170)

insanity (p. 170)
incompetency (p. 170)
bifurcated trial (p. 171)
M'Naghten test (p. 172)
irresistible impulse test (p. 173)
MPC test (p. 174)
federal test for insanity (p. 174)
diminished capacity (p. 175)

Review Questions

1. Explain how the burden of proof defines the prosecutor's task, and how defenses shift the burden of proof to the defendant.
2. What are the retreat rule and the castle exception, and how are they related?
3. What is considered to be a reasonable defense of habitation and property? When can deadly force be used?
4. What are the MPC's three requirements in order to maintain nondeadly mechanical security devices?
5. Under what four conditions may police officers use nondeadly force?
6. Are citizen's arrests legal? If so, under what circumstances? If not, why?
7. Give some examples of cases in which the necessity defense would be valid.
8. Compare the MPC's choice of evils defense with the common law necessity defense.
9. Under what noteworthy situations does the MPC, but not the common law, allow the duress defense?
10. What is a bifurcated trial, and how is it used in a trial where the insanity defense is raised?
11. Explain the two ways in which the diminished capacity defense may be used, and give an example of each.

Problem-Solving Exercises

1. **Duress Defense** A police officer has just arrested a male defendant for armed bank robbery. At the station, he agrees to speak to the officer without a lawyer present. He confesses to the offense but claims that he was under duress, stating that if he did not carry out the robbery he would be killed. The defendant goes on to say that an old enemy of his from Ecuador wrote him a letter and sent it to his home. The letter stated that the old friend desperately needed $5,000 for an operation, and if the defendant did not rob a bank, he would find a way to travel to New York and kill the defendant and his entire family. Answer the following questions:
   a. What problems will the defendant have with the duress defense in this case?
   b. What are some additional questions the officer should ask him to find out whether he has a chance at a defense?
   c. How might different factual circumstances affect the defendant's chances of getting acquitted by arguing duress?

2. **Voluntary Intoxication** Mark is on trial for double homicide, committed with the specific intent to kill. He maintains that extreme intoxication rendered him physically incapable of committing the murders and also accounted for his inability to recall the events on the night in question. The jury was instructed that the intoxicated condition was not a legitimate factor in considering the existence of the specific intent to kill as an element of the offenses charged. Answer the following questions:
   a. Assuming the defendant is being tried in a common law state, can the defendant's voluntary intoxication provide either an excuse or a justification for his crimes?
   b. Can the defendant even present such evidence to a jury?
   c. Does the due process clause give the defendant the right to present and have the jury consider all relevant elements to rebut the state's evidence?

3. **Insanity Defense** A local business owner has been arrested for the nonfatal shooting of a competitor, who he said taunted him and destroyed his business reputation. The defendant is from a culture in which people who commit social wrongs make public apologies; in some cases, they commit suicide to show remorse. The defendant stated that his competitor slandered him to vendors and to customers. In addition, he refused to apologize when confronted, and only laughed at the defendant. The defendant said that he was "out of his mind" with rage when he pulled the trigger.
   a. Can the defendant use any affirmative defenses? Why or why not?
   b. Should the defendant be charged with any crime? Why or why not? What crime?

Workplace Applications

1. **Involuntary Intoxication** You are a patrol officer and have just arrested a defendant for vehicular manslaughter. He was driving his car when he drove off the road, hitting and killing a pedestrian. The defendant is clearly under the influence of some substance, although you do not know what it is. Later that evening, when the defendant sobers up, he tells you that he was at a party and drank only one soda the entire night. He claims that he does not drink alcohol or take drugs and that the only possible explanation he can give is that someone drugged his soda. Answer the following questions:
   a. What steps should you take at the crime scene to secure a conviction?
   b. How should you carry on this investigation?
   c. What information do you need from the defendant to find out whether there is any validity to his story?

2. **Diminished Capacity** You are a juror hearing a case in which a young man is being tried for several counts of aggravated battery and one count of murder. One night, he consumed alcohol and violently attacked his co-residents in the group home in which he lives. The defense raises the diminished capacity defense for all charges, stating that the defendant's IQ is 83, he has fetal alcohol syndrome, and he functions at the emotional level of an 11-year-old. You live in a state in which the diminished capacity defense can be used as a true partial responsibility defense. Can he use this defense? If so, in what specific way? If not, explain why.

3. **Self-Defense** You are a police detective investigating a homicide case in which the defendant shot and killed a man who had broken into her apartment and threatened to rape her. He was eight inches taller and 60 pounds heavier than she is, and she stated that she feared for her life.

   a. In such a case, is lethal force justified for self-defense? Why or why not?

   b. What other factors would you consider in a case such as this?

Ethics Exercises

1. **Defense of Habitation** You are a detective in charge of investigating a homicide that involves a homeowner who shot and killed an alleged burglar. During an in-office interview, the homeowner gave you an oral and written statement indicating that he shot the burglar when he came at him with a knife after the homeowner discovered him in the kitchen. The homeowner states that he was afraid for his own safety and for that of his family, who were also at home during this time. You discover from the state data bank that the deceased victim had an extensive record of committing burglaries and fencing stolen property, but no record of violent crime.

   The day before the case against the homeowner is to be presented to the grand jury with a possible recommendation for dismissal, you receive some startling information. Apparently the homeowner lied, because his family was not present in the house on the night of the burglary, and the decedent's fingerprints were not on the knife that he allegedly brandished in his bare hands on the night of the alleged attempted burglary. Do you bring this information to the attention of the district attorney or let the case go to the grand jury without it? Why?

2. **Defense of Duress** A defendant who has been charged with embezzlement is using the affirmative defense of duress to justify her actions. She states that her boyfriend, who was also her supervisor, blackmailed her and threatened to show people pornographic photographs of her if she did not steal cash from the company safe on a regular basis. They split the money, which she spent to pay off a credit card, buy clothing, and have her car painted.

   a. Can she claim a defense of duress? Why or why not?

   b. Does it matter that she kept half of the money and spent it on nonessential items?

Notes

1. Paul H. Robinson, *Criminal Law Defenses: A Systematic Analysis*, 82 Colum. L. Rev. 199, 203 (1982).
2. These examples mainly come from Joshua Dressler, Understanding Criminal Law § 16.02, at 218 (4th ed. 2006).
3. In re Winship, 397 U.S. 358 (1970).
4. Mullaney v. Wilbur, 421 U.S. 684 (1975).
5. Patterson v. New York, 432 U.S. 197 (1977).

6. George F. Fletcher, *Justification: Theory, in* Encyclopedia of Crime and Justice 883 (Joshua Dressler ed., 2d ed. 2002).

7. 4 William Blackstone, Commentaries *180.

8. *See* Joshua Dressler, Understanding Criminal Law § 17.05, at 233–36 n.38 (4th ed. 2006). Dressler relies upon his own works and works by George P. Fletcher in describing the reasons for distinguishing between justification and excuse defenses, particularly George P. Fletcher, Rethinking Criminal Law 664–70, 759–69 (1978).

9. Joshua Dressler, Understanding Criminal Law § 17.05[B], at 233 (4th ed. 2006).

10. *Id.* at 234–36.

11. George E. Dix, *Justification: Self-Defense, in* Encyclopedia of Crime and Justice 946–47 (Sanford H. Kadish ed., 1983).

12. Wayne R. LaFave, Criminal Law § 10.4(e), at 546–47 n.59 (4th ed. 2003) (citing Rowe v. United States, 164 U.S. 546 (1896)).

13. Joshua Dressler, Understanding Criminal Law § 18.02[B][2], at 241 (4th ed. 2006).

14. *See* Joshua Dressler, Understanding Criminal Law § 18.05[B][2], at 260 (4th ed. 2006).

15. *Id.* at n.133 (citing People v. Yaklich, 833 P.2d 758 (Colo. Ct. App. 1991)).

16. *See* Menendez v. Superior Court, 834 P.2d 786 (Cal. 1992).

17. Paul Harris, Black Rage Confronts the Law 1–2 (1997).

18. Model Penal Code § 3.05 cmt.1 (1985).

19. Model Penal Code § 3.06 cmt.7(c)(i) (1985).

20. Wayne R. LaFave, Criminal Law § 10.6(c), at 556 (4th ed. 2003) (citing State v. Barr, 39 P. 1080 (Wash. 1895)).

21. Model Penal Code § 3.06(5) (1985).

22. *See* Paul G. Chevigny, *Justification: Law Enforcement, in* Encyclopedia of Crime and Justice 889–93 (Joshua Dressler ed., 2d ed. 2002).

23. Joshua Dressler, Understanding Criminal Law § 21.03[A], at 297–98 (4th ed. 2006).

24. 4 William Blackstone, Commentaries *31.

25. Joshua Dressler, Understanding Criminal Law § 21.03[B][2], at 299–300 (4th ed. 2006).

26. *Id.* at § 21.05[B][2], at 305 (citing Model Penal Code § 3.07(5)(a)(ii)(A) (1985)).

27. 4 William Blackstone, Commentaries *30; *see also* Glanville Williams, Criminal Law: The General Part § 234, at 733 (2d ed. 1961) ("Self-defense can be regarded as a part of necessity that has attained relatively fixed rules.").

28. This definition, though a distillation of many sources, is a paraphrase of language appearing in Wayne R. LaFave, Criminal Law § 10.1(a), at 523 (4th ed. 2003).

29. Model Penal Code § 3.02 (1985).

30. Joshua Dressler, Understanding Criminal Law § 22.02, at 311–14 (4th ed. 2006).

31. Model Penal Code § 3.02, cmt.3 (1985).

32. *See* Joshua Dressler, Understanding Criminal Law § 22.03, at 265 (4th ed. 2006).

33. Model Penal Code § 2.11(1) (1985).

34. For a review of the cases going both ways on criminal liability for injury inflicted during a sporting event, see Charles Harary, *Aggressive Play or Criminal Assault? An In Depth Look at Sports Violence and Criminal Liability*, 25 Colum. J.L. & Arts 197 (2002).

35. United States v. Bailey, 444 U.S. 394, 410 (1980).

36. This example comes from Joshua Dressler, Understanding Criminal Law § 23.01[C], at 275 (4th ed. 2006).

37. Leo Katz, *Excuse: Duress, in* Encyclopedia of Crime and Justice 647 (Joshua Dressler ed., 2d ed. 2002) (citing Regina v. Hudson, 2 All E.R. 244, 246 (C.A. 1971)).

38. Model Penal Code § 2.09(1) (1985).

39. Herbert Fingarette & Ann Fingarette Hasse, *Excuse: Intoxication, in* Encyclopedia of Crime and Justice 742 (Sanford H. Kadish ed., 1983).

40. City of Minneapolis v. Altimus, 238 N.W.2d 851, 856 (Minn. 1976), *as cited in* Joshua Dressler, Understanding Criminal Law § 24.06[A], at 357 (4th ed. 2006).

41. Altimus, 238 N.W.2d 851 at 856 (citing Model Penal Code § 2.08(5)(c) (1985)).

42. Model Penal Code § 2.09(4)–(5) (1985).

43. *See* Michael L. Perlin, *Excuse: Insanity, in* Encyclopedia of Crime and Justice 650 (Joshua Dressler ed., 2d ed. 2002).

44. M'Naghten's Case, 8 Eng. Rep. 718 (1843).

45. Wayne R. Lafave, Substantive Criminal Law § 7.3 (2d ed. 2007).

46. Model Penal Code § 4.01(1) (1985).

47. 18 U.S.C. § 17(a) (2000).

48. Durham v. United States, 214 F.2d 862 (D.C. Cir. 1954), *overruled by* United States v. Brawner, 471 F.2d 969 (D.C. Cir. 1972).

49. Joshua Dressler, Understanding Criminal Law § 26, at 393–404 (4th ed. 2006).

50. Model Penal Code § 210.3(1)(b) (1985).

51. Massachusetts Mut. Life Ins. Co. v. Woodall, 304 F. Supp. 2d 1364, 1377 n.7 (S.D. Ga. 2003).

52. *See* United States v. Walls, 70 F.3d 1323 (D.C. Cir. 1995); United States v. Shepherd, 857 F. Supp. 105 (D.D.C. 1994).

Punishment and Sentencing

CHAPTER OUTLINE

7.1 Punishment in the Criminal Justice System

Definition of Punishment

Retributive Rationale for Punishment

Utilitarian Justification for Punishment

Modern Views on Punishment

7.2 Sentencing

Types of Sentencing

Alternatives to Imprisonment

Death Penalty

CHAPTER OBJECTIVES

After reading and studying this chapter, you should be able to:

1. Identify the principal purpose of laws that make certain acts punishable by society in the form of criminal prohibitions.

2. Name the two justifying theories of punishment that underlie modern criminal law.

3. Explain the retributive theory of punishment.

4. State the hallmarks of the utilitarian theory of punishment.

5. Define the types of sentences that may be imposed.

6. Explain indeterminate sentencing.

7. Define determinate sentencing.

8. Explain sentencing guidelines.

9. Describe the alternatives to imprisonment.

10. State when the death penalty cannot be imposed.

7.1 Punishment in the Criminal Justice System

The question of what sanction to impose on those who should be sanctioned raises questions relating to punishment. The feature of the criminal law that distinguishes it from other types of law is the imposition of punishment for its violation. The stigma attached to conviction for a crime is itself often sufficient to constitute a "punishment" in the eyes of society. Nonetheless, the criminal law "consists of prohibitions of antisocial behavior backed by serious sanctions."[1] Although not every person who suffers a criminal conviction is punished, a meaningful set of mandatory rules of conduct must provide for punishment of those who violate the rules. Thus, the meaning, theories, and possible justifications of criminal punishment are closely related to the meaning, theories, and possible justifications of the criminal law itself.[2]

Definition of Punishment

Punishment is not meted out exclusively through the criminal justice system, or the law, for that matter. Parents, teachers, religious leaders, and club presidents, to name a few, regularly punish their children, students, parishioners, and fellows. **Punishment** in the criminal justice system exists when an agent of the government, using authority granted by virtue of a legal criminal conviction, intentionally inflicts pain, loss of liberty, or some other unpleasant consequence on the person who has been convicted.[3]

Punishment is relative; thus, any definition of it may be criticized as arbitrary. If the punishment is payment of a fine that the convict can afford, then the punishment may seem inadequate. The same could be said for minimal sentences of imprisonment, probation, or community service. Conversely, noncriminal penalties such as payment of a large civil judgment or loss of a license to practice one's profession may be very painful, but do not constitute punishment. They merely represent civil penalties.

Punishment is an integral part of the criminal justice system, "where governments consciously and intentionally seek to condemn individuals" for violating those social norms that are prohibited by the definition of the criminal law.[4] Moreover, punishment must actually be delivered, at least enough of the time to make the threat meaningful. Thus, even though there are many reasons why threatened punishment may not be carried out—prosecutors may not pursue the case, or the jury may acquit the accused—actual punishment is required in most cases.

Two dominant justifying theories of punishment underlie modern criminal law,[5] though mixed theories of punishment have developed:[6]

1. The **retributive justification** is that a wrongdoer deserves punishment. The retributive view is expressed in the phrase "just deserts."
2. The **utilitarian justification** is predicated on the notion that a social practice is desirable if it promotes human happiness more effectively than any other alternatives. Although it is a simplification, the hallmarks of the utilitarian view are general deterrence, individual deterrence, incapacitation, reform, and vengeance.

The moving force in American criminal law theory from approximately 1900 to 1970 was the utilitarian justification. Since the 1970s, however, the retributive justification has reemerged as a significant factor.

punishment
When an agent of the government, using authority granted by virtue of a legal criminal conviction, intentionally inflicts pain, loss of liberty, or some other unpleasant consequence on the person who has been convicted.

retributive justification
A justification for punishment based on the theory that a wrongdoer deserves punishment for punishment's sake.

utilitarian justification
A justification for punishment based on the theory that a social practice is desirable if it promotes the greatest good for the largest number of people.

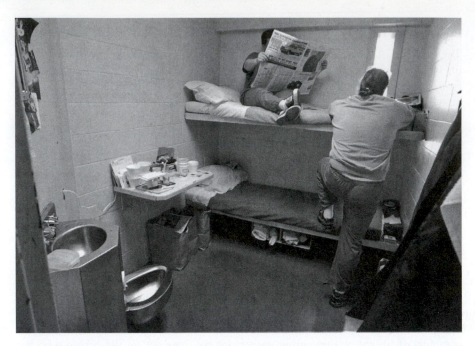

A Modern Prison Cell

**rehabilitative
justification**

A justification for
punishment based on the
theory that if an offender
is reformed, the offender
will not commit any more
crimes.

A third theory of punishment, the **rehabilitative justification**, is to reform the offender so that he or she will not commit any more crimes. Rehabilitation was popular before the 1970s but is less so today. Many critics do not believe that criminals can in fact be reformed.

Retributive Rationale for Punishment

The simplest retributive justification is that one who has violated the rights of others should be penalized. Punishment restores the moral order that has been breached by the original wrongful act. The eighteenth-century German philosopher Immanuel Kant made the point in stating that an island society about to disband should still execute its last murderer. Society's duty is to punish, or else the guilt remains upon society. Punishment of the deserving honors free will. Moreover, the imposition of a punishment in proportion to the degree of wrongdoing sets matters right. These retributive theories are all predicated on principles of moral wrong.[7]

A different retributive approach is that criminals deserve punishment because they violate social norms. By avoiding questions of morality, this theory fits better with modern approaches to criminal punishment. It avoids the criticism that the criminal law should not be in the business of correcting moral wrongs.[8] Furthermore, this theory does not impose upon public officials the impossible task of deciding subtle degrees of moral guilt.

Utilitarian Justification for Punishment

The utilitarian justification is based on Jeremy Bentham's test for moral desirability of an act or social practice: whether the act or practice promotes human happiness better than possible alternatives. The greatest good for the greatest number was the goal of this test. In modern usage, utilitarianism usually refers to the theory that likely consequences determine the morality of action. Thus, the varieties of beneficial consequences that can be realized by punishment according to utilitarian theory include general deterrence, individual deterrence, incapacitation, reform, and vengeance.

General Deterrence

General deterrence is the effect that punishment of the offender will have in causing other people in the community to refrain from committing the same crime. The offender cannot be reached, but the potential future offender can. A rational person will see that the benefits to be gained from criminal activity will be outweighed by the harms of punishment, even when those harms are discounted by the possibility of avoiding detection. On this theory, the greater the temptation to commit the crime and the less the chance of detection, the more severe the penalty should be.

Individual Deterrence

Individual deterrence is the effect that the imposition of punishment on the wrongdoer will have in causing him or her to refrain from repeating the act. To achieve this result, the punishment must be severe enough to outweigh the benefits of the crime. More severe punishment for repeat offenders is justified because the first penalty was ineffective.

Incapacitation

Incapacitation is the removal or restriction of freedom of those who have violated criminal laws. The primary means used to achieve incapacitation is imprisonment. Intolerance for recidivist offenders and a desire to incapacitate them have led to the development of **three-strikes laws**, which impose sentences of 25-years-to-life for those convicted of certain serious offenses three times. Another development has been **zero tolerance**, or one-strike laws, which impose maximum penalties for certain crimes, such as particular sex offenses.

Reform

Reform, or rehabilitation, of the offender so that he or she will no longer desire to commit crimes and will be a useful citizen may be sought as a by-product of punishment. Usually, conviction and imprisonment alone have been thought not to be enough to achieve reform; rehabilitative therapy and education have been considered essential. Drug treatment, psychiatric treatment, and vocational training are examples of rehabilitation. In recent years, reform has fallen out of favor as an achievable beneficial consequence of punishment. Here is a recent description of that process:

> [R]ehabilitation as a general justifying theory came under a sustained attack in the 1960s and 1970s, as illustrated by Professor Francis Allen's famous book, *The Decline of the Rehabilitative Ideal: Penal Policy and Social Purpose* (1981). These attacks were capped by Robert Martinson's widely discussed short paper What Works?—Questions and Answers About Prison Reform, *The Public Interest* (1974), which reviewed numerous studies evaluating efforts at penal rehabilitation. Martinson's conclusions, which were generally discouraging, quickly became

incapacitation

The removal or restriction of freedom of those who have violated criminal laws, usually by imprisonment.

three-strikes laws

Laws that impose sentences of 25-years-to-life for those who have been convicted of certain serious offenses three times.

zero tolerance

Laws that impose maximum penalties for certain crimes, such as particular sex offenses; also known as one-strike laws.

oversimplified into the assertion that "nothing works." Commentators and others have tended to overstate the prior dominance of rehabilitation, as well as the modern findings of rehabilitative efforts and the general decline of rehabilitation in sentencing. Indeed, though different theories of punishment have been expressly favored or disfavored in different eras, a thoughtful observer can probably identify the impact of each classic theory in nearly every punishment or sentencing system throughout history.[9]

Vengeance

vengeance

The imposition of punishment in the context of an "eye for an eye" or a "tooth for a tooth"; usually associated with retribution, though the utilitarian may see a benefit in vengeance.

Vengeance is the imposition of punishment in the context of an "eye for an eye" or a "tooth for a tooth." It is usually associated with retribution. The utilitarian, however, may see a benefit in vengeance, whereas the retributivist believes that the wrongful act deserves punishment for punishment's sake: "just deserts," as it is known. Vengeance is a beneficial consequence in that it satisfies victims, their families and friends, and members of the public. More specifically, the frustration generated in such people by the failure of punishment makes the imposition of punishment for their sake a worthwhile justification.

Modern Views on Punishment

Most commentators agree that modern punishment theory, though actively debated, cannot be classified into any one of the categories discussed above. One commentator refers to "mixed or hybrid theories," stating that "some mixture of utilitarian and retributive elements provides the most cogent approach to punishment."[10] Another commentator refers to another alternative theory of punishment, "denunciation," also referred to as the "expressive" view of punishment, which he describes as justifying punishment "as a means of expressing society's condemnation, and the relative seriousness of the offense."[11] Yet another commentator notes: "Some scholars assert that a dominant modern rationale has emerged through the idea of 'limiting retributivism' in which retribution sets the upper and lower boundaries of just punishment, within which other purposes can hold sway, including utilitarian theories of deterrence, incapacitation, and rehabilitation."[12]

In any event, the prevalent punishment practices in the United States from the mid-twentieth century to the 1960s and 1970s were predicated upon the utilitarian theories, but also consistent with "important retributive limits on severity."[13] The focus on general deterrence and individual aims led to the widespread development of systems of indeterminate sentencing. For a particular offense, for example, the judge could impose a term of from, say, one to five years. Thus, the determination of the offender's progress toward rehabilitation, the ultimate goal, could be made by the parole board. Reform and rehabilitation through a "medical model" treating offenders as "antisocial" and in need of treatment were never fully accepted, however, and by the 1970s "there was a sharp reaction against the emphasis on rehabilitation."[14] The result was a reformation of sentencing practices, which, while not "rejecting general deterrence" entirely, focused the "'just deserts' model" on the achievement of "proportionality and uniformity."[15] To achieve these goals, prison terms would be set firmly at the time of sentencing, and rehabilitation practices, though still employed, would "no longer be relevant to the time of release."[16]

The result of the reform movement of the 1970s, emphasizing fixed term sentencing, was the development of the sentencing guidelines legislative model, discussed in the next section. Most recently, the courts have found that sentencing guidelines violate constitutional principles, thus putting the criminal justice system in a state of redevelopment with respect to the application of punishment theories to the practices of sentencing discussed next.

CRITICAL THINKING 7.1

1. What is the status of the Federal Sentencing Guidelines?
2. What can a federal judge do who wants to deviate from the Guidelines?

7.2 Sentencing

If the accused is convicted of a crime, he or she will be sentenced. Sentencing is a huge and very controversial area in criminal law. Many of the procedural protections that an accused has before conviction do not exist during sentencing.[17] There is a wide variety of ways to sentence criminal offenders. The death penalty, the harshest possible sentence, is discussed later in the chapter. Judges in the federal criminal law system have the Federal Sentencing Guidelines available to assist them in determining what sentence is appropriate.

Types of Sentencing

States may use an indeterminate system, a determinate sentencing system, or a combination of the two systems. Judicial discretion plays a role in both federal and many state courts.

Indeterminate Sentencing

Indeterminate sentencing systems were once the predominant approach to sentencing in the United States. The principal features of **indeterminate sentencing** systems are (1) the grant of great discretion to the trial judge to fashion a sentence for an individual defendant based on information obtained in a sentencing hearing after conviction, and (2) parole boards and other correctional authorities with the power to release a prisoner before completion of the maximum sentence imposed by the judge if, in the view of those authorities, rehabilitative goals have been achieved.[18] Such systems are predicated on the view that criminals can be reformed, and this method of sentencing looks closely at the individual offender to determine his or her sentence. This approach still exists in some states today. However, "by the year 2000, nearly every state in the country had adopted some form of structured sentencing; though a number of states did so through a few mandatory sentencing statutes, many states created sentencing commissions to develop comprehensive guideline schemes."[19] Trial courts in an indeterminate system look at a variety of factors, including "the life history, behavioral deficits, and 'treatment' needs of each offender."[20] The judge has the discretion to impose almost any punishment, ranging from no punishment to the maximum penalty.

indeterminate sentencing
A sentencing system in which the trial judge has great discretion and correctional authorities have the power to release a prisoner before completion of the maximum sentence imposed by the judge if, in the view of those authorities, rehabilitative goals have been achieved.

Determinate Sentencing

Many states, disappointed with the results of indeterminate sentencing, turned to determinate sentencing in the 1970s. The change was a result of many factors, including recidivism, politics, pressure from society to increase prison sentences, and dissatisfaction with judicial discretion in sentencing. Triggered by a powerful criticism of determinate sentencing by Judge Marvin Frankel,[21] by the 1980s a few state legislatures (most notably California and North Carolina) adopted **determinate sentencing** statutes that "abolished parole boards and created presumptive sentencing ranges for various classes of offenses."[22] The first state to fulfill the vision of Judge Frankel was Minnesota in 1978 when the legislature established the Minnesota Sentencing Guidelines Commission to establish **sentencing guidelines**. Other states followed, and in 1984 the federal government enacted the Sentencing Reform Act establishing the U.S. Sentencing Commission, which created federal sentencing guidelines. With determinate sentencing, judges have less discretion, and the offender's sentence is determined at the time he is sentenced. A well-known determinate sentencing system is California's, where serious offenses carry three terms that an offender can be sentenced to and the judge must pick one of those terms. For example, sentencing terms for first-degree burglary are "imprisonment in the state prison for two, four, or six years."[23] The judge generally starts off with the middle term and can consider mitigating factors to give the low term or aggravating factors to give the high term. California also abolished the parole board's authority to decide release dates, though "prison terms are subject to limited reduction at the discretion of corrections authorities."[24]

Like indeterminate sentencing, determinate sentencing has been criticized by many commentators. Proponents of rehabilitation complain that it gives the judge no discretion in sentencing. They argue that someone who may truly deserve a lesser sentence will not get it because by law the judge cannot impose a lesser term. The prison populations are larger in states that have determinate sentencing, which burdens state resources.

Mandatory Sentencing

Mandatory penalties have become quite popular among the states in recent years. Through such **mandatory sentencing** laws, the state's legislature fixes either the exact penalty for the crime or a minimum number of years that the defendant must serve.[25] Mandatory sentences may be found in either determinate or indeterminate sentencing systems.

Habitual Offender Laws

For many years, most states have had **habitual-felon laws**, providing for enhanced sentencing of repeat offenders. But "between 1993 and 1995, three strikes laws effected a sea change in criminal sentencing throughout the Nation."[26] In response to widespread public concern about crime, legislators enacted three strikes and you're out laws. Under these laws, a person convicted of a third felony, having previously been convicted of a serious or violent felony, will likely be sentenced to life in prison. The three strikes and you're out laws effectively adopt the incapacitation justification for punishment. The statutes that determine what types of felonies count as strikes

---

determinate sentencing

A sentencing system that abolishes parole boards and creates presumptive sentencing ranges for various classes of offenses, thereby limiting trial judges' discretion; such a system typically has sentencing guidelines for judges to follow.

sentencing guidelines

A set of standards for sentencing, set by a commission legislatively established for that purpose, that judges in a determinate sentencing system must or may follow.

mandatory sentencing

Laws by which the state's legislature fixes either the exact penalty for the crime or a minimum number of years that the defendant must serve.

habitual-felon laws

Laws that provide for enhanced sentencing of repeat offenders.

as well as the length of the sentence, from one year to life imprisonment without the possibility of parole, vary from state to state. The judge has little or no discretion to effect a deviation from the outcome, once the predicate and triggering crimes have been alleged and proven. The prosecutor has some discretion in deciding whether to charge a triggering felony, and sometimes the judge has some ability to decide that a previous felony can be reduced to a misdemeanor, thus eliminating the necessary predicate felony. These strike laws have consistently been found to be constitutional over claims that they inflict cruel and unusual punishment prohibited by the Eighth Amendment to the U.S. Constitution.[27] (See Application Case 7.1.)

⚖️ Application Case 7.1

Ewing v. California

Lockyer v. Andrade

In March 2003, the U.S. Supreme Court decided two companion cases in which a majority of the Court approved the application of California's recidivist three-strikes law. In *Ewing*, the defendant had stolen three golf clubs, valued all together at about $1,200. He had previously been convicted of one robbery and three burglaries and thus qualified under the law for a sentence of 25-years-to-life. In a 5–4 decision, the Court upheld the conviction, sentence, and law against a claim of violation of the Eighth Amendment's cruel and unusual punishment clause, though the majority could not agree on a single theory or test to support the result.

In *Lockyer*, the defendant, Andrade, was convicted of two counts of petty theft and was sentenced to two consecutive life terms of 25-years-to-life under the same law. This was a *habeas corpus* appeal, and the issue before the Court was whether defendant's conviction was contrary to, or an unreasonable application of, clearly established federal law. The same majority as in the *Ewing* case concluded that the sentences did not violate those principles, and the convictions, sentences, and application of the law were upheld.

SOURCE: Ewing v. California, 538 U.S. 11 (2003); Lockyer v. Andrade, 538 U.S. 63 (2003).

Perhaps as many as half the states have enacted three-strikes laws, but they are not uniform in their terms. Some states have adopted two-strikes laws, and others have four-strikes laws.[28] There is also a federal three-strikes law, which uses predicate convictions in state or federal courts for serious or violent crimes.[29]

The California three-strikes law is the strongest in the country. First, the law defines the predicate crimes in such a way that many prior convictions qualify as strikes. A "third felony results in a minimum sentence of 25 years to life even if the third felony is neither violent nor serious, and sentences are doubled even for offenders with only one strike."[30] Though the impact of three-strikes laws, especially in terms of deterrent effect, is hotly debated, one sure thing is that it has increased the prison population, particularly in California.[31]

Federal Sentencing Guidelines

Before the Federal Sentencing Guidelines, federal judges had substantial discretion in choosing a sentence and could impose a wide variety of sentences. This discretion was sharply criticized by many commentators, with the biggest criticism being that similarly situated defendants were receiving different sentences. Fed up with these sentencing disparities,[32] Congress passed the Sentencing Reform Act of 1984, which created the U.S. Sentencing Commission that developed the Federal Sentencing Guidelines. Although the guidelines were originally upheld as constitutional,[33] the U.S. Supreme Court later held, in *United States v. Booker*,[34] that "the presumptive guideline system in the federal courts violated the Sixth Amendment jury trial guarantee."[35] In *Booker*, the Court remedied this constitutional error by "excising only those portions of the federal statutes that gave the guidelines binding force on the sentencing judge."[36] (See Application Case 7.2.) This effectively renders the federal sentencing guidelines merely advisory and not binding on the trial judges. Despite this, federal judges still adhere very closely to the guidelines. In fact, federal sentences conformed to the guidelines in 86 percent of cases in 2006, and "sentence severity has not changed substantially, though average sentence length has increased."[37]

⚖ Application Case 7.2

Blakely v. Washington

United States v. Booker

The issue for the Court in *Blakely* was whether Washington's sentencing guidelines violated the Sixth Amendment by allowing the judge to impose a sentence that exceeded the maximum authorized under the guidelines based on facts not admitted by the defendant or presented to the jury. The defendant entered a guilty plea to kidnapping his estranged wife, a second-degree class B felony that the state argued was subject to the statutory maximum of 10 years although the standard range maximum was 53 months. The trial judge, however, imposed a sentence of 90 months (37 months beyond the standard range maximum), based on his conclusion that the kidnapping involved deliberate cruelty. In a 5–4 decision the Supreme Court declared the sentencing guidelines unconstitutional in order to give intelligible content to the right of jury trial. Additionally, by eviscerating Washington's sentencing guidelines, the *Blakely* Court cast severe uncertainty on the vitality of mandatory guideline schemes, including the Federal Sentencing Guidelines.

Within a few months of the Court's *Blakely* decision came *Booker*, in which the Court declared the Federal Sentencing Guidelines unconstitutional because the guidelines as applied to Booker violated his Sixth Amendment right to a jury trial by allowing a judge to make factual findings that increased his sentence. But the Court declared a remedy for this by severing the portions of the law making the guidelines mandatory, thus declaring the Federal Sentencing Guidelines to be advisory only.

SOURCE: Blakely v. Washington, 542 U.S. 296 (2004); United States v. Booker, 543 U.S. 220 (2005).

States' Sentencing Guidelines

The *Booker* case declaring federal sentencing guidelines advisory to avoid Sixth Amendment violations extended some previous rulings by the Supreme Court dealing with the validity of states' sentencing guidelines and enhanced penalty sentencing laws. Beginning with *Apprendi v. New Jersey*[38] in 2000, the Court addressed enhanced sentencing with an eye to requiring the states to afford a convicted defendant a right to trial by jury on "any fact that increases the penalty for a crime beyond the prescribed statutory maximum" other than the fact of a prior conviction. In 2004, the Court reaffirmed this principle in invalidating a sentence imposed under the guidelines of the state of Washington, in *Blakely v. Washington*,[39] a case that suggested that nondiscretionary sentencing procedures were constitutionally suspect, as was ultimately declared in *Booker* a few months later.

In response to this line of decisions by the U.S. Supreme Court, some states have decided that their determinate sentencing laws violated jury trial rights as held in *Blakely*, but other states have claimed that their sentencing laws leave enough discretion to the trial judge to avoid such problems.[40] In 2007, the Supreme Court again reaffirmed the *Apprendi-Blakely* rule in *Cunningham v. California*[41] when the Court found that the California determinate sentencing law violated that line of cases. Though there are a number of exceptions to the *Blakely* holding,[42] the result of the decision is to cast substantial doubt on the mandatory nature of such sentencing schemes.

Even though the sentencing guidelines were put in place to counter criticism of disparity in sentencing, the guidelines themselves have been harshly criticized by commentators. Some have stated that the cure is worse than the disease.[43] Others have criticized the guidelines for racial disparities in federal sentences, longer sentences (though many applaud this result), and giving less discretion to federal judges and more to prosecutors, who are not impartial.[44]

Alternatives to Imprisonment

Problems with Imprisonment

With the rise of determinate sentencing systems and mandatory sentences, the prison population has exploded. According to one report, the state and federal prison population has increased 628 percent since 1970. At the end of 2005, a total of 2,193,798 prisoners were incarcerated in federal and state prisons and jails.[45] More than 1.5 million people "were incarcerated in U.S. prisons on any given day, and an additional 750,000 were incarcerated in local jails" according to a report published in January 2007.[46] That same report noted that nearly 3 percent of the living population had spent time in either state or federal prison. As a result of this explosion, the cost of corrections has skyrocketed into billions of dollars, and many are searching for alternatives to imprisonment.

Probation and Parole

By the end of 2005, more than 4.9 million people in the United States were under the supervision of either probation or parole, with approximately 4,162,500 people on probation and 784,400 people on parole.[47] While probation and parole are both considered to be community corrections, there are differences between the two, and

7.1 On the Job

Probation Officer

Description and Duties: Supervise offenders who have been placed on probation through personal contact with offenders and their families. May meet offenders at their homes or places of employment or therapy. May arrange for substance abuse rehabilitation or job training. Usually work with either adults or juveniles exclusively. Also spend time working for the courts, investigating defendants' backgrounds, writing pre-sentencing reports, and recommending sentences. Review sentencing recommendations with offenders and their families before submitting them to the court. May be required to testify in court as to their findings and recommendations. Also attend hearings to update the court on offenders' efforts at rehabilitation and compliance with the terms of their sentences.

Salary: Middle 50 percent earn approximately $32,000 to $52,000, with a median of $40,000; higher in urban areas.

SOURCE: U.S. Department of Labor, Bureau of Labor Statistics, Occupational Outlook Handbook, http://www.bls.gov/oco/ocos265.htm#nature.

---

probation
The suspension of a sentence of incarceration, allowing the offender to return to the community with conditions under the supervision of a probation officer.

parole
The release of an offender from incarceration prior to the expiration of the full term of incarceration, to carry out the rest of the sentence with conditions under the supervision of a corrections officer.

restorative justice
A process through which all the parties with a stake in a particular offense come together to resolve collectively how to deal with the aftermath of the offense and its implications for the future.

many people get them mixed up. **Probation** is the suspension of a sentence of incarceration, allowing the offender to return to the community with conditions set by the court.[48] The conditions may include obeying all laws, staying away from specific persons or types of persons, finding employment, and doing community service. The offender is under the supervision of a probation officer while on probation. Violation of the conditions of probation can result in the offender's being sentenced to what the prison term would have been had it been imposed in the first place.

Parole is the release of an offender from incarceration prior to the expiration of the full term of incarceration. The offender is allowed back into the community under the supervision of a corrections officer to carry out the rest of the sentence with conditions.[49] The rules and conditions for parole differ widely among the states. With the increase in determinate sentencing and mandatory minimum sentencing, many prisoners are not eligible for parole for many years, despite good behavior. Many of the same conditions of probationers are often applied to parolees.

Restorative Justice

Restorative justice is "a process through which all the parties with a stake in a particular offense come together to resolve collectively how to deal with the aftermath of the offense and its implications for the future."[50] Unlike most other forms of punishment, in which the victim sits back and watches the state or government take action against the offender, the victim is very involved here and plays an important role in holding the offender accountable for his actions. In criminal cases, a victim can tell the offender how the crime has changed the victim's life and can ask the offender questions about the crime. The offender can say why the crime occurred and describe the effect of the punishment. An offender may also be given an opportunity to make things right with the victim, usually by some form of compensation, such as money. Restorative justice techniques include sentencing circles, "offender mediation, family group conferencing, citizen panels, and various restitution initiatives."[51]

Wrongful Convictions

Unfortunately, the criminal justice system is not perfect, and sometimes gross injustice results. One of the most prominent examples of gross injustice is the wrongful criminal conviction of an innocent person. In recent years, DNA evidence and other advancements in science have exonerated a growing number of prisoners. One study has suggested that there are thousands of innocent people in prison today.[52] Even if that study overstates the number,[53] the fact remains that our prisons have housed, and may continue to house, a number of innocent inmates.

A DNA Strip
DNA testing can exonerate the wrongfully convicted.

Wrongful convictions can result from a number of factors, including prosecution misconduct, ineffective assistance of defense counsel, police corruption, vengeful juries, racism, junk science, wrong eyewitness identifications, false confessions, and many others.[54] Sadly, there are few remedies for those who are wrongly imprisoned. They cannot get back the years of their lives that they lost. Usually, wrongly convicted individuals sue the city, the state, and sometimes the prosecutor (if prosecutorial misconduct is alleged) for monetary compensation. Of course, the worst scenario for the wrongly convicted, one that can never be corrected, is the imposition of the death penalty.

Death Penalty

The ultimate punishment is death. It is also the most controversial punishment in the United States and in many other countries. According to one source, 111 countries do not impose the death penalty, including most European countries, while 84 countries do impose the death penalty, including the United States and number of countries in the Middle East and Asia.[55] In those countries that do impose the death penalty, the crimes for which it is imposed varies: some countries impose the death penalty only in murder cases; other countries use it for other crimes, including adultery and robbery.

Within the United States, most states (35 as of October 2007), the federal government, and the military impose the death penalty in certain cases and circumstances.[56] Many of these states authorize the death penalty only for certain homicides, and many use lethal injection as the method of execution.[57] Twelve states and the District of Columbia have abolished the death penalty. (See Figure 7.1.) The controversy surrounding the death penalty is not likely to end. Some people believe that it should be abolished, some believe that it should be used more, and some believe that the death penalty should only be used for certain crimes or certain offenders.

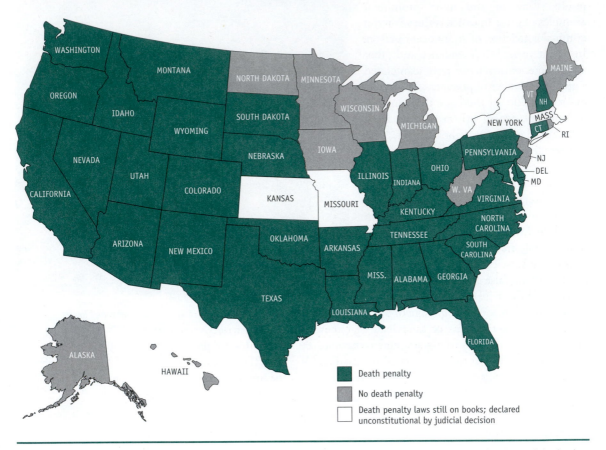

> **FIGURE 7.1**

States That Do and Do Not Have the Death Penalty

Legend:
- ■ Death penalty
- ■ No death penalty
- □ Death penalty laws still on books; declared unconstitutional by judicial decision

SOURCE: http://deathpenaltyinfo.org/state; Thomson West, 50 State Statutory Surveys, Capital Punishment (2005) (available in Westlaw "Surveys" database).

History and Evolution of the Death Penalty

The death penalty has existed throughout history all over the world from the earliest days of civilization. In England, the death penalty went in and out of fashion, but it is important to discuss this because many of the people who settled in America were English, and America derived its common law from England's common law. People were executed for a wide variety of crimes in England, and even some famous people were executed, such as Mary, Queen of Scots and Sir Walter Raleigh. The idea was deterrence; many of these executions were public and sought to humiliate the offender. England eventually began to limit the death penalty and abolished it in 1965.

The death penalty came to the American colonies along with the English common law. Over time, application of the death penalty was limited to certain types of crimes. As the states developed, each developed its own law with respect to the death penalty, and even today there remains variation in application and scope. As in England, the death penalty has gone in and out of fashion in the United States, but it has remained strong in particular areas, such as in the southeast and in Texas.[58] Texas is often singled out, for good reason: Texas has accounted for 35 percent of the executions in the United States since 1977.[59] The twelve states that have abolished the death penalty are mostly in New England and the upper Midwest.

Some states have imposed moratoriums on the death penalty, which means that all scheduled executions in the state come to a halt. A famous example was in California in 1972, when the California Supreme Court declared the death penalty unconstitutional and reduced all death sentences to life imprisonment. This was extremely controversial because mass murderer Charles Manson, who brutally murdered seven people including actress Sharon Tate, had his death sentence reduced to life imprisonment. Other states, such as Illinois and Maryland, have imposed temporary moratoriums to address problems with the death penalty.[60]

The Death Penalty Today

Since 1910 the imposition of the death penalty has come under judicial scrutiny, principally by the Supreme Court of the United States, under the "cruel and unusual punishment" clause of the Eighth Amendment to the U.S. Constitution. In *Weems v. United States*,[61] the Court, in a noncapital case, found implicit in the concept of cruel and unusual punishment the principle of **proportionality**. "Proportionality can be calculated by use of either utilitarian or retributive tools of analysis, and results may differ depending upon the approach followed."[62] Beginning in 1972, the Court has considered the constitutionality of the death penalty. In that year, in *Furman v. Georgia*,[63] the Court held that the death penalty in three cases from Georgia and Texas was unconstitutional as applied. Though there was no one reason that all the justices adhered to in the case, the "dominant theme" among the five-justice majority was the "arbitrary and capricious imposition of the death penalty."[64] Another theme among the justices was that imposition of the death penalty failed to further a goal of punishment and was, for that reason, excessive.[65] Four years later, after 35 states had revised their death penalty statutes in response to *Furman*, three more cases came before the Court, and the Court upheld the validity of the statutes. The principal case was *Gregg v. Georgia*,[66] in which the Court held that the death penalty itself did not violate the Constitution.

Most death penalty case challenges since 1976 have focused on proportionality of a sentence of death for a particular crime or as applied to a particular class of defendants. The Supreme Court developed a two-pronged test to determine the constitutional question, "containing the acceptability and human dignity analyses from *Gregg*."[67] Over the years, the Court has considered the death penalty related to certain crimes and classes of defendants in a number of areas, the most important decisions covering: "1) a nonkiller accomplice to a felony murder, 2) juveniles, 3) a person who is mentally retarded, or 4) a crime that does not involve the taking of life."[68]

In the category of accomplice to felony murder, through two successive decisions, *Enmund v. Florida*[69] and *Tison v. Arizona*,[70] the Court established a test

proportionality
A principle that has been read into the cruel and unusual punishment clause of the Eighth Amendment to measure the validity of punishment, including the death penalty.

7.1 Web Exploration

Death Penalty Information Center

Visit the Death Penalty Information Center's "Methods of Execution" page at http://www.deathpenaltyinfo.org/article.php?scid+8&did=245. Pick a link to learn more about one of the related topics. Did anything you learned from visiting this site change your views on the death penalty?

requiring that the "government must show that the defendant either intended to kill or was a major participant in the crime and demonstrated a reckless indifference to human life. Absent this showing, the accomplice will be ineligible" for the death penalty.[71] In the category of juveniles, in 2005, in *Roper v. Simmons*,[72] the Supreme Court held that a state cannot execute a defendant who was under the age of 18 when the crime was committed. In *Atkins v. Virginia*,[73] in 2002, the Court held that the death penalty cannot be imposed on a defendant who is mentally retarded. The Court declared the death penalty unconstitutional when applied to a conviction for rape of an adult woman in *Coker*[74] in 1977. Since then, it has not addressed the question of whether crimes other than murder may be punished by death, so in such a case, "the courts will have to decide its constitutionality."[75]

Given the change in composition of the Supreme Court—Justice O'Connor retired, as did Chief Justice Rehnquist before he died—it is likely that death penalty law will be revisited by the Court. The likelihood is that the role of proportionality in death penalty doctrine will be subject to change.

In January 2008, the case of *Baze v. Rees* was argued before the U.S. Supreme Court, testing the constitutionality of execution using lethal injection by the methods employed for that purpose in Kentucky.[76] No state today relies on hanging as a method of execution, though two states allow the condemned to choose hanging.[77] Today, no state relies on electrocution as a method of execution,[78] although nine states "allow inmates sentenced to death before a certain date to choose electrocution."[79] Nebraska used electrocution until February 2008, when the Supreme Court of Nebraska declared that method of execution unconstitutional as cruel and unusual punishment under the state constitution.[80] No state today relies on lethal gas as a method of execution, though four states provide for lethal gas as an alternative method of execution.[81] The use of lethal injection, which is the subject of dispute in *Baze v. Rees*, is used in every state but one that has the death penalty.[82] The U.S. Supreme Court's decision in *Baze v. Rees* may significantly affect the constitutional status of the death penalty. We can only wait and see what lies ahead in this highly volatile area of criminal law and punishment.

CRITICAL THINKING 7.2

1. What is the purpose of mandatory sentencing?
2. Should a trial judge have the ability to impose a lesser sentence than mandated? If so, when?

REVIEW AND APPLICATIONS

Summary by Chapter Objectives

1. **Identify the principal purpose of laws that make certain acts punishable by society in the form of criminal prohibitions.** The principal purpose of the criminal law is to sanction, usually by punishment, behavior by an individual that violates the rules of acceptable conduct within a community. The question of criminalization or decriminalization is largely answered with what most people think of as crime—offenses such as murder, rape, assault, robbery, burglary, and traditional forms of theft. The modern focus of debate on the question of criminalization is in other areas, such as offenses designed to protect public morality, the economy, the environment, or generally to promote public welfare.

2. **Name the two justifying theories of punishment that underlie modern criminal law.** The two justifying theories of punishment underlying modern criminal law are the retributive justification and the utilitarian justification. The retributive justification is that a wrongdoer deserves punishment.

3. **Explain the retributive theory of punishment.** The simplest retributive justification is that one who has violated the rights of others should be penalized. Punishment restores the moral order that has been breached by the original wrongful act. A different retributive approach is that criminals deserve punishment because they violate social norms.

4. **State the hallmarks of the utilitarian theory of punishment.** The hallmarks of the utilitarian view are general deterrence, individual deterrence, incapacitation, reform, and vengeance.

5. **Define the types of sentences that may be imposed.** States may use an indeterminate system, a determinate sentencing system, or a combination of the two systems.

6. **Explain indeterminate sentencing.** In an indeterminate sentencing system, the trial judge has great discretion, and correctional authorities have the power to release a prisoner before completion of the maximum sentence imposed by the judge if, in the view of those authorities, rehabilitative goals have been achieved.

7. **Define determinate sentencing.** A determinate sentencing system abolishes parole boards and creates presumptive sentencing ranges for various classes of offenses, thereby limiting trial judges' discretion; such a system typically will have sentencing guidelines for judges to follow.

8. **Explain sentencing guidelines.** Sentencing guidelines are a set of standards, set by a commission legislatively established for that purpose, that judges in a determinate sentencing system must or may follow.

9. **Describe the alternatives to imprisonment.** The alternatives to imprisonment are probation and parole. Probation is where a sentence of incarceration is suspended and the offender is allowed to return to the community with

conditions under the supervision of a probation officer. Parole is where an offender is released from incarceration prior to the expiration of the full term of incarceration, to carry out the rest of the sentence with conditions under supervision of a corrections officer.

10. **State when the death penalty cannot be imposed.** The death penalty cannot be imposed when to do so would violate the cruel and unusual punishment clause of the Eighth Amendment to the U.S. Constitution, particularly in cases involving (1) a nonkiller accomplice to a felony murder, (2) a juvenile, (3) a person who is mentally retarded, or (4) a crime that does not involve the taking of life.

Key Terms

punishment (p. 185)
retributive justification (p. 185)
utilitarian justification (p. 185)
rehabilitative justification (p. 186)
incapacitation (p. 187)
three-strikes laws (p. 187)
zero tolerance (p. 187)
vengeance (p. 188)
indeterminate sentencing (p. 189)

determinate sentencing (p. 190)
sentencing guidelines (p. 190)
mandatory sentencing (p. 190)
habitual-felon laws (p. 190)
probation (p. 194)
parole (p. 194)
restorative justice (p. 194)
proportionality (p. 197)

Review Questions

1. How is the criminal law different from other types of law?
2. What is the difference between retributive and utilitarian theories of punishment?
3. Into what category does modern punishment theory fit?
4. What are the differences between determinate and indeterminate sentencing?
5. What is the current legal status of sentencing guidelines?
6. What is the current legal status of habitual offender laws, such as three-strikes laws?
7. What is the difference between probation and parole?
8. What is the constitutional basis on which courts have found the death penalty to be unlawful in some instances?

Problem-Solving Exercises

1. **Learning a Lesson** Judy was single and depressed because she had just broken up with her boyfriend. She went to a neighborhood bar with some friends so they could cheer her up. At the bar she met Peter, a tall, good-looking, friendly guy. He said he was interested in "partying" with her. They went back to her place, after she described it as being in a great building near a posh girls' school. Judy had a small amount of cocaine in her apartment, and when she offered to share it with Peter, he arrested her. Peter was an undercover police officer. Judy had no prior arrests or convictions. It turns out her apartment was 800 feet from a private girls' school. In Judy's state, there is a mandatory minimum

three-year sentence for any offender who sells illicit drugs within 1,000 feet of a school.

   a. If you were the trial judge, would you nevertheless sentence Judy to less than three years?

   b. How could you explain your decision?

Workplace Applications

1. **Three-Strikes "Wobbler"** George Jones is a 45-year-old who has two felony convictions, one for robbery and one for assault with a deadly weapon. In 2007, he stole some items worth about $100 from a Walmart. Jones has admitted stealing the merchandise. Under the state's criminal code, his conduct qualifies as petty theft, which is a felony. There is, however, another provision in the code for misdemeanor theft.

   a. If you were the prosecuting attorney in the case against Jones, would you file felony charges against him?

   b. Would your answer to (a) change if you knew that charging a felony would count as a third strike under the criminal code so that Jones would be subject to a sentence of 25-years-to-life?

   c. If you were the judge in Jones's case, would you grant the defendant's motion to dismiss the felony charge and accept a proposed guilty plea for misdemeanor theft (which could result in a sentence of up to one year in the county jail)?

2. **Sentencing Guidelines Downward Departure** David Dove, a 25-year-old man living with his two children, fiancée, and her parents has pled guilty in federal district court to one count of distributing cocaine base. Dove has one prior arrest, but has never been incarcerated. At 16, he was charged with possession of marijuana, but the charge was dismissed. He was convicted of assault and battery at age 18, resulting in six months probation. After that, Dove learned his girlfriend was pregnant, dropped out of school, became a member of a union, and maintained steady employment until his arrest on the current charge. He supports his children, his fiancée, and her parents, all of whom say that Dove is a wonderful father and person. His family says that his incarceration would have an extreme detrimental effect on them. Under the sentencing guidelines, Dove would be sentenced to 77 months in prison. He has asked for a downward departure to 60 months.

   a. If you were the judge, would you grant Dove's request for a downward departure?

   b. What punishment purposes should guide you in making that decision?

Ethics Exercises

1. **If I Can't Have You** Bertha shot and killed her husband and his lover after discovering them having sex in his car. When an officer came to her house to

inform Bertha that her husband had been shot, Bertha broke down and admitted she did it. She also admitted that she had purchased a gun illegally because she suspected her husband of cheating. This confession took place before the officer read Bertha her *Miranda* rights, although when he went to the house the officer had suspected Bertha. Bertha was convicted of manslaughter because her confession was suppressed.

a. You are the trial judge at the sentencing hearing. If you wish, you can rely on the suppressed confession for a sentence enhancement, in effect imposing the same sentence Bertha would have received for second-degree murder. Should you do so? Why or why not?

b. If you were on the appellate court reviewing Bertha's sentence imposed as described in (a), would you rule that this sentence is fair?

Notes

1. Kent Greenwalt, *Punishment, in* Encyclopedia of Crime and Justice 1282, 1273 (Joshua Dressler ed., 2d ed. 2002).
2. *See* Richard S. Frase, *Criminalization and Decriminalization, in* Encyclopedia of Crime and Justice 347 (Joshua Dressler ed., 2d ed. 2002).
3. Joshua Dressler, Understanding Criminal Law § 2.02[A], at 12–13 (4th ed. 2006).
4. Nora Demleitner, Douglas Berman, Marc Miller & Ronald Wright, Sentencing Law and Policy, Cases, Statutes, and Guidelines 2 (2d ed. 2007).
5. *See* Kent Greenwalt, *Punishment, in* Encyclopedia of Crime and Justice 1282, 1284 (Joshua Dressler ed., 2d ed. 2002).
6. *See* Joshua Dressler, Understanding Criminal Law § 2.05, at 23–24 (4th ed. 2006).
7. Kent Greenwalt, *Punishment, in* Encyclopedia of Crime and Justice 1282, 1284 (Joshua Dressler ed., 2d ed. 2002).
8. *Id.* at 1285.
9. Nora Demleitner, Douglas Berman, Marc Miller & Ronald Wright, Sentencing Law and Policy, Cases, Statutes, and Guidelines 8 (2d ed. 2007).
10. Kent Greenwalt, *Punishment, in* Encyclopedia of Crime and Justice 1282, 1289 (Joshua Dressler ed., 2d ed. 2002).
11. Joshua Dressler, Understanding Criminal Law § 2.05, at 19 (4th ed. 2006).
12. Nora Demleitner, Douglas Berman, Marc Miller & Ronald Wright, Sentencing Law and Policy, Cases, Statutes, and Guidelines 8 (2d ed. 2007), citing Richard Frase, *Limiting Retributivism: The Consensus Model of Criminal Punishment, in* The Future of Imprisonment (Michael Toney ed., 2004).
13. Kent Greenwalt, *Punishment, in* Encyclopedia of Crime and Justice 1282, 1290–91 (Joshua Dressler ed., 2d ed. 2002).
14. *Id.*
15. *Id.*

16. *Id.*

17. Joshua Dressler, Understanding Criminal Procedure Volume 2: Adjudication § 15.01[A], at 345 (4th ed. 2006).

18. Joshua Dressler, Understanding Criminal Law § 2.06, at 26 (4th ed. 2006).

19. Nora Demleitner, Douglas Berman, Marc Miller & Ronald Wright, Sentencing Law and Policy, Cases, Statutes, and Guidelines 147 (2d ed. 2007).

20. Kevin R. Reitz, *Sentencing: Allocation of Authority, in* Encyclopedia of Crime and Justice 1400, 1401 (Joshua Dressler ed., 2d ed. 2002).

21. Marvin E. Frankel, Criminal Sentences: Law Without Order (1973), *as cited and quoted in* Nora Demleitner, Douglas Berman, Marc Miller & Ronald Wright, Sentencing Law and Policy, Cases, Statutes, and Guidelines 140 (2d ed. 2007).

22. Nora Demleitner, Douglas Berman, Marc Miller & Ronald Wright, Sentencing Law and Policy, Cases, Statutes, and Guidelines 148 (2d ed. 2007).

23. Kevin R. Reitz, *Sentencing: Allocation of Authority, in* Encyclopedia of Crime and Justice 1400, 1403 (Joshua Dressler ed., 2d ed. 2002) (quoting Cal. Penal Code § 461 (West 1997)).

24. *Id.*

25. *Id.* at 1404–05.

26. Ewing v. California, 538 U.S. 11, 24 (2003).

27. *Id. See also* Lockyer v. Andrade, 538 U.S. 63 (2003).

28. Nora Demleitner, Douglas Berman, Marc Miller & Ronald Wright, Sentencing Law and Policy, Cases, Statutes, and Guidelines 348 (2d ed. 2007).

29. 18 U.S.C. § 3559 (2007).

30. Nora Demleitner, Douglas Berman, Marc Miller & Ronald Wright, Sentencing Law and Policy, Cases, Statutes, and Guidelines 348 (2d ed. 2007).

31. *Id.* at 349.

32. Joshua Dressler, Understanding Criminal Procedure Volume 2: Adjudication § 15.03[A], at 360 (4th ed. 2006).

33. Mistretta v. United States, 488 U.S. 1361 (1989).

34. United States v. Booker, 543 U.S. 220 (2005).

35. Nora Demleitner, Douglas Berman, Marc Miller & Ronald Wright, Sentencing Law and Policy, Cases, Statutes, and Guidelines 453 (2d ed. 2007).

36. *Id.*

37. Joshua Dressler, Understanding Criminal Procedure Volume 2: Adjudication § 15.03[A], at 361 (4th ed. 2006).

38. Apprendi v. New Jersey, 530 U.S. 466 (2000).

39. Blakely v. Washington, 542 U.S. 296 (2004).

40. Nora Demleitner, Douglas Berman, Marc Miller & Ronald Wright, Sentencing Law and Policy, Cases, Statutes, and Guidelines 453 (2d ed. 2007).

41. Cunningham v. California, 127 S. Ct. 856 (2007).

42. Nora Demleitner, Douglas Berman, Marc Miller & Ronald Wright, Sentencing Law and Policy, Cases, Statutes, and Guidelines 455 (2d ed. 2007).

43. Joshua Dressler, Understanding Criminal Procedure Volume 2: Adjudication § 15.03[C], at 363 (4th ed. 2006) (citing Albert A. Alschuler, *Disparity: The Normative and Empirical Failure of the Federal Guidelines*, 58 Stan. L. Rev. 85 (2005)).

44. Joshua Dressler, Understanding Criminal Procedure Volume 2: Adjudication § 15.03[A], at 361 (4th ed. 2006).

45. Bureau of Justice Statistics, Prison Statistics, available at http://www.ojp.usdoj.gov/bjs/prisons.htm.

46. Reconsidering Incarceration: New Directions for Reducing Crime, available at http://www.vera.org/publication_pdf/379_727.pdf.

47. Bureau of Justice Statistics, Probation and Parole Statistics, available at http://www.ojp.usdoj.gov/bjs/pandp.htm.

48. Doris Layton MacKenzie, *Probation and Parole: History, Goals, and Decision-Making, in* Encyclopedia of Crime and Justice 1210, 1210–11 (Joshua Dressler ed., 2d ed. 2002).

49. *Id.* at 1211–12.

50. Nora Demleitner, Douglas Berman, Marc Miller & Ronald Wright, Sentencing Law and Policy, Cases, Statutes, and Guidelines 20 (2d ed. 2007).

51. *Id.* at 28.

52. Samuel R. Gross et al., *Exonerations in the United States 1989 Through 2003*, 95 J. Crim. L. & Criminology, 523, 551 (2005).

53. http://truthinjustice.org/exoneration-study.htm.

54. *See* http://www.truthinjustice.org.

55. Linda E. Carter & Ellen Kreitzberg, Understanding Capital Punishment Law § 1.01, at 1 (2004).

56. Thirty-nine states had death penalty laws on the books as of October 2007, as indicated in Figure 7.1; however, four of those states' courts (Kansas, Massachusetts, Missouri, and New York) had declared the death penalty statutes unconstitutional and no legislative action had been taken to cure the law. *See* http://deathpenaltyinfo.org/state and Thomson West, 50 State Statutory Surveys, Capital Punishment (2005) (available in Westlaw "Surveys" database).

57. Linda E. Carter & Ellen Kreitzberg, Understanding Capital Punishment Law § 1.01, at 2 (2004).

58. Victor Streib, Death Penalty in a Nutshell 6–8 (2d ed. 2005).

59. *Id.* at 8.

60. Linda E. Carter & Ellen Kreitzberg, Understanding Capital Punishment Law § 1.01, at 2 (2004).

61. Weems v. United States, 217 U.S. 349 (1910).

62. Joshua Dressler, Understanding Criminal Law § 6.05 [A], at 60 (4th ed. 2006).

63. Furman v. Georgia, 408 U.S. 238 (1972).

64. Linda E. Carter & Ellen Kreitzberg, Understanding Capital Punishment Law § 4.02 [B], at 23 (2004).

65. *Id.* at 24.

66. Gregg v. Georgia, 428 U.S. 153 (1976).

67. Linda E. Carter & Ellen Kreitzberg, Understanding Capital Punishment Law § 4.02 [B], at 27 (2004) (footnotes omitted).

68. *Id.* § 8.01 [A], at 61.

69. Enmund v. Florida, 458 U.S. 782 (1982).

70. Tison v. Arizona, 481 U.S. 137 (1987).

71. Linda E. Carter & Ellen Kreitzberg, Understanding Capital Punishment Law § 8.02 [A], at 64 (2004) (footnotes omitted).

72. Roper v. Simmons, 543 U.S. 551 (2005).

73. Atkins v. Virginia, 536 U.S. 304 (2002).

74. Coker v. Georgia, 433 U.S. 584 (1977).

75. Linda E. Carter & Ellen Kreitzberg, Understanding Capital Punishment Law § 8.05 [A], at 86 (2004).

76. Baze v. Rees, ___ U.S. ___, 128 S. Ct. 34 (2007) (grant of *certiorari*). For a transcript of the oral argument before the Supreme Court, see 2008 W.L. 63222 (Jan. 7, 2008).

77. Brief of Petitioners at 2, Baze v. Rees, No. 07-5439 (U.S. Nov. 5, 2007), 2007 W.L. 3307732 (citing Deborah W. Denno, *When Legislatures Delegate Death: The Troubling Paradox Behind State Uses of Electrocution and Lethal Injection and What It Says About Us*, 63 Ohio St. L.J. 63, 129 (2002)).

78. *Id.* at 3 (citing Deborah W. Denno, *The Lethal Injection Quandary: How Medicine Has Dismantled the Death Penalty*, 76 Fordham L. Rev. 49, 93 (2007)).

79. *Id.* at n.2 (citing U.S. Department of Justice, Bureau of Justice Statistics, Table 2, *available at* http://www.ojp.usdoj.gov/bjs/pub/pdf/cp05.pdf (last visited Feb. 10, 2008)).

80. State v. Mata, ___ N.E.2d ___, ___, 275 Neb. 1, 67 (2008).

81. *Id.* at 4 n.3 (citing U.S. Department of Justice, Bureau of Justice Statistics, Table 2, *available at* http://www.ojp.usdoj.gov/bjs/pub/pdf/cp05.pdf (last visited Feb. 10, 2008)).

82. *Id.* at 7 (citing Deborah W. Denno, *The Lethal Injection Quandary: How Medicine Has Dismantled the Death Penalty*, 76 Fordham L. Rev. 49, 93 (2007)).

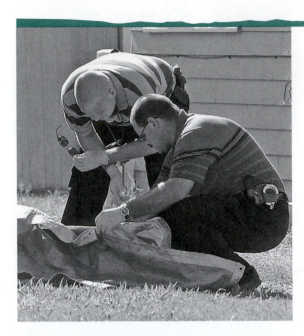

Criminal Homicide

CHAPTER OBJECTIVES

After reading and studying this chapter, you should be able to:

1. Distinguish between homicide and criminal homicide.
2. List the rules defining when life begins and ends for criminal homicide.
3. List the essential elements of murder.
4. Explain the felony murder rule.
5. Distinguish between first-degree and second-degree murder.
6. Describe the Model Penal Code's definition of murder.
7. Explain the difference between justification and excuse defenses.
8. Describe the differences in voluntary manslaughter, involuntary manslaughter, and murder.

8.1 Homicide

The law defines **homicide** as the killing of one human being by an act, procurement, or omission of another.[1] Not all killings are considered criminal, and not all mandate punishment and criminal liability. A **criminal homicide** is any act that causes the death of another person with criminally culpable *mens rea* and without a lawful justification or excuse. To illustrate the difference, consider the following examples of homicides:

- A death intentionally caused by a serial killer.
- An accidental death caused by an automobile driver striking a pedestrian on a rainy day.
- A state's execution of a convicted serial killer.

Of these examples, only the first could clearly be considered criminal. In the first example, the actor has a criminally culpable *mens rea* and would be criminally responsible for the killings unless he or she can provide a legal excuse. In the second example, if the driver was exercising caution while driving in the wet conditions, his or her criminal intent is lacking with reference to the death. In the final example, in those states that have enacted a death penalty statute, the government is justified under the law to execute any defendant convicted of a capital crime.

At early common law, criminal homicide consisted of two types: murder and manslaughter. In modern times, criminal homicide is generally divided into three categories: murder, voluntary manslaughter, and involuntary manslaughter. An essential element distinguishing murder from the two types of manslaughter is **malice aforethought**, which is the *mens rea* (or mental state) of the accused at the time of the act. Within these categories, some states further distinguish and divide criminal homicide into varying levels of seriousness based on the circumstances under which the death occurred. For instance, in various states murder is divided by degrees, including first-degree and second-degree; this practice is known as *gradation of offenses*. These types of criminal homicide, as well as *mens rea* and the gradation of offenses, will be discussed in detail later in this chapter. Remember that all of the general principles of criminal liability discussed and analyzed in the previous chapters also apply to the offense of criminal homicide.

The Beginning of Life

A basic requirement for assessing liability for criminal homicide is that the victim was alive at the time the act was committed. This requirement raises issues about when life legally begins, such as in the case of an unborn child, and when it legally ends. If, by definition, a criminal homicide requires the killing of a human being, the critical question becomes, "What constitutes a human being?"

Feticide and Criminal Abortions

Is the killing of an unborn fetus legally considered a homicide? The answer is *sometimes* and *in some places*. Some states allow prosecution for homicide for the killing of an unborn fetus (with or without the consent of the mother) under certain circumstances. Thus, the definition of a human being is not *always* limited to a child born alive.

homicide
The killing of one human being by another.

criminal homicide
Any act that causes the death of another person with criminal intent and without lawful justification or excuse.

malice aforethought
Under modern law, any one of four mental states that reveal the intent to (1) kill, (2) inflict grievous bodily injury, (3) show extreme reckless disregard for human life, or (4) commit a felony that results in another's death.

At common law, an unborn child could not be the subject or victim of criminal homicide.[2] Neither a fetus *in utero* (within the mother's uterus, or womb) nor a stillborn child was considered alive for legal purposes. Only a person who caused the death of a child "born alive" could be guilty of criminal homicide. Under the **born-alive rule**, a child would have to be physically separated from the mother in order to be considered a human being. In other words, the fetus would have to be outside of the mother's body with the umbilical cord severed, showing clear signs of independent respiration and heartbeat. Although many states have abolished various common law rules, some states have maintained the born-alive rule by writing it into their current statutes.

Modern statutes that allow prosecution for the death of fetuses generally include four types of fetal homicide. These are defined by the stage of fetal development at which the death occurs. (For feticide definition by state, see Figure 8.1.) These four stages are:

born-alive rule

The common law rule defining the beginning of life, for purposes of criminal homicide, as the birth of a live child.

FIGURE 8.1

Definition of Person for Purposes of Homicide, by State

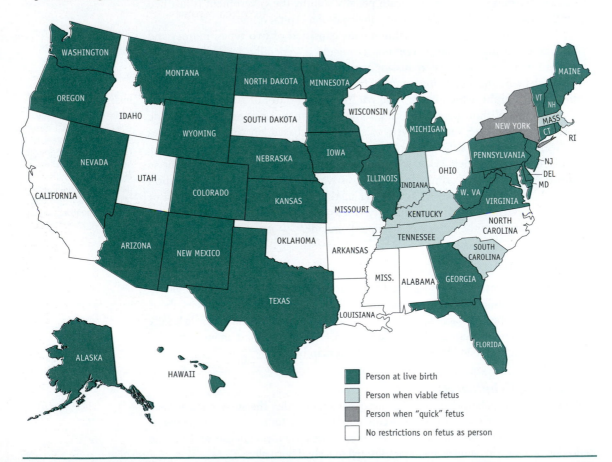

■	Person at live birth
■	Person when viable fetus
■	Person when "quick" fetus
□	No restrictions on fetus as person

1. Viability, when the fetus is developed enough to survive outside the womb; usually about five to six months after conception.
2. Quickening, or first movement, of the fetus; usually about four to five months after conception.
3. Seven to eight weeks after conception, or when an embryo (an earlier stage of pregnancy) becomes a fetus.
4. Conception.[3]

With the development of modern medical technology, a medical professional can tell whether a fetus *in utero* is alive by evidence of heartbeat and blood circulation. Through ultrasound and other techniques, a medical professional can detect the presence and condition of the fetus far earlier and more accurately than ever before.

To adapt to these technological advances, many states have developed alternative legal definitions of when life begins in relation to criminal homicide. After the decision in *Keeler v. Superior Court* (see Application Case 8.1), the state of California specifically modified the wording of its penal code to include the death of fetuses as criminal homicide.[4] Under this revised statute, the purposeful killing of a fetus without the mother's consent is murder, and this criminal liability is in effect for the entire fetal stage of pregnancy. In *People v. Davis* (1994), a California court held that a fetus could be the victim of murder if it has progressed beyond the embryonic stage of seven to eight weeks.[5]

⚖️ Application Case 8.1

Keeler v. Superior Court

In the 1970 case of *Keeler v. Superior Court*, the Supreme Court of California held that the defendant could not be convicted of murder for the intentional killing of a fetus. Keeler physically attacked his recently divorced wife, who was pregnant by another man. During the attack, Keeler stated to his wife, "I'm going to stomp it out of you," and then proceeded to shove his knee into her abdomen. Shortly after the attack, an examination of the fetus *in utero* revealed that its skull was severely fractured. The child, a five-pound girl, was delivered stillborn by Caesarian section. It was determined by medical evidence that prior to the attack, the fetus was viable; the viability of the fetus was terminated by the skull fracture and consequent cerebral hemorrhaging. The medical examiner concluded further that the skull fracture was a result of force applied to the mother's abdomen.

Given the defendant's obvious intent to harm the fetus and given the fact that the fetus was, in fact, conclusively harmed by the defendant's actions, the prosecution charged and convicted Keeler of criminal homicide. The indictment charged that Keeler did "unlawfully kill a human being." Keller appealed his conviction, claiming that since the child was stillborn, he had only caused harm to a fetus, not to a human being as required by the statute. The Supreme Court of California reversed Keeler's conviction for murder. It noted that at the time Keeler attacked his ex-wife, California law defined a "human being" in the same way as common law did, under the born-alive rule. The court reasoned that when the legislature passed the law in 1850, there was no intent to include a fetus within the meaning of human being. Therefore, in order for Keeler to be guilty for the death of the infant, under the criminal homicide statute charged, she would have had to be born alive. Although the California legislature subsequently reworded the statute to include the death of a fetus as criminal homicide, the change in the law could not be applied retroactively to Keeler.

SOURCE: Keeler v. Superior Court, 470 P.2d 617 (Cal. 1970).

feticide

The unlawful killing of a fetus.

In other states, such as Iowa,[6] killing a fetus is a criminal homicide called a **feticide**. It is important to understand the distinction between a legal abortion and a feticide. Legal abortion is generally protected by the mother's right to privacy until the fetus is viable,[7] so a mother's consent to such an abortion prior to viability is *not* a criminal act. In certain circumstances, state law also permits abortions after viability, with the mother's consent. These typically involve a medical emergency to protect the life of the mother. A feticide, in contrast, may be defined as an abortion performed after viability and when the mother's health is not at risk. Again, a feticide can be prosecuted as a criminal homicide, depending on the developmental stage of the fetus at the time of the act.

Criminal homicide liability may also apply in cases where the fetus is not yet viable. A Minnesota court held in *State v. Merrill* (1980) that the legislature can create liability and punish as murder the killing of a nonviable fetus.[8] In 2004, Congress enacted the Unborn Victims of Violence Act of 2004.[9] The Act makes a violent attack on a pregnant women two different crimes: one against the woman and the other against the fetus she is carrying. It is commonly known as Laci and Conner's Law. Laci Peterson and her unborn son, Conner, were killed by Scott Peterson, Laci's husband and Conner's father.

Infanticide

In cases involving the death of newborns, particularly in settings other than hospitals, officials always question whether the child was born and was alive during the act (or omission) that caused his or her death. In cases such as these, both prosecutors and defense attorneys must collect and examine all of the evidence related to the child's condition. Most of this evidence will be of a medical nature and will help to establish or disestablish (1) whether the child was born alive and thus physically separated from the mother's womb, and (2) whether the child showed independent respiration and heartbeat at the time of death. Evidence of this nature is particularly important in states where killing a fetus is not considered criminal homicide. *All* states consider the killing of a newborn child, known as an *infanticide*, a homicide. Even in states that prosecute the illegal killing of a fetus as a criminal homicide or feticide, close examination of medical evidence to determine the victim's stage of development is still required for prosecution.

The End of Life

In order to consider an act a homicide, the defendant's conduct must have *caused* the death of somebody who was alive at the time of the act. It is important to determine that death occurred and that it occurred as the result of the defendant's conduct. For example, if the victim was already dead at the time of the defendant's conduct, the defendant cannot be prosecuted for criminal homicide with reference to the death.

At common law, a person was considered dead when there was a permanent cessation of respiration and heartbeat. However, in light of advancements in technology, including life support systems, the common law definition is no longer adequate and has been replaced with the concept of brain death, which is the permanent cessation of all brain functions which, absent mechanical support, would result in the cessation of other body functions as well. Reflecting this change, 32 states have adopted the Uniform Determination of Death Act. The act provides that "An individual who has sustained either (1) irreversible cessation of circulatory and respiratory functions, or (2) irreversible cessation of all functions of the entire brain, including the brain stem, is dead. A determination of death must be made in accordance with accepted medical standards." The remaining states each have their own definition of death, which generally includes brain death and some other alternative measure.

The Right to Die

As courts expand individual rights to privacy and autonomy, the question arises whether an individual has the right to end his or her life. This issue has been the basis of great legal, moral, and ethical debate. At common law, suicide was a felony punishable by forfeiture, or legal seizure by the government of the deceased's property.[10] Under modern American law, neither suicide nor attempted suicide is a crime, as these acts do not involve the killing of another. However, assisted suicide—the act of aiding or abetting another to commit suicide—has been made criminal by statute in 39 states, and it is still punishable as a common law crime in approximately six states.[11] A small number of states have not affirmatively addressed the issue, but Oregon is the only state that has explicitly legalized physician-assisted suicide in certain circumstances.[12] Other states have no such protection from prosecution for physicians who engage in assisted suicide of terminally ill patients.

It is important to note the distinction between euthanasia—the act or practice of painlessly putting to death persons suffering from a terminal and distressing disease as an act of mercy[13]—and physician-assisted suicide. In physician-assisted suicide, a medical doctor provides the necessary means, information, or both to enable the patient to accomplish death. The physician cannot administer the medication, or he or she can be found guilty of criminal homicide. The patient must get the physician's prescription, then self-administer it. In cases where the patient is too weak to self-administer, serious legal issues may arise if someone other than the physician becomes involved in the suicide attempt. If a medical assistant is aware of the nature and purpose of the medication and administers it nonetheless, he or she runs the risk of criminal prosecution because, legally, a homicide has occurred. Given that the actor specifically intends to bring about death, a murder prosecution is likely.

For example, in *People v. Cleave* (1991), the defendant was found guilty of murder in the second degree for participating in the death of a friend suffering from AIDS.[14] Similarly, in *People v. Hearn* (1998), the defendant was sentenced to

8.1 Web Exploration

Assisted Suicide

You can learn more about the particulars of Oregon's "Death with Dignity" Act that allows physician-assisted suicide without creating criminal liability for participating doctors by visiting the Oregon Health Division Web site at http://www.oregon.gov/DHS/ph/pas/index.shtml. Review the limitations to the applicability of the act and the statistics regarding patient characteristics and the number of times the act has been utilized since its enactment. Do you think the act should be adopted in other states? Why or why not? Should only doctors be exempt from criminal liability in assisted-suicide cases? What about family members?

one-and-a-half to four years in prison for shooting her terminally ill husband in a murder-suicide pact.[15]

Dr. Jack Kevorkian, the well-known advocate of euthanasia who admittedly performed more than 100 assisted suicides, was convicted following a televised *60 Minutes* recording of him administering a lethal injection to a terminally ill patient in Michigan. Prior to 1998, Dr. Kevorkian had been acquitted of murder several times. However, in 1996, the Michigan legislature enacted laws that affirmatively banned assisted suicide. A few days following the televised recording, Dr. Kevorkian was charged with first-degree murder. He was subsequently convicted of second-degree murder in the death of Thomas Youk, a terminally ill patient suffering from Lou Gehrig's disease. Dr. Kevorkian was sentenced to 10 to 25 years' imprisonment for causing the death and 3 to 7 years' imprisonment for delivery of a controlled substance.[16] Cases such as these reveal the ongoing controversy associated with assisted suicide, an issue that is not likely to be resolved in the near future.

 CRITICAL THINKING 8.1

1. Why are the definitions of the beginning and end of life so important in criminal homicide cases?

2. If you could change one or two elements of the current definitions, what would be the legal consequences of such changes? Why?

8.2 Elements of Criminal Homicide

As noted previously, the offense of criminal homicide can be understood as consisting of five basic elements:

1. An act or omission.
2. That causes the death.
3. Of another human being.

4. With criminally culpable *mens rea.*
5. Without lawful justification or excuse.

As with all criminal offenses, the prosecution must prove all of the elements that constitute criminal homicide beyond a reasonable doubt. It must be proven that a person committed an act or failed to perform an act that he or she was legally required to perform, and that the accused person's act or failure to act was the legal or *proximate cause* of another's death. There must also be proof that, at the time of the killing, the accused had a criminally culpable *mens rea* regarding the death or the acts leading to the death and cannot offer a reason for the killing that the law would recognize as justifying or excusing his or her conduct. If these elements are not proven, the prosecution will not be able to gain a conviction.

The highest level of culpability in criminal homicide is reserved for killings where the actor specifically intends to cause death and achieves that goal through **premeditation and deliberation**. However, a killing can still be charged as a criminal homicide even if the actor does *not* have the specific intent to kill. Those whose extremely reckless behavior indicates a *depraved indifference* to the well-being of others, and those who commit a killing during the commission of another felony such as rape or robbery, are also traditionally believed to deserve the most severe punishment. Because of the seriousness of these crimes, legislatures and courts have attempted to define their elements very carefully and comprehensively.

> **premeditation and deliberation**
>
> The mental state that raises second-degree murder to first-degree murder in jurisdictions that classify murder into two or more levels. It implies a cold-blooded killing.

Corpus Delicti **Requirement**

A basic requirement for a homicide prosecution under American law is that of the *corpus delicti*, which means the body or substance of the crime. The *corpus delicti* requirement exists for every crime, but in homicide it is especially important. It has two parts:

> **corpus delicti**
>
> The required proof that a crime has been committed. In homicide cases, this usually means the corpse of the victim.

1. The prosecution cannot use the defendant's statements or confession alone to prove that a crime has been committed. As unbelievable as it may sound, some people confess to crimes they have not committed, for a variety of reasons including mental infirmity. An example is John Karr, who confessed to killing JonBenét Ramsey, when DNA evidence exonerated him.
2. There must be proof that the victim died as a result of the accused person's criminal act. However, the prosecution does not have to produce a corpse to obtain a murder conviction. If no body is recovered, the fact of death can be proven circumstantially.

There are occasional exceptions to these strict requirements. The 1959 California case of *People v. Scott* was the first to hold that a murder conviction could be upheld when the evidence disclosed only the unexplained disappearance of the victim. In the *Scott* case, circumstantial evidence pointed to the defendant's husband as the perpetrator. Although the victim's body was not recovered, the U.S. Supreme Court refused to reverse Scott's murder conviction. As a result, its principle has become part of American jurisprudence.[17] (See Application Case 8.2.)

⚖️ Application Case 8.2

People v. Kimes and Kimes

On July 5, 1998, an 82-year-old millionaire vanished less than a month after renting an apartment in her mansion to Kenneth Kimes. Although the victim's body had not been recovered, prosecutors were successful in proving that Kenneth Kimes and his mother Sante Kimes had murdered Irene Silverman to steal her Manhattan townhouse worth $10 million. During a 15-week trial that included 130 witnesses, the prosecutors presented a trail of evidence that provided a roadmap of the detailed plans to kill the victim and dispose of her body. It was alleged that the victim had been strangled, wrapped with duct tape in a shower curtain and garbage bags, and placed in the trunk of the defendants' vehicle.

During the trial, prosecutors presented dozens of notebooks with incriminating entries of the defendants' plans and references made to the items used in the killing. Kenneth Kimes's fingerprints were recovered from tangled duct tape found in the apartment he rented from the victim. A critical piece of evidence was the deed to the mansion containing the victim's forged signature. The forged deed transferred ownership of the mansion to a company controlled by the Kimeses.

Following their convictions of second-degree murder, fraud, and conspiracy, Kenneth Kimes, 25, was sentenced to 125 years' imprisonment. His mother, Sante Kimes, 66, received 120 years. Approximately six months after his conviction, Kenneth

Evidence of Criminal Homicide In the prosecution of a criminal homicide case, a defendant's testimony is not enough. Investigators must be able to find corroborating evidence that proves that a murder did take place and that a particular person murdered a particular victim.

Kimes confessed to killing Irene Silverman and to throwing her body into "a ditch at a New Jersey construction site."

SOURCE: Barbara Ross and Alice McQuillian, *Missing Body of Evidence*, DAILY NEWS, May 14, 2000; Alice McQuillian, *Kimes Admits to Killing*, DAILY NEWS, Nov. 16, 2000.

Actus Reus

As with all criminal offenses, in order to create liability for criminal homicide, the act that produces death must be voluntary. (See Application Case 8.3.) Death to others that occurs while the actor is unconscious (for instance, suffering from a heart attack or an epileptic seizure) or during a genuine case of sleepwalking would therefore be excluded unless the actor somehow caused the involuntary condition. Examples of how an actor may cause such an involuntary condition include:

- Knowingly driving while sleepy.
- Knowingly drinking to the point of passing out.
- Disregarding advice from doctors by driving or operating dangerous equipment knowing that one is subject to heart failure or epilepsy.
- Driving or operating dangerous equipment while knowingly on any kind of psychoactive substance.

⚖ Application Case 8.3

People v. Newton

An example of a nonvolitional killing is the case of *People v. Newton*, in which the defendant, Huey Newton, a reputed member of the Black Panther organization, was involved in an altercation with police officers during a traffic stop. During the altercation, the defendant was shot in the midsection, and immediately thereafter the defendant shot and killed a police office at point-blank range. The defense was successful on appeal in arguing that his loss of consciousness, as a result of being shot in the midsection, could have made his conduct involuntary. In that case, if the jury believed his act was nonvolitional, he could not be held responsible for the shooting. The California Court of Appeal agreed, reversed his conviction, and held that Newton was entitled to a jury instruction on the subject of unconsciousness.

SOURCE: People v. Newton, 87 Cal. Rptr. 394 (Cal. Ct. App. 1970).

In these cases, although the actor may not be acting voluntarily at the actual time of the victim's death, the actor can still be held liable for placing himself or herself in the position where his or her involuntary conduct might be dangerous to others.

Finally, a person can also be held criminally liable for failure to act. In the case of criminal homicide, if the person has a legal duty to act on behalf of another but fails to do so, and death results, the person can be prosecuted for the death.

Mens Rea

Determining a defendant's state of mind at the time of a killing is a critical element in criminal homicide prosecutions. Not every criminal homicide is a murder, and it is the element of *mens rea*, or state of mind, that distinguishes murder from lesser forms of criminal homicide. Consequently, it also determines the amount of potential punishment to which a defendant may be sentenced.

The determination of a defendant's mental state at the time of the killing is sometimes difficult to establish for two main reasons: (1) the determination is made at some later point, and (2) the defendant's state of mind can only be established by circumstantial evidence (that is, facts outside of the defendant's mind). Hence, inferences (logical deductions) must be made about the defendant's thoughts based on statements, events, or both that occurred before, during, and after the killing.

As mentioned previously, not all forms of criminal homicide require an intent to kill. Even murder, which is considered the most serious form of criminal homicide, can be committed intentionally or unintentionally. Given this fact, legislatures and courts have developed highly refined principles concerning the mental state required to prove a particular criminal homicide charge.

murder
The killing of another with the mental element of malice aforethought.

manslaughter
The killing of another without the mental element of malice aforethought.

Generally, criminal homicides are divided into two categories: murder and manslaughter. Under the common law definitions, **murder** is the killing of another *with* malice aforethought, and **manslaughter** is the killing of another *without* malice aforethought. The specific elements of murder and manslaughter, and the various forms of malice aforethought, will be discussed later in this chapter. For now, it is important to note that under the revised common law, under which some felonies ceased to be punishable by death, the presence or absence of malice aforethought affected punishment. It became the sole determinant of whether one was guilty of murder, which remained a capital offense and thus punishable by death, or the non-capital offense of manslaughter.

Model Penal Code

The MPC has adopted a different method of classifying criminal homicides, but still uses the important *mens rea* element. The mental states specified in the MPC are designed to be more concise and understandable than the vague common law term "malice." Under the MPC, a person is guilty of criminal homicide if he or she purposely, knowingly, recklessly, or negligently causes the death of another human being.[18] Therefore, the MPC names three categories of criminal homicide: murder, manslaughter, and negligent homicide. In addition, the MPC holds a person guilty of criminal homicide if he or she purposely caused a suicide by force, duress, or deception. The MPC also makes aiding or soliciting suicide (but not assisted suicides, which were discussed earlier) punishable as an independent second-degree felony if one's conduct causes a suicide or suicide attempt.[19]

Inference of Mens Rea from Circumstantial Evidence

Rarely will an accused person admit to intentionally or purposefully causing someone's death. And even if the person does make such a confession, that evidence alone is legally insufficient to bring about a conviction. In order to secure a homicide conviction, a prosecutor must introduce evidence of the circumstances surrounding the death. Such circumstances might include the actor's presence at the scene of the killing, conduct in relation to the killing, or statements made about the killing to the police, friends, or others.

Other forms of circumstantial evidence of *mens rea* may be more difficult for the prosecution to argue, but may certainly be just as effective as a confession. The act of pointing a gun and shooting someone dead is evidence of an intent to kill. Such a circumstance, known as the deadly weapon doctrine, allows, but does not require, the jury to infer from the fact that the defendant used a deadly weapon upon the deceased that he intended to kill the deceased. This is circumstantial evidence of the accused's mental state through conduct. Another example is the accused's stalking the victim prior to the crime, with witnesses called to testify to the accused's behavior. A mutilated photograph of the victim in the defendant's possession can also be a form of circumstantial evidence of *mens rea*. A motive to kill is frequently used to prove intent. If the prosecution can trace back evidence of a disagreement or "bad blood" between the victim and the accused, this fact can lend itself to the inference of an intent to kill.

Although a motive (or reason) for committing the crime is not an essential legal requirement for any charge of criminal homicide, or any crime for that matter, identifying a particular reason why a particular defendant would kill a particular victim is extremely useful to the prosecution, which needs to convince a jury of guilt beyond a reasonable doubt. Investigators working on homicide cases should always be on the lookout for the possibility that someone has a motive to kill the victim. Typical criminal homicide motives include revenge, jealousy, financial gain, or concealment of damaging information. Investigators should also consider the possibility that someone may have made some incriminating statement implicating himself or herself in the killing and/or indicating whether the killing was intentional or unintentional. Confessions or partial admissions of guilt might be made to friends or family members of either the accused or the victim. Confessions are also overheard at police stations or courtrooms, or the accused may make statements to cellmates while in a jail or holding facility. It is important to investigate each of these avenues. If any of these are successful, any witness who has information about the motive or confession should be asked to give a formal (preferably written) statement and called as a witness at the trial.

Causation

As noted earlier in this chapter, in order for a defendant to be held criminally responsible for causing the death of another human being, the victim must be alive at the time of the defendant's actions. If, at the time of the defendant's actions, the victim is not yet alive or has already died, the defendant cannot be prosecuted for criminal homicide. Except in jurisdictions that consider "abuse of corpse" a crime, a defendant is not guilty of a crime if he inflicts injury on a victim who is already dead.

Determining death might appear to be a simple proposition. In fact, with widely varying definitions of death, legal issues surrounding what constitutes death may produce different criminal law outcomes from state to state. In the following sections, you will examine some of the different rules that are used.

Year-and-a-Day Rule

With advances in medical science, a victim may not die immediately following fatal injuries. Death may not occur until months or even years after the injury. At common law, in order to prevent a prolonged and uncertain threat of prosecution, and in order to prevent the potential for an unjust conviction, the year-and-a-day rule was created. The **year-and-a-day-rule** holds that if the victim does not die within a year and a day of the time the injury was inflicted by the defendant, the defendant cannot be convicted of being the legal cause of the victim's death. This time limit is an *absolute rule* of criminal liability. If a victim dies after this specified period of time, the defendant cannot be prosecuted for any form of criminal homicide in relation to that death. However, depending on the circumstances under which the injuries occurred, the accused may still be charged with and convicted of attempted murder.

Although this common law rule currently remains in effect in a number of states, other states have extended the time period to three years and a day. The change has occurred for the same reason that the definition of the end of life has—advancements in medical technology. Figure 8.2 indicates the current status of the year-and-a-day rule by state.

year-and-a-day rule
The causation rule that requires that, in order to classify a killing as a homicide, the victim must die within a year and a day after the act causing death occurred.

The "But For" Test and Multiple Causes

Questions of causation arise even if a long period of time does not pass between infliction of injury by the defendant and the victim's death. In the ordinary course of events, a defendant will be held criminally liable for a death if the other elements of criminal homicide are met *and* if without the defendant's conduct the victim would not have died at that point in time. If the defendant's conduct shortened the victim's life even by a minute, that defendant is guilty of criminal homicide. Put another way, "but for" the actions of the defendant, the victim would not be dead.

In modern times, even this seemingly simple test has become difficult to apply in cases where the defendant's conduct is not the direct cause of the victim's death. Events that occur after the defendant's conduct but before the victim's death, and which directly contribute to the death, have raised special concerns. These events, legally termed *intervening acts*, may or may not terminate the original defendant's criminal liability for the death. Over time, the courts have determined that in situations involving intervening acts, the defendant will be considered the initial actor and will not be relieved of legal responsibility for causing the death. An exception to this rule is when the intervening act was totally unforeseeable, highly abnormal, completely independent of the defendant's actions, or any combination of these circumstances.

Through case law, courts have determined that complications such as medical malpractice and the intervening criminal acts of others are foreseeable consequences of subjecting an innocent victim to injury. These courts hold the initial perpetrator responsible for all subsequent injuries, including death, that occur to the victim at the hands of third parties. Other courts use a fairness analysis. The jury is instructed to decide whether or not, in light of the intervening act, it is still fair to hold the initial actor liable for the death. (See Application Case 8.4.) If an intervening actor meets the five required elements of criminal homicide, that person can also be held responsible for the death. Hence, a single death can create criminal liability for multiple perpetrators.

⚖️ F I G U R E   8 . 2

Current Status of the Year-and-a-Day Rule, by State

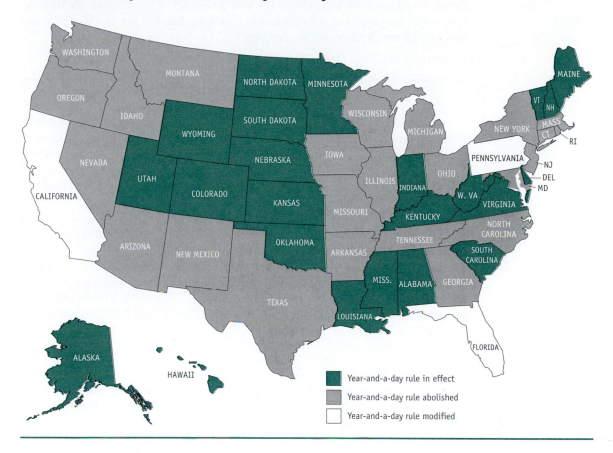

Year-and-a-day rule in effect

Year-and-a-day rule abolished

Year-and-a-day rule modified

⚖️ Application Case 8.4

Kibbe v. Henderson

Two defendants met the victim in a bar and decided to rob him. Although the victim was already so drunk that two bartenders refused to serve him, the defendants took him to yet another bar where they were all served drinks. The defendants then drove the victim to a rural area, stole his money, and left him on the side of an unlit highway. The victim was left without his eyeglasses and with his trousers down around his ankles. Shortly thereafter, a college student struck and killed the victim, who by that time was sitting in the middle of the road waving his arms in a drunken stupor. The surprised driver never applied his brakes before running the victim over.

Despite the defendants' objections, the Court of Appeals confirmed murder convictions against the two of them. The court found sufficient evidence to support a jury's conclusion that but for their actions that put the victim in harm's way, the victim would not have been killed. The intervening act of the student (striking the victim with his truck) was not sufficient to terminate their liability. The United States Supreme Court also affirmed the decision.

SOURCE: Kibbe v. Henderson, 534 F.2d 493 (C.A.N.Y. 1976); Kibbe v. Henderson, 431 U.S. 145 (1977).

Causation may become a critical issue when the *actus reus* of the criminal homicide is an omission, which means that a death is caused by the defendant's failure to act. Assume, for example, that the victim's grandson, who is heir to his grandmother's fortune, purposely withholds his grandmother's medication and causes her to die of a heart attack. A critical issue for the prosecution is to prove that the victim died due to the absence of the heart medication and not of natural causes.

Another important factor is any individual characteristic of the victim that contributes to his or her death. Although some of these are the victim's choice, the defendant must accept the risk that a selected victim may have such characteristics. In the English case *Regina v. Blaue* (1975), the defendant sexually attacked a woman who was a Jehovah's Witness. During the attack, the defendant stabbed the woman, who subsequently died when she refused to accept a blood transfusion. Her refusal of the transfusion did not relieve the defendant of responsibility for criminal homicide.[20]

The "Substantial Factor" Test

On relatively rare occasions, two or more forces sufficient to cause death may occur simultaneously. In this instance, the "but for" test of causation fails. Even if one of the perpetrators had not acted, the victim would still be dead at that moment in time. To avoid fruitless finger-pointing and to insure that equally guilty people are subject to punishment, the substantial factor test was devised. An applicable example is a drive-by shooting in which three perpetrators shoot the same victim. If medical records demonstrate that bullets from all three guns struck vital organs while the victim was still alive, the law does not require that the medical examiner also determine how much blood was lost from each wound. If the medical examination establishes that each shooter's conduct was a "substantial factor" in bringing about the victim's death, each may be held liable for causing the victim's death. As an alternative, these codefendants may also be held liable for the death under accomplice liability, which you read about in Chapter 4.

Without Lawful Justification or Excuse

Under the law, if a killing occurs under circumstances that are legally justified, the actor is not guilty of criminal homicide. *Justification*, as a defense to a criminal homicide charge, means that the actor had a right or privilege to engage in conduct that otherwise would have been criminal. Usually, the defense of justification focuses on the circumstances of the incident, including the conduct of the accused and the victim. An example of a justifiable homicide is a situation in which a person kills someone who he or she reasonably believes poses an imminent threat of serious physical injury or death to himself or herself, or to another individual. The rules regarding the use of force in self-defense, in defense of others, and in the prevention of a crime are somewhat complex and tend to vary from state to state; they were discussed more fully in Chapter 6. In general, it is accepted that lethal force is justified in the defense of human life, but not for the sole purpose of protecting property.

A person can have a legal *excuse* as a defense to a criminal homicide charge when the death occurs under circumstances that the law recognizes as lacking moral culpability. This type of defense, also discussed in Chapter 6, focuses on the status or condition of the defendant. For example, a person who is too young to understand the consequences of his or her actions, as well as an individual suffering from mental illness or involuntary intoxication, may be excused from liability for acts that cause death.

In most states, the defense must present evidence to support a justification or excuse. If the jury accepts this evidence, the defendant will be acquitted. These complete defenses that result in acquittal should not be confused with partial or mitigating defenses, discussed later in this chapter. Partial or mitigating defenses only reduce murder to voluntary manslaughter and still carry a penalty.

CRITICAL THINKING 8.2

1. Why is the concept of *actus reus,* or voluntary action, crucial in proving criminal homicide?

2. If the *actus reus* of a crime can also prove *mens rea,* have you then proven criminal homicide? Why or why not?

8.3 Types and Degrees of Criminal Homicide

At early common law, the commission of any felony was punishable by death. Since criminal homicide was a felony, degrees of criminal homicide were unnecessary. As punishment for crimes became more graduated, it became necessary to distinguish between crimes that warranted the death penalty and those that did not. Quite simply, the common law definition of criminal homicide provides that, unless there are circumstances that excuse or justify the killing, all killings with malice are murder, and all killings without malice are manslaughter.

Today, many states have decided that a number of factors, primarily related to the actor's mental state, can be used to distinguish between different levels of culpability (and the punishment deserved) in homicide cases. The various types and degrees of homicide include murder, voluntary manslaughter, and involuntary manslaughter. The distinctions among these different kinds of homicide, as well as the applicable defenses, are explained throughout the next two sections.

8.2 Web Exploration

Homicide Trends

Y ou can learn more about trends in criminal homicide, including statistical information about victims, perpetrators, types of homicides, arrest rates, and more, by visiting the Bureau of Justice Statistics Web site at http://www.ojp.usdoj.gov/bjs/homicide/homtrnd.htm. Review statistics and descriptive information on crimes, victims, and criminal offenders.

CRITICAL THINKING 8.3

1. How do common law and modern laws differ in regard to criminal homicide?

8.4 Murder

The crime of murder requires the five basic elements of all criminal homicides: *actus reus, mens rea*, causation, death of the victim, and a lack of lawful justification or excuse. Under both common law and modern American law, any killing done with the intent to kill is murder, and any killing accomplished when the actor intends to maim or seriously injure the victim is also murder, even if the accused did not intend to kill the victim. An example of this would be a killing that resulted from a bar fight when the accused attacked the victim with a broken bottle, intending only to hurt him badly.

Any killing that results from extreme reckless conduct is also murder, even if the accused did not intend to kill but was aware that someone's death would be likely. As another example, a workman who throws a heavy beam from the top of a skyscraper onto the busy street below is culpable for murder if the beam strikes and kills a passing pedestrian.[21] The fact that the workman did not specifically desire to cause anyone's death is irrelevant.

Finally, if the accused causes a death in the course of committing a felony (or, at common law, in an attempt to resist a legal arrest), the law implies that the *mens rea* for murder is present from the intent to commit the felony. This form of implied malice, which is discussed in the next section, gives rise to a prosecution for murder under the felony murder rule, which is also discussed later in this section.

Malice Aforethought

Malice aforethought, as you have already learned in this chapter, is a special legal term that refers to the *mens rea* element of murder at common law. As previously noted, this element distinguishes murder from the lesser homicides of voluntary and involuntary manslaughter. Contrary to popular belief, malice is *not* synonymous with intent. The term **malice** connotes an "abandoned and malignant heart"; it is not limited to intentional killings, since even a wanton or reckless state of mind may constitute malice. Moreover, the word *aforethought* is misleading, since the mental state required for murder can be formed at the moment of the action causing death, or at least immediately

malice

A state of mind connoting an "abandoned and malignant heart." It is not limited to the specific intent to kill, since even a wanton or reckless state of mind may constitute malice.

beforehand. For example, a defendant can be found to have killed with malice afore-thought without having planned the killing or taken any other previous action.[22]

Malice aforethought is not a single state of mind, but five distinct states of mind that sometimes overlap. Each form existing alone is sufficient to support a murder conviction. The common law defines malice aforethought as any one of the following five mental states:

1. The specific intent to kill another human being.
2. The intent to inflict grievous bodily injury or harm upon another.
3. The intent to act in a manner that shows extreme reckless disregard for the value of human life.
4. The intent to commit a felony that results in the death of another human being.
5. The intent to resist a known lawful arrest.

Causing a death with the specific intent to kill constitutes *express malice*, but malice aforethought may be either express or implied. In the five states of mind listed above, only the first defines express malice; the other four define different types of implied malice. Under common law definitions and the current laws of many states, *implied malice* occurs when the actor causes death without intending to kill, but with a state of mind that is extremely dangerous to other persons.

The Felony Murder Rule

At common law, a person was guilty of murder if he or she killed another person, even accidentally, during an attempt or perpetration of a felony or while in flight from the perpetration of the felony. Since all murders and felonies were punishable by death at common law, it was unnecessary to distinguish between intentional killings and those caused unintentionally. Since most felonies and many types of murder are no longer punishable by death under modern criminal law, modern felony murder statutes vary considerably from the original common law.

The common law **felony murder rule** originally created murder liability for all deaths that occurred as a result of the felony participants' perpetrating, attempting, or fleeing the felony. Potential victims of felony murder included:

- The intended victim of the underlying felony.
- Innocent bystanders.
- Law enforcement officers.
- Non-law enforcement persons attempting to rescue the victim.
- All co-felons.

Deterrence, which you learned about in Chapter 7, is the primary purpose behind application of the felony murder rule. Deterrence is seen as justifying the most severe punishment. In those states that divide murder into degrees, even if an individual's death was unintentional and unforeseeable, the law may authorize imposition of the death penalty for deaths resulting from the commission of certain felonies.

Whether or not the felony murder rule acts as a deterrent, it does lessen the burden on the prosecution by requiring only proof of the defendant's intent to commit the underlying felony that resulted in the death. Under this rule, the prosecution does not have the burden of proving specific intent to kill. It must only prove that the accused intended

felony murder rule
The rule that when the accused kills in the course of committing a felony, the *mens rea* for murder is present in the intent to commit the felony, and therefore murder has been committed.

to commit a felony, such as a robbery, and that a person died as a consequence of the robbery, the attempted robbery, or flight from having attempted or committed the robbery.

The felony murder rule imposes a form of strict liability: It applies as long as there was intent to commit the felony and a death resulted.[23] The rule is applicable whether the victim is killed accidentally, negligently, or recklessly. Again, no *specific* intent to cause death is necessary.

Given the severity of the potential punishment and given that most felonies are no longer punishable by death, modern statutes have placed some limitations on the felony murder rule. For example, most states restrict the application of the rule to **inherently dangerous felonies**, also known as *forcible felonies*, which are those that pose a significant threat to human life. These felonies typically include residential burglary, arson, rape, robbery, kidnapping, and forcible sodomy. In states such as California and Pennsylvania, where murder is divided into degrees, killings that occur as a result of these enumerated (or specified) felonies often constitute first-degree murder, whereas killings that occur during the commission of other dangerous felonies constitute second-degree murder. In short, although felony murder liability was limited to unintentional killings at common law, in a number of modern jurisdictions the felony murder rule can be applied to both intentional and unintentional killings, even if the death was unforeseeable, unintended, or accidental. (See Application Case 8.5.)

inherently dangerous felonies

Felonies involving conduct that is inherently dangerous to human life, such as rape, arson, and armed robbery.

⚖ Application Case 8.5

People v. Stamp

During a robbery, one defendant remained in the car outside while the other two felons forcibly robbed the victims. During the robbery, the felons forced the victims to lie down on the floor and ordered them to stay in that position until after they left the location. A short time after the felons left, one of the victims died of a heart attack as a result of shock. All three defendants were convicted and sentenced to life imprisonment. The court of appeals reasoned that under the felony murder rule, the defendants were responsible for "all killing committed by him or his accomplices in the course of the felony."

SOURCE: People v. Stamp, 2 Cal. App. 3d 203, 209–11 (Cal. Ct. App. 1969).

Another major distinction between the felony murder rule at common law and its modern-day variations is the scope of vicarious liability for participating co-felons. As originally formulated, under agency theory, a person driving the getaway car for an armed bank robbery in which a teller is shot and killed by one of the robbers would have the same liability as the shooter. Even co-felons who are not present at the bank but who participated in the planning of the robbery could be held liable for the death. In addition, co-felons shot by the police during the course of the attempt, commission, or flight from the robbery could be seen as victims of felony murder and their deaths charged against the surviving felons as murder.

Several states, Pennsylvania being among the first, were troubled by the fact that a single death could be both a murder and justifiable homicide. In response, they

8.1 On the Job

Forensic Scientist

Description and Duties: Work in a crime laboratory. Perform routine analytical and experimental work, participate in the search and collection of physical evidence, and prepare reports of findings. May include analyzing blood specimens collected from convicted offenders for DNA identification; comparing footwear, tool, and tire impressions; identifying gunshot residue from subjects and victims; and identifying and grouping blood and seminal stains.

    Salary: Salaries range from approximately $24,000 to $60,000, depending on the level of experience.

    Other Information: Education requirements include graduation from an accredited four-year college with a major in criminalistics, biology, chemistry, biochemistry, or a related field. Some positions will substitute work experience for college education, and previous work experience is either preferred or required for all positions. In addition, most employers prefer some graduate work, such as a master's degree in criminalistics, and recommend that forensic scientists make an effort to keep updated on developments in this field.

SOURCE: Southern Association of Forensic Scientists, http://www.southernforensic.org/employment_opportunities.htm.

began excluding from felony murder liability the deaths of co-felons killed by police during the felony attempt, commission, or flight. In *Commonwealth v. Redline* (1958), the court held that the felony murder rule did not apply to the death of a codefendant who was shot by a police officer during an attempt to apprehend the defendants.[24]

    In virtually all cases, courts will find felony murder liability if death was a foreseeable outcome in carrying out the felony. For example, the courts have held that an accused who intentionally sets fire to a building can be convicted of murder on the basis of felony murder if a firefighter dies while trying to put out the blaze. Similarly, courts have found felony murder liability in cases where the victim is killed as a result of being shot during an armed robbery.

    Under modern law, there is much controversy surrounding the application of the felony murder rule. Some states evaluate the facts of the particular case to determine the dangerousness of the felony and apply the felony murder rule on a case-by-case basis. Common forms of inherently dangerous felonies include escape from lawful custody and sexual abuse of children. On the other hand, the Michigan Supreme Court has abolished the rule,[25] and the MPC originally proposed its elimination. Instead, the MPC decided to propose that the felony murder rule should not apply if the defendant can establish that he did not cause an unintentional killing with an "indifference to the value of human life."[26]

Reckless Disregard for the Value of Human Life

In the absence of felony murder liability, prosecution for murder can still be pursued on the theory of reckless indifference to the value of human life. As noted earlier, even when the defendant does not intend to kill, his or her actions may be so outrageous that they provide evidence of a strong disregard for the well-being of others. A defendant acts *recklessly* when he or she consciously disregards a substantial and unjustifiable risk that criminal harm will occur. In situations evidencing inherent danger, the charge of killing by wanton recklessness or depraved indifference is commonly pursued in place of the charge of felony murder. (See Application Case 8.6.)

⚖️ Application Case 8.6

Taylor v. Superior Court

In *Taylor v. Superior Court*, the defendant was charged with first-degree murder when a botched robbery caused the death of one his accomplices. The defendant was waiting in a getaway car while two other accomplices robbed a liquor store. During the robbery, the other two accomplices acted in a reckless manner by provoking and repeatedly threatening to execute the storeowner they held at gunpoint. The storeowner shot and killed one of the robbers in self-defense. While the defendant was unaware at the time of what transpired in the liquor store, under accomplice liability, he was held liable for the natural and probable consequences of the acts of the other accomplices. The defendant was charged with first-degree murder instead of second-degree murder because the conduct of his accomplices was so extreme as to constitute aggravating circumstances.

SOURCE: Taylor v. Superior Court, 477 P.2d 131 (Cal. 1970).

Examples of conduct that the courts have recognized as wantonly reckless include drag racing on public streets and games of Russian roulette. Because these activities create a high risk of death and are not legally justifiable, defendants involved in them may face murder convictions. Like the rationale behind the felony murder rule, the high level of potential punishment is expected to deter such behaviors. Any dangerous behavior that results in an unintended death can be evaluated to see if it fits a wantonly reckless standard. The question of whether the defendant's conduct is merely reckless, and thus liable for a conviction for involuntary manslaughter, or is wantonly reckless and liable for a murder conviction, is a question of fact for a jury.

The Division of Murder into Degrees

Many states assign first-degree and second-degree levels for the offense of murder, and others have divided the degrees even further. In both cases, they divide murder into degrees based on the level of culpability of the accused, the severity of the crime, or special circumstances under which the killing was committed. Other states follow the MPC.

Where the death penalty is allowed, first-degree murder is usually a capital offense. **Capital murder** is a charge of murder with the maximum punishment of

capital murder
A charge of murder with the maximum punishment of death, often called murder in the first degree.

death, which is usually only applicable to murder in the first degree. Murder in the first degree is committed under the following circumstances:

- An intentional killing that is aggravated by premeditation and deliberation.
- An unintentional killing committed by poison, torture, ambush, or bomb.
- A killing occurring during the commission of specifically enumerated or inherently dangerous felonies (felony murder rule).

In those states that distinguish between first- and second-degree murder, second-degree murder is any form of murder committed with malice aforethought, either express or implied, which does not amount to murder in the first degree. The following statutes provide some specific examples of how to determine whether a murder is in the first degree.

Pennsylvania

In Pennsylvania, a person is guilty of criminal homicide if he or she intentionally, knowingly, recklessly, or negligently causes the death of another human being. There are three ways in which a killing can constitute murder in the first degree:

1. Willful, deliberate, and premeditated killings.
2. Killings perpetrated in one of a number of specific ways, such as by means of poison or torture.
3. Killings that occur during the perpetration or attempt of an enumerated felony.

All other unlawful killings are considered second-degree murder.[27]

California

Current California law defines murder as the unlawful killing of a human being or fetus with malice aforethought.[28] First-degree murder is any murder committed in a specific manner, such as by poisoning or lying in wait, or any other kind of willful, deliberate, and premeditated killing, or any killing committed while in the act of certain enumerated felonies.[29]

In *People v. Anderson* (1968), a California court developed three elements that would show deliberation (see Application Case 8.7). The court concluded that proof of any one, or any combination, of the following elements was necessary:

1. Planning activity prior to the killing.
2. Evidence of a motive.
3. A manner of killing "so particular and exacting that the defendant must have intentionally killed according to a 'preconceived design.'"

⚖️ Application Case 8.7

People v. Anderson

The defendant killed the 10-year-old daughter of his live-in girlfriend, and the victim's body was found with 60 stab wounds. There was evidence that the defendant had been drinking and may have been drunk at the time of the murder. In addition, the defendant had told conflicting stories to the victim's mother and brother about her whereabouts. The court found that the facts surrounding the murder were insufficient to support first-degree murder on premeditation and deliberation, because there was no evidence of any planning activity by the defendant. In addition, there was no evidence of a motive, nor was the stabbing committed in such a way that would indicate a "preconceived design."

SOURCE: People v. Anderson, 447 P.2d 942 (Cal. 1968).

In California, as in Pennsylvania, all unlawful, unjustified, and unexcused killings that are not first-degree murder are considered second-degree murder.

Elevation to First-Degree Murder

One way that second-degree murder can be elevated to first-degree murder is by premeditation and deliberation, which implies a cold-blooded killer who plans and plots to end the life of another. The law seeks to separate the individual who kills spontaneously or impulsively from the individual who kills after deliberation or reflection. The required length of time the accused thought about and reflected on the killing varies from state to state. (See Application Case 8.8.)

⚖️ Application Case 8.8

State v. Gounagias
People v. Berry

In *State v. Gounagias*, the victim had committed sodomy on the defendant while the defendant was unconscious. For nearly a month, the victim bragged about the incident to others, and the defendant finally killed the victim because of the severe humiliation. The appellate court held that too much time had elapsed between the provocation and the killing and denied the defendant the legal right to take the provocation issue to the jury.

In contrast to *Gounagias*, the defendant in *People v. Berry*, who strangled his wife with a telephone cord after waiting 20 hours in the apartment for her to return, was still allowed to claim heat of passion. The defendant appealed his conviction of murder in the first-degree. The California court stated that there was sufficient evidence of a two-week period of provocation by defendant's wife who had taunted him with her infidelity, possible pregnancy by the person she claimed to be in love with, and demands for a divorce. The court found that although the defendant had waited in the apartment for 20 hours, because of the long course of provocation he did not have time to cool off and killed in an uncontrolled rage when his wife returned to the apartment and started screaming. In short, the defendant's passions were rekindled by the victim's behavior when she returned to the apartment.

SOURCE: State v. Gounagias, 153 P. 9 (Wash. 1915); People v. Berry, 556 P.2d 777 (Cal. 1976).

There is no particular time needed to establish premeditation and deliberation. Some courts have held that premeditation can be accomplished by a brief moment of thought and that the term does not imply any particular duration of thought or consideration.[30] Others have held that premeditation and deliberation require more than momentary consideration. Many modern courts require a reasonable period of time of deliberation, but some require a significant period of actual reflection.

It has been suggested that jurors evaluating prior calculation and design should consider the following important factors:

- Whether the accused knew the victim before the killing.
- Whether the accused and the victim were on bad terms with each other or had a strained relationship.
- Whether the accused gave careful thought and preparation to the weapon used and to the place where the killing occurred.[31]

The elevation of murder in the second degree to murder in the first degree focuses on the manner or method of killing and assesses a higher level of criminal culpability. For example, California Penal Code § 188 specifies that murder perpetrated by means of "destructive device or explosive, knowing use of ammunition designed primarily to penetrate metal or armor, poison, lying in wait, torture . . ." is murder in the first degree. In addition, as previously discussed under the felony murder rule, the laws of some states designate specific felonies (including inherently dangerous felonies) as so likely to endanger human life that a killing committed during the perpetration of such a felony constitutes murder in the first degree. Finally, numerous states consider a killing committed under any of the following circumstances murder in the first degree:

- The killing occurred during an attempt to escape lawful custody.
- The person killed was a police officer or prison guard.
- The killer was serving a life sentence in prison.

Degrees of Murder under the Model Penal Code

As you know, the MPC specifies the mental states or *mens rea* of criminal conduct as purposeful, knowing, reckless, or negligent. Consistent with this classification, killing done purposely, knowingly, or with extreme recklessness is murder; killing done negligently is manslaughter, which is discussed in the next section. In addition, murder is any killing accomplished during the perpetration of typical enumerated felonies, such as robbery and rape.

The MPC does not distinguish between first-degree and second-degree murder. It simply notes that "murder is a felony of the first degree," and specifies the circumstances under which a person convicted of murder may be sentenced to death.[32]

Defenses to Murder

As previously stated, not all homicides are criminal. A killing done with a justification or excuse, which you read about earlier in this chapter and in Chapter 6, releases the individual from criminal liability. Both justifications and excuses are affirmative defenses to murder, which means that the accused person who raises the defense is required to prove it. The standard of proof is usually a *preponderance of the evidence*, which is considerably lower than *beyond a reasonable doubt*. On the other hand, the prosecution has the burden of proving all of the elements of the crime beyond a reasonable doubt *and* disproving the existence of the accused person's defense.

As noted earlier in this chapter, some killings can be justified and some actions can be excused through circumstances. Although it may seem that all killings should result in criminal punishment, there are many common exceptions:

- Soldiers who kill enemies during wartime.
- A warden who approves the lawful electrocution of a convicted serial killer.
- A person who kills an armed assailant in self-defense, if he or she is rightfully protecting self or family. (See Application Case 8.9.)

⚖️ Application Case 8.9

Law v. State

The defendant was convicted for mistakenly shooting and killing a police officer whom he believed to be a burglar. The defendant, who was black, had had his home burglarized soon after moving into a predominately white neighborhood. Following the first break-in, the defendant purchased a shotgun. Shortly thereafter, a neighbor called the police believing that a second break-in was in progress. The police attempted to enter the house from where they believed the burglar had gained entrance. The defendant heard the sounds made by the police officers and thought that they were burglars. He shot through the closed door twice, killing one of the responding police officers. On appeal from his conviction for murder, the defendant argued that he was allowed to use deadly force to defend his home. The court disagreed and held that, even defending one's own home, the use of deadly force must be necessary under the circumstances.

SOURCE: Law v. State, 318 A.2d 859 (Md. 1974).

In certain instances, the existence of a mitigating factor (partial defense) may justify a reduction of the charge from murder to voluntary manslaughter, which you will read about in the following discussion.

CRITICAL THINKING 8.4

1. Why do you think provocation can be a mitigating factor in a case of voluntary manslaughter?

2. Do you think that the felony murder rule should be used in all states or rejected by them (as in Michigan)? Why?

8.5 Manslaughter

Voluntary manslaughter is an intentional, unlawful killing of a human being without malice aforethought. Although early common law did not distinguish between voluntary and involuntary manslaughter, and only intentional killings were mitigated to manslaughter at common law, many states have modified the common law rule. Today, many provide for involuntary manslaughter to include killings that are unintentional.

Voluntary Manslaughter

At common law, there was only one form of manslaughter, which is now often referred to as voluntary manslaughter. **Voluntary manslaughter** is, by definition, killing committed *without malice aforethought*. This means that the killing would ordinarily be considered murder, but because of some mitigating factor the actor did not have the requisite state of mind for murder. The absence of malice aforethought thus makes manslaughter a lesser offense than murder. It is therefore considered one of the partial defenses, or mitigating defenses, to the charge of murder.

voluntary manslaughter
An intentional, unlawful killing of a human being without malice aforethought.

A person is guilty of voluntary manslaughter if the accused had an intent to kill or to cause great bodily harm, under any one (or any combination) of the following circumstances. Although the accused in these cases had an intent to kill or to cause great bodily harm, the law recognizes the three following circumstances as negating (taking away) those guilty states of mind.

Provocation

At common law, before a killing could be downgraded from murder to manslaughter, the actor must have been provoked in a way that caused him or her to act in the *heat of passion*. Many modern statutes allow similar mitigation if the defendant acts in a state of *extreme emotional distress* or disturbance. Under the common law rule, which still exists in some jurisdictions, in order to successfully make a provocation defense, the accused is required to show that at the time of the killing he or she:

- Acted in the *heat of passion*
- Caused by *legally sufficient provocation*
- Of such a degree as would cause a person of *reasonable, ordinary temperament* to lose normal self-control.

In addition, the accused must not have had sufficient time to cool off before engaging in the killing act.

Under any provocation claim, in order for a killing to be mitigated from murder to manslaughter, the provocation must involve a sudden and intense passion, and the defendant must have been in a state of passion when the killing occurred. The common law requirement for such **mitigation** is very strict, and it limits the situations in which a killer can claim heat of passion.

mitigation
The reduction, or lessening, of a penalty or punishment imposed by law.

At common law, an accused could claim a heat of passion defense only if he had legally sufficient provocation. Legally sufficient provocation was limited to the following categories:

- Harmful battery.
- An assault with the intent to kill or seriously injure.

- Infidelity of a spouse.
- Serious injury to a close relative.
- A known illegal arrest.

Claims of provocation that fell outside of these categories were unlikely to be successful.

It is important to note these additional provocation issues:

- In states that continue to follow the common law today, the last category above no longer has legal relevance.
- At common law, verbal insults alone, no matter how vile or abusive, were not considered legally sufficient provocation.
- At common law, an accused person who was not present at the provoking event could still claim a heat of passion defense. For instance, somebody who knew from a reliable source that an enemy had shot his or her mother, then in turn shot and killed this enemy, could claim this defense.
- No single emotion constitutes the state of passion. Many emotions can be involved, such as fear, jealousy, severe humiliation, or some other intense emotion.

The trend in modern criminal law is to make the heat of passion less restrictive. In fact, in order to claim heat of passion as a defense, specific circumstances of provocation are no longer required. For instance, under the MPC and New York State law, killing can be downgraded to voluntary manslaughter if it was the result of extreme emotional disturbance for which there is reasonable explanation or excuse. Hence, an accused can claim a provocation defense under any set of circumstances, as long as there is a reasonable explanation or excuse for his or her emotional state at the time of the killing. A jury will ultimately weigh the reasoning of the defendant's response to the provoking event.

At common law, a heat of passion claim was assessed by an *objective test*, which showed that the defendant suffered adequate provocation before committing the act. **Adequate provocation** means that the acts or conduct of the person killed would be sufficient to cause a person of reasonable, ordinary temperament to lose self-control. Obviously, an accused person with a short temper cannot use this personal trait as part of his or her heat of passion claim. Today, the test used by New York and the MPC allows for consideration of both objective and subjective factors when a claim of provocation is made.[33]

adequate provocation
When the acts or conduct of the person killed would be sufficient to cause a person of reasonable, ordinary temperament to lose self-control.

The accused cannot claim heat of passion if he or she had sufficient time to cool off. Again, the objective "reasonable person" standard is used to determine whether or not a reasonable person could have cooled off from the intense passion in the time span between the provocation and the killing. Unlike the provocation element, which may be subjectively measured to assess a defendant's mental state, the cooling-off period is measured from an objective standpoint. Therefore, it does not take into account the defendant's mental state or characteristics; the time period is strictly measured by the time it would take the ordinary person to cool off. In addition, some courts have allowed a provocation claim where original passions had cooled off but were rekindled by subsequent actions by the victim.

In summary, the courts have determined that the cooling-off period for a heat of passion defense should be evaluated on a case-by-case basis under the circumstances presented by each individual case.

Mistaken Justification (Imperfect Self-Defense)

In some states, a private citizen who mistakenly uses deadly force can be held criminally liable for the death of the victim. For instance, Nino killed Melanie when Nino believed that Melanie was about to rob him. If Nino was wrong in his assessment of the facts, and it is later determined that he was not justified in the use of deadly force, he can be held criminally liable. A few states will not hold an individual liable if his or her belief that a felony was being committed is reasonable. In contrast, if the accused unreasonably believed that deadly force was necessary in self-defense or in defense of others, the accused will not be charged with murder but may still be charged with voluntary manslaughter. However the individual state statute is drafted, an **imperfect self-defense** claim such as this is sufficient to reduce murder to manslaughter. In light of the potential exposure to some criminal liability, private citizens who use deadly force to protect themselves or to prevent a crime do so at their own risk.

Diminished Mental Capacity

Finally, if an accused is suffering from *diminished capacity* at the time of the killing, he or she may be entitled to have a murder charge reduced to voluntary manslaughter. Diminished capacity can be demonstrated by evidence of extreme voluntary intoxication, such as from drugs or alcohol, or it may be due to mental illness that does not rise to the level of insanity. In the case of voluntary intoxication, because the defendant is willfully in a situation where his or her conduct is harmful to others, he or she cannot completely escape criminal liability. On the other hand, since the effects of the drugs or alcohol may impede a person's ability to form the clear-minded intent to kill, the intoxication negates the higher level of intent. One type of exception to this is that some courts will allow a murder conviction anyway if the level of intoxication and the conduct accompanying it evidences a reckless disregard for life. (See Application Case 8.10.)

imperfect self-defense
A partial defense that reduces a murder charge to voluntary manslaughter, where the claim of self-defense fails because it is not objectively reasonable but is honestly believed by the accused.

⚖️ Application Case 8.10

Montana v. Egelhoff

In *Montana v. Egelhoff*, the state prosecuted the defendant for murder, but the defendant Egelhoff claimed that he was too intoxicated to have formed the necessary mental state to be guilty of murder. Since Montana's statute prohibited a criminal defense based on voluntary intoxication, the defendant argued that he had a constitutional right to present this defense to the jury. The state court disagreed and refused his request to present a defense of intoxication to the jury. He was convicted of murder.

On appeal, the U.S. Supreme Court held that submitting the defense of voluntary intoxication to the jury is not a "fundamental principle of justice." Therefore, the Court upheld Montana's statutory ban, ruling that it did not violate the U.S. Constitution. This Supreme Court decision has a substantial impact on an accused person's ability to claim intoxication as a defense to murder, because any state can employ the same type of statutory ban as Montana's on voluntary intoxication as a defense.

SOURCE: Montana v. Egelhoff, 518 U.S. 37 (1996).

Involuntary Manslaughter

involuntary manslaughter

A criminal homicide that encompasses a killing done without intent to kill, and without such indifference to human life as to constitute implied malice, as a result of criminally negligent conduct on the part of the defendant.

Some states divide manslaughter into involuntary and voluntary manslaughter. An actor is guilty of **involuntary manslaughter** if he or she causes an unintentional killing while acting in a criminally negligent or nonwantonly reckless manner, which is defined as creating a high and unreasonable risk of death or great bodily harm. Criminally negligent conduct is also referred to as *culpable negligence* or *gross negligence*. Mere negligence, or carelessness, is sufficient to create civil liability, which could result in a lawsuit, but insufficient to create criminal liability. For criminal negligence, the defendant's conduct must be so different from that of the ordinarily careful person that it shows an indifference to the consequences. This is different from recklessness as a *mens rea*, which requires that the defendant must be aware of the risk of harm but nonetheless disregard it. Rather, a defendant can be held liable under a gross negligence *mens rea* standard even if he or she did not specifically consider the possible harm that would result from his or her conduct—if an ordinarily careful person would have, under the same circumstances. Therefore, like provocation, criminal negligence is measured against an objective standard.

There are sometimes fine lines separating criminally wantonly reckless, negligent, and merely reckless behavior. The following two examples are helpful in distinguishing the degrees of recklessness necessary to determine whether the charge will be murder, manslaughter, or civil negligence.

Commonwealth v. Welansky

In *Commonwealth v. Welansky* (1944), the defendant owned a nightclub. While the defendant was hospitalized, a 16-year-old employee used a lighted match to view a burned-out lightbulb in the nightclub, but accidentally set fire to some flammable decorations. The fire spread throughout the nightclub, killing several hundred patrons. The defendant was convicted of manslaughter for allowing dangerous conditions (overcrowding, faulty wiring, and insufficient exits) to exist in his nightclub, and his conviction was upheld on appeal.[34]

Commonwealth v. Malone

In this 1946 case, the defendant and his friend agreed to play Russian roulette. Exercising his turn at the game, the defendant shot and killed his friend. The 17-year-old defendant was convicted of murder, which was affirmed on appeal on the ground that his pulling the trigger manifested such extreme recklessness that malice may be implied. In short, drawing the line between the level of recklessness that warrants a charge of murder and that which justifies a lesser charge of manslaughter can be very difficult.[35]

Criminal Negligence behind the Wheel Drivers with or without passengers have a special duty to make sure that their driving is safe to themselves and to others.

An accused can also be convicted of involuntary manslaughter if an unintentional death occurs from the commission of a misdemeanor or nonforcible felony. This basis of involuntary manslaughter liability is often referred to as the *misdemeanor manslaughter rule*. It can be thought of as a lesser form of the felony murder rule. An example of the application of this rule would be a defendant who is charged with involuntary manslaughter when he intentionally pushes the victim and the victim accidentally falls, striking his head on a hard object. The blow to his head causes his death. "But for" the push (the misdemeanor charge of simple assault), the victim would not have hit his head. Thus, the defendant is guilty of causing his death and can be charged with involuntary manslaughter under the misdemeanor manslaughter rule. The fact that the death was not intended is legally irrelevant.

Some states have a category separate from involuntary manslaughter called **negligent homicide**. This is a criminal homicide committed by a person who has neglected to exercise the degree of care that an ordinary person would have exercised under the same circumstances. In addition, some states have created a separate category of homicide termed **vehicular manslaughter**, which imposes criminal sanctions for causing a death while operating a motor vehicle, either by gross negligence or while under the influence of alcohol or other drugs.

negligent homicide
A criminal homicide committed by a person who has neglected to exercise the degree of care that an ordinary person would have exercised under the same circumstances.

vehicular manslaughter
A criminal homicide in which the perpetrator caused a death while operating a motor vehicle, either by gross negligence or while under the influence of alcohol or other drugs.

▲ **CRITICAL THINKING 8.5**

1. What elements of the *mens rea* of criminal liability apply to voluntary manslaughter? To involuntary manslaughter?

2. How do you differentiate wanton recklessness, negligence, and mere recklessness?

REVIEW AND APPLICATIONS

Summary by Chapter Objectives

1. **Distinguish between homicide and criminal homicide.** Homicide is the killing of one human being by another; criminal homicide is the unlawful killing of one human being by another (that is, without justification or excuse). Criminal homicide has been classified into three categories: murder, voluntary manslaughter, and involuntary manslaughter. In addition, some states also have statutes for negligent homicide and vehicular manslaughter.

2. **List the rules defining when life begins and ends for criminal homicide.** Common law provides that life begins with the birth of a live child. Many modern laws provide that life begins at different times of pregnancy, depending on the jurisdiction. For example, California law provides that life begins when a fetus has reached seven or eight weeks of gestation.

   Common law provides that life ends with the cessation of circulatory and respiratory functions, but the modern rule is that brain death marks the end of life.

3. **List the essential elements of murder.** The essential elements of murder are:
   • The killing of one human being by another.
   • Without justification or excuse.
   • By doing a voluntary act (or omitting an act when under a legal duty to act).
   • When the act is accompanied by the mental state of malice aforethought, and
   • The death of the human being is caused by the act.

4. **Explain the felony murder rule.** There are actually two felony murder rules:
   • The first-degree felony murder rule, in those states that have graded murder, provides that any act that causes death while committing an enumerated felony (such as rape, robbery, or arson) constitutes murder in the first degree, whether or not the perpetrator intended to kill.
   • The common law felony murder rule, which is the second-degree felony murder rule in states that grade murder, provides that any act that causes death while committing *any* felony (or any dangerous felony) constitutes murder, whether or not the perpetrator intended to kill.

5. **Distinguish between first-degree and second-degree murder.** First-degree murder is an intentional killing that is accomplished with premeditation and deliberation; any killing perpetrated by certain means such as poison, lying in wait, or torture; or any killing that occurs during the perpetration of certain enumerated, highly dangerous felonies, such as arson, rape, or robbery. In states with a grading system, second-degree murder is any other killing with malice aforethought.

6. **Describe the Model Penal Code's definition of murder.** Under the MPC, murder is a killing done purposely, knowingly, with extreme recklessness, or

during the perpetration of certain enumerated felonies, such as robbery or rape. This does not cover negligent killings, which are a form of manslaughter.

7. **Explain the difference between justification and excuse defenses.** Justification defenses focus on the victim's conduct. Excuse defenses focus on the status or condition of the defendant.

8. **Describe the differences in voluntary manslaughter, involuntary manslaughter, and murder.** Voluntary manslaughter is the intentional killing of another without malice aforethought, or killing in the heat of passion on sudden provocation. Involuntary manslaughter is an unintentional killing in which the killer has been reckless or negligent enough to be charged with criminal homicide. Murder is the killing of another with malice aforethought and, in the case of intentional murder, with intent to kill.

Key Terms

homicide (p. 207)
criminal homicide (p. 207)
malice aforethought (p. 207)
born-alive rule (p. 208)
feticide (p. 210)
premeditation and deliberation (p. 213)
corpus delicti (p. 213)
murder (p. 216)
manslaughter (p. 216)
year-and-a-day rule (p. 218)
malice (p. 222)

felony murder rule (p. 223)
inherently dangerous felonies (p. 224)
capital murder (p. 226)
voluntary manslaughter (p. 231)
mitigation (p. 231)
adequate provocation (p. 232)
imperfect self-defense (p. 233)
involuntary manslaughter (p. 234)
negligent homicide (p. 235)
vehicular manslaughter (p. 235)

Review Questions

1. What is malice aforethought, and how does it distinguish murder from manslaughter?
2. What is feticide?
3. What is the difference between the common law and modern law definitions of death?
4. What is the difference between express and implied malice?
5. Explain the difference between the felony murder rule and the misdemeanor manslaughter rule.
6. What is the Model Penal Code's definition of murder?
7. What is a capital offense, and are all murders capital offenses?
8. What are the possible defenses to murder?
9. What role does negligence play in determining whether a killing is voluntary or involuntary manslaughter?
10. What are negligent homicide and vehicular manslaughter?

Problem-Solving Exercises

1. **Prom Mom: Criminal Homicide?** On June 6, 1997, high school senior Melissa Drexler gave birth to a healthy baby boy in the bathroom of the catering hall of her prom. Melissa admitted that after giving birth, she removed the baby from the toilet and cut the umbilical cord, thus separating herself from the baby. She wrapped the baby in a series of garbage bags, then placed the baby into another garbage bag and tied that bag closed. This bag was thrown into a trash can and Melissa returned to the dance floor. The baby's body was later discovered by a janitor, but efforts to resuscitate him were unsuccessful. The medical examiner's autopsy revealed that there was air in one of his lungs and blood on one of his feet, indicating possible circulatory function. Answer the following questions:
   a. Should Drexler be charged with criminal homicide? Why or why not?
   b. What are some possible mitigating and aggravating circumstances in this case that could affect Drexler's conviction and sentence?
   c. What excuse, if any, could Drexler offer for this act?

2. **Evidence of a Crime?** Peter is suspected of killing David, who was found bludgeoned to death in his home. In Peter's residence, the police discover a love letter from David to Peter's girlfriend. In addition to the love letter, a floor plan of David's home was found lying next to a crowbar that was apparently used to gain entry to David's home. You are the prosecutor preparing to present the case to the grand jury. Answer the following questions:
   a. What crime or crimes will you ask them to consider in the indictment against Peter?
   b. What facts will you use to support the various charges?
   c. Will you need a confession from Peter in order to prove your case? Why or why not?

3. **School Violence** Joshua has repeatedly teased and harassed Colin at their high school. On one occasion, Joshua and some other people abducted Colin and tied him to the flag post, partially nude, for everyone to see. Colin wanted to get even, so he decided to scare Joshua. One morning before school, Colin drove his car at high speed directly at Joshua, intending to stop just before hitting him. Colin couldn't stop in time, however, and Joshua was killed instantly.
   a. Could Colin be charged with murder, voluntary manslaughter, or involuntary manslaughter? Why?
   b. Suppose that this occurred in a state where Colin is still considered a minor, but can be transferred to adult court if the offense is serious enough to warrant it. Is Colin's age a mitigating defense, or should he be treated as an adult?
   c. Could the length of time between the ongoing provocation and Joshua's killing be a factor in this? Why or why not?

Workplace Applications

1. **Police Investigation** You are a police officer called to investigate a reported gunshot. When you arrive at the scene, inside a residence you find a dead body with a gunshot wound to the head. It appears that the victim was shot while she

was sleeping. In addition, several valuable items are missing from the residence, such as a VCR, stereo system, and television. Write a report indicating what charges could be brought against the perpetrator. If you conclude that the perpetrator could be charged with first-degree murder, explain the primary basis on which such a charge could be brought.

2. **Decisive Factors** In the preceding exercise, assume the perpetrator is apprehended. Further, assume that the victim and the perpetrator were married and living together before the victim had a restraining order issued against the perpetrator. The perpetrator, while in custody, tells an officer that if he couldn't have the victim, then no one else would. Under these facts, would your conclusion change from the previous example? If so, explain why, and state what charges you would choose to bring against this perpetrator.

Ethics Exercises

1. **Infanticide, Feticide, or Neither?** You are the prosecutor in *People v. Grossberg and Petersen*. In the case, an 18-year-old female gave birth to a full-term baby boy in a Delaware motel room. The 18-year-old father of the child was also present at the time the baby was born. Sometime after the baby was delivered, it was wrapped in a garbage bag and thrown into a dumpster behind the motel. The baby's body was not discovered until more than 12 hours later. Medical examination revealed that the umbilical cord had been severed prior to the baby's being placed in the dumpster. The baby's head showed signs of two skull fractures and some brain injury. The medical examiner concludes that the baby died from being shaken, from multiple skull fractures from blunt trauma, or perhaps from both. She also notes that the baby may have sustained the injuries postmortem (after death) from the force of being thrown into the dumpster; also, the brain abnormalities may have developed while the child was still in the uterus. Answer the following questions:
   a. Must you consider all of the medical examiner's findings in determining whether to prosecute the teen parents for criminal homicide? Why or why not?
   b. What is the minimum amount of information that the medical examiner must find to determine criminal homicide? What else can she find in addition to this?
   c. As a matter of professional ethics, are you obligated to share all of the medical examiner's statements with the defense?

Notes

1. BLACK'S LAW DICTIONARY 751–52 (8th ed. 2004).
2. WAYNE R. LaFAVE, MODERN CRIMINAL LAW 251 (4th ed. 2006).
3. *See* Bicka A. Barlow, *Severe Penalties for the Destruction of "Potential Life"—Cruel and Unusual Punishment?*, 29 U.S.F.L. REV. 463 (1995).
4. CAL. PENAL CODE §187 (a) (West 2007).
5. People v. Davis, 872 P.2d 591 (Cal. 1994).
6. IOWA CODE § 707.7 (2003).

7. Roe v. Wade, 410 U.S. 113 (1973).

8. State v. Merrill, 450 N.W.2d 318 (Minn. 1990).

9. 18 U.S.C. 1841 (West 2007).

10. David A. Pratt, *Too Many Physicians: Physician–Assisted Suicide After Glucksberg/ Quill*, 9 Alb. L.J. Sci. & Tech. 161, 167 (1999).

11. *Id.*

12. Oregon Rev. Stat. 127.805 (2005).

13. Black's Law Dictionary 594 (8th ed. 2004).

14. People v. Cleave, 280 Cal. Rptr. 146, 151 (Cal. Ct. App. 1991).

15. People v. Hearn, 669 N.Y.S.2d 984 (N.Y. App. Div. 1998).

16. Dirk Johnson, *Kevorkian Sentenced to 10 to 25 Years in Prison*, N.Y. Times, Apr. 14, 1999, at A1.

17. People v. Scott, 1 Cal. Rptr. 600 (Cal. Ct. App. 1959).

18. Model Penal Code § 210 (1985).

19. Model Penal Code § 210.5(2) (1985).

20. Regina v. Blaue, 1 W.L.R. 1411, 3 All E.R. 446 (C.A.) (Ct. of App. England, 1975).

21. Oliver Wendell Holmes, The Common Law 47 (1963), citing 4 William Blackstone, Commentaries *192.

22. Joshua Dressler, Understanding Criminal Law § 31.02[B][1], at 544 n.34 (4th ed. 2006), citing State v. Heidelberg, 45 So. 256, 258 (La. 1907).

23. Rudolph J. Gerber, *The Felony Murder Rule: Conundrum Without Punishment*, 31 Ariz. St. L.J. 763, 770 (1999).

24. Commonwealth v. Redline, 137 A.2d 472 (Pa. 1958)

25. People v. Aaron, 299 N.W.2d 304 (Mich. 1980).

26. Model Penal Code § 210(1)(b) (1985).

27. 18 Pa. Cons. Stat. § 2502 (2007).

28. Cal. Penal Code §187(a) (West 2007).

29. Cal. Penal Code § 188 (West 2007).

30. United States v. Brown, 518 F.2d 821 (7th Cir. 1975).

31. Wayne R. LaFave, Modern Criminal Law 271 (4th ed. 2006).

32. Model Penal Code § 210.2(2) & 210.6 (1985).

33. *See* Model Penal Code § 210.3(1)(b) (1985).

34. Commonwealth v. Welansky, 55 N.E.2d 902 (Mass. 1944).

35. Commonwealth v. Malone, 47 A.2d 445 (Pa. 1946).

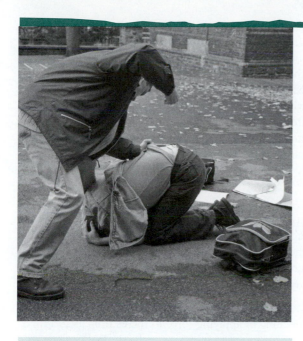

Crimes against Persons: Other Offenses

CHAPTER OBJECTIVES

After reading and studying this chapter, you should be able to:

1. State the elements of battery.
2. List the elements of assault.
3. State the elements of mayhem.
4. List the essential elements of robbery.
5. State the elements of rape, and explain the difference between rape and statutory rape.
6. Describe Megan's Law.
7. Define child abuse.
8. Distinguish between the elements of false imprisonment and kidnapping.

9.1 Physical Crimes

This section will cover the crimes of assault, battery, mayhem, and robbery. Often, the terms *assault* and *battery* are used in conjunction with one another. Both were common law misdemeanors, and both exist today as statutory crimes in every American jurisdiction. Legally, however, the terms apply to separate and distinct crimes, distinguishable by the presence or absence of physical injury or offensive physical contact. The common law felony of mayhem is perhaps less well known than assault and battery, perhaps because it applies to specialized injuries. It appears in fewer jurisdictions than the other two crimes; many jurisdictions do not carry it in their statutes and prefer to charge defendants with aggravated assault instead.

Battery

battery

A misdemeanor consisting of the unlawful application of force that actually and intentionally causes the touching of another person against his or her will.

Battery is the unlawful application of force that actually and intentionally causes the touching of another person against his or her will. "Touching," in this context, refers to any physical contact that either directly or indirectly causes bodily injury or that is offensive to the victim. A battery is a completed assault, and assault is an attempted battery. This close relationship explains why the terms are often used together. Thus, the elements of battery are:

- The actor's conduct of touching or applying force to the victim.
- The actor's mental state (either intent to injure, or with criminal negligence, or, in some jurisdictions, while committing an unlawful act).
- The harm done to the victim (bodily injury or offensive touching).

Direct application of force is clearly battery. For example, shoving another person could be enough to constitute battery. The minimum conduct required for a battery conviction is simply the direct touching or the indirect application of force upon another person. The defendant may set in motion a force that indirectly causes bodily injury or that is offensive to the victim. For example, if the defendant places some kind of poison in the victim's drink, resulting in injury to the victim, the defendant is guilty of battery. The act of placing poison in the victim's drink resulted in injury. The fact that no actual contact occurred between the defendant and the victim is immaterial.

A defendant will be culpable for battery if he or she possesses the intent to inflict injury by touching the victim. However, the accused does not have to possess a specific intent to inflict bodily injury or an offensive touching in order to be guilty of battery. In many jurisdictions, battery only requires that the defendant act with criminal negligence; in some jurisdictions, the defendant will be guilty of battery if he or she commits an unlawful act while engaged in the conduct, regardless of mental state. The defendant only needs to know that his or her actions could cause the application of force on another; therefore, it is not required that the defendant batter the person he or she intended to batter in order to be guilty. For example, if a man swung his arm at an enemy with the intention of striking him, but accidentally punched an innocent bystander, the accused could still be guilty of battery.

If the defendant's culpability for battery is based on criminal negligence, the negligence required must be distinguished from negligence in noncriminal settings. Criminal negligence in general, which also applies to the case of battery, requires that the actor create an unreasonable and high risk of harm to others by his or her actions.

In order for a defendant to be guilty of battery, not only must he or she intend to cause harmful or offensive touching, he or she must actually cause such a result to the victim. The result could be something obvious, such as broken bones, stab wounds, or a bullet wound. It could also be pain without physical signs of a wounding: spitting in another's face or touching a member of the opposite sex in an inappropriate manner, such as touching a woman on her breast or kissing her without her consent. The conduct does not have to cause pain in order for a person to be guilty of battery. Currently, however, most jurisdictions follow the MPC guidelines, which limit battery offenses to physical injuries. Unwanted sexual touching is usually addressed in other statutes covering sexual offenses.[1]

Aggravated battery is a felony in many states. This crime is usually reserved for conduct accompanied by intent to kill or rape. Therefore, it is usually a specific intent crime and carries greater penalties. Even in states where it is not a felony, it is classified in a different category of misdemeanors than is simple battery.

aggravated battery
A battery accompanied by an intent to kill or rape—thus, usually a specific intent crime. A felony in many states.

Assault

Assault has two definitions: (1) attempted battery, or (2) the intentional frightening of another person. Any willful attempt or threat to inflict injury upon the person of another, when coupled with an apparent present ability to do so, or any intentional display of force that would give the victim reason to be fearful of immediate bodily harm constitutes an assault.

The elements of the crime of assault are: an attempt to batter, or conduct that is threatening, menacing, or otherwise designed to intentionally frighten the victim, with the intent to commit a battery upon the victim or to frighten the victim and that in fact does frighten the victim and would reasonably cause the average person to fear physical injury.

The first type of assault is *attempted battery*, in which the actor actually intends to commit a battery. Attempted battery is committed by any gesture or movement that threatens future physical harm to a victim. In most jurisdictions, assault can also be committed by *intentional frightening*. Any conduct that is designed to frighten another will suffice—a menacing movement or pointing a gun, for example. Words alone are usually not enough to constitute the required conduct to sustain the charge; however, in some situations words may meet the requirement. Usually, the *actus reus* is satisfied when a defendant makes a movement with his body or with a weapon that indicates future harm. In some states, an assault committed by attempted battery must be accompanied by the actor's present ability to commit a battery.[2]

An assault may be committed without actually touching, striking, or doing bodily harm to the person of another. Nonetheless, an essential element of the crime in most states, which must be proven by the prosecution, is that the defendant intended to use force on the victim or intended to put the victim in fear of actual harm. A negligent but inadvertent imposition of fear—that is, when the defendant's behavior unintentionally frightens a victim—usually will not suffice for a charge of

assault
A misdemeanor consisting of either an attempted battery or an intentional frightening of another person.

assault. If the defendant is wildly flailing his or her arms and nearly strikes the victim, but does nothing to indicate that he or she intends to cause harm to the victim, the defendant is not guilty of assault. His or her actions, although perhaps reckless, were not intended to cause harm to another. Therefore, an assault charge would not be warranted.

The second type of assault is the intentional frightening of another person. A victim of the threat must reasonably fear immediate personal harm, or must view the defendant's actions as a threat that could cause such harm. If the defendant intended to put the victim in fear, and the victim experienced an apprehension of immediate harm, most jurisdictions would hold the defendant culpable for assault. At the time of the act, the victim must fear that a physical injury will result from the defendant's actions.

Where intent is present, the defendant's movement does not need to cause an actual harm to the victim in order for the defendant to be criminally culpable of assault. The defendant only needs to take some action that will bring him or her reasonably close to successfully completing the injury or harm, such as making a fist and waving an arm while walking toward a victim. From the victim's perspective, it is likely that the defendant will take a punch at him; therefore, this could constitute assault. This victim has actually been assaulted because there was a physical act by the defendant—a movement toward the victim likely to result in physical harm. In addition, all other elements of the crime were present.

conditional assault

An assault in which the actor threatens harm only under certain conditions, such as the failure of the victim to act a certain way demanded by the actor.

Although mere words are usually not enough to charge a person with assault, words accompanied by some movement may be sufficient. If a defendant approaches a victim from behind and whispers in his ear, "Don't turn around or I'll shoot you," and the victim then feels a gunlike object shoved into his back, the victim has reason to believe that the defendant does have a gun, or some other deadly weapon, and can fulfill his threat. It is likely that this defendant would be charged with the crime of assault.

A prosecutor must prove that the victim was aware of the assault and was placed in fear or apprehension of immediate danger. This must be determined by sight or by another sense, such as hearing or touch. If a defendant approached a blind man from behind and pointed a gun at him without saying anything, the defendant would not be guilty of assault because the victim would be unaware—and therefore not fearful—of any intent on the part of the defendant to harm him.

Another form of assault is **conditional assault**, in which the actor threatens harm only under certain conditions, such as the failure of the victim to act in a certain way demanded by the actor. If a defendant

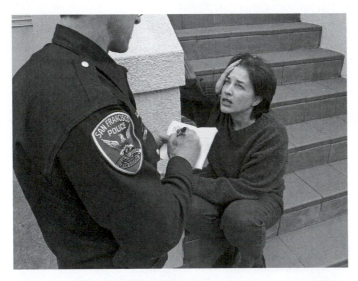

Differences between Assault and Battery Contrary to popular belief, assault and battery have different legal definitions. It is unlikely that this person has been assaulted; from the extent of the injuries, battery appears more likely.

threatens to shoot the victim unless the victim leaves, this would be a conditional assault. In most instances, the defendant is guilty of assault, even though the victim complied with the condition. Still another form is **aggravated assault**, which, like aggravated battery, is a felony in most jurisdictions. Assault with intent to kill, rob, or rape and assaults with specified deadly weapons qualify as aggravated assault under most of these laws.

aggravated assault

Assault with intent to kill, rob, or rape, or assault with specified deadly weapons. A felony in most states.

Mayhem

Mayhem is assault with intent to maim. A common law felony, it is defined by historical legal commentator William Blackstone as "the violently depriving of another of the use of such of his members, as may render him the less able in fighting, either to defend himself, or to annoy his adversary."[3] This crime was created to deter acts that tended to make one of the king's subjects less able to render the king "aid and assistance."

The law of mayhem in the United States developed to protect the physical integrity of the person. The injuries prohibited by the crime of mayhem can be characterized as "dismemberment, disablement, or disfigurement."[4] Although state laws vary, those that designate the specific crime of mayhem generally define it by types of prohibited injury. Uniformly, state laws on mayhem prohibit the infliction of a permanent injury upon a victim that disables a limb or an eye. Some states also define mayhem as an injury that causes "grievous bodily harm," and a number include specific types of disfigurement within a prohibited injury. The most prevalent of these is the slitting of an ear or nose; scarring may also be included.

The elements of the crime of mayhem are subject to variation, even among those states that still have it as a separate crime. Still, they may be stated generally as the infliction of a specified injury constituting dismemberment, disablement, or disfigurement, and the intent to maim or disfigure. Though it is possible for an actor to be held culpable for mayhem when the injury was inflicted by accident or with negligence, in the absence of specific statutory provision, it is not likely.

The *actus reus* requirement of mayhem is that the defendant cause bodily injury that permanently dismembers, disables, or disfigures the victim.

mayhem

The felony of assault with intent to maim.

- *Dismemberment* means the severing of a body part.
- *Disablement* requires the loss of use of a major part of the body, such as an arm, leg, eye, or testicle, although the part need not be actually removed. To constitute mayhem, disablement must cause permanent injury to the victim. If a defendant jams his finger in the victim's eye, causing the victim to be permanently blind in that eye, the victim's eye is disabled.
- *Disfigurement* requires an alteration of the victim's face or body that changes its normal appearance. Like disablement, disfigurement must cause permanent injury to constitute mayhem. If the defendant slashes a victim's lip and the lip cannot be restored to the way it was prior to the incident, the victim's lip has been permanently disfigured. If, however, the lip is stitched and heals, leaving no mark, the defendant most likely will not be convicted of mayhem but will be charged with another offense, such as battery or attempted murder. (See Application Case 9.1.)

⚖️ Application Case 9.1

People v. Keenan

In *People v. Keenan* (1991), the defendant entered the apartment of a woman at night. He tied her up and burned both of her breasts with a lit cigarette, leaving permanent scars. He also raped and sodomized her and stole property from her home. In addition to other charges, the defendant was convicted of mayhem for permanently scarring the victim's breasts with the lit cigarette. On appeal, he challenged the mayhem conviction, arguing that mayhem is only an appropriate charge for the most disfiguring or disabling attacks and claiming that the harm to the victim was minor.

The appellate court upheld the mayhem conviction. It ruled that the disfigurement of the victim's breasts was within the definition of the mayhem statute, and although the scars could not be seen by others, the impact they had on the victim was as serious as if the scars had been on her face.

SOURCE: People v. Keenan, 227 Cal. App. 3d 26 (Cal. Ct. App. 1991).

The *mens rea* requirement for mayhem depends on the particular statute in a jurisdiction. Some states only require that the defendant intended to commit harm, and this intent resulted in the maiming. Others require that the defendant specifically intended to cause the particular type of disfigurement or disablement that he or she did in fact cause. Should a defendant intend to maim in one way and cause a different maiming through his actions, however, he or she will still be culpable for this crime. If a defendant jabs a knife at a victim attempting to slash his face, but instead gouges his eye, he or she will still be guilty of mayhem.

Because of this crime's origins, it has outlived its purpose and has been all but eliminated from American criminal law. Today many jurisdictions, as well as the MPC, have eliminated mayhem and treat it as maiming, assault with intent to maim, or the highest level of assault or aggravated assault. At present, only a handful of states treat the crime separately.

Robbery

robbery

The taking of property by the use of force or fear, where the property is taken either from the person of the victim or in his or her immediate presence.

Robbery is a common law crime that consists of the taking of property by the use of force or fear, where the property is taken either from the person of the victim or in his or her immediate presence. Although the wording of the elements of robbery may vary from jurisdiction to jurisdiction, the essential elements of Florida's statute is typical: the taking of property from a person or the person's custody with the intent to either permanently or temporarily deprive the person or the owner of the property when in the course of the taking there is the use of force, violence, assault, or putting in fear.[5] If force or fear is missing, a theft or larceny has taken place. These elements are explained in greater detail in the following paragraphs.

Taking of Property

The taking of property element of robbery is the same element found in larceny: the taking and carrying away of property of another, without consent, with the purpose of stealing or permanently depriving the owner of possession.

Taking from a Person

The crime of robbery requires that the property be taken either from the person or from the person's immediate presence. The victim's immediate presence is considered to be the area within his or her immediate control; therefore, the property may not be at some distance away in order for robbery to occur. If a threat of force were used to cause a victim to telephone another location to have property delivered to the perpetrator, the property would not be sufficiently within the victim's presence to satisfy the traditional definition of robbery.

Intent to Deprive the Owner

One difference between robbery and larceny is that in modern robbery statutes, such as the Florida statute described above, the intent to deprive the owner temporarily, rather than permanently, is enough to create criminal liability.

Use of Force or Fear

The element of the use of force or fear is the primary distinction between robbery and larceny. If a larceny occurs with force or fear, then a robbery has taken place. Force is the actual use of physical power to aid in obtaining money or property from the victim. The use of fear or intimidation is the use of threats to do immediate bodily injury or harm to the victim, a family member, or someone else who is present. Threats can be explicit or implied, and they can be verbal or nonverbal. When force, fear, or intimidation is used, the victim is not required to actually be fearful as long as he or she is aware of the impending force or threat.

Whether the force, fear, or intimidation occurred in order to take property, or merely in an attempt to retain or escape with it, makes a difference in some states in determining whether the crime is robbery rather than merely larceny. In some states, there is a question of whether a robbery occurs when the property is obtained peacefully but force or fear is subsequently used to retain possession or allow escape. Some jurisdictions rationalize that if force or fear is used only subsequent to the taking, it does not satisfy the robbery element. In one case, the court stated that the test was whether or not the defendant had completed the taking of the property by the time he used the force or fear.[6]

On the other hand, the MPC and some states define robbery as using force or fear at any time during the attempt or commission of theft, including the escape after committing the theft. In *Santilli v. State* (1990), the court held that robbery had occurred, and the element of force or fear satisfied, when the perpetrator hit a police officer with his car as he attempted to flee after completing the act of shoplifting a greeting card.[7]

Purse snatching is a crime that can be considered either a larceny or a robbery, depending on two factors: the circumstances and the jurisdiction. As with other takings of property, if the purse snatching includes the use of force or fear, it is robbery; absent force or fear, it is larceny or larceny from the person. Several states make purse snatching a robbery, but the majority of jurisdictions consider it to be larceny or larceny from the person if the snatching in itself does not involve enough force or fear. Some statutes draw fine lines. For example, if the taking is unnoticed and accomplished by stealth, with no resistance, it will be classified as larceny from the person. However, if the victim resists, even slightly, then the crime will be considered a robbery. For example, robberies occurred in cases where the defendant grabbed money from the victim's hands and beat the victim before leaving with the money,[8] and where the victim struggled with the defendant to retain possession of her purse.[9] In another case, in which a victim testified that she was very scared when her purse was taken at gunpoint, the crime of robbery by fear from threat of force was shown.[10]

There is one common circumstance that affects punishment for robbery: the use of a dangerous or deadly weapon. Another, less common circumstance affecting punishment is the act of robbing persons over the age of 65.

Armed Robbery

Most robbery statutes are divided into different degrees based on one important factor—whether the defendant was armed with a dangerous or deadly weapon.

Some jurisdictions require that the defendant actually be armed with a deadly weapon for purposes of armed robbery. Most jurisdictions, however, only require that the perpetrator cause the victim to believe that the robber is armed with a deadly weapon, regardless of whether he or she is so armed. For example, South Carolina's Code of Laws provides: "A person who commits robbery while armed with a . . . deadly weapon, or while alleging, either by action or words, he was armed while using a representation of a deadly weapon or any object which a person present during the commission of the robbery reasonably believed to be a deadly weapon, is guilty" of the offense.[11]

armed robbery
Robbery accomplished by means of a dangerous or deadly weapon; often classified as robbery in the first degree or aggravated robbery.

The actual amount of force used is not relevant. **Armed robbery** has different meanings in different jurisdictions, but usually is defined as robbery accomplished by means of a dangerous or deadly weapon. It is often classified as robbery in the first degree or aggravated robbery. Armed robbery cases are always treated as more serious offenses than unarmed robbery cases.

Whether an instrumentality is a dangerous weapon for purposes of armed robbery is a question for the jury to decide. Numerous cases have determined that a wide variety of instrumentalities other than a loaded gun can be dangerous weapons. A toy gun or a simulated gun, such as an object in a coat pocket intended to look like a gun, may be a dangerous weapon. Pepper spray, BB guns, pocket knives, hands, feet, a car, scissors, and a bottle are all objects that can be dangerous or deadly weapons if used in a manner to intimidate and evoke fear. Even an unloaded gun can qualify as a dangerous weapon because it can still evoke considerable fear in the victim or can be used as a bludgeon to inflict serious bodily injury. Almost no jurisdictions require that a weapon must be loaded or that the prosecution must prove that the gun was loaded at the time of the robbery.

Robbing the Elderly

Robbing the elderly is not a separate or more serious offense than the same type of robbery committed against a younger person, but in at least one jurisdiction it carries

9.1 Web Exploration

Bankguys

Visit the Bankguys Web site at http://bankguys.us to learn about recent unsolved bank robberies in the Pittsburgh, western Pennsylvania, and West Virginia areas. What information does this site provide? How does it help investigators?

sentence enhancements that make the minimum punishment considerably greater. Georgia, recognizing that persons over the age of 65 are more likely to be robbed and to have serious bodily injuries as a result of the robbery, has created a statute that enhances the penalty for robbery of a person age 65 or older. The punishment for robbery of a person 65 or over is at least five years' imprisonment, whereas the minimum sentence for robbery of a person under 65 is one year.[12]

 CRITICAL THINKING 9.1

1. What is the difference between assault and battery, and why are the two sometimes confused with each other?

2. Describe the trend to eliminate the charge of mayhem.

9.2 Sex Crimes

This section will cover four sexual offenses: rape, statutory rape, spousal rape, and child molestation. Child molestation will also receive some coverage in the following section, under the topic of child abuse. You will also learn about effective ways in which you, as a criminal justice professional, can deal with victims of the highly personal crime of rape.

Rape

Rape is a common law felony that is defined as "the carnal knowledge of [i.e., sexual intercourse with] a woman forcibly and against her will."[13] Sexual penetration by the penis of the vulva was necessary to constitute rape at common law; sexual emission, or ejaculation, was neither sufficient nor necessary. Therefore, a man who ejaculated without penetration did not commit rape, but a man who penetrated someone without ejaculation did. Today, rape is defined differently in many jurisdictions, including sexual intercourse by drugging or by fraud. Some states have adopted gender neutral definitions of rape. Some jurisdictions, for example, have changed the name of the offense to sexual assault and have included all other forced sexual activity within the definition of the crime.[14]

Today the crimes of rape, attempted rape, and sexual assault continue to be a widespread problem. According to the 2005 National Crime Victimization Survey (NCVS), the total number of rapes, attempted rapes, and sexual assaults was tallied at more than 190,000.[15]

rape
A felony defined as "the carnal knowledge of a woman forcibly and against her will."

9.2 Web Exploration

Rape Awareness at RAINN

Visit the Web site for RAINN (Rape, Abuse, and Incest National Network) at http://www.rainn.org. Read their home page and the sections titled "Counseling Centers" and "What Should I Do?" How does this information and the 800 number help victims? How could criminal justice and medical professionals benefit from such information?

In general, rape is sexual intercourse by a male defendant with a female victim that is committed under one of the following circumstances:

- Forcibly.
- By means of some specific forms of deception.
- While the victim was asleep or unconscious.
- Under circumstances in which the victim was not competent to give consent (e.g., under the influence of drugs, mental disability, or being too young).

These definitions do not include sexual offenses committed by a man against his wife. A new category of statutes covers *spousal rape*, discussed later in this chapter.

The most prevalent form of rape is forcible rape. Although the law is changing in this area, forcible rape traditionally requires proof that the victim did not consent *and* "that the sexual act was 'by force' or 'against her will.'"[16] The problem with this requirement is that it appears self-contradictory. When force is used, consent is typically not an issue for two reasons:

1. Any consent could be coerced through the use of force.
2. If the defendant had to use force to carry out the rape, the victim was obviously not a willing or consensual participant.

Traditionally, the victim must physically "resist to the utmost," "resist until exhausted or overpowered," or "resist the attack in every way possible. She was expected to continue such resistance until she was overcome by force, insensible through fright, or ceased resistance out of exhaustion, fear of death, or great bodily harm."[17] Alternately, she must have been prevented from physically resisting by threats to her safety.

When a victim does not resist out of fear that she will be physically harmed, the trier of fact will look at both the victim's belief that she faces harm and the defendant's conduct in determining whether the defendant can be convicted of forcible rape.[18] For example, suppose that Raelene is five feet tall and weighs 105 pounds. As she is walking alone at night, a six-foot-tall man weighing 250 pounds grabs her and tells her that if she does not allow him to have sexual intercourse with her, he will kill her. Raelene does not see a weapon, nor does the perpetrator tell her he has a weapon, but she chooses not to fight and allows the perpetrator to have sexual intercourse with her. Under these circumstances, the defendant would still be guilty of forcible rape. It is reasonable for a small woman who is alone at night to fear harm from a large man who grabs her. Raelene most likely felt that if she didn't allow the sex to occur, the perpetrator would be able to kill her even without a weapon. Therefore, forcible rape has occurred. (See Application Case 9.2.)

⚖️ Application Case 9.2

Rusk v. State

In *Rusk v. State*, the victim met the defendant in a bar and agreed to give him a ride home. Once at his home, the defendant asked the victim to come up to his apartment. When the victim refused, the defendant took her car keys from the ignition and asked her again to come up. Feeling as though she had no choice because she was in an unfamiliar neighborhood late at night, she entered the apartment. The defendant began taking off the victim's clothes and, at his request, the victim finished removing her clothing on her own. The defendant performed various sexual acts over a period of several hours, even though the victim repeatedly begged him to allow her to leave. At one point, the defendant lightly placed his hands on her throat. In response, the victim asked him if she did what he said, would he let her go without killing her? Once the defendant agreed, the victim told him to do whatever he wanted.

The defendant was found guilty of forcible rape. On appeal, the court affirmed the conviction, holding that the reasonableness of the victim's fear was a question for the trier of fact. In this case, a jury had found that the defendant's actions warranted a forcible rape conviction.

SOURCE: Rusk v. State, 434 A.2d 720 (Md. 1981).

Rapes that are the product of nonconsent, but not the result of force, threat, or bodily injury, are still punishable as rape but receive a lesser penalty. In addition, some jurisdictions have expanded their forcible rape statutes to include acts where force is inferred through the circumstances, or where a rape has occurred solely because the victim did not give permission. For example, the New Jersey Supreme Court has held "that a person is guilty of forcible rape if he commits an act of sexual penetration of another person in the absence of affirmative and freely given permission, either express or implied, for the specific act of penetration. Without such permission, any force used, even the force inherent in the sexual act itself, justifies a forcible rape prosecution."[19]

Rape is a general intent offense. The defendant does not have to have the specific intent to have nonconsensual sex in order to be guilty of rape, but is guilty "if he possessed a morally blameworthy state of mind regarding the victim's lack of consent."[20] This means that a defendant is not guilty of rape if he had a reasonable and genuine belief that the victim consented. A reasonable and genuine belief of consent is hard to argue where the defendant used some type of force to achieve his goal, but it does arise in date rape cases, especially where the victim and the defendant have had prior sexual relations.

Rape and the Law

Traditionally, rape statutes have only addressed the scenario where a male is the perpetrator and the female is the victim. That is why the language "against her will" still exists in many rape statutes. Recently, some states have expanded their rape statutes

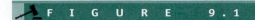

F I G U R E   9 . 1

Wyoming Statute on Sexual Assault

6-2-302. Sexual assault in the first degree.

(a) Any actor who inflicts sexual intrusion on a victim commits a sexual assault in the first degree if:

    (i) The actor causes submission of the victim through the actual application, reasonably calculated to cause submission of the victim, of physical force or forcible confinement;

    (ii) The actor causes submission of the victim by threat of death, serious bodily injury, extreme physical pain or kidnapping to be inflicted on anyone and the victim reasonably believes that the actor has the present ability to execute these threats;

    (iii) The victim is physically helpless, and the actor knows or reasonably should know that the victim is physically helpless and that the victim has not consented; or

    (iv) The actor knows or reasonably should know that the victim through a mental illness, mental deficiency or developmental disability is incapable of appraising the nature of the victim's conduct.

SOURCE: http://legisweb.state.wy.us/statutes/compress/title06.doc.

to provide for same-sex rape, as well as rape by a female against a male. Statutes involving nonconsensual sex against a grown woman or a child are sometimes divided into categories depending on the circumstances of the case. For example, a man who rapes while holding a loaded gun to a woman's head may be punished more severely than a man who rapes without a weapon. (See Figure 9.1.)

Because the men who created rape laws feared that women could falsely claim rape too easily, the common law crime was predicated on the fact that rape was a capital offense, and inordinate burdens were placed upon the victim. For the successful prosecution of rape, the common law required proof that the victim made a fresh complaint, was of chaste character, and could provide corroboration, among other things. For centuries, the prosecution of a rape case involved grave difficulties for the victim, who often was on trial as much as or more than the accused. The victim, while on the witness stand, was subject to intrusive personal interrogations pertaining to her reputation, personal characteristics, and frequently her race and economic class. As a result, women today still fear reporting rape. Unfortunately, rape is still the most underreported violent crime.[21]

To deal with the problems faced by sexual assault victims, including their low report rates, legislators enacted *rape shield statutes* that offered rape victims protection of their privacy. These statutes deny a defendant the opportunity to cross-examine the victim with respect to her sexual history and general moral character. One exception is that a victim's past sexual history *with the defendant* may be allowed into evidence, but only to the extent it may relate to the defense of consent.

Statutory Rape

At common law, sexual intercourse between a man and a "woman child under the age of 10 years" was considered rape regardless of whether "consent" was given. Today, the age of the victim has generally been raised to 17 and under, with some variation from state to state, and the crime is known as **statutory rape**. Many states divide statutory rape offenses into two categories; statutory rape involving a very young girl usually carries a stiffer penalty than cases involving girls in their late teens.

Spousal Rape

The common law did not consider sexual intercourse forced upon a wife by her husband to be rape. Recently, laws have been passed prohibiting **spousal rape**, which can be defined as "non-consensual sexual acts between a woman and her husband, former husband or long term partner, and . . . any unwanted, humiliating and painful sexual activity."[22] Lack of consent can be determined by the use of intimidation or threats. Spousal rape is a serious problem: Approximately 28 percent of all rape victims are raped by an intimate.[23]

Currently, all 50 states and federal territories have passed laws that make spousal rape a crime. In most jurisdictions, it is a crime only when accompanied by force. As another legal option, a wife may also sue her husband in civil court for pain, suffering, and medical and other costs incurred as a result of spousal rape.[24]

Dealing with Rape Victims

Although it is somewhat beyond the scope of this book, some note should be taken of this topic. Because rape is an extremely intrusive offense, it is crucial that a rape victim be treated with sensitivity, compassion, and respect regardless of the circumstances. Due to the intrusive nature of the offense, victims' reactions will differ, ranging from an extremely subdued state—almost a state of shock—to an excited and animated state. Whenever possible, when a police department receives a call for help from a female rape victim, female personnel will be designated to speak to the victim, to provide a more comfortable atmosphere for the victim.

Often, victims will want to shower immediately because they feel dirty. It is *critical* that they do not shower until they have been properly examined by medical personnel. Showering will remove fingerprints, semen, and other physical evidence that is needed to ensure conviction of a perpetrator. Usually, medical personnel will perform a series of exams on the victim, and will collect evidence using a rape kit, which contains sealable plastic bags and other items to help preserve evidence.

Police or medical personnel should find out if there is someone close to the victim whom she would like to be with her during this time. Nearly always, a familiar face will make the process more comfortable. They should also provide the victim with resources that can assist in her recovery, such as rape hotlines, counseling centers, and rape survivor support groups that can assist the victim during this difficult period. Again, it is important, regardless of one's personal impression of the victim, that the victim always be treated with respect.

Rape Trauma Syndrome

In recent years, an ailment unique to rape victims has become noticeable in the prosecution of rape cases in the United States. **Rape trauma syndrome** is a condition observed in some rape victims. Immediately after an attack, the victim may appear

statutory rape
A form of rape involving sexual intercourse between an adult and a child, usually between the ages of 13 and 17.

spousal rape
Nonconsensual sex between a woman and her husband, ex-husband, or partner.

rape trauma syndrome
A condition observed in some rape victims, in which the victim develops phobias and physical problems as a result of having been raped.

calm and subdued; over time, however, the victim exhibits physical symptoms such as tension headaches, fatigue, and sleeplessness, leading to the development of phobias related to the circumstances of the rape.[25] Increasingly, courts in various states are allowing expert testimony in rape trials to explain the behavior of a rape victim based on rape trauma syndrome. Such a move is intended to allow juries to better understand the long-term physical and psychological damage caused to rape victims.

Child Molestation

According to various sources, many millions of child molesters reside in the United States. Of the 400,000 registered sexual offenders in the United States, an estimated 80,000 to 100,000 are missing. More than half of all convicted sex offenders are sent back to prison within a year. Within two years, more than 77 percent are back.[26] Child molesters often seek employment where they will have the most contact with children. They may work at summer camps, day care centers, and schools, as these jobs provide the easiest opportunities to target children. (See Application Case 9.3.)

⚖ Application Case 9.3

Buckey v. County of Los Angeles

One of the most publicized and time-consuming criminal trials in the United States involved teachers at the McMartin Preschool in Manhattan Beach, California. Virginia McMartin, several of her family members (including Peggy McMartin Buckey) who taught at the school, and other caregivers were charged with several counts of child molestation. In 1993, a parent who was known to be paranoid and mentally ill alleged to the police that her child had been sexually molested at the school. The police sent letters to all McMartin parents, which resulted in a wave of allegations regarding atrocious sexual acts against the children. In addition, a therapist who interviewed many of the children used manipulative tactics to get the children to say they had been molested. As a result, children fabricated their testimony at trial.

In all instances of the case, either the charges were dropped or the defendant was acquitted. The irresponsible tactics used by therapists and law enforcement officers demonstrate the strong animosity that many people feel toward child molesters. Unfortunately, in this case the well-meaning outrage of the police and therapists backfired.

SOURCE: Buckey v. County of Los Angeles, 968 F.2d 791 (9th Cir. 1992).

---

child molestation
Any sexual conduct by an adult with a child.

Generally, an adult person is guilty of **child molestation** if he or she engages in any sexual conduct with a child. This includes, but is not limited to:

- Exposing the genitals to a child.
- Having a child touch the perpetrator's genitals.

- Removing the child's clothing.
- Taking nude pictures of a child.
- Having a child touch the perpetrator or another child in an inappropriate fashion.

Many jurisdictions have general child molestation statutes providing that a perpetrator can be convicted of child molestation for almost any kind of sexual contact with a child, which is usually defined as an individual under the age of 13. In some states, such as Arizona, the age can be as high as 15. In almost all state statutes, the *mens rea* requirement for child molestation is established by showing that the molester intended to have sexual contact with a child. This is fairly easy to prove because if the molestation occurred, the intent to cause the act or harm is usually a given.

Child molestation statutes are often divided between first-degree and second-degree offenses, depending on the age of the victim. In Missouri, first-degree child molestation occurs when the child is under the age of 14 and the contact between the victim and perpetrator was sexual in nature. A second-degree charge involves a child who is less than 17. When a child is over the age of 17, the perpetrator is usually charged with rape or some type of sexual assault.[27]

Unfortunately, sexual abuse of children often goes undetected or unreported. Because so many children are abused by adults whom they know and are encouraged to respect, the children may not be willing to talk about it with another adult. In many instances, the molester will tell the child not to talk about what happened and may threaten further harm. Therefore, children often do not tell anyone about the abuse because of:

- A desire to protect the molester, who is often a family member or close family friend.
- A feeling that they were at fault, especially if they have been taught to look up to the molester.
- Fear of punishment.
- Difficulty in verbally expressing what has occurred.

Another possible problem is that once a nonoffending parent does learn of the events, that parent may not be inclined to push the issue because of the relation to the molester.

A serious issue in dealing with sexual abuse of children is the recidivist nature of the offender—in other words, offenders usually continue to molest each time they are released from prison. Upon release from prison, they move to communities in which their neighbors are unaware of their past history. In July 1994, convicted sex offender Jesse K. Timmendequas sexually assaulted and murdered seven-year-old Megan Kanka, who lived across the street from him in Hamilton Township, New Jersey. Megan's family was completely unaware of his prior record of sexual offending. As a result, Megan's Law was enacted in New Jersey later that year. **Megan's Law** requires community notification by authorities when a convicted sex offender is released from prison. The identities of these offenders are placed in a database, to which parents and other concerned community members have access. This database can perform a search by zip code to determine if convicted molesters reside in a given community. Megan's Law has now been adopted in all 50 states.

Megan's Law
A statute that has been enacted in all 50 states that requires community notification by authorities when a convicted sex offender is released from prison.

In California, all residents over the age of 18 who are not registered sex offenders have access to the database, and only need to state their reason for viewing it in order to do so. The information provided includes the names of sex offenders in a particular zip code (but not addresses), the crime committed, and (if available) a photograph of the perpetrator. Sexual offenders are added to the database for the following crimes: sexual abuse of a child, penetration of a genital or anal opening by a foreign object, kidnapping for purposes of lewd conduct, and sodomy.[28]

⚖ CRITICAL THINKING 9.2

1. How have recent laws changed the ways in which rape victims are treated at trials?

2. How does Megan's Law protect a community from recidivism among sexual offenders?

9.3 Crimes against the Person in the Home

This section will discuss historical and current issues regarding:

- Criminal abortion, which continues the discussion of feticide that began in Chapter 8.
- Child abuse, which can be physical, emotional, sexual, or the result of neglect.
- Spousal abuse, problems with prosecuting spousal abuse cases, and ways in which criminal justice personnel can learn to deal effectively with these cases.
- Elder abuse, which only recently has gained attention as a widespread form of family violence.

Criminal Abortion

Abortion is defined "as the spontaneous or artificially induced expulsion of an embryo or fetus."[29] Before 1973, abortion was a crime at common law, but the killing of an unborn child was a different offense than homicide. Early American criminal statutes included the crime of abortion, most of them punishing only the person performing the abortion. Later American laws in the mid- to late-nineteenth century made abortion a felony. These new laws punished the pregnant woman as well as the abortionist, and criminalized attempted abortion to eliminate the former legal necessity of proving pregnancy.

In *Roe v. Wade* (1973), the U.S. Supreme Court recognized the right to a legal abortion if the woman had not yet reached the third trimester of pregnancy. The decision in *Roe v. Wade* and in companion cases largely ended the criminal law of abortion as stated in the MPC and many state penal statutes. Current laws governing criminal abortion are enforceable only with respect to requirements that abortions must be performed by licensed physicians and with respect to abortions during the final trimester of pregnancy, when the fetus is usually viable. The law relating to abortion continues to be an area of considerable controversy in the United States.

criminal abortion
The artificially induced expulsion of a fetus by illegal means, such as spousal abuse.

Criminal abortion is very different from legal abortion. It involves the act of feticide, which is the killing of a fetus, or unborn child, other than by legal abortion. In any jurisdiction where feticide is not defined as homicide, the terms *criminal abortion* and *feticide* can be used interchangeably. (See Figure 9.2.) In

F I G U R E   9 . 2

Tennessee Criminal Abortion Statute

39-15-201. **Criminal abortion and attempt to procure miscarriage; lawful abortion; distinguished.**

(a)   For the purpose of this section:

  (1)   "Abortion" means the administration to any woman pregnant with child, whether the child be quick or not, of any medicine, drug, or substance whatever, or the use or employment of any instrument, or other means whatever, with the intent to destroy the child, thereby destroying the child before the child's birth; and

  (2)   "Attempt to procure a miscarriage" means the administration of any substance with the intention to procure the miscarriage of a woman or the use or employment of any instrument or other means with such intent.

(b)   (1)   Every person who performs an abortion commits the crime of criminal abortion, unless such abortion is performed in compliance with the requirements of subsection (c). Criminal abortion is a Class C felony.

  (2)   Every person who attempts to procure a miscarriage commits the crime of attempt to procure criminal miscarriage, unless the attempt to procure a miscarriage is performed in compliance with the requirements of subsection (c). Attempt to procure a criminal miscarriage is a Class E felony.

  (3)   Every person who compels, coerces, or exercises duress in any form with regard to any other person in order to obtain or procure an abortion on any female commits a misdemeanor. A violation of this section is a Class A misdemeanor.

SOURCE: Tenn. Code Ann § 39-15-201 (West 2007).

jurisdictions whose definitions of a person, for purposes of homicide, include fetuses, anyone who kills a fetus with the requisite intent of murder may be charged with feticide as the criminal homicide of a fetus. In this case, the killer must commit the act with malice. Whether the fetus was the intended victim is irrelevant because transferred intent is sufficient to meet the *mens rea* requirement. This means that if the defendant intended to kill another, such as a pregnant woman carrying the fetus, but killed the fetus instead, he or she can still be criminally liable for murder.

Although some states, such as California, will charge a person with feticide long before the fetus has reached viability, most states require that the fetus reach the point of viability before a person can be charged with the offense. **Viability** is the point at which a fetus can reasonably live outside its mother's womb, with or without artificial support. The point of viability may be reached as early as 22 weeks (about five months) of development. At this point, tests can be used to determine whether the fetus is actually viable. For example, suppose that a man accosts a woman who is three months pregnant at gunpoint, beats her until she is unconscious, and rapes her. As a result of the trauma from the attack, she suffers a miscarriage. In this case, the fetus was not viable at the time of the miscarriage and could not have survived outside of the womb. As a result, the perpetrator would

viability
The point at which a fetus can reasonably live outside its mother's womb, with or without artificial support.

not be charged with feticide in states that require the viability test. However, if the attack took place in a state where viability is not a necessary element, the man would be charged with feticide in addition to the crimes against the woman. (See Application Case 9.4.)

⚖️ Application Case 9.4

State v. Horne

In *State v. Horne*, a man violently beat his wife, which not only resulted in serious injuries to her but also caused the death of their nine-month-old fetus. Following the beating, the woman was rushed to the hospital, but the fetus had already suffocated because the mother's blood supply to the fetus had been cut off during the beating. The child, therefore, was born dead.

The prosecution was able to prove beyond a reasonable doubt that (1) the defendant had the requisite malice because he beat his wife, which transferred to the fetus, and (2) the fetus was viable at the time of the beating. As a result, the defendant was charged with and convicted of feticide.

SOURCE: State v. Horne, 319 S.E.2d 703 (N.C. 1984).

Child Abuse

child abuse

An intentional or neglectful physical or emotional injury imposed on a child, including sexual molestation.

Child abuse is an intentional or neglectful physical or emotional injury imposed on a child. This includes sexual molestation, which you learned about earlier in this chapter. According to a study from Administration for Children and Families, 872,000 children were victims of child abuse or neglect in 2004.[30] In addition, it is estimated that millions more cases go unreported each year. Moreover, 68 percent of all abuse occurs at the hands of the child's father or stepfather.[31] Child abuse can range from failure to supervise a child resulting in harm to actual physical abuse. In other words, a parent or guardian does not need to hit a child to be guilty of child abuse, but hitting can be considered child abuse in certain circumstances.

Child abuse often takes place in the home; whether the abuse is an act or an omission, parents are usually the perpetrators. Like many states, Maryland requires that in order to be convicted of felony child abuse in the first degree, the abuser must be either a parent, a person acting as the parent (a legal responsibility referred to as *in loco parentis*), or another person responsible for the supervision of the minor child.[32] Parents and guardians have an inherent duty that no other person has to care for, protect, and provide for their child. If the parent is the abuser, an observer of the abuse, or knows that the child is being abused, but fails to intervene, that parent will be punished by the child abuse laws of any state.

A person who does not have a special duty as a parent or guardian is still culpable for actual abuse, but does not have the same obligations if he or she is only a witness to abuse or is aware that abuse is occurring. If a child is being beaten continually by his father, and his live-in mother and next-door neighbor are both aware of the abuse, the mother must intervene or face punishment. On the other hand, the neighbor arguably has a moral obligation to intervene, but will not be criminally prosecuted for failing to do so. One exception is that, in almost all states, professionals who perform guardian-like roles, such as teachers and school nurses, are required to report the possible abuse of a child.

There are four general types of child abuse: neglect, physical abuse, sexual abuse, and emotional maltreatment.

Neglect

Neglect of a child can take various forms, such as:

- Denying a child proper nutrition.
- Failing to enroll a child at school.
- Leaving a young child alone.
- Residing with a child in an unsanitary home.

For example, Colorado's child abuse statute provides that "a person commits child abuse if such person [among other things] . . . engages in a continued pattern of conduct which results in malnourishment, [or] lack of proper medical care."[33] Suppose that a married couple has two children ages six and eight. They reside together in a one-bedroom apartment that has not been cleaned for several months. It is infested with cockroaches because of unwashed dishes and food scraps left throughout the home. Both parents work at night, and they leave the children at home by themselves for up to 10 hours. At times, there is no food in the house for the children to eat. There is no telephone, so that if there is an emergency, the children cannot call for help.

In such a situation, a social worker who visits the home and discovers the situation will most likely remove the children from the home because the parents' neglect could have serious consequences. Even when neglect does result in injury to a child, the punishment may not be as severe as if the parent directly injured the child. If a child who is left alone is hospitalized for malnutrition, the parent may only be charged with a misdemeanor, whereas a parent who physically harms a child may be charged with a felony. (See Application Case 9.5.)

⚖️ Application Case 9.5

State v. Williams

In *State v. Williams*, a husband and wife breached their duty of care to their 17-month-old baby by failing to get medical help when the baby became ill. An abscessed tooth had gone untreated and developed into an infection of the mouth and cheeks, which eventually became gangrenous. This condition left the child unable to eat, which caused malnutrition and lowered the child's resistance until the child contracted pneumonia, which was the actual cause of death. The couple had neglected to seek medical help because they were afraid that when a doctor saw the child's swollen cheeks, the child would be removed from the home. By the time they finally sought help, it was too late.

Although the parents were not well educated, the court found no evidence that they were either physically or financially unable to take the child to a doctor. The autopsy surgeon testified that the odor from the gangrene would have been noticeable 10 days prior to the child's death, so the parents had considerable warning that their child was in grave danger. As a result, both parents were convicted of manslaughter.

SOURCE: State v. Williams, 484 P.2d 1167 (Wash. Ct. App. 1971).

Physical Abuse

Physical abuse normally involves hitting, striking, beating, or in some way injuring the child by direct or indirect physical force. Indirect physical force includes using a belt or throwing an object with the intent to cause injury to a child. Direct physical abuse involves extreme forms of corporal punishment. Often, a parent will attempt to justify his or her actions by stating that the punishment was for the good of the child. California's child abuse statute provides that "'child abuse' means a physical injury which is inflicted by other than accidental means on a child by another person."[34]

Occasionally, it is hard to distinguish between child abuse, which is unlawful, and punishment by the parent, which is not. For example, many parents believe that spanking is an effective disciplinary tool, and spanking is normally not a criminal offense; however, a social worker may feel that a parent's use of spanking is excessive and beyond the bounds of reasonable parenting. To determine whether the action is excessive, a social worker will typically consider the following criteria:

- Permanent injuries, such as scarring.
- The amount of physical force used.
- How often the child is spanked.
- The age of the child when the incident occurs.

Sexual Abuse

Sexual abuse includes rape and child molestation. It ranges from improper touching of the child's genitalia to sexual intercourse. Although sexual abuse is often repetitive and ongoing, after one incident an abuser can be charged with child abuse. California's child abuse statute, for example, provides that sexual abuse of a child is considered child abuse.

Emotional Maltreatment

Emotional maltreatment involves what is often referred to as *verbal abuse*, which may include berating the child for his or her appearance, intelligence, or what a disappointment he or she is. Verbal abuse is not normally included in child abuse statutes, but a social worker may determine that excessive verbal attacks create an unhealthy environment for a child and remove the child from the home. In addition, a court may order a parent to attend parenting classes to learn how to parent without verbal abuse.

9.3 Web Exploration

Children's Defense Fund

Go to the Web site for the Children's Defense Fund, located at http://www.childrensdefense.org. Click the link to go to the main Web site, and click the About Us link. Place your cursor over the text in the center of the page and read the different pages that are linked, highlighting the goals of the CDF. What does CDF mean by "A Healthy Start," "A Head Start," and the other items that you see listed? Overall, what is the goal of the CDF?

There has emerged in the area of child abuse a recognized pattern known as **battered child syndrome**, originating from a theory developed by Dr. Henry C. Kempe in 1962 as a physical diagnosis for describing abuse.[35] It is described as a clinical condition suffered by young children who have been the victims of prolonged serious physical abuse. The syndrome has two components: clinical manifestations and psychiatric aspects. Clinical manifestations include occurrence at any age, but generally in children age three or younger; medical findings conflicting with parents' explanations of the children's injuries; and a history of physical injury indicative of intentional abuse. Psychiatric aspects, often used to determine whether the parent intentionally injured the child, include parental history of abuse as a child, low intelligence level, and lack of maturity; parental denial of involvement in the injury; and a pattern of alcoholism, sexual promiscuity, unstable marriages, and minor criminal acts. The theory of child abuse syndrome has evolved to refer to both physiological and psychological effects of long-term abuse, analogous to battered woman syndrome. Courts have recognized both physiological and psychological explanations, generally permitting physiological explanation as evidence of intent to abuse. However, courts rarely allow psychological explanation as a defense to criminal acts perpetrated by the abused person as a justification for killing the abuser.[36]

battered child syndrome
A clinical condition suffered by young children who have been the victims of prolonged serious physical abuse.

Spousal Abuse

Spousal abuse usually involves long-term physical abuse by a man against his wife or girlfriend, although occasionally it involves abuse of a man by a woman and can also happen in homosexual relationships. Spousal abuse raises different concerns than other types of abuse because of the preexisting relationships involved. In spousal abuse cases, the person being abused often does not feel free to leave the relationship, because she fears for her physical safety or feels financial and emotional dependence on the abuser.

spousal abuse
Long-term physical abuse by the victim's spouse or partner.

In recent years, psychologists have recognized a pattern exhibited by many abused women who endure long-term abuse. **Battered woman syndrome**, in which the victim of abuse eventually "snaps" and kills the abuser, is now recognized as a valid defense in many jurisdictions. A victim of domestic abuse may raise the defense of battered woman syndrome if charged in the death of her husband or boyfriend. The defense is usually allowed only in a particular set of circumstances, in which a woman believes that if she does not kill her spouse, he will kill her. This unique defense

battered woman syndrome
A defense in many jurisdictions, in which the victim of abuse eventually "snaps" and kills the abuser.

creates unique problems because usually when a defendant claims self-defense, he or she must show that there were no reasonable alternatives. However, battered women often stay in abusive relationships long after the beating begins and are physically capable of escaping, but do not for complex psychological reasons.

The following provides a brief overview of the battering cycle:

- *Phase one* is the tension-building stage, in which the batterer engages in minor incidents of verbal abuse or physical incidents. At this stage, the victim begins to fear that she will be harmed. Often she tries to be as passive as possible to avoid further abuse, but by not taking action she is actually setting herself up for the next phase.
- *Phase two* is the acute battering incident, in which something provokes the perpetrator, and he acts out physically.
- In *phase three*, the abuser regrets his actions and promises to get help in stopping the abuse, whether by refraining from alcohol or seeking out anger management assistance. This phase is what gets women to stay, because they believe the abuser's remorse and think that the abuse has ended. This cycle repeats indefinitely for months or years, until the victim either is killed or leaves.[37]

Even if a woman kills her abuser while he sleeps or several hours after he has abused her, experts in the field believe that a woman suffering from the syndrome reasonably believes that her life is in jeopardy at the time she commits the killing. Therefore, in these cases, this defense can be used successfully.

Unfortunately, law enforcement officers come across countless incidents of domestic violence. Often, the batterers are drunk; equally often, victims of domestic violence call the police when being beaten but refuse to press charges or testify in court. This pattern can become frustrating for officers who respond to these calls, because their efforts to help the victim can go nowhere.

The officer should always try to be sympathetic, regardless of the situation or the history of the couple's behavior. Even if the woman refuses to press charges, the officer should try to separate the couple for the time being so that the abuse will not continue at that time. The officer should see if the victim has a friend or relative whom the officer can call to assist the victim. The officer should refer the victim to the emergency shelters in her community and any hotline numbers available for her to call when being abused. Depending on the jurisdiction, the officer may be able to arrest the perpetrator, and even gain a conviction, without the victim's assistance. To facilitate convictions for domestic violence, some states are using expert witnesses to testify to abuse when victims refuse to do so.

Elder Abuse

elder abuse
The abuse, neglect, or financial exploitation of elderly persons.

Abuse of the elderly may bring to mind news stories of horrific conditions in nursing homes: residents left for days in their beds, lying in their own urine, and enduring physical abuse from caregivers or nurses. In reality, **elder abuse**, which is the abuse, neglect, or financial exploitation of elderly persons, usually occurs in the home. Furthermore, the perpetrators are frequently the victim's spouse or children. When an older person requires another to take care of him or her, he or she is at the mercy of

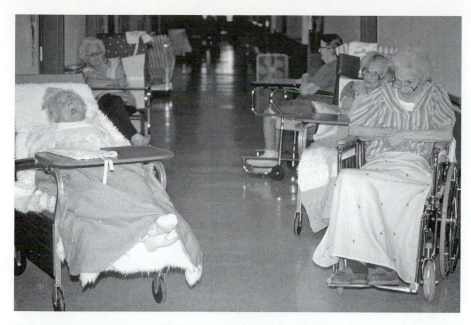

Elder Abuse   Although most elder abuse occurs in the home, it can also occur in nursing homes like this.

the caregiver; all too often, the burden is overwhelming, and the elder does not get the care and attention he or she needs.

Because elder abuse often occurs after the victim has become incapacitated and requires the assistance of another person for basic living, reporting the abuse can be difficult. The victim may not have access to a telephone, may be unable to communicate, or may not know whom to contact. Because the abuse is usually committed by a family member, the victim may not want to report the abuse or may hope it will eventually end on its own.

Financial exploitation is a common form of elder abuse. A common action is for the abuser to take advantage of the victim's possible memory loss or inability to organize and manage his or her own possessions and assets. Often, a victim will request help in managing finances, and this leads to manipulation or outright theft by the perpetrator.

Females represent more than 52 percent of abusers, which is quite different from other abuse profiles, as well as 65 percent of those who suffer from elder abuse.[38] As medical progress makes it possible for people to live longer despite chronic health conditions and overall deterioration, older adults will continue to need assistance for longer periods of time. As a result, family members may experience additional emotional and financial pressures, and this may continue to trigger elder abuse.

CRITICAL THINKING 9.3

1. How does viability affect the prosecution of feticide cases?

2. What are the differences in how social workers and prosecutors treat emotional abuse, physical abuse, sexual abuse, and neglect of children?

9.4 False Imprisonment and Kidnapping

False imprisonment and kidnapping are discussed together in this chapter because most jurisdictions currently view them similarly. Although there is a correlation between the two offenses, it is important to recognize that the elements of these crimes are different. These elements are discussed throughout this section.

False Imprisonment

false imprisonment

Knowingly and unlawfully restraining a person so as to substantially interfere with his or her liberty.

False imprisonment is defined as knowingly and unlawfully restraining a person, and thus substantially interfering with his or her liberty. Therefore, the elements of the crime are (1) the act of unlawfully restraining a person so as to substantially interfere with his or her liberty, and (2) the specific intent to restrain that person. Prior to the adoption of the MPC in the 1960s, few states considered false imprisonment a crime. After the introduction of the MPC, many states revised their penal codes, and a majority of them included the offense for the first time.

Most false imprisonment statutes punish the crime as a misdemeanor, but a felony charge is possible when aggravated circumstances are involved. An example of false imprisonment would be a situation in which two friends are arguing over money that one friend owes the other. Suppose the person owing the money is at the other person's residence and wants to leave without paying. If the person who lives at the residence blocks the exit and refuses to allow his friend to leave unless he pays the money, he may be charged with false imprisonment regardless of whether he is rightly owed the money. There are other courses of action he could take to get the money back, such as suing his friend in civil court, but he does not have the right to hold his friend against his will.

The *actus reus* requirement of false imprisonment is that the defendant compel the victim to remain in a place where he or she does not want to remain or compel the victim to go where he or she does not want to go. There is no requirement that the defendant make threats of physical injury or harm. The defendant need only confine the person in some place against his or her will and without his or her consent. The place of confinement may be as small as a closet or as large as a house, or may even be on a public street. The length of time required can be as short as a few seconds or as long as days or weeks.

What determines whether actual confinement has taken place is whether the victim had alternate ways of leaving. Suppose that a man traps a woman in a room with only one locked door and no windows. Since there is no alternate way for the woman to leave the room, and assuming that she did not consent to being in the room, she has been falsely imprisoned. If there were a window through which the woman could safely escape without harm, the woman would be obligated to do so, and the defendant would likely not be found guilty of false imprisonment. If, however, the woman were 80 years old, in poor health, and with little mobility, the defendant would probably not be able to defend his actions by arguing that she had an alternate means of escape. In determining whether a victim had a safe alternate way of escape, a fact-finder must determine whether the average reasonable person in the same situation would feel that he or she could escape safely. A reasonable

80-year-old woman would probably not be able to crawl out of a window and jump to safety.

Most jurisdictions require a showing of specific intent in order for someone to be guilty of false imprisonment. This means that the defendant must have intended to confine the victim. (See Application Case 9.6.) Suppose that Jim invites his friend Bonnie to his house to watch a movie. As he leaves the house to go rent the movie, he accidentally locks a door that can only be opened from the outside. When Bonnie attempts to go outside to get something from her car, she cannot get out; in a panic, she calls 911. In most jurisdictions, Jim would not be guilty of false imprisonment because he had no intention of restraining Bonnie.

⚖️ Application Case 9.6

In the Matter of the Welfare of R.W.C.

In the Minnesota case *In the Matter of the Welfare of R.W.C.* (1997), the defendant was a high school student who, with three of his friends, wrapped duct tape around another student until he was unable to move. Before leaving the student in an isolated stairwell, the defendant shoved the student, causing him to fall and sustain injuries. The defendant argued that he did not know he was not allowed to engage in "taping" because it was a tradition at his high school.

The court interpreted the *mens rea* requirement of Minnesota's false imprisonment statute only as acting with intention to produce a specific *result*; it did not require acting with knowledge that the conduct was wrongful. Whether or not the defendant knew he was not allowed to tape the other student had no bearing on the defendant's guilt because he acted to produce a specific result—to restrain the student by taping him and leaving him immobile. The appellate court affirmed the defendant's conviction for false imprisonment.

SOURCE: In the Matter of the Welfare of R.W.C., 1997 WL 3366 (Minn. Ct. App. 1997).

There are some unique situations in which a person may be held by lawful restraint. The two main lawful restraint categories are the "shopkeeper's rule" and law enforcement.

Lawful Restraint: The Shopkeeper's Rule

The **shopkeeper's rule** provides that a shopkeeper, defined as an owner or manager of a store or restaurant, may restrain a person if the shopkeeper possesses a reasonable belief that the customer has not paid a bill or has shoplifted an item. In this situation, a shopkeeper may restrain the customer in order to ascertain whether the bill or item has been paid for. As long as the restraint does not last an inordinate amount of time and no physical force is used, the owner will not be charged with or convicted of false imprisonment even if the customer has actually paid the bill or paid for the item.

shopkeeper's rule
An exception to false imprisonment laws that gives a shopkeeper the right to restrain a person if the shopkeeper possesses a reasonable belief that the customer has not paid a bill or has shoplifted an item.

Lawful Restraint by Law Enforcement

The second and most common type of lawful restraint involves restraint by law enforcement. If a police officer detains or arrests a person, such imprisonment is not against the law. If a driver is speeding, the police officer is within his or her lawful right to sound the siren, flash the lights, and force the driver to pull over. The time the driver spends waiting for the officer to check for registration and write a ticket is a form of restraint because the driver has to remain in his or her car, but the restraint is lawful. If an officer restrains a person unlawfully, the officer could be charged with false imprisonment. Suppose that a male officer notices an attractive female driver and pulls her over without any legal cause to do so. Once he pulls her over, he makes up a reason for doing so, asks for her license, and goes to his car to run a computer check. He then returns to her car and admits that the only reason he pulled her over was to ask for her phone number. In this situation, an officer can be charged with and convicted of false imprisonment.

Kidnapping

At common law, kidnapping was a rather obscure misdemeanor defined as "the unlawful confinement and transportation of another out of the country."[39] Today, **kidnapping** is a serious major felony, defined as "[t]he act or an instance of taking or carrying away a person without consent, by force or fraud, and without lawful excuse—and often with a demand for ransom."[40] The common law requirement of transporting the victim out of the country, which was also known as *asportation*, established the basic element of removing the victim from the protection of the law. Modern kidnapping statutes retain this element to some extent. They usually involve the forcible movement of a person from one place to another, or confining the victim secretly. It is important to note that common law asportation involved removing an individual from a place of more security to a place of less security. Kidnapping, however, does not require extensive movement. With kidnapping, the issue is not the distance moved, but the change in security.

For example, Illinois's kidnapping statute provides that kidnapping occurs when a person (1) knowingly and secretly confines another against his will, or (2) by force or threat of imminent force carries another from one place to another with intent secretly to confine him against his will, or (3) by deceit or enticement induces another to go from one place to another with intent secretly to confine him against his will.[41]

Most jurisdictions require that a perpetrator specifically intend to move a person from a particular locale and to confine that person for some period of time against his or her will. Kidnapping is often committed in tandem with another, usually violent crime. In some instances, it is incidental to the commission of another crime. Suppose that Gerry walks into a liquor store to rob it. The store clerk hits the alarm, and Gerry hears police sirens coming closer while he is still in the store. He panics and holds a gun to the clerk's head, demanding that she come with him. He then drives her to his house, where he holds her for 12 hours while deciding what to do. Gerry would be guilty of kidnapping in addition to the robbery.

kidnapping
A felony defined as taking or carrying away a person without consent, by force or fraud, without lawful excuse, and often with a demand for ransom.

9.1 On the Job

Certified Victim Assistance Specialist

Description and Duties: Provide victim assistance and advocacy immediately following the crime and for several months following. Provide telephone support. Provide referral assistance to crime victims in their homes. Develop and update resource and referral contacts files. In some positions, dispatch locksmiths to secure the homes of victims of domestic violence, robbery, burglary, sexual assault, harassment, and other types of crimes.

Salary: Many specialist positions are filled by volunteers. A typical specialist position does not pay more than $30,000.

Other Information: Victim assistance specialists must complete certification training, which can include the following elements:

- One year of experience in a trauma-related field.
- Associate's degree, two years of trauma services or crisis response training, or two years of trauma services or support work.
- Letters of recommendation from one supervisor and one colleague.
- Current resume with documented experience in trauma service field.
- Recertification every three years.
- Thirty hours of continuing education.
- Six days of training designed to enhance the knowledge, skills, and effectiveness of victim assistants.

SOURCE: Association of Traumatic Stress Specialists (ATSS), http://www.atss-hq.com; Victim Assistance Institute at the University of South Carolina, http://www.sc.edu/cosw/center/vai.html; and Safe Horizon, http://www.safehorizon.org.htm.

According to the American Bar Association, more than 300,000 children are abducted each year. About half of these cases involve parents kidnapping their own children and taking them out of state—usually because the kidnappers are unhappy with child custody decisions. In response to the growing number of children being abducted by their parents, Congress enacted legislation that responds to the specific crime of parental kidnapping and child abduction. The Parental Kidnapping Prevention Act requires states to enforce child custody decisions entered by a court of another state if the custody decision is consistent with provisions of the act.

The other federal law involving child kidnapping is the Lindbergh Act. Although this act is not specific to children, it was passed in 1934 in response to the kidnapping and murder of Charles Lindbergh, Jr., the 20-month-old son of aviator Charles Lindbergh. This law specifically addresses kidnapping for ransom or reward when the victim is transported to another state or to a foreign country.[42]

CRITICAL THINKING 9.4

1. How have laws changed regarding kidnapping?
2. Explain the Parental Kidnapping Prevention Act.

REVIEW AND APPLICATIONS

Summary by Chapter Objectives

1. **State the elements of battery.** The three elements of battery are:
   - The actor's conduct of touching or applying force to the victim.
   - The actor's mental state (intent to injure, or criminal negligence, or, in some jurisdictions, while committing an unlawful act).
   - The harm done to the victim (bodily injury or offensive touching).

2. **List the elements of assault.** The three elements of the crime of assault are:
   - An attempt to batter, or conduct that is threatening, menacing, or otherwise designed to frighten the victim (intentional scaring).
   - The intent to commit a battery upon the victim or to frighten the victim.
   - The result that the conduct in fact does frighten the victim and would arouse a reasonable apprehension of bodily harm in the average person.

3. **State the elements of mayhem.** The elements of mayhem are the infliction of a specified injury constituting dismemberment, disablement, or disfigurement, and the intent to maim or disfigure.

4. **List the essential elements of robbery.** The elements of robbery are:
   - The taking of property.
   - From a person.
   - With the intent to deprive the owner of the property.
   - By the use of force, fear, or intimidation.

5. **State the elements of rape, and explain the difference between rape and statutory rape.** In general, rape is sexual intercourse by a male defendant with a female victim that is committed in any one of the four following ways:
   - Forcibly.
   - By means of some specific forms of deception.
   - While the victim was asleep or unconscious.
   - Under circumstances in which the victim was not competent to give consent (e.g., under the influence of drugs, mental disability, or being too young).

   Rape is sexual intercourse without consent. Statutory rape consists of sexual contact, with or without consent, between an adult and a minor. In most states, the age range for statutory rape is 13 to 17. An individual who has reached the age of sexual consent, which is often 18, is considered an adult, and an individual below the minimum age is considered a child; an adult who has sexual contact with anyone below this minimum age will be tried for child molestation.

6. **Describe Megan's Law.** Megan's Law is a statute that requires community notification by authorities when a convicted sex offender is released from prison and moves into that community. It originated in New Jersey in 1994 but has since been adopted in all other states.

7. **Define child abuse.** Child abuse is any intentional or neglectful harm done to a child; in other words, child abuse can be inflicted either by an action or by an

omission. The four main categories of child abuse are neglect, physical abuse, sexual abuse, and emotional maltreatment. Prosecution varies depending on the nature and the extent of the abuse, but all states have laws that make parents and legal guardians liable for committing, witnessing, or even knowing about the abuse of their child without notifying authorities.

8. **Distinguish between the elements of false imprisonment and kidnapping.** The elements of false imprisonment are the act of unlawfully restraining a person so as to substantially interfere with his or her liberty, and the specific intent to restrain that person. Modern elements of kidnapping usually involve the forcible movement of a person from one place to another or confining the victim secretly.

Key Terms

battery (p. 242)
aggravated battery (p. 243)
assault (p. 243)
conditional assault (p. 244)
aggravated assault (p. 245)
mayhem (p. 245)
robbery (p. 246)
armed robbery (p. 248)
rape (p. 249)
statutory rape (p. 253)
spousal rape (p. 253)
rape trauma syndrome (p. 253)

child molestation (p. 254)
Megan's Law (p. 255)
criminal abortion (p. 256)
viability (p. 257)
child abuse (p. 258)
battered child syndrome (p. 261)
spousal abuse (p. 261)
battered woman syndrome (p. 261)
elder abuse (p. 262)
false imprisonment (p. 264)
shopkeeper's rule (p. 265)
kidnapping (p. 266)

Review Questions

1. Name some ways in which assault and battery differ from mayhem.
2. How do aggravated assault and aggravated battery differ from simple assault and battery?
3. Why is rape considered a general intent offense?
4. Explain how the laws regarding statutory rape have changed over time.
5. Define spousal rape, and explain recent legislation to outlaw it.
6. Name some reasons why child molestation frequently goes unreported.
7. Why are parents and guardians more liable for child abuse than others?
8. What are some ways that social workers can respond to child neglect? To child physical abuse? To child emotional maltreatment?
9. Who is usually the perpetrator in elder abuse cases, and why?
10. How did the MPC affect laws regarding false imprisonment?
11. Explain how the shopkeeper's rule works. What are its limitations?
12. Name and define the two legal responses to child abduction discussed in this chapter.

Problem-Solving Exercises

1. **Assault and Battery** A police officer responds to a call to a park late at night and finds eight young men huddled around one 18-year-old male, who is lying on the ground. He is bleeding from his nose and mouth and is cupping his right eye, screaming, "I can't see! I can't see!" From what the officer learns, there had apparently been a "meeting" of two rival gangs, and one member from each gang fought each other. The victim lying on the ground had taken the first punch, but threw the last punch. Answer the following questions:

   a. What crimes have been committed against the young man lying on the ground?

   b. What crimes has the young man committed?

   c. How would you recommend that the prosecutor handle the case?

2. **Spousal Abuse** An officer responds to a 911 dispatcher's call that a man has been bludgeoned to death with a shovel. When the officer arrives on the scene, the officer finds a woman on the ground, holding her husband's lifeless body in her arms 100 yards from their home. After speaking to a neighbor who witnessed the events leading up to the man's death, the officer learns that the couple had been married for three years and, almost from the beginning, had a very tumultuous relationship. The police had been called to the house twice before, both times for domestic disturbances. On this particular day, the couple had fought for approximately an hour—both screaming at the top of their lungs. The man apparently chased his wife out of their home and down the street. He then turned around and began walking home, as though nothing had happened. The wife picked up a shovel lying on another neighbor's front lawn, charged at her husband from behind, and hit him over the head. He immediately dropped to the ground, and although his wife tried to resuscitate him, he had obviously died the moment he was hit with the shovel. At the wife's trial, could the battered woman syndrome be successfully used as a defense? Why or why not? Based on what you have read in this and the previous chapter, could another defense be used successfully?

3. **Sex Crimes and False Imprisonment** A man and woman are set up on a blind dinner date and arrive at the restaurant in their own cars. During dinner, the woman is totally turned off by the man's sick sense of humor and bad eating habits, but the man finds the woman extremely entertaining and attractive. When they finish dinner, the woman intends to leave, but the man insists that she go for a ride in his car to the beach, which is just a mile away. The woman really doesn't want to go and tells the man this, but he repeatedly asks her and she finally gives in, only because she really loves the beach and hasn't been in a long time. They get into his car, begin a conversation, and arrive at the beach parking lot. The woman begins to unbuckle her seatbelt, but the man grabs her hands, holds her down, and eventually forces the woman to have sexual intercourse against her will. Can the man be charged with kidnapping? False imprisonment? Rape?

4. **Assault** You are a parole officer. One of your clients has been arrested for waving around a large cattle bone, which he said that he found in the trash of a nearby meat packing plant. He was arrested when he waved the bone around in a

crowded public place and the bone brushed against someone's head. At the time of his arrest, he was heavily intoxicated.

a. Should your client's parole be revoked? Why or why not?

b. Was the client's arrest justified? Why or why not? With what crimes could he be charged?

Workplace Applications

1. **Child Abuse** You are a social worker responding to a report of an anonymous caller who stated that the three children next door had not been seen in 10 days. When you arrive, you meet a woman who is apparently the mother. You tell her the station received an anonymous call and wanted to make sure everything was okay. The woman invites you to come in, where you see children's toys on the floor. When you ask if her children are home, she responds that they are in their rooms and have been punished for being bad. She goes on to tell you that they are not good in school, so she has pulled them from their school and is thinking about homeschooling them. Answer the following questions:

    a. What questions should you ask the mother to determine if abuse is occurring?

    b. What evidence should you look for?

    c. Could the mother be charged with child abuse?

    d. What other facts might be helpful in making this determination?

2. **Domestic Violence** Contact your local domestic violence shelter and ask to speak to someone who works as a counselor or in a counseling role (most of the employees at these shelters are volunteers). Ask him or her to describe the services that the shelter provides, as well as the typical outcome for women who come to this shelter. Do many return to their husbands, or do they stay separated? How many of them have children, and how does this affect a woman's decision to leave an abuser? Write your findings in a one-page report.

3. **Crime on Campus** You are a police officer answering a service call near the local university. A woman comes out of her apartment crying and states that her roommate intimidated her and wouldn't let her leave the bedroom until she gave her money. When the woman gave her roommate $40 in cash, the roommate shoved her onto the bed and ran out of the room.

    a. With what crimes could the roommate be charged?

    b. Do you need other information before you make an arrest? Why or why not?

Ethics Exercises

1. **Abuse** A young homeless woman and her baby arrive at a church for shelter. An older woman who lives alone and is a member of the church offers to take them in and provide them with food and shelter until the young mother can find a job and get back on her feet. After about one week, the young woman begins to act strangely and tells the old woman that she is possessed by the devil. The old woman starts to be concerned, but assumes that her head is just "a little messed up from living on the streets." During the next week, the old woman hears the

young girl chanting in her room while the baby is crying. Two days after that, she hears what sounds like the woman beating the baby and the baby crying continually. The old woman questions the young woman, who replies, "I have to beat the Devil. I can't let him take over my life. Those who are bad must be punished." Answer the following questions:

a. What kind of abuse seems to be occurring?
b. If physical abuse is occurring, what legal options could she exercise?
c. Does the woman have a duty to protect the child from further abuse, as she was giving food and shelter to the mother and baby?
d. Could she be charged for the abuse that has already occurred? What about the mother?

Notes

1. WAYNE R. LAFAVE, SUBSTANTIVE CRIMINAL LAW § 16.2(a), n.5 (2003), citing MODEL PENAL CODE § 211.1 and comment (1985).
2. *Id.* at § 16.3(b), nn.38 & 40.
3. 4 WILLIAM BLACKSTONE, COMMENTARIES *205.
4. WAYNE R. LAFAVE, SUBSTANTIVE CRIMINAL LAW § 16.5(c) (2003).
5. FLA. STAT. ANN. § 812.13(1) (West 2007).
6. State v. Aldershof, 556 P.2d 371, 375 (Kan. 1976). The principle stated in that case was reconsidered and reaffirmed in State v. Bateson, 970 P.2d 1000 (Kan. 1998).
7. Santilli v. State, 570 So. 2d 400 (Fla. Dist. Ct. App. 1990).
8. Andre v. State, 431 So. 2d 1042 (Fla. Dist. Ct. App. 1983), overruled by Robinson v. State, 431 So. 2d 883 (1997), but effectively reinstated by enactment (effective 1999) of FLA. STAT. ANN. § 812.131.
9. Jefferson v. State, 840 P.2d 1234 (Nev. 1992).
10. People v. Freeman, 157 Cal. Rptr. 454 (Cal. Ct. App. 1979).
11. S.C. CODE § 16.11-330(A) (2006).
12. GA. CODE ANN. §16-8-40(b), (c) (West 2007).
13. 4 WILLIAM BLACKSTONE, COMMENTARIES *210.
14. *See* JOSHUA DRESSLER, UNDERSTANDING CRIMINAL LAW § 33.01[B], at 618 (4th ed. 2006).
15. BUREAU OF JUSTICE STATISTICS, NATIONAL CRIME VICTIMIZATION SURVEY (2005); *see* http://www.ojp.usdoj.gov/bjs/pub/pdf/cvus/current/cv0502.pdf. *See also* JOSHUA DRESSLER, UNDERSTANDING CRIMINAL LAW § 33.02[B], at 620 (4th ed. 2006).
16. JOSHUA DRESSLER, UNDERSTANDING CRIMINAL LAW § 33.04[B][1][a], at 625 n.49 (4th ed. 2006), citing Commonwealth v. Berkowitz, 641 A.2d 1161, 1164 (Pa. 1994); State v. Alston, 312 S.E.2d 470 (N.C. 1984).
17. *Id.* at 628, n.63, citing People v. Dohring, 59 N.Y. 374, 386 (1874).
18. *Id.* n.64, citing King v. State, 357 S.W.2d 42, 45 (Tenn. 1962).
19. *Id.* § 33.04[B][2][b], at 634–35, nn.94–99, citing and quoting State in the Interest of M.T.S., 609 A.2d 1266 (N.J. 1992).
20. *Id.* § 33.05, at 637.

21. *Id.* § 33.02, at 619–20, n.26.

22. Flora Guillory, *The Trap of Marital Rape*, http://suite101.com/article.cfm/
    rape_prevention_survival/51294.

23. *See* Bureau of Justice Statistics, National Crime Victimization
    Survey (2005), *available at* http://www.rainn.org/statistics/index
    .html?gclid=CLSurd27-IsCFSBhgQod-mNeVw.

24. Sexual Harassment and Rape Prevention Program [SHARPP], *The Wife
    Rape Information Page*, http://www.unh.edu/sharpp/stats_facts_folder/
    marital_rape.htm.

25. See Paul C. Giannelli & Edward J. Imwinkelried, *Scientific Evidence*, in
    Encyclopedia of Crime and Justice 1375–76 (Joshua Dressler ed.,
    2d ed. 2002).

26. Child Predator Statistics, http://www.yellodyno.com/html/childabusestatistics
    .html.

27. Mo. Ann. Stat. § 566.040 (sexual assault); § 566.067 (child molestation in the
    first degree); § 566.068 (child molestation in the second degree) (West 2006).

28. Cal. Penal Code § 290.4 (West 2007). For an explanation of the law available
    on the World Wide Web, go to http://www.familywatchdog.us. Many states
    also have Web sites where the public can find out where sex offenders live in
    their community. Just type your state's name and "sex offender" into a search
    engine such as Google.com or Yahoo.com. For example, see http://www.
    meganslaw.ca.gov (California); https://az.gov/webapp/offender/main.do
    (Arizona).

29. Black's Law Dictionary 6 (8th ed. 2004).

30. Administration for Children and Families, *available at* http://www.acf.dhhs
    .gov/programs/cb/pubs/cm04/summary.htm.

31. Thomas Roesler & Tiffany Weissman Wind, *Telling the Secret: Adult Women
    Describe Their Disclosures of Incest*, 9 J. Interpersonal Violence 327–38
    (1994).

32. Md. Code Ann., Fam. Law § 5-701(b)(1) (West 2007).

33. Colo. Rev. Stat. Ann. §18-6-401(1) (West 2007) (amendment to this statute
    pending as of May 2007).

34. Cal. Penal Code §11165.6 (West 2007).

35. See Kristi Baldwin, *Battered Child Syndrome as a Sword and a Shield*, 29 Am. J.
    Crim. L. 59 (2001).

36. *Id.* at 79–80.

37. Joshua Dressler, Understanding Criminal Law § 18.05[B][3][b],
    at 261 (4th ed. 2006) (citing Lenore E. Walker, The Battered Woman
    Syndrome 75–85 (1984)).

38. National Center on Elder Abuse, http://www.elderabusecenter.org/pdf/
    2-14-06%2060FACT%20SHEET.pdf.

39. Model Penal Code § 212.1, cmt. 1 (1985).

40. Black's Law Dictionary 886 (8th ed. 2004).

41. 720 Ill. Comp. Stat. § 5/10-1(a) (2007).

42. 18 U.S.C. § 1201 (2007).

Crimes against Habitation

CHAPTER OBJECTIVES

After reading and studying this chapter, you should be able to:

1. Understand the difference between common and modern law arson.
2. Explain the difference between specific intent and general intent arson.
3. List the three elements of burglary.
4. Explain how a burglary can be committed without actual entry by the perpetrator.
5. Understand the intent required to commit a burglary.
6. Explain the difference between simple and aggravated burglary.
7. State the difference between burglary and breaking and entering.
8. Name the elements of the crime of possession of burglar's tools.

10.1 Arson

This chapter categorizes arson and burglary not as crimes against property, but by their common law distinction of being crimes against habitation. At common law, the felonies of arson and burglary developed to provide special protection and security to people's dwellings. This distinction existed for several reasons, one of the most important being that crimes against dwellings could lead to serious violent crimes against the residents of the house. Although modern statutes do not retain the same strict dwelling requirements as before and have broadened their scope considerably, it is still useful to categorize arson and burglary separately, as we have done here.

Common law arson was the malicious and willful burning of another's house. A house was defined as the dwelling of the occupant and any buildings located in the **curtilage**—the land immediately surrounding and associated with the home—such as a barn, outhouse, or milk house. Arson was considered a crime against habitation only, and not a crime against property. Therefore, the burning of an unoccupied house or dwelling was not considered arson.

For the burning of the dwelling to constitute arson, charring of the wood, no matter how minor, was required. Scorching, discoloration, or smoking of the wood did not constitute arson unless charring also occurred. The law also required that the burning be malicious and willful. *Malice*, as you have learned in previous chapters, is the desire to injure a victim by means of a crime. **Willfulness** was a separate element that required proof that the arsonist set the fire intentionally.

Under modern law, most jurisdictions consider arson to be a violent crime against *both* habitation and property. **Modern arson** is generally defined as the malicious, willful burning, or attempted burning, of one's own or another person's property. The Model Penal Code, for example, provides that a person is guilty of arson:

> [I]f he starts a fire or causes an explosion with the purpose of:
> (a) destroying a building or occupied structure of another; or
> (b) destroying or damaging any property, whether his own or another's, to collect insurance for such loss.[1]

Prior to the MPC, there was a "vast legislative development" in the United States that changed the definition of arson to include the burning of almost any property. At the time the MPC was drafted, its drafters noted that three legislative patterns had developed in the United States:

1. Classifying the offense in relation to the types of property involved.
2. Classifying the offense in relation to the danger to persons involved.
3. Following the influence of the Model Arson Law proposed by the National Board of Fire Underwriters in 1953. This proposal introduced the definition of arson as the burning of any property of any type, no matter by whom owned, for the purpose of defrauding an insurer.

States are still divided on how property is defined. Generally speaking, most states have expanded the definition of property from the limited "dwelling house" definition under the common law rule to include virtually any structure and, in some instances, personal property. The definition of a dwelling house has been expanded to include structures that people do not use regularly as a place to sleep. For example,

common law arson

The malicious and willful burning of another's house.

curtilage

The land immediately surrounding and associated with the home, including such structures as a barn, outhouse, or milk house.

willfulness

The voluntary, intentional nature of a crime; required as a separate element of arson.

modern arson

The malicious, willful burning of, or attempted burning of, one's own or another person's property.

Florida statutes define arson in the first degree as the willful and unlawful damage by fire or explosion of:

- Any dwelling, whether occupied or not, or its contents.
- Any structure where persons are normally present, such as jails, hospitals, department stores, office buildings, or churches.
- Any structure that the arsonist knew or had reasonable grounds to believe was occupied by a human being.[2]

Moreover, this statute defines a structure "as any building of any kind, any enclosed area with a roof over it, any real property and appurtenances thereto, any tent or other portable building, and any vehicle, vessel, watercraft, or aircraft."[3]

Only a handful of states still follow the narrow common law definition of arson as a crime against habitation only, especially when defining levels of arson (see Figure 10.1). For example, Maryland law provides that arson in the first degree is the burning of an inhabited structure, but the burning of any other structure constitutes

---

FIGURE   10.1

Vermont Statutes Defining Arson

502. First degree arson.

A person who wilfully and maliciously sets fire to or burns or causes to be burned, or who wilfully and maliciously aids, counsels or procures the burning of any dwelling house, whether occupied, unoccupied or vacant, or any kitchen, shop, barn, stable or other outhouse that is parcel thereof, or belonging, or adjoining thereto, whether the property of himself or of another, shall be guilty of arson in the first degree, and shall be imprisoned not more than ten years nor less than two years or fined not more than $2,000.00, or both.

503. Second degree arson.

A person who wilfully and maliciously sets fire to or burns or causes to be burned, or who wilfully and maliciously aids, counsels or procures the burning of any building or structure of whatsoever class or character, whether the property of himself or of another, not included or described in section 502 of this title, shall be guilty of arson in the second degree, and shall be imprisoned not more than five years nor less than one year or fined not more than $1,000.00, or both.

504. Third degree arson.

A person who wilfully and maliciously sets fire to or burns or causes to be burned, or who wilfully and maliciously aids, counsels or procures the burning of any personal property of whatsoever class or character, not less than $25.00 in value and the property of another person, shall be guilty of arson in the third degree, and shall be imprisoned not more than three years nor less than one year, or fined not more than $500.00, or both.

505. Fourth degree arson.

A person who wilfully and maliciously attempts to set fire to or wilfully and maliciously attempts to burn or to aid, counsel or procure the burning of any of the buildings or property mentioned in sections 502–504 of this title, or who wilfully and maliciously commits any act preliminary thereto, or in furtherance thereof, shall be guilty of arson in the fourth degree, and shall be imprisoned not more than two years nor less than one year or fined not more than $500.00, or both.

SOURCE: 13 Vт. Coɒᴇ R. §§ 502–05 (West 2007).

arson in the second degree.[4] The original statute did not define "dwelling house"; it was defined by judicial decision in the case of *Poff v. State* (1968) (see Application Case 10.1). The current statute does define "dwelling."[5]

⚖️ Application Case 10.1

Poff v. State

This case applies to both crimes discussed in this chapter. Although it involves the definition of *dwelling house* for the purposes of the laws relating to burglary, the same definition is applicable to the crime of arson.

In *Poff v. State* (1968), a Maryland court stated that the test for determining whether a structure is a *dwelling house* is whether it is used "regularly as a place to sleep." In *Poff*, police officers rented an apartment and moved personal property there for the purpose of enticing burglars. The officers occupied the apartment only during the daytime. The court held that the defendant, who was apprehended while breaking into the apartment, could be properly convicted only of breaking into a storehouse rather than a dwelling.

SOURCE: Poff v. State, 241 A.2d 898, 900 (Md. 1968).

Intent Required for Arson

At common law, and almost universally today, arson is a general intent crime. In other words, only the intent to burn is required for guilt, even though some forms of the crime require specific intent. For example, arson statutes that require only general intent define the crime as the voluntary or "willful" setting of a fire. As previously explained in Chapter 3, when a crime requires a *mens rea* of general intent, a person can be culpable if he or she voluntarily commits the underlying criminal act or acts without accident, mistake, or negligence, but not necessarily with the purpose of achieving any particular result. When a crime requires a *mens rea* of specific intent, a person is culpable only if he or she voluntarily commits the underlying criminal act or acts without accident, mistake or negligence, *and in addition* has the intent to achieve a particular result.

The California arson statutes provide a good example of this distinction. Under the statutes, a person commits the felony of arson who "willfully and maliciously sets fire to or burns . . . any structure, forest land, or property." This provision requires only a general intent for the crime of arson to be committed. It is a more serious felony if the burning results in any level of bodily injury to any person.[6]

Another provision of the California statute specifies that arson may also be committed with specific intent when a person, "willfully, maliciously, deliberately, with premeditation, and with intent to cause injury to one or more persons . . . sets fire to . . . any residence [or] structure." This form of the crime requires two types of intent simultaneously:

1. The general intent to set fire to or burn property.
2. The additional specific intent to cause injury to one or more persons. This is an aggravated form of arson, punishable more harshly.[7]

Elements and Degrees of Arson

Many states have degrees, or levels of severity, of arson in their statutes. Each different level of arson ranges in severity of punishment, and each includes elements that are not included in other levels. For example, Alaska law provides for arson in the first and second degree:

- Arson in the first degree is defined as when a "person intentionally damages any property by starting a fire or causing an explosion and by that act recklessly places another person in danger of serious physical injury."
- Arson in the second degree occurs "if the person intentionally damages a building by starting a fire or causing an explosion."[8]

Other factors specified in statutes punishing higher levels of arson include:

- The type of property burned.
- A previous conviction for arson.
- The value of the loss caused by the fire.
- An attempt to commit arson while other people are present inside the building.[9]

A rash of racially motivated church fires, primarily targeting southern African American churches, led federal lawmakers in the 1990s to enact arson statutes that carry much greater penalties for those people convicted of setting such church fires. In 1997, three white defendants were the first to be prosecuted and convicted under the federal arson statute. They were convicted of the racially motivated burning of a

Accidental Fire or Arson? Investigators will look for several different clues to determine if a fire is accidental or intentional.

10.1 Web Exploration

Arson Investigators

Check out the International Association of Arson Investigators (IAAI) at http://www.firearson.com. What is their focus, and how do they educate the public about arson?

predominately black church, the St. Joe Baptist Church in Alabama, and did receive the harsher penalties.[10]

Usually, fire departments have an arson investigator who will respond to a burning building call to determine whether the fire was accidental or intentional. In addition, when an officer responds to the scene of a fire, there are several things he or she can do to help determine the fire's origin:

- Look for incendiary devices, fuel cans, broken door locks, or any other signs of forced entry.
- Interview all available witnesses at the scene, asking questions that may help determine the financial stability of the building owner or occupants. Any financial instability might indicate a motive to collect on an insurance policy.
- Seek to learn of any enemies of the owner or occupant, who might have set the fire for revenge.
- Scan the crowd for any known firebugs or known arsonists. Many arsonists get a psychological rush by watching the fires they have set and often are present at the fire.

These early efforts, coupled with the work of an arson investigator, will provide valuable aid in catching the arsonist.

10.1 On the Job

Fire/Arson Investigator

Description and Duties: Investigate fire origins and causes; determine arson cases and provide reports. Determine accidental and intentional fires. Work with law enforcement and insurers in cases of arson. Enforce compliance with city and state fire prevention codes.

Salary: Salaries range from approximately $35,000 to $48,000.

Other Information: Requires state inspection certificate, as well as any accreditation from state firefighter standards councils. Also usually requires a two-year degree in fire science, criminal justice, public administration, or related area, and three to five years' experience in local or state government fire inspections.

SOURCE: Florida Fire Marshals and Inspectors Association, http://www.ffmia.org/employment.htm.

> **CRITICAL THINKING 10.1**
>
> 1. How have laws regarding arson changed since common law?
> 2. What are the steps that officers need to take to investigate a fire, in order to determine if it was accidental or intentional?

10.2 Burglary

At common law, burglary was viewed as a forcible invasion and disturbance of a person's right of habitation, and was likely to be punished by death. The law comes to the aid of the inhabitant and designates acts against habitation as a crime. Thus, **common law burglary** was defined as the breaking and entering, in the nighttime, of the mansion or dwelling house or curtilage of another, with the intent to commit a felony.[11]

The purpose of the burglary laws was not to protect persons merely against unlawful trespass (also called breaking and entering), which does not require the intent to commit a crime beyond the actual trespass or entering. Rather, their purpose was to protect the habitation.

Today, this common law perspective of burglary has been statutorily expanded beyond the dwelling house and its curtilage to include other places that are susceptible to burglary. The modern definition of burglary, brought about by judicial decision and legislation, has substantially enlarged the scope of the offense. Under the most comprehensive definitions of **modern burglary**, the offense can be committed by entry alone, in the daytime as well as night, in any building, structure, or vehicle with the intent to commit any criminal offense. The MPC defines burglary as the entry of a "building or occupied structure, or separately secured or occupied portion thereof," with the purpose to commit a crime, "unless the premises are at the time open to the public or if the actor is licensed or privileged to enter."[12]

Elements of Burglary

Generally, burglary requires three elements:

1. An entry.
2. Of a dwelling or building.
3. With intent to commit a crime inside.

In addition, some statutes differentiate between burglaries committed during the daytime and those committed at night, with the latter carrying a heavier penalty.

Entry

An entry of some sort, no matter how slight, is required into a structure for there to be a burglary. Entry can be accomplished through many different means, such as forcing open a door or window, entering through a partially opened door or window, or entering through a closed inner door. (See Application Case 10.2.) Contrary to popular belief, entry with consent can also be an element of burglary.

---

common law burglary
Breaking and entering, in the nighttime, of the mansion or dwelling house or curtilage of another, with the intent to commit a felony.

modern burglary
Entering, whether in the daytime or at night, of any building, structure, or vehicle, with the intent to commit any criminal offense.

⚖️ Application Case 10.2

Youthful Burglars

In 1986, two nine-year-old California boys were arrested and later convicted of several residential burglaries. They were caught when one of them got stuck in a chimney as he was attempting to enter a house. The chimney had been the point of entry for all of the burglaries, and unfortunately for the boy, this particular chimney was too small for him to slip through. Entry through the chimney met the necessary breaking and entering element requirement to constitute burglary.

SOURCE: Patricia Klein, *Boy Pulled from Chimney, Friends Are Charged in Home Burglaries*, L.A. Times, Jan. 1, 1986, Valley Edition, at 6.

Some states follow the common law definition of burglary and require that the entry occur "at night." Today, though, the distinction between commission of the offense at night and during the day is most frequently a matter of defining the degree of the crime, rather than defining the basic offense. For example, under the MPC, burglary is a felony of the second degree if it is committed at night in the dwelling of another.

The usual method of gaining entry of a structure is to break open a closed door or window. From this comes the term *breaking and entering*, which you will learn more about later in this chapter. Many jurisdictions have eliminated the burglary requirement of a breaking, and others have changed their statutes to read "breaking *or* entering." If there is no requirement for a breaking, burglary can occur when a person enters an open business with the intent to commit a crime inside, even if the entry is not trespassory in nature. In these jurisdictions, a person is guilty of burglary if he or she walks into a store open for business with the intent to steal.[13] In contrast, the MPC does not classify such an entry into a public place as a burglary.

In those jurisdictions where the requirement of "breaking" remains, the further opening of an already partially opened door or window is sufficient to constitute a burglary. The slightest removal of an obstruction to the burglar's entry into the dwelling is enough for a breaking—in other words, the amount of force needed to remove an obstacle to the entry is immaterial. Therefore, raising a partially opened bedroom window or pushing open a hotel room door that was ajar three to four inches is considered a "breaking."[14]

In *Green v. Commonwealth* (1972), for example, an on-duty police officer was found guilty of a storehouse breaking when he entered an unlocked back door of a barber shop. Other officers had "staked out" the shop prior to the officer's entry and observed Green take a bottle of shampoo, some pocket combs, $25 in cash, and a bottle of hair oil. The court held that Green had a right to be in the store for purposes of protecting the owner's property, but if he entered with the intent to steal, he "shed his official immunity at the door" and therefore broke and entered feloniously.[15]

An **inner door** is any door that is inside a building and does not lead directly outside; one must already be inside to gain entry. It could be a bedroom, bathroom, suite, or office door. Even if one achieved entry through an open outer door with consent, breaking into an inner door of a building is still burglary. In

inner door
A door inside a building that does not lead directly to the outside.

State v. Edell (1935), the court instructed the jury that a burglary has occurred if a thief enters an open outer door or window, and later turns a knob or key, or lifts a latch.[16] Opening an attached garage door and cellar door have also been held to constitute burglary. In *People v. Davis* (1959), the defendant entered a service station and hid until after the station closed and was locked up for the evening. The defendant then opened an unlocked inner office door, and this act made the entry burglary.[17]

It may be difficult to prosecute for burglary someone who enters a business that is open to the public, but with the intent to commit a crime. For example, how do you charge a person who enters a grocery store and buys $100 worth of groceries, but after entering the store decides to put a candy bar in her pocket and walks out without paying for it? Such a person would probably argue that she never had the requisite intent to commit a crime because she entered the store only to shop and did not have a plan to steal the candy bar at the time of entry. Even if a prosecutor does not have enough evidence to obtain a burglary conviction, there are other crimes for which the defendant can be charged, such as shoplifting.

To commit an entry for purposes of burglary, the defendant does not have to physically enter. Instead, he or she can enter by using an instrumentality, such as another person, an animal, or a physical object. This is called **constructive entry**. An instrumentality, such as a hook, can be pushed through an open window to retrieve an item inside the structure. Also, a trained monkey or dog can be used to make the entry for the defendant.

constructive entry

An entry effected by using an instrumentality, such as another person, an animal, or a physical object.

For example, Carol and Victor plan to burglarize a jewelry store. Carol breaks open the back door and enters the store. Victor goes to the roof and lowers a basket on a string through an open skylight. Victor has committed burglary by constructive entry, even though he has not entered the store. In fact, he has effected constructive entry in two ways: (1) Carol made entry on Victor's behalf to steal the jewelry, and (2) Victor used an instrumentality under his control to effectuate entry into the building.

Consent can be a valid defense to a burglary charge in jurisdictions where a breaking is required, either under the common law rule or under a statute. For example, in *People v. Carstensen* (1966), the defendant could not be found guilty of burglary because he had permission to enter an apartment to paint it and was still engaged in painting when he stole a television set from the apartment. Therefore, there was no breaking to enter.[18] However, even entry with consent will not preclude a burglary prosecution in many instances (see Application Cases 10.3, 10.4, and 10.5).

⚖️ Application Case 10.3

State v. Cochran

In *State v. Cochran*, Cochran spent the night at his niece's house, which she shared with two other women. The next morning, he entered the locked room of one of the women and stole several items. In affirming Cochran's burglary conviction, the court found that the locked bedroom was a "building" and that, although Cochran had permission from his niece to be within the house, no consent was given to enter the locked bedroom.

SOURCE: State v. Cochran, 463 A2d 618 (Conn. 1983).

⚖️ Application Case 10.4
People v. Czerminski

In *People v. Czerminski*, a police officer was convicted of burglary when he stole several items while investigating a warehouse break-in. The court upheld the conviction on the grounds that the consent for the officer to be on the premises was to perform a public duty only, and when the officer remained on the property to commit a theft, he exceeded the scope of that consent.

SOURCE: People v. Czerminski, 464 N.Y.S.2d 83 (App. Div. 1983).

⚖️ Application Case 10.5
K.P.M. v. State

In *K.P.M. v. State*, the defendant made an agreement with a store clerk to pay the clerk to receive groceries with a retail value of more than the amount he paid. The court upheld the defendant's conviction for burglary and rejected the defendant's argument that the clerk had consented to the agreement. The court reasoned that the clerk had no authority to give such consent and the defendant could not in good faith have reasonably believed the transaction was legal.

SOURCE: K.P.M. v. State, 446 So. 2d 723 (Fla. Dist. Ct. App. 1984).

Time of Day Requirements

The common law and some current state laws require that for an entry to be a burglary, the act must be committed at night. **Nighttime** was defined under common law as the period between sunset and sunrise when there is not enough daylight to discern a man's face. For states following this common law definition, the time of day, amount of sunlight, and use of sunlight to see become important in establishing whether or not it is nighttime. The existence of moonlight, streetlights, or building lights does not count as "daylight." Alternatively, many states define burglary without a time requirement, so that it can occur during the day or at night. The jury has the right to apply common sense and knowledge to determine when the burglary occurred.

nighttime
At common law, the period between sunset and sunrise when there is not enough daylight to discern a man's face.

Dwelling or Building Requirements

Burglary requires the entering of a dwelling, building, or structure. The absence or presence of an occupant may make a difference in whether a structure is considered a "dwelling." Some jurisdictions require for the highest degree of burglary not only that the structure be used as a dwelling, but also that a person be physically present in the dwelling at the time of the burglary. In other jurisdictions, a person does not have to be physically present in the home at the time of the burglary, but to be considered a dwelling the structure must be "inhabited." A temporary absence does not necessarily make the dwelling uninhabited. In *State v. Hicks* (1973), the court upheld a conviction of aggravated burglary of an inhabited dwelling where the defendant entered a dwelling with no one home and fled when he heard the occupants return.[19]

sleep test

Whether the dwelling is used regularly as a place to sleep determines whether a dwelling is occupied.

Some states apply a **sleep test** in determining whether a dwelling is occupied. According to this test, if a dwelling is used regularly as a place to sleep, it is inhabited. Occasional sleeping on the premises is usually not enough to satisfy the sleep test. Nonetheless, in one case, a summer vacation home in Maine that was entered in the winter was held to be a "dwelling place," even though the house did not have heat or other utilities and was therefore uninhabitable during the winter months.[20] Usually, residences that are under construction and have never been occupied are held to be uninhabited. If the sole owner and occupant of the dwelling is deceased or in a mental hospital at the time of the burglary, most jurisdictions will consider the house uninhabited.

The MPC states that a person commits burglary who "enters a building, occupied structure, or separately secured or occupied portion thereof with [the] purpose to commit a crime therein, unless the premises are at the time open to the public or the actor is licensed or privileged to enter." The MPC defines "occupied structure" as "any structure, vehicle, or place adapted for overnight accommodation of persons, or for carrying on business therein, whether or not a person is actually present." A person does not have to be physically present in the dwelling for the crime to be burglary, because it is only a coincidence that the burglar happened to miss the residents at that particular time.[21]

To assist the investigation, a burglary report taken from a victim should state how the crime was committed. The reporting officer should look for the burglar's *modus operandi* (mode of operation), as well as any other details that will assist in ultimately identifying and convicting the perpetrator. The list and description of stolen property should be as detailed as possible, including information such as serial and model numbers, initials, or noticeable scratches. Here is a sample narrative of a burglary report:

> Between 7 a.m. and 5 p.m. on 5-29-08, one or more unknown suspects obtained entry from the northwest window of 123 Westmoreland Avenue, a two-story house, by using approximately a half-inch pry tool, possibly a flathead screwdriver. The suspect(s) popped open the latch on the window and slid the window open. Fresh sneaker marks were found on the dirt outside the window, and the dust on the windowsill had been disturbed. The suspect(s) then proceeded to ransack the bedroom, living room, and dining room, taking the items listed in the attached property report. The suspect(s) exited out the living room patio door, leaving it slightly ajar. Latent prints were discernable on both the window and the sliding door and were lifted and sent to the crime laboratory under the above property number for analysis. The victim was interviewed and stated that she left the house secured and she was not present during the burglary.

10.2 Web Exploration

The Burgled Helpline

Visit http://www.burgled.com, a UK-based Web site, and read "Recently been burgled?" and "Making your home safer." Which of these suggestions have you already implemented? Which should you implement to increase your safety?

The report should also include a list of the items taken, make, model, and serial numbers, and approximate value.

Intent

In most jurisdictions, the specific intent to commit a crime must be present at the time of entry in order for the crime to be a burglary. The burglar does not actually have to remove or even touch an item from the structure to be guilty of burglary. If the intent is formed after the entry is made, or there is no intent to commit a crime at all, the crimes of theft or trespass may have been committed, but not burglary.

The intent to commit a crime can be inferred from the circumstances surrounding the entry. Examples include:

- If the defendant enters a business open to the public with a shopping bag that is lined with aluminum foil, it is reasonable to infer that the suspect intended to place stolen merchandise in the bag and avoid detection from the electronic security devices at the store's entrance.
- Intent can also be inferred from the time of entry. For instance, if one enters a stranger's residence or a closed place of business at midnight, intent to steal could be reasonably inferred.
- The type of building entered, such as a warehouse not open to the public, can imply intent.
- Possession of a weapon or burglar's tools can determine intent.
- When applied to the crime of shoplifting, specific intent can also be shown if the suspect went shopping and selected items with no money or credit cards in his or her possession, possessed a shopping bag with a false bottom, or wore baggy clothes to hide stolen items.

Thus, the elements of the crime of burglary are complete when the entry is made with the requisite intent.

Breaking and Entering

Breaking and entering, or unlawful forced entry, is very similar to burglary, except it is lacking one element—the specific intent to commit a theft or felony inside the structure. Therefore, if a homeless person breaks into a structure to get out of the rain and forms the intent to steal after entry, or never even steals, he or she has not committed burglary, but rather the lesser crime of breaking and entering. The breaking and entering offense can be an effective tool for prosecutors to use because they may offer this charge to a defendant, rather than burglary, in the hope of a plea bargain.

breaking and entering
Unlawful forced entry; similar to burglary, but without the specific intent to commit a theft or felony inside the structure.

Breaking and Entering Breaking and entering does not require the specific intent to commit a felony that burglary does.

Degrees of Burglary

Burglary is divided into degrees in two ways. Some states divide burglary offenses into simple and aggravated burglary. For example, Louisiana defines **simple burglary** as "the unauthorized entering of any dwelling, vehicle, water craft, or other structure, movable or immovable, with the intent to commit a felony or any theft therein." Simple burglary is a lesser included offense of **aggravated burglary**, which consists of the added elements of entering an inhabited dwelling, or any structure or vehicle, while armed with a dangerous weapon, or by committing a battery after or upon the entry.[22]

Other states classify burglary offenses into degrees or grades. California has two degrees of burglary: first and second degree. Under the California classification, "every burglary of an inhabited dwelling house, trailer coach as defined by the Vehicle Code, or inhabited portion of any other building, is burglary of the first degree. All other kinds of burglary are of the second degree."[23]

Arizona divides burglary into three categories:

1. First-degree burglary occurs when a person or accomplice commits second- or third-degree burglary "and knowingly possesses explosives, a deadly weapon or a dangerous instrument in the course of committing any theft or any felony."
2. Second-degree burglary is committed when a person enters or remains unlawfully "in or on a residential structure with the intent to commit any theft or any felony therein."
3. A person commits third-degree burglary "by entering or remaining unlawfully in or on a nonresidential structure or in a fenced commercial or residential yard with the intent to commit any theft or any felony therein."[24]

Whether a structure is residential or nonresidential also affects the degree of burglary in Arizona.

simple burglary

The unauthorized entering of any dwelling, vehicle, watercraft, or other structure, movable or immovable, with the intent to commit a felony or any theft therein.

aggravated burglary

Simple burglary with the added elements of entering an inhabited dwelling, or any structure or vehicle, while armed with a dangerous weapon, or by committing a battery after or upon the entry.

Possession of Burglar's Tools

Most states make it illegal to possess **burglar's tools**—tools and instruments that are designed, adapted, or commonly used to commit burglaries. The possession of burglar's tools is a separate crime, not an element of the crime of burglary. Therefore, a person can be convicted of burglary even though he or she is not in possession of these tools, and a person can be convicted of possession of burglar's tools even if he or she is nowhere near a structure to burglarize. The typical elements of this crime are:

- Possession of the burglar's tools, or instruments that are adapted, designed, or commonly used for committing any burglary.
- The intent to use the tools in the commission of a burglary.[25]

A person does not have to own the burglar's tools to be criminally culpable. The person need only possess the tools with the requisite intent—that is, the specific intent to burglarize—to be convicted of possession of burglar's tools. The prosecution does not need to establish that the defendant intended to commit a particular burglary, only that he or she intended to commit some burglary. Intent can be established by the time of day, location of possession, employment of the possessor, or the possessor's trying to get rid of the tools when confronted by police.

All of the items that could be burglar's tools can have legitimate uses. For example, even if a tool is commonly used or originally designed for a lawful purpose, it can still be a burglar's tool. Lug wrenches, lock-picking devices, screwdrivers, slim jims, bolt cutters, porcelain chips from spark plugs, crowbars, wire, and nitroglycerin or other explosives all have legitimate uses—but can still be burglar's tools.

Remember, possessing such tools is just one part of this crime. A person must also have the requisite intent to commit burglary. Some states, therefore, require that there be lack of a lawful excuse for the possession of the tools to be illegal. This requirement would be satisfied if the defendant could not give a legitimate explanation of what the tools were used for or why he or she was in possession of them. A law enforcement officer has to use discretion to determine if the suspect has a lawful reason for possessing these items. If someone is discovered outside of a closed business, late at night, wearing black, inference of the requisite intent would probably be justified.

Vehicular Burglary

The basic burglary statute of many states creates the crime of vehicular burglary by defining vehicles as a type of structure that can be the subject of breaking and entering. The definition of breaking, for purposes of committing the crime of vehicular burglary, is adapted for the nature of vehicles. For example, using the slightest force to turn a vehicle's unlocked door handle, or using a coat hanger to open the trunk, may be sufficient to constitute a breaking. Additionally, the slightest intrusion or entry into the vehicle by a body part or instrument is sufficient to constitute burglary. Some states, like California, require that the vehicle be locked, although case law does not require the state to prove that every door was locked—the owner's testimony that the doors were locked is usually sufficient.[26]

A **motor vehicle** is generally defined as "a vehicle proceeding on land by means of its own power plant and free of rails, tracks, or overhead wires."[27] Each state defines vehicle and motor vehicle for burglary and for breaking and entering. For example, a

burglar's tools
Tools and instruments that are designed, adapted, or commonly used to commit burglaries.

motor vehicle
A vehicle proceeding on land by means of its own power plant and free of rails, tracks, or overheard wires.

van that has flat tires and is used for storage is considered a vehicle under the breaking and entering statute in Michigan. Under this statute, "vehicle" includes all vehicles that could be moved on the state's public highway with mechanical power.[28] The court reasoned that the van could be easily repaired and that thousands of vehicles in need of repair sit in repair lots, yards, and garages, yet are still considered vehicles. In *Trevino v. State* (1985), a vehicle sitting in a car lot without an engine was still a vehicle under Texas statutory language, which defines "vehicle" as any device that could be moved, propelled, or drawn by a person in the normal course of commerce or transportation. The court found that the temporary condition of the vehicle was less important than its mechanism, design, and construction.[29]

joyriding
The illegal driving of someone else's automobile without permission, but with no intent to deprive the owner of it permanently.

There are only a few crimes that a person might intend to commit when he or she breaks and enters a vehicle: stealing the vehicle, stealing something out of the vehicle, or joyriding. **Joyriding** is defined as the illegal removal and driving of someone else's car, but with the intention of keeping it only temporarily. Although joyriding is a felony in many jurisdictions, it is not considered as serious as burglary and may be the tool necessary for a defendant to accept a plea bargain and not go to trial. Sometimes, and under certain circumstances, a prosecutor may reduce the original charge of vehicular burglary to joyriding. For example, if a very young person steals a car and uses it to drive around with friends, then returns the car unharmed, the prosecutor might not charge burglary.

⚖ CRITICAL THINKING 10.2

1. What are the differences between burglary and breaking and entering?
2. What are the three general purposes of vehicular burglary?

REVIEW AND APPLICATIONS

Summary by Chapter Objectives

1. **Understand the difference between common law and modern law arson.**
   Common law arson required that the burning occur at night and the dwelling be occupied. The common law definition of dwelling was narrowly defined, to include only the dwelling of the occupant and any buildings located in the curtilage surrounding the dwelling. Under the definition of modern law arson, most structures qualify as a dwelling, arson does not have to occur at night, and the dwelling need not be occupied. Another modern element concerning arson, which is covered under many statutes, is the intent to defraud insurers through arson.

2. **Explain the difference between specific intent and general intent arson.**
   Specific intent arson statutes include the lesser intent requirement of general intent and go one step further by requiring an additional intent of a definite and actual purpose to accomplish some particular thing. Specific intent statutes

usually include the specific words "with intent to" effect a certain result. One example of this is the intent to defraud insurers by making a fire appear accidental.

3. **List the three elements of burglary.** The three elements are:
   - The entry
   - Of a dwelling
   - With intent to commit a crime inside.

4. **Explain how a burglary can be committed without actual entry by the perpetrator.** Entry can be made *constructively*, which means that the burglar uses an instrumentality—such as another person, an animal, or a physical object such as a tool—to actually break into the structure.

5. **Understand the intent required to commit a burglary.** The specific intent to commit a crime must be present at the time of entry in order for it to constitute a burglary. If the intent is formed after the entry is made, or there is no intent to commit a crime at all, the crimes of theft or trespass may have been committed, but not burglary.

6. **Explain the difference between simple and aggravated burglary.** A simple burglary is the unauthorized entering of any dwelling with the intent to commit a felony or any theft therein. Simple burglary is a lesser offense than aggravated burglary, which adds the elements of entering an inhabited dwelling, or any structure or vehicle, while armed with a dangerous weapon, or by committing a battery upon or after entry.

7. **State the difference between burglary and breaking and entering.** A breaking and entering, or unlawful forced entry, is very similar to burglary, except that it is lacking one element—the specific intent to commit a theft or felony inside the structure.

8. **Name the elements of the crime of possession of burglar's tools.** The typical elements to this crime are possession of tools or instruments that are adapted, designed, or commonly used for committing any burglary, and the intent to use the tools in the commission of a burglary. Although all burglar's tools can be used for legal purposes, police look at the totality of the circumstances— including the suspect's explanation for possessing such tools—to determine whether a crime has taken place.

Key Terms

common law arson (p. 275)
curtilage (p. 275)
willfulness (p. 275)
modern arson (p. 275)
common law burglary (p. 280)
modern burglary (p. 280)
inner door (p. 281)
constructive entry (p. 282)

nighttime (p. 283)
sleep test (p. 284)
breaking and entering (p. 285)
simple burglary (p. 286)
aggravated burglary (p. 286)
burglar's tools (p. 287)
motor vehicle (p. 287)
joyriding (p. 288)

Review Questions

1. What level of burning is required to constitute arson? What levels of burning do not constitute arson?
2. Under modern law, what is the definition of *dwelling house* in most jurisdictions?
3. What are some of the differences between first-degree and second-degree arson?
4. State the common law purpose of the burglary law.
5. What is an inner door, and what is its meaning in relation to burglary?
6. What is the difference between the common law and modern definitions of nighttime and its relevance to the crime of burglary?
7. What is the sleep test?
8. How can the offense of breaking and entering be used as a prosecutor's tool, and why?
9. What are some general and specific definitions of a motor vehicle, as given in your text?
10. What is joyriding, and how can this offense be used as a prosecutor's tool?

Problem-Solving Exercises

1. **Burglar's Tools** It is 5 p.m. on a Saturday when an officer pulls over a vehicle for a missing taillight. The officer notices a bunch of tools on the passenger floorboard. The officer gets permission from the driver to inspect the tools and inventory the items. There are two large flathead screwdrivers, a small pry bar, a flashlight, a knife, a large crescent wrench, and a pair of plastic gloves. The officer runs the driver's name on the computer database and discovers that he has been convicted of burglary, breaking and entering, and theft. The driver says he was coming from his contracting job, where he was laying some carpet. He says he cannot remember the address where he was working because he followed his boss there.
   a. Does he appear to be telling the truth regarding carpet tools? Why or why not?
   b. What else can you ask him to gain pertinent information?
   c. Should the officer arrest the driver for possession of burglar's tools? Why or why not?
2. **Arson Investigation** You are investigating a fire at a hardware store that has been in your community for nearly 40 years. It is located in a neighborhood that, because of a growing industrial presence, receives little business. When you arrive at the scene, you see in front of the building the owner, his wife, some neighbors, and a small group. Among those in the group is a young man who is talking excitedly about the fire and is apparently oblivious to the owner's obvious grief. Answer the following questions:
   a. Whom do you question first, and whom do you question afterward? Why?
   b. Who appears to be a suspect? Why?
   c. What else can you do to investigate this fire properly?

Workplace Applications

1. **Burglary Statutes**   Look up the burglary statute in your jurisdiction. Under the statute, which of the following are dwellings?
   a. A motorcycle.
   b. A dog house.
   c. An empty house that is for sale.
   d. A tool shed next to a house.
   e. A corn crib.
   Explain why each one is or is not a dwelling. What additional information would you need in order to determine if they are dwellings?

2. **Theft or Burglary?**   On a Saturday morning, an officer responds to a burglary call. When he arrives, he finds beer cans and bottles strewn all over the living room. The victim denies having a party the night before and says he and his roommate are bad housekeepers. The victim claims that he keeps the back door closed, but unlocked, because he and his roommate often forget their keys. He reports some jewelry and cash was stolen the night before, while he was at the movies. The officer suspects the victim had a party and one of the guests took the items. The officer also knows that the victim's roommate has a history of thefts and may have taken the property. Answer the following questions:
   a. Should the officer take the victim's word at face value, or should he question the victim's report?
   b. If the officer believes the victim is lying, should he still make a report of the crime as stated by the victim? Why or why not?
   c. What other information should the officer gather from the victim, roommates, and from investigatory activities?

Ethics Exercises

1. **Blue Wall of Silence**   Assume that you are a newly assigned police officer and you respond to a burglary call with your training officer. No one is at the house when you get there, and the back door is wide open. The house is totally ransacked, and it is immediately apparent that the television, VCR, and stereo are missing. In addition, a jewelry case in one of the bedrooms is almost empty. You glance at the jewelry case and see that the burglars left behind a woman's gold watch and some rings. After you clear the house for suspects, you go back to take pictures of all of the rooms for your report. As you take a picture of the jewelry case, you notice that the watch is missing.
   a. What do you do first?
   b. Whom do you speak to about this?
   c. What possible repercussions concern you?

Notes

1. MODEL PENAL CODE § 220.1(1) (1985).
2. FLA. STAT. ANN. § 806.01(1) (West 2007).

3. Fla. Stat. Ann. § 806.01(3) (West 2007).

4. Md. Code Ann., Crim. Law § 6-102 & 6-103 (West 2007).

5. Md. Code Ann., Crim. Law § 6-101(b) (West 2007).

6. Cal. Penal Code § 451 (West 2007).

7. Cal. Penal Code § 451.5 (West 2007).

8. Alaska Stat. § 11.46.400 & § 11.46.410 (2006).

9. See, e.g., Cal. Penal Code § 451.5 (West 2007).

10. Church Arson Prevention Act of 1996, amending 18 U.S.C. § 241 (2000); *see also Whites Convicted of Burning Church*, L.A. Times, Nov. 4, 1997, at A11.

11. 4 William Blackstone, Commentaries *224.

12. Model Penal Code § 221.1 cmt. 1 (1985); Model Penal Code § 221.1(1) (1985).

13. Emile F. Short, Annotation, *Breaking and Entering of Inner Door of Building as Burglary*, 43 A.L.R. 3d 1147 (1996).

14. State v. Rosencranz, 167 P.2d 170 (Wash. 1946).

15. Green v. Commonwealth, 488 S.W.2d 339 (Ky. 1972).

16. Emile F. Short, Annotation, *Breaking and Entering of Inner Door of Building as Burglary*, 43 A.L.R. 3d 1147 at § 9(a) (1996) (citing State v. Edell, 183 A. 630 (Del. 1935)).

17. *Id.* at § 10 (1996) (citing People v. Davis, 346 P.2d 248 (Cal. App. 1959)).

18. People v. Carstensen, 420 P.2d 820 (Colo. 1966).

19. State v. Hicks, 286 So. 2d 331 (La. 1973).

20. State v. Albert, 426 A.2d 1370 (Me. 1981).

21. Model Penal Code § 221.1 (1985); Model Penal Code § 221.0(1) (1985); Model Penal Code § 221.0(1) cmt. 2 (1985).

22. La. Rev. Stat. Ann. § 14:62 & § 14:60 (West 2007).

23. Cal. Penal Code § 460 (West 2007).

24. Ariz. Rev. Stat. Ann. § 13-1506, § 13-1507 & § 13-1508 (2007).

25. *See, e.g.*, People v. Pesce, 239 N.Y.S.2d 651 (N.Y. App. Div. 1963); Ariz. Rev. Stat. Ann. § 13-1505 (2007).

26. People v. Blalock, 98 Cal. Rptr. 231 (Cal. Ct. App. 1971); People v. Lombardi, 23 Cal. Rptr. 35 (Cal. Ct. App. 1962).

27. Jeffrey F. Ghent, *Annotation: Burglary, Breaking, or Entering of Motor Vehicle*, 72 A.L.R. 4th 710 § 1(a) (1990).

28. People v. Matusik, 234 N.W.2d 517 (Mich. Ct. App. 1975), discussing Mich. Comp. Laws § 750.412 (West 2007).

29. Trevino v. State, 697 S.W.2d 476 (Tex. App. 1985), discussing Tex. Penal Code Ann. § 30.01 (Vernon 2007).

Crimes against Property

CHAPTER OBJECTIVES

After reading and studying this chapter, you should be able to:

1. List the elements of larceny.
2. Explain the difference between larceny from a person and robbery.
3. List the elements of embezzlement.
4. State the difference between embezzlement and larceny.
5. Differentiate among extortion, blackmail, and bribery.
6. State the essential elements of forgery.

11.1 Forms and Variations of Theft

It is often confusing to officers, prosecutors, defense attorneys, and even judges to determine if a theft is larceny, stealing, shoplifting, or something else. The common law definitions of all of the crimes under the broad category of theft are very narrowly drawn, but still can be difficult to distinguish. To remedy this, many states have eliminated these common law distinctions and have instead created a single term to cover everything. For example, Maine's criminal code states: "Conduct denominated theft in this chapter constitutes a single crime embracing the separate crimes such as those heretofore known as larceny, larceny by trick, larceny by bailee, embezzlement, false pretenses, extortion, blackmail, shoplifting and receiving stolen property."[1] Similarly, the California Penal Code says: "Wherever any law or statute of this state refers to or mentions larceny, embezzlement, or stealing, said law or statute shall hereafter be read and interpreted as if the word "theft" were substituted therefor."[2] However, many states have kept the distinctions between the different crimes of theft. For that reason, you will learn about each type and variation of theft in more detail.

Theft

Theft is a broad category of crimes against property that includes:

- Larceny.
- Embezzlement.
- Theft by false pretenses.
- Shoplifting.
- Robbery.
- Receiving stolen goods.

Theft can be divided into **grand theft**, a felony charge for thefts of property worth more than a statutorily determined amount of money (such as $1,000); and **petit or petty theft**, a misdemeanor charge for thefts of property worth less than the minimum required for grand theft.

The common ingredient in all theft crimes is a thief. A **thief** is the original unlawful taker of the property of another person. This term does not apply to persons who are merely subsequent receivers of the property; hence, the intent to deprive the owner of his or her property is *not* required for all theft crimes. (See Application Case 11.1.)

theft
A broad category of misconduct against property that includes the crimes of larceny, embezzlement, theft by false pretenses, shoplifting, robbery, and receiving stolen goods.

grand theft
The felonious taking of property valued above a set monetary amount, or the theft of a motor vehicle. More serious than petty or petit theft.

petit or petty theft
The misdemeanor taking of property under a set monetary amount. Less serious than grand theft.

thief
The original unlawful taker of the property of another person.

⚖️ Application Case 11.1

Quarterman v. State

In *Quarterman v. State* (1981), a reporter parked his vehicle on an interstate highway in anticipation that it would be stolen so that he could film the theft in progress. A court found that this did not mean that he consented to having his vehicle stolen. Since the reporter neither suggested the theft to anybody nor urged the defendant to commit it, and since the criminal plan originated with the defendant, the court considering this case held that the car was indeed stolen.

SOURCE: Quarterman v. State, 401 So. 2d 1159 (Fla. Dist. Ct. App. 1981).

Larceny

Larceny has four elements:

1. The taking and carrying away.
2. Of the property of another.
3. Without consent.
4. And with the purpose of stealing or permanently depriving the owner of possession.[3]

larceny
The taking and carrying away of property of another, without consent, with the purpose of stealing or permanently depriving the owner of possession.

The first element, of taking and carrying away, occurs when a thief exercises control over the property. The thief must begin to move, or actually move, the property for at least a brief period of time. Only the slightest movement of the property is required for the thief to exercise dominion and control over it. Therefore, a person who slides a computer monitor across the top of a computer desk has satisfied the taking and carrying element of larceny.

The property taken (1) must be tangible, or concrete, such as a ring or a check; (2) must have value; and (3) must have an owner. In addition, the owner of the property must be able to positively identify the property as his or hers, such as by providing the serial number for a stolen item, identifying unique marks or scratches on the item, or otherwise proving that he or she owns it. It can be very difficult to prove positive ownership of property such as money, nondescript jewelry like a gold chain, or other everyday objects.

In larceny cases, the prosecution must establish that the owner of the property did not give the defendant permission to take the item. (See Application Case 11.2.) This is usually easily accomplished by having the owner testify to that fact. In addition, the prosecution must show that the defendant possessed the specific intent to permanently deprive the owner of the property, not merely to borrow it temporarily. This can be proven through direct evidence, such as the defendant's stating that he or she intended to keep the property. It can also be proven through circumstantial evidence, such as the length of time the defendant had possession of the item, or if the defendant tried to scratch out the owner's name on the property or replace it with his own name.

⚖️ Application Case 11.2

Fussell v. United States

If the owner of the property gives the possessor permission to use the property and the possessor misappropriates or steals it, the crime is not larceny. In the case of *Fussell v. United States* (1986), the defendant approached a plainclothes police officer and offered to sell the officer a fake subway pass. Although the officer gave the defendant $10 for the pass, the defendant could not be convicted of larceny because the defendant took the $10 with the officer's consent.

SOURCE: Fussell v. United States, 505 A.2d 72 (D.C. 1986).

As with theft and other offenses, many jurisdictions classify larceny according to degrees of seriousness of the offense. For example, West Virginia law divides charges into grand larceny and petit (or petty) larceny. The distinction is simple: If the loss of goods is less than $1,000, it is the misdemeanor offense of petit larceny. If the loss is greater than $1,000, it is the felony offense of grand larceny.[4]

Two types of larceny deserve special attention: larceny from a person, which is the offense of taking property from the person of another; and shoplifting, which is defined by a specific theft statute to address thefts of merchandise, concealment of merchandise, altering of price tags, and retail theft.

Larceny from a Person

larceny from a person
Statutory offense of taking property from the person of another; the penalty is usually greater than that for simple larceny.

Some states have a statutory offense called **larceny from a person**. Larceny from a person differs from robbery in that robbery requires the additional element of taking by fear or force. The rationale for larceny from a person statutes is to prevent crimes such as pickpocketing, purse snatching, and similar offenses where there is a greater risk of the victim's being injured because of the close contact between the victim and the perpetrator. The penalties for taking property from the person of another are usually greater than those provided for simple larceny.

Different states have adopted two different definitions of this offense, depending on the definition of "from a person." Some states define the term to mean that the victim must have actual possession of the property on his or her person when the larceny occurs; other states require only that the property be within the person's immediate presence.

Property that is "on" a person must be actually on the person, attached to the person, or held or carried by the person. This would include items such as jewelry, clothing, purses, wallets, and shopping bags that a person is actually touching. Courts in Colorado and Texas have found that larceny from a person was committed when a purse was taken from a shopping cart that the victim was pushing.[5] In a California case, two perpetrators fought with a victim while trying to take his wallet from his pocket. During the struggle, the victim's pants were torn off and his wallet fell to the ground. Although the perpetrators picked up the wallet and pants from the ground, not directly from the victim's person, the perpetrator's actions caused those items to fall to the ground in the first place. Therefore, they were guilty of larceny from a person.[6] On the other hand, larceny from a person did not occur in a case in which the defendant took $250 worth of gaming chips from a craps table rack that was immediately in front of the victim.[7]

To constitute larceny from a person in other states, the only requirement is that the property lie within a person's "actual and immediate physical control," not that it be attached to or on the person. For example, a purse taken from a car seat next to a victim or from beneath a victim's car seat are within the immediate control of the

Larceny from a Person Larceny from a person occurs when an object is taken either from the victim's immediate person or from the area within his or her immediate control.

victim. Therefore, such offenses constituted larceny from a person. Larceny from a person was also committed when the perpetrator took $350 from a wallet that was placed under the sleeping victim's pillow.[8]

11.1 On the Job

Fingerprint Technician

Description and Duties: Enter fingerprints and information such as case identification number, race, sex, and birth date into automated information system for examination and retention. Initiate computer searches for suspects. Compare new finger, palm, and foot prints with prints on file for points of identification to determine a match. Verify positive identification through comparisons of recidivist (second or more) prints to existing prints in criminals' folders. Work with local, state, and federal police.

Salary: Trainee salaries range from approximately $18,000 to $23,000. Technician salaries range from $23,000 to $35,000.

Other Information: High school diploma required. Some positions require one to two years' experience; others require experience in classifying fingerprints with the Henry system, the Modified Henry System, and/or the Automated Fingerprint Identification System (AFIS).

SOURCE: Delaware State Police, http://www.state.de.us/dsp/recruiting/fptrain.htm; Hillsborough County Sheriff's Office (Tampa, FL), http://www.crime-scene-investigator.net/JOB01028.html; and State of Virginia, http://www.dpt.state.va.us/services/compens/70000/descrip/71091.html.

Shoplifting

Most states have created specific theft statutes for thefts of merchandise, concealment of merchandise, altering of price tags, and retail theft. All of these offenses are known as **shoplifting**. The essential elements of shoplifting are:

shoplifting
A crime defined by a specific theft statute to address thefts of merchandise, concealment of merchandise, altering of price tags, and retail theft.

- The willful taking of possession of merchandise of another.
- Without consent of the seller.
- With the intention of converting the goods and without paying for the goods.

In addition, some shoplifting statutes do not require that the shoplifter intend to permanently deprive the store of its merchandise.

Since larceny covers many types of theft, it is also important to understand what larceny does not usually cover. Two common examples are (1) lost and abandoned property and (2) the crime of joyriding.

Lost or Abandoned Property

If property is lost or abandoned, the issue becomes who owns the property. An object becomes **abandoned property** when the person who owns it voluntarily gives up permanent possession or ownership of it, such as by throwing it away. To prevent thieves from claiming that every item that they "found" was lost or abandoned and that they are entitled to it by right of "finders keepers," courts generally hold that the "finder" has an obligation to give the item back to the owner if three conditions are met:

abandoned property
Property over which a person voluntarily gives up permanent possession or ownership.

1. The owner of the property can be identified.
2. The item can be easily given back to the owner.
3. The item has substantial value.

Failure to give back the item under these conditions can result in the "finder" being found to be guilty of some form of theft.

For example, the Maryland code, Criminal Law, § 7-104(d), under the heading "general theft provisions" states:

> A person may not obtain control over property knowing that the property was lost, mislaid . . . if he (1) knows or learns the identity of the owner or knows, or is aware of, or learns of a reasonable method of identifying the owner; and (2) fails to take reasonable measures to restore the property to the owner; and (3) intends to deprive the owner permanently of the use or benefit of the property either when the person obtains the property, or at a later time.[9]

Thus, although a $20 bill found lying on the sidewalk has substantial value, the owner cannot be easily identified, and the finder may keep the money. In contrast, if a person finds a purse lying on the sidewalk containing cash and a driver's license, the finder is required to return all of the property because the owner can easily be identified.

Joyriding

If a defendant merely borrows an item and intends to return it to the owner, then larceny has not occurred even if the borrowing was without permission. A common example is joyriding—the unlawful taking, using, or operating of a motor vehicle without the consent of the owner. Joyriding, discussed in Chapter 10, is usually committed by juveniles, who take a car without permission and drive it for a short period of time before abandoning it.

The exact definition of joyriding depends on the exact wording of each state's statute. In some states, joyriding is a lesser included offense of larceny, having all the elements of larceny except the intent to permanently deprive the owner of the vehicle. Other states have separate statutes for joyriding and unauthorized use. Under these statutes, joyriding requires the taking of a vehicle without the owner's permission. Unauthorized use occurs if the defendant has been given consent to drive the vehicle but exceeds that consent, or if the defendant is not driving the vehicle at the time, such as by being a passenger.

Unauthorized use of a motor vehicle generally requires that a person:

- Knowingly takes control.
- Without authority.
- Of another person's vehicle.

The state does not need to prove the defendant took the property "without intent to permanently deprive." In addition, the motor of the vehicle does not have to be running or the car in motion to satisfy this element. For example, in *People v. Roby* (1976), the defendant was convicted of unauthorized use when he sat in the front passenger seat of a stolen car and his companion sat behind the driver's seat, attempting to put a key in the ignition.[10]

Embezzlement

The crime of **embezzlement** consists of two elements: (1) the misappropriation (2) of the property of another. The element of theft requiring that the perpetrator have the intent to permanently deprive the owner is not an element of embezzlement. Therefore, an employee who fraudulently "borrows" property entrusted to him or her, but does so with the intent to return it, can still be found guilty of embezzlement.

Embezzlement is not a common law crime, but a statutory crime created to resolve common law inadequacies. Since embezzlers do not meet the theft or larceny requirement of wrongfully obtaining the property, their misdeeds were not covered in the common law definitions of larceny. As a solution, the crime of embezzlement was created to deal with people, typically employees, who lawfully come into possession of property and then take it for their own use. Unlike the crime of theft by initial wrongful taking, embezzlement involves a violation of trust. Today, some states include embezzlement under their theft or larceny statutes (see Figure 11.1), and others have separate statutes.

Misappropriation is the key element of embezzlement, just as taking is the key element of a larceny. **Misappropriation** is the wrongful misuse or taking of another's property that has been entrusted to the embezzler. The property of another can include real or personal property, securities, or negotiable instruments such as notes that are promises to pay, drafts that are an order to pay, checks that are payable on demand, and certificates of deposit. The same issues that arise in connection with larceny also arise in connection with embezzlement, such as proving that the

embezzlement
The unlawful taking or misuse of property by persons, typically employees, who lawfully come into possession of the property and therefore do not meet the theft or larceny requirement of wrongfully obtaining the property.

misappropriation
The wrongful misuse or taking of another's property that has been entrusted to the accused.

FIGURE   11.1

Wisconsin Statute Concerning Theft

943.20. Theft.

(1) Acts. Whoever does any of the following may be penalized as provided in sub. (3):

(a) Intentionally takes and carries away, uses, transfers, conceals, or retains possession of movable property of another without the other's consent and with intent to deprive the owner permanently of possession of such property.

(b) By virtue of his or her office, business or employment, or as trustee or bailee, having possession or custody of money or of a negotiable security, instrument, paper or other negotiable writing of another, intentionally uses, transfers, conceals, or retains possession of such money, security, instrument, paper or writing without the owner's consent, contrary to his or her authority, and with intent to convert to his or her own use or to the use of any other person except the owner. A refusal to deliver any money or a negotiable security, instrument, paper or other negotiable writing, which is in his or her possession or custody by virtue of his or her office, business or employment, or as trustee or bailee, upon demand of the person entitled to receive it, or as required by law, is prima facie evidence of an intent to convert to his or her own use within the meaning of this paragraph.

(c) Having a legal interest in movable property, intentionally and without consent, takes such property out of the possession of a pledgee or other person having a superior right of possession, with intent thereby to deprive the pledgee or other person permanently of the possession of such property.

(d) Obtains title to property of another person by intentionally deceiving the person with a false representation which is known to be false, made with intent to defraud, and which does defraud the person to whom it is made. "False representation" includes a promise made with intent not to perform it if it is a part of a false and fraudulent scheme.

(e) Intentionally fails to return any personal property which is in his or her possession or under his or her control by virtue of a written lease or written rental agreement after the lease or rental agreement has expired. This paragraph does not apply to a person who returns personal property, except a motor vehicle, which is in his or her possession or under his or her control by virtue of a written lease or written rental agreement, within 10 days after the lease or rental agreement expires.

SOURCE: Wis. Stat. § 943.20 (West 2007).

property actually belongs to someone, was not lost or abandoned, and can be positively identified.

In the embezzlement case of *Gwaltney v. Commonwealth* (1995), the defendant was a bank teller who took $1,000 from another teller's cash drawer. The defendant claimed that since she was not placed in a position of trust over the other teller's drawer, she did not misappropriate the bank's property and thus was not guilty of embezzlement. She argued that she could only be found guilty of larceny. The court rejected this argument, finding that the defendant was in fact in a position of trust even though she was only indirectly responsible for the cash drawer not assigned to her.[11]

False Pretenses

The theft crimes discussed so far deal only with crimes in which property is taken or misappropriated from the owner. The crime of **false pretenses**, on the other hand, involves the owner's being tricked by misrepresentation into voluntarily transferring title to the property. (See Application Case 11.3.) Technically, there is no *taking* of the property from the owner, but the owner is nonetheless deprived by illegal means. As with embezzlement, the common law did not consider obtaining property by false pretenses to be a crime. Therefore, the crime of false pretenses is also strictly a statutory offense.

false pretenses
A crime in which title or ownership of the property is passed to the defendant in reliance on the defendant's misrepresentation.

⚖️ Application Case 11.3

People v. Lorenzo

In *People v. Lorenzo* (1976), a market manager observed the defendant switch price tags on merchandise, pay less for the items than they were previously marked, and leave the store. The court found that theft by false pretenses was not committed because the market manager was aware that the defendant had switched the price tags and did not rely upon the defendant's conduct.

SOURCE: People v. Lorenzo, 135 Cal. Rptr. 337 (Cal. App. Dep't Super. Ct. 1976).

The elements of false pretenses are:

- The making of a material misrepresentation of fact.
- With intent to defraud the owner of the property.
- And thereby inducing the owner to part with both possession of and title to the property.

Note that false pretenses is not committed if the defendant only obtains possession of the property and not title. When the perpetrator gains *possession* alone of the property, the crime is *larceny by trick*.

Receiving Stolen Property

Receiving stolen goods or property is a separate and distinct offense from theft, although it is sometimes included in the same statute. Theft is not an element of receiving stolen goods, nor does the prosecution usually have to prove that the defendant did not steal the goods. **Receiving** means acquiring goods or property that has been stolen. A "fence" is a professional receiver of stolen property.

The offense of receiving stolen property has three essential elements:

receiving
Acquiring possession, control, or title, or lending on the security of, property that has been stolen.

1. The accused bought, received, or otherwise came into possession of the property.
2. The property was stolen.
3. At the time of possession of the property, the accused knew the property had been stolen.

Some jurisdictions do not require that a person other than the accused steal the property. This provision allows a thief to be prosecuted for receiving his or her own stolen goods when the prosecution does not have sufficient evidence to prove that the defendant stole the goods, but only enough to prove that he or she possessed them.

constructive possession

A relationship between the defendant and the stolen goods such that it is reasonable to treat the extent of the defendant's dominion and control over the property as if it were actual possession.

Possession is easily shown when the perpetrator is caught in actual physical possession of the property. A person need not be in actual physical control of stolen property to be guilty of receiving it, however, as long as he or she has constructive possession. **Constructive possession** is a relationship between the defendant and the stolen goods such that it is reasonable to treat the extent of the defendant's dominion and control over the property as if it were actual possession. In *Nelson* v. *State* (1981), one male defendant and one female defendant were convicted of receiving stolen property, even though only one defendant was present in the trailer when the police discovered stolen property inside. Although the court did not find any evidence that both defendants had actual, physical control over the property, the court held that there was ample evidence that constructive possession existed because letters and other items had the defendants' names on them, both male and female clothes were found in the trailer, and there was testimony that both defendants lived in the trailer.[12]

Constructive possession can also exist when stolen property is in close proximity to the accused. In *State v. Bozeyowski* (1962), police saw the defendant on top of a stolen truck, attempting to unload stolen cases of beer from the truck. The court ruled that there was enough evidence of the defendant's actions to infer the defendant's intentional control over the stolen truck, which satisfied the requirement of possession.[13]

Mere possession or unexplained possession of stolen property is not enough to constitute the crime of receiving stolen property; the crime also requires that the perpetrator know that the property was stolen. Knowledge can be shown by actual knowledge, such as the defendant's saying, "I knew it was stolen." It can also be shown by knowledge of circumstances that would alert any reasonable person that goods were stolen, such as the defendant's buying the property for a price far below its real value. Other circumstances could also show knowledge. In one case, contradictory statements made by the defendant as to where he got the stolen fur coats, from whom, and other circumstances surrounding obtaining the fur coats were sufficient to prove that the defendant knew the coats were stolen.[14] In *Hurston v. State* (1991), the defendant was found guilty of receiving a stolen car when he rode in a recently stolen vehicle for two hours as a passenger. The car was being driven without keys and had steering wheel damage, and the defendant attempted to flee from the police. All of these factors clearly indicated that the defendant had knowledge that the car was stolen.[15]

CRITICAL THINKING 11.1

1. What is larceny, and how is it distinguished from the other types of theft discussed here?

2. How is receiving stolen goods related to, but not a part of, theft?

11.2 Extortion, Blackmail, and Bribery

These three crimes are related. The common law treated extortion and blackmail as separate crimes, whereas modern statutes frequently use the terms interchangeably. You will note in the following separate discussions that many issues relating to extortion also relate to blackmail and bribery. A number of jurisdictions define the crime of extortion without limiting it to action by a public official, as described in the next section.[16]

Extortion

The common law crime of **extortion** is the gaining of property by threat of physical harm to a person or property by a public official under color of his or her office. The common law crime of extortion had five elements: (1) seeking of an unlawful fee, (2) by a public officer, (3) collected under color of office, (4) where the fee is actually received, and (5) where the fee was taken corruptly.[17] A good example of modern extortion laws can be found in the current New Jersey statute, which provides:

> A person is guilty of theft by extortion if he purposely and unlawfully obtains property of another by extortion. A person extorts if he purposely threatens to:
>
> - Inflict bodily injury on or physically confine or restrain anyone or commit any other criminal offense;
> - Accuse anyone of an offense or cause charges of an offense to be instituted against any person;
> - Expose or publicize any secret or any asserted fact, whether true or false, tending to subject any person to hatred, contempt or ridicule, or to impair his credit or business repute;
> - Take or withhold action as an official, or cause an official to take or withhold action;
> - Bring about or continue a strike, boycott or other collective action, if the property is not demanded or received for the benefit of the group in whose interest the actor purports to act;
> - Testify or provide information or withhold testimony or information with respect to another's legal claim or defense;
> - Inflict any other harm which would not substantially benefit the actor but which is calculated to materially harm another person.[18]

A defendant can claim an affirmative defense based on the elements described above by stating that the property obtained was honestly claimed as restitution or indemnification, either for harm done or as lawful compensation for property or services.

When the crime of extortion is based on the acts of a public official, one of the elements usually is that the perpetrator act **under color of authority or office**. This element requires that the action taken by the perpetrator be in his or her capacity as a public official; therefore, services performed in a private capacity usually do not amount to extortion. Public officials are forbidden from misusing their title and position to obtain services or property to which they are not otherwise entitled. In *United States v. Tillem* (1990), health department officials were guilty of extortion under federal law for exchanging favorable health inspections for money or free food from restauranteurs.[19] (See Figure 11.2.)

The definition of property for purposes of committing modern extortion (and blackmail) is very broad and includes both tangible and intangible property. The

extortion

The gaining of property by threat of physical harm to a person or property by a public official under color of his or her office.

under color of authority or office

The requirement at common law for the crime of extortion that the action taken by the perpetrator be in his or her capacity as a public official.

F I G U R E   1 1 . 2

District of Columbia Code on Extortion

22-3251. Extortion.

(a) A person commits the offense of extortion if:

  (1) That person obtains or attempts to obtain the property of another with the other's consent which was induced by wrongful use of actual or threatened force or violence or by wrongful threat of economic injury; or

  (2) That person obtains or attempts to obtain property of another with the other's consent which was obtained under color or pretense of official right.

(b) Any person **convicted** of **extortion** shall be fined not more than $10,000 or imprisoned for not more than 10 years, or both.

SOURCE: D.C. CODE § 22-3251 (West 2007).

property does not need to have actual cash value to be extorted; it can be a particular right belonging to the individual victim. In one case, a defendant was found guilty of grand larceny by means of extortion when he threatened the victim with bodily harm if the victim did not give up a business customer to the defendant. The victim gave up the customer, whom the court determined was "property" delivered to the defendant under threat of physical harm.[20] In another case, a real estate agent was found guilty of extortion for refusing to testify honestly in a malpractice lawsuit against an attorney unless the victim paid her for appearing at the deposition and trial. The court determined that the "property" was her interest in the malpractice lawsuit.[21]

Extortion and blackmail are also related to robbery. The distinction is that robbery is committed by a threat to do immediate bodily harm, whereas extortion (or blackmail) is committed by a threat to do harm in the future. Whereas a robber merely seeks to gain money by physical threat or intimidation, extortion and blackmail usually involve a threat to expose the victim's involvement in a crime or a shameful act unless the victim pays money or does some other act.[22] (See Application Case 11.4.)

⚖ Application Case 11.4

United States v. Jackson

A high-profile case of extortion was the conviction of Autumn Jackson for scheming to extort $40 million from actor Bill Cosby. (Under federal law, 18 U.S.C. § 875, the crime is called extortion, rather than blackmail.) She threatened to tell the tabloids that she was Cosby's illegitimate daughter unless Cosby gave her the money. Jackson had the right to tell her story to the media. However, the element that made her action extortion was her demand for money in return for not telling the "secret" to the media, which would harm Cosby's reputation and publicly disgrace the famous TV father.

SOURCE: United States v. Jackson, 196 F.3d 383 (2d Cir. 1999).

Bribery Bribers attempt to use payoffs to pass inspections, avoid criminal liability, and otherwise avoid legal responsibilities.

Blackmail

The crime of **blackmail** is a threat by a private citizen seeking "hush money"—payment to remain silent about a crime or a shameful act. As mentioned previously, today this crime is labeled extortion in many jurisdictions, and the crime of blackmail does not exist in those jurisdictions.[23] Although it is easy to see the moral reprehensibility of blackmail, the fact that it is a crime presents a legal paradox. This is because blackmail involves the threat to do something that the threatener has a legal right to do. For example, if one threatens to expose a businessman's tax evasion unless he gives the threatener a lucrative contract, the threatener has committed blackmail. Yet the blackmailer has a legal right to expose and threaten to expose the tax evasion, and a legal right to seek a lucrative contract. Nonetheless, combining the two legal rights constitutes a crime.[24] This specific combination of elements—using the threat of public shame to obtain something desirable—constitutes the crime of blackmail.

blackmail

A threat by a private citizen seeking hush money, or payment, to remain silent about a crime or a shameful act.

Bribery

The crime of **bribery** is a payment by a person to a public official in order to gain an advantage that the person is not otherwise entitled to, in which case both parties are guilty of the crime. The aforementioned case of *United States v. Tillem*, in which the defendant was found guilty of extortion, involved circumstances similar to bribery.

bribery

Payment by a person to a public official in order to gain an advantage that the person is not otherwise entitled to; both parties are guilty of the crime.

⚖ CRITICAL THINKING 11.2

1. How do you determine whether enough force or fear was used to justify a charge of robbery, as opposed to larceny or larceny from a person?

2. In your own words, how are extortion, blackmail, and bribery similar? How are they different?

11.3 Forgery and Uttering

Forgery is a common law crime that has been codified in most states. Generally speaking, a person who, with the purpose of deceiving or injuring, makes or alters a writing in such a way as to convey a false impression concerning its authenticity is guilty of **forgery**. The Indiana forgery statute is a typical example of the modern statement of the essential elements of forgery:

forgery

Making or altering a writing, with the purpose of deceiving or injuring, in such a way as to convey a false impression concerning its authenticity.

A person commits forgery who, with intent to defraud, makes or utters a written instrument in such a manner that it purports to have been made:

- By another person.
- At another time.
- With different provisions.
- By authority of one who did not give authority.[25]

Forgery can occur when a person signs a name other than his or her own on a writing and claims that the signature belongs to the other person. It can also occur by signing a writing using a fictitious or assumed name, by falsely signing a credit charge or sales slip, or by falsifying a money order. In some states, a person who uses trick, artifice, or other fraudulent devices to procure a genuine signature on a writing that has legal significance is guilty of forgery.

Falsifying another person's name on a credit charge or sales slip is forgery. It is immaterial whether the writings are orders for merchandise or merely receipts for delivery, as long as the writing, if taken as genuine, would have the effect to defraud. In one case, the defendant signed his "guest check" at an oyster bar with the name of another person. The court rejected the defendant's argument that a "guest check" was not subject to forgery, stating that the person whose name had been forged would have been obligated to pay for the amount of the "guest check" had it been genuine.[26]

The subject matter of forgery under the law in most jurisdictions must be a writing; therefore, contrary to popular belief, there cannot be a forgery of an object such as a work of art. The writing in a forgery needs to appear sufficiently convincing to be used to fool others. A forgery cannot occur if the writing does not deceive an ordinary, prudent person with ordinary observational skills.[27] Thus, a $3 bill that is larger than an authentic paper bill, made from a different shade of green, and with the face of Jim Carrey on it would not deceive an ordinary, prudent person with ordinary observation skills and, thus, could not be the subject of a forgery.

uttering

Presenting a forged writing and attempting to use it to deceive or cheat.

In addition, a person who merely has a forged writing in his or her possession is not guilty of forgery until he or she "utters" it, or attempts to pass it off. **Uttering** occurs when a person presents the writing and attempts to use it. The intent required for forgery is the intent to defraud, or with the "purpose to deceive or cheat another person or entity out of his or its legal due."[28] The intended act does *not* need to be successfully completed for the intent element to be satisfied.

fraudulent making

Creating a document that is not authentic.

Forgery is different from **fraudulent making**, which is defined as the creation of documents that are not authentic. If a writing is full of false statements, the author is not guilty of forgery but of fraudulent making. In contrast, if a document is full of truths, but is signed by a person using another person's name without permission, the writing is a forgery.

> ### CRITICAL THINKING 11.3
>
> 1. What, in your opinion, is the most common type of forgery? Why?
> 2. Give an example of the crime of fraudulent making, and explain why this behavior satisfies the elements of a crime.

REVIEW AND APPLICATIONS

Summary by Chapter Objectives

1. **List the elements of larceny.** Larceny is:
   - The taking and carrying away.
   - Of the property of another.
   - Without consent.
   - But with the purpose of stealing or permanently depriving the owner of possession.

2. **Explain the difference between larceny from a person and robbery.** Larceny from a person differs from robbery in that robbery requires the additional element of taking by fear or force.

3. **List the elements of embezzlement.** The crime of embezzlement has two elements:
   - Misappropriation.
   - Of the property of another.

4. **State the difference between embezzlement and larceny.** Embezzlement is the taking of property by persons, typically employees, who have the property lawfully put in their possession by the owner, and therefore do not meet the theft or larceny requirement of wrongfully obtaining the property. Embezzlement occurs when the accused is given considerable control over the property and violates that trust by appropriating the property.

5. **Differentiate among extortion, blackmail, and bribery.** Extortion is the gaining of property by threat of future harm to a person or property by a public official under color of his or her office. Blackmail is a threat by a private citizen seeking hush money. (In many jurisdictions today, a threat by anyone to do harm in the future in exchange for money is classified as extortion.) Bribery is a payment by a person to a public official in order to gain an advantage that the person is not otherwise entitled to, in which case both parties are guilty of the crime.

6. **State the essential elements of forgery.** A person commits forgery who, with intent to defraud, makes or utters a written instrument in such a manner that it purports to have been made:
   - By another person.
   - At another time.
   - With different provisions.
   - By authority of one who did not give authority.

Key Terms

theft (p. 294)
grand theft (p. 294)
petit or petty theft (p. 294)
thief (p. 294)
larceny (p. 295)
larceny from a person (p. 296)
shoplifting (p. 298)
abandoned property (p. 298)
embezzlement (p. 299)
misappropriation (p. 299)
false pretenses (p. 301)

receiving (p. 301)
constructive possession (p. 302)
extortion (p. 303)
under color of authority or office
 (p. 303)
blackmail (p. 305)
bribery (p. 305)
forgery (p. 306)
uttering (p. 306)
fraudulent making (p. 306)

Review Questions

1. Name the different crimes listed under theft, and explain why there is so much confusion in distinguishing among these different crimes.
2. What are the elements of shoplifting?
3. How can a person be convicted of larceny of "found" property?
4. What is the difference between joyriding and larceny?
5. State the difference between false pretenses and larceny.
6. List the essential elements of receiving stolen property.
7. Explain the difference between extortion, blackmail, and bribery.
8. What is uttering, and how does it relate to the crime of forgery?
9. What are the differences between forgery and fraudulent making?

Problem-Solving Exercises

1. **Shoplifting** A woman looking at cosmetics in a drug store was noticed by the store manager because she was not carrying a purse. She was pushing a shopping cart and put several cosmetic items into the cart. She went to the checkout stand and paid for all the items but one lipstick, which remained in the shopping cart. The manager noticed the lipstick in the cart and followed the female to her car. As the manager approached the female, she was picking the lipstick up from the cart. When the manager told her he was arresting her for shoplifting, she said that she did not see the lipstick in the cart until she got to her car and picked it up to return it to the store. The lipstick cost $5.99, and the female had $1.09 on her person. Answer the following questions:
   a. Was there any responsibility on the part of the clerk or manager to ensure that all items were paid for because she left the store? Why or why not?
   b. Should she be arrested? If so, on what charges and why? If not, why not?
   c. Write a statement reflecting your decision as though you were filling out a police report.
2. **Embezzlement** A jail guard is working on the night shift all alone. He locks himself out of his office, leaving all the jail keys in the office. He remembers

an inmate brought in earlier in the day who had lock-picking devices in his possession when he was booked. He goes to the evidence locker, retrieves the lock-picking devices, opens the locked door, and returns the devices to the locker. The lock-picking devices were gone for less than five minutes. Answer the following questions:

a. Has he embezzled the devices?

b. Does it make a difference that he put the property back within five minutes?

c. If you were his supervisor, how would you handle this situation?

Workplace Applications

1. **Burglary** A homeowner entered her home and saw a burglar unplugging her television. The burglar ran off without the television, but grabbed the homeowner's purse from her as he left. The woman tried holding on to the purse, but did not succeed. The purse contained credit cards, a box of new checks from her bank, and $80 cash. Answer the following questions:

   a. What crime(s) has the burglar committed? What crime(s) has the burglar attempted?

   b. Regarding the television, has the burglar committed a sufficient act for the taking and carrying away element of larceny?

   c. How can the monetary value of the checks and credit cards be ascertained to determine the degree of the crime?

2. **Shoplifting without Larceny** Your state has a law that provides that a person can commit shoplifting without committing larceny. Remember that for larceny, only the slightest movement is required to satisfy the taking and carrying away element. Answer the following questions:

   a. How can this law justify the fact that shoplifters move items when they conceal them on their person?

   b. Does it have anything to do with proving intent to permanently deprive the owners of the property?

   c. Would you change this law if you could? If so, how and why? If not, why not, and how would you address this current apparent contradiction?

Ethics Exercises

1. **Cheeseburger Bribes?** Janene, a volunteer for her suburban town's Police Explorer program, takes a break from her shift to eat lunch at Burgerland, a fast food restaurant. When the Burgerland manager sees her in full uniform, he groans and says, "You Explorers and cops are always coming in here, at least a dozen times a day. I know if I don't feed you I won't get adequate police responses the next time we get robbed again. I'll do it, but I'm sick of it." Janene is surprised and insists on paying for her meal, but the manager refuses to take the money. She finally agrees to accept the free meal. Answer the following questions:

   a. Is the Explorer extorting the restaurant or manager for food for police protection, even if she accepted the meal reluctantly? Why or why not?

b. Does it matter that no threats were ever made by anyone?

c. If the manager has reason to believe that police protection will be withheld if free food is not given, what is a better course of action for him to take?

Notes

1. Me. Rev. Stat. Ann. tit. 17-A, § 351 (West 2007).
2. Cal. Penal Code § 490a (West 2007).
3. Louis B. Schwartz & Dan M. Kahan, *Theft*, Encyclopedia of Crime and Justice 1556 (Joshua Dressler ed., 2002).
4. W. Va. Code § 61-3-13 (West 2007).
5. People v. Evans, 612 P.2d 1153 (Colo. Ct. App. 1980); Mack v. State, 465 S.W.2d 941 (Tex. Crim. App. 1971).
6. People v. Smith, 73 Cal. Rptr. 859 (Cal. Ct. App. 1968).
7. Terral v. State, 442 P.2d 465 (Nev. 1968).
8. Banks v. State, 40 S.E.2d 103 (Ga. Ct. App. 1946).
9. Md. Ann. Code, Crim. Law § 7-104(d) (West 2007).
10. People v. Roby, 346 N.E.2d 540 (N.Y. 1976).
11. Gwaltney v. Commonwealth, 452 S.E.2d 687 (Va. Ct. App. 1995).
12. Nelson v. State, 628 P.2d 884 (Alaska 1981).
13. State v. Bozeyowski, 185 A.2d 393 (N.J. Super. 1962), *cert. denied,* 374 U.S. 851 (1963).
14. People v. Boinus, 314 P.2d 787 (Cal. Ct. App. 1957).
15. Hurston v. State, 414 S.E.2d 303 (Ga. Ct. App. 1991).
16. *See* Model Penal Code § 223.4 (1985).
17. James Lindgren, *Blackmail and Extortion*, Encyclopedia of Crime and Justice 102 (Joshua Dressler ed., 2002).
18. N.J. Stat. Ann. § 2C:20-5 (West 2007).
19. United States v. Tillem, 906 F.2d 814 (2d Cir. 1990).
20. People v. Spatarella, 313 N.E.2d 38 (N.Y. 1974).
21. State v. Manthey, 487 N.W.2d 44 (Wis. Ct. App. 1992).
22. Floyd Feeney & Dan M. Kahan, *Robbery*, Encyclopedia of Crime and Justice, 1354 1356–57 (Joshua Dressler ed., 2002).
23. Wayne R. LaFave, Substantive Criminal Law § 20.4 (West 2007).
24. This hypothetical comes from James Lindgren, *Blackmail and Extortion*, Encyclopedia of Crime and Justice 102, 104–105 (Joshua Dressler ed., 2002).
25. Ind. Code Ann. § 35-43-5-2 (West 2007).
26. People ex rel. Arter v. Foster, 104 N.Y.S.2d 39 (N.Y. Sup. Ct. 1951).
27. Peter Goldberger & Dan M. Kahan, *Forgery*, Encyclopedia of Crime and Justice 719 (Joshua Dressler ed., 2002).
28. *Id.* at 720.

CHAPTER 12

White-Collar Crimes

CHAPTER OBJECTIVES

After reading and studying this chapter, you should be able to:

1. Define white-collar crime.
2. List the elements of tax evasion.
3. List the elements for a civil action for false advertising.
4. List the elements of mail fraud.
5. List the elements of securities fraud.
6. List the elements of an FDCA action.
7. List the main federal antitrust acts and the elements of an antitrust action.
8. Explain a monopoly.

12.1 Understanding White-Collar Crime

white-collar crime
A broad category of nonviolent misconduct involving commercial and financial fraud.

White-collar crime is a term that describes a broad category of nonviolent misconduct involving commercial and financial fraud. Examples are:

- Tax evasion.
- False advertising.
- Mail fraud.
- Securities fraud.
- Crimes against the Food and Drug Act.
- Monopolies and antitrust crimes.

White-collar crimes are more often perpetrated by corporations than by individuals. At common law, however, a corporation could not be held liable for criminal activity. This is because most crimes required the element of *mens rea* at the time of commission or omission; since corporations do not have minds, it was virtually impossible under common law to hold corporations accountable for their misdeeds. Instead, individuals acting on behalf of the corporation were indicted. In modern times, however, legislatures have been adopting statutes that allow corporations to be penalized for white-collar criminality.

CRITICAL THINKING 12.1

1. What issues arise when the government or consumers try to prosecute corporations for white-collar crimes?

12.2 Tax Evasion

tax evasion
The willful attempt to avoid paying legally due taxes; a specific intent crime. Also called *tax fraud*.

Tax evasion, also called *tax fraud*, is the willful attempt to avoid paying legally due taxes. One can evade paying federal, state, or local taxes. However, because evasion of federal taxes is the most commonly prosecuted tax offense, this part of the chapter will focus on it.

Tax evasion generally involves three elements:

1. The existence of a tax deficiency.
2. An affirmative act constituting an evasion or attempted evasion of a tax.
3. Willfulness in the commission of the affirmative act.

The element of willfulness indicates that tax evasion is a specific intent crime.

To obtain a conviction for tax evasion, the government must prove all three elements of the tax offense beyond a reasonable doubt. The following sections examine each of these three elements in detail.

Existence and Proof of a Tax Deficiency

tax deficiency
When the proper amount of tax to be paid is greater than the amount shown on a taxpayer's tax return.

A **tax deficiency** exists when the proper amount of tax to be paid is greater than the amount shown on a taxpayer's tax return. For example, if a taxpayer owes $5,000 in taxes but manipulates his or her tax return to state that he should pay only $4,000, a $1,000 tax deficiency exists. Most courts require proof of deficiencies of any size, but others require that the deficiency be substantial. What is "substantial" is a question of fact to be determined by the fact-finder (judge or jury).

To prove the existence of a tax deficiency, the government must show the following:

- The defendant received income in addition to what was reported.
- The unreported income was taxable.

The burden of the second element does not fall on the prosecution if it can prove a deficiency with direct evidence.

The government can use several methods to prove a tax deficiency, involving both direct and circumstantial evidence.

Direct Evidence

Using direct evidence to prove a tax deficiency involves examining and searching through the defendant's records for all taxable income, then comparing it to the tax return filed. This procedure is commonly known as the *specific items method* because it requires the government to produce evidence of specific items of reportable income that do not appear, or appear in a diminished amount, on the defendant's income tax returns. Examples include evidence of taxable income from checks the defendant received for services rendered, or checks made out to the defendant from the defendant's corporation for personal use that were not reported. In such cases, the checks themselves would be considered the specific items of taxable income.

Although the use of direct evidence is the ideal way to prove a tax deficiency, it is often extremely difficult to obtain such evidence in criminal tax offense trials. Obtaining direct evidence depends on the taxpayer's retaining all records of income, and a defendant who intends to evade paying income taxes is likely to conceal the existence of any unreported income, not retain it.

Circumstantial/Indirect Evidence

As an alternative to direct evidence, the prosecution may opt to use circumstantial or indirect evidence to establish a tax deficiency. There are three main indirect methods of proving a tax deficiency:

1. *Net worth method*, which requires the government to establish that during the year for which the defendant is accused of evading taxes, the defendant's net worth increased by more than what is reflected on his or her income tax return for that year. A person's net worth is the value of everything owned (assets), less the total amount owed (debts). (See Application Case 12.1.)
2. *Cash expenditures method*, in which the prosecution establishes to a reasonable certainty that the expenditures the defendant made within the fiscal year under examination exceed the amount of income reported on his or her tax return.
3. *Bank deposits method*, in which the prosecution merely examines the deposits the defendant made into a bank account within the relevant year. If the total amount of the deposits exceeds the amount reported on the income tax return, the excess is presumed to be unreported income.

⚖️ Application Case 12.1

Friedberg v. United States

In *Friedberg v. United States* (1954), the defendant claimed that he had been saving cash over the course of several years, and accordingly his net worth was much higher than reported on income tax returns. Cash held over from previous years has already been taxed, and therefore need not be reported. Although the government was unable to establish with complete certainty whether or not this cash on hand existed, it showed that it was unlikely. The government showed that (1) the defendant's property was foreclosed upon because he could not make minimum payments of $30 a month; (2) he lost his business because of inability to pay basic bills; and (3) the defendant claimed in a loan application to have only $150 in cash. The evidence was sufficient to satisfy the government's burden of negating alternative sources of nontaxable income.

SOURCE: Friedberg v. United States, 348 U.S. 142 (1954).

Affirmative Act

The second element that generally must be satisfied to obtain a conviction of tax evasion is that the accused must have performed an affirmative act toward the evasion or attempted evasion of taxes. This is a critical element because it can make the difference between conviction of a felony and a misdemeanor. Although performing an affirmative act toward the evasion of taxes constitutes a felony, mere neglect to file a tax return or pay require taxes results in a misdemeanor conviction. (See Application Case 12.2.)

⚖️ Application Case 12.2

Spies v. United States

In the landmark case of *Spies v. United States* (1943), the defendant simply did not file his tax return, nor did he pay the required taxes. The U.S. Supreme Court held that for a felony conviction of tax evasion, the defendant must commit an act, whereas an omission will only result in a misdemeanor, even if this omission is willful. In this case, the defendant's behavior constituted an omission, not an affirmative act. The Court held that for a felony conviction, the government must prove that the taxpayer did not merely neglect to file a return, but that he affirmatively attempted to evade paying the tax or filing the return. For a misdemeanor conviction, it is enough if the taxpayer willfully failed to file the return.

SOURCE: Spies v. United States, 317 U.S. 492 (1943).

What are considered affirmative acts for purposes of tax evasion? Examples include:

- Filing false tax returns.
- Keeping a double set of books.
- Concealing assets.
- Placing assets in the name of a third party.
- Lying to IRS agents.

Many courts, including the U.S. Supreme Court, have held that any practice designed to mislead the government, or to conceal funds or income, can be categorized as an affirmative act. Additionally, some courts hold that if the government can show a pattern of failure to file tax returns, this pattern of omissions might be collectively viewed as an affirmative act in an attempt to evade taxes.

Willfulness

The third and final element that the government must prove for a tax evasion conviction is willfulness. *Willfulness*, for tax evasion purposes, is the voluntary, intentional violation of a known legal duty—that is, the taxpayer knows that he or she should have reported more income than he or she actually did. It is required by both the felony and misdemeanor tax statutes, and there is no difference in the definition of the word *willful* when it is used in either statute. The main issue is what state of mind, or *mens rea*, must be shown to satisfy this willfulness requirement. To prove willfulness, the government must show that:

- The law imposed a duty on the defendant.
- The defendant knew of this duty.
- The defendant voluntarily and intentionally violated this duty.

In other words, if the government can establish that the defendant was aware of his or her legal duty as a taxpayer, the willfulness requirement is satisfied. Conversely, if the defendant was unaware of his or her duty, then the willfulness requirement is not satisfied.

Unlike other crimes, the Supreme Court has established that ignorance of the law is a defense when it comes to tax evasion. The Court noted that tax laws are extremely complex and difficult to understand. Therefore, several tax evasion offenses, including both felonies and misdemeanors, require a specific intent. This has the result of making the government's burden of proving willfulness much heavier.

Defenses

A taxpayer can offer several defenses to negate one or more of the three elements discussed above.

Cash Hoard Defense

This defense attacks the showing of a tax deficiency by asserting that although there may seem to be a tax deficiency (i.e., unreported income), in actuality the alleged unreported income is not taxable for some reason. For example, taxpayers often claim that they had saved-up cash on hand.

Defense against the Element of Willfulness

A second defense attacks the willfulness element. Remember that the government must show that the act or omission of tax evasion was done with an awareness of its illegality. Therefore, even if the defendant's good faith lack of knowledge or awareness is objectively unreasonable, the government's burden of proof is not satisfied.

Third-Party Defense: Defense against the Element of Affirmative Act

This defense shifts the blame of the alleged evasion to a third party, such as an accountant or attorney.

 CRITICAL THINKING 12.2

1. What is the difference between an affirmative act and an omission in tax evasion, and how does the difference affect penalties?

2. What are some common defenses against charges of tax evasion?

12.3 False Advertising

Like tax evasion, false advertising can be a violation of both state and federal laws. Unlike tax evasion, it can lead to both criminal and civil liability.

Federal Law

Two main federal laws target false advertising: the Trademark Law Revision Act (Lanham Act) and the Federal Trade Commission Act.

Trademark Law Revision Act of 1988 (Lanham Act)

This statute allows anyone who "is or is likely to be damaged" by a false advertisement to sue the advertiser. The courts have interpreted this provision to cover the rights of competitors, but have not considered consumers and other noncompetitors as falling within the category of those "likely to be damaged." Under the original provisions of this law, a plaintiff was only able to bring a claim alleging that the defendant misrepresented the defendant's own product, injuring the plaintiff.[1] Under the more recent Trademark Law Revision Act of 1988, liability falls on anyone who makes a false or misleading advertisement regarding his or her own goods, services, or commercial activities *or* regarding someone else's goods, services, or commercial activities. This act imposes only civil liability, not criminal penalty; therefore, only plaintiffs can bring legal action, not prosecutors.

A plaintiff must make five showings to succeed in a suit based on this act:

1. The advertiser made a false or misleading statement or representation about his or her or another person's goods, services, or commercial activity.
2. The statement or representation actually deceived, or has the capacity to deceive, a substantial segment of the targeted audience.

3. The deception is material, in that it is likely to influence purchasing decisions.
4. The advertising is made in connection with goods or services that travel in interstate commerce.
5. The deception has resulted or is likely to result in injury to the plaintiff.

As stated above, the defendant must have made a *representation* or an *advertisement*. Hence, the first task is to understand what constitutes a representation or advertisement. A representation or advertisement can be in either words or pictures, and it must be about a product or service. (See Application Case 12.3.) For example, if a company advertises to sell shelves and displays a picture of a shelf on a brochure, a representation has been made about the shelves for sale. If the company subsequently sells a shelf of a quality inferior to the one pictured, the representation may be deemed to be false.[2]

⚖️ Application Case 12.3

Truck Components, Inc. v. K-H Corp.

There have been cases in which a plaintiff tried to sue under the Trademark/Lanham Act, but the court held that the defendant's representation was not made about any good or service. In *Truck Components, Inc. v. K-H Corp.* (1991), the defendant agreed not to compete with the plaintiff in the sale of certain truck components. When the defendant breached this agreement, the plaintiff sued under the Trademark Act. The plaintiff claimed that the defendant's promotions were misleading because they "constitute representations that defendants are legally entitled and empowered to design, manufacture and market such products," when in fact, under the agreement, the defendant was not "legally entitled" to sell such products.

The court, however, disagreed with the plaintiff and held that the defendant's alleged representation did not fall within the Act. The court stated that the Act was limited to representations about "nature, characteristics, qualities, or geographic origin of his or her or another person's goods." In this case, the debate focused on the defendant's legal right to sell or manufacture the components. This is not enough to constitute legal liability, as the representation must be made about an actual *good* or *service*, and no representation regarding the production or quality of the goods in question (i.e., the components) was made.

SOURCE: Truck Components, Inc. v. K-H Corp., 776 F. Supp. 405 (N.D. Ill. 1991).

An important issue regarding the nature of a representation is whether the "representation" must always be in the affirmative. Does the Act also apply to omissions or nondisclosures that may mislead? Originally, it was proposed that such an omission of material information should be actionable. However, this proposed amendment was deleted, and the answer was left to the courts. The reason for its deletion was to prevent the likely misreading that an advertisement must contain every single material fact that may or may not influence a consumer's decision to buy a service or product.[3] As of now, there is a split in the courts as to whether a "representation," as used in the Trademark/Lanham Act, includes omissions or nondisclosures. See Application Case 12.4 for an example of this ongoing and complex debate.

⚖️ Application Case 12.4

American Home Products Corporation v. Johnson & Johnson

This 1987 case is a good example of how a failure to disclose certain material facts may render the representation misleading. The defendant, the makers of Tylenol, made a list as part of its marketing scheme that compared the side effects of its drug to those of Advil, manufactured by the plaintiff. The plaintiff claimed that the defendant omitted one negative effect that the defendant's drug had, but that the plaintiff's drug did not. The court held in favor of the plaintiff. Although it recognized that the Lanham Act does not require that all facts be disclosed, it held that a caption used in the advertisement implied that the list was comprehensive, which would mislead the targeted audience. In addition, because the defendant is in an industry that can pose many risks to consumers, court policy held that the defendants were held to a higher standard of care.

SOURCE: American Home Products Corporation v. Johnson & Johnson, 654 F. Supp. 568 (S.D.N.Y. 1987).

Federal Trade Commission Act

This act provides that it is illegal for any person or business to create or cause to be created any false advertisement that:

- By the U.S. Mail or by any means, is used for the purpose of inducing, or is likely to directly or indirectly induce, the purchase of food, drugs, devices, services, or cosmetics.
- By any means is used for the purpose of inducing, or is likely to directly or indirectly induce, the purchase of commerce relating to food, drugs, devices, services, or cosmetics.
- The creation of, or the causing to be created, any false advertisement within the provisions of this section shall be an unfair or deceptive act or practice in or affecting commerce.[4]

The Federal Trade Commission Act will be briefly covered again later, in the section on antitrust laws.

State Laws

A defendant may be civilly or criminally liable under state laws prohibiting false or misleading advertisements. Unlike the federal acts, however, these laws are passed mainly to protect consumers from being misled regarding products or services offered for sale.

Although the laws vary from state to state, the falsity generally must be material, and proof of an actual intent to sell the product is necessary. Many times in criminal false advertisement cases, however, it is not necessary for the prosecution to show that there has been an actual victim who made a purchase based on the deceptive ad.

For example, under California's false advertisement laws, a criminal violation must satisfy four elements:

1. A statement
2. Made by the disseminator in connection with the sale or disposition of goods or services
3. Which is untrue or misleading
4. And which statement is known, or should have been known, to be untrue or misleading.[5]

California courts have employed a "capacity to deceive" test: As long as the ad is capable of deceiving the public, a violation can be established. Further, it is the general, overall impression of the ad that determines the violation. Finally, the *mens rea* requirement is negligence: The California law requires only that the defendant knew, or with reasonable care should have known, the ad to be false.

CRITICAL THINKING 12.3

1. When defending charges of false advertising, what legally constitutes a representation or advertisement?

12.4 Mail Fraud

Mail fraud is a form of fraud that uses a mail service to disseminate materials that deceive people. To obtain a conviction for mail fraud, the government must establish beyond a reasonable doubt four basic elements:

1. A scheme to defraud.
2. With the intent to defraud.
3. While using the U.S. Postal Service or any private interstate commercial carrier.
4. In furtherance of that scheme.

This statute has a very broad reach. Furthermore, it is an offense often charged in conjunction with other crimes. In the landmark case *United States v. Weatherspoon* (1978), a conviction of both mail fraud and false statements was upheld.[6] Most courts also allow a mail fraud conviction for mailing a fraudulent tax return, and mail fraud is often charged together with securities fraud.

The following sections discuss the four elements of mail fraud in detail.

Scheme to Defraud

Of all the elements of mail fraud, this one has resulted in the most litigation because the federal statute neither defines what constitutes a "scheme" nor states what types of schemes fall within the purview of the statute. Thus, courts are given wide discretion in shaping this element. It is understood, though, that the government need

mail fraud
A form of fraud that uses a mail service to disseminate materials that deceive people.

12.1 Web Exploration

Mail Fraud Tips

Read "What you need to know about mail fraud" at http://www.howtoadvice.com/ MailFraud. How can mail fraud affect you? How can you protect yourself from mail fraud?

not show that the scheme or plan was successful or completed. In other words, it is not necessary that the government show that an individual has actually suffered an economic loss or deprivation of property.

Originally, the statute was used only to prosecute "schemes" that consisted of traditional common law fraud—that is, defrauding someone of tangible property or interest in property. Later, it was interpreted to prosecute schemes defrauding individuals out of intangible property as well. A congressional statute now expressly allows mail fraud to encompass fraudulent schemes involving intangible property rights.

Schemes involving traditional fraud deprive one of money or other tangible property through misrepresentations, including omissions, that are reasonably calculated to deceive. The courts apply an objective standard in determining whether a reasonable person would rely upon the representations made. Some examples of traditional fraud cases involving mail fraud are false loan applications and fraudulent investment schemes.

intangible rights theory

A type of prosecution under mail fraud that was primarily used to protect citizens from dishonest public officials.

The **intangible rights theory** covers a type of prosecution under mail fraud that was primarily used to protect citizens from dishonest public officials. A public official using the mail as part of a scheme to "deprive the citizenry of the right to good government" was actionable under the mail fraud statute. This theory, however, has undergone some testing over the years. (See Application Case 12.5.)

⚖ Application Case 12.5

McNally v. United States

In *McNally v. United States* (1987), the U.S. Supreme Court restricted the reach of the federal mail fraud statute. The Court found that the statute could no longer be used to convict individuals engaged in political corruption, because the interest or right involved did not fall within the definition of "scheme to defraud."

In this case, the chairman of the Democratic Party of Kentucky, Howard Hunt, was given the authority to select the insurance companies that were to provide the commonwealth with its workmen's compensation policy. Hunt chose a certain insurance agent on condition that this agency share its commissions with other specified insurance agencies, one of them owned by McNally. The selected insurance company mailed commission checks to the other specified agencies, which served as the basis for one of the mail fraud counts: that a "scheme" was devised "to defraud the citizens of Kentucky of their right to have the Commonwealth's affairs conducted honestly."

The prosecution argued that the commonwealth's public officials owe a fiduciary duty to the public, and to "misuse . . . [the public] office for private gain is a fraud." The Court held, however, that although the statute protects property rights, a "scheme to defraud" does not include protection of intangible rights to honest government.

In any case, Congress subsequently overturned the *McNally* decision by passing section 1346, defining "scheme to defraud" to include "a scheme or artifice to deprive another of the intangible right of honest services." In addition, when the prosecution is trying to establish a "scheme" involving the intangible rights doctrine (as distinguished from a traditional fraud scheme), there must be a fiduciary duty between the parties.

SOURCE: McNally v. United States, 483 U.S. 350 (1987); 18 U.S.C. § 1346.

Intent to Defraud

This element of mail fraud is the same as any fraud case: that the defendant intended to defraud the victim through the defendant's scheme. Some courts have found intent if the defendant was merely reckless. Therefore, the defendant is criminally liable even with only a reckless disregard for the truth.

Use of the Post Office or Private Interstate Carrier

Originally, the federal mail fraud statute applied only to cases in which the defendant used the U.S. Post Office to carry out the scheme to defraud. As can be seen from the modern mail fraud statute, however, a violation can also arise from use of any private carrier. A private carrier, however, must be an *interstate* carrier, whereas if the defendant is using the U.S. Postal Service, it is enough if the defendant merely mailed something down the block. This is because Congress has complete power over the Postal Service, as granted by the Constitution, whereas Congress's control over private carriers is limited to the power to regulate interstate commerce.[7]

Furtherance of the Scheme to Defraud

To support a conviction of mail fraud, the prosecution must prove that the use of mail was "in furtherance," or for the purpose, of executing or completing the scheme to

Mail Fraud   Mail fraud can be committed either through the U.S. Postal Service or through private carriers.

defraud. Using the mail must be part of at least one key element of the mail fraud scheme. Therefore, if the scheme is undermined or ruined by mail use, the mail use is not "in furtherance" of the scheme, and the element is therefore not satisfied.

Additionally, if the mailing occurred after the scheme was completed, the mailing element is usually not satisfied. In *United States v. Maze* (1974), the defendant used a stolen credit card. Thereafter, several mailings occurred between the bank and the vendor. The government argued that this was enough to satisfy the mailing element. The U.S. Supreme Court rejected this argument, because the scheme was complete once the defendant used the stolen credit card.[8] Nonetheless, the Court has also held that there are certain times when the mailing could occur even after the defendant defrauded the victim of his or her money and still satisfy the "in furtherance" element.

A defendant has two main defenses to a mail fraud charge:

1. A good faith defense, which is merely an assertion that there was no fraud intended.
2. A statute of limitations defense. The statute of limitations is generally 5 years on a mail fraud charge and 10 years if it involves a financial institution. The statute of limitations begins running from the time of the final overt act made in furtherance of the scheme to defraud.

 CRITICAL THINKING 12.4

1. What are some schemes to defraud, and why has there been difficulty in defining a "scheme"?

2. What is the intangible rights doctrine, and how has the debate surrounding it been resolved?

12.5 Securities Fraud

With the crash of the stock market in 1929, Congress enacted the Securities Act of 1933 and the Securities Exchange Act of 1934 to promote integrity in the stock market. The Securities Exchange Act is most widely used to prosecute defendants for securities fraud. It protects both purchasers and sellers of securities, whereas the Securities Act of 1933 protects only the purchaser.

A **securities fraud** can be criminal, civil, or administrative. There are four main elements for every type of securities fraud action:

securities fraud
A criminal, civil, or administrative offense with the following elements: substantive fraud that is found in the offer, purchase, or sale of a security or in connection therewith; the use of interstate commerce or the mails; and willfulness.

1. Substantive fraud—including material omissions/misrepresentations, insider trading, parking, and broker-dealer fraud, each of which has its own elements.
2. Such fraud is found in the offer, purchase, or sale of a security or in connection therewith.
3. The use of interstate commerce or the mails.
4. Willfulness.[9]

The sections that follow will discuss the first three of these four elements in greater detail. The last, willfulness, has been covered in previous discussions that generally apply here as well.

The Sarbanes-Oxley Act of 2002 created a new crime, "securities fraud," codified in the federal criminal code.[10] "The mens rea under the statute is knowledge, as compared with the willfulness requirement of the securities fraud statutes."[11] The Act, passed in response to a wave of corporate and accounting scandals, including Enron, Tyco, and Worldcom, is probably the most significant securities legislation implemented since the New Deal. The Act provides enhanced standards for the executives and boards of public companies and public accounting firms. It created a new public agency to oversee compliance with the Act and to regulate, inspect, and discipline public accounting firms acting as auditors of public companies. Also included in the Act are provisions pertaining to issues of auditor independence, corporate governance, and financial disclosure.

Substantive Fraud

As noted above, there are four different ways this element can be satisfied, each with elements unique to that particular type of fraud.

Material Omissions and Misrepresentations

Liability for this most common type of securities fraud stems from the Securities Exchange Act of 1934. The Act states that it is illegal for anyone "to make any untrue statement of a material fact or to omit to state a material fact necessary in order to make the statements made . . . in connection with the purchase or sale of any security." To prove this crime, the government must prove the following four (or five) elements:

1. The defendant made a false statement or omission.
2. That is material.
3. That is made with knowledge.
4. And that caused the injured party's damages.
5. And (in the case of an omission only) the defendant had a duty to disclose the information.[12]

Insider Trading

Insider trading is a type of substantive fraud that involves the purchase and sale of securities based on material, nonpublic information. Insider trading usually deals with cases in which one insider, quasi-insider, or misappropriator who has inside information tips off another individual regarding certain material, nonpublic information. At times the tipper is liable, and at other times the tippee is liable. The Securities Exchange Act of 1934 prohibits certain trades by corporate officers, directors, and majority shareholders. It also prohibits misrepresentations and other "fraudulent, deceptive, or manipulative acts or practices" specifically with regard to tender offers.

> **insider trading**
> A type of substantive fraud that involves the purchase and sale of securities based on material, nonpublic information.

One of the more famous insider trading cases in recent years involved Martha Stewart. In 2002, charges were brought against Martha Stewart when she sold her shares of ImClone stock just days before the company's application for a new drug was denied. Stewart was presumed to be actively complicit in the alleged insider trading, given her extensive background as stockbroker and president of the NYSE Board of Governors. She pled guilty to lying to federal investigators and served a five-month prison sentence. She also settled the insider trading charges by paying the maximum penalty.

An important question in regard to insider trading is who qualifies as an insider. Many different individuals have been classified as insiders, including directors, officers, major shareholders, lower-level employees obtaining information because of their jobs, outside professionals and advisers (e.g., accountants and lawyers), press, companies and firms of the above-mentioned individuals, and even their families. (See Application Case 12.6.)

⚖️ Application Case 12.6
Dirks v. SEC

In *Dirks v. SEC* (1983), a financial analyst discovered that an insurance company was involved in a major fraud resulting in an overstatement of the company's assets. Before the information became public, the analyst disseminated this information to his clients, who subsequently sold their shares in the insurance company.

The Court held that the analyst could not be held liable as a tippee, one who receives the information regarding the fraud from the tipper, because liability requires that the tipper breach a fiduciary duty. In other words, the tippee does not invariably inherit the insider's duty. The Court held that the analyst's tipper breached no duty, but was merely reporting a fraud.

SOURCE: Dirks v. SEC, 463 U.S. 646 (1983).

Parking

parking
Any sale of securities that are purchased with the understanding that they will be repurchased by the seller at a later time, to manipulate stock prices or avoid reporting requirements.

A third method of securities fraud is known as parking. **Parking** can be defined as any sale of securities that are purchased with the understanding that they will be repurchased by the seller at a later time. Although parking is a criminal violation in and of itself, it is often part of a larger scheme. Parking is used to:

- Manipulate the supply and demand of stock, which will affect its price.
- Circumvent margin rules and minimum net capital requirements.
- Avoid the reporting requirements of the 1934 Act. [13]

Broker–Dealer Fraud

churning
When a stockbroker excessively purchases and sells securities for a client without regard or concern for the client's investment objectives but rather to advance the stockbroker's own interests, usually by generating commissions.

A final practice found under the substantive fraud element of a securities fraud action is a type of broker-dealer fraud known as churning. **Churning** occurs when a stockbroker excessively purchases and sells securities for a client without regard or concern for the client's investment objectives but rather to advance the stockbroker's own interests, usually by generating commissions.

For a conviction, the government (or investor) must establish that:

- The broker exercised control over trading in the account.
- The trading was excessive in light of the character of the account.
- The broker showed an intent to defraud or showed willful and reckless disregard for the investor's interests.

Offer, Purchase, or Sale of a Security

The 1933 and 1934 Acts require that the substantive fraud discussed above be "in the *offer or sale*" or "in connection with the *purchase or sale*" of a security. The 1933 Act defines an offer for sale, or offer, as "every attempt or offer to dispose of, or solicitation of an offer to buy, a security or interest in a security, for value." A transfer of title is not required for a sale to occur. The 1934 Act defines purchase as "any contract to buy, purchase or otherwise acquire" a security. A sale includes "any contracts to sell or otherwise dispose of" a security. These definitions include a corporation's purchase or sale of its own securities, mergers, and acquisitions.[14]

Use of Interstate Commerce or Mails

This third element of the crime requires that a securities fraud scheme include the "use of any means or instrumentality of interstate commerce or of the mails, or of any facility of any national securities exchange."[15] In some situations, an intrastate use of an interstate means of communication is sufficient, such as the use of a telephone to call someone within the same state. Further, use of interstate commerce or mails need only be incidental, so long as it was in furtherance of the fraud (similar to the mail fraud requirement).

Defenses

There are three common defenses to securities fraud:

1. *No Knowledge*: The defendant can argue that he or she did not have knowledge of the substantive law. This does not mean that the defendant asserts that he or she was not aware of the applicable securities laws, but rather did not know that his or her actions were contrary to the laws. Note that this is not a complete defense; it only lessens the penalties.
2. *Good Faith*: In a case where the substantive fraud entails a misstatement or omission, the defendant can claim that he or she had a good faith belief that the statement was true and accurate, or that the omission was unintentional or immaterial.
3. *Reliance on Counsel*: The defendant can also assert that his or her actions were a result of a good faith reliance on the advice of counsel. This defense requires the defendant to show (a) a request for counsel's advice regarding the legality of the proposed action, (b) full disclosure to counsel of all relevant facts, (c) counsel's assurance that the action was legal, and (d) good faith reliance on counsel's advice. This defense is not available if counsel is an interested party.[16]

CRITICAL THINKING 12.5

1. What is insider trading, and who qualifies as an insider?
2. What are common defenses against charges of securities fraud?

12.6 Crimes against the Food and Drug Act

According to the Federal Food, Drug, and Cosmetic Act (FDCA), committing or causing the following acts is prohibited:

- The introduction, or delivery for introduction, into interstate commerce of any food, drug, device, or cosmetic that is adulterated or misbranded.
- The adulteration or misbranding of any food, drug, device, or cosmetic in interstate commerce.
- The receipt in interstate commerce of any food, drug, device, or cosmetic that is adulterated or misbranded, and the delivery or proffered delivery thereof for pay or otherwise.
- The refusal to permit entry or inspection.
- The manufacture within any territory of any food, drug, device, or cosmetic that is adulterated or misbranded.

The underlying purpose of this act is to protect the health and safety of the public by prohibiting all adulterated and misbranded goods from entering the stream of interstate commerce. Any violation of the FDCA can be either a misdemeanor or a felony, and can result in criminal liability, injunctions, or seizure of the illegal merchandise.

12.1 On the Job

Food and Drug Inspector

Description and Duties: Investigate and inspect facilities, procedures, and products to ensure that they comply with required standards. Collect and evaluate evidence. Enforce restrictions on unacceptable products to prevent their sale or distribution. Supervise the destruction or reconditioning of restrained products. Investigate, evaluate, and take appropriate action on consumer complaints and illegal or fraudulent practices in the advertisement, manufacture, or sale of products.

Salary: Salaries for federal inspectors are by federal government pay grades and vary depending on experience and supervisory level. State jobs are similar. Starting pay is approximately $35,000 and can reach $65,000.

Other Information: Generally requires a B.S. degree in bacteriology, biology, chemistry, food technology, pharmacology, environmental health, biomedical engineering, or other biological or chemical science. Job experience and at least 30 semester hours of college courses in an appropriate field can also be combined to substitute.

SOURCE: California State Personnel Board, http://www.dpa.ca.gov/textdocs/specs/s1/s1589.txt.

The elements of FDCA violations differ depending on the level of criminality and on who the defendant is. For a misdemeanor conviction, three (or four) elements must be satisfied:

1. There must be a "food," drug," "cosmetic," or "device."
2. The object must be "adulterated" or "misbranded."
3. The object must be introduced into interstate commerce.
4. When defendant is a corporate officer, the officer must bear a "responsible relation" to the violation.

A felony conviction requires, in addition to these three (or four) misdemeanor elements, either intent or evidence of a prior FDCA violation.

Definitions

The FDCA definitions of key terms are summarized in the following paragraphs.

Food

The definition of food includes:

- Articles used for food or drink for humans or other animals.
- Chewing gum.
- Articles used for components of any such article.

Drug

A drug includes any "articles intended for use in the diagnosis, cure, mitigation, treatment, or prevention of disease in man or other animals."

Cosmetic

Cosmetics include "articles intended to be rubbed, poured, sprinkled, or sprayed on, introduced into, or otherwise applied to the human body or any part thereof for cleansing, beautifying, promoting attractiveness, or altering the appearance."

Device

A device is any "instrument, apparatus, implement, machine, contrivance, implant, in vitro reagent, or other similar or related article, including any component, part, or accessory, which is:

- Recognized in the official National Formulary.
- Intended for use in the diagnosis of disease or other conditions, or in the cure, mitigation, treatment, or prevention of disease.
- Intended to affect the structure or any function of the body.[17]

Adulterated Goods

An item has been subject to **adulteration** when its ingredients are poisonous, filthy, putrid, otherwise unsanitary, or have been contaminated.[18] In *United States v. Park* (1975), the Court held that food that comes into contact with rodents can be considered "adulterated."[19] Some courts have held that a food can be labeled "adulterated"

adulteration
When the ingredients of a food, drug, cosmetic, or device are poisonous, filthy, putrid, otherwise unsanitary, or have been contaminated.

Food Adulteration Adulteration occurs when food is contaminated in any way, such as by improper handling, improper storage, or outside contaminants.

if there is a reasonable possibility that the method or place of storage and/or processing may result in contamination.

Misbranding

misbranding

Any branding of a food, drug, cosmetic, or device that includes the use of false or misleading information, labels, packaging, or containers.

Misbranding means any branding of a food, drug, cosmetic, or device that includes the use of false or misleading information, labels, packaging, or containers. An example is labeling an item as "sterile" when it is actually not sterile.

Interstate Commerce

FDCA violations require that the adulterated or misbranded food, drug, cosmetic, or device be introduced into interstate commerce. Such interstate commerce is not limited "to the actual transportation of articles across state lines, but includes the whole transaction of which such transportation is a part."[20]

Felony: Intent or Prior Violation

For a felony conviction under the FDCA, the government has an additional burden of proving either:

- That the defendant had the intent to introduce adulterated or misbranded foods, drugs, cosmetics, or devices into interstate commerce.
- That the defendant has done this in the past and is now being prosecuted again.

Defenses

Two main defenses have been asserted in connection with FDCA violations: the Fourth Amendment and impossibility.

Fourth Amendment

The Fourth Amendment protects the people against unreasonable searches and seizures. This provision applies to administrative searches as well. Administrative searches, however, may be valid without a warrant if:

- The inspection is made pursuant to a regulatory scheme for which there is a substantial government interest.
- The owner of the premises is aware of the periodic inspections, and the inspection furthers this regulatory scheme.
- The scheme's predictable regularity leads the owner to expect it, which creates an awareness that substitutes for a warrant.[21]

Impossibility

The U.S. Supreme Court requires the government to show that a corporate officer whose business violated the FDCA had the authority or power to prevent or correct the FDCA violation. If it was objectively impossible for the officer to do so, then liability cannot be found. Therefore, many defendants assert an "impossibility" defense, which is a claim that the defendant did not have the authority to prevent or rectify the violative situation, and therefore had no liability. If such a defense is made, the government then has the burden of establishing that the defendant did in fact have the necessary control or authority to prevent or correct the situation. (See Application Case 12.7.)

⚖️ Application Case 12.7

United States v. Dotterweich

United States v. Park

In *United States v. Dotterweich* (1943), a company purchased drugs from their manufacturer, relabeled them, and shipped them out into interstate commerce. Dotterweich was found guilty of violating the FDCA. They took no part in shipping the misbranded and adulterated goods into interstate commerce, but because they had the "responsible share in the furtherance of the transaction," they were found liable.

More than 30 years later, the U.S. Supreme Court clarified this finding in *United States v. Park* (1975). In *Park*, the president of a national retail food chain was held strictly criminally liable under the FDCA for failing to prevent his company from storing food in an area where rodent contamination was a reasonable possibility. In other words, the *Dotterweich* strict liability standard was still upheld, in that no intent is required for a misdemeanor conviction.

A "responsible relation" test had been used in *Dotterweich*, but there were some questions about its application. This test was used again in *Park*, but to prevent any controversy it was articulated as follows: In addition to the usual elements, it must be established with "evidence sufficient to warrant a finding by the trier that the defendant had, by reason of his position in the corporation, responsibility and authority either to prevent in the first instance, or promptly correct, the violation complained of, and that he failed to do so." In sum, the Court stated that strict liability will be applied to individuals who fail to prevent, detect, or correct the adulteration or misbranding when the authority or power to do so is available to them.

SOURCE: United States v. Dotterweich, 320 U.S. 277, 281 (1943); United States v. Park, 421 U.S. 658 (1975).

⚖ CRITICAL THINKING 12.6

1. For a felony conviction under the FDCA, one of two requirements must be satisfied. Name these requirements.

12.7 Antitrust Crimes and Monopoly

antitrust laws
Laws that protect trade and commerce from restraints, monopolies, price-fixing, and price discrimination, to ensure and preserve a competitive economy.

Antitrust laws protect trade and commerce from restraints, monopolies, price-fixing, and price discrimination. These laws are designed to ensure and preserve a competitive economy, to allow free enterprise to prosper, and to allow everyone an equal opportunity to engage in business, trade, and commerce.

Key Federal Acts

Both the federal government and the state governments have their own antitrust laws with which companies must comply. This section focuses on the four main federal antitrust laws: the Sherman Act, Clayton Act, Robinson-Patman Act, and Federal Trade Commission Act. Many state laws follow the same outline as these federal laws.

The Sherman Act

The Sherman Act is the primary statute used to prosecute antitrust cases. Section 1 generally criminalizes unreasonable restraints on interstate commerce. It specifically makes illegal "[e]very contract, combination in the form of trust or otherwise, or conspiracy, in restraint of trade or commerce among the several States, or with foreign nations." A violation can result in a felony conviction. Section 2 criminalizes monopolizing, attempting to monopolize, or conspiring to monopolize a market through unfair practices.[22]

Under section 1 of the Sherman Act, the government must satisfy three elements for a civil judgment and four for a criminal conviction:

1. Two or more entities formed a combination or conspiracy.
2. The combination or conspiracy produces, or potentially produces, an unreasonable restraint of trade or commerce.
3. The restraint is on interstate trade or commerce.
4. General intent (for criminal charges only).

Penalties for violations of the various antitrust laws can be severe, including a three-year prison sentence for *each* offense, several millions of dollars in fines imposed on both the corporation and the individuals involved, injunctions, and various other fees and damages.

The Robinson–Patman Act

Under the Robinson-Patman Price Discrimination Act, one "engaged in commerce" can be subjected to criminal liability if he or she is involved in any sale of goods "at unreasonably low prices for the purpose of destroying competition or eliminating a competitor."[23] This practice, known as *pricing*, creates a high risk of being sued. Nevertheless, because this seems to negate the underlying purpose of the antitrust laws—to preserve a competitive economy—the government usually does not bring criminal charges for it.

The Clayton Act

The Clayton Act prohibits certain types of activities that harm competition, such as exclusive dealing arrangements and mergers damaging competition. Furthermore, this Act provides a private citizen's right to sue for injury caused by violation of the antitrust laws.

The Federal Trade Commission Act

The FTCA, which you have already learned about in the section on false advertising, is mainly used to prosecute unfair and deceptive practices. In that capacity, it has provisions that apply to antitrust and monopoly issues as well. Specifically, it prohibits practices similar to those mentioned in the Sherman and Clayton Acts that relate to harm done to competition.

Other Issues

Price-Fixing

In general, price-fixing refers to an agreement to raise, lower, fix, peg, or stabilize commodity prices entering interstate commerce. There are two main types of price-fixing. **Horizontal price-fixing** agreements are direct or indirect agreements made between market participants at the *same level* within a given market, regarding the prices they will charge for a similar product they both sell. **Vertical price-fixing** agreements are direct or indirect agreements made between market participants at *different levels* within a given market, regarding the price at which their product will be resold.

horizontal price-fixing
Direct or indirect agreements made between market participants at the same level within a given market, regarding the prices they will charge for a similar product they both sell.

vertical price-fixing
Direct or indirect agreements made between market participants at different levels within a given market, regarding the price at which their product will be resold.

Market Allocation Agreements

Agreements involving market allocation are those made between competitors within a given market to divide up markets by territory, product line, or customers. Such an agreement is usually done to minimize competition, and is thus an automatic violation of the antitrust laws.

Boycotts

In *Klor's, Inc. v. Broadway-Hale Stores* (1959), the U.S. Supreme Court defined *boycotts* as "concerted refusals by traders to deal with other traders." As an anticompetitive measure, such boycotts are considered illegal.[24]

Tying Arrangement

A **tying arrangement** is an agreement that a purchaser must buy additional (or tied) products along with the one product that he or she desires. At the very least, the purchaser

tying arrangement
An agreement that a purchaser must buy additional (or tied) products along with the one product that he or she desires; at the very least, the purchaser must agree to not buy this tied product from any other supplier.

must agree to not buy this tied product from any other supplier. Tying arrangements have the anticompetitive effect of denying competitors "free access to the market for the tied product, not because the party imposing the tying requirements has a better product or lower price, but because of his power or leverage in another market. At the same time buyers are forced to forego their free choice between competing products."[25]

Tying is illegal if (1) there are actually two separate products, and (2) the seller has a substantial market share in one of the products and, thus, has "leverage" to force the purchase of the second product. If it is economically impractical to sell two items separately, there is no tying violation. Additionally, some tying arrangements actually have pro-competitive effects, in which case the agreement will only be found unlawful under the "rule of reason" analysis.

Government actions against Microsoft in *United States v. Microsoft Corp.* (1998) involved both federal and state claims for antitrust violations. The federal government found a violation of both sections 1 and 2 of the Sherman Act. The section 1 violation, which is not the main claim, is that Microsoft engaged in a tying arrangement by tying their Internet explorer to Windows 95 and to Windows 98—two separate offenses.

Price Discrimination (Robinson–Patman Act)

As stated above, the Robinson-Patman Act generally deals with pricing. It also prohibits other practices, such as discriminatory promotional allowances, unlawful brokerage payments, and the unlawful inducement of a discriminatory price. More specifically, it prohibits *price discrimination* that does either one of the following:

- Unfairly eliminates competition by another manufacturer.
- Unfairly causes one or more customers to go out of business.[26]

The first arrangement is intended to drive the defendant's competitors out of business, whereas the second is intended to drive competitors of the defendant's customer out of business. In both scenarios, the idea is basically the same: The idea is for a business to charge one distributor a lower price than another, in order to drive either the business's competition out of business or the distributor's competition out of business.

Monopolies

monopolize
To jointly acquire and maintain the power to control and dominate interstate trade and commerce in a commodity sufficient to exclude actual or potential competitors from the field.

attempt to monopolize
Engaging in behavior and business practices that, if successful, would create a monopoly and that come close enough to so doing to create a dangerous probability that it would have occurred.

Obtaining or attempting to obtain a monopoly are both prohibited under the antitrust laws. To **monopolize** means to obtain the joint acquisition and maintenance "of the power to control and dominate interstate trade and commerce in a commodity to such an extent that they are able, as a group, to exclude actual or potential competitors from the field, accompanied with the intention and purpose to exercise such power."[27] An **attempt to monopolize** means engaging in behavior and business practices that, if successful, would create a monopoly and that come close enough to so doing as to create a dangerous probability that it would have occurred.

A monopolization conviction requires satisfaction of two elements:

1. The possession of monopoly power, which includes the power to control or fix prices and unreasonably restrict or exclude competition in a relevant market.
2. The willful acquisition or maintenance of such power through unlawful means, and not from fair competitive practices such as high-quality products, business acumen, or historical accident.[28]

Thus, if a company achieves a monopoly share of a market through lawful, pro-competitive means, there is no antitrust violation. In certain circumstances, however, a company can equally lower prices to all its customers and be subject to the laws of monopolization and attempted monopolization.

An attempted monopoly conviction requires satisfaction of three elements:

1. Specific intent to obtain monopoly power in a given market.
2. Use of unlawful means to increase market share.
3. Dangerous probability that a monopoly will be obtained.

As discussed earlier under tying arrangements, in *United States v. Microsoft Corp.* (1998), the U.S. government's lawsuit against Microsoft revealed violations of both sections 1 and 2 of the Sherman Act. The section 2 violation, which was the government's main claim, is that of monopolization and attempted monopolization, with the aforementioned tying allegations playing a role in the monopolization charges. The monopolization counts alleged that Microsoft abused its monopoly power in the market for PC-compatible computers, for the purpose of maintaining its monopoly power in that market. It also alleged that Microsoft attempted to monopolize the Internet browser market through several anticompetitive means.[29]

CRITICAL THINKING 12.7

1. How does price-fixing harm competition? Do vertical price-fixing and horizontal price-fixing affect it differently?
2. Why is an attempt to monopolize a crime?

REVIEW AND APPLICATIONS

Summary by Chapter Objectives

1. **Define white-collar crime.** *White-collar crime* is a term that describes a broad category of nonviolent misconduct involving commercial and financial fraud. Examples are tax evasion, false advertising, mail fraud, securities fraud, crimes against the Food and Drug Act, and monopolies and antitrust crimes. White-collar crimes are more often perpetrated by corporations than by individuals.

2. **List the elements of tax evasion.** To obtain a conviction for tax evasion, the government must prove all three elements of the tax offense beyond a reasonable doubt:
   • The existence of a tax deficiency.
   • An affirmative act constituting an evasion or attempted evasion of a tax.
   • Willfulness.
   The element of willfulness indicates that tax evasion is a specific intent crime.

3. **List the elements for a civil action for false advertising.** To succeed in a suit based on this act, a plaintiff must make five showings:
   - The advertiser made a false or misleading statement or representation about its own or another person's goods, services, or commercial activity.
   - The statement or representation actually deceived, or has the capacity to deceive, a substantial segment of the targeted audience.
   - The deception is material, in that it is likely to influence purchasing decisions.
   - The advertising is made in connection with goods or services that travel in interstate commerce.
   - The deception has resulted or is likely to result in injury to the plaintiff.

4. **List the elements of mail fraud.** To obtain a conviction for mail fraud, the government must establish beyond a reasonable doubt these four basic elements:
   - A scheme to defraud.
   - With the intent to defraud.
   - While using the U.S. Postal Service or any private interstate commercial carrier.
   - In furtherance of that scheme.

5. **List the elements of securities fraud.** Every type of securities fraud action has four main elements:
   - Substantive fraud—including material omissions/misrepresentations, insider trading, parking, and broker-dealer fraud, each of which has its own elements.
   - Such fraud is found in the offer, purchase, or sale of a security or in connection therewith.
   - The use of interstate commerce or the mails.
   - Willfulness.

6. **List the elements of an FDCA action.** For a *misdemeanor* conviction, three elements must be satisfied (four when the defendant is a corporate officer):
   - There must be a "food," "drug," "cosmetic," or "device."
   - The object must be "adulterated" or "misbranded."
   - The object must be introduced into interstate commerce.
   - When the defendant is a corporate officer, the officer must bear a "responsible relation" to the violation.

   A *felony* conviction requires, in addition to these three (or four) misdemeanor elements, either intent or evidence of a prior FDCA violation.

7. **List the main federal antitrust acts and the elements of an antitrust action.** The four main federal antitrust laws are the Sherman Act, Clayton Act, Robinson-Patman Act, and Federal Trade Commission Act. Under the Sherman Act, the government must satisfy three elements for a civil judgment and four for a criminal conviction:
   - Two or more entities formed a combination or conspiracy.
   - The combination or conspiracy produces, or potentially produces, an unreasonable restraint of trade or commerce.
   - The restraint is on interstate trade or commerce.
   - General intent (for criminal charges only).

8. **Explain a monopoly.** To monopolize means to obtain the joint acquisition and maintenance "of the power to control and dominate interstate trade and commerce in a commodity to such an extent that they are able, as a group, to exclude actual or potential competitors from the field, accompanied with the intention and purpose to exercise such power."

Key Terms

white-collar crime (p. 312)
tax evasion (p. 312)
tax deficiency (p. 312)
mail fraud (p. 319)
intangible rights theory (p. 320)
securities fraud (p. 322)
insider trading (p. 323)
parking (p. 324)
churning (p. 324)

adulteration (p. 327)
misbranding (p. 328)
antitrust laws (p. 330)
horizontal price-fixing (p. 331)
vertical price-fixing (p. 331)
tying arrangement (p. 331)
monopolize (p. 332)
attempt to monopolize (p. 332)

Review Questions

1. Define tax deficiency and give an example.
2. What are the various defenses for tax evasion?
3. What are the different methods, direct and indirect, of proving a tax deficiency?
4. What is the difference between a misdemeanor violation and a felony violation for tax evasion?
5. When is an act in furtherance of a scheme to defraud?
6. Explain the role of material omissions and misrepresentations according to the Securities Exchange Act of 1934.
7. List and explain the elements of "churning."
8. What are the four major elements of securities fraud?
9. What is the difference between horizontal and vertical price-fixing?

Problem-Solving Exercises

1. **Mail Fraud** You are in charge of investigating mail fraud for the U.S. Postal Service. You are handling a case that involves several cases of mail fraud using the U.S. Postal Service, UPS, and Federal Express. Some of the shipping was interstate, and some was intrastate. With prosecutors, you must establish what qualifies as mail fraud under federal laws. Answer the following questions:
   a. What is the difference in the requirements for interstate shipping for the U.S. Postal Service and for private carriers? Why?
   b. Which intrastate mail can be used as evidence, and what intrastate mail cannot? Why?

   c. Suppose that international shipping was involved, too. Based on what you have learned, do you think that it could be used as evidence? Do you think that it would be used? Why or why not?

2. **Drug Inspection** You are a food and drug inspector working with a large pharmaceutical company that produces several types of drugs for children with "behavioral" problems. They are an extremely successful company, but lately they have been riddled with lawsuits from parents claiming that their children were given drugs unnecessarily. While eating at the company lunchroom, you overhear some salespeople talking. Evidently, they are paying doctors and psychiatrists kickbacks (illegal payments) in exchange for their promise to stop prescribing drugs from other manufacturers. They are also paying doctors to falsify information that can be used in marketing and advertising materials, as well as in journal articles read by other members of the medical community. Answer the following questions:

   a. What crimes appear to be taking place? How?

   b. Although you are a food and drug inspector, can you get involved in this legal issue? Why or why not? If so, how? If not, how can it be resolved?

   c. What additional consumer or public health issues should be addressed?

3. **Tax Deficiency** You are a federal judge hearing the case of a defendant who is being charged with tax evasion. The defendant is a musician who has earned a large amount of money over the last two years and who has paid some taxes, but not enough to cover her total income. She pleads ignorance of the tax laws and explains that she had hired an inept accountant who misinformed her about her total income. She provides proof that the accountant told her she would have to pay a much smaller amount than what she actually owed. She is willing to pay what she owes, but does not feel that she should be penalized in any way.

   a. Is ignorance of tax law an adequate defense? Why or why not?

   b. Is the accountant liable in any way, and does his inefficiency contribute to her defense?

4. **False Advertising** You are a judge in a trial in which the defendant is accused of false advertising. According to the prosecutors, he gave misleading information about a free CD that he was offering people who visited his store. The CD was advertised as containing popular dance songs by famous artists, but in fact contained versions of these songs sung by an unpopular local band. The CD was given away during a weekend sale, and many customers who got a copy of the CD also made purchases at the store.

   a. Does the fact that the CD was free matter in this case? Why or why not?

   b. How could the CD giveaway be said to influence people's purchasing decisions in this case?

Workplace Applications

1. **Food Inspection** You are a restaurant inspector who is conducting a regular inspection of a new, popular restaurant. You are concerned because you have received three phone calls from customers who reported cases of food poisoning over the last two weeks. As you examine the dry goods storage area, you notice

a long pink tail coming from behind a bag of rice. You move the bag and find a dead rat. Answer the following questions:

   a. What Act is being violated by this dead rat's presence?

   b. In what exact way is it being violated?

   c. Is all of the food in the area affected or just the bag of rice? Why?

2. **Tying Arrangements** You are a federal prosecutor who is part of a team that is bringing charges against a large software company. Over the years, this company is alleged to have forced distributors to buy its products in quantities that are dictated by the company, to refuse to buy from other companies, and to install only its products on computers that they sell. As a result, countless other companies have gone bankrupt, and many others are suffering irreparable damage. In its defense, this company states that it is only "winning fairly" and that it charges everyone a uniform low price. Answer the following questions:

   a. What specific laws are being violated by this company?

   b. In what way are these laws being violated?

   c. Does the fact that the company is charging uniform low prices have any legal bearing on the case?

Ethics Exercises

1. **Insider Trading** You are a broker and financial consultant who works both with large businesses in your community and with first-time investors. Many of the first-time investors in your community are elderly people who are interested in supplementing their income with low to moderate risk. A client comes in and asks your opinion about whether he should purchase stock in a local company that manufacturers parts for industrial vehicles. From all appearances, the company seems to be thriving and is a good investment. However, you know from a friend who works in their accounting department that their CEO is very close to being indicted for embezzlement and that the company is in serious financial trouble as a result of the CEO's actions. When this becomes public, stock values are expected to dip sharply. Answer the following questions:

   a. Should you advise your client to not purchase this stock? Why or why not?

   b. How much can you tell your client about the situation regarding this company? Why?

   c. Would you be liable if you, knowing this information, advised your client to purchase this stock and then it dropped? Why or why not?

2. **FDA Searches** You are an FDA inspector making a routine semiannual inspection of a pharmaceutical laboratory. Upon arrival, you are surprised at the disarray. The supervisor has just quit, and the employees are extremely careless in their handling and preparation of drug mixtures. You write them up for several violations, which the pharmaceutical company promptly rejects. They take the FDA to court and accuse you of violating their Fourth Amendment rights, since you did not contact the interim supervisor to make her aware of your visit.

   a. Does this company have a case? Why or why not?

   b. What would be the best way for the company to handle this situation?

Notes

1. 15 U.S.C. § 1125(a) (2000); *see also* Bruce P. Keller & Tiffany D. Trunko, *Consumer Use of RICO to Challenge False Advertising Claims*, C674 A.L.I.-A.B.A. 51 (1991).
2. Kenneth A. Plevan & Miriam L. Siroky, Advertising Compliance Handbook 2–3 (Practicing Law Institute 1991). *See also* Professional Product Research, Inc. v. LTD Commodities, No. 90-C-2078, 1991 U.S. Dist. LEXIS 1876 (E.D.N.Y. Feb. 6, 1991).
3. S. Rep. No. 100–515, at 41 (1988), *as reprinted in* 1988 U.S.C.C.A.N. 5577, 5603.
4. Federal Trade Commission Act, 15 U.S.C. § 52(a) (2000).
5. Cal. Bus. & Prof. Code § 17500 (West 2007); *see also* Thomas A. Papageorge, *State Regulations—California: The False Advertising Statute—An Overview: B. California False Advertising Law*, 1010 P.L.I./Corp. 97, 105 (1997).
6. United States v. Weatherspoon, 581 F.2d 595 (7th Cir. 1978).
7. U.S. Const., art. I, § 8.
8. United States v. Maze, 414 U.S. 395, 402 (1974).
9. James J. Armstrong, Deidre Corkery, E. Michael Karol, Kevin Lombardi & Paul Secunda, *Securities Fraud*, 33 Am. Crim. L. Rev. 973, 975 (1996).
10. 18 U.S.C. § 1348. *See* J. Kelly Strader, Understanding White Collar Crime §5.05, at 105–06 (2d ed. 2006).
11. J. Kelly Strader, Understanding White Collar Crime § 5.05, at 106.
12. Scott J. Davis, *Liability Under Sections 10, 18 and 20 of the Securities Exchange Act of 1934*, 1073 P.L.I./Corp. 179, 189 (1998).
13. Armstrong et al., *Securities Fraud*, 33 Am. Crim. L. Rev. 973, 989, *quoting* Kenneth J. Bialkin et al., *Counseling the Client in Enforcement Inquiries: The Criminalization of "Parking*,*"* 15 U.C. San Diego Sec. Reg. Inst. 2 (1988).
14. Armstrong et. al., *Securities Fraud*, 33 Am. Crim. L. Rev. 973, 1003.
15. 15 U.S.C. § 78j (1994).
16. C.E. Calson, Inc. v. SEC, 859 F.2d 1429, 1436 (10th Cir. 1988).
17. 21 U.S.C. §§ 321(f), 321(g)(1)(B), 321(i)(1), 321(h) (1998).
18. Erica L. Niezgoda & Maureen M. Richardson, *Federal Food and Drug Act Violations*, 35 Am. Crim. L. Rev. 767, 770 (1998).
19. United States v. Park, 421 U.S. 658, 660 (1975).
20. 21 U.S.C. §§ 331(a), 331(k) (1998).
21. New York v. Burger, 482 U.S. 691, 702 (1987).
22. 15 U.S.C. §§ 1 and 2 (1994).
23. 15 U.S.C. § 13a (1994).
24. Klor's, Inc. v. Broadway-Hale Stores, 359 U.S. 207, 212 (1959).
25. Northern Pacific Ry. v. United States, 356 U.S. 1, 5–6 (1958).
26. *See* Kirk S. Jordan, *Model Antitrust Compliance Manual*, C900 A.L.I.-A.B.A. 283, 299 (1994).
27. American Tobacco Co. v. United States, 328 U.S. 781, 785 (1946).
28. United States v. Grinnell Corp., 384 U.S. 563 (1966).
29. *See generally* United States v. Microsoft Corp. and State of New York v. Microsoft Corp., transcripts from Microsoft trial, 1998 W.L. 735825 (D.D.C. Trans).

Crimes against Public Order, Safety, and Morality

CHAPTER OBJECTIVES

After reading and studying this chapter, you should be able to:

1. Define the crimes that encompass breaching the peace.
2. State the purpose and elements of nuisance crimes.
3. Understand the most common traffic offenses and explain their distinctions.
4. Name typical circumstances that could constitute a weapons offense.
5. Explain and understand obscenity offenses.
6. Understand the crime of prostitution and the parties involved.
7. Explain the crime of sodomy.
8. Distinguish legal from illegal gambling.

13.1 Public Order and Safety Offenses

public order and safety offenses

Offenses designed to protect the general public by dealing with behavior that is not necessarily immoral, but nonetheless affects the peace and safety of the community.

mala prohibita

Crimes defining conduct that is wrong only because the law says it is wrong, in order to protect the general public.

mala in se

Crimes (such as rape and murder) that are inherently wrong.

Public order and safety offenses are designed to protect the general public by dealing with behavior that is not necessarily morally wrong, but nonetheless affects the peace and safety of the community. They are a modern outgrowth of common law crimes aimed at keeping peace that evolved after the onset of the industrial revolution, when lawmakers found it necessary to update the legal approach to addressing such problems.

These offenses are considered *mala prohibita* crimes. This means that the acts are not inherently bad, but are considered crimes only because the law dictates them to be for various reasons. In contrast are *mala in se* crimes, a designation that covers conduct that is prohibited because it is inherently wrong. Common examples of *mala in se* crimes are murder, rape, and kidnapping.

Public order and safety offenses are distinguishable from other crimes because most of them do not require a particular *mens rea* in order for a defendant to be guilty. Rather, they are usually strict liability offenses, which means that if the defendant committed the *actus reus* of the crime, his or her *mens rea*, or intent, to cause harm is irrelevant. In short, if the act is committed, the defendant will be found guilty. In this area, lawmakers generally believe that the need to protect the public from potentially harmful action outweighs the defendant's usual right to a higher standard of blame, especially since the penalties for such offenses are usually light.

Offenses That Create a Public Disturbance

At common law, any voluntary action that disturbed a community's peace without lawful justification or excuse was considered a crime. These actions were generally categorized under the offense of *breach of the peace*. Breach of the peace offenses included unlawful assembly, rout, riot, disorderly conduct, and vagrancy. Each of these offenses is discussed in detail below.

Unlawful Assembly

unlawful assembly

A gathering together of three or more persons with the common intent to achieve a lawful or unlawful purpose in a tumultuous manner.

An **unlawful assembly** is a gathering together of three or more persons with the common intent to achieve a lawful or unlawful purpose in a tumultuous manner. A common intent need not have been formed prior to the assembly. Therefore, a meeting can begin as a lawful assembly but develop into an unlawful one.

For example, suppose that a group of students have gathered in front of a government building to protest military action by the government. Initially, the students are peacefully holding signs and handing out literature to those passing by. As the day progresses, however, the students begin blocking the entrance to the government building so that the employees cannot leave work. This would constitute unlawful assembly, and the students could be arrested.

Rout

rout

An unlawful assembly that is escalating toward, but does not reach, the level of a riot; an attempted riot.

The definition of **rout** is an unlawful assembly that is escalating toward, but does not reach, the level of a riot. In short, a rout is an attempted riot: It requires a specific intent to riot and conduct that falls short of a riot. Today, rout is usually not a separate crime. Instead, it has been either eliminated or merged with the crime of unlawful assembly.

Riot

A **riot** is an unlawful assembly that fulfills the participants' common purpose of violently breaching the peace and terrorizing the public. Because of the number of people involved in a riot, the group behavior is potentially more dangerous to the public than other activity, thus posing special problems for law enforcement. For this reason, many police departments, especially in large cities, have trained riot units and protective riot gear with which to handle such occurrences.

riot

A tumultuous disturbance of the peace by three or more persons assembling together in the execution of a lawful or unlawful act and committing it in a violent and turbulent manner.

Disorderly Conduct

At common law, there was no offense known as disorderly conduct. The closest offense was *breach of the peace*, which covered many public disturbances. Modern **disorderly conduct** laws include behavior that disturbs the safety, health, or morals of others, or that is intended only to annoy another person.

The MPC defines disorderly conduct rather narrowly, but its definition contains the essential elements of the crime:

> A person is guilty of disorderly conduct if, with purpose to cause public inconvenience, annoyance or alarm, or recklessly creating a risk thereof:
>
> - Engages in fighting or threatening, or in violent or tumultuous behavior.
> - Makes unreasonable noise or offensively coarse utterance, gesture or display, or addresses abusive language to any person present.
> - Creates a hazardous or physically offensive condition by any act that serves no legitimate purpose of the actor.[1]

disorderly conduct

A loosely defined offense addressing behavior that disturbs the safety, health, or morals of others, or that is intended only to annoy another person.

Vagrancy

The largely outdated crime of **vagrancy** historically was vaguely defined as being idle, or wandering, without a visible means of support.[2] Although all states once had anti-vagrancy laws, many states today have repealed these laws because the U.S. Supreme Court has issued decisions that effectively rendered them unconstitutional.

In the 1972 case *Papachristou v. City of Jacksonville*, the Court struck down the defendants' convictions on charges that stemmed from a fairly typical vagrancy law (see Application Case 13.1). The Court based its decision on two grounds: (1) the vagueness of the ordinance, and (2) the overly broad scope of the ordinance, such that it criminalized many modern innocent activities. After the *Papachristou* case, many states repealed or revised their vagrancy and disorderly conduct laws.

vagrancy

A crime that is vaguely defined as being idle or wandering without visible means of support; no longer a crime in most jurisdictions because of the unconstitutionality of past vagrancy laws.

⚖ Application Case 13.1

Papachristou v. City of Jacksonville

In *Papachristou v. City of Jacksonville* (1972), the following ordinance was declared unconstitutional by the U.S. Supreme Court:

> Rogues and vagabonds, or dissolute persons who go about begging, common gamblers, persons who use juggling or unlawful games or plays, common drunkards, common night walkers, thieves, pilferers or pickpockets, traders in stolen property, lewd, wanton

and lascivious persons, keepers of gambling places, common railers and brawlers, persons wandering or strolling around from place to place without any lawful purpose or object, habitual loafers, disorderly persons, persons neglecting all lawful business and habitually spending their time by frequenting houses of ill fame, gaming houses, or places where alcoholic beverages are sold or served, persons able to work but habitually living upon the earnings of their wives or minor children shall be deemed vagrants.

In striking down this ordinance, the Court found it void on account of vagueness for two reasons. First, it failed to give a person of ordinary intelligence fair notice that his contemplated conduct is forbidden. Second, it encouraged arbitrary and erratic arrests and convictions. The Court also noted that the ordinance imposed criminal sanctions on activities that by modern standards are lawful.

SOURCE: Papachristou v. City of Jacksonville, 405 U.S. 156 (1972).

Nuisances

nuisance

Anything that endangers life or health, gives offense to the senses, violates laws of decency, or obstructs the reasonable and comfortable use of property.

A **nuisance** encompasses anything that endangers life or health, gives offense to the senses, violates laws of decency, or obstructs the reasonable and comfortable use of property. For example, the California Penal Code defines a public nuisance as follows:

> Anything which is injurious to health, or is indecent, or offensive to the senses, or an obstruction to the free use of property, so as to interfere with the comfortable enjoyment of life or property by an entire community or neighborhood, or by any considerable number of persons, or unlawfully obstructs the free passage or use, in the customary manner, of any navigable lake, or river, bay, stream, canal, or basin, or any public park, square, street, or highway, is a public nuisance.[3]

abatement

The ending or eliminating of a nuisance.

Anyone who maintains, permits, or allows a public nuisance will receive a notice for **abatement**, which means ending or eliminating the nuisance. If the person fails to abate the nuisance, he or she is guilty of a misdemeanor. Although criminal prosecution is one remedy for a nuisance, the most common approach is through a civil action on behalf of the community, either for damages or to abate the nuisance.

The historical development of the public nuisance concept did not result from a desire to deal harshly with nuisance offenders. Instead, it was intended for the protection of both the public and the individual committing the nuisance. If every member of the community who was annoyed by a public nuisance could maintain an action, the result would be disastrous to the person who had caused it. The king, therefore, would maintain one action on behalf of the community, and individuals could not bring a private action for public nuisance.

Today, even though criminal nuisance statutes still exist in many jurisdictions, behavior that otherwise might be charged as a nuisance may also be the subject of action for disorderly conduct. Criminal prosecution may also be brought for other types of nuisances, such as the maintenance of a disorderly house (a dwelling where people conduct criminal or immoral activities, such as prostitution), the manufacture or storage of explosives, nuisances in streets or highways, liquor nuisances, and interference with the uses to which property has been dedicated. Nuisance statutes have also been used to close crack houses and other establishments related to drug use. In addition, courts routinely find that massage parlors constitute a nuisance subject to abatement or other remedies. Although administering massages is a legitimate occupation, massage parlors and similar establishments that specialize in sexually oriented massages administered by members of the opposite sex have led many municipalities to enact ordinances regulating or prohibiting massage parlors or to pursue common law remedies.[4] (See Application Case 13.2.)

⚖️ Application Case 13.2
Arcara v. Cloud Books, Inc.

Some laws provide that buildings may be declared either public or private health nuisances. An example is the case of *Arcara v. Cloud Books, Inc.* (1986), where solicitation for prostitution was taking place in a New York adult bookstore and, under a court order, the premises were declared a nuisance and closed for one year. In affirming this action, the U.S. Supreme Court held that the nuisance law "sought to protect the environment of the community by directing the sanction at premises knowingly used for lawless activities." As a result, the nuisance statute was constitutionally permissible. The public good of eliminating the behavior that took place in the bookstore outweighed the need to protect the rights of the individuals running the bookstore.

SOURCE: Arcara v. Cloud Books, Inc., 478 U.S. 697 (1986).

Behavior with serious criminal implications is sometimes charged as a nuisance and prosecuted through civil courts so that it can be prosecuted with the lowered burden of proof found in civil courts. In the case of *Gallo v. Acuna*, the city of San Jose, California, obtained an injunction against members of an alleged criminal street gang under the provisions of California's civil public nuisance statutes. The California Supreme Court upheld the injunction, rejecting claims that the court order violated the defendant's constitutional rights.[5]

Traffic Violations

Traffic violations are usually strict liability offenses that, in most jurisdictions, are criminal in nature. A few jurisdictions have decriminalized traffic violations, but the overwhelming majority of American states still treat such violations as criminal.[6] They usually carry light penalties, such as a fine, an order to attend traffic school, or possibly some jail time. If a person is sentenced to jail for a traffic violation, the time served is usually very short.

The most common types of traffic offenses are speeding, reckless, driving, failure to stop, hit and run, driving with a suspended or revoked license, driving under the influence, DUI manslaughter, vehicular manslaughter, and vehicular homicide.

Speeding

The traffic violation of *speeding* exists to ensure a safe and orderly flow of traffic on streets and highways. Drivers are provided with the speed laws by the local department of motor vehicles, to whom they must show an understanding of traffic laws before receiving a license to drive, and by posted signs. Therefore, all drivers have received notice of the law. If they are speeding, they are usually guilty. Because of the strict liability of the offense, a defense that the car's speedometer was broken will have no effect on the outcome.

Reckless Driving

reckless driving

Driving with voluntary and wanton disregard for the safety of persons or property.

Another traffic violation is **reckless driving**, which can be defined as voluntary and wanton disregard for the safety of persons or property. This offense requires a purpose or willingness to commit an act as a free agent, but does not require an evil intent. It includes the following elements:

- Consciousness of one's conduct.
- The general intent to do or omit the act in question.
- Realization of the probable injury to another.
- Reckless disregard for the consequences.

In a prosecution for reckless driving, the prosecution must prove that the defendant would have reasonably foreseen that death or injury might occur as a result of his or her driving. Suppose that Tom, a 19-year-old driver, has just bought his first car and is excited to take it out for a spin. Tom lives in Michigan, where snow and ice storms are frequent during the winter. Tom knows that the streets are covered with black ice, and he has heard radio warnings that motorists should avoid the roads unless absolutely necessary. Tom ignores the warnings, drives his car at 10 mph over the legal limit, spins out of control, and hits another vehicle. Tom would likely be charged with reckless driving, although in other circumstances, driving 10 mph over the speed limit alone would probably not warrant such a charge.

Failure to Stop

An individual violates the law if he or she is directed to stop by a duly authorized law enforcement office but willfully refuses or fails to do so. Another violation occurs when a driver stops in compliance with the direction of an officer, then willfully flees in an attempt to elude law enforcement. For example, if Lucy pulls over after being signaled by an officer, but gets frustrated because the officer takes so long looking up her registration and leaves without waiting for the officer to return to her vehicle, she will likely be guilty of fleeing a police officer.

Hit and Run

Leaving the scene of an accident involving death, personal injury, or property damage is more commonly referred to as *hit and run*. The elements of hit and run include:

- Involvement in an accident resulting in injury or death of a person or damage to a vehicle.
- Failure to stop and furnish information about one's identity and that of the vehicle.
- Failure to render assistance to any persons injured and give immediate notice of the accident to the police.

Hit and run statutes exist to ensure that people will stop, exchange information, and render aid (if necessary) in the event of an accident. These requirements usually exist regardless of who is at fault. Even if a driver is not to blame for an accident, by failing to stay at the scene he or she prevents the other driver from getting insurance information, license information, and anything else needed to resolve any future problems.

Driving with a Suspended or Revoked License

Another common traffic violation is driving on a suspended or revoked license. Most states require that their departments of motor vehicles notify drivers when their driving privileges have been revoked, suspended, or canceled. A person caught driving with a suspended license may receive an additional suspension or revocation period, or perhaps a stiffer penalty such as jail time or the impounding of the vehicle.

Driving under the Influence

The elements of **driving under the influence (DUI)** are the same in most jurisdictions:

- The defendant operated a motor vehicle on a roadway within the jurisdiction of the court.
- The operation occurred while the defendant was under the influence of an intoxicant, narcotic, or hallucinogenic to the extent that his or her normal faculties were impaired; or
- The operation occurred while the defendant was driving with a blood or breath alcohol concentration above a prohibited level—the current limit for all U.S. states being .08 percent.

Even though the "D" in DUI stands for driving, a defendant does not have to actually drive the car in order to be convicted. Many statutes provide that DUI may be proved if the defendant is in actual physical control of the vehicle at the time it was stopped. *Actual physical control* can be defined as the legitimate inference that when a DUI defendant places himself or herself behind the wheel, he or she could start the car and drive away at any time.[7] This can be proven when an officer approaches a vehicle in which the lights and ignition are on, but the driver has fallen asleep at the wheel. Therefore, the crime rests upon the defendant's readiness to operate the car while under the influence.

Although most traffic offenses are tried as summary offenses, which means that they are tried in front of a judge rather than a jury, almost every state specifically allows DUI cases to be tried before a jury of one's peers because of the seriousness of the penalties.

DUI Manslaughter

The crime of **DUI manslaughter** occurs when an individual is driving under the influence and, by reason of the operation of a motor vehicle, causes the death of a human being. Many statutes on DUI manslaughter declare that the defendant is guilty of manslaughter if:

- Someone was killed by the defendant's vehicle
- While the defendant was under the influence of alcohol or another intoxicant or drug
- And either the defendant's faculties were impaired or he or she had an unlawful blood alcohol level.

driving under the influence (DUI)
Operating a motor vehicle while under the influence of a substance or with a blood or breath alcohol concentration above a prohibited level.

DUI manslaughter
Causing the death of a human being by reason of operation of a motor vehicle while under the influence of alcohol or drugs.

13.1 On the Job

Chemical Dependency Counselor

Description and Duties: Meet with residents individually, and work out ways to combat reversion tendencies. Establish an understanding and cooperative relationship with residents. Arrange for released residents to join local Alcoholics Anonymous chapters or other appropriate aftercare resources. Meet with family or others close to the resident while he or she he is in treatment to keep them informed of progress toward recovery.

Salary: $18,000 to $35,000, depending on location and experience.

Other Information: Should have considerable knowledge of the habits and actions of alcoholics and other drug abusers, the techniques employed in Alcoholics Anonymous type of recovery work, and comprehensive programs for recovery of alcoholics and other drug abusers. Many positions require at least a bachelor's degree, and some require a master's or doctorate degree in a mental health field.

SOURCE: State of Kansas, http://da.ks.gov/ps/specs/specs/4034d2.htm; State of Minnesota, http://www.doer.state.mn.us/stfcs-ac/cspcs-c/c-1027.htm.

Vehicular Manslaughter

The crime of vehicular manslaughter, as we saw in Chapter 8, is the killing of a human being by the operation of a motor vehicle in a reckless manner likely to cause death or great bodily harm to another. Alternatively, vehicular manslaughter occurs when one drives a vehicle in the commission of an unlawful act, not amounting to a felony, and with gross negligence. In any event, this offense requires proof of death as a result of the operation of a motor vehicle in a reckless manner.

DUI Dangers Individuals who choose to drive drunk risk the possibility not only of being pulled over and losing their licenses, but also of the far more serious offense of DUI manslaughter.

Vehicular Homicide

In contrast to the lesser offense of vehicular manslaughter, a person can be convicted of murder with a motor vehicle if the required elements of the offense are present. These elements are satisfied if the driver of a motor vehicle essentially uses the vehicle as the murder weapon and, with deliberation and premeditation and with malice aforethought, drives over or strikes a person with the specific intent of killing him or her. In the absence of any statute to the contrary, no degree of negligence, no matter how gross, will suffice to make the unlawful killing murder.

Weapons Offenses

In many circumstances, an adult is legally entitled to purchase and possess weapons, including firearms. However, a variety of circumstances may constitute a weapons offense. These include, but are not limited to:

- An underage possessor.
- The use of an illegal or legal but unregistered weapon.
- The location where the weapon was discovered, such as in one's vehicle or on one's person, without permission to carry a weapon there.
- The possession or transportation of an explosive, firearm, or ammunition, with intent that it be used or with knowledge that it may be used to commit a crime.
- Placing another person in fear of a harmful weapon.
- Offensive bodily contact with a weapon.
- Using a firearm as a weapon (such as a club), whether it is loaded or not.

The case of *Figueroa v. Kirmayer* (1969) illustrates the different ways in which weapons offenses may be used to prosecute defendants. In this case, the defendant testified that he drew his pistol, pointed it at one victim, and fired one shot in the general direction of each of the victims. He argued that he did not intend to shoot either of the two victims, and therefore was not guilty of assault. The court disagreed and established liability for both assault and battery.[8]

Unlike most assault or battery charges, an assault or battery with a dangerous or deadly weapon is usually classified as a felony. The charge will be higher or lower in degree depending on whether the defendant acted intentionally, recklessly, or only negligently; whether serious physical injury or only physical injury resulted; and whether a deadly or only dangerous weapon was used.

In regard to weapons offenses, an unintended killing is one that results from the reckless or criminally negligent use of a firearm. Such a killing constitutes manslaughter. The following three examples show the variety of circumstances in which this may occur:

- A defendant points a gun that he or she believes to be unloaded at another person and pulls the trigger, causing the gun to be discharged and resulting in the other person's death.
- A hunter shoots and kills another person, believing him to be an animal.
- A defendant shoots at the occupants of a boat and so terrifies them that they overturn the boat and are drowned.

The following paragraphs discuss the types of weapons that are most relevant to weapons offenses, as well as federal and state laws regulating the use of firearms and assault weapons.

Deadly or Dangerous Weapons

Because some weapons are clearly lethal, it is the duty of the court to declare them to be such as a matter or law. The most obvious weapons in this class are guns, as well as swords and the like when used within striking distance of the victim. Objects that are considered deadly or dangerous weapons include bowie knives, pocket or folding knives, chisels (when used for stabbing), large stones or rocks, heavy iron weights, heavy pistols (when used for clubbing), and automobiles.

Firearms

firearm

Any weapon that can, is designed to, or may readily be converted to expel a projectile by the action of an explosive; the frame or receiver of any such weapon; any firearm muffler or firearm silencer.

A **firearm** is defined under federal law[9] as:

- Any weapon, including a starter gun, that can, is designed to, or may readily be converted to expel a projectile by the action of an explosive.
- The frame or receiver of any such weapon.
- Any firearm muffler or firearm silencer.

Assault Weapons

assault weapon

One of the prohibited weapons named by federal legislation, such as rifles with conspicuous pistol grips, pistols with shrouds, and shotguns with a higher ammunition capacity.

The definition of **assault weapon** includes rifles with conspicuous pistol grips, pistols with shrouds, and shotguns with a higher ammunition capacity. Federal law has three basic definitions of assault weapons:

1. A list of specific assault weapon models.
2. A list of duplicates.
3. A generic, all-included category that covers certain assault weapon characteristics.

Assault weapon legislation, which began with a 1989 California law and culminated in the Federal Crime Act of 1994, marked a new trend in firearms law. The federal assault weapon prohibition included in this act made it unlawful for a person to manufacture, transfer, or possess a semiautomatic assault weapon. However, this prohibition did not apply to any semiautomatic assault weapon otherwise lawfully possessed under federal law on the date of enactment.

Firearms Owners Protection Act of 1986

The Firearms Owners Protection Act of 1986, also known as the National Firearms Act (NFA), comprehensively amended the Gun Control Act of 1968, the first comprehensive federal statute regulating commerce in firearms. The 1986 act regulates traditional firearms such as rifles, pistols, and shotguns. One section regulates defined firearms, including machine guns, short-barreled shotguns, rifles, destructive devices such as hand grenades, bazookas, silencers, and deceptive weapons. NFA firearms must be registered with the Bureau of Alcohol Tobacco and Firearms (BATF) and are subject to regulation.

For a conviction under the NFA, the prosecution must prove that the violation was willful or intentional. Thus, the government must prove that the defendant voluntarily and intentionally violated a known legal duty. The extent to which a weapon clearly is or is not an NFA firearm, and was known to be so by the defendant, may determine whether the defendant has a defense, depending on the charges.

FIGURE 13.1

Various States' Assault Weapons Laws

	Texas	California	Montana	New York
Carrying concealed weapons laws	Shall issue; with restrictions	May issue	Shall issue; with restrictions	May issue
Juvenile possession laws	None	Yes, age minor	Yes, age 14	Yes, age 21
Juvenile sales laws	Yes, age 18	Yes, 18 for firearm, 21 for handgun	No	Yes, age 21
Permit to purchase required	No	No	No	Yes, background check required
One-gun-per-month laws	No	Yes	No	No
Record-of-sale laws	No	Yes, sent to state agency	No	Yes, sent to state agency
Registration laws	No	No	No	No
Statewide waiting period	None	Yes	None	Yes

SOURCE: http://www.stategunlaws.org.

State Firearms Laws

Firearms laws greatly vary from state to state, but most states have constitutional provisions guaranteeing the right of its citizens to keep and bear arms. Almost all states restrict possession of firearms by convicted felons. More urbanized states such as New Jersey, Massachusetts, and California have stricter prohibitions, such as license or permit requirements for mere possession of a firearm. Southern and western states, with the exception of California, tend to regulate the carrying of concealed weapons but otherwise have few restrictions.

In California, it is unlawful for anyone convicted of a felony, a drug addict, a present or former mental patient, anyone ever committed for mental observation, or anyone ever acquitted of criminal charges by reason of insanity to own or possess any firearm. People with certain misdemeanor convictions involving force or violence may not possess or own any firearm within 10 years of the conviction. A person who has been adjudicated as a juvenile offender or delinquent for any offense that would be classified as a felony or misdemeanor involving force or violence if committed by an adult may not own or possess any firearm until the age of 30. A minor may not possess a handgun except with written permission or under the supervision of a parent or guardian. (See Figure 13.1.)

CRITICAL THINKING 13.1

1. What types of firearms are prohibited under the NFA?
2. What federal agency handles the registration and control of firearms?

13.2 Public Morality Offenses

This section covers a wide variety of offenses that are considered to be affronts to public morality. Some issues, such as what constitutes indecent exposure, change in the public's eyes over time; others, such as child pornography, do not. Some public morality offenses, such as prostitution and gambling, are geographically restricted to certain areas of the United States. There is considerable public debate about whether some of these offenses, such as gambling, prostitution, and sodomy, are victimless crimes and thus should be decriminalized. You will learn about the history of these laws, changes to them that have occurred over time, and their current application by the courts.

Obscenity

The term *pornography* refers to sexually explicit material that is generally protected by First Amendment guarantees of freedom of speech and freedom of the press. Although the law may regulate pornography, it does not make the sale, possession, or distribution of it a crime. On the other hand, the law punishes the sale, possession, and distribution of obscene material. The term **obscenity** refers to the legal definition of certain materials that are not protected under the First Amendment. Obscenity may take the form of a book, magazine, newspaper, picture, drawing, photograph, motion picture, statue, or recording. Therefore, although obscenity is very similar to pornography, these terms are not legally synonymous.

obscenity
Sexually explicit material that falls outside the protection of the First Amendment and therefore may be punished under a criminal statute.

Obscenity was first held to be an offense under English common law as early as 1729. In the United States, the first federal obscenity law resulted from the circulation of French postcards in the mid-nineteenth century. The Customs Law of 1842 barred the importation of indecent and obscene prints, paintings, lithographs, engravings, and transparencies. Later, the Federal Comstock Act of 1873, named after the anti-vice crusader Anthony Comstock, prohibited use of the mail to convey obscene material. The Comstock Act survives today with alterations and additions.

Federal Law and Obscenity Tests

Through the early twentieth century, American courts applied the standard of obscenity articulated by an English court in the 1868 decision *Regina v. Hicklin*. The *Hicklin* court made its decision based on the content of isolated passages of the book rather than the book as a whole, and this standard was known as the *Hicklin* test. In 1933, however, a federal district court rejected the "isolated passages" approach established in *Hicklin*. Instead, in determining whether the material was obscene, it focused on the dominant effect the entire book would have on the average person.[10]

In 1957, a new test evolved to determine whether material was obscene. That year, the U.S. Supreme Court held in *Roth v. United States* that because the First Amendment protected material with even the slightest redeeming social importance, obscenity was defined as material that is utterly without redeeming social importance. The Court established what has become known as the *tripartite test* for obscenity. In this three-part test, the Court focused on whether an average person, applying contemporary community standards, would think that the dominant theme of the material taken as a whole appeals to *prurient interest*, which means that it has a tendency to excite lustful thoughts and its only appeal is to a shameful or morbid interest in sex.

This standard was the applicable law until 1966, when the Court was asked again to define obscenity. In *Memoirs v. Massachusetts*, the Court held that for a book or other publication to be outside the protection of the First Amendment, it must be utterly without redeeming social interest.[11]

In 1973, the Court overturned its previous decisions of 1957 and 1966 and abandoned its previous requirement of "utterly without redeeming social value." It established the test that is used today in determining whether material is obscene. The Court provided the following guidelines for determining whether material was obscene:

- Whether the average person, applying contemporary community standards, would find that the work, taken as a whole, appeals to prurient interest.
- Whether the work depicts or describes, in a patently offensive way, sexual conduct specifically defined by the applicable state law.
- Whether the work, taken as a whole, lacks serious literary, artistic, political, or scientific value.[12]

The U.S. Supreme Court held that obscene material is an exception to the First Amendment, and the burden of deciding whether or not something is obscene rests with the U.S. Supreme Court. Today, both the federal and state governments have enacted laws that make it a criminal offense to produce, distribute, or exhibit obscene material.

Obscenity and the Model Penal Code

Obscenity statutes cover many areas. The MPC provides that material is obscene if its predominant appeal is to a shameful or morbid interest in nudity, sex, or excretion; and if, in addition, it goes substantially beyond customary limits of candor in describing or representing such matters. Undeveloped photographs, molds, printing plates, and other unfinished items can also be deemed obscene, even though processing or other acts may be required to create and disseminate the finished product. Under the MPC, the concept of *predominant appeal* is judged with reference to ordinary adults. An exception occurs when material appears, from its character or the circumstances of its dissemination, to be designed for children or other especially susceptible audiences.

The MPC establishes an affirmative defense to a charge of obscenity if dissemination was restricted to noncommercial dissemination to personal associates of the actor. Thus, the code attempts to prevent the commercial exploitation of ordinary members of society caught between normal sex drives and curiosities, while on the other hand providing powerful social and legal restraints on overt sexual behavior.

Obscenity and the Internet

Regulating indecent material on the Internet has proven a very difficult task. There is much concern over how to prevent children from encountering sexually explicit materials and discussions through their computers, yet still protect the First Amendment rights of adults to engage in constitutionally protected indecent speech. Most states have laws prohibiting the production, distribution, display, and possession with intent to sell of obscene or pornographic materials, and in many instances, the laws are written in such a manner as to encompass computer transmissions. There are also federal laws making it a federal crime to distribute obscene material across state lines, particularly by computer.[13] The history of the federal laws underscores the tension between such attempted regulation and First Amendment rights.

As part of the Telecommunications Act of 1996, the Communications Decency Act (CDA) of 1996 banned the transmission of obscene materials to minors via broadcast media, including the Internet. In *Reno v. ACLU*, 521 U.S. 844 (1997), the Supreme Court struck down portions of the Act as unconstitutional in application. Subsequently, Congress enacted the Child Online Protection Act (COPA), which sought to remedy the deficiencies of the CDA. The Supreme Court, however, found, in *Ashcroft v. ACLU*,[14] that COPA was likely to fail a First Amendment challenge. In March 2007, the trial court issued a permanent injunction against enforcement of COPA.[15] It is likely that some provisions of the law will continue to be enforceable and that Congress will take steps to remedy deficiencies in the law with respect to any provisions that may continue to be declared unconstitutional.[16]

Currently, federal law prohibits the interstate and foreign transportation of obscene materials for sale or distribution by mail, importation or transport via common carrier, broadcast, and private conveyance. In regard to the Internet, there have already been many obscenity prosecutions (see Application Case 13.3 for two examples).

⚖️ Application Case 13.3

United States v. Thomas
Unites States v. Maxwell

In *United States v. Thomas* (1996), a couple living in California was convicted by a Tennessee jury for transmitting obscene computer-generated images to Tennessee via interstate commerce. In *Unites States v. Maxwell* (1995), the U.S. Air Force Court of Military Appeals ruled that the electronic transmission of visual images through an online computer service is a statutory violation. The court found that Congress clearly intended to stem the transportation of obscene material in interstate commerce, regardless of the means used to effect that end.

SOURCE: Jonathon Rosenoer, CyberLaw: The Law of the Internet 182 (1997), citing United States v. Thomas, No. 94-6649, 1996 FED App. 1069 (6th Cir.) and United States v. Maxwell, 42 M.J. 568 (A.F. Ct. Crim. App. 1995).

Child Pornography

Child pornography is a highly organized, multimillion-dollar industry. Its distribution operates on an international scale and is now making disturbing inroads on the Internet.

In 1977, Congress held hearings on child pornography. Witnesses told nightmarish tales about small children who were kidnapped by pornographers or sold to pornographers by their parents. After these hearings, Congress passed the Protection of Children from Sexual Exploitation Act of 1977. This Act prohibited the production of any sexually explicit material using a child under the age of 16 if such material was destined for, or had already traveled in, interstate commerce. Violation of this Act incurred penalties of up to 10 years in prison and/or a $10,000 fine. The law was

applicable to parents or other custodians who knowingly permitted a child to participate in the production of sexually explicit material.

This law was revised under the Child Protection Act of 1984, which extended
criminal sanctions for child pornography. The 1984 Act:

- Eliminated the requirement that child pornography distribution be
  undertaken for commerce, criminalizing distribution for any reason.
- Eradicated former obscenity test requirements so that any pornography can
  be prosecuted.
- Raised the age of protected persons to 18.

In addition, current federal law prohibits employing, using, persuading,
inducing, enticing, or coercing a minor to engage in any sexually explicit conduct
for the purpose of producing any visual depiction of such conduct. (See Application
Case 13.4.) Also barred is the knowing transmission or receipt by computer of
visual depictions involving the use of a minor engaged in sexually explicit conduct,
as well as the knowing publication of a notice or advertisement seeking or offering
to receive, exchange, buy, produce, display, distribute, or reproduce such visual
depictions. Possession with intent to sell visual depictions that have been transmitted
by computer, or possession of three or more items containing such depictions that
may have been transmitted by computer, is a criminal offense.[17]

⚖️ Application Case 13.4

United States v. United States District Court

In 1989, several pornographic movie producers were charged with violating federal
child pornography laws after law enforcement discovered that porn star Traci Lords
was only 16 years old at the time that she made many adult movies. In the original
trial, the defendants were denied the right to raise the defense and provide evidence
that they had a reasonable belief that Lords was actually 18 at the time the movies
were made. The Court of Appeals reversed this decision, stating that the defendants
have an affirmative defense if they establish by clear and convincing evidence that
they did not know, and could not know, that she was not 18 years of age.

SOURCE: Sanford H. Kadish & Stephen J. Schulhofer, Criminal Law and Its Processes 253–254 (6th ed.
1995), citing United States v. United States District Court, 858 F.2d 534 (9th Cir. 1988).

Indecent Exposure

Under common law and early statutes, indecent exposure was referred to as *lewdness*.
The elements required to convict a person of lewdness were (1) intentionally,
indecently, and offensively exposing the sex organs (2) in the presence of another.
Prior to the drafting of the Model Penal Code, indecent exposure and related crimes
were covered under a multitude of statutes and given widely varying titles, such
as Lewd and Lascivious Behavior, Public Lewdness, and even Appearing on the
Highway in Bathing Garb.

indecent exposure

An offensive display of one's body in public, especially the genitals or the female breasts.

Under modern law, **indecent exposure** involves the unlawful exposure of the human body, particularly a person's genitals or the female breasts. The purpose of indecent exposure statutes is to protect public sensibilities and prevent public lewdness. Public exposure may occur on a street, in a building, on the beach, or even within a private location, provided that the exposure can be viewed from another public or private place.

Almost every jurisdiction recognizes indecent exposure as a criminal offense, and a general criminal intent is usually required to hold a person criminally liable for this offense. Some jurisdictions have adopted the common law approach of requiring that the conduct be committed in a public place, and others only require knowledge on the part of the defendant that his or her exposure is likely to cause affront or alarm.

exhibitionism

Repeated intentional acts of exposing the genitals to an unsuspecting stranger for the purpose of achieving sexual excitement.

Persons who practice this type of offense are often called exhibitionists. **Exhibitionism** is the repeated intentional act of exposing one's genitals to an unsuspecting stranger or strangers, for the purpose of achieving sexual excitement. Exhibitionists are intentional in what they do and do not include people who occasionally and accidentally expose themselves, such as by undressing in their own homes and forgetting to close the blinds. (See Application Case 13.5.)

⚖️ Application Case 13.5

People v. Garrison

In *People v. Garrison* (1980), the defendant stood behind a storm door in his home, exposing his penis to a woman standing outside. The Supreme Court of Illinois held that this conduct was not private and that the defendant could not claim a right of privacy. It held that if a jury found that the defendant exposed his or her body with intent to arouse or to satisfy his or her sexual desire, the defendant could be found guilty of the Illinois Public Indecency Statute.

SOURCE: People v Garrison, 412 N.E.2d 483 (1980).

Many states have specific statutes dealing with exhibitionism; others classify it as disorderly conduct. The MPC provides that a person commits a misdemeanor when, for the purpose of arousing or gratifying the sexual desire of himself or of any person other than his spouse, exposes his genitals under circumstances in which he knows his conduct is likely to cause affront or alarm.

Many state laws and municipal ordinances contain provisions that permit exceptions to indecent exposure statutes, such as partial or full nudity during public entertainment to which only adults are invited. Local communities usually set standards for what exceptions they will tolerate. One community might allow total nudity, whereas another may only allow topless dancing. Again, the distinction between this and indecent exposure is that indecent exposure crimes usually involve perpetrators exposing themselves for personal gratification, and without consent of the people witnessing the exposure. Where nudity is part of a form of entertainment between adults in a private place, indecent exposure is usually not an issue.

Prostitution, Solicitation, and Pandering

Prostitution is committed when one person agrees to engage in sexual or deviate sexual intercourse in return for something of value, usually money. It is often referred to as the world's oldest profession and is described in history's earliest written records. Prostitution was not specifically a crime under common law, but when a woman solicited men on the street, her conduct was punishable as a public nuisance.

Prostitution today is a statutory crime. Modern statutes forbid several types of sexual intercourse and sexual contact when done in exchange for money. It is important to note that the offense of prostitution often does not consist of the sexual act itself; rather, it is the agreement to participate in sexual activity for compensation.[18] Moreover, members of either sex may be convicted of prostitution, as distinguished from past laws that applied only to women. As long as there is an agreement for pay, prostitution is criminal regardless of whether the agreement to perform sex is within a heterosexual or homosexual context.[19]

Although state and local statutes generally prohibit prostitution, the crime may also be applicable in a federal context. The **Mann Act** is a federal statute that was originally enacted to prohibit:

- The interstate transportation of any woman or girl for the purpose of prostitution, debauchery, or any other immoral purpose.
- The interstate transportation of any woman or girl with the intent and purpose to induce, entice, or compel her to become a prostitute, give herself up to debauchery, or engage in any other immoral practice.

An amendment to the act prohibits the knowing transportation in interstate or foreign commerce of any individual, male or female, with the intent that such individual engage in prostitution or in any sexual activity for which any person can be charged with a criminal offense. The conduct constitutes a felony punishable by fine and/or imprisonment of not more than 10 years.[20] In addition, another federal statute prohibits travel in interstate or foreign commerce, or the use of the mails, in aid of state or federal prostitution offenses.

Efforts to decriminalize prostitution have met with limited success. Only one state, Nevada, has legalized prostitution under certain conditions. Nonetheless, prostitution and its related activities flourish and remain a nationwide public morality issue despite fears of AIDS. It probably will continue to flourish as long as customers are willing to pay money for sexual favors and as long as there are persons willing to perform those favors in return for compensation.

Solicitation

Some jurisdictions make soliciting a prostitute an offense. A person is guilty of **solicitation** when he or she offers to pay another (as a customer) or to receive payment from another (as a prostitute) for sex. The purpose of statutes forbidding soliciting is to prevent prostitutes from standing in public places, trying to entice passersby into paying for sex. Since the crime of solicitation punishes both actors, the patron who solicits a prostitute is also found guilty under these laws.

When a prospective patron propositions an undercover agent posing as a prostitute, this person is usually charged with soliciting. Indeed, most prostitution

prostitution
A crime that is committed when one person agrees to engage in sexual or deviate sexual intercourse in return for something of value, usually money.

Mann Act
A federal act that prohibits the knowing transportation in interstate or foreign commerce of any individual, male or female, with the intent that such individual engage in prostitution or in any sexual activity.

solicitation
The act of offering to pay another, or receive payment from another, for sex.

cases that go to court today involve police decoys that use solicitation as the basis of the criminal charge. Defendants in such cases are women who solicit male undercover officers, men who proposition female officers, and male prostitutes offering sex for a fee. (See Application Case 13.6.)

⚖️ Application Case 13.6

State v. Tookes

In *State v. Tookes* (1985), a civilian police volunteer engaged in sexual intercourse with women in order to obtain evidence for their prostitution convictions. The Supreme Court of Hawaii affirmed the convictions of the prostitutes, holding: "While we question whether the actions of [the defendant] Fox and the police in this case comport to the ethical standards which law enforcement officials should be guided by, we cannot say that they constituted outrageous conduct in the constitutional sense. Neither are we able to find a due process violation because Fox's conduct, if undertaken by a police officer, would have violated an internal department rule against engaging in sex with a prostitute in order to obtain evidence sufficient for a conviction."

Although this procedure might be legal, most law enforcement agencies and communities probably would not tolerate it in this day of AIDS and other diseases.

SOURCE: State v. Tookes, 699 P.2d 983 (Haw. 1985).

Patronizing a Prostitute

If the prospective patron agrees to purchase sexual favors, he or she may bear the criminal responsibility for the separate offense known as *patronizing a prostitute*. Ordinarily, the offense of patronizing a prostitute is punishable to the same extent as prostitution, which is usually a misdemeanor.

As an example of laws covering this offense, a Connecticut statute provides that a person is guilty of patronizing a prostitute when:

- Pursuant to a prior understanding,
- The patron pays or agrees to pay a fee to another person as compensation for such person or a third person having engaged in sexual conduct with him, or
- The patron pays or agrees to pay a fee to another person pursuant to an understanding that in return therefore such person or a third person will engage in sexual conduct with him, or
- The patron solicits or requests another person to engage in sexual conduct with him in return for a fee.[21]

Pimping and Pandering

The real force behind prostitution is not the prostitute, but the person who promotes prostitution. Since the promoter makes prostitution a growing business, his or her activity is usually punished more severely than that of a prostitute. These promoters are commonly known as *pimps*, and their activity is called **pimping**. Pimps live off of the earnings of prostitutes, and the prostitute works for the pimp. Because of the financial gains, pimps have a motive to encourage and coerce young persons into prostitution. They increase the volume and extent to which prostitution is practiced and often gain a strong emotional hold over the prostitutes who work for them.

Pandering consists of either procuring a female for a place of prostitution or procuring a place for a prostitute to ply her trade. A person who has engaged in either of these two activities is guilty of pandering even if no sexual activity has yet taken place. The principal difference between pimping and pandering is that a pimp solicits patrons for the prostitute and lives off her earnings, whereas a panderer recruits prostitutes and sets them up in business.

Promoting, pimping, and pandering are generally forbidden by state statutes. In California, a person is guilty of pimping when, knowing another person is a prostitute, he or she:

- Lives in whole or in part from the earnings or proceeds of the person's prostitution, or
- Lives from money loaned or advanced to or charged against that person by any keeper or manager or inmate of a house or other place where prostitution is practiced or allowed, or
- Solicits or receives compensation for soliciting for the person.[22]

In Utah, there are three basic offenses: aiding prostitution, exploiting prostitution, and aggravated exploitation of prostitution. They are broken down as follows:

- A person is guilty of *aiding prostitution* when he solicits a patron for a prostitute, procures a prostitute for a patron, allows a place to be used for prostitution, or receives or agrees to receive a benefit for doing any of the acts prohibited.
- A person is guilty of *exploiting prostitution* when he procures an inmate for a house of prostitution, causes another person to become or remain a prostitute, transports or pays for the transportation of another person into or within the state for the purpose of prostitution, shares the proceeds of prostitution with a prostitute, or keeps a house of prostitution.
- A person is guilty of *aggravated exploitation of prostitution* when he, in committing an act of exploiting prostitution, uses any force, threat, or fear against any person; or when the person procured or transported, or with whom the proceeds of prostitution are shared, is under 18 years of age or is the wife of the accused.[23]

Adultery, Fornication, and Illicit Cohabitation

At common law, adultery and fornication were not crimes unless the conduct was open and notorious, in which case it was punishable as a public nuisance. Today, **adultery** requires only a single act of sexual intercourse; each adulterous act constitutes a crime.[24] The elements of adultery are (1) voluntary sexual intercourse, (2) by persons not married to each other, and (3) where one party is in a lawful

pimping
Promoting prostitution, living off of the earnings of prostitutes, and in some cases coercing individuals to work as prostitutes.

pandering
Either procuring a prostitute for a place of prostitution or procuring a place for a prostitute to engage in prostitution.

adultery
Sexual relations with someone other than a spouse when the person is married.

fornication

Voluntary, unlawful sexual intercourse under circumstances not constituting adultery.

marriage. **Fornication** is unlawful sexual intercourse that is consensual by both parties and is committed under circumstances not constituting adultery. To constitute intercourse, all that is necessary is that there be some penetration.

Today, these crimes are misdemeanors, if they are treated as crimes at all. In some states, fornication is no longer a recognized offense but adultery is. Here are a few examples of states that still carry such laws:

- In Utah, any unmarried person who voluntarily engages in sexual intercourse with another is guilty of fornication. If the other person is married, he or she is guilty of adultery. Both are class B misdemeanors.[25]
- In Idaho, any unmarried person who has sexual intercourse with an unmarried person of the opposite sex is guilty of fornication.[26]
- In Minnesota, sexual intercourse constitutes adultery only when the woman is the married party. If the woman is unmarried, neither party is guilty of adultery even if the man is married; instead, each party is guilty of fornication.[27]

Recognizing that many of the statutes against fornication and adultery that still exist are no longer enforced, the Model Penal Code omits any provisions relating to these offenses.

Sodomy and Related Offenses

sodomy

The unlawful sexual penetration of the anus of one person by the penis of another.

The term **sodomy** has been defined in many ways and in many jurisdictions over many years. At common law, sodomy was much narrower in its scope, and was only committed when a male person penetrated his penis into the anus of another male or female person. In its broadest terms under modern law, sodomy required an act of *deviate sexual intercourse*, which under most statutes occurred whenever a male penetrated his penis into the anus or mouth of another male or female person. Under most statutes, also, deviate sexual intercourse occurred whenever a male penetrated the vagina of a female animal or the anus of a male or female animal.

Few sexual acts have created as much controversy throughout history as the act of sodomy, even when it applies only to consensual relations between adult humans. The term sodomy was derived from the ancient city of Sodom. According to some biblical interpretations, the residents of Sodom engaged in certain deviant sexual acts; in response, God allegedly destroyed their city. Early English statutes made sodomy a capital offense, and this act was considered so vile that the famous English legal commentator William Blackstone refused to name it.

This early revulsion continued in American culture, and some sodomy laws existed until as recently as 2003. Modern sodomy was defined as the unlawful sexual penetration of the anus or mouth of one person by the penis of another, committed by use of force or fear. The crime of sodomy had three elements: unlawful sexual penetration of the anus or mouth of one person by the penis of another by use of force or fear. Some states, however, punished sodomy even if it was a consensual act between consenting adults in the privacy of their bedroom.[28] In 2003, the U.S. Supreme Court in *Lawrence v. Texas* declared state sodomy laws to be a violation of due process.[29] (See Application Case 13.7.)

⚖ Application Case 13.7

Lawrence v. Texas

In *Lawrence v. Texas*, the U.S. Supreme Court overruled its decision in *Bowers v. Hardwick*, holding Texas's sodomy statute to be unconstitutional. Texas's statute criminalized sodomy between two individuals of the same sex. Responding to reports of a weapons violation, Houston police entered a man's apartment and observed two men engaging in anal sex. The police arrested the men, and both were convicted of violating Texas's sodomy statute. The men appealed the conviction, and the Supreme Court held that the Texas statute demeaned the private lives of consenting homosexual adults. The state is not permitted to interfere in the private lives of these individuals by criminalizing their private sexual conduct.

Lawrence is not a statement on homosexuality per se. The Court's purpose was to state unequivocally that moral disapproval alone is an insufficient justification to intrude upon the private sexual lives of consenting adults. Legal scholars predict, however, that the *Lawrence* decision will call into question statutes prohibiting same-sex marriage, prostitution, adultery, fornication, and obscenity.

SOURCE: Lawrence v. Texas, 539 U.S. 558 (2003). See also James W. Paulson, Features: The Significance of Lawrence v. Texas, 41 Houston Lawyer 32 (2004).

Gambling

A person engages in **gambling** when he or she stakes or risks something of value on the outcome of a contest of chance or on a future event of chance that is not under his or her control or influence. Gambling usually involves an agreement that a person will win something based on a certain outcome of events. There are many forms of gambling, including track racing, state lotteries, video machines, commercial sweepstakes, gambling tournaments, charity, Indian bingo, and the rapid growth of legal card rooms, particularly for the game of poker.

gambling
The act of staking or risking something of value on the outcome of a contest of chance, or on a future event of chance that is not under the gambler's control or influence.

Betting and wagering are used interchangeably, and they apply only to forms of gambling that are not lotteries. Betting or wagering is a promise to give something of value upon the determination of an uncertain event, whether or not skill is involved. A common example is horse racing. When people bet money at the races, they do so in the hope of increasing the amount if their horse wins. There is no guarantee that this will happen, and often people who bet at the races lose their money.

Under common law, gambling was not a crime unless it became a public nuisance. All games were considered legal, and a loser had to pay off his debts. Courts would close down any gambling establishment only if it caused a breach of the peace or of public morals. Today, gambling is supported by a large segment of the population that enjoys it. Additionally, many states use lotteries as a legal form of gambling to raise public revenues.

In order for gambling to be illegal, there must be a specific law or ordinance prohibiting it. All states have at least some laws prohibiting gambling, and they vary by jurisdiction. Most forms of gambling are legal in Nevada; in Atlantic City,

Illegal Gambling Even where gambling is legal, some forms of betting and gambling are nonetheless prohibited. Most often this involves betting on animals that have been bred for aggression and are subjected to deadly fights.

New Jersey; and on Indian reservations in several states. In these areas, gambling is legal only in licensed establishments, although the definition of "licensed establishment" can be quite broad. For example, some grocery stores surrounding Las Vegas offer slot machines for any member of the general public over the age of 21.

In most jurisdictions, the only forms of gambling that are lawful are state-operated lotteries, racing, and bingo or other contests sponsored on a nonprofit basis by social organizations. In jurisdictions such as these, gambling establishments sometimes open on "off-shore" premises such as riverboats to circumvent laws about gambling on state land. This is commonly seen in Mississippi.

Although state and local governments regulate most gambling activities, several federal statutes also limit gambling. Federal gambling statutes are similar to state statutes but usually target large-scale operations involving a significant amount of money with many individuals working the operation. These statutes regulate gambling via interstate transportation, wire communications, the U.S. Postal Service, or any other way in which gambling is conducted between the states.

In contrast to the types of gambling discussed above, friendly gambling such as an office pool, a football pool, or a neighborhood poker game is generally legal. Friendly gambling can be distinguished from commercial gambling by factors such as where the game is played, who the players are, the size of the pot, and whether the house takes a percentage of each pot. Suppose that four friends who work together have a weekly poker game at one of their houses. They look at the game as a good social outlet and a way to have fun. They bet with pocket change and one-dollar bills, and no one ever loses or wins more than $20. It is unlikely that this type of gambling would be considered illegal under a statute.

CRITICAL THINKING 13.2

1. Should society continue to enforce laws regulating private sexual activities between consenting adults?
2. How can illegal gambling be tracked down and eradicated?

REVIEW AND APPLICATIONS

Summary by Chapter Objectives

1. **Define the crimes that encompass breaching the peace.** Crimes that breach the peace can be defined as follows:
   - Unlawful assembly is the gathering of three or more persons with a common intent to achieve a purpose, unlawful or lawful, by committing disorderly acts.
   - Rout is an attempted riot.
   - Riot is an unlawful assembly in which people act in a violent and turbulent manner.
   - Disorderly conduct is misconduct that constitutes a public nuisance.
   - Vagrancy is idle wandering or a variety of other vaguely defined acts.

   Today, vagrancy laws have generally been declared unconstitutional.

2. **State the purpose and elements of nuisance crimes.** Nuisance crimes exist in order to protect the public from acts or omissions that may cause physical, emotional, or personal harm. The elements vary from jurisdiction to jurisdiction, but generally the laws criminalize any conduct that:
   - Endangers life or health.
   - Gives offense to the senses.
   - Violates laws of decency.
   - Obstructs the reasonable and comfortable use of property.

3. **Understand the most common traffic offenses and explain their distinctions.** The most common traffic offenses can be defined as follows:
   - Speeding, which is driving faster than the posted speed limit.
   - Reckless driving, which is the voluntary and wanton disregard for the safety of persons or property.
   - Driving with a suspended or revoked license.
   - Leaving the scene of an accident, whether or not the individual is at fault.
   - Driving under the influence of an intoxicant.

   These offenses exist to protect drivers and passengers and to keep the roads and highways safe.

4. **Name typical circumstances that could constitute a weapons offense.** Circumstances can include any of the following:
   - An underage possessor.
   - The use of an illegal or legal but unregistered weapon.
   - The location where the weapon was discovered, such as in one's vehicle or on one's person, without permission to carry a weapon there.

- The possession or transportation of an explosive, firearm, or ammunition, with intent that it be used or with knowledge that it may be used to commit a crime.
- Placing another person in fear of a harmful weapon.
- Offensive bodily contact with a weapon.
- Using a firearm as a weapon (such as a club), whether it is loaded or not.

5. **Explain and understand obscenity offenses.** Obscenity offenses address certain materials that are not protected under the First Amendment. These materials may take the form of a book, magazine, newspaper, picture, drawing, photograph, motion picture, statue, or recording. Courts today use the following guidelines in determining whether material is obscene:
   - Whether the average person, applying contemporary community standards, would find that the work, taken as a whole, appeals to prurient interest.
   - Whether the work depicts or describes, in a patently offensive way, sexual conduct specifically defined by the applicable state law.
   - Whether the work, taken as a whole, lacks serious literary, artistic, political, or scientific value.

6. **Understand the crime of prostitution and the parties involved.** Prostitution is committed when one person agrees to engage in sexual or deviate sexual intercourse in return for something of value, usually money. The parties involved usually include:
   - The prostitute.
   - The person paying for sex.
   - Usually, the person managing the activities of the prostitute, such as a pimp or a panderer.

7. **Explain the crime of sodomy.** Under its broadest modern definition, sodomy was defined as the unlawful sexual penetration of the anus of one person by the penis of another. Other sexual acts, such as bestiality, were often included in these sodomy statutes. Sodomy has a history of controversy and was formerly a capital offense. Today, though, sodomy statutes are held to be unconstitutional.

8. **Distinguish legal from illegal gambling.** Legal gambling includes gambling in certain licensed establishments and in certain geographic areas, such as gambling establishments in Nevada or on some Indian reservations. It also includes activities that are regulated by the state, such as lotteries. Unlawful gambling is any gambling activity that is either specifically prohibited by statute or that does not fall under a validly recognized form of gambling in a particular jurisdiction.

Key Terms

public order and safety offenses
   (p. 340)
mala prohibita (p. 340)
mala in se (p. 340)
unlawful assembly (p. 340)

rout (p. 340)
riot (p. 341)
disorderly conduct (p. 341)
vagrancy (p. 341)
nuisance (p. 342)

Review Questions

1. Why do public order offenses exist, and how do they differ from more serious crimes?
2. What is the history of vagrancy laws, and why are they no longer in common use today?
3. Why is speeding a strict liability offense?
4. What are the characteristics that define firearms, and what commonly used weapons do not qualify as firearms?
5. What is a DUI offense, and how is DUI manslaughter different from vehicular manslaughter?
6. What are the elements and required culpability for indecent exposure?
7. What are the differences among prostitution, solicitation, and patronizing a prostitute?
8. What is the difference between pimping and pandering?
9. What forms of legal gambling exist today, and under what circumstances?

Problem-Solving Exercises

1. **Vagrancy Statutes** You work for the prosecutor's office in a fairly large midwestern city. A big political convention is coming to your city, and your police chief has been getting pressure from the mayor to "crack down" on homeless people and prostitutes. As a result, the police initiated a comprehensive sweep by using a vagrancy ordinance that prohibits, among other things, "common night walkers, persons wandering or strolling around from place to place without any lawful purpose or object, and habitual loafers." Four people who were arrested are protesting that this ordinance is unconstitutional. Answer the following questions:
   a. Is this ordinance unconstitutional? Why or why not?
   b. What are your options in dealing with these four defendants, and what would be the wisest move? The easiest move?
   c. How should this situation be resolved to avoid similar future occurrences? Why?
2. **Consensual Sodomy** You are a state supreme court judge hearing a case in which two adult male homosexuals, who have been in a relationship for more

than 12 years, are being charged under state sodomy laws. They were arrested when police officers obtained arrest warrants based on probable cause that they were committing sodomy in their home. The men argue that their sexual relations are private and consensual and that these charges violate their rights under the First and Fourth Amendments. Answer the following questions:

a. Are their First Amendment rights being violated? Why or why not?

b. What about their Fourth Amendment rights? Why or why not?

c. What are your options as a judge in your state's highest court? Which option will you choose, and why?

3. **Traffic Violations** You are a federal law enforcement officer testifying at an important trial. Your alarm fails to go off, and you are speeding to reach the courtroom when you are pulled over by the state highway patrol. The state officer does not care about who you are or why you are speeding and is exceptionally slow in processing your ticket. You know that the judge in whose courtroom you are testifying is extremely impatient with people who are late or who fail to show up to testify. After waiting about 20 minutes, you start your car and leave.

a. Have you committed any violations? Why or why not?

b. Are any of the other factors relevant to your case? Why or why not?

Workplace Applications

1. **Unlawful Assembly** You are a municipal police officer working foot patrol in a public commons area during a large protest. The organizers of the protest have obtained the necessary city permits to be there, and the police department has received advanced notice of the event. This particular protest is in response to the shooting of a young black woman by local officers. The woman was unarmed when she was shot and killed, and she had no criminal history; nonetheless, the officer involved in the shooting was acquitted. The protesters today are angry that he is not going to be punished. As the protest progresses, one speaker hollers, "If we are not going to get any justice, we've got to take justice into our own hands." The next three speakers urge the listeners to disobey the police. You are aware of the speakers' First Amendment rights, but because of their specific messages you are concerned that the crowd will become violent and will direct their violence at you and your fellow officers. Answer the following questions:

a. Do you allow the protest to continue, or do you shut it down early?

b. What steps should you take to avoid the possibility of violence?

c. What other information do you need before making a decision?

2. **Indecent Exposure** You are a local prosecutor, and you receive a report filed by a homeowner complaining that her next-door neighbors are sunbathing nude and violating public decency laws. Because the homeowner has small children, she wants her neighbors to stop doing this. To date, however, they have refused. Local police have spoken to the sunbathers, who responded that they are allowed to sunbathe naked on their own property in their backyard. They argue that it would be different if they were out on the street or in the front of the house.

The only divider between the two homes is a four-foot picket fence. Answer the following questions:

a. Are the sunbathers guilty of indecent exposure? Why or why not?

b. Are there any other crimes for which they could be found guilty?

c. What are the various solutions available for this problem?

3. **Gang Nuisances** You are a city prosecutor whose city has cracked down on gang violence by issuing nuisance abatement orders to known gang members. Under these orders, these individuals are forbidden to sell drugs, congregate in public for longer than 10 minutes, carry papers, or engage in other activities. As everyone knows, these orders forbid certain illegal actions, as well as certain actions that otherwise would be legal.

a. Are such orders constitutional? Why or why not?

b. Which is more important in this case, the good of the individuals or the good of the community?

Notes

1. Model Penal Code § 250.2(1) (1985).

2. See Debra Livingston, *Vagrancy and Disorderly Conduct*, in Encyclopedia of Crime and Justice 1613, 1614 (Joshua Dressler ed., 2d ed. 2002).

3. Cal. Penal Code § 370 (West 2007).

4. Deborah Tussey, Annotation, *Massage Parlor As Nuisance*, 80 A.L.R.3d 1020 (1978).

5. People ex re Gallo v. Acuna, 929 P.2d 596 (1997).

6. *See* 7A Am. Jur. 2d *Automobiles and Highway Traffic* § 244 (2006).

7. Griffin v. State, 457 So. 2d 1070, 1072 (Fla. Dist. Ct. App. 1984). See also State v. Smelter, 674 P.2d 690 (Wash. Ct. App. 1984).

8. Figueroa v. Kirmayer, 303 N.Y.S.2d 349 (N.Y. App. Div. 1969).

9. 18 U.S.C. § 921 (a) (3) (2006).

10. Margaret C. Jasper, The Law of Obscenity and Pornography 3 (1996); *see also* U.S. v. One Book Called "Ulysses," 5 F. Supp. 182 (D.S.D. 1933).

11. Harvey Wallace & Cliff Roberson, Principles of Criminal Law 225 (1996) (citing Roth v. United States, 354 U.S. 476 (1957) & A Book Named "John Cleland's Memoirs of a Woman of Pleasure" v. Massachusetts, 383 U.S. 413 (1966)). *See also* Charles E. Torcia, Wharton's Criminal Law 138 (15th ed. 1995).

12. David A. Jones, Crime and Criminal Responsibility 359 (1978).

13. For a summary of state and federal laws relating to pornography and the Internet, see 61 Am. Jur. 3d §§ 9 & 10 (2007).

14. Ashcroft v. ACLU, 542 U.S. 656 (2004).

15. ACLU v. Gonzales, Final Adjudication, Mar. 22, 2007, http://www .paed.uscourts.gov/documents/opinions/07d0346p.pdf.

16. See discussion in Simmons v. State, 944 So. 2d 317 (Fla. 2006).

17. Jonathon Rosenoer, CyberLaw: The Law of the Internet 179–80 (1997), citing 18 U.S.C. § 2252 (a)(2), (a)(4).

18. 63C Am. Jur. 2d *Prostitution* § 1, n.10.

19. *Id.*, n.16.
20. 18 U.S.C. § 2421 (West 2007).
21. Conn. Gen. Stat. Ann. § 53a-83 (West 2007).
22. Cal. Penal Code § 266h (West 2007).
23. Utah Code Ann. §§ 76-10-1304, 1305 & 1306 (West 2007).
24. 2 Charles E. Torcia, Wharton's Criminal Law 529 (15th ed. 1995), citing Burns v. State, 17 Okla. Crim. 26 (1919), 182 P. 738 (1919).
25. Utah Code Ann. §§ 76-10-103, 1304 (West 2007).
26. Idaho Code Ann. § 18-6603 (2007).
27. Minn. Stat. §§ 609.36 & 609.34 (2007).
28. Harvey Wallace & Cliff Roberson, Principles of Criminal Law 141 (1996), citing 4 William Blackstone, Commentaries *215, and Phillips v. State, 248 Ind. 150, 222 N.E.2d 821 (1967).
29. Lawrence v. Texas, 539 U.S. 558 (2003).

Drug- and Alcohol-Related Crimes

CHAPTER OBJECTIVES

After reading and studying this chapter, you should be able to:

1. Identify the five major categories of controlled substances.

2. State the purposes and effect of the Uniform Controlled Substances Act.

3. Recognize and describe the difference between actual and constructive possession of a controlled substance.

4. State the difference between the offense of possession and the offense of possession with intent to deliver.

5. Define the drug offenses of delivery, drug conspiracy, drug loitering, and possession of drug paraphernalia.

6. Understand when drug addiction is and is not a defense to drug offenses.

7. State the elements of driving under the influence.

8. Define the extent to which alcoholism can be a defense in a criminal case.

14.1 Types of Psychoactive Drugs

In the United States, some drugs that affect mental states and behavior have been subject to little or no regulation, and others have been targets of extremely punitive legislation and a "war on drugs." There is disagreement about what substances are drugs, and which are harmful. Although nicotine and caffeine stimulate the central nervous system, many Americans do not consider smoking cigarettes or drinking coffee to be drug use. Although Ritalin, Valium, Xanax, and the like are clearly addictive and have controversial medical value, they are legally prescribed to thousands of people with little question.

controlled substance

Any substance that is strictly regulated or outlawed because of its potential for abuse or addiction.

psychoactive drug

A drug that has the ability to alter mood, anxiety, behavior, cognitive processes, or mental tension.

Under federal law, a **controlled substance** is any *psychoactive* (affecting mind or behavior) or *bioactive* (affecting the body) chemical substance that is strictly regulated or made illegal because of its potential for abuse or addiction. Overall, drugs are classified as controlled substances based on medical use, potential for abuse, and probability of creating dependence.

From a biochemical standpoint, a **psychoactive drug** is a drug that has the ability to alter mood, anxiety, behavior, cognitive processes, or mental tension.[1] Psychoactive drugs are generally classified according to their principal or usual affects on human beings.

Stimulants

Stimulant drugs directly affect the central nervous system and tend to produce arousal, alertness, or excitation. They may also reduce fatigue. They include amphetamines, methamphetamines, cocaine, caffeine, nicotine, and the prescription drug Ritalin.

Crack cocaine is most commonly associated with the urban poor because it is available in strong but small and low-priced doses. Powder cocaine, on the other hand, is associated with privileged middle- and upper-class white Americans and is glamorized in and by the entertainment industry. Crack pipes are used to smoke crack cocaine. They are commonly small glass tubes that measure a quarter of an inch in diameter and are on average four inches in length. Soda cans, with small holes punched in the side near the bottom, are also used as crack pipes.

Depressants

Depressants are drugs that depress or slow down the activity of the central nervous system and tend to produce drowsiness, relaxation, or sleep. These are divided into narcotics (drugs derived from opium or opium-like compounds) and non-narcotic general depressants. Opiates are powerful pain-relieving depressant drugs that may induce sleep and that commonly become physically addictive after prolonged use. Opiates, including opium, morphine, heroin, and codeine, are derived from unripe poppy seed capsules. Heroin kits differ with the method of drug use. If the drug is being injected, a heroin kit would include hypodermic needles, cotton balls, water, and spoons or bottle caps. If heroin is being smoked or inhaled, a kit would include razor blades, straws, rolled dollar bills, and/or pipes. Synthetic narcotics include Percodan and Demerol (used for pain relief) and methadone (used to treat heroin addiction). Non-narcotic general depressants include alcohol, barbiturates, and tranquilizers such as Librium, Valium, and Xanax.

Hallucinogens

Hallucinogenic drugs act on the central nervous system to cause visual or auditory hallucinations. They include LSD (lysergic acid diethylamide), PCP (phencyclidine), mescaline and peyote (derived from a small cactus, the mescal button), psilocybin (derived from a fungus), and numerous synthetic drugs. LSD is commonly sold in vials as a liquid or sprayed and soaked into a distribution medium such as a sugar cube or blotter paper. Because only small quantities are required for an effective dose, LSD is easy to conceal and smuggle. Fortunately for law enforcement officers, use of the drug has declined sharply since 2000.

Marijuana

Marijuana consists of the dried leaves and "tops" of *cannabis sativa*, the common hemp plant. This drug has been classified as a hallucinogen, a stimulant, and a depressant. Some argue that it should be in a separate category because it does not closely resemble the other types of drugs. Hashish and hashish oil are derivatives of cannabis.

Recent controversy has arisen as doctors and patients, particularly those undergoing cancer treatment, wish to use marijuana for medicinal purposes. The Marijuana Tax Act of 1937 made marijuana prescriptions illegal in the United States. In recent years, many advocacy groups have argued for the legalization of marijuana use for (at least) these limited purposes. The effectiveness of marijuana for medicinal purposes is widely contested, and efforts to legalize have met with little success. In 2005, the U.S. Supreme Court, in *Gonzales v. Raich*, upheld the federal ban against medical marijuana use pursuant to the commerce clause, thus striking down the validity of medical use laws in California and at least eight other states.[2]

Inhalants

These drugs are classified by their method of use rather than by their effects. They have stimulating but very short-lived effects. They include amyl nitrite ("poppers") and nitrous oxide ("laughing gas"). Other household chemicals are used as inhalants but are not legally considered drugs.[3]

Designer Drugs

Designer drugs are synthetic drugs that mimic the effects of known illegal drugs but are not specifically listed as controlled substances by the Drug Enforcement Administration. The best-known designer drug, Ecstasy (3,4-methylenedioxy-N-methylamphetamine or MDMA), is chemically related to the family of amphetamines and also to mescaline. It was first synthesized in the early 1900s but was not used as a psychoactive drug until the 1970s. Some psychiatrists and psychologists began experimenting with it as a psychotherapeutic tool, claiming that it decreased anxiety, removed defenses, and facilitated communication between therapist and client. In the 1980s, it became popular at large, all-night dance parties, known as raves, in both England and the United States. The FDA classified it as a controlled substance in 1985, but it has continued to grow in popularity. Users say that it has amphetamine-like properties and produces positive feelings of relaxation, empathy, and confidence. Other designer drugs include Rohypnol (known as a "date rape" drug), China White, and New Heroin.

Steroids

Steroids are not really classifiable as a psychoactive drug, but deserve mention in any discussion of modern drug use problems. Steroids consist of natural and synthetic hormones that promote cell and muscle growth. They are routinely used for numerous medical purposes. Steroid abuse is commonly found by athletes at all levels, who value the increased strength and athletic performance. Such uses, however, lead to risk of increased blood pressure, fluctuating cholesterol levels, premature baldness, and prostate cancer, among other conditions. One of the side effects of steroid use is steroid rage, which can lead to aberrant behavior.

CRITICAL THINKING 14.1

1. Which category of drugs seems the most dangerous? The most addictive? Why?

14.2 History of Drug Legislation in the United States

According to historians and archaeologists, marijuana and the opium poppy have been used as intoxicants and in rituals in many societies for thousands of years. The use of alcohol is, for the most part, "a human cultural universal."[4] World trade in such substances, however, began only after the European colonization of America.

Drug Use in Nineteenth-Century America

The classification of various drugs in the United States as legal or illegal has also changed over time.[5] Narcotics and cocaine are good examples.

Narcotics

During the nineteenth century, it was legal to distribute, promote, and sell narcotics. Opium was used to treat everything from teething pain to tuberculosis, and it was also a potent source of recreational pleasure. It had been used in home remedies and patent medicines since the latter part of the eighteenth century. Morphine was isolated in the early nineteenth century, and it became widely used as an anesthetic. After using it as a painkiller on the battlefields of the Civil War, tens of thousands of soldiers returned home addicted to the drug. By the end of the nineteenth century, both physicians and the general public became concerned about the addictive potential of opiates.[6] Heroin, a powerful derivative of morphine, was first introduced by the Bayer Company in 1898 as a cough medicine. It was also seen as a cure for morphine addiction and alcoholism.

Cocaine

Cocaine, too, was widely used in the United States after it was chemically extracted from the coca leaf in 1844. Many patent medicines of the late nineteenth century contained cocaine, and until 1903 it was an ingredient in Coca-Cola.[7] Its medical uses included the treatment of depression, narcolepsy (excessive sleepiness), and more mundane ailments such as hay fever, sinus troubles, and runny noses.

Other products that could be purchased over the counter at local drugstores and variety stores contained cocaine, opium, and morphine. During the 1800s, the use of opium, morphine, cocaine, and heroin was so extensive that by 1900 there were approximately 250,000 narcotic addicts in the United States. Some estimates put the number at 8 million.[8] The widespread use of drugs gave rise to demands by the medical community, the media, and the general public for government regulation.

Drug Legislation from the 1800s to the Present

Drug legislation began at a local, rather than a national, level. In 1875, the City of San Francisco enacted the first drug law in the United States. The law did not outlaw the use of opium, but it prohibited smoking in opium dens. Whites used over-the-counter drugs containing opium in powder, liquid, and pill form, but opium smoking was associated with Chinese immigrants.

Beginnings of Federal Legislation

In 1888, federal legislation placed certain restrictions on smoking opium. Smoking opium was banned in 1909, but drinking it remained legal. The law was one of the few restrictions on drug use in effect in the United States at the time. In 1906, in an attempt to control opiate addiction, Congress passed the Federal Pure Food and Drug Act. This law required that product labels specify the amount of drugs (opium, morphine, and heroin) in the product. The same was required for products containing alcohol, marijuana, and cocaine.

The Harrison Narcotics Act of 1914

In 1914, Congress passed the Harrison Narcotics Act of 1914, which took effect March 15, 1915. It was not intended to prohibit the use or sale of narcotics, but was primarily an economic regulation. It required persons dealing in narcotics or cocaine to register with the government and pay a tax; however, anyone was allowed to engage in such trade. The Harrison Act was in part a response to international pressures to regulate the opium trade; the law also provided revenue for the federal government. The Treasury Department was given the responsibility of enforcing the law.

Under the Harrison Act, it was still legal to use cough medicine that contained a restricted amount of heroin, and physicians could still prescribe opiates for medical treatment. However, in 1919, the United States Supreme Court held, in the case of *Webb v. United States*, that physicians could not maintain addicts on morphine. The Court ruled that such prescriptions prolonged addiction and thus could not be considered medical treatment.[9] As a result of the increased numbers of individuals addicted to drugs, the United States grew fearful and intolerant of recreational drug use.

The Marijuana Tax Act

The use and sale of marijuana was legal in the United States until the 1930s. Harry Anslinger, head of the Federal Bureau of Narcotics from its founding in 1930 until his retirement in 1962, led an anti-marijuana campaign that portrayed it as a "killer drug." With the aid of anti-marijuana stories run in mass circulation newspapers and magazines, including claims that marijuana would lead to the destruction of the youth of America, 46 of 48 states banned marijuana. The Women's Christian Temperance Union and the General Federation of Women's Clubs launched campaigns to ban marijuana.

At the federal level, the first law regulating marijuana was the Marijuana Tax Act of 1937. The law imposed taxes on marijuana, declared cannabis (hemp) a narcotic, and penalized its use and distribution. In 1951, Congress passed the Boggs Act, which made marijuana illegal and also removed heroin from the list of medically useful drugs.

Drug Use and Legislation in the 1950s and 1960s

During the 1950s, organized crime began to play a much larger role in the distribution and sale of drugs. Heroin addiction increased sharply during this time, especially among youth in the inner cities.[10] During the 1960s, drug use expanded from the cities to suburbia, and the use of heroin by U.S. soldiers in Vietnam became a national concern.

In addition, although legal in the 1950s, the drug LSD became illegal in 1967 because of its association with a generation whose values at the time were different from the general population. Laws were also created to regulate the availability and use of depressants.

The Uniform Controlled Substances Act of 1970

In 1970, the U.S. Congress enacted the Comprehensive Drug Abuse and Prevention Act, also called the Controlled Substances Act of 1970. It replaced the 1933 Uniform Narcotic Drug Act and the 1966 Model State Drug Abuse Control Act. A majority of the states enacted parallel legislation.

The goals of the Uniform Act were to achieve uniformity between the laws of the several states and those of the federal government and to complement the new federal narcotic and dangerous drug legislation.[11] Nevertheless, conflicts between federal and state laws sometimes arise, and there is significant variation among state drug laws. For example, Minnesota treats marijuana possession in small amounts as a petty misdemeanor that may result in a maximum fine of $200 and participation in a drug education program. In contrast, Florida makes marijuana possession a first-degree misdemeanor, and possession of up to 20 grams can result in a fine of up to $1,000 and/or a prison term of up to one year.

The Uniform Controlled Substances Act forbids and makes it a crime to engage in the following conduct:

- Manufacture or deliver a controlled (forbidden) substance.
- Possess with the intent to manufacture or deliver a controlled substance.
- Create, deliver, or possess with intent to deliver a counterfeit substance.
- Offer or agree to deliver a controlled substance and deliver or dispense a controlled substance.
- Possess a controlled substance.

F I G U R E   1 4 . 1

Schedule of Drugs under the Controlled Substances Act of 1970

Schedule I	Controlled substances that have no established medical usage, cannot be used safely, and have great potential for abuse.	Heroin, LSD, mescaline, peyote, Quaaludes, psilocybin, marijuana, hashish, and some hallucinogens.
Schedule II	Drugs with a high potential for abuse (and addiction) but for which there is a currently accepted pharmacological or medical use.	Opium, morphine, codeine, cocaine, phencyclidine (PCP), some stimulants such as methylphenidate (Ritalin) and phenmetrazine (Preludin), and some barbiturates.
Schedule III	Substances with some potential for abuse, with an accepted medical use, but which may lead to a high level of psychological dependence or a low to moderate level of physical dependence.	Anabolic steroids (added in 1991), cold medicines, and pain relievers containing codeine.
Schedule IV	Substances with relatively low potential for abuse, useful in established medical treatment, and involving only limited risk of psychological or physical dependency.	Depressants and minor tranquilizers such as Valium, Librium, and Equanil, and some stimulants.
Schedule V	Prescription drugs with a low potential for abuse and a very limited possibility of psychological or physical dependence.	Cough medicines and antidiarrheals containing small amounts of opium, morphine, or codeine.

- Knowingly keep or maintain a store, dwelling, building, vehicle, boat, aircraft, or other facility resorted to by persons illegally using a controlled substance.
- Acquire or obtain possession of a controlled substance by misrepresentation, fraud, forgery, deception, or subterfuge.

The Uniform Controlled Substances Act divides controlled substances into five categories or "schedules" (see Figure 14.1), graded according to their potential for abuse, relative physical danger to the abuser, and degree of accepted medical use. The drugs in Schedule I are the most tightly controlled, and possession of them results in the severest penalties.

The three criteria for placing a drug into Schedule I are that the drug must:

- Have a high potential for abuse.
- Have no currently accepted medical use.
- Lack safety even under medical supervision.

The War on Drugs

Despite the enactment of anti-drug laws, drug use by Americans increased significantly from the 1960s until 1980. In response to this increase in drug usage, President Ronald Reagan launched the "War on Drugs" in the 1980s. Underlying this campaign was the belief that the nation should take a punitive approach to the possession and sale of illicit drugs. The War on Drugs was an attempt to create a uniform scheme for identifying, regulating, and prohibiting the use and possession of potentially dangerous drugs. Federal funds for drug treatment programs were sharply reduced, and tough mandatory sentencing laws were passed for possession of relatively small amounts of cocaine and other drugs. Supporters of the War on Drugs advocate long prison sentences for users, dealers, suppliers, smugglers, and manufacturers of these drugs. The most extreme advocates of this view argue that harsher penalties are the only solution to the drug problem.

Enacted after basketball star Len Bias died from a cocaine overdose, the Anti-Drug Abuse Act of 1986[12] enhances penalties for drug use and distribution with weight-based minimums, extending civil liability to small-time offenders.

Current Drug Use

Although overall rates of illicit drug use leveled out the late 1990s, U.S. Bureau of Justice data indicate that the rate of drug abuse violations remains high. According to FBI data for 2005, there were 1.8 million arrests for drug abuse violations.[13] Although use of the majority of illicit drugs has decreased since the highs of the 1970s, the following drug trends are apparent:

- The use of inhalants and of the synthetic drug Ecstasy has increased among youth.
- Illicit use of prescription psychotherapeutics, especially pain relievers, for nonmedical purposes has also increased among adolescents. In 1990, there were 6.3 new users per 1,000 potential users in the 12–17 age group. By 1998, the number of new users of prescription pain relievers in that age group increased to 32.4 per 1,000 potential users.
- Illicit use of anabolic steroids has increased.
- The increase in the rate of new users of marijuana between 1990 and 2000 seems due primarily to the increasing rate of new users among youth ages 12 to 17. In 1977, the rate of new users per 1,000 potential users was at a high of 3.4. It had declined to 1.4 by 1990, but reached 2.6 in 1996, then fell again to 2.3 in 1998.[14]

Current Drug Policy

Today, opponents of the War on Drugs argue that criminalization is not the solution to the drug problem. In their view, the 74 years of federal prohibition, the attempt to enforce zero tolerance for drugs in the 1980s, and the harsher penalties for drug violations have had limited success and have created important civil rights problems. They argue that drug laws and their implementation have been enormously expensive and have served mainly to create enormous profits for drug dealers and traffickers, overcrowded jails, corruption among police and other government employees, a distorted foreign policy, and urban areas harassed by street-level drug dealers and terrorized by violent drug gangs.[15]

One criticism is that the War on Drugs has created racial disparities regarding use, arrest, and convictions for possession and distribution of illegal substances.[16] Studies have revealed that black and white Americans use drugs at the same or similar rates. Therefore, because there are more white than black Americans, there are more white users. Black Americans, however, are 13.4 times more likely to be arrested

14.1 Web Exploration

Punishing Drug Offenders

Read "Jailhouse Blues" on MetroActive.com, at http://www.metroactive.com/papers/sonoma/08.03.00/drugs-0031.html. Then write a half-page report discussing whether you think incarceration is the correct response for nonviolent drug offenders. Should they be punished? If so, why and how? If not, why not?

and prosecuted for drug violations. One explanation offered for the disparity is that drug arrests are easier to make in inner-city neighborhoods where drug exchanges are conducted more openly than in middle-class neighborhoods.

Some opponents of the War on Drugs say that the United States should emphasize medical and therapeutic approaches to the drug problem. Others believe that legalization would stop the violent crime associated with drug sales. Still others hold that the United States should remove all criminal penalties for the possession and sale of all psychoactive substances, allowing a free market to operate.[17]

By the dawn of the twenty-first century, many authorities on drug use had developed more complex proposals that recognize the many factors that affect an individual's choice to use drugs. Some advocate "harm reduction," not as a policy or program but as a principle suggesting that it is more reasonable to manage drug misuse rather than attempt to stop it altogether. Proposals for harm reduction can include any of the following:[18]

- Advocacy for changes in drug policies: legalization, reduction of criminal sanctions for drug-related crimes.
- HIV/AIDS-related interventions: needle exchange programs, HIV prevention programs.
- Broader drug treatment options, including methadone maintenance by primary care physicians.
- Drug abuse management for those who wish to continue using drugs.
- Ancillary programs such as support and advocacy groups.

Drugs and Religious Freedom

Peyote has been used in certain Native American rituals for at least 400 years. Until 1990, the First Amendment's guarantee of the free exercise of religion or its prohibition against the establishment of religion had been held to exempt the use of peyote in Native American religious ceremonies from drug laws.[19] In 1990, however, in *Employment Division, Department of Human Resources of Oregon v. Smith*,[20] the U.S. Supreme Court held that Native American religious use of peyote was not to be afforded First Amendment protection under the Free Exercise Clause. The Court rejected the claim by Native Americans that the religious basis for their use of peyote placed them beyond the reach of a criminal statute directed at use of peyote for nonreligious purposes.

As the only Supreme Court decision on the issue, *Oregon v. Smith* was immediately accepted as controlling authority—to the dismay of the executive and legislative branches of the federal government, which had a well-established relationship with Native American tribes to protect their rights as dependent sovereign nations. In order to halt the impact of the *Smith* decision, Congress passed the American Indian Religious Freedom Act Amendments in October 1994. This bill stripped *Smith* of its authority over peyote use in Native American religious ceremonies.

This federal exemption served two important functions:

1. It provided uniformity in the varying state laws governing peyote use by Native Americans.
2. It exempted Native Americans from penalty under the federal Controlled Substances Act, as well as under any state statutes that criminalized peyote use.[21]

Prior to the federal exemption, the diversity of state laws caused fragmented treatment of Native Americans engaged in peyote use and transportation.

CRITICAL THINKING 14.2

1. For what reasons was the Uniform Controlled Substances Act created?
2. In general, have efforts to fight and criminalize the use of psychoactive substances been successful in the United States? Why or why not?

14.3 Drug Offenses

Both federal and state systems have, in general, set up two penal categories for controlled substances: offenses involving possession and offenses involving the sale, distribution, and manufacture of controlled substances. In this section, we first discuss possession and then cover more serious drug offenses such as drug transportation and drug conspiracy.

Possession

The offense of (mere, simple, or straight) possession of a controlled substance is the most common criminal drug charge. The *actus reus* of the crime of criminal possession is the actual or constructive possession of a controlled substance.

Actual Possession

actual possession
When the controlled substance is on the defendant's person or in a container that the defendant is carrying.

Actual possession is the charge when the controlled substance is recovered on the defendant's person. For example, a suspect who is apprehended while holding a marijuana joint in his or her hands, lips, or pocket will be charged with actual possession. This offense may also occur when the controlled substance is found in a container (such as a bag) that the defendant is carrying.

Constructive Possession

constructive possession
When illegal drugs are in a place immediately accessible to the accused and subject to his or her domination and control.

Constructive possession of an illegal item (including controlled substances, guns, stolen goods, or other contraband) occurs when the item is in a place immediately accessible to the accused and he or she is able to exercise "dominion and control" over it. Hence, constructive possession does not require actual physical possession, but only that the accused be in a position to move the illegal substance from one place or another or have a knowing ability and intent to do so ("guide its destiny"). Constructive possession is frequently proven by showing that the controlled substance was located in an area or container in the accused's house or car, backpack, or other container that was accessible to the accused. In addition, the prosecution can prove constructive possession even if more than one individual had the ability to exercise dominion and control over the illegal substance. (See Application Case 14.1.)

⚖️ Application Case 14.1
Wheeler v. United States

In *Wheeler v. United States*, the defendant was convicted of possession of heroin on the theory of constructive possession. Detectives executed a search warrant for a hotel room, based on information that female occupants had been selling heroin from the room. When the detectives knocked on the door, they received no response but could hear a lot of "scurrying" noises in the room. A minute later, after no one opened the door, the detectives broke the door down. They discovered the defendant and two other women coming out of the bathroom and leaving a toilet that had just been flushed. A fourth woman was sitting next to the bathroom in a chair. Two women were in regular street clothing, while the defendant and the other female were wearing sleeping attire.

Further examination of the room revealed luggage and clothing belonging to the defendant. The defendant and the other female admitted to living in the room, but they gave aliases (false names) to the detectives. The other female retrieved some slippers from under one of the two beds in the room. At the opposite end of the room, where the other bed was located, the detectives recovered 3,550 milligrams of 2.7 percent heroin from under the pillow. Both the defendant and the other female who admitted to living in the room were arrested. The charges against the other female were later dismissed. Following a bench trial, the defendant was convicted of possession of heroin. She appealed her conviction on the basis that the drugs were not recovered on her person, but in a room where three other female individuals were present at the time. The defendant argued that the drugs could have belonged to any one of the other females and could have been placed under the pillow by any one of them.

The court refused to reverse the defendant's conviction. It held that even though the evidence was circumstantial, it supported a finding of constructive possession. The defendant's mere presence in the room by itself might not have been sufficient; however, evidence of an ongoing criminal enterprise, the defendant's admission that she lived in the room, the fact that the heroin was recovered from the bed that the defendant appeared to have occupied, the defendant's giving an alias to the detective, and her failure to open the door for the detectives, requiring them to break it down while a toilet was being flushed, together permitted an inference that the defendant knew of the presence of the drugs and had a measure of control over the heroin. Thus, a finding of constructive possession was justified.

SOURCE: Wheeler v. United States, 494 A.2d 170 (D.C. 1995).

Knowing Possession

More than mere proximity to the illegal substance is required to prove constructive possession. Even when there is actual possession, most states require that a "knowing" state of mind (*mens rea*) accompany the act of possession. In order to be lawfully convicted, the accused must know (be consciously aware) that he or she is in possession of the substance and must know that the substance is of a contraband (illegal) nature. Even if the accused is not actually knowledgeable about the illegal character of the item, many states will uphold a conviction if there is sufficient circumstantial evidence indicating that the accused was aware of the presence of the contraband and knew or should have known that the item possessed was a controlled substance.

In particular, virtually every state allows suspects to be punished when there is proof that they "willfully blinded" themselves to actual knowledge of the illegal character of items in their possession (see Application Cases 14.2 and 14.3). However, under most state laws, a conviction will not result from situations in which a defendant has a white powdery substance on his or her person but honestly believes it to be sugar even though it is cocaine.

⚖️ Application Case 14.2

United States v. Civelli

In *United States v. Civelli*, the defendant, Oscar Civelli, received a call from one Diego Bedoya, who asked the defendant to drive to Bedoya's home to make a delivery for him. Civelli was in the commercial delivery and moving business, and he had moved household items for Bedoya several times before. Civelli left his apartment and drove to Bedoya's home, which was under surveillance as a suspected center of narcotics distribution. Civelli was observed emerging from the house with four large tan envelopes.

Two officers followed Civelli as he drove away. After driving some distance, Civelli stopped to make a call from a public telephone. The officers approached the defendant and asked him what was in the packages in the van. He pulled one of the envelopes from the van to show the officers. The officers discovered 8.5 kilograms of cocaine in the four envelopes. Each envelope was folded shut but not sealed, and each had a name written on the outside. The officers also recovered from Civelli a beeper and a list of four names. The list was in his handwriting, and the names on the list corresponded to the names on the envelopes. There was a telephone number next to each name on the list, and a circled digit beside the name and number corresponded to the number of bricks of cocaine in one of the labeled envelopes.

Civelli was indicted for conspiracy to possess cocaine with intent to distribute and for possession of more than five kilograms of cocaine with intent to distribute. The key question at trial was whether the defendant knew he was carrying narcotics. The defendant testified that he never knew what was inside the envelopes until the officers opened them. He conceded that he had prepared the list of names, but he stated that he had transcribed the list verbatim at Bedoya's direction and that Bedoya was to pay him only $100 to deliver the packages. At trial, the judge instructed the jury that in order to find the defendant guilty on either the conspiracy or the substantive count, they had to find that the government had "prove[d] beyond a reasonable doubt that the defendant knew the packages in the van contained cocaine."

During deliberations, the jury sent the judge a note asking: "If Oscar Civelli suspected that he was carrying cocaine, but didn't look in the package, would that have constituted conspiracy?" The judge responded that a defendant's knowledge of a fact may be inferred from his willful blindness to the existence of the fact. The jury returned guilty verdicts on both counts. Civelli was sentenced to 10 years' imprisonment. The appellate court affirmed the conviction.

SOURCE: United States v. Civelli, 883 F.2d 191 (2nd Cir. 1989).

⚖ Application Case 14.3

United States v. Jewell

In *Jewell*, the defendant was convicted of "knowingly" transporting marijuana in his car from Mexico to the United States. The defendant entered the United States driving an automobile in which 110 pounds of marijuana had been concealed in a secret compartment between the trunk and rear seat. The defendant testified that he did not know that the marijuana was present, although he knew of the presence of the secret compartment and had knowledge of facts indicating that it contained marijuana.

The court found that the defendant deliberately avoided positive knowledge (actual knowledge) of the presence of the marijuana in an attempt to avoid responsibility in the event of discovery. The court found the defendant's "deliberate ignorance" equally as culpable of the crime as positive knowledge of the presence of marijuana would have been. The court held that "[defendant's] narrow interpretation of 'knowingly' is inconsistent with the Drug Control Act's general purpose to deal more effectively with the growing menace of drug abuse in the United States."

SOURCE: United States v. Jewell, 532 F.2d 697 (9th Cir. 1976).

Irrelevance of Amount

In many states, a conviction for simple possession of a controlled substance does not require possession of any minimum amount of the drug. An accused person may be convicted of possession for even a minute amount of an illegal substance. Some states, such as New York, hold that possession of a controlled substance can be based on the presence of even a residue of a substance such as cocaine.

Other jurisdictions hold that a person can be convicted for the possession of a "trace" amount of a controlled substance. A trace amount is an amount that is so small it is unusable. What is required is that the trace amount of the controlled substance be "reflected in such form as reasonably imputes knowledge to the defendant."[22] In still other states, simple possession cannot be established when there are only minuscule amounts of drug amounting to "lint" or "dust" that often innocently adheres to commonly used objects in the environment. (See Application Case 14.4.)

⚖️ Application Case 14.4

Jones v. State

In *Jones v. State*, the defendant was convicted of possession of a controlled substance. The basis for this conviction was an infinitesimal "residue" of cocaine on a small piece of metal ribbon, or screen, that is commonly used in smoking the drug. Because this screen was found in Jones's jacket pocket, he was convicted of possession of cocaine. The defendant contended that the cocaine, which was visible on the screen and detectable both by field and laboratory tests but was not "realistically weighable," was, as a matter of law, of insufficient quantity to justify a possession charge.

The appeal court disagreed and affirmed the conviction. It referred to the rule that one cannot be found guilty of possession when there are *only* trace amounts of *only* drug "lint" or "dust," but explained that this rule was inapplicable to this case. The reason was that the cocaine was found on an implement that is usable only for the obviously knowing use of the drug.

SOURCE: Jones v. State, 589 So. 2d 1001 (Fla. Dist. Ct. App. 1991).

Possession with Intent to Deliver

possession with intent to deliver

A drug offense that may be proven circumstantially by proof of a monetarily valuable quantity of drugs, possession of manufacturing or packaging implements, and the activities or statements of the person or persons in possession of the substance.

Possession with intent to deliver is another prevalent drug-related offense. Possession with intent to deliver is referred to as "possession for sale" or "possession with intent to sell or distribute" in some jurisdictions. This offense may be shown circumstantially by evidence such as possession of a large quantity of drugs or a quantity of drugs worth a lot of money; possession of manufacturing or packaging equipment, such as measuring scales or large quantities of small glassine envelopes; or the activities or statements of the person or persons in possession of the substance. In contrast to the crime of simple possession of a controlled substance, possession with intent to sell is treated as a felony under both federal and state statutes. Because of the stiffer penalties imposed for possession with intent, many states forbid the inference of intent to deliver merely on the basis of possession of a controlled substance. (See Application Case 14.5.)

⚖️ Application Case 14.5

State v. Brown

In *State v. Brown*, the defendant, a young man, was found with a baggie containing 20 pieces of rock cocaine. There was no other evidence of intent to deliver, other than the quantity of the drug possessed. In reversing his conviction for possession with intent to deliver, the appellate court stated,

> The courts must be careful to preserve the distinction and not to turn every possession of a minimal amount of a controlled substance into a possession with intent to

Possession with Intent to Sell   Unlike mere possession, possession with intent to sell carries severe penalties.

deliver without substantial evidence as to the possessor's intent above and beyond the possession itself. Convictions for possession with intent to deliver are highly fact specific and require substantial corroborating evidence in addition to the mere fact of possession.

SOURCE: State v. Brown, 843 P.2d 1098 (Wash. Ct. App. 1995).

In order to obtain a conviction for possession with intent to sell, the state must prove that the defendant intended to sell controlled substances to another person or persons, either immediately or at some time in the future. Evidence of intent to sell must be sufficiently compelling that the specific criminal intent of the accused may be inferred from conduct in which the intent to transfer the drug to others is a clearly indicated logical probability. However, in some cases, such proof may be no easy task for the prosecution (see Application Case 14.6).

⚖️ Application Case 14.6

State v. Davis

In *State v. Davis*, Leroy Davis was convicted of possession of marijuana with the intent to deliver. The evidence against him included possession of a bread sack with six individually wrapped baggies of marijuana, two baggies of marijuana seeds, a film canister containing marijuana, a baggie with marijuana residue in it, a box of sandwich baggies, a pipe used for smoking marijuana, a number of knives, and a police officer's testimony that it was not customary for people who simply use marijuana to have that "quantity with that packaging." The question presented on appeal was whether the evidence presented by the state was sufficient to infer an intent to deliver marijuana.

The Court of Appeals of Washington found that it was not and reversed the conviction. It reasoned that there was no evidence Mr. Davis had bought or sold marijuana or was in the business of buying or selling. No quantity of money was found, nor were any weighing devices. The marijuana obtained from Mr. Davis totaled 19 grams, an amount that, the court found, could certainly be consumed in the course of normal personal use. The packaging was also consistent with personal use. Therefore, the court found that there was not enough evidence to infer the specific criminal intent to deliver as required by statute. The intent to deliver did not follow as a matter of logical probability.

SOURCE: State v. Davis, 904 P.2d 306 (Wash. Ct. App. 1995).

Other Drug Offenses

Other than possession, a person can be convicted for several other drug violations in the United States, including:

- Delivery of a controlled substance.
- Drug conspiracy.
- Drug loitering.
- Drug transportation.
- Cultivation of marijuana.
- Drug paraphernalia.

Delivery of a Controlled Substance

delivery of a controlled substance

The transfer of a controlled substance from one person to another.

Delivery of a controlled substance is defined as the voluntary transfer of a controlled substance from one person to another. Delivery, like possession, can be proven constructively, as well as through the actual delivery of the controlled substance. Delivery statutes are geared toward the suppliers of controlled substances. The Controlled Substances Act attaches the same felony penalties to delivery as it does to possession with intent to deliver.

simulated controlled substance

A substance representing a controlled substance in its nature, packaging, or appearance, which would lead a reasonable person to believe it to be a controlled substance.

Some states also have statutes that make the delivery or possession of a **simulated controlled substance** a crime. A simulated controlled substance (or imitation) is a substance represented to be a controlled substance, which, because of its nature, packaging, or appearance, would lead a reasonable person to believe it to be a controlled substance.

Often a person engaged in selling controlled substances is also charged with the crimes of possession, possession with intent to deliver, and conspiracy, because there is a group effort to distribute the controlled substances. The case of *United States v. Civelli* (Application Case 14.2) illustrates the crimes of delivery of a controlled substance, drug conspiracy, and possession with intent to deliver.

Drug Conspiracy

A **drug conspiracy** is an agreement between two or more persons with the intent to manufacture and/or distribute drugs. In order to establish this offense, the state must show that an agreement existed, that the defendant had knowledge of the agreement, and that the defendant voluntarily participated in the agreement. An agreement may be inferred from a concert of action, participation from a totality of the circumstances, and knowledge from surrounding circumstances. (See Application Cases 14.2 and 14.7.)

drug conspiracy

An agreement between two or more people to commit a criminal or unlawful drug-related act, or to commit a lawful drug-related act by criminal or unlawful means.

⚖️ Application Case 14.7

United States v. Eastman

A case that demonstrates a drug conspiracy is *United States v. Eastman* (1998), in which a jury convicted William Eastman of one count of conspiring to distribute cocaine and methamphetamine and two counts of conspiring to launder drug proceeds. In April 1990, one Lawrence Lawler in Minnesota began receiving cocaine and methamphetamine from his cousin, Joe Sakel, in California. For the next four years, Lawler periodically wired money to Sakel. Sakel and other suppliers shipped distribution quantities of drugs to Lawler by Federal Express. Lawler distributed about one-third of the drugs to a Robin Birk and two-thirds to the accused, William Eastman. Birk and Eastman supplied the money that Lawler wired for drugs. Over the course of the conspiracy, $250,000 was sent to California to purchase cocaine and methamphetamine for distribution in the Duluth area of Minnesota.

In June 1994, Lawler was arrested and agreed to cooperate with authorities. He arranged controlled buys from his sources in California and a controlled sale of two ounces of cocaine to Eastman in July 1994. Eastman was then arrested. At his trial, Lawler and Sakel testified against him for the government. Robin Birk also testified that she occasionally purchased drugs directly from Eastman.

To sustain Eastman's conviction for conspiracy to distribute drugs, the evidence had to establish that a conspiracy existed to distribute the drugs, and that Eastman knew of and intentionally joined the conspiracy. Eastman argued that he was a mere customer of the conspiracy. The Eighth Circuit Court disagreed and affirmed Eastman's conviction. It found that the testimony of the other conspirators was sufficient for the jury to find that Eastman knowingly participated in a conspiracy.

SOURCE: U.S. v. Eastman, 149 F.3d 802 (8th Cir. 1998).

Drug Loitering

The crime of "drug loitering" or "loitering for the purposes of engaging in drug-related activity" is another category of drug-related offenses. The crime of **drug loitering** consists of an action done in public that manifests the intent to engage in illegal drug activity. Proof of the presence of a controlled substance, its possession, or its delivery is not required under most ordinances to support a charge of drug loitering; however, the action must occur in public. (See Application Case 14.8.)

drug loitering

An action done in public that manifests the intent to engage in illegal drug activity.

⚖ Application Case 14.8

City of Tacoma v. Luvene

A case that illustrates the elements necessary to sustain a drug loitering conviction is *City of Tacoma v. Luvene* (1988). One Friday evening, a Tacoma (Washington) police officer watched three men in their mid-20s, including defendant Luvene, standing on a street corner. They were pacing two to three steps in all directions and continually surveying their surroundings. The men stood in the middle of the intersection waving at and trying to flag down vehicles, several of which stopped. The officer observed the defendant in the middle of the street and on the sidewalk for nearly one hour, in an area known for drug trafficking. He was waving his arms at passing cars and standing by a car while another exchanged what looked to be rock cocaine for money.

After these observations, the officers approached and arrested five persons, including Luvene, for drug loitering. Glass tubing, commonly used to smoke crack cocaine, was found on one of the persons arrested. Although no drugs or drug paraphernalia were found on Luvene, the Supreme Court of Washington found there was sufficient evidence to sustain the conviction, considering the "totality of the circumstances."

SOURCE: City of Tacoma v. Luvene, 827 P.2d 1374 (Wash. 1992).

Drug Transportation

drug transportation
Transporting a controlled substance in a vehicle; a crime in every state.

Every state prohibits the transportation of a controlled substance in a vehicle, which is the offense of **drug transportation**. The case of *United States v. Jewell*

Drug Loitering Drug loitering occurs when individuals take public action, such as selling drugs from a street corner, which indicates the intent to engage in illegal drug activity.

14.1 On the Job

Chemical Dependency Manager

Description and Duties: Provide supportive counseling to adults (or youths, depending on the position) in a clinical setting and through community outreach. Act as advocate and coach in building daily living skills and in crisis prevention and intervention. Provide one-on-one counseling, assessments, treatment plans, and some group work. Some positions prefer previous experience with women, with youths, or in residential settings.

Salary: Salaries range from approximately $30,000 to $55,000.

Other Information: Many positions, especially full-time positions with benefits, require a bachelor's degree and certification as an alcohol and drug counselor. Most positions require or prefer one to two years of work experience.

SOURCE: Community Psychiatric Clinic of Seattle, http://www.cpcwa.org/cnslgjob.htm; Loma Linda University Medical Center, Community Medical Center, and Children's Hospital, http://www.llu.edu/lluch/services; NationJob.com, http://www.nationjob.com.

(Application Case 14.3) demonstrates how the offense of transporting the controlled substance marijuana can be proven.

Cultivation of Marijuana

It is also a crime to cultivate or "dry" marijuana. Conviction of cultivating, drying, or processing marijuana is a felony punishable by a year or more in prison. In most states, in order to prove the crime of cultivating, drying, or processing marijuana, the prosecution must prove that the person:

- Knew plants were growing on his or her property.
- Knew the plants were cannabis.

A person cannot be sentenced for both cultivation and possession of the same plants. The prosecution must elect one crime or the other.

Drug Paraphernalia

The possession or sale of drug paraphernalia is another prevalent drug-related offense. **Drug paraphernalia** is defined as "any equipment, product or material of any kind that is primarily intended or designed for use . . . [in connection with] a controlled substances."[23] Examples of drug paraphernalia include bongs, pipes, rolling papers, scales, and hypodermic needles. Drug paraphernalia charges and convictions are most often obtained when the item or paraphernalia are seized at the same time that drugs such as marijuana or cocaine are seized. However, possessing drug paraphernalia is a crime without possession of the illegal substance itself.

In response to the spread of AIDS, some cities, such as Baltimore, have amended paraphernalia laws to accommodate needle exchange programs. Under these programs, hypodermic needles are provided to addicts in an attempt to prevent the spread of the disease through needle sharing by intravenous drug users.

drug paraphernalia
Any equipment, product, or material that is primarily intended or designed for use with a controlled substance, such as bongs, pipes, rolling papers, scales, and hypodermic needles.

Narcotics or Drug Addiction as a Defense

Narcotics addiction is the repeated or uncontrolled use of controlled substances. Although possession or use of controlled substances is a crime, being a drug addict is not. Addiction to drugs is a disease, which cannot be punished criminally under the cruel and unusual punishment clause of the Eighth Amendment to the U.S. Constitution, applicable to the states through the due process clause of the Fourteenth Amendment. This was the holding in the U.S. Supreme Court case of *Robinson v. California* (see Application Case 14.9).

⚖️ Application Case 14.9

Robinson v. California and United States v. Moore

In *Robinson v. California*, the defendant was convicted of being a drug addict in violation of a municipal ordinance of the City of Los Angeles. The Court overturned the Los Angeles ordinance, which made it a criminal offense for a person "to be addicted to the use of narcotics." It reversed the conviction, holding that a person cannot be punished criminally simply for having the status of drug addict. The Court noted that addiction is a "status" and not an "act," and that to punish an individual for mere status was to inflict cruel and unusual punishment in violation of the Eighth and Fourteenth Amendments.

However, the Court did emphasize that states were free to punish such criminal acts as the sale, purchase, or possession of narcotics. Thus, an addict can be convicted for possession of a controlled substance, and addiction to drugs is not a defense to the possessory offenses or delivery offenses. In *United States v. Moore*, the U.S. Court of Appeals affirmed a heroin addict's conviction for possession of heroin, noting that the "particular nature of the problem of the heroin traffic makes certain policies necessary that should not be weakened by the creation of this defense."

SOURCE: Robinson v. California, 370 U.S. 660 (1962); United States v. Moore, 486 F.2d 1139 (D.C. Cir. 1973).

⚖ CRITICAL THINKING 14.3

1. Why does possession with intent to deliver need more proof than mere possession?
2. How can police officers determine if people are drug loitering or just loitering?

14.4 Alcohol Legislation and Offenses

Alcohol was widely used in early America; indeed, the per capita consumption has been estimated at five times that of today.[24] Until the eighteenth century, there were no attempts to prohibit the manufacture, sale, or consumption of alcohol, although there were regulatory fines, excise taxes, and license fees.

Temperance and Prohibition

Toward the end of the eighteenth century, a temperance movement began to develop, and during the early nineteenth century, religious leaders such as Cotton Mather and John Wesley galvanized public opinion against alcohol. The first prohibition law in America went into effect in 1843 in the territory of Oregon (it was repealed five years later), and in 1846 Maine became the first state to enact a prohibition statute. By 1855, 12 other states had followed suit; by the end of the Civil War, however, 9 of these states had either repealed their laws or had them ruled unconstitutional. At the federal level, legislation continued to be regulatory in nature. In 1862, the federal government imposed a tax on liquor and beer of 20 cents per gallon. The tax increased to $2 per gallon by 1868, but was decreased to 50 cents per gallon in 1869.[25]

With the end of the Civil War, the temperance movement gained momentum, and women assumed a prominent role with the founding of the Women's Christian Temperance Union (WCTU) in 1874. The National Prohibition Party was formed in 1869 and fielded its first presidential candidate in 1872. The Anti-Saloon League, formed in 1893, joined its efforts to the prohibition movement. In the late nineteenth century, there was a second wave of state prohibition laws. In 1880, Kansas became the first state to incorporate prohibition into its constitution. By 1917, 13 states were totally dry, and another 13 had local option or other limited prohibition laws.[26]

With the entry of the United States into World War I, prohibitionists raised additional arguments that a ban on alcohol would stop the waste of grain and molasses and make workers more productive. In December 1917, Congress approved the Eighteenth Amendment, prohibiting the manufacture, sale, and transportation of alcohol. Eleven months later, the amendment was ratified, and in 1919 Congress passed the Volstead Act, which contained the enforcement procedures needed to implement prohibition.

Prohibition was in part a response to high levels of alcohol production and consumption and to social problems related to drinking and alcoholism. However, in practice, "enforcement proved to be a national scandal that gave rise to bootleggers and gang wars, police corruption, 'speakeasies,' and general disrespect for law and order."[27]

With the outbreak of the Great Depression, a movement to repeal the Eighteenth Amendment gained strength, and in 1933 Congress passed the Twenty-First Amendment, repealing prohibition. Congress also established the Federal Alcohol Control Administration (FACA) to regulate the alcoholic beverage industry.

Changing Views on Alcohol Use and Abuse

Today FACA is an agency of the Department of the Treasury, responsible for enforcing laws concerning liquor taxes and penalties for unauthorized commerce in alcohol.[28] In addition, many states have passed **dram shop laws**, which hold alcohol servers responsible for harm that intoxicated or underage patrons cause to other people.[29] In American culture during the twentieth century, the concept of alcoholism gradually changed to focus on treatment, based on the view that the fault is in the man, not the bottle, and that alcoholism afflicts individuals based on vulnerability—genetic, biochemical, psychological, or social/cultural.

A great number of arrests were made, however, for alcohol-related offenses. According to Bureau of Justice data for 2005, a total of 1,371,900 persons were

dram shop acts
Legislative acts that impose strict liability on the seller of intoxicating beverages when the sale results in harm to a third party's person, property, or means of support.

arrested for drunk driving, 556,200 were arrested for drunkenness, and 556,200 were arrested for other liquor law violations, adding up to more than 2 million arrests for violating laws regulating alcohol use.[30] Drug or alcohol treatment was a sentence condition for 41 percent of adults on probation, and 32 percent of adults on probation were subject to mandatory drug testing.

Alcohol is often associated with a wide range of criminal offenses. One of the most common is the offense of driving under the influence. Prior to 1980, drunk driving was seen not as a serious criminal problem, but as a behavior associated with drinking problems. In 1996, there were 17,126 alcohol-related traffic fatalities[31] and hundreds of thousands of injuries, raising awareness of the seriousness of drunk driving. As a result, federal and state legislatures have enacted laws with stiffer penalties.

Drunk Driving Offense (Driving under the Influence)

drunk driving

The offense of driving while drunk, known as DWI, DUI, DWAI, or DUBAL.

The offense of **drunk driving** is essentially the same in most states. Generally the offense is referred to as DWI (driving while intoxicated), DUI (driving under the influence, of alcohol or drugs), DWAI (driving while ability is impaired), or DUBAL (driving with an unlawful blood alcohol level). Some states distinguish between intoxication and impairment.

Intoxication

Under most state laws today, intoxication (or being under the influence) occurs when a person has ingested enough alcohol (or other drug) so that his or her physical and mental control is diminished or judgment and ability to operate a motor vehicle are adversely affected to some degree. Most U.S. states prohibit operating a motor vehicle with a specified level of alcohol in the person's system. Alternatively, a driver may be prohibited from driving while impaired. An example is the Michigan DWI law, which prohibits the operation of a motor vehicle by a person who is intoxicated, as determined by specified blood or urine alcohol content, or if the "person's ability to operate the motor vehicle is visibly impaired."[32]

BAC Levels

The BAC (blood alcohol content) level that determines when a driver is legally drunk is almost uniform across the country at .08 percent; a few states retain a 0.10 percent level. This uniformity resulted from Congress's conditioning receipt of federal funding assistance for local law enforcement on states' acceptance of a .08 percent BAC national standard. In addition, some states, such as Maine, have lowered the legal BAC level to .05 percent for drivers previously convicted of a DUI.

Finally, states have lowered the BAC specifically for drivers of commercial vehicles. For instance, the driver of a commercial vehicle in New York can be convicted of driving while intoxicated with a BAC of .04 percent.

Elements of a DUI Offense

The elements of the drunk driving offense are similar in every jurisdiction. Those elements are:

- The defendant operated a motor vehicle on a roadway within the jurisdiction of the court.

- The operation occurred while the defendant was under the influence of an intoxicant, narcotic, or hallucinogenic to the extent that his or her normal faculties were impaired; or
- The operation occurred while the defendant was driving with a blood or breath alcohol concentration above a prohibited level.

Operation, the first element of a DUI offense, is rarely at issue because operation is generally easy to establish. The arresting officer usually observes the operation. The arrest may have resulted from a sobriety checkpoint or an automobile accident that resulted in police intervention. In addition, the accused may have admitted operating the motor vehicle. Finally, a private citizen may have observed the incident and given consistent testimony.

DUI Traffic Stops

The arresting officer's observations of the erratic operation of the vehicle or the behavior of a driver will often lead to a stop for investigating DUI/DWI. These observations serve as evidence of being under the influence, the second element of a DUI/DWI offense. After the stop, the officer will take note of the physical appearance of the driver to determine whether he or she may be intoxicated. For example, bloodshot or watery eyes, the smell of alcohol, and slurred speech are indicative of being under the influence. In addition, during the investigation, the officer will ask the driver questions and observe the driver's demeanor.

If the officer is still suspicious, the officer will administer a series of field sobriety tests (FSTs). These consist of physical exercises, such as walking toe to heel and walking a straight line, and verbal exercises, such as counting backward. All of the officer's observations may confirm the officer's suspicion that the suspect is under the influence. This determination provides the constitutional foundation for a breath, blood, or urine test to determine the driver's BAC. The officer's right to demand that the suspect submit to such tests depends on a valid Fourth Amendment justification for the search and seizure related to the activity.

DUI Statutes

DUI/DWI statutes in most states provide that a driver who is arrested for driving under the influence must submit to a blood, breath, or urine test to determine the blood alcohol level. Most states base this provision on the theory that by obtaining the privilege of driving, the driver can be "deemed to have given consent" to a chemical test of the level of alcohol when arrested for DUI.[33] Every state has laws specifying penalties for refusal to submit to a forensic test that detects the presence of a controlled substance. These include a fine and imprisonment, if convicted of DUI, and automatic suspension of driving privileges for one year.[34]

Variation in State Laws

The states vary greatly with respect to the specific test that is required and whether to provide the accused with a choice of tests. Some states give an accused the right to refuse to take a test for alcohol. In many states, however, a jury can be told to draw a negative inference from a driver's refusal to be tested. Hence, if the driver refuses to submit to the test, he or she will be presumed to have been driving under the influence. (See Application Case 14.10.)

⚖️ Application Case 14.10

Schmerber v. California

In *Schmerber v. California* (1966), the defendant had been driving an automobile involved in an accident and was taken to the hospital for treatment of his injuries. A police officer arrested him while he was in the hospital and directed a physician to draw blood from the defendant to determine the level of alcohol in his blood. The evidence of the result of this blood test was admitted against Schmerber at his trial for DUI. He was convicted, but appealed to the Supreme Court of the United States, claiming that the drawing of blood without his permission violated his constitutional rights. Specifically, he argued that his right to due process, his privilege against self-incrimination, his right to counsel, and his right to be free from unreasonable search and seizure were all violated. The Court rejected all of these claims and affirmed Schmerber's conviction.

SOURCE: Schmerber v. California, 384 U.S. 757 (1966).

Intoxication and Alcoholism as Defenses

Alcohol and drugs have been linked to violent crimes, including murder, rape, robbery, and domestic violence. They also play a role in other criminal offenses such as child abuse and neglect cases. In criminal law, voluntary intoxication is no defense against crimes of general intent, but may operate to disprove the existence of *mens rea* necessary for crimes of specific intent.

For instance, an individual who is accused of larceny (a crime requiring specific intent) can use intoxication as a defense, arguing that intoxication rendered him or her unable to form the necessary intent. It should be noted, however, that although assault is a specific intent crime, intoxication may not be a defense to assault. Under the rationale that many assaults occur as a result of intoxication or drunkenness, some states have held that voluntary intoxication is not a defense to assault.

Since general intent crimes such as trespass do not require specific intent but can be committed recklessly or negligently, intoxication is not usually a defense to them. In addition, since *mens rea* is not an element of strict liability crimes, intoxication is not a defense to them. Hence, intoxication is not a defense to statutory rape or serving alcohol to a minor.

On the other hand, intoxication may be a mitigating factor reducing punishment for certain crimes. For instance, an individual accused of committing murder while intoxicated cannot be convicted of murder with premeditation and deliberation, because his or her ability to deliberate may have been negated by the intoxication. In such cases, the defendant's criminal responsibility is diminished, though not eliminated, and the punishment will correspondingly be less serious. Involuntary intoxication (e.g., being forced or tricked into ingesting an intoxicating substance) will render an actor's conduct involuntary and thereby allow him or her to avoid criminal liability.

There are several ways in which an alcoholic's intoxication might be relevant to his or her criminal liability. The state of voluntary intoxication might be offered to show that the alcoholic defendant was so drunk that he or she was physically incapable of the crime charged. It could also demonstrate an absence of voluntary conduct. Finally, it might negate the mental state required for the crime. This subject is discussed in more detail in Chapter 6.

The question of whether alcoholics may be punished for certain acts attributable to their disease is often discussed in terms of the constitutional prohibition against cruel and unusual punishment as it applies to the voluntary act requirement. The foremost case on this issue is *Robinson v. California* (Application Case 14.9), in which the Supreme Court held that a minimal requirement of some voluntary behavior was constitutionally necessary as a basis for criminal liability. *Robinson's* prohibition against prosecution for status crimes was soon extended to the prosecution of alcoholics (see Application Case 14.11).

⚖️ Application Case 14.11

Driver v. Hinnant

In *Driver* v. *Hinnant*, the defendant appealed his most recent of (at least) 200 convictions for public intoxication. The Fourth Circuit Court agreed that he was a chronic alcoholic and classified alcoholism as a disease. Relying on a liberal interpretation of *Robinson v. California*, the court held that it was constitutionally prevented from convicting the defendant for behavior that was "compulsive as symptomatic of the disease." The court stated that "[t]he alcoholic's presence in public is not his act for he did not will it."

SOURCE: Driver v. Hinnant, 356 F.2d 761, 763 (4th Cir. 1966).

Nevertheless, in 1968, in *Powell v. Texas,*[35] the U.S. Supreme Court refused to extend the holding of *Robinson* to public intoxication. The defendant, Powell, had been convicted of public intoxication. His attorneys, relying on the *Robinson* rationale, argued that Powell was afflicted with the disease of alcoholism, that his appearance in public while drunk was not of his own volition, and that to convict and punish him for that conduct would be cruel and unusual punishment in violation of the Eighth and Fourteenth Amendments. A majority of the justices assented to the proposition that irresistible conduct caused by a condition not in itself punishable could not constitutionally be subjected to criminal sanctions. However, only four of those justices believed that the defendant actually suffered from the disease of alcoholism to such a degree as to be incapable of controlling his conduct. Therefore, Powell's conviction was permitted to stand, and the impact of the *Robinson* decision has since remained limited.

Although alcoholics, like drug addicts, cannot be punished for their condition, they can legally be punished for appearing in public while they are in an intoxicated condition. Many local municipalities have ordinances prohibiting public drunkenness. However, as illustrated in *State ex rel. Harper v. Zegeer* (see Application Case 14.12), some states have opted to allow alcoholism as a defense to public intoxication charges under their own constitutions, despite the Supreme Court's decision in *Powell*.

⚖ Application Case 14.12

State ex rel. Harper v. Zegeer

An example of how the disease of alcoholism serves as a defense to the crime of public intoxication is illustrated by the case of *State ex rel. Harper v. Zegeer*. The defendant was arrested and incarcerated for public intoxication. He petitioned by *habeas corpus* to test the constitutionality of jailing chronic alcoholics who are intoxicated in public.

The Supreme Court of Appeals of West Virginia held that criminal punishment of chronic alcoholics for public intoxication violated the state constitutional prohibition against cruel and unusual punishment. The court in *Harper* agreed with medical experts and professional groups, including the World Health Organization, that alcoholism is a disease. The court reasoned that on the evidence presented, the defendant was no more able to make a free choice as to when or how much he would drink than a person would be who is forced to drink under threat of physical violence.

The *Harper* court specifically opposed two prevalent schools of thought that have been endorsed by other courts to uphold the convictions of alcoholics for public intoxication:

1. That drinking is a voluntary act.
2. That if alcoholism is allowed to be a defense to public intoxication charges, it might become a defense to other crimes.

The *Harper* court ruled that to hold that alcoholics can control their drinking and appearances in public contradicts all recognized medical evidence about alcoholics' overwhelming compulsion to drink. Further, alcoholism is only a defense to those acts that are compulsive and symptomatic of the disease, so the rationale that it will extend as a defense to other crimes is unfounded.

SOURCE: State *ex rel.* Harper v. Zegeer, 296 S.E.2d 873 (W. Va. 1982).

⚖ CRITICAL THINKING 14.4

1. What are some legal actions that can be taken against a drunk driver?

2. When can alcohol be used as a defense? When is it not an acceptable defense?

REVIEW AND APPLICATIONS

Summary by Chapter Objectives

1. **Identify the five major categories of controlled substances.** Classifications of controlled substances ordinarily fall into the following five categories:
   - Narcotics: opiates such as heroin, morphine, and cocaine, and non-opiate synthetics such as Demerol and methadone.
   - Stimulants: cocaine, amphetamine, methamphetamine, and others.
   - Depressants: barbiturates and tranquilizers.
   - Cannabis: marijuana and hashish.
   - Hallucinogens: includes LSD, mescaline, and peyote.

2. **State the purposes and effect of the Uniform Controlled Substances Act.** The Uniform Act was drafted to achieve uniformity between the drug laws of the several states and those of the federal government. It forbids the manufacture, delivery, possession, storage, or sale of controlled substances. It has five schedules of controlled substances, graded according to their potential for abuse, relative physical danger to the abuser, and degree of accepted medical use.

3. **Recognize and describe the difference between actual and constructive possession of a controlled substance.** Actual possession is when the controlled substance is on the defendant's person, or within an area of his or her immediate control and reach. It may also occur when the controlled substance is within a container that the defendant is carrying or has within his or her reach. Constructive possession occurs when illegal drugs are in a place immediately accessible to the accused and are subject to his or her domination and control.

4. **State the difference between the offense of possession and the offense of possession with intent to deliver.** In contrast to crimes of mere possession of controlled substances, possession with intent to deliver is treated as a felony under both federal and state statutes. Because of the stiffer penalties imposed for possession with intent to deliver, many states forbid the inference of intent to deliver based on mere possession of controlled substances. Convictions for possession with the intent to deliver are highly fact-specific and require substantial corroborating evidence in addition to the mere fact of possession.

5. **Define the drug offenses of delivery, drug conspiracy, drug loitering, and possession of drug paraphernalia.** Delivery of controlled substances is defined as the voluntary transfer of a controlled substance from one person to another. Drug loitering crimes require some action be taken in public that manifests the intent to engage in illegal drug activity. Possession of drug paraphernalia is the possession of any equipment, product, or material that is primarily intended or designed for use with a controlled substance. Drug conspiracies are agreements between two or more persons that form a shared intent to manufacture and/or distribute drugs.

6. **Understand when drug addiction is and is not a defense to drug offenses.**
Drug addiction is a defense only against prosecution for the offense of being a drug user. An addict can be convicted for possession of a controlled substance, and addiction to the drug is not a defense to the possessory offenses or delivery offenses.

7. **State the elements of driving under the influence.** The elements of DUI are:

   • Operation of a motor vehicle on a public roadway.
   • Such operation occurs while the driver is under the influence of any alcoholic beverage or drug.

8. **Define the extent to which alcoholism can be a defense in a criminal case.**
Voluntary intoxication is not a defense against crimes of general intent, but may operate to disprove the existence of *mens rea* for crimes of specific intent. Involuntary intoxication will render an actor's conduct involuntary and thereby allow him or her to avoid criminal liability.

Key Terms

controlled substance (p. 368)
psychoactive drugs (p. 368)
actual possession (p. 376)
constructive possession (p. 376)
possession with intent to deliver
   (p. 380)
delivery of a controlled substance
   (p. 382)

simulated controlled substance (p. 382)
drug conspiracy (p. 383)
drug loitering (p. 383)
drug transportation (p. 384)
drug paraphernalia (p. 385)
dram shop acts (p. 387)
drunk driving (p. 388)

Review Questions

1. Explain the differences between marijuana and hallucinogens.
2. Explain the U.S. Supreme Court's findings on the use of peyote in traditional Native American religious ceremonies.
3. Outline the history and outcome of the "War on Drugs."
4. What does the Uniform Controlled Substances Act forbid? Give at least five examples.
5. What is a simulated controlled substance? Is possession of this a crime?
6. What elements are required to convict a person of cultivating marijuana?
7. Define drug paraphernalia, and provide three examples.
8. What is narcotics addiction? Is it legal or illegal? What constitutional amendment is relevant to this discussion, and why?
9. What procedures does an officer use after pulling over a suspect whom he or she believes is driving drunk?
10. What are dram shop acts?

Problem-Solving Exercises

1. **Possession and Intent to Sell** Because of the stiffer felony penalties imposed for possession with the intent to sell versus mere possession, many states forbid prosecutors from assuming that there is an intent to sell based on the defendant's mere possession of a controlled substance. If a suspected drug dealer is arrested with nine baggies of marijuana in his possession, a marijuana pipe, a bag of marijuana seeds, but only $20 in cash on his person, what are the chances that he could be charged with possession with the intent to sell? Why?

2. **Drug Loitering** A police officer on patrol comes upon a group of six youths one night. They are gathered on a corner in a high-crime area known for its drug dealing and gang activities. The officer observes the youths for about 10 minutes and sees a number of other persons approach the group, seeming to engage in some transactions involving the exchange of money for something in bags. Describe what other evidence, if any, the officer would need in order to arrest the youths for drug loitering.

3. **Probation and DUI** A defendant who is on probation for a drug-related offense is required to refrain from drug use during his probationary period. He is required to submit to a urine test once a month to determine whether he has used drugs within the last 30 days. During a casual conversation, prior to the test, the defendant tells his probation officer that he drove his car to the probation office. The test reveals traces of a controlled substance in the defendant's bloodstream. Upon questioning by the probation officer, the defendant admits to having used crack cocaine a few hours prior to the visit.
   a. Should the defendant be charged with violating his probation? Why or why not?
   b. Should he be charged with driving under the influence? Why or why not?

Workplace Applications

1. **Peyote in Religious Ceremonies** As a state parole officer, you staunchly support your state's drug control laws. Any parolees on your caseload that test positive for any controlled dangerous substance are promptly taken into custody and set for a parole revocation hearing. Harold Running Bull, a Native American, has recently been assigned to you. His first urine sample tests positive for the presence of the hallucinogen peyote. You call the authorities and have Running Bull arrested when he reports to your office. As the police are taking him away, Running Bull shouts that he only uses peyote as part of his religious ceremonies. Answer the following questions:
   a. Do you investigate this claim? Why or why not?
   b. Do you ask the police to release him until you investigate the claim? Why or why not?
   c. Do you remain silent and let the police take him away? Why or why not?
   d. What are the ramifications if his assertions are correct?

2. **Pregnancy and Addiction** You are a nurse working at a county hospital, and in recent years you have noticed a surge in babies born with drug addictions, especially crack cocaine addiction. Your hospital is considering taking legal

action against women who deliver babies born with drug or alcohol addiction, as well as the host of neurological and physical disorders that most addicted babies have. Answer the following questions:

a. Should a pregnant woman who smokes crack cocaine hours before giving birth be charged with delivery of narcotics to a newborn baby via the umbilical cord?

b. Does the fact that the drug was taken five hours before birth constitute delivery if the mother could not predict the time of birth precisely enough to know that the drug would be delivered to the child?

c. What other drug charges and child abuse charges could be used in such instances? What about any other charges?

d. To what authorities could you report these crimes?

3. **Drug Transportation** You are a U.S. customs agent. During a routine search of a passenger's luggage, you recover a quantity of cocaine inside a small sealed package. The passenger tells the agent that the cocaine is not his. You have heard this before, but the passenger is adamant that he is as shocked as you are and has never seen the package before in his life.

a. Should the passenger be arrested immediately? What questions could you ask first?

b. What issues may arise if the passenger was doing someone a favor by taking the package to a relative or friend?

Ethics Exercises

1. **Probation and Drugs** You are a county probation officer who believes that only the most serious offenders belong in prison or jail. You are particularly disturbed by the fact that more and more people on your caseload are on probation for drug offenses. Although you personally believe that marijuana is a harmless recreational drug, you know that it continues to be outlawed in your state and can bring substantial terms in the county jail. One day, a probationer reports to your office. Up until now, he has been a model probationer; he is employed and has paid all of his fines. Today, however, he has very bloodshot eyes and smells like marijuana. One of the conditions of his probation is that he refrain from all illegal activity. It is at your discretion whether or not to request a urine sample from him. If he tests positive, he can be sent to jail. If you fail to report your observations about his physical appearance when he arrived at your office, you can be fired. The probationer reveals to you that he "may have smoked a little 'something'" because he was depressed about the death of this mother. He begs you not to ask for a urine sample because he has only one month remaining on probation.

a. What are your options at this time? What should you do?

b. How can you show him that you are serious about his committing no more offenses?

c. Assume that his statement about the death of his mother seems genuine, and that you as a probation officer have a strong intuitive sense about when people are lying to you. Does this drug use seem as though it will be a growing problem, or that it will end here?

2. **Medical Marijuana** You are a doctor who lives in a state where medical marijuana has been made legal, but a recent Supreme Court decision has declared your state's measure invalid. Nonetheless, the practice of prescribing medical marijuana has continued in your state as if nothing has happened. Several of your terminally ill patients are asking you to continue to prescribe it because it relieves their pain.
   a. What decision will you make, and why?
   b. What are the legal repercussions when people continue to follow a state measure that has been declared invalid at the federal level?

Notes

1. STEDMAN'S MEDICAL DICTIONARY 1475 (27th ed. 2000).
2. Gonzales v. Raich, 545 U.S. 1 (2005).
3. STEVEN B. DUKE & ALBERT C. GROSS, AMERICA'S LONGEST WAR: RETHINKING OUR TRAGIC CRUSADE AGAINST DRUGS 15–16 (1993).
4. THE DRUG LEGALIZATION DEBATE 3 (James A. Inciardi ed., 1999).
5. *Id.*
6. DANIEL K. BENJAMIN & ROGER LeRoY MILLER, UNDOING DRUGS: BEYOND LEGALIZATION 254 (1991).
7. *Id.* at 255–56. In 1903, the Coca-Cola Company began using caffeine as the main ingredient in its product.
8. THE DRUG LEGALIZATION DEBATE 3 (James A. Inciardi ed., 1999).
9. DANIEL K. BENJAMIN & ROGER LeRoY MILLER, UNDOING DRUGS: BEYOND LEGALIZATION 93–94 (1991), citing Webb v. United States, 249 U.S. 96 (1919).
10. THE DRUG LEGALIZATION DEBATE 4 (James A. Inciardi ed., 1999).
11. UNIF. CONTROLLED SUBSTANCES ACT, 9 Pt. II U.L.A. 1 (1997).
12. Pub. L. No. 99-570, 100 Stat. 3207 (1986) (codified in part as amended in 21 U.S.C. § 841 *et seq.* (2000)).
13. Bureau of Justice data, http://www.ojp.usdoj.gov/bjs/dcf/enforce.htm.
14. Bureau of Justice data and statistics are available at http://www.ojp.usdoj.gov/bjs; the latest drug use statistics are available at http://www.ojp.usdoj.gov/bjs/dcf/du.htm.
15. THE DRUG LEGALIZATION DEBATE 16 (James A. Inciardi ed., 1999).
16. For a discussion of prosecution and sentencing disparity, *see* Steven J. Chanenson, *Booker on Crack: Sentencing's Latest Gordian Knot*, 15 CORNELL J. L. & PUB. POL'Y 551 (2006).
17. Erich Goode, *Thinking About the Drug Policy Debate, in* THE DRUG LEGALIZATION DEBATE 111, 112–13 (James A. Inciardi ed., 1999).
18. THE DRUG LEGALIZATION DEBATE 6–7 (James A. Inciardi ed., 1999).
19. *Id.;* John T. Bannon, Jr., *The Legality of the Religious Use of Peyote by the Native American Church: A Commentary on the Free Exercise, Equal Protection, and Establishment Issues Raised by the Peyote Way Church of God Case*, 22 AM. INDIAN L. REV. 475, 476 (1998).
20. Employment Division, Department of Human Resources of Oregon v. Smith, 494 U.S. 872 (1990).

21. *See* Autumn Gray, *Effects of the American Indian Religious Freedom Act Amendment on Criminal Law: Will Peyotism Eat Away at the Controlled Substances Act?*, 22 Am. J. Crim. L. 769 (1995).
22. *See* People v. Aguilar, 35 Cal. Rptr. 516, 519 (Cal. Dist. Ct. App. 1964).
23. 21 U.S.C. § 863(d) (2000).
24. Daniel K. Benjamin & Roger LeRoy Miller, Undoing Drugs: Beyond Legalization 195 n.5 (1991).
25. Schaffer Library of Drug Policy, http://www.druglibrary.org/schaffer/library/studies/nc/nc2a.htm.
26. John D. Buenker, *Prohibition and the Volstead Act, in* Handbook of American Women's History 451–52 (Angela M. Howard & Frances M. Kavenik eds., 2d ed. 2000).
27. *Id.* at 452.
28. Shaffer Library of Drug Policy, http://www.druglibrary.org/schaffer/library/studies/nc/nc2a_6.htm.
29. Black's Law Dictionary 531 (8th ed. 2004).
30. Bureau of Justice data: http://www.ojp.usdoj.gov/bjs/dcf/enforce.htm.
31. Bureau of Justice data: http://www.ojp.usdoj.gov/bjs/pub/ascii/ac.txt.
32. Mich. Comp. Laws § 257.625(1) (West 2008).
33. *See, e.g.*, People v. Selby, 608 N.E.2d 961, 963 (Ill. App. Ct. 1993), relying upon what is now 625 Ill. Comp. Stat. 5/11-501.1 (1999).
34. *See, e.g.*, Cal. Veh. Code § 23612(D) (West 2007).
35. Powell v. Texas, 392 U.S. 514, 517 (1968).

Crimes against the Administration of Justice

CHAPTER OBJECTIVES

After reading and studying this chapter, you should be able to:

1. Recognize the difference between the offenses of bribery and commercial bribery.

2. Define the elements of perjury.

3. Understand the offense of obstruction of justice and recognize the scope of crimes it covers.

4. Describe the crime of resisting arrest.

5. Recognize the offense of compounding a felony, and explain why it is different from the offense of misprision of a felony.

6. Define the elements of the crime of escape.

7. Recognize when constructive contempt takes place and how it differs from direct contempt.

8. Differentiate between the offenses and penalties for civil contempt and criminal contempt.

15.1 Obstruction of Justice

This chapter covers two different types of offenses: (1) offenses that are committed by citizens who try to disrupt the legal system; and (2) offenses that are committed by those in positions of authority, such as government officials and law enforcement officers, who injure citizens by abusing their power. These offenses, also called crimes against the administration of justice, can be defined as any offenses that hinder or prevent the effective operation of the criminal justice system, such as law enforcement, the civil and criminal court systems, and the corrections system.

At common law, the crimes of bribery, perjury, resisting arrest, and contempt of court were all recognized as offenses that threatened the administration of justice. Today, however, many of these crimes have been combined into the single crime of obstruction of justice. **Obstruction of justice** is the act by which one or more persons attempt to or actually prevent the execution of a lawful process. Crimes under this modern definition include:

obstruction of justice
The act by which one or more persons attempt to or actually prevent the execution of a lawful process.

- Bribery and the attempt or conspiracy to commit bribery or extortion. An example of bribery would be paying off a police officer so as not to be arrested. An example of extortion would be threatening to accuse someone of a crime or to file criminal charges unless money is paid.
- Perjury, false testimony, and interfering with a law enforcement officer in the performance of his or her official duties. An example of this would be lying under oath.
- Tampering with the jury process, such as by threatening jurors, attempting to harm jurors, or actually causing harm to them or to their families.
- Suppressing or refusing to produce evidence relevant to a grand jury investigation, such as by destroying papers or other evidence after receiving notice of such an investigation.

These crimes require a particular form of intent. The intent element of an obstruction of justice offense is referred to as the *nexus requirement*. The term *nexus* means a link or relationship; in legal terms, it means that a defendant's obstruction of justice must have a relationship with the legal proceedings against him or her in order to show intent. In other words, the act must have an effect of interfering with the due administration of justice.[1]

⚖ CRITICAL THINKING 15.1

1. Which do you think are more serious, crimes committed by citizens who try to disrupt the legal system or crimes committed by those in positions of authority? Why?

15.2 Bribery

Common Law Bribery

For the past 700 years in England and later in the United States, extortion was the most common public offense, but in recent years bribery prosecutions have become more prevalent. There is some overlap between the nature of the two offenses, for the principles that underlie extortion are similar to those of bribery.[2] At common law, as we saw in Chapter 11, *bribery* was voluntarily giving or receiving anything of value as unlawful payment for the commission of an official act. In other words, if a private citizen who will be a defendant in an upcoming trial pays a prosecutor something of value, both are guilty of bribery.

According to the first English bribery statute in 1384, judges may not take "robe, fee, pension, girt, nor reward of any but the King, except reward of meat and drink, which shall be no great value."[3] Later, when the founders of the United States wrote the U.S. Constitution, they determined that bribery, along with treason, constituted serious grounds for the impeachment of a president or any civil officer of the United States.

Modern Bribery

Bribery today exists in many forms. In general, the exploitation of public power for personal gain defines the modern concept of bribery. Modern statues have extended the crime of bribery to include both the party who offers the bribe and the party who receives it. For example, a prosecutor could commit bribery by receiving compensation in return for not filing or pressing charges, and the defendant who paid the bribe would also be guilty.

Modern statutes are balanced to fulfill their aim of controlling undue influence while avoiding a "chilling" or deterring effect on the right of private citizens to properly influence government action. An ideal bribery statute must distinguish between acts of undue influence, which constitute bribery, and appropriate acts that are intended to legally influence governmental action. (See Application Case 15.1.) In short, as the Supreme Court has stated, bribery laws should "deal with only the most blatant and specific attempts of those with money to influence governmental action."[4]

⚖️ Application Case 15.1

Florida v. Saad

In *Florida v. Saad* (1983), the defendant attempted to deliver $1,000 each to two police officers to secure the return of $20,700 in cash, which had been taken from him in the course of a prior arrest. The defendant was charged with bribery. The trial judge granted a motion to dismiss the bribery charges on the grounds that the initial seizure had been unlawful and that the defendant was entitled to his $20,700 money in any case. An appeals court reversed this decision and found that the defendant was still guilty of bribery for unlawfully offering money to the police officers, regardless of whether he was entitled to have his money returned to him. The court stated, "In our system at least, the end does not justify the means. The effectuation of Saad's intent to get his money by short-circuiting and subverting that system may, and must, be held accountable to the criminal law."

SOURCE: Florida v. Saad, 429 So. 2d 757 (Fla. Dist. Ct. App. 1983).

Some states have extended the crime of bribery to include people other than public officials whose functions are nonetheless considered important to the public welfare. This offense is known as **quasi-bribery** because although it has the same essential effect as standard bribery, its recipients are private citizens. Officers of political conventions, officers or employees of public institutions, and representatives of labor organizations are considered positions important to the public that could be unduly influenced by quasi-bribery.

Under modern law, bribery forbids not just the result of influencing a public official, but also the act itself, whether the attempt to bribe is successful or not. In addition, the MPC forbids:

- Law enforcement and public officials to receive gifts from individuals subject to their jurisdiction.
- A public servant who has the authority and discretion over contracts or transactions to accept or solicit gifts from any person "known to be interested or likely to become interested" in such contract or transaction.[5]

Under the MPC, it is also forbidden to accept or agree to accept a gift from an individual in one's custody as a prisoner.

Sometimes bribery overlaps considerably with extortion. To compel or induce a person to provide a bribe by instilling fear that criminal charges will be filed against that individual is larceny by extortion.[6] In other words, threatening a person into paying someone to avoid criminal charges is always a crime.

On the other hand, should the law prevent individuals from entering into voluntary private agreements to avoid criminal prosecution when no threats or coercive actions are made? Suppose that Tom assaults Paul, and then offers Paul money not to file charges against him. Should the law prevent this type of agreement? There are two things to consider before answering this question. On one hand, recall what you learned in Chapter 3, that while the person assaulted is a victim, criminal prosecutions are brought on behalf of the people of the state. Hence, the decision whether to prosecute or not belongs to the prosecutor, not to the complainant.

On the other hand, an agreement by which a plaintiff or victim agrees to *drop charges*, whether criminal or civil, in exchange for money does not constitute receiving a bribe. This is because the plaintiff of a civil suit and the victim of a crime are not government officials with special responsibilities to their trials. In addition, they are not being asked to lie, alter their testimony, or avoid appearing at an action or proceeding, all of which are criminal actions that are generally *not* considered the same as the act of dropping charges. A plaintiff in a civil suit need not consult a prosecutor because civil suits are actions between private parties. A victim of a crime cannot determine whether or not a prosecutor files charges, but his or her unwillingness to help in the prosecution can create enough of a deterrent to the prosecutor that charges will not be filed.

Commercial Bribery

Commercial bribery is a statutory expansion of the crime of bribery. The types of bribery that you have just learned about pertain to officials and private citizens who can influence official action in a way that gives the briber better treatment than he or she deserves. In contrast, **commercial bribery** entails the giving, receiving, or soliciting of anything of value to influence an employee or professional in the performance of his or her duties. The purpose is usually to influence the employee to breach his or her duty to the employer in order to give some undeserved or inappropriate benefit or information to the briber. This crime often occurs when business is conducted through agents. Unlike the principal in an agreement, an agent may have no direct interest or benefit in the contract and may be tempted to transact side deals for payments known as *kickbacks*. In large commercial cities such as New York, one out of every seven dollars exchanging hands involves or hints of commercial bribery.[7]

commercial bribery
The giving, receiving, or soliciting of anything of value to influence an employee or professional in the performance of his or her duties.

The following Alaska statute is an example of a commercial bribery statute:

> A person commits the crime of commercial bribery if, knowing that another is subject to a duty described in AS 11.46.660(a) and with intent to influence the other to violate that duty, the person confers, offers to confer, or agrees to confer a benefit on the other.
>
> A person commits the crime of commercial bribe receiving if the person solicits, accepts, or agrees to accept a benefit with intent to violate a duty to which that person is subject as:
>
> - an agent or employee of another;
> - a trustee, guardian, or other fiduciary;
> - a lawyer, physician, accountant, appraiser, or other professional advisor;
> - an officer, director, partner, manager, or other participant in the direction of the affairs of an organization, or;
> - an arbitrator or other purportedly disinterested adjudicator or referee.[8]

There is a distinction in the business community between legal favors and bribery. Most businesses today will give campaign contributions, gratuities, and entertainment of some sort to an entity with the hope of receiving favorable treatment. This practice is acceptable. However, it becomes bribery when there is an agreement between the payer and the recipient that there will be a *quid pro quo* payoff; in other words, "contributions" become bribery when the briber expects "something for something."

A number of states have created statutes to address various problems connected with commercial bribery.[9] In addition, courts today examine acts of commercial bribery under the Sherman Act to determine whether commercial bribery may be a combination, a conspiracy, or another illegal action in restraint of trade.[10] To have a *combination* or *conspiracy*, which you learned about in Chapter 12, there must be an agreement between two or more independent companies in a bribery scheme.[11] Such a conspiracy negatively affects free trade if the briber creates a monopoly through payoffs.[12]

Many contracts have some semblance of this practice, but the companies who engage in it are rarely prosecuted. Therefore, this practice occurs often and usually goes undetected. Courts will, however, impose liability if this unfair trade practice creates an unreasonable restraint on competition.

CRITICAL THINKING 15.2

1. What are some ways in which bribery is different from quasi-bribery?
2. Should commercial bribery carry different penalties than regular bribery or quasi-bribery? Why or why not?

15.3 Perjury

perjury
Making false statements under oath or affirmation.

Perjury is the criminal offense of making false statements under oath or affirmation. Under common law, perjury was considered a willfully corrupt sworn statement that was:

- Made without sincere belief in its truth.
- Made in a judicial proceeding regarding a *material* (important or substantive) matter.

Common law perjury had to be proven by the testimony of two witnesses. The two-witness rule has largely been abandoned under modern law; most courts now require only one witness plus independent corroboration, such as documents or other evidence that proves that the statement made was false. This helps prevent the problem of lying witnesses and being forced to decide solely on the basis of one person's word against another's.

Proof of the element of intent in a perjury case requires proof that the witness believes that his or her given testimony is false. Juries are instructed to apply the objective standard to determine the witness's intent to commit perjury, then ask themselves, "Would a reasonable person believe that the witness believed that his or her testimony was false?" The prosecution carries the burden of proving this falsity beyond a reasonable doubt.

false swearing
The giving of a false oath during a proceeding or matter in which an oath is required by law.

At common law, if a false statement did not take place in a judicial proceeding, it was considered a **false swearing**, which was only a misdemeanor. Modern statutes in some jurisdictions have broadened the offense of perjury so that a false swearing or statement made in *any* legal setting is perjury, even if it is not material and even though it is not presented in a judicial proceeding. Most jurisdictions, however, require that the matter be material. *Materiality* is a major aspect of perjury, and the concept rests on whether a witness's false testimony has a natural effect or tendency to influence, impede, or dissuade a jury from making the correct decision.

As a typical example of a modern statute, the federal perjury statute states:

Whoever:

- having taken an oath before a competent tribunal, officer, or person, in any case in which a law of the United States authorizes an oath to be administered, that he will testify, declare, depose, or certify truly, or that any written testimony, declaration, or certificate by him subscribed, is true, willfully and contrary to such oath states or subscribes any material matter which he does not believe to be true; or
- in any declaration, certificate, verification, or statement under penalty of perjury as permitted under section 1746 of title 28, USC, willfully subscribes as true any material matter which he does not believe to be true.[13]

Compare this with the MPC's definition of the felony of perjury. Under the MPC, a person commits perjury "if in any official proceeding he makes a false statement under oath or equivalent affirmation, or swears or affirms the truth of a statement previously made, when the statement is material and he does not believe it to be true."[14] Hence, an essential element of perjury is the belief in the accused's mind that the statement is false. Again, the statement must be material.

subornation of perjury
The crime of procuring another person to make a false oath.

Subornation of perjury is the crime of procuring another person to make a false oath. At common law, anyone who procured the making of false statements or intentionally caused another to commit perjury could be charged with subornation of perjury. Proof of guilt required that the perjurer be convicted of perjury as well as the actor charged with subornation of perjury. It also required that the perjurer knew or should have known that his or her actions would be considered perjury.[15]

Proof of subornation of perjury requires three elements:

1. Perjury in fact.
2. The perjured statements were procured by the accused.
3. Proof that the suborner, the person who procures the perjury, knew or should have known that such oaths or testimony would be false.

For example, federal law states: "Whoever procures another to commit any perjury is guilty of perjury, and shall be fined not more than $2,000 or imprisoned not more than five years, or both."[16] Hence, not only will an accused be held liable for his or her knowingly false statement. If the accused causes another to make false statements under oath, he or she can be guilty of a distinct and separate crime of subornation of perjury.

Under the MPC, it is a crime to make a false report to law enforcement with the purpose of implicating another. Under the Code, a person commits a misdemeanor if the person gives information about a crime to a law enforcement officer when he or she knows the crime did not occur, or pretends to provide genuine information relating to a crime, which, in reality, he or she knows is false. [17] (See Application Case 15.2.)

⚖️ Application Case 15.2

People v. Sharpe

In *People v. Sharpe* (1950), the defendant was convicted of perjury, conspiracy to commit perjury, and subornation of perjury. His criminal cohort Charles Barrett was convicted of subornation of perjury and conspiracy to commit perjury. The defendants were charged based on testimony given by Sharpe and one William Gould before a grand jury. This testimony, which was false, stated that a local probation officer solicited and accepted bribes from Sharpe. The subornation of perjury charges against both defendants was based on the fact that they procured Gould to give false testimony. On appeal, the defendants argued that their convictions should have been reversed because the special prosecutor allegedly committed misconduct. They also argued that the trial court erred by sentencing them to consecutive rather than concurrent terms for the crimes of conspiracy to commit perjury and subornation of perjury.

The court of appeals found that even if the special prosecutor's actions rose to the level of misconduct, there was still substantial evidence to support the judgment against the appellants. The court also found that there was no merit to the appellants' contention that the trial court erred by sentencing them to consecutive rather than concurrent terms for their crimes. The convictions were affirmed.

SOURCE: People v. Sharpe, 96 Cal. App. 2d 943 (1950).

---

1. Why do you think that the laws regarding false swearing have changed since common law?
2. What elements are required for subornation of perjury?

15.4 Obstruction of Justice

Obstruction of justice, as mentioned earlier, is the act by which one or more persons attempt to prevent, or actually prevent, the execution of lawful process. As you have learned, the intent element is referred to as the *nexus* requirement. This means that the act that is considered to obstruct justice must have some relationship to the act of justice that the defendant is seeking to avoid.

An example of obstruction of justice occurs when an individual attempts to prevent a law enforcement officer from arresting someone, whether that person is a relative, a friend, or even a total stranger. Suppose that Renata pushes or physically gets in the way of a police officer who is attempting to handcuff her friend Jerome, who has committed a crime and is about to be placed under arrest. Since the officer is attempting to carry out his official duty by making an arrest, and since Renata is attempting to prevent him from doing so, Renata has committed the crime of obstruction of justice.

It should be noted, however, that if Jerome were resisting arrest, Jerome would not be charged with obstructing justice. This is because under the MPC, the obstruction of justice does not apply to those resisting arrest or fleeing from a crime.[18] This may seem like a contradiction: If a person is resisting arrest, isn't it logical to say that he or she is preventing an officer from carrying out official duties? The answer to that question will come later in this chapter, in the discussion of the crime of resisting arrest.

Other types of obstruction of justice include:

- Attempting to influence, intimidate, or impede any juror, witness, or officer in any court regarding the discharge of his or her duty.
- The actual impeding or obstructing of the due administration of justice.

When a statute addressing this subject encompasses more than interference with police officers and other such administrative officials, it is sometimes called *obstruction of governmental administration* or *obstructing governmental operations*.

Witness Tampering

witness tampering
Illegal conduct with the intent to influence witness testimony, such as by approaching a potential witness with threats or other means to prevent the witness from testifying.

Laws that define obstruction of justice include provisions for illegal conduct with the intent to influence witness testimony, a crime that is commonly called **witness tampering**. Some of these laws were designed to address actions by organized criminals, who are known for attempting to intimidate witnesses or otherwise influence the outcome of trials and prosecutions.

An example of such a law is the Victim and Witness Protection Act, which Congress enacted in 1982. This act addresses a variety of problems faced by victims and witnesses, including harassment and threats from defendants or former criminal associates. Prior to the act, victims and witnesses received minimal governmental protection. Because prosecutors realized how necessary victims and witnesses are to the successful prosecution of felons, Congress acted to provide more thorough protection. The Victim and Witness Protection Act now provides protection that lasts through the duration of the judicial proceedings.

To prove witness tampering charges, the government has the burden of proving that the defendant knowingly engaged in intimidation, physical force, threats, misleading conduct, or corrupt persuasion with the intent to influence, delay, or prevent testimony or cause any person to withhold a record, object, or document from an official proceeding.[19] Although typical witness tampering cases involve approaching a potential witness with threats or other means in an attempt

Federal Victim and Witness Protection Witness protection programs allow prosecutors considerable leverage in obtaining helpful witnesses, especially in organized crime cases. Here, Sammy "The Bull" Gravano prepares to testify against his former boss, mobster John Gotti.

to prevent the witness from testifying, a defendant who attempts to frustrate a government plan to infiltrate his or her operation can also face witness tampering charges (see *United States v. Baldyga*, Application Case 15.3).

⚖ Application Case 15.3

United States v. Baldyga

In the case of *United States v. Baldyga* (2000), the defendant was convicted of several charges: (1) multiple counts of possession of cocaine with the intent to distribute, (2) distribution of cocaine, and (3) witness tampering. During an investigation of the defendant, the DEA arranged for a cooperating witness who had purchased drugs from the defendant in the past to purchase cocaine from the defendant. During the transaction, the cooperating witness wore a wiretap device so that the DEA agents could safely monitor him.

Although the three previous sales were successful, this one was not. When the witness attempted to make the fourth sale, the defendant gave the witness a note instructing him to remain quiet and to put his hands on the wall. The witness testified that when he finished reading the note, the defendant was standing in front of him pointing a "gold-colored double gun at his face." The defendant searched the witness, discovered the listening device on his person, disabled it, and told him to leave the premises. The officers who had been monitoring the transaction approached the premises when the listening device went dead, and the defendant was arrested as he was attempting to flee the area.

The defendant appealed his conviction on the basis that his actions in confronting the witness were insufficient to support the charge of witness tampering. In affirming the defendant's conviction, the court held that although the defendant did not explicitly threaten to harm the witness, the jury could have reasonably inferred beyond a reasonable doubt that the defendant's brandishing a gun and holding it to the head of the witness was an intent to deter the witness from discussing the cocaine deals with the federal authorities.

In addition, the court held that the jury could have concluded that the defendant was aware of the witness's cooperating with federal agents when the defendant stated to the witness that the defendant heard that the witness would be wearing a wire and proceeded to search for it. Moreover, the jury could have further concluded that the defendant's act of ripping the wire away from the transmitter was intended to prevent or discourage the witness's cooperation with the federal agents. Hence, the defendant's actions of disconnecting the listening device satisfied the requirements under the statute because "the possibility existed that such communication would occur with the federal officials, especially in light of his prior communications with the officers."

SOURCE: United States v. Baldyga, 233 F.3d 674 (1st Cir. 2000). *See also* 18 U.S.C. § 1512(b)(3).

The reasoning in *United States v. Baldyga* indicated the court's intent to broadly apply and even extend the statute on witness tampering. The court held the statute to include circumstances that might be interpreted as actions taken by the defendant to prevent and frustrate undercover operations. Clearly, the court used this broad application as a warning to others who might consider the same tactics as used by the defendant in *Baldyga*.

Suppressing Evidence

suppressing evidence
A crime that occurs when a defendant, or a person working on behalf of the defendant, suppresses (hides), destroys, or refuses to produce evidence relevant to a grand jury investigation.

Suppressing evidence occurs when a defendant, or a person working on behalf of the defendant, suppresses (hides), destroys, or refuses to produce evidence relevant to a grand jury investigation. Federal law states that a defendant, in order to be convicted of obstruction of justice for the concealment of subpoenaed documents in a federal proceeding, must:

- Have knowledge of the pending grand jury investigation. Therefore, concealing or changing documentation after receiving notification of a pending grand jury investigation is a violation of this law.
- Know that particular documents are covered by a subpoena.
- Willfully conceal or endeavor to conceal them from a grand jury.[20]

An example of this occurred in the case of *United States v. Brooks*, in which the Fourth Circuit Court upheld a conviction for obstruction of justice where testimony indicated that subpoenaed corporate minutes had been altered after the date of subpoena, and some original minutes remained missing.[21]

1. Should the federal witness tampering statute apply only to witnesses who are *not* involved in undercover operations? Should it apply only to classic cases of intimidating or threatening witnesses?

2. What are some ways that evidence can be suppressed? Among the participants in a trial, who seems most likely to suppress evidence?

15.5 Resisting Arrest

An old saying holds that "Freedom is a man's natural power of doing what he pleases, so far as he is not prevented by force or law." One way that the law can restrict a person's freedom is through arrest, and resisting arrest is considered a crime. At common law, the offense of **resisting arrest** involved physical efforts to oppose a lawful arrest. It amounted to a trespass against the police officer that was similar to battery. The reasoning was that when an officer has a legal right to arrest or restrain a private citizen, that citizen "can have no right to resist since the two rights cannot coexist."[22] Therefore, those who resisted lawful arrests could not claim self-defense, because the officer's right to arrest them superceded their right to resist.

Since an officer at common law was not authorized to make an arrest without a warrant for a misdemeanor not committed in his presence, a defendant who killed an officer who did not have the right to arrest him or her (and was thus making an unlawful arrest) could claim the lack of a warrant as a partial defense. The result was that the offense would be reduced from murder to manslaughter.

A question that arises today, and that has not been answered in the same way by current laws throughout the United States, is how an individual should be allowed to react if he or she believes that an arrest is unlawful. Is such an individual allowed to resist an unlawful arrest?

Some laws forbid resisting arrest in any circumstances. The MPC and statutes in a number of states specify that an individual does not *ever* have the right to use force in resisting a law enforcement officer who is making an arrest. For example, California's Penal Code states: "If a person has knowledge, or by the exercise of reasonable care should have knowledge, that he is being arrested by a peace officer, it is the duty of such person to refrain from using force or any weapon to resist such arrest."[23]

resisting arrest
Physical efforts to oppose a lawful arrest.

15.1 Web Exploration

LawInfo.com

Read "Resisting Arrest" on LawInfo.com at http://www.legalmatch.com/law-library/article/resisting-an-unlawful-arrest.html. What is their general advice about resisting arrest, and why?

As another example, in the case of *People v. Volition*, a court affirmed the defendant's conviction of resisting arrest even though it found that the officers had engaged in an unlawful seizure. The court stated that a defendant could not use physical force to resist an arrest by a police officer, whether "authorized or unauthorized . . . when it reasonably appeared that the individual is a police officer."[24] Thus, even if the underlying charge or seizure is deemed illegal, if the defendant knowingly resists an arrest by a police officer, he is still guilty of resisting arrest. In addition, a few statutes specify that an individual may not resist an arrest even if the arrest is unlawful.

At common law and in those states that still follow the common law rule, however, force is allowed to prevent an unlawful arrest. In such a case, a suspect may use only a reasonable amount of force to ward off the arresting official. (See Application Case 15.4.) Since law enforcement personnel are rarely authorized to use deadly physical force to arrest a suspect, self-defense would prohibit an individual from the use of deadly physical force to resist an arrest. Police response to an individual's actions is supposed to be proportionate to the action. Officers are guided by a use of force continuum that sets the appropriate level of force when directly responding to an individual's behavior. Police perception of, and attitude toward, different groups and communities in society may affect their response and result in a disproportionate and excessive use of force. A famous example of excessive use of force can be found in the case of Rodney King. When King refused to comply with police orders to remain face down on the ground, LAPD officers struck him repeatedly with their batons.

⚖️ Application Case 15.4
United States v. John Bad Elk

One of the earliest cases regarding the common law right to resist an unlawful arrest was *United States v. John Bad Elk* (1900). Law enforcement officers attempted to arrest the defendant without a warrant and without an official charge being filed against him. It was alleged that the defendant, who was also a police officer, fired his gun in the air and refused to accompany the officers when requested. He then advised them that he would go to the police department the next morning. After some more disagreements, the defendant shot and killed one of the police officers when the officer made a move as if reaching for his gun.

The defendant was convicted of murder. At trial and on appeal, the defendant argued that since the officers were not justified in arresting him, he had the right to use such force as a reasonable, prudent person might use in resisting the arrest. The appellate court agreed with the defendant that it was the lower court's error to instruct the jury that the officer had a right to arrest the defendant and the defendant had no right to resist the unlawful arrest. In fact, the jury should have been instructed that the defendant had the right to use such force as was absolutely necessary to resist an attempted illegal arrest.

The appellate court held that the officer had no right to arrest the defendant without a warrant, but also stated that the defendant had no right to unnecessarily injure or kill his assailant. In the end, the court remanded the case for the correct instructions to be given the jury and to consider whether the defendant's actions were reasonable under the circumstances.

SOURCE: United States v. John Bad Elk, 177 U.S. 529 (1900).

There are two main reasons for this ongoing disagreement regarding resisting unlawful arrests:

1. The accused rarely knows at the time of the arrest whether it is lawful or not.
2. The unlawfully arrested individual has other recourses or remedies post-arrest, including civil remedies for wrongful arrest.

Citizens who fear unlawful arrests should know that unlawful arrests can and do have effects upon both the civil and criminal justice system. Individuals who are wrongfully arrested can sue for damages in a civil court. In a criminal matter, an illegal seizure or unlawful arrest will result in the suppression of any evidence recovered in connection with such unlawful arrest. In other words, if officers find evidence during an unlawful arrest, that evidence cannot be admitted at trial no matter how valuable it may be to the prosecution. This rule exists to prevent police officers from benefiting in any way from illegal searches and seizures that are in violation of the individual's constitutional rights.[25]

 CRITICAL THINKING 15.5

1. Should individuals have the right to resist unlawful arrest? Why or why not?

15.6 Compounding and Misprision of a Felony

Compounding a felony is an offense that occurs when someone refuses to report or prosecute a felony in exchange for a benefit or reward of some value. As a result, the defendant escapes conviction and punishment, which may cause greater harm to society. Public policy has always favored prosecuting all violations, and therefore a single individual should not have the sole right to overlook the harm done to society as a whole. In addition, when a felon is not held accountable for the crime, he or she is not deterred from engaging in further criminal conduct. Rather, one could argue that he or she is encouraged by the prosecution's failure to take action.

The essence of the crime of compounding a felony is the making of the unlawful agreement that causes one to decline prosecution. The MPC gives the following example regarding compounding a crime:

> A person commits a misdemeanor if he accepts or agrees to accept any pecuniary benefit in consideration of refraining from reporting to law enforcement authorities the commission or suspected commission of any offense or information relating to an offense. It is an affirmative defense to prosecution under this Section that the pecuniary benefit did not exceed an amount which the actor believed to be due as restitution or indemnification for harm caused by the offense.[26]

compounding a felony
An offense that occurs when someone refuses to report or prosecute a felony in exchange for a benefit or reward of some value.

For example, Patty's car is stolen. In exchange for not reporting the crime, Patty accepts a cash payment from Carol, the mother of the person who stole the car, because Carol knows that her son is a habitual criminal, and she is afraid that he will go to prison again. Ordinarily, Patty's acceptance of money as part of an agreement not to report a felony would automatically be considered a crime. Under the MPC, however, she may have a defense: If she accepted a sum equal to the value of the car, this money can be considered restitution for the stolen vehicle. If she took a much larger sum than the amount at which the car could reasonably be valued, though, restitution would not be a valid defense.

misprision of a felony

The act of failing to report or prosecute a known felony and taking positive steps to conceal the crime.

Compounding a crime differs from the offense of misprision of a felony. **Misprision of a felony** refers to the act of failing to report or prosecute a known felony and taking positive steps to conceal the crime. The offense is defined under federal law as follows: "Whoever, having knowledge of the actual commission of a felony cognizable by a court of the United States, conceals and does not as soon as possible make known the same to some judge or other person or military authority under the United States, shall be fined under this title or imprisoned not more than three years, or both."[27]

The example of Carol, the mother of the felon, can be used again here. If Carol failed to report the crimes of her son with which she was familiar, and took steps to conceal that they had occurred, such as by paying hush money to victims in exchange for not reporting the crime, she would be guilty of misprision of a felony.

CRITICAL THINKING 15.6

1. Why is misprision of a felony considered a more serious crime than compounding a felony? Do you agree that it should be?

2. Should society be more concerned about felonies and insist that all felonies be prosecuted, rather than prosecuting misdemeanors?

15.7 Escape

escape

A crime that occurs when a person who is lawfully detained or imprisoned leaves custody before he or she is entitled to freedom by due process of law.

Escape occurs when a person who is lawfully detained or imprisoned leaves custody before he or she is entitled to freedom by due process of law. A person is guilty of this crime if, without lawful authority, he or she commits one of the following acts:

- Removes or attempts to leave official detention.
- Fails to return to official detention following a temporarily granted leave.

The crime of escape covers individuals who escape while in the custody of a police officer, a jail or lockup, or any type of correctional facility. For instance, an accused who is officially under arrest and escapes from the holding cell of a local police station has committed the crime of escape.

Before a conviction for escape can be sustained, the prosecution must first prove that the person was actually under arrest. If the arrest was not completed, such as due to resistance, the accused is not guilty of the crime of escape. An accused who flees just as he or she is about to be arrested or placed in handcuffs has not escaped within the meaning of the statute.

Escape from Prison Escape from prison is a serious offense and can add years to a person's sentence.

One important exception to the elements that form the crime of escape can be found in cases that have interpreted escape statutes to exclude inmates who escape custody as the result of reasonable fears for their safety while incarcerated. (See Application Case 15.5.) Generally, though, court decisions that have precluded convictions for escape in these types of situations have required the escapees to turn themselves in to authorities within a reasonable time after the escape.

⚖ Application Case 15.5

People v. Trujillo

In *People v. Trujillo* (1978), the defendant claimed that he escaped from prison because he had been previously gang-raped by six inmates and was again being threatened by inmates who demanded sexual favors. He claimed that he reported the attack to prison officials, but nothing was done to protect his safety. At trial, the judge excluded all evidence pertaining to the gang rape, and the defendant was convicted. On appeal, the conviction was reversed on the grounds that the defendant should have been allowed to introduce the evidence in support of his defense. Thus, the courts have recognized that an accused may be justified in escaping a correctional facility when he or she reasonably fears for his or her physical safety.

SOURCE: People v. Trujillo, 585 P.2d 235 (Colo. App. 1978).

 CRITICAL THINKING 15.7

1. Under what circumstances are escape statutes interpreted to exclude certain inmates? Do you agree with this? Why or why not?

15.8 Contempt of Court

contempt of court

Any affirmative act or omission that obstructs justice or attempts to negate the dignity and authority of the court.

Contempt of court is any affirmative act or omission that obstructs justice or attempts to negate the dignity and authority of the court. Courts may cite or issue summonses to individuals for contempt and civil disobedience of court orders, disruption of court proceedings, and other affronts to the courts' dignity and authority.[28] Contempt is generally divided into four categories: direct contempt, constructive or indirect contempt, criminal contempt, and civil contempt.

direct contempt

A criminal form of contempt of court that occurs in the presence of the court when a person resists the court's authority.

Direct contempt occurs in the presence of the court when a person resists the court's authority. Such contempt is criminal in nature. One example of direct contempt is the use of profane language toward an officer of the court. A criminal trial would be unnecessary in this case, because the judge would usually be a witness to the contemptuous behavior. In cases of direct contempt, the court has the option to impose a fine or imprisonment for a specified period of time.

As with any crime, if the potential punishment for contempt is six months or more, the defendant is entitled to a jury trial. In *Bloom v. Illinois*, the Supreme Court found:

> Serious contempts of court are so nearly like other serious crimes that they are subject to the jury trial provisions of the Constitution. We accept the judgment of our earlier cases that criminal contempt is a petty offense unless the punishment makes it a serious one; but, in our view, dispensing with the jury in the trial of contempt subjected to severe punishment represents an unacceptable construction of the Constitution.

The Court went on to find that because the defendant was given a relatively severe sentence of two years in prison, he was entitled to a jury trial.[29]

constructive contempt

Contempt of court that results from matters outside the court, such as failure to comply with court orders.

Constructive contempt, also known as *indirect contempt*, results from matters outside the court. An example of constructive contempt would be the failure to comply with a judicial order. In such a case, the judicial officer who issued the order will be called upon to enforce it against a disobedient party. This type of contempt does not present the same issues as does direct contempt because it does not attempt to openly disrupt or interfere with court proceedings as they occur.

15.1 On the Job

Judge

Description and Duties: Apply the law to citizens and companies within one's jurisdiction. Oversee legal processes in courts of law. Sentence convicted criminals. Manage courtroom staff and budget. Interact with other judges, lawyers, defendants, victims, police officers, and court staff. Interact with the public, including people from different cultures.

Salary: Federal judges earn approximately $97,000 to $145,000. State judges earn approximately $63,000 to $122,000.

Other Information: Most judges were previously employed as lawyers. Contrary to popular belief, however, a law degree is not required to hold some lower court judgeships in 40 states. Judges can work relatively long hours, and about one-third of all judges work 50 hours per week.

According to David Carruthers, Chief District Court Judge, "Laws and social policies are changing all the time, and society's perceptions of things are always changing. These changes tend to work themselves out in the legal system. So being a judge is stimulating and challenging, and the challenges you face change as society does."

SOURCE: http://www.kiwicareers.govt.nz/default.aspx?id0=1050103&id1=J11510&id2=5FAFC011-4A63-4557-AB2C-5F589B40F320.

15.2 Web Exploration

Contemptuous?

An individual can be held in contempt of court even if his or her act was not intended to obstruct the orderly administration of justice. If your cell phone rings while court is in session, can the judge hold you held in criminal contempt of court? To learn more about instances involving criminal contempt, visit http://www.commercialappeal.com/news/2008/apr/03/lawyer-held-in-criminal-contempt.

Constructive contempt may be either civil or criminal. **Criminal contempt** is an act of disrespect toward the court or its procedures, other than direct contempt, that obstructs the administration of justice. The penalty for criminal contempt is intended as punishment, and is usually a fine or imprisonment for a specified period of time. Again, if post-conviction contempt proceedings impose sentences exceeding an aggregate of six months, a trial by jury is required. **Civil contempt** consists of the failure to do something ordered by the court for the benefit of another party to the proceedings. The penalty for civil contempt is usually payment of a fine or imprisonment for an indefinite period of time until the party in contempt agrees to perform his or her legal obligation.

criminal contempt
An act of disrespect toward the court or its procedures, other than direct contempt, that obstructs the administration of justice.

civil contempt
The failure to do something ordered by the court for the benefit of another party to the proceedings.

CRITICAL THINKING 15.8

1. Can constructive contempt be as harmful as direct contempt in some circumstances? Why or why not?

REVIEW AND APPLICATIONS

Summary by Chapter Objectives

1. **Recognize the difference between the offenses of bribery and commercial bribery.** Bribery is the voluntary giving of something of value to influence performance or official duty; its essential elements are offering a gift, with the purpose to influence, and the official status of the recipient. Commercial bribery is a breach of duty by an employee, in which he or she accepts secret compensation from a nonemployee and in return gives the briber information or rewards that he or she does not deserve.

2. **Define the elements of perjury.** The three key elements of perjury are:
   - Making false statements.
   - Under oath or affirmation.
   - In a legal setting.

3. **Define the offense of obstruction of justice and recognize the scope of crimes it covers.** Obstruction of justice can be generally defined as interference with law enforcement officials or the civil and criminal courts. It includes the crimes of bribery, perjury, subornation of perjury, witness tampering, suppression of evidence, and contempt.

4. **Describe the crime of resisting arrest.** Resisting arrest is the offense of using physical efforts to resist a lawful arrest. Although the common law and states that still follow the common law rule permit an individual to resist an unlawful arrest, some state statutes do not allow an individual to resist an arrest even if it is unlawful.

5. **Recognize the offense of compounding a felony, and explain why it is different from the offense of misprision of a felony.** Compounding a felony is an offense that occurs when someone refuses to report or prosecute a felony in exchange for a benefit or reward of some value. As a result, the defendant escapes conviction and punishment, which may cause greater harm to society. Misprision of a felony refers to the act of failing to report or prosecute a known felony and taking positive steps to conceal the crime. It does not involve the exchange of a benefit or reward.

6. **Define the elements of the crime of escape.** Escape occurs when a person who is lawfully detained or imprisoned leaves custody before he or she is entitled to freedom by due process of law. A person is guilty of this crime if, without lawful authority, he or she commits one of the following acts:
   - Removes or attempts to leave official detention.
   - Fails to return to official detention following a temporarily granted leave.

7. **Recognize when constructive contempt takes place and how it differs from direct contempt.** Constructive contempt, also called indirect contempt, takes place outside of the courtroom. It results from matters concerning the court, such as a failure to comply with judicial orders. This type of contempt does not present the same issues as direct contempt because it does not attempt to openly disrupt or interfere with court proceedings as they occur.

8. **Differentiate between the offenses and penalties for civil contempt and criminal contempt.** The penalty for civil contempt is usually imprisonment for an indefinite period of time, until the party in contempt agrees to perform his or her legal obligation, or a fine. The penalty for criminal contempt is imprisonment for a specified period of time that is intended to punish, or a fine.

Key Terms

obstruction of justice (p. 400)
quasi-bribery (p. 402)
commercial bribery (p. 403)
perjury (p. 404)
false swearing (p. 404)
subornation of perjury (p. 404)
witness tampering (p. 406)
suppressing evidence (p. 408)
resisting arrest (p. 409)

compounding a felony (p. 411)
misprision of a felony (p. 412)
escape (p. 412)
contempt of court (p. 414)
direct contempt (p. 414)
constructive contempt (p. 414)
criminal contempt (p. 415)
civil contempt (p. 415)

Review Questions

1. What are the elements of the offense of bribery?
2. What is quasi-bribery, and how does it differ from regular bribery? Give an example.
3. What is subornation of perjury, and how are the defendant and the perjurer punished for it?
4. In what situations does the obstruction of governmental administration occur?
5. What is witness tampering, and what are two examples of it?
6. What are the ways in which evidence can be suppressed?
7. What are the laws regarding resisting lawful arrests? What about unlawful arrests?
8. In what situations may the crime of escape occur? In what situations, discussed in your text, is it deemed to have not occurred or excused by the courts?
9. When and where can direct contempt take place?
10. Identify and analyze the difference between the offenses of criminal contempt and civil contempt.

Problem-Solving Exercises

1. **Police Perjury** A police officer arrives at the scene of a report of an assault and observes a woman crying with a bruised eye and a bloody nose. She tells the

officer that her boyfriend beat her up. The officer asks the boyfriend, who is present, if he assaulted the woman. The boyfriend refuses to answer, but there is blood on his hand and nobody else in the apartment. At the trial, during the police officer's testimony, he is asked by the prosecutor, "Did you see who assaulted the woman?" The police officer replies, "Yes, it was her boyfriend," and points to the defendant. Answer the following questions:

a. Is this perjury? Why or why not?

b. In a situation such as this, where guilt can be proven circumstantially, does it matter if perjury is committed? Why or why not?

c. In a situation such as this, where guilt can be proven circumstantially, are there any unnecessary risks in making the type of statement that the officer did? Why or why not?

2. **Compounding a Felony** You are a police investigator. During a routine investigation of burglaries in the neighborhood, you learn that Clyde, a 32-year-old who still lives at home, burglarized his neighbor's home. Clyde's father, Darrell, offers the neighbor $10,000 to replace the property stolen by Clyde, which the neighbor accepts because it is considerably more than what the property was worth. Darrell then says to the neighbor, "I hope this is the end of it and that you're not going to the police." Answer the following questions:

a. What crime, if any, has Darrell committed?

b. If there were no physical threats made to the neighbor, has Darrell committed a crime?

c. Is it illegal for the neighbor to accept the money and not report the burglary to the police?

d. What if the neighbor tells Darrell that he wants $20,000 for his "trouble and inconvenience," and that if he does not receive it, he is going to the police?

3. **Witness Tampering** You are prosecuting a defendant who stole a diamond ring worth $250,000. Your key witness overheard the defendant on the telephone, stating how and when he stole the ring. The defendant knows that this witness overheard his statement and says to his lawyer, "I am going to mess him up if he testifies that I stole the ring." The defendant then telephones the witness and says, "How are the wife and kids? I hope we all survive this mess."

a. Is this a form of witness tampering? Why or why not?

b. What factors influenced your decision?

Workplace Applications

1. **Resisting Arrest** During an abortion protest, the police officer orders Teresa and her friends to refrain from blocking the entrance of the clinic. Teresa and her friends refuse to leave and sit on the steps in front of the entrance. The officer decides to place Teresa under arrest. Answer the following questions:

a. Is Teresa resisting arrest if she remains sitting and refuses to move at all, forcing the officer to lift and carry her away from the demonstration?

b. Is Teresa resisting arrest if she hooks her clothing or body around a stair rail in such a way that the officer has more difficulty in pulling her away?

c. What if the police officer is in plain clothes and does not identify himself as a police officer?

2. **Perjury** A prosecutor charged Hosea with committing perjury when he denied giving Steve $1,000 on February 2, 2001. In fact, Hosea gave Steve $1,000 on February 3, 2001. Answer the following questions:

a. Has Hosea committed perjury? Should Hosea's statement be considered truthful or false?

b. Does it make a difference what day the money was given?

c. Should Hosea be required to voluntarily give the correct date?

3. **Resisting Arrest versus Escape** You recently arrested a suspect who committed an assault in your presence. As you drove the suspect to the precinct, he somehow managed to open the back door of the squad car and run. You chased and apprehend him a few blocks away.

a. Should the defendant be charged with resisting arrest or escape? (You must first determine whether the accused escaped while under arrest.)

b. Does it make a difference that the accused was immediately apprehended a few blocks away and that he escaped from a police vehicle and not a holding cell?

Ethics Exercises

1. **Bribery** You work for your county's sheriff's department, and your primary duties are at the county jail. Today you are processing new inmates who have just been brought in and are awaiting their initial appearance before the judge. Just before you go off duty, the last inmate that you process offers you two free tickets to a basketball game that evening. He says that since he obviously has no use for them, you can have them instead. Answer the following questions:

a. Should you refuse or accept the tickets? Why or why not?

b. Should you accept the tickets but offer to pay for them? Why or why not?

c. What if you accept the tickets, pay for them, and explain that you cannot give him any favors or preferential treatment in return?

Notes

1. Nancy M. Ro, *Obstruction of Justice*, 36 AM. CRIM. L. REV. 929 (1999).

2. Extortion consists of two types: extortion by threats or fear (i.e., coercive extortion or blackmail) and extortion under the color of office. If public officials are involved or the threats are of physical violence, the term *extortion* is commonly used, rather than *blackmail*. In the past, extortion under the color of office was defined as the seeking or receipt of a corrupt payment by a public official or someone pretending to be one.

3. 8 Rich 2, c. 3 (1384) (Eng.) (repealed by the Statute Law Revision Act, 1881, 44 & 45 Vict., c. 59 (Eng.) (based on 18 Edw. 3, stat. 4 (1344) (Eng.) (oath of justices)); *see also* Royal Proclamation of Oct. 20, 1258, 3 ENG. HIST. DOC. 369 (H. Rothwell ed., 1975).

4. Buckley v. Valeo, 424 U.S. 1, 28 (1976).

5. Model Penal Code § 240.5 cmt. 1–2 (1985).

6. N.Y. Penal Law § 155.05 (2)(e)(iv) (McKinney 1998).

7. August Bequai, White Collar Crime: A 20th Century Crisis 42 (1978).

8. Alaska Stat. § 11.46.660 & § 11.46.670 (1998).

9. An example of statutes that have made commercial bribery a crime is N.Y. Penal Law §§ 180.00–180.08 (McKinney 1998). Federal statutes have also made commercial bribery a crime in certain instances, *e.g.*, 18 U.S.C. § 215 (2000), bribery of bank employees; 27 U.S.C. § 205(c) (2000), commercial bribery in the alcoholic beverage industry. *See also* United States v. Beckley, 259 F. Supp. 567 (N.D. Ga. 1986): bribing an employee of a telephone company to allow uncharged use of long-distance service may violate the wire fraud statute.

10. 15 U.S.C. §§ 1–7 (2000). "Commercial bribery is an agreement or combination that has the effect of increasing prices and depriving consumers of the advantages of free competition." Section 1 of the Sherman Act was designed to prohibit this practice. *See also* Franklin A. Gevurtz, *Commercial Bribery and the Sherman Act: The Case for Per Se Illegality*, 42 U. Miami L. Rev. 365–66 (1997).

11. Continental Ore Co. v. Union Carbide & Carbon Corp., 370 U.S. 690, 702 (1962) (holding that evidence was sufficient for a jury to decide whether parties violated the Sherman Act by conspiring to monopolize commerce in certain ore products); *see also* United States v. Sisal Sales Corp, 274 U.S. 268, 276 (1927) (holding that parties in a combination violated the Sherman Act by monopolizing the local and foreign sisal commerce).

12. Bribery can destroy competition and have a ripple effect, once it affects consumer pricing in the market, on services provided by the non-bribing party, which then cannot participate in free competition.

13. 18 U.S.C. § 1621 (2000).

14. Model Penal Code § 241.1 (1) (1985).

15. United States v. Standifer, 40 M.J. 440 (C.M.A. 1994) (discussing the elements of the crime of subornation of perjury under the UCMJ and quoting the *Manual for Courts-Martial*, United States (1984)).

16. 18 U.S.C. § 1622 (2000).

17. Model Penal Code § 241.5 (1)–(2)(a)(b) (1985).

18. Model Penal Code § 242.1 (1985).

19. 18 U.S.C. § 1512(b) (2000).

20. 18 U.S.C. § 1503 (2000).

21. United States v. Brooks, 111 F.3d 365, 373 (4th Cir. 1997).

22. State v. Van Wormer, 173 P. 1076, 1080 (Kan. 1918).

23. Cal. Penal Code § 834(a) (West 2007).

24. People v. Volition, 630 N.E.2d 641 (N.Y. 1994).

25. *See* Wong Sun v. United States, 371 U.S. 471 (1963), a landmark case pertaining to the exclusionary rule, or the "fruit of the poisonous tree" doctrine. The U.S. Supreme Court held that an unlawful arrest predicated upon mistakes made by non-law enforcement officials will not suppress the evidence in court.

26. Model Penal Code § 242.5 (1985).

27. 18 U.S.C. § 4 (2000).

28. Margit Livingston, *Disobedience and Contempt*, 75 Wash. L. Rev. 345 (2000).

29. Bloom v. Illinois, 391 U.S. 194 (1968).

Organized Crime, Gangs, and Terrorism

CHAPTER OBJECTIVES

After reading and studying this chapter, you should be able to:

1. Understand the historical development of organized crime.
2. List some typical organized crime activities.
3. List the elements of a RICO violation.
4. Understand and differentiate various laws aimed at targeting organized crime.
5. Understand the structure and activities of modern street gangs.
6. Explain the laws that target street gangs.
7. Understand the types of criminal activity that constitute terrorism.
8. Describe the various laws that target terrorism.

CHAPTER OUTLINE

16.1 Organized Crime
  Historical Development
  Elements and Participants of Organized Crime
  Typical Organized Crime Activities
  Laws That Target Organized Crime

16.2 Street Gangs
  The Structure of a Modern Street Gang
  Crimes Committed by Gangs
  Identifying Gang Organizations
  Laws That Target Gangs

16.3 Terrorism
  Terrorism Distinguished from Other Crimes
  Laws That Target Terrorism

16.1 Organized Crime

Most people base their understanding of organized crime on movie and television images that glamorize the Mafia lifestyle and create an illusion. This illusion is that organized crime is an exciting and somehow honorable way of life, in which the only people who get hurt are the ruthless gangsters who choose to be in the Mafia. In reality, organized crime syndicates such as the Mafia have murdered countless innocent people, have brought an endless supply of drugs into the United States, and have terrorized many innocent people who are forced to live among these organizations.

Another common illusion is that only persons of Italian descent, or Mafia members, are involved in organized crime. Again, the reality is very different. The idea of a Mafia usually brings to mind the Italian Mafia, but almost every ethnic group in America contains organized crime syndicates. There is a Russian Mafia, a Chinese Mafia, a Jewish Mafia, and countless other ethnically distinct criminal organizations. Organized crime includes drug gangs from Latin America and the Caribbean, Chinese Tongs, and street gangs of various ethnic backgrounds. These crime syndicates pursue a multitude of criminal activities, including but not limited to drug trafficking, gambling, extortion, prostitution, pornography, and fraud.[1] In other words, organized crime is a highly dangerous crime problem that creates and contributes to numerous social problems.

organized crime

Individuals who associate together for the purpose of engaging in criminal activity on a sustained basis, with an emphasis on the life of the organization.

Historical Development

Organized crime consists of individuals who associate together for the purpose of engaging in criminal activity for a sustained period of time, with an emphasis on the life of the organization. It has existed in the United States for centuries. In addition, there is a direct correlation between (1) the development of laws that criminalize a particular type of organized criminal behavior or activity and (2) the expansion of criminal enterprises.

The earliest example of this is the *lottery*. During the eighteenth and nineteenth centuries, lotteries were quite popular and, as in many states today, completely legal. States used lotteries to raise revenue for public expenditures. For example, one lottery was used to raise more than a million dollars to help fund the Revolutionary War.

Over time, though, the public grew concerned that hardworking men were losing their wages because of lotteries and were left unable to provide for their families. By 1878, lotteries were illegal in most states. At this time, a syndicate of New York gamblers began to keep alive the Louisiana lottery by selling its lottery tickets by mail. From then until the end of the nineteenth century, many legal battles were fought over lotteries in the United States. Finally, in *Champion v. Ames* (1903),

The Mafia Myth The Mafia lifestyle is presented in film as a glamorous lifestyle dominated by persons of Italian descent.

also known at the *Lottery Case*, the U.S. Supreme Court upheld Congress's power to ban lotteries under the commerce clause.[2] This case attempted to disable the organized criminals who were keeping lotteries alive illegally.

The early 1900s, however, saw the creation of many crime organizations throughout the country, many of which became very powerful and grew significantly in numbers. For example, this period marked the beginning of the Italian Mafia. The reason for this growth was the criminalization of drugs and then alcohol. Rather than eradicating existing drug problems, criminalization actually created a demand for an illegal drug trade. For example, when drugs such as morphine and opium grew in popularity during this period and many people became addicted, Congress reacted by banning the importation of opium. In 1914, Congress acted further with the Harrison Narcotics Act, which limited the lawful trade of specified narcotics such as morphine to physicians and druggists. The effect of these prohibitions was disastrous: Opium and morphine use and addiction continued as always, and criminals found an easy market in which to ply their trade.

The criminalization of drugs, however, did not help organized crime nearly as much as the prohibition of alcohol. Although it may seem hard to believe now, for decades during the late nineteenth and early twentieth century the United States had a strong *temperance*, or anti-alcohol, movement. This movement's ultimate goal was to completely outlaw the brewing, distilling, selling, and use of alcohol anywhere in the country. In 1919, this goal was achieved with the passage of the Eighteenth Amendment to the U.S. Constitution and the Volstead Act.[3] Overnight, the legitimate brewing and distilling industry became illegal. The demand for alcoholic beverages, however, continued as before, and those willing to break the law in order to provide the public with drugs and alcohol prospered. Rather than curbing the American desire for alcohol, the era of Prohibition allowed organized crime to create hugely profitable enterprises in *bootlegging*, the manufacture and sale of illegal alcohol.

Additionally, the need to drink and use drugs in secret locations known as speakeasies, where people could enjoy alcohol and entertainment, created a growing number of other illicit enterprises. Because of the secret nature of speakeasies, gambling and prostitution businesses flourished for many criminal organizations. Although the era of Prohibition ended in 1933, organized crime did not. It merely found other criminal ventures to pursue, and continued to grow and prosper throughout the country.

Elements and Participants of Organized Crime

Individuals in organized crime engage in *enterprise crime*, which usually consists of providing illegal goods and services such as drugs and prostitution. The more sophisticated groups have several different levels throughout their organization, and each is distinguished by different amounts of power and control. Most of these organizations use violence and corruption to facilitate their economic activities and have a dangerous reputation within their community, where others are aware of their capability of committing violence.[4]

Typical Structure

A classic example of organized crime, which illustrates the elements and partici-pants of a typical organized crime group, would be as follows: In a neighborhood in

St. Louis, Missouri, a criminal organization makes money through cocaine distribution and illegal gambling. Everyone who works for the organization must vow to protect the group at all costs, putting the group's interests before one's own. When a member hears about a profit opportunity, he or she must go to his or her supervisor and report it so that the organization can decide whether to pursue the activity.

The organization consists of three different groups:

1. Mike, the boss, and his underboss Julio.
2. About 10 men and women who work directly below those two and oversee the street operations of the group. Among this group are two of Julio's brothers, one of Mike's brothers, and Mike's girlfriend Keisha. They report to Mike and, at times, Julio.
3. About 40 young men and women who work on the streets distributing the cocaine. They report directly to the 10 men and women above them.

When the group is faced with the threat of competition, everyone is encouraged to do whatever it takes to protect the group's members and territory, including murdering the competitors. Everyone in the neighborhood knows about the group, and also knows never to get anyone in the organization upset because they will risk being beaten or killed.

As you can see from the basic structure shown above, a very important aspect of an organized crime syndicate is the hierarchy, or many-leveled structure, that characterizes these organizations. Each member has a role to play within the group, each member works for a particular person, and each follows the instructions of that person in carrying out criminal activities. In this way, the organized crime structure can be compared to any type of legitimate business or organization. For example, consider a typical police department. Beat officers report to an immediate supervisor such as a sergeant for instructions or guidance, but do not usually go directly to their chief of police. In the same way, police detectives usually go to the head of detectives for their supervision. The same structure applies within organized crime groups.

The Boss and Underboss

At the very top of the crime organization is the **boss**. This person is the head of the crime "family," but usually does not involve himself in the day-to-day operations of the group. Only certain people are considered qualified to be bosses. Depending on the person's family, ethnic group, prior history with the group, and commitment to the group, a boss may be selected years before the current boss has died or stepped down. In some cases, a current boss's son may be chosen to succeed him when he dies.

Below the boss is the **underboss**. The underboss is the second in command and is usually the person being groomed to be the next boss. Below the underboss is a group of middle managers and supervisors, sometimes referred to as **captains and soldiers**. These people are usually responsible for overseeing the day-to-day operations of the organization.[5]

Crews and Other Members

Most organized crime groups consist of **crews**—men and women who perform the lower, street-level work by carrying out the actual operations of the group. Crew

boss
The head or leader of an organized crime family. Usually, this person does not involve himself in the day-to-day operations of the group but is the ultimate decision maker.

underboss
The second in command of an organized crime family, who is usually the person being groomed to take over for the boss in the event of his death or possible incarceration.

captains and soldiers
A group of middle managers and supervisors below the underboss of an organized crime family.

crews
The men and women in an organized crime organization who work out on the street carrying out the actual operations of the group.

members are not usually in a higher, decision-making position. For instance, in any drug-dealing organization, crew members usually sell and distribute the drugs. Crews usually have a crew boss who coordinates the objectives of the crew, supervises crew members, and disciplines them if necessary. A crew boss is also the person who reports the crew's activities, progress, and any problems to a higher-level person within the organization, usually a captain or soldier.

There are also people involved with the organization who maintain legitimate jobs outside of the group but help the organization pursue its goals. These people, sometimes referred to as **protectors**, consist of law enforcement, lawyers, bankers, and accountants who use their skills to protect the organization from government interference or criminal prosecution. Often a crime organization establishes legitimate businesses in order to make the organization look legal. One of the most important functions of these businesses is finding a way to legitimize the money obtained from illegal activities. This crime, called money laundering, will be discussed later.

An accountant, for example, may be used to set up a system that will accomplish these goals, change the books, and make it hard for the government to detect any wrongdoing. The accountant may be a willing participant in this operation because his or her services are very well paid; or the person may be participating out of fear of the organization. Sometimes, a crew member or captain will approach legitimate businesspeople and let them know that if they choose not to help, there will be severe consequences. This type of threat, known as a **shakedown**, occurs when a member of the organization uses the threat of violence to get someone to do something for the group. Shakedowns can also include forcing a legitimate business owner to pay protection money to the group. For example, a crew member who offers protection services may approach the owner of a restaurant. Although the restaurant does not have security problems and the owner has no need for such services, he realizes that if he refuses, his business may be destroyed and he may by physically harmed. Therefore, he feels he has no choice but to agree.

Typical Organized Crimes Activities

Organized crime groups pursue all types of criminal activity, including large-scale drug operations, gambling networks, prostitution rings, and financial crimes such as money laundering and loan sharking. These crimes can be grouped under the label of **racketeering**, a system of organized crime that traditionally involves the extortion of money from businesses by intimidation, violence, or other illegal methods. It can also refer to activity in any fraudulent scheme or enterprise. (See Figure 16.1.) The crimes that will be discussed here are drug operations, prostitution rings, loan sharking, bookmaking, and money laundering.

Drug Operations

The structure and size of a crime organization allows a family to carry out crimes that require many people to play many different roles. In a drug operation, some members may be responsible for actually bringing the drugs into the country, and others for distribution and sales. Organizations may work with other people who are already involved with the sale of narcotics as a way to gain control of the market and distribute

protectors

Law enforcement officers, lawyers, bankers, and accountants who use their skills to protect a crime organization from government interference or criminal prosecution.

shakedown

When a member of a crime organization uses the threat of violence to get someone to do something for the group.

racketeering

A system of organized crime traditionally involving the extortion of money from businesses by intimidation, violence, or other illegal methods; the practice of engaging in a fraudulent scheme or enterprise.

▲ F I G U R E   1 6 . 1

Racketeering Offenses

Racketeering activities include:

- Hobbs Act violations (extortion).
- Travel Act violations (interference with interstate commerce).
- Bribery.
- Sports bribery.
- Counterfeiting.
- Embezzlement from union funds.
- Loan sharking.
- Mail fraud.
- Wire fraud.
- Obstruction of state or federal justice.
- Contraband cigarettes.
- Prostitution (Mann Act).
- Bankruptcy fraud.
- Drug violations.

SOURCE: 18 U.S.C. 1961(1)(A) (1994).

---

drugs throughout the country. Suppliers and dealers of drugs may not be members of the family, but may work for the family and help carry out its goals.

As you learned earlier, the underworld narcotics trade erupted after the passage of the Harrison Narcotics Acts of 1914, which imposed criminal sanctions for narcotics abuse. Many narcotics such as heroin cannot be grown or manufactured within the borders of the United States. Because of the need to import large quantities of drugs to meet U.S. demand, investigators believe that significant organized crime financial resources are dedicated to maintaining a network of importers and suppliers of these drugs.

Prostitution Rings

One of the oldest organized crime activities is prostitution. In the past, this activity consisted primarily of importing foreign women for purposes of prostitution, which was known as the "white slave trade." The public believed that organized crime was responsible for bringing the women into the country and organizing the prostitution rings. The U.S. Immigration Commission reported in 1909 that this importation was actually worse than prostitution alone, because the women coming to the United States as prostitutes were particularly disease-riddled.

In 1875, Congress invoked its power to regulate immigration and enacted a statute that made it illegal to import women into the United States for the purpose of prostitution. In 1907, Congress went further and enacted a statute that made it a crime for anyone to keep any foreign woman "for the purpose of prostitution or any other immoral purpose" for three years after she entered the United States. In addition, those found guilty of this offense were forced to provide for the woman's deportation to her home country.[6]

Today, organized crime groups control prostitution, particularly in large cities and around areas where they have other interests, such as casinos. Even in Las Vegas, Nevada, the only location in the United States where prostitution and gambling are both legal, organized criminals are heavily involved in controlling and profiting from both activities.

Loan Sharking

The crime of **loan sharking**, also known as *criminal usury*, is the practice of lending money at excessive rates and using threats or extortion to enforce repayment. A loan shark normally supplies the money in cash and attaches a very high interest rate to the loan—much higher than if the person went though a bank or credit union. Unfortunately, the people who are most in need of loan sharking services are usually people with poor or no credit, so the possibility of getting a legitimate loan is slim. They are forced to use the services of loan shark as a way to survive.

Many people involved in the loan sharking business have no connection to organized crime. The benefit of being a loan shark associated with a crime organization is that borrowers are far more likely to take the threat of violence seriously should they fail to repay the loan. Loan sharks often resort to violence not only because the money is not paid back, but also so that future borrowers will realize the importance of paying off their debts.

Suppose that a family living in a working-class neighborhood of Chicago has just found out that their youngest daughter has cancer. The family does not have health insurance, there is no additional income to pay for expensive chemotherapy treatments, and the nearest hospital with adequate cancer treatment is unwilling to give them reasonable payment options. The father of the family has started a second job, but will not have the income from that job for a month, which will be too late.

Knowing that a neighborhood crime organization loans money at an interest rate of 23 percent, the father goes to the crime organization family and requests a loan. They give him the money and a month to pay it back with interest. If he fails to pay the money back, he will likely be seriously hurt or even killed. The loan shark is not concerned with the circumstances of why the father needs the money. If he does not repay it on time, he will face serious consequences.

loan sharking
The practice of lending money at excessive rates and using threats or extortion to enforce repayment.

Bookmaking

The crime of **bookmaking** is a form of illegal gambling in which customers use bookies to place bets on horse and dog races, professional sporting competitions, and other events. A bookmaker, or bookie, charges or accepts a percentage, fee, or "vig" on the wager.

Bookmaking operations involve complicated procedures, such as using scratch sheets and other documents to keep track of the betting and determine how much the bettor owes the bookie. Crime organizations set up bookmaking operations where residents of the community can place their bets with the organization. Like loan sharking, bookmaking is a good industry for organized crime because people are aware of the consequences of not paying on the bet. Should a person place a bet with a bookie and lose, that person will be compelled to pay the money back or face serious consequences.

bookmaking
The promotion of gambling by unlawfully accepting bets on the outcomes of future contingent events from members of the public, as a business rather than in a casual or personal fashion.

Bookmaking is a multimillion-dollar industry that usually involves a complicated system for delivery of betting information and payoffs. The process usually requires establishing a physical location where the bookie can work, taking and placing bets. Although a small-time criminal without a lot of resources would find it difficult to work in the industry, a crime organization could easily set up the necessary tools.[7] Bookmakers may face charges under both state and federal laws.

Money Laundering

The money received through illegal activities such as drug sales and gambling is known as **dirty money**. When large amounts of illegally obtained money are spent, it is usually possible for law enforcement to detect that fact—someone with no legitimate source of income could only have acquired such large amounts of money illegally. If such expenditures are detected, this can lead to arrest and prosecution for the illegal activities that generated the money. Crime organizations seek to avoid such detection by **money laundering**, which is filtering money through legitimate sources until it appears to be derived from these sources. Money laundering is a crime under federal law, and is a serious crime problem. Recent studies report that more than $300 billion is laundered through legitimate American businesses each year.[8]

Money laundering can be accomplished in a number of ways. An organization can take dirty money and give it to a legitimate business, so that it looks as if the money was actually received through the business. For example, a Mafia organization that obtains large profits through drug sales may take those profits and channel them through a car wash or restaurant owned by the group. The profits from the legitimate business will be much larger than what the legitimate business actually earned, but the group may be able to wash their money for some time without detection. Law enforcement, however, may become suspicious of a small business reporting a disproportionately huge income. This may lead to an investigation and, possibly, money laundering convictions.

Another way to cleanse the money is for an organization to pay someone else to do it. The Colombian-based Cali Cartel, one of the largest drug organizations in the world, launders its money this way. Once a large-scale drug operation is complete, the Cartel holds an auction for professional money launderers who bid on the job. The successful launderer usually has about two weeks to return the cleansed money.[9]

To avoid detection, laundering money involves several steps. The first step is changing the money derived from criminal activities into an easily manipulated and less suspicious form. Organized criminals must figure out how to move huge quantities of cash without detection. Imagine showing up at a small, family-run restaurant with suitcases full of $100 bills and asking them to launder it. Doing so would likely raise suspicions, and observers might tip off law enforcement officers that laundering is going on.

To avoid this, crime organizations may disperse the money through several different channels, each involving smaller, less detectable amounts. Organizations may funnel some money through legitimate businesses, convert some into other instruments such as money orders, and transfer the rest to offshore or overseas accounts, where detection by U.S. law enforcement is difficult. To complicate matters, many foreign countries have strict secrecy laws that make it very difficult for American law enforcement to investigate possible money laundering.

---

dirty money

The money received through illegal activities such as drug sales and gambling.

money laundering

Transferring illegally obtained money through legitimate persons or accounts so that its original source cannot be traced; a federal crime.

Once dirty money has been turned into clean money, it can be freely used, spent, and transformed into financial instruments such as letters of credit, bonds, other securities, bank notes, and guarantees that can be used and accessed anywhere in the world. Once this happens, the money, now appearing legitimate, is virtually impossible to detect as laundered money.[10]

Money laundering allows organized crime syndicates not only to prosper through illegal means, but also to hide the profits from the illegal activity. Therefore, these profits are not taxed, and the people who make the money do not have to contribute to the government like the rest of us. As a result of the growing problem of money laundering, Congress and many states have enacted statutes that directly target the crime and provide stiff penalties. These various laws will be discussed fully later in this chapter.

Laws That Target Organized Crime

As organized crime continued to grow throughout the twentieth century, the federal government and individual state jurisdictions enacted laws that directly targeted organized crime syndicates and the activities they pursue. In 1986, the President's Commission on Organized Crime expanded the definition of organized crime to include outside organizations that protect or render services to the criminal group itself.[11] These laws provide stiff penalties for any convictions related to organized crime. Thus, a defendant may be convicted of a substantive offense, such as murder or drug distribution, and also for being part of a particular type of group criminal behavior. (See Application Case 16.1.)

⚖️ Application Case 16.1

United States v. Gotti

In *United States v. Gotti* (1990), notorious boss John Gotti of New York's Gambino crime family in New York was arrested with crime family members Salvatore Gravano, Frank Locascio, and Thomas Gambino. They were charged with racketeering, murder, obstruction of justice, racketeering conspiracy, conspiracy to commit murder, illegal gambling, conspiracy to obstruct justice, and conspiracy to defraud the United States by obstructing its collection of income taxes. Gotti was also charged with racketeering violations, including a loan sharking conspiracy.

About 10 weeks before the trial began, Salvatore ("Sammy the Bull") Gravano entered into a cooperation agreement with the government and provided valuable evidence to assist its case. In 1992, the jury found John Gotti guilty on all counts. Gotti received multiple life sentences for his violations of RICO and other crimes. While serving his time at a maximum security federal penitentiary, Gotti filed countless appeals to his convictions, but higher courts upheld the convictions on all grounds. John Gotti died in prison of throat cancer in 2002.

SOURCE: United States v. Gotti, 171 F.R.D. 19 (E.D.N.Y. 1997).

16.1 Web Exploration

CrimeLibrary.com

Read the entire story of John Gotti and his eventual demise on CrimeLibrary.com, at http://www.crimelibrary.com/gangsters_outlaws/mob_bosses/gotti/index_1.html. What obstacles did the FBI have to overcome in bringing him to trial? How did they succeed in having him convicted?

Racketeer Influenced and Corrupt Organizations (RICO)

A federal law that criminalizes illegal activities committed by organized crime members.

Racketeer Influenced and Corrupt Organizations (RICO)

In 1970, Congress enacted the landmark **Racketeer Influenced and Corrupt Organizations (RICO)** law. RICO is a federal law that criminalizes illegal activities committed by organized crime members and was enacted to eradicate sophisticated organized crime syndicates. At the time of its creation, its focus was on large, East Coast Mafia families that were controlling major criminal activity throughout the country. Federal prosecutors successfully used RICO to break down the structure and sophistication of these groups by convicting and severely sentencing its leaders.[12]

Congress made RICO elastic so that it could continuously apply to the evolving reality of organized crime in the United States. As a result, RICO's elements are fairly broad, allow for criminal prosecutions of various groups involved in a wide range of activities, and include both criminal and civil provisions. The five elements of a criminal violation under RICO are:

1. Unlawful activity involving an enterprise.
2. Two or more qualifying acts of racketeering activity.
3. A showing of a pattern of such activity.
4. An effect upon interstate commerce.
5. The commission of the prohibited acts.[13]

For purposes of RICO, the U.S. Supreme Court has defined *enterprise* as any "union or group of individuals associated in fact . . . [and] associated together for a common purpose of engaging in a course of conduct."[14] For example, if three men associate together every day by having lunch and playing pool, and all of them are involved in criminal activity, this does not create an enterprise for purposes of the RICO statute because they must be working together on the same criminal pursuit.

When prosecuting someone for a RICO violation, the government must also show a pattern of two or more racketeering activities. A *racketeering activity* includes violating certain specified provisions of either federal or state criminal statutes. RICO generally defines racketeering activity as "Any act or threat involving murder, kidnapping, gambling, arson, robbery, bribery, extortion, dealing in obscene matter, or dealing in narcotic or other dangerous drugs, which is chargeable under State law and punishable by imprisonment for more than one year." In addition, the statute lists several other violations of specific criminal statutes that constitute racketeering activity, including various acts of bribery, theft, extortion, and fraud.[15]

To prove a pattern of conduct, the prosecutor must show both relationship and continuity as separate elements. This means that the government must prove that a

F I G U R E   1 6 . 2

Activities Prohibited by RICO

1962. Prohibited activities.

(a) It shall be unlawful for any person who has received any income derived, directly or indirectly, from a pattern of racketeering activity or through collection of an unlawful debt in which such person has participated as a principal within the meaning of section 2, title 18, United States Code, to use or invest, directly or indirectly, any part of such income, or the proceeds of such income, in acquisition of any interest in, or the establishment or operation of, any enterprise which is engaged in, or the activities of which affect, interstate or foreign commerce. A purchase of securities on the open market for purposes of investment, and without the intention of controlling or participating in the control of the issuer, or of assisting another to do so, shall not be unlawful under this subsection if the securities of the issuer held by the purchaser, the members of his immediate family, and his or their accomplices in any pattern or racketeering activity or the collection of an unlawful debt after such purchase do not amount in the aggregate to one percent of the outstanding securities of any one class, and do not confer, either in law or in fact, the power to elect one or more directors of the issuer.

(b) It shall be unlawful for any person through a pattern of racketeering activity or through collection of an unlawful debt to acquire or maintain, directly or indirectly, any interest in or control of any enterprise which is engaged in, or the activities of which affect, interstate or foreign commerce.

(c) It shall be unlawful for any person employed by or associated with any enterprise engaged in, or the activities of which affect, interstate or foreign commerce, to conduct or participate, directly or indirectly, in the conduct of such enterprise's affairs through a pattern of racketeering activity or collection of unlawful debt.

(d) It shall be unlawful for any person to conspire to violate any of the provisions of subsection (a), (b), or (c) of this section.

SOURCE: 18 U.S.C. § 1962 (2000).

relationship existed between the defendants, and that they were working together to achieve a common criminal goal.[16]

To prove that the criminal act had an effect on interstate commerce, the government only needs to show that the illegal activity was in some way related to interstate commerce. It does not have to involve a defendant's physical presence in another state; using a telephone, computer, or fax to contact someone in another state during the course of an illegal activity is sufficient. It is very easy for the government to prove this element because almost all organized crime syndicates involve some aspect of interstate commerce.

Finally, to prove a RICO violation, the government must prove that at least one specific prohibited act has taken place. The statute sets forth four such prohibited acts (see Figure 16.2):

1. Investing income from a pattern of racketeering activity.
2. Acquiring or maintaining an interest in an enterprise through a pattern of racketeering activity.

3. Conducting the affairs of an enterprise through a pattern of racketeering activity.
4. Conspiring to do any of the above.[17]

In addition to stiff prison terms, persons convicted under RICO may face forfeiture of all property, heavy fines, and, under the RICO civil provisions, lawsuits brought by individuals who suffered from the RICO activity.[18] (See Application Case 16.2.)

⚖ Application Case 16.2

United States v. Andrews

In *United States v. Andrews*, more than 80 members of the El Rukn Street gang were convicted of various RICO charges. The El Rukn gang was a highly disciplined and organized association that existed solely for the purpose of perpetrating crime. Between the late 1960s and the late 1980s, the El Rukns committed countless acts of racketeering, including 20 murders, 12 attempted murders, 11 conspiracies to murder, 1 kidnapping, wide-scale drug trafficking, and numerous obstructions of justice. To protect their business, the El Rukns found it necessary to murder several rival drug dealers and rival gang members. To protect members from prosecution for some of these murders and other crimes, the El Rukns killed, intimidated, and kidnapped witnesses. These activities were carried out through a formal chain of command that was headed by Jeff Fort, an unindicted co-conspirator. Five of the defendants held positions at the second and third levels of command and were known as either generals or officers in the organization.

In addition to the RICO charges, 37 of the defendants were convicted of conspiring to possess with intent to distribute multikilogram quantities of heroin and cocaine, hundreds of pounds of marijuana, thousands of amphetamine pills, and other narcotics. Several of the defendants challenged their convictions on appeal, arguing that RICO was not applicable to the conduct of a street gang and that RICO was unconstitutionally vague.

The appellate court upheld all convictions, finding that the conduct of the El Rukn gang was precisely what Congress intended to criminalize when RICO was created. The court also held that the statute was not constitutionally vague and that the government had met its burden of proving an "enterprise" for purposes of the statute. This is an important case because it was one of the first instances in which federal prosecutors used the RICO statute to prosecute gangs and to recognize gangs as organized crime syndicates.

SOURCE: United States v. Andrews, 749 F. Supp. 1520 (N.D. Ill. 1990).

State Versions of RICO

In addition to the federal RICO statutes, many states have enacted their own legislation to combat organized crime in their jurisdiction. The obvious benefit in creating

16.2 Web Exploration

Interpol.int

To learn more about the increasingly international nature of organized crime, visit the Web site of Interpol, an organization that coordinates international law enforcement, at http://www.interpol.int. What information did you find on international efforts against organized crime, white-collar crime, and terrorism?

such laws is that they can be used to prosecute intrastate, as opposed to interstate, commerce. In other words, organized criminal activity that is confined to a single state cannot escape prosecution simply because it lacks the element of interstate commerce. For example, Oregon's "little RICO" law defines racketeering essentially the same as the federal RICO law and contains the same elements as the federal statute, except for the requirement for interstate commerce. Under Oregon's RICO statute, a person violates this law if he or she launders money, uses threats to illegally take over a business, runs a criminal business, operates a legitimate business through criminal means, or conspires to do any of the above.[19]

Continuing Criminal Enterprise (CCE)

The Continuing Criminal Enterprise statute, or CCE, is similar to RICO but applies only to organized criminal activity involving drugs. This statute provides that a criminal enterprise exists when a continuing series of federal drug-related felonies is committed in concert with other crimes (1) in which the defendant occupies a managerial role and (2) from which he or she obtains a substantial income.

A continuing criminal enterprise consists of five elements:

1. A felony violation of federal narcotics laws.
2. As part of a continuing series of violations.
3. In concert with five or more persons.
4. For whom the defendant is an organizer or supervisor.
5. From which the defendant obtains a substantial income.[20]

As with RICO violations, a defendant can be charged with both a substantive crime (in this case, a drug crime) and a violation of the CCE. For example, an organized crime leader would likely be charged with CCE if he or she were involved in a national drug operation with distribution centers throughout the country. He or she would likely be charged with a federal drug crime, such as possession or distribution of narcotics, in addition to the CCE charge.

Anti-Drug Abuse Act

In addition to the various federal and state laws that target organized crime, there are specific statutes that target money laundering. For example, the Anti-Drug Abuse Act of 1986 holds people criminally liable for knowingly participating in money laundering schemes, and provides stiff penalties for monetary manipulation that involves (1) disguising the source of proceeds of unlawful activities or (2) the failure to report income. This act also allows the government to seize and forfeit any cash or property related to such a scheme. The penalties provided are fines up to $500,000, imprisonment up to 20 years, or both.[21]

Bank Fraud Act and Bank Secrecy Act

The Bank Fraud Act and the Bank Secrecy Act require mandatory reporting provisions for financial institutions with regard to large sums of money. This legislation allows the government to monitor money laundering operations and to ensure that the money passing through these institutions is made legitimately.[22]

Money Laundering Control Act (MLCA)

The Money Laundering Control Act of 1986 (MLCA) was enacted in response to two problems that were experiencing significant growth:

1. Money laundering that resulted from the booming cocaine trade of the 1980s.
2. Widespread noncompliance with the banking reporting statutes.

Clearly, prior statutes were not working in combating the growing money laundering industry. Under the MLCA, the act of money laundering itself is criminalized, regardless of whether any reporting statutes are violated. Provisions of this act hold individuals criminally liable for knowingly spending money that is laundered even if they were not involved in the laundering process. A person can be convicted under the statute for conspiring to launder money, even if the person does not actually go through with it. Like RICO, the MCLA also provides for both civil and criminal forfeitures of funds or property implicated in money laundering.[23]

Criticisms

Critics of RICO and similar laws have several complaints about these laws, including the following:

- Although RICO is intended to target high-ranking organized crime figures, it could apply to almost anyone as long as the elements have been established.
- RICO has "federalized" virtually all criminal activities, even those normally within the jurisdiction of states' criminal statutes.
- Under RICO and similar laws, convicted persons are punished multiple times for the same offense or offenses, in violation of the prohibition against double jeopardy.
- RICO and similar offenses are too vague, and their elements are unclear.

Regarding the double jeopardy claim, a number of people convicted under these statutes have argued a violation of double jeopardy to challenge the validity of their convictions. Federal courts have consistently upheld their convictions on two separate grounds. First, the doctrine of dual sovereignty holds that a state prosecution does not bar a subsequent federal prosecution of the same person for the same act. This applies to people convicted under a state substantive offense and a federal organized crime offense.[24] Second, multiple offenses are valid as long as one element of the crime is different for each of the offenses.[25]

Regarding arguments about the vagueness of these laws, the federal courts have consistently rejected this argument. Federal courts have upheld these convictions and stated that an ordinary person would know that the activities of an organized crime family fell within the range of conduct, and as such could be prosecuted under RICO. In other words, Congress's original intent that these statutes cover a broad range of criminal conduct has been upheld, thus allowing for more people to be convicted under the statutes.[26]

CRITICAL THINKING 16.1

1. Why did the criminalization of drugs and, for a time, alcohol benefit criminals? Can this be undone? Why or why not?

2. Why do organized criminals need to launder money, and how is this done?

16.2 Street Gangs

Although street gangs have existed in the United States since the nineteenth century, they have grown tremendously in the last 20 years. Throughout the country, in big cities and small rural communities, street gangs have developed into large, organized crime syndicates that have influenced illegal activity in almost every state. A number of states and cities, seeking to address gang problems, have enacted laws aimed at such groups, some even specifically defining and criminalizing street gangs. An example is an Iowa statute, defining a **criminal street gang** as any formal or informal ongoing group of three or more persons:

- Whose primary activity is the commission of one or more criminal acts.
- Which has an identifiable name or identifying sign or symbol.
- Whose members individually or collectively engage in or have engaged in a pattern of criminal gang activity.[27]

The Structure of a Modern Street Gang

A modern-day street gang exhibits several consistent traits. In order for a gang to maintain itself and prosper, there must be frequent contact between gang members. Typically, the neighborhood or area from which someone comes determines membership, which makes it easier for members to have constant interaction. A gang usually controls a specific neighborhood or territory, and members of the community are aware that the area belongs to the gang. Members may mark their territory by using graffiti to put the gang's names on local buildings, and gang members will be quick to defend their territory should another gang try to lay claim to it.

Another typical characteristic is that a gang faces problems or conflicts as a united group, rather than individually. For instance, if one member is being bothered or harassed by someone, the whole gang will come to his or her side and lend support.

criminal street gang
Any formal or informal ongoing organization whose primary activity is the commission of one or more criminal acts, which has an identifiable name or identifying sign or symbol, and whose members individually or collectively engage in or have engaged in a pattern of criminal gang activity.

Like other organized crime groups, gangs typically have a hierarchical system. Usually, this structure is determined by the length of time a person has been in the gang, the person's age, and the person's family ties to gang leaders or organizers. Sometimes, leadership will be determined by the dedication a member has shown to the group. For example, a gang member who has committed a number of crimes for the group, or who is the first to physically defend the neighborhood or the gang, may quickly rise to a leadership position.

Crimes Committed by Gangs

In the past, street gang behavior was fairly innocent and usually lawful, despite occasional instances of rival gang fistfights and small-scale criminal activity. Today, however, many street gangs are involved in all kinds of criminal activity, ranging from drug dealing and distribution to gambling operations, murder, bank robberies, financial crimes, extortion, bribery, racketeering, kidnapping, and even terrorism. As the gangs become more sophisticated, their level of criminal activity becomes more sophisticated as well. The crack cocaine boom of the 1980s and 1990s "is primarily responsible for transforming many fraternal, juvenile organizations into highly sophisticated organized crime entities."[28]

The level of development of a gang's drug operation may be an accurate measure of the overall level of sophistication of the gang. The amount of drug activity engaged in by any individual gang is "directly related to the size of its membership and the degree of organizational sophistication achieved by the gang. The smaller, less organized gangs are generally only involved in selling drugs at the street level. As the gang grows and becomes more structured, it develops more specialized distribution methods and expands its product."[29]

Some of the largest street gangs have made millions of dollars in drug profits through an organized system of narcotics distribution. The El Rukns, a notorious Chicago gang that has existed since the 1960s, reportedly brings in between $50,000 and $70,000 *per day* from narcotics sales alone.[30] In order for the El Rukns to maintain power and control over their drug monopoly, members have systematically killed rival drug dealers. If they don't kill witnesses who are going to testify against them in court, their intimidation tactics usually dissuade them from testifying.

Identifying Gang Organizations

Although there are thousands of gangs throughout the United States, a small handful of groups have gained notoriety because of their size, power, ruthlessness, or monopoly on crime. Most people have some recognition of the notorious Los Angeles street gangs, the Bloods and the Crips. What they may not know is that there are hundreds of different Crips and Bloods gangs throughout Los Angeles, as well as Crips and Bloods scattered throughout the country.

A common misconception about street gangs relates to gender. Most people think that only males are gang members, but in fact girls have joined gangs in larger numbers. The U.S. Justice Department has identified 650,000 gang members nationwide, and 10 to 15 percent of them are female. In Los Angeles County, the active gang population is 10 to 15 percent female.[31]

Latino Gangs

Latino gangs are located primarily in the *barrios*, or Mexican American slums, of Southern California. Most members of these gangs are either first-generation Americans or were actually born in Mexico or Central America, then immigrated to the United States as children. As with most gang organizations, Latino gangs are created based on certain neighborhoods, housing projects, or communities. By joining a gang, a young person living in a gang-infested area will have others to protect him or her. Upon admission into a Latino street gang, he or she will become a **cholo** or **chola**. In some circumstances, entire cholo families, including one or both parents as well as their children, are all members of the same gang.[32]

cholo/chola
A member of a Latino (especially Mexican American) street gang.

Latino gangs have grown in membership and power over the last few decades. The largest of these gangs, particularly the Mexican Mafia, have been responsible for large-scale drug operations throughout the country. Additionally, many of these gangs run their criminal operations inside the toughest California prisons. Although many of the Mexican Mafia's leaders are serving life sentences, they are able to designate responsibilities to members on the outside and continue to expand their operations. Additionally, members of Hispanic gangs are able to use their command of the Spanish language to facilitate the importation of drugs from Mexico and Central America.[33] (See Application Case 16.3.)

⚖️ Application Case 16.3

Mexican Mafia Crackdown

In 1999, more than 200 law enforcement agents conducted raids throughout Los Angeles County and arrested 13 Mexican Mafia leaders on charges of murder and drug trafficking; 27 other members, including some already in prison, were charged in connection with 4 murders, 3 attempted murders, and 13 counts of conspiracy to distribute narcotics. One of the lead officers in the crackdown stated that the effort to bring down the Mexican Mafia was comparable to the 30-year effort by federal agencies to dismantle the Cosa Nostra.

During the trial, prosecutors relied heavily on the testimony of former gang members, some of whom turned to the government when they feared they would be killed by others in the gang. The jury reached its verdict after six weeks of testimony by more than 150 witnesses and five days of deliberations. During the reading of the verdicts, heavily armed federal marshals and state troopers surrounded the courthouse, and police helicopters circled over the courthouse as the defendants were taken into court. Ten Mexican Mafia members, including several high-ranking leaders, were convicted of federal racketeering and conspiracy related to multiple robberies, drug deals, and 15 murders.

SOURCE: Karen Low, *Authorities Arrest 13 Alleged Mexican Mafia Members*, Associated Press, Feb. 3, 1999.

Crips and Bloods

The Crips and Bloods gangs, which evolved in Los Angeles but are now established throughout the country, have existed for more than 30 years. It is believed that the Crips were first organized in 1969, and the Bloods soon after. As mentioned earlier, each group is comprised of hundreds of "sets," which are like gangs within the gangs. In Los Angeles County alone, officials have identified 219 different Crips gangs and 84 different Bloods gangs. Examples of the various sets comprising the Bloods and Crips in Los Angeles include the Hoover Crips, the Harlem Crips, the Grape Street Bloods, the Bounty Hunter Bloods, and the Swan Bloods. Some of these gangs are friendly and have established ties with each other, but others hold the same vindictiveness toward each other as they do toward rival gangs.[34]

The Crips and Bloods have many identifying characteristics that are unique to their gangs and the sets within them. For example, the Crips's color is blue, and Crips tend to wear blue clothing and other attire. Likewise, the Bloods's color is red, so Bloods tend to wear red clothing and accessories. In addition, low-waisted khaki pants with oversized T-shirts are typical gang clothing, and certain tennis shoes or jewelry may identify gang membership or association. Depending on the individual gang, members may wear a particular sports jersey or baseball cap with a team that the group adopts as being representative of the gang.

Each gang is an independent entity that does not answer to a centralized Crips or Bloods leader. Instead, leaders known as shot-callers represent their gang when interacting with other groups. In 1993, after Los Angeles experienced the worst rioting in its history as a result of the Rodney King verdict, shot-callers throughout Los Angeles County, as well as specialized police gang units and community leaders, met to discuss the possibility of a gang truce between the Crips and the Bloods. Even before the Rodney King trial aftermath riots, the gangs were moving toward a truce.[35] Although gang rivalry continues in Los Angeles, and Crips and Bloods continue to war in a few communities as if nothing has changed, many believe that this gang truce was successful overall. In some areas of Los Angeles, the truce is credited with erasing two decades of violence. In others, gangs have agreed not to initiate combat, but still end up killing in the course of robberies, drug deals, dice games, and parties.

Although the Los Angeles gang problem may not be as serious as before, the gang problem in California is far from over. There are still countless shootings and other crimes related to gang associations. Both the Los Angeles County Sheriff's Department and the Los Angeles Police Department have specialized gang units that focus all of their attention on gang members and the crimes they commit. These officers become experts in identifying gang members, understanding which gangs are rivals, knowing the various turfs the gangs control, and recognizing graffiti, clothing, and other marks that may categorize an individual as a gang member.

In addition, Crips and Bloods have spread throughout the country and are now visible in the Midwest and on the East Coast. Former Los Angeles gang members who have moved out of state are responsible for creating these new gang sets. As a result, crime has increased in those areas. Former Los Angeles gang members have been found in all regions of the United States.

Chinese Gangs

Chinese gangs have experienced rapid growth since the passage of an immigration act in the 1960s that allowed many immigrants to come to the United States. These gangs, like all others, were formed as a way to make money through illegal means. Chinese gangs usually have between 25 and 50 members, with a hierarchical system based around a leader, middle supervisors, and lower ranks who commit the actual crimes. Several characteristics distinguish a Chinese gang from other groups, including a close relationship with community organizations, investment in legitimate businesses, international connections, and control over large amounts of money. Women and girls are not usually admitted into Chinese gangs, but do associate with them and lend support.

Chinese gangs in the United States prey on people's weaknesses in their recruiting methods. They target new immigrants with limited education and skills who need the gang's assistance to earn money. Their initiation rituals usually involve a ceremony in which the new member takes an oath, then drinks a combination of blood and wine in front of the leader.

Vietnamese Gangs

Vietnamese gangs began to organize at the end of the Vietnam War, when hundreds of thousands of immigrants poured into Southern California. These groups tend to focus their criminal activities on theft, robbery, carjacking, and extortion. Vietnamese immigrants often distrust legitimate banks, and as a result are known to keep large quantities of cash in their homes. Gang members often target these homes and steal the money.[36]

Laws That Target Gangs

As gangs have evolved and become more and more violent over the last few decades, many jurisdictions have enacted legislation directly targeting gang members and their crimes. Just as RICO was established as a way to break down and destroy organized crime syndicates, gang legislation works toward the same purpose. These laws provide additional penalties for gang members convicted of crimes, prohibit gang members from associating with one another, and restrict areas where gang members can associate. Some of this legislation has become quite controversial in recent years because opponents argue that many of the laws violate constitutional rights, such as freedom of association and freedom of expression. For example, the Chicago City Counsel enacted an ordinance aimed at gang activities. The U.S. Supreme Court, however, struck down that ordinance in 1999, in the *Morales* case.[37] (See Application Case 16.4.) One of the more serious problems that the Court had with the ordinance was its focus on "loitering" by a street gang member as the trigger of the offense. In the aftermath of *Morales*, similar ordinances have been held unconstitutional in Georgia and Nevada.[38] Many of these laws are still on the books, and lawmakers have been struggling to continue to address the problem of street gangs with criminal penalty responses.

⚖ Application Case 16.4

City of Chicago v. Morales

In the 1999 case of *City of Chicago v. Morales*, the U.S. Supreme Court called into question the validity of recent anti-gang laws. In 1992, the Chicago City Council enacted the Gang Congregation Ordinance, which prohibits "criminal street gang members" from "loitering" with one another or with other persons in any public place. Commission of the offense involves four predicates:

1. The police officer must reasonably believe that at least one of the two or more persons present in a "public place" is a "criminal street gang member."
2. The persons must be "loitering," which the ordinance defined as "remain[ing] in any one place with no apparent purpose."
3. The officer must then order "all" of the persons to disperse and remove themselves "from the area."
4. A person must disobey the officer's order. If any person, whether a gang member or not, disobeyed the officer's order, that person is guilty of violating the ordinance.

The Court found the ordinance was void for vagueness on two grounds: (1) It was unconstitutionally vague in failing to provide fair notice of prohibited conduct, and (2) it was also impermissibly vague in failing to establish minimal guidelines for enforcement.

SOURCE: City of Chicago v. Morales, 527 U.S. 41 (1999).

Under federal sentencing laws, a defendant who is convicted of a narcotics offense may be given additional prison time if the prosecutor can prove that he or she is a serious gang member. This law's purpose is to enhance the sentences of defendants who participate in groups, clubs, organizations, or associations that use violence to further their ends.[39]

More than a dozen states have passed laws that make it an offense to aid or conspire to aid crimes intended to further the activities of a street gang. An Iowa statute, for example, provides: "A person who actively participates in or is a member of a criminal street gang and who willfully aids and abets any criminal act committed for the benefit of, at the direction of, or in association with any criminal street gang, commits a class D felony."[40]

Because California has one of the largest gang populations of any state, and because it has experienced a tremendous amount of gang-related crime in its cities and rural areas, it has also become one of the toughest states in the creation of legislation to combat gangs. The Street Terrorism Enforcement and Prevention Act (STEP) is an all-inclusive anti-gang law, the purpose of which is to eradicate gangs in the state.[41]

STEP provides, in part:

- Any adult who utilizes physical violence to coerce, induce, or solicit another person who is under 18 years of age to actively participate in any criminal

16.1 On the Job

Federal Prosecutor

Description and Duties: Enforce federal laws, including the RICO statute. Many positions are through different federal agencies or special prosecution teams. For example, the Tobacco Litigation Team handles the lawsuit against the cigarette manufacturers to recover federal health care costs associated with tobacco use and equitable relief, including disgorgement of proceeds, under the RICO statute. Federal prosecutors for the DEA provide legal advice and support to DEA management and field offices worldwide, with an emphasis on federal criminal drug laws and related issues. Federal prosecutors for the Southern District of California may work with the Border Crimes Section, where they prosecute felony immigration and border drug smuggling cases.

Salary: Salaries are within the range of a government pay scale, but these pay levels have some flexibility. Salaries can range from GS-11 ($44,352–57,656) to GS-15 ($87,864–114,224).

Other Information: Federal prosecutors generally must possess a J.D., be an active member of the bar in any jurisdiction, and have at least two years of post-J.D. legal experience. Excellent legal research, writing, and analytical skills are required. Prosecutorial experience, especially in the federal courts, is desirable.

SOURCE: U.S. Department of Justice, http://www.usdoj.gov/oarm/arm/hp/hpsalary.htm and http://www .usdoj.gov/oarm/arm/hp/condemp.htm.

street gang, as defined in subdivision (f) of Section 186.22, the members of which engage in a pattern of criminal gang activity, as defined in subdivision (e) of Section 186.22, shall be punished by imprisonment in the state prison for one, two, or three years.

- Any adult who threatens a minor with physical violence on two or more separate occasions within any 30-day period with the intent to coerce, induce, or solicit the minor to actively participate in a criminal street gang, as defined in subdivision (f) of Section 186.22, the members of which engage in a pattern of criminal gang activity, as defined in subdivision (e) of Section 186.22, shall be punished by imprisonment in the state prison for one, two, or three years or in a county jail for up to one year.
- A minor who is 16 years of age or older who commits an offense described in subdivision (a) or (b) is guilty of a misdemeanor.

STEP requires that, to obtain a conviction, the prosecutor must show a pattern of gang activity. This is defined in the statute as:

the commission of, attempted commission of, or solicitation of, sustained juvenile petition for, or conviction of two or more of the following offenses, provided at least one of these offenses occurred after the effective date of this chapter and the last of those offenses occurred within three years after a prior offense, and the offenses were committed on separate occasions, or by two or more persons: [there follows an enumeration of 23 offenses, including homicide, robbery, and rape].[42]

Prior to *Morales*, although several cases challenged the constitutionality of the STEP statute arguing that it infringes on gang members' right to associate, the courts upheld the validity of the law.[43]

In another type of anti-gang legislation, several cities in California have enacted legislation banning gang members from associating in certain areas, such as parks. The San Fernando City Council, for example, passed an ordinance to this effect after a mother and her three children were killed by the crossfire of a gang shooting. This law provides that "gang members who are formally classified under STEP based on their criminal records, associates, street names, tattoos and other signs of gang involvement, and who are then served with papers notifying them of the classification, are banned from using the park for sports or other non-gang activities."[44]

Arkansas, a state hard hit by Los Angeles gang transplants, enacted a statute that is modeled on RICO but applies particularly to gang members. The Arkansas Criminal Gang, Organization, or Enterprise Act provides additional penalties for gang members convicted of crimes. This law goes beyond other state gang laws and punishes people who are acting in concert. Notably, the law specifically provides that it is not a defense to the enhanced penalty to argue that the people involved were not gang members.[45]

In addition, another part of Arkansas's gang legislation goes a step further and provides:

(1) A person commits the offense of engaging in a continuing criminal gang, organization, or enterprise in the first degree if he:
   A. Commits or attempts to commit or solicits to commit a felony predicate criminal offense; and
   B. That offense is part of a continuing series of two (2) or more predicate criminal offenses which are undertaken by that person in concert with two (2) or more other persons with respect to whom that person occupies a position of organizer, a supervisory position, or any other position of management.
(2) A person who engages in a continuing criminal gang, organization, or enterprise in the first degree is guilty of a felony two (2) classifications higher than the classification of the highest underlying predicate offense referenced in subdivision (a)(1)(A) of this section.[46]

CRITICAL THINKING 16.2

1. Why, in your opinion, have gang activities changed so much over the years? Are drugs solely to blame?

2. Why do you think that girls and women are now more involved in gang activities?

16.3 Terrorism

When most people picture terrorists or terrorist activity, they imagine religious extremists blowing up buildings or airplanes. In actuality, terrorism is much more that. People commit terrorist acts for all types of reasons, including political, religious, and social beliefs. Broadly defined, **terrorism** is any deliberate use or threat of violence by groups seeking to achieve political, social, or religious objectives. Terrorism has also been defined to include:

- The unlawful use or threatened use of force or violence by a revolutionary organization against individuals or property with the intention of coercing or intimidating governments or societies, often for political or ideological purposes.
- The unlawful use of force or violence against persons or property to intimidate or coerce a government, the civilian population, or any segment thereof, in furtherance of political or social objectives.
- Premeditated, politically motivated violence perpetrated against noncombatant targets by subnational groups or clandestine state agents.[47]

terrorism
The deliberate use or threat of violence by groups seeking to achieve political, social, or religious objectives.

Terrorism Distinguished from Other Crimes

The main difference between terrorist crime and other types of crime is that the motive behind terrorism is political, as opposed to economic. Other criminal groups, such as gangs or organized crime syndicates, are usually only trying to achieve economic gain. For example, a gang may distribute cocaine in order to make money, but a terrorist may bomb a building or kidnap innocent hostages in order to get the government's attention, draw focus to their cause, or get a law changed. As another example of terrorism, a group may blow up a bus carrying innocent passengers and then tell the government that unless some of its members are released from prison, a second bus will be blown up.

Terrorist acts may include any type of criminal behavior that is used to further a political or religious goal. Well-known examples include:

- **Bombings.** Two of the more extreme examples of terrorist bombings are the 2004 Madrid train bombings and the July 7, 2005, London bombings. On March 11, 2004, a series of bombs went off on Madrid trains at the peak of rush hour, killing 191 people and wounding 2,050. Responsibility has been attributed to a group of Moroccan, Syrian, and Algerian Muslims that was believed to have been inspired by al-Qaeda. On July 7, 2005, a series of bombs exploded on London's public transportation system during morning rush hour, killing 52 people. Numerous Islamic terrorist cells were quick to claim responsibility for the attacks.
- **Hijacking airplanes or other vehicles.** On September 11, 2001, four airplanes were hijacked by Islamic extremists affiliated with al-Qaeda. Two of the planes were flown into the North and South Towers of the World Trade Center in New York City. One was flown into the Pentagon. And the fourth crashed in a field in Pennsylvania. A total of 2,973 individuals were killed in the attacks.
- **Kidnapping or taking hostages.** On January 23, 2002, on his way to what he thought was an interview with Sheikh Mubarak Ali Gilani at the Village restaurant in Karachi, Danny Pearl, a United States journalist, was kidnapped by a militant group calling itself the National Movement for the Restoration of Pakistani Sovereignty. This group claimed Pearl was a CIA agent and, via

The 9/11 Terrorist Attack The attack of September 11, 2001, changed the face of terrorism in many people's minds.

e-mail, sent the United States a range of demands, including the freeing of all Pakistani terror detainees and the release of a halted U.S. shipment of F-16 fighter jets to the Pakistani government. The message read: "We give you one more day. If America will not meet our demands we will kill Daniel. Then this cycle will continue and no American journalist could enter Pakistan." Nine days later, Pearl was murdered and beheaded.

Individuals resort to terrorist behavior for all types of reasons. They may be demanding territory for their ethnic or religious group, objecting to government authority, or protesting that they are not getting the political rights they deserve. Whatever the reasons for these acts or the means of carrying them out, terrorism is a serious threat and can take place almost anywhere. Until a few years ago, many Americans believed that terrorism only occurred overseas. Unfortunately, with the Oklahoma City bombing in 1995, Americans witnessed firsthand a horrible act of violence committed for political or religious reasons. (See Application Case 16.5.) As a result, laws have been enacted to combat terrorism and its attacks on innocent people.

⚖ Application Case 16.5

United States v. McVeigh

In 1995, in one of the worst cases of domestic terrorism in United States history, Timothy McVeigh blew up the Alfred Murrah Federal Building in Oklahoma City, Oklahoma. The bombing killed 168 innocent people, including 19 children at the federal building's day care center. McVeigh was tried and convicted of 168 counts of murder, as well as other charges related to the nature of the crime.

McVeigh appealed his case to both the federal Court of Appeals and the U.S. Supreme Court, raising a total of nine separate challenges to his conviction. His attorneys argued that a new trial was warranted because of juror misconduct, an unfair exclusion of evidence, prejudicial pretrial publicity, and inflammatory testimony by victims' relatives. The Tenth Circuit Court of Appeals rejected all of McVeigh's arguments that he deserved a new trial, as did the U.S. Supreme Court. McVeigh, the first federal prisoner to be executed since 1963, was executed by lethal injection on Monday, June 11, 2001.

SOURCE: United States v. McVeigh, 153 F.3d 1166 (10th Cir. 1998), *cert. denied*, 526 U.S. 1007, 119 S. Ct. 1148 (1999). *See also* Andrew Cohen, *Legal Fight Won from Trenches*, DENVER POST, June 3, 1997, at A9.

Laws That Target Terrorism

Congress has created several statutes that criminalize terrorist-related activity and provide stiffer penalties when a perpetrator uses violence to carry out a political agenda. Federal law defines **international terrorism** as acts of violence that "appear to be intended to intimidate or coerce" people, a government policy or conduct, and that "occur primarily outside the territorial jurisdiction of the United States, or transcend national boundaries." In 1996, Congress adopted new anti-terrorist legislation that provides:

international terrorism
The deliberate use or threat of violence that is politically motivated and crosses national borders.

   A.   Prohibited Acts
      1.   Offenses. Whoever, involving conduct transcending national boundaries and in a circumstance described in subsection (b)—
         a. kills, kidnaps, maims, commits an assault resulting in serious bodily injury, or assaults with a dangerous weapon any person within the United States; or
         b. creates a substantial risk of serious bodily injury to any other person by destroying or damaging any structure, conveyance, or other real or personal property within the United States or by attempting or conspiring to destroy or damage any structure, conveyance, or other real or personal property within the United States;
       in violation of the laws of any State, or the United States, shall be punished as prescribed in subsection (c).[48]

Under the penalty provisions of this law, punishment can be as much as life imprisonment or death if the criminal conduct results in a killing. Punishment can result in various other serious terms for conduct that results in less than a killing.

After the September 11 terrorist attacks, Congress enacted the Uniting and Strengthening America by Providing Appropriate Tools Required to Intercept and Obstruct Terrorism Act of 2001 (USA PATRIOT Act).[49] The act greatly expanded law enforcement authority for the purpose of detecting and fighting terrorist activity. Key provisions included "the ease with which the federal government could conduct electronic surveillance, including roving wiretaps; the FBI's access to certain private records; the ability to detain immigrants suspected of terrorism for up to a week without being charged with a crime; and the requirement that banks find the sources of money in certain large private accounts."[50]

Some of the more controversial provisions were due to sunset in December 2005, but President Bush signed a renewal of the Act in March 2006. With the application of controversial provisions of the Patriot Act in the years since 9/11, debate has continued to rage over the balance between national security and individual rights.[51]

1. How have American perceptions regarding terrorism changed since the Oklahoma City bombing?

2. Which do you feel is a bigger threat to the United States, international or domestic terrorism?

REVIEW AND APPLICATIONS

Summary by Chapter Objectives

1. **Understand the historical development of organized crime.** Organized crime grew out of the criminalization of lotteries and prostitution and the prohibition of drugs and alcohol. Since its beginning in the United States, it has evolved into a sophisticated operation that uses illegal means to accomplish a variety of economic goals.

2. **List some typical organized crime activities.** Typical organized crime activities include:
   • Loan sharking.
   • Gambling.
   • Prostitution rings.
   • Money laundering.
   • Drug distribution.
   • Bookmaking.
   • Extortion.

3. **List the elements of a RICO violation.** The five elements of a criminal violation under RICO are:
   • Unlawful activity involving an enterprise.
   • Two or more qualifying acts of racketeering activity.
   • A showing of a pattern of such activity.
   • An effect upon interstate commerce.
   • The commission of the prohibited acts.

4. **Understand and differentiate various laws aimed at targeting organized crime.** Crimes such as the Racketeers Influenced and Corrupt Organization Statute (RICO) and the Continuing Criminal Enterprise Statute (CCE) were created as a way for the legislature to break down and put an end to organized crime. These statutes add stiffer penalties for people who commit crimes as part of a criminal enterprise and make the very act of participation in these groups a criminal violation.

5. **Understand the structure and activities of modern street gangs.** Like many organized crime organizations, many modern street gangs have a leader, members in middle management roles, and lower-level members who

commit the actual crimes. In addition, gangs also have shot-callers, who act as liaisons with other gangs. Typical activities of modern street gangs include all kinds of criminal activity, ranging from drug dealing and distribution to gambling operations, murder, bank robbery, financial crimes, extortion, bribery, racketeering, kidnapping, and even terrorism.

6. **Explain the laws that target street gangs.** Several jurisdictions have created laws that specifically address gang-related activity. One well-known example is STEP, which provides stiffer penalties if a person commits a crime in association with his or her gang membership. Several cities have also enacted legislation that prohibits gang members from associating in certain areas, such as in parks or on sidewalks.

7. **Understand the types of criminal activity that constitute terrorism.** Terrorism occurs when a group or person uses violence or other criminal means for a political or religious purpose rather than for economic reasons. Examples of common terrorist activities include:
   • Bombing.
   • Hijacking.
   • Kidnapping.
   • Hostage taking.

8. **Describe the various laws that target terrorism.** Congress has enacted several statutes that criminalize terrorist-related activity and provide stiffer penalties when a perpetrator uses violence in pursuit of a political or religious agenda. In 1996, Congress adopted new anti-terrorist legislation, which provides that anyone who transcends national boundaries and kills, kidnaps, maims, commits an assault resulting in serious bodily injury, or assaults with a dangerous weapon any person within the United States can receive a punishment as severe as the death penalty. Lesser acts of terrorism receive lesser, but still severe, penalties. The USA PATRIOT Act, enacted after the terrorist attack on September 11, 2001, grants strong weapons to federal law enforcement to protect the country against another similar attack. Some provisions of the PATRIOT Act have been controversial, with opponents claiming that they deprive citizens of their individual rights.

Key Terms

organized crime (p. 422)
boss (p. 424)
underboss (p. 424)
captains and soldiers (p. 424)
crews (p. 424)
protectors (p. 425)
shakedown (p. 425)
racketeering (p. 425)
loan sharking (p. 427)

bookmaking (p. 427)
dirty money (p. 428)
money laundering (p. 428)
Racketeer Influenced and Corrupt
    Organizations (RICO) (p. 430)
criminal street gang (p. 435)
cholo/chola (p. 437)
terrorism (p. 443)
international terrorism (p. 445)

Review Questions

1. How did the prohibition of drugs and alcohol help in the development of organized crime?
2. What role have lotteries played in organized crime, and how has the role of lotteries changed over the years?
3. What is loan sharking?
4. What is bookmaking, and how does a bookie make a profit?
5. Describe money laundering and the two main ways in which this crime is committed.
6. What is RICO? How do CCE and state versions of RICO differ from federal RICO?
7. Summarize the various laws aimed at combating money laundering.
8. How have the activities of gangs changed over the last century?
9. What is the main difference between organized crime and terrorism?
10. What are some reasons why individuals resort to terrorism?

Problem-Solving Exercises

1. **Organized Crime** You have just arrested Lonnie, 25, for possession with intent to distribute cocaine. Lonnie has a large amount of drugs on him when he is caught and is charged with distribution. At the station, you ask him if he would like to call a lawyer. Lonnie replies, "Man, I can't do no more time. I could be a big help to you if we can work something out." He then goes on to say that he is working for the Williams crime family, a notorious and ruthless crime syndicate that has dominated part of your city for nearly 20 years. Authorities have been trying for years to arrest and charge one of the leaders. Lonnie offers to wear a wire when he is to meet with his supervisor, who has direct contact with Tracy Williams, the boss. Lonnie wears the wire, and the captain is taped while giving specific instructions related to pickup points, quantities of cocaine, distribution areas, and a number of other crimes that the family has committed. Lonnie names several men who are known to be high-ranking members of the gang and describes their roles in the various operations. Lonnie, as well as several others, has two prior felony convictions for organized crimes. Answer the following questions:
   a. Should criminal charges be considered against Lonnie? Why or why not?
   b. What additional information does the officer need to know before making an arrest of the other crime family members?
   c. Who can be arrested, and why?
2. **Terrorism** You are working at the reception desk of the Nebraska state capitol building when you receive a call from a man with a foreign accent. He warns that in two hours a bomb will explode in your building, where hundreds of people work. The caller says that the Mission Fighters organization has planted the bomb as a way to draw attention to their cause, which is to have Montana declared a separate country where United States law doesn't apply, and leaders of the Mission Fighters run the government. If their demands are not met, they will

proceed to bomb a different state capitol each week, starting with yours. Answer the following questions:

a. If a bomb is discovered, what are some possible charges the perpetrators could be convicted of?

b. If the bomb explodes and kills one or more people, what charges could be brought?

c. Considering the organization that is threatening these attacks, but also considering the fact that the caller has a foreign accent, is it likely that international terrorists are involved as well? Why or why not?

Workplace Applications

1. **Kids and Gangs** You have worked as a beat officer in the same neighborhood for several years. As a result, you are very familiar with most of the families, in particular a young single mother and her 11-year-old son, Jacob. The mother is working full-time and pursuing a bachelor's degree at night, and she tells you that she is concerned. She worries that her son is getting involved with the wrong crowd, will join a gang, and will pursue a life of crime. Because she works and goes to school, she is unable to monitor Jacob's activities on a regular basis. Answer the following questions:

   a. Should you get involved?

   b. What are some of the measures an officer can take to protect Jacob and make sure he doesn't join a gang?

   c. Even if the mother is gone frequently, what can she do to prevent Jacob from joining a gang?

2. **Organized Crime and Extortion** You are a prosecutor who lives in the quietest, most pleasant suburb of your county. Every Thursday, you eat dinner with a friend from work at a family-run Mexican restaurant in the neighborhood. You know the family and like them very much. Tonight, the owner asks if he can speak with you. He explains that he has been approached by a local crime family that is demanding money for "protection." He does not have enough money to pay them, but is terrified that they will kill his only son in retaliation. He also states that he doesn't believe the local police will do anything, because they all seem to be paid off by the crime family. Although he wants to protect his family, he assures you that he will do anything he can personally to help you end this crime ring. Answer the following questions:

   a. Is there anything he can do to help, such as wear a wiretap device? Why or why not?

   b. Suppose that the charges of police corruption are true. What can you do about this? Where can you start?

   c. For now, what can you do to protect his family against a criminal attack?

3. **RICO and Gangs** You are a federal prosecutor and are beginning to charge local large-scale gangs with violating the RICO statute. You bring a case against 62 members of your city's most notorious gang, who have been distributing cocaine and crack for years. Attorneys for the defendants argue that the RICO statutes are meant to attack organized criminals such as the Mafia and not street gangs.

   a. Does this argument have any merit? Why or why not?

b. As a federal prosecutor, do you think street gangs are a worthwhile target of RICO statutes? Why or why not?

Ethics Exercises

1. **Terrorism and the Media** The newspaper you own has received a phone call from an extremist who has been responsible for at least five deaths nationwide. He asks you to publish his writings; in exchange, he promises not to kill any more people. State and federal government leaders have urged you never to negotiate with terrorists. On the other hand, he has been on the loose for more than 12 years, and police have very few leads with which to find him.
   a. What do you think your newspaper should do, and why?
   b. Is the newspaper legally liable in any way for publishing the work of this terrorist? Why or why not?

Notes

1. Craig M. Bradley, *Racketeering and the Federalization of Crime*, 22 Am. Crim. L. Rev. 213 n.1 (1984) (citing *Organized Crime in America: Hearings Before the S. Comm. on the Judiciary*, 98th Cong. 3 (1983) (letter from Pres. Reagan to Sen. Thurmond, Jan. 26, 1983)).
2. *Id.* at 215 (citing John S. Ezell, Fortune's Merry Wheel: The Lottery in America 249 (1960)); *see also* Stone v. Mississippi, 101 U.S. 814 (1879) & Champion v. Ames, 188 U.S. 321 (1903).
3. National Prohibition Act, ch. 85, 41 Stat. 305 (1919).
4. Dorean Marguerite Koenig, *The Criminal Justice System Facing the Challenge of Organized Crime*, 44 Wayne L. Rev. 1351, 1355 (1998) (citing Darrell J. Steffensmeier, *A Public Policy Agenda for Combating Organized Crime*, in Crime and Public Policy 269–70 (Hugh D. Barlow ed., 1995)).
5. Lesley Suzanne Bonnie, *The Prosecution of Sophisticated Urban Street Gangs: A Proper Application of RICO*, 42 Cath. U. L. Rev. 579, 584 (1993).
6. Law of Mar. 3, 1875, ch. 141 § 3, 18 Stat. 477 (1875), *superseded by* Law of Mar. 3, 1903, ch. 1012, §2, 32 Stat. 1213 (1903), and Law of Feb. 20, 1907, ch. 1134, § 3, 34 Stat. 89 (1907).
7. Craig M. Bradley, *Racketeering and the Federalization of Crime*, 22 Am. Crim. L. Rev. 213, 252 (1984).
8. Scott Sultzer, *Money Laundering: The Scope of the Problem and Attempts to Combat It*, 63 Tenn. L. Rev. 143, 146 n.4 (1995) (citing *Federal Government's Response to Money Laundering: Hearings Before the H. Comm. on Banking, Finance, & Urban Affairs*, 103d Cong. 546 (1993) (statement of John P. LaWare, Governor of the Board of Governors, U.S. Federal Reserve System (citing Federal Bureau of Investigation (FBI) estimates)).
9. *Id.* at 147 n.12 (citing Timothy L. O'Brien, *Cash-Flow Woes: Law Firm's Downfall Exposes New Methods of Money Laundering*, Wall Street Journal, May 26, 1995, at A1). This article explains that the Cali Cartel uses an "international network" of white-collar professionals to launder its revenues.

10. *Money Laundering Legislation: Hearing of the S. Comm. on the Judiciary*, 99th Cong. 190 (1985) and *Federal Government's Response to Money Laundering: Hearings Before the H. Comm. on Banking, Finance, & Urban Affairs*, 103d Cong. 200–01 (1993).

11. Dorean Marguerite Koenig, *The Criminal Justice System Facing the Challenge of Organized Crime*, 44 Wayne L. Rev. 1351, 1355 (1998) (citing President's Commission on Organized Crime, Report to the President and the Attorney General, The Impact: Organized Crime Today 25 (1986)).

12. 18 U.S.C. § 1961 (2000) (Congressional Statement of Findings and Purpose); *see also* Dorean Marguerite Koenig, *The Criminal Justice System Facing the Challenge of Organized Crime*, 44 Wayne L. Rev. 1351, 1364 (1998) (citing Glenn Beard et al., *Racketeer Influenced and Corrupt Organizations*, 33 Am. Crim. L. Rev. 929 (1996)).

13. 18 U.S.C. §§ 1961–1968 (2000).

14. United States v. Turkette, 452 U.S. 576, 580–81, 583 (1981).

15. 18 U.S.C. § 1961(1)(a)–(f) (2000).

16. Dorean Marguerite Koenig, *The Criminal Justice System Facing the Challenge of Organized Crime*, 44 Wayne L. Rev. 1351, 1365 (1998) (citing Glenn Beard et al., *Racketeer Influenced and Corrupt Organizations*, 33 Am. Crim. L. Rev. 929, 935 (1996)).

17. 18 U.S.C. § 1962(a)–(d) (2000).

18. 18 U.S.C. § 1964(c) (2000).

19. Or. Rev. Stat. §§ 166.715–166.735 (1998).

20. 21 U.S.C. § 848(c) (2000); *see also* Susan W. Brenner, *RICO, CCE, and Other Complex Crimes: The Transformation of American Criminal Law*, 2 Wm. & Mary Bill Rts. J. 239 (1993).

21. 18 U.S.C. § 1956 (2000).

22. 18 U.S.C. § 1344 (2000) & 31 U.S.C. §§ 1829, 1951–59, 5311–26 (2000).

23. 18 U.S.C. § 1956 (2000).

24. United States v. Wheeler, 435 U.S. 313, 316–17 (1978).

25. Blockburger v. United States, 284 U.S. 299 (1932); *see also* United States v. Dixon, 509 U.S. 688 (1993).

26. Lesley Suzanne Bonnie, *The Prosecution of Sophisticated Urban Street Gangs: A Proper Application of RICO*, 42 Cath. U. L. Rev. 579, 598 (1993) (citing United States v. Angiulo, 897 F.2d 1169, 1180 (1st Cir. 1990)).

27. Iowa Code Ann. § 723A.1 (West 2007).

28. Lesley Suzanne Bonnie, *The Prosecution of Sophisticated Urban Street Gangs: A Proper Application of RICO*, 42 Cath. U. L. Rev. 579, 584 (1993).

29. *Id.*

30. United States v. Andrews, 749 F. Supp. 1520 (N.D. Ill. 1990).

31. Rachelle Q. Ayuyang, *Hard Girls: Filipino Girls in Gangs*, Filipinas Magazine, Aug. 31, 1998.

32. *Id.*

33. Karen Low, *Authorities Arrest 13 Alleged Mexican Mafia Members*, Associated Press, Feb. 3, 1999.

34. Louis Holland, *Can Gang Recruitment Be Stopped? An Analysis of the Social and Legal Factors Affecting Anti-Gang Legislation*, 21 J. Contemp. L. 259, 271 (1995).

35. Jesse Katz, *Violence Punctuates Truce Between Bloods and Crips Gangs: Rivalry-Based Killings Have Declined Since the Spring Accord, But Other Reasons Can Lead to Slayings*, L. A. TIMES, Sept. 13, 1992, Part A, Metro Desk.

36. Louis Holland, *Can Gang Recruitment Be Stopped? An Analysis of the Social and Legal Factors Affecting Anti-Gang Legislation*, 21 J. CONTEMP. L. 259, 274 (1995).

37. City of Chicago v. Morales, 529 U.S. 41 (1999).

38. *See* Johnson v. Athens-Clarke County, 529 S.E.2d 613 (Ga. 2000) and Silvar v. District Court, 129 P.3d 682 (Nev. 2006); *see also* Kim Stronsnider, *Anti-Gang Ordinances After City of Chicago v. Morales: The Intersection of Race, Vagueness Doctrine, and Equal Protection in Criminal Law*, 39 AM. CRIM. L. REV. 101 (2002), *all cited in* SANFORD H. KADISH, STEPHEN J. SCHULHOFER & CAROL S. STEIKER, CRIMINAL LAW AND ITS PROCESSES 165–66 (8th ed. 2007).

39. 18 U.S.C. § 521 (2000).

40. IOWA CODE ANN. § 723A.2 (West 2007).

41. CAL. PENAL CODE §§ 186.20–186.33 (West 2007).

42. CAL. PENAL CODE § 186.22(f) & (e) (West 1998).

43. *See* Beth Bjerregaard, *The Constitutionality of Anti-Gang Legislation*, 21 CAMPBELL L. REV. 31, 40 n.51 (1998) and cases cited therein.

44. Alexander Molina, *California's Anti-Gang Street Terrorism Enforcement and Prevention Act: One Step Forward, Two Steps Back?*, 22 SW. U. L. REV. 457, 477 n.139 (1993) (citing Sebastian Rotella, *Gangs Question Their Exile From Park*, L.A. TIMES (Valley ed.) Sept. 18, 1991, at B3).

45. ARK. CODE ANN. § 5-74-108 (West 2007).

46. ARK. CODE. ANN. § 5-74-104 (West 2007).

47. *See* Austin T. Turk, *Terrorism*, *in* ENCYCLOPEDIA OF CRIME AND JUSTICE 1549–55 (Joshua Dressler ed., 2d ed. 2002).

48. 18 U.S.C. § 2332b(a)–(c) (1996).

49. Uniting and Strengthening America by Providing Appropriate Tools Required to Intercept and Obstruct Terrorism Act (USA PATRIOT Act) of 2001, Pub. L. No. 107-56, 115 Stat. 272 (2001) (codified in scattered sections of the U.S.C.).

50. Eugene Kim, *The New York Police Department's Random Bag Search Policy: Withstanding Fourth Amendment Scrutiny Is Only the First Step in Combating Terrorism*, 37 SETON HALL L. REV. 561, 564 (2007).

51. *See, e.g.*, Patricia Mell, *Big Brother at the Door: Balancing National Security with Privacy Under the USA Patriot Act*, 80 DENV. U. L. REV. 375 (2002); Brett A. Shumate, *From "Sneak and Peek" to "Sneak and Steal": Section 213 of the USA Patriot Act*, 19 REGENT U. L. REV. 203 (2006).

Glossary

A

abandoned property   Property over which a person voluntarily gives up permanent possession or ownership.

abandonment   An affirmative defense to the crime of attempt that exists only if the defendant voluntarily and completely renounces his or her criminal purpose.

abatement   The ending or eliminating of a nuisance.

accessory   One who aids in the commission of a crime without being present when the crime is committed.

accessory after the fact   One who intentionally aids another whom he or she knows has committed a felony, in order for the person assisted to avoid criminal prosecution and punishment.

accessory before the fact   One who intentionally counsels, solicits, or commands another in the commision of a crime.

accomplice   Someone who knowingly and willingly associates with the commision of a criminal offense, and who intentionally assists another in the commission of a crime.

accomplice liability   The accountablity of one individual for the criminal act or acts of another.

actual possession   When the controlled substance is on the defendant's person or in a container that the defendant is carrying.

actus reus   A willed unlawful act; the wrongful deed that comprises the physical component of a crime.

adequate provocation   When the acts or conduct of the person killed would be sufficient to cause a person of reasonable, ordinary temperament to lose self-control.

adulteration   When the ingredients of a food, drug, cosmetic or device are poisonous, filthy, putrid, otherwise unsanitary, or have been contaminated.

adultery   Sexual relations with someone other than a spouse when the person is married.

affirmative defense   A defense in which the defendant admits to the existence of all of the necessary legal elements for criminal liability, but offers one or more legally recognized reasons why he or she should nonetheless be acquitted.

agency theory   The theory that all conspirators act as the agents of (and represent) their co-conspirators involved in the criminal scheme and are liable for all criminal acts commited by any of their co-conspirators.

agent provocateur   Someone who intends for the principal to fail in his or her illegal venture and, because of this lack of causation, is not an accomplice.

aggravated assault   Assault with intent to kill, rob, or rape, or assaults with specified deadly weapons. A felony in most states.

aggravated battery   A battery accompanied by an intent to kill or rape—thus, usually a specific intent crime. A felony in many states.

aggravated burglary   Simple burglary with the added elements of entering an inhabited dwelling, or any structure or vehicle, while armed with a dangerous weapon, or by committing a battery after or upon the entry.

aggressor   One who first employs hostile force, either by threatening or striking another, which justifies like response.

aid and abet   To assist or faciliate a person in accomplishing a crime.

antitrust laws   Laws that protect trade and commerce from restraints, monopolies, price-fixing, and price discrimination, to ensure and preserve a competitive economy.

armed robbery   Robbery accomplished by means of a dangerous or deadly weapon; often classified as robbery in the first degree or aggravated robbery.

arraignment and plea   The defendant's appearance to respond formally to the charges.

assault   A misdemeanor consisting of either an attempted battery or an intentional frightening of another person.

assault weapon   One of the prohibited weapons named by federal legislation, such as rifles with conspicuous pistol grips, pistols with shrouds, and shotguns with a higher ammunition capacity.

attempt   When a person, with the intent to commit an offense, performs any act that constitutes a substantial step toward the commission of that offense.

attempt to monopolize   Engaging in behavior and business practices that, if successful, would create a monopoly and that come close enough to so doing to create a dangerous probability that it would have occurred.

B

bail   A deposit of cash, other property, or a bond, guaranteeing the accused will appear in court.

battered child syndrome   A clinical condition suffered by young children who have been the victims of prolonged serious physical abuse.

battered woman syndrome   A defense in many jurisdictions, in which the victim of abuse eventually "snaps" and kills the abuser.

battery   A misdemeanor consisting of the unlawful application of force that actually and intentionally causes the touching of another person against his or her will.

bifurcated trial   The division of a criminal trial into two parts, the first part leading to a verdict of guilty or not guilty, and the second relating to another issue, such as the sanity of the accused (or the penalty phase of a death penalty case).

bill of attainder   A special legislative enactment that declares a person or group of persons guilty of a crime and subject to punishment without trial.

Bill of Rights   The first 10 amendments to the U.S. Constitution, especially those portions that guarantee fundamental individual rights vis-à-vis the government.

blackmail   A threat by a private citizen seeking hush money, or payment, to remain silent about a crime or a shameful act.

bond   A written promise to pay the bail sum, posted by a financially responsible person, usually a professional bondsman.

bookmaking   The promotion of gambling by unlawfully accepting bets on the outcomes of future contingent events from members of the public, as a business rather than in a casual or personal fashion.

born-alive rule   The common law rule defining the beginning of life, for purposes of criminal homicide, as the birth of a live child.

boss   The head or leader of an organized crime family. Usually, this person does not involve himself in the day-to-day operations of the group but is the ultimate decision maker.

breaking and entering   Unlawful forced entry; similar to burglary, but without the specific intent to commit a theft or felony inside the structure.

bribery   Payment by a person to a public official in order to gain an advantage that the person is not otherwise entitled to; both parties are guilty of the crime.

burden of proof   The onus of producing evidence and also of persuading the jury with the required level of proof, which in a criminal case is "beyond a reasonable doubt."

burglar's tools   Tools and instruments that are designed, adapted, or commonly used to commit burglaries.

but-for test   The test that asks whether the result would have occurred if the defendant had not acted.

C

capital murder   A charge of murder with the maximum punishment of death, often called murder in the first degree.

captains and soldiers   A group of middle managers and supervisors below the underboss of an organized crime family.

cause-in-fact   The cause of the social harm in a criminal act, as determined by the but-for test.

child abuse   An intentional or neglectful physical or emotional injury imposed on a child, including sexual molestation.

child molestation   Any sexual conduct by an adult with a child.

cholo/chola   A member of a Latino (especially Mexican American) street gang.

churning   When a stockbroker excessively purchases and sells securities for a client without regard or concern for the client's investment objectives but rather to advance the stockbroker's own interests, usually by generating commissions.

civil contempt   The failure to do something ordered by the court for the benefit of another party to the proceedings.

civil law   Law that deals with matters considered to be private concerns between individuals.

clear and present danger test   A test to determine whether a defendant's words pose an immediate danger of bringing about substantive evils that Congress has the right (and duty) to prevent.

commercial bribery   The giving, receiving, or soliciting of anything of value to influence an employee or professional in the performance of his or her duties.

common law   Law created by judicial opinion. Historically, law from America's colonial and English past, which has set precedents that are still sometimes followed today.

common law arson   The malicious and willful burning of another's house.

common law burglary   Breaking and entering, in the nighttime, of the mansion or dwelling house or curtilage of another, with the intent to commit a felony.

compounding a felony   An offense that occurs when someone refuses to report or prosecute a felony in exchange for a benefit or reward of some value.

concurrence of elements   Requirement for criminal liability that the accused performed a voluntary act *accompanied by* the required mental state that actually and proximately caused the prohibited social harm.

conditional assault   An assault in which the actor threatens harm only under certain conditions, such as the failure of the victim to act a certain way demanded by the actor.

consent   A defense, in certain circumstances, in which the victim agrees to the actor's conduct. The consent negates an element of the offense or precludes infliction of the harm to be prevented by the law defining the offense.

conspiracy   A partnership in crime, defined as an agreement between two or more people to achieve a criminal purpose or to achieve a lawful purpose using unlawful means. Also called a common criminal enterprise.

constructive contempt   Contempt of court that results from matters outside the court, such as failure to comply with court orders.

constructive entry   An entry effected by using an instrumentality, such as another person, an animal, or a physical object.

constructive possession (drugs)   When illegal drugs are in a place immediately accessible to the accused and subject to his or her domination and control.

constructive possession (stolen goods)   A relationship between the defendant and the stolen goods such that it is reasonable to treat the extent of the defendant's dominion and control over the property as if it were actual possession.

constructive presence   When an individual is within the vicinity of the crime and is able to assist the primary actor if necessary.

contempt of court   Any affirmative act or omission that obstructs justice or attempts to negate the dignity and authority of the court.

controlled substance   Any substance that is strictly regulated or outlawed because of its potential for abuse or addiction.

corpus delicti   The required proof that a crime has been committed. In homicide cases, this usually means the corpse of the victim.

crews   The men and women in an organized crime organization who work out on the street carrying out the actual operations of the group.

crime   An act or omission that the law makes punishable, generally by fine, penalty, forfeiture, or confinement.

criminal abortion   The artificially induced expulsion of a fetus by illegal means, such as spousal abuse.

criminal contempt   An act of disrespect toward the court or its procedures, other than direct contempt, that obstructs the administration of justice.

criminal facilitation   When an individual knowingly aids another, but does not truly have a separate intent to aid in the commission of the underlying offense.

criminal homicide   Any act that causes the death of another with criminal intent and without lawful justification or excuse.

criminal law   Law that involves the violation of public rights and duties, creating a social harm.

criminal street gang   Any formal or informal ongoing organization whose primary activity is the commission of one or more criminal acts, which has an identifiable name or identifying sign or symbol, and whose members individually or collectively engage in or have engaged in a pattern of criminal gang activity.

curtilage   The land immediately surrounding and associated with the home, including such structures as a barn, outhouse, or milk house.

D

dangerous proximity test   A test that determines that an attempt has occurred when the perpetrator's conduct is in dangerous proximity to success, or when an act is so near to the result that the danger of its success is very great.

deadly force   Force likely or intended to cause death or great bodily harm.

defense   Either a failure of proof by the prosecution, or a defendant's statement of a reason why the prosecutor has no valid case against him or her.

delivery of a controlled substance   The transfer of a controlled substance from one person to another.

determinate sentencing   A sentencing system that abolishes parole boards and creates presumptive sentencing ranges for various classes of offenses, thereby limiting trial judges' discretion; such a system typically has sentencing guidelines for judges to follow.

diminished capacity   A term used to describe two circumstances in which a mental condition short of insanity will lead to an acquittal or lessened charges: (1) where the accused raises the condition as a failure of proof defense, and (2) a true partial defense, whereby the crime of murder can be mitigated to manslaughter.

direct contempt   A criminal form of contempt of court that occurs in the presence of the court when a person resists the court's authority.

dirty money   The money received through illegal activities such as drug sales and gambling.

disorderly conduct   A loosely defined offense addressing behavior that disturbs the safety, health, or morals of others, or that is intended only to annoy another person.

dram shop acts   Legislative acts that impose strict liability on the seller of intoxicating beverages when the sale results in harm to a third party's person, property, or means of support.

driving under the influence (DUI)   Operating a motor vehicle while under the influence of a substance or with a blood or breath alcohol concentration above a prohibited level.

drug conspiracy   An agreement between two or more people to commit a criminal or unlawful drug-related act, or to commit a lawful drug-related act by criminal or unlawful means.

drug loitering   An action done in public that manifests the intent to engage in illegal drug activity.

drug paraphernalia   Any equipment, product, or material that is primarily intended or designed for use with a controlled substance, such as bongs, pipes, rolling papers, scales, and hypodermic needles.

drug transportation   Transporting a controlled substance in a vehicle; a crime in every state.

drunk driving   The offense of driving while drunk, known as DWI, DUI, DWAI, or DUBAL.

due process   The multiple criminal justice procedures and processes that must be followed before a person can be legally deprived of his or her life, liberty, or property.

DUI manslaughter   Causing the death of a human being by reason of operation of a motor vehicle while under the influence of alcohol or drugs.

duress   A defense that arises when a person commits an unlawful act because of a threat of imminent death or serious bodily injury to himself or another, unless the actor intentionally kills an innocent third person.

E

elder abuse   The abuse, neglect, or financial exploitation of elderly persons.

embezzlement   The unlawful taking or misuse of property by persons, typically employees, who lawfully come into possession of the property and therefore do not meet the theft or larceny requirement of wrongfully obtaining the property.

entrapment   When officers or agents of the government, for the purpose of instituting a criminal prosecution against a person, induce an otherwise innocent person to commit a crime that he or she had not contemplated.

equal protection   The constitutional provision that all people should be treated equally with respect to the practice dealt with by the law.

escape   A crime that occurs when a person who is lawfully detained or imprisoned leaves custody before he or she is entitled to freedom by due process of law.

ex post facto law   A law that (1) makes criminal an act done before passage of the law against it, and punishes such action; (2) aggravates a crime, or makes it greater than it was when committed; or (3) inflicts a greater punishment than the law imposed or allows evidence of guilt that is less than what the law required at the time the offense was committed.

excuse   A defense in which the criminal actor has committed an unjustified crime, but there is a reason for not holding him or her personally accountable for it.

exhibitionism   Repeated intentional acts of exposing the genitals to an unsuspecting stranger for the purpose of achieving sexual excitement.

extortion   The gaining of property by threat of physical harm to a person or property by a public official under color of his or her office.

F

factual impossibility   When a person's intended end constitutes a crime, but the person fails to consummate the offense because of an attendant circumstance that is unknown or beyond his or her control, making commission of the crime impossible.

failure of proof   A defense in which the defense counsel either makes a motion for judgment of acquittal or the defendant introduces evidence that shows that the prosecution's case is lacking.

fair notice   The due process requirement that people are entitled to know what they are forbidden to do so that they may shape their conduct accordingly.

false imprisonment   Knowingly and unlawfully restraining a person so as to substantially interfere with his or her liberty.

false pretenses   A crime in which title or ownership of the property is passed to the defendant in reliance on the defendant's misrepresentation.

false swearing   The giving of a false oath during a proceeding or matter in which an oath is required by law.

federal test   The federal statutory definition of insanity, which provides that a person is excused by reason of insanity if he or she proves by clear and convincing evidence that at the time of the offense, as a result of a severe mental disease or defect, he or she was unable to appreciate the nature and quality of his or her act, or the wrongfulness of his or her conduct.

federalism   The system of government of the United States whereby all power resides in the state governments unless specifically granted to the federal government.

felony   A serious crime that is usually punishable by imprisonment for more than one year or by death.

felony murder rule   The rule that when the accused kills in the course of committing a felony, the *mens rea* for murder is present in the intent to commit the felony, and therefore murder has been committed.

feticide   The unlawful killing of a fetus.

firearm   Any weapon that can, is designed to, or may readily be converted to expel a projectile by the action of an explosive; the frame or receiver of any such weapon; any firearm muffler or firearm silencer.

forgery   Making or altering a writing, with the purpose of deceiving or injuring, in such a way as to convey a false impression concerning its authenticity.

fornication   Voluntary, unlawful sexual intercourse under circumstances not constituting adultery.

fraudulent making   Creating a document that is not authentic.

G

gambling   The act of staking or risking something of value on the outcome of a contest of chance or on a future event of chance that is not under the gambler's control or influence.

general intent   The intent only to do the *actus reus* of the crime, without any of the elements of specific intent.

genuine legal impossibility   Where the law does not define as criminal the goal the defendant sought to achieve. This is a valid defense to the crime of attempt.

grand jury   A panel of persons chosen through strict court procedures to review criminal investigations and, in some instances, to conduct criminal investigations. Grand juries decide whether to charge crimes in the cases presented to them or investigated by them.

grand theft   The felonious taking of property valued above a set monetary amount, or the theft of a motor vehicle. More serious than petty or petit theft.

H

habeas corpus   Literally, "you have the body." A legal action separate from the criminal case, it can only be brought by a prisoner who has exhausted all the usual appellate remedies.

habitual-felon laws   Laws that provide for enhanced sentencing of repeat offenders.

homicide   The killing of one human being by another.

horizontal price-fixing   Direct or indirect agreements made between market participants at the same level within a given market, regarding the prices they will charge for a similar product they both sell.

"hybrid" legal impossibility   An ambiguous case in which impossibility could be considered either legal or factual, as distinguished from cases of true legal impossibility.

I

imperfect self-defense   A partial defense that reduces a murder charge to voluntary manslaughter, where the claim of self-defense fails because it is not objectively reasonable but is honestly believed by the accused.

incapacitation   The removal or restriction of freedom of those who have violated criminal laws, usually by imprisonment.

inchoate crime   A criminal act that is detected and punished before the ultimate or intended crime actually occurs. The principal modern inchoate crimes are attempt, conspiracy, and solicitation.

incompetency   An accused person's inability to rationally consult with an attorney or to understand the nature of the proceedings against him or her.

indecent exposure   An offensive display of one's body in public, especially the genitals or the female breasts.

indeterminate sentencing   A sentencing system in which the trial judge has great discretion and correctional authorities have the power to release a prisoner before completion of the maximum sentence imposed by the judge if, in the view of those authorities, rehabilitative goals have been achieved.

indictment   The paper issued by a grand jury that charges an accused with a felony.

indispensable element test   A test that determines that no attempt has occurred when a suspect has not yet gained control over an indispensable instrumentality of the criminal plan.

information   The paper issued by a prosecutor that charges an accused of a felony.

inherently dangerous felonies   Felonies involving conduct that is inherently dangerous to human life, such as rape, arson, and armed robbery.

inner door   A door inside a building that does not lead directly to the outside.

innocent agent or instrumentality   An object, animal, or person who cannot be culpable under the law, such as an insane person or a child, that is used by a principal to commit a crime.

insanity   A defense in which the law recognizes that the accused was suffering from mental disease when the crime occurred, and thus may be relieved of criminal responsibility.

insider trading   A type of substantive fraud that involves the purchase and sale of securities based on material, nonpublic information.

intangible rights theory   A type of prosecution under mail fraud that was primarily used to protect citizens from dishonest public officials.

international terrorism   The deliberate use or threat of violence that is politically motivated and crosses national borders.

intervening cause   A cause other than the defendant's conduct that contributes to the social harm.

intoxication   A disturbance of mental or physical capacities resulting from the introduction of any substance into the body.

involuntary intoxication   Intoxication that occurs when the actor does not consume drugs or alcohol voluntarily or if the actor is not to blame for becoming intoxicated because, for example, he or she has an unanticipated reaction to drugs or alcohol.

involuntary manslaughter   A criminal homicide that encompasses a killing done without intent to kill, and without such indifference to human life as to constitute implied malice, as a result of criminally negligent conduct on the part of the defendant.

irresistible impulse test   A test for insanity that permits a verdict of not guilty by reason of insanity if the fact-finder concludes that the accused had a mental disease that kept him or her from controlling his or her conduct.

J

joyriding   The illegal driving of someone else's automobile without permission, but with no intent to deprive the owner of it permanently.

jurisdiction   The power or authority of a court to act with respect to any case before it.

justification   A defense that, because of the circumstances, renders criminal conduct lawful and therefore exempts the actor from criminal sanctions.

K

kidnapping   A felony defined as taking or carrying away a person without consent, by force or fraud, without lawful excuse, and often with a demand for ransom.

knowingly causes a result   Commits an act in the awareness that one's conduct will almost certainly cause this result.

knowingly with respect to conduct and attendant circumstances   Aware that one's actions are criminal or that attendant circumstances make an otherwise legal act a criminal one.

L

larceny   The taking and carrying away of property of another, without consent, with the purpose of stealing or permanently depriving the owner of possession.

larceny from a person   Statutory offense of taking property from the person of another; the penalty is usually greater than that for simple larceny.

last act test   A test that determines that an attempt has occurred when a person has performed all of the acts that he or she believed were necessary to commit the underlying offense.

law   The federal, state, or local enactments of legislative bodies; the known decisions of the courts of the federal and state governments; rules and regulations proclaimed by government bodies; and proclamations by executives of the federal, state, or local government.

legal impossibility   When the intended acts, even if completed, would not amount to a crime. Legal impossibility is a common law defense to the crime of attempt.

legality   The principle that no one can be punished for an act that was not defined as criminal before the person did the act.

loan sharking   The practice of lending money at excessive rates and using threats or extortion to enforce repayment.

M

mail fraud   A form of fraud that uses a mail service to disseminate materials that deceive people.

mala in se   Crimes (such as rape and murder) that are inherently wrong.

mala prohibita   Crimes defining conduct that is wrong only because the law says it is wrong, in order to protect the general public.

malice   A state of mind connoting an "abandoned and malignant heart." It is not limited to the specific intent to kill, since even a wanton or reckless state of mind may constitute malice.

malice aforethought   Under modern law, any one of four mental states that reveal the intent to (1) kill, (2) inflict grievous bodily injury, (3) show extreme reckless disregard for human life, or (4) commit a felony that results in another's death.

mandatory sentencing   Laws by which the state's legislature fixes either the exact penalty for the crime or a minimum number of years that the defendant must serve.

Mann Act   A federal act that prohibits the knowing transportation in interstate or foreign commerce of any individual, male or female, with the intent that such individual engage in prostitution or in any sexual activity.

manslaughter　The killing of another without the mental element of malice aforethought.

mayhem　The felony of assault with intent to maim.

Megan's Law　A statute that has been enacted in all 50 states that requires community notification by authorities when a convicted sex offender is released from prison.

mens rea　A guilty mind, or intent; the state of mind that the prosecution, to secure a conviction, must prove that a defendant had when committing a crime.

misappropriation　The wrongful misuse or stealing of another's property that has been entrusted to the accused.

misbranding　Any branding of an item that includes the use of false or misleading information, labels, packaging, or containers.

misdemeanor　A crime that is less serious then a felony and is usually punishable by fine, penalty, forfeiture, or confinement in a jail for less than one year.

misprision of a felony　The act of failing to report or prosecute a known felony and taking positive steps to conceal the crime.

mitigation　The reduction, or lessening, of a penalty or punishment imposed by law.

M'Naghten test　The rule used to establish an insanity defense. Under this rule, it must be clearly proved that, at the time of the offense, the accused was laboring under such a mental illness as not to know the nature and quality of what he or she he was doing or, if he or she did know it, did not know that it was wrong.

Model Penal Code (MPC)　A comprehensive recodification of the principles of American criminal responsibility.

modern arson　The malicious, willful burning of, or attempted burning of, one's own or another person's property.

modern burglary　Entering, whether in the daytime or at night, of any building, structure, or vehicle, with the intent to commit any criminal offense.

money laundering　Transferring illegally obtained money through legitimate persons or accounts so that its original source cannot be traced; a federal crime.

monopolize　To jointly acquire and maintain the power to control and dominate interstate trade and commerce in a commodity sufficient to exclude actual or potential competitors from the field.

motive　The emotion that prompts a person to act. It is not an element of a crime that is required to prove

criminal liability, but it often may be shown in order to identify the perpetrator of a crime or explain his or her reason for acting.

motor vehicle　A vehicle proceeding on land by means of its own power plant and free of rails, tracks, or overheard wires.

MPC test　A test for insanity that provides that a person is not responsible for criminal conduct if he or she is found to lack substantial capacity to appreciate the criminality of the conduct, or to conform his or her conduct to the requirements of the law.

murder　The killing of another with the mental element of malice aforethought.

N

natural and probable consequences doctrine　A doctrine that holds an accomplice liable not only for the offense he intended to facilitate or encourage, but also for any natural and foreseeable additional offenses committed by the principal to whom he or she is an accomplice.

necessity　A defense in which a person, faced with a choice between two courses of action, chooses the lesser of evils, as long as the harm produced is less than the harm that would have occurred without the action.

negligent homicide　A criminal homicide committed by a person who has neglected to exercise the degree of care that an ordinary person would have exercised under the same circumstances.

negligently　Acting in a manner that ignores a substantial and unjustified risk of which one should have been aware.

nighttime　At common law, the period between sunset and sunrise when there is not enough daylight to discern a man's face.

nonproxyable offense　A crime that can only be committed through the actor's own conduct and cannot be committed by an agent.

nuisance　Anything that endangers life or health, gives offense to the senses, violates laws of decency, or obstructs the reasonable and comfortable use of property.

O

obscenity　Sexually explicit material that falls outside the protection of the First Amendment and therefore may be punished under a criminal statute.

obstruction of justice　The act by which one or more persons attempt to or actually prevent the execution of a lawful process.

omissions   Narrowly defined circumstances in which a failure to act is viewed as a criminal act.

organized crime   Individuals who associate together for the purpose of engaging in criminal activity on a sustained basis, with an emphasis on the life of the organization.

P

pandering   Either procuring a prostitute for a place of prostitution or procuring a place for a prostitute to engage in prostitution.

parking   Any sale of securities that are purchased with the understanding that they will be repurchased by the seller at a later time, to manipulate stock prices or avoid reporting requirements.

parole   The release of an offender from incarceration prior to the expiration of the full term of incarceration, to carry out the rest of the sentence with conditions under the supervision of a corrections officer.

perjury   Making false statements under oath or affirmation.

petty offense   A minor or insignificant crime, also known as a violation or infraction.

petty or petit theft   The misdemeanor taking of property under a set monetary amount. Less serious than grand theft.

physical proximity test   A test that determines that an attempt has occurred when the perpetrator's conduct, though not having advanced so far as the last act, approaches sufficiently near to the completed crime as to be a substantial step toward commission of the offense.

pimping   Promoting prostitution, living off of the earnings of prostitutes, and in some cases coercing individuals to work as prostitutes.

Pinkerton **doctrine**   The doctrine that holds a person associated with a conspiracy responsible for any criminal act commited by a co-conspirator if the act is within the scope of the conspiracy and is a forseeable result of the criminal scheme.

possession with intent to deliver   A drug offense that may be proven circumstantially by proof of a monetarily valuable quantity of drugs, possession of manufacturing or packaging implements, and the activities or statements of the person or persons in possession of the substance.

possessory offenses   Criminal offenses in which the law defines possession as an act.

preliminary hearing   A post-arrest, pretrial judicial proceeding, at which the judge decides whether there is probable cause to prosecute the accused. In some jurisdictions, the preliminary hearing is minimal; in others, it is a mini-trial.

premeditation and deliberation   The mental state that raises second-degree murder to first-degree murder in jurisdictions that classify murder into two or more levels. It implies a cold-blooded killing.

principal   One who is present at and participates in the crime charged or who procures an innocent agent to commit the crime.

principal in the first degree   Usually the primary actor or perpetrator of the crime.

principal in the second degree   One who intentionally assists in the commission of a crime in his or her presence; such presence may be either actual or constructive.

probable cause   Evidence that there is a fair probability that the suspect committed a crime; required for an arrest of a suspect by a law enforcement officer.

probation   The suspension of a sentence of incarceration, allowing the offender to return to the community with conditions under the supervision of a probation officer.

procedural criminal law   The rules governing how the criminal law is administered.

proportionality   The constitutional principle that the punishment should fit the crime, expressed in the Eighth Amendment's cruel and unusual punishment clause.

prostitution   A crime that is committed when one person agrees to engage in sexual or deviate sexual intercourse in return for something of value, usually money.

protectors   Law enforcement officers, lawyers, bankers, and accountants who use their skills to protect a crime organization from government interference or criminal prosecution.

proximate cause   That cause, from among all of the causes-in-fact that may exist, that is the legal cause of the social harm.

psychoactive drug   A drug that has the ability to alter mood, anxiety, behavior, cognitive processes, or mental tension.

public order and safety offenses   Offenses designed to protect the general public by dealing with behavior that is not necessarily immoral, but nonetheless affects the peace and safety of the community.

punishment   When an agent of the government, using authority granted by virtue of a legal criminal conviction, intentionally inflicts pain, loss of liberty, or some other unpleasant consequence on the person who has been convicted.

purposely with respect to attendant circumstances   When the actor is aware of conditions that will make the intended crime possible, or believes or hopes that they exist.

purposely with respect to result or conduct When the actor has a voluntary wish to act in a certain way or produce a certain result.

Q

quasi-bribery An extension of the crime of bribery to include people other than public officials whose functions are considered important to the public.

R

Racketeer Influenced and Corrupt Organizations (RICO) A federal law that criminalizes illegal activities committed by organized crime members.

racketeering A system of organized crime traditionally involving the extortion of money from businesses by intimidation, violence, or other illegal methods; the practice of engaging in a fraudulent scheme or enterprise.

rape A felony defined as "the carnal knowledge of a woman forcibly and against her will."

rape trauma syndrome A condition observed in some rape victims, in which the victim develops phobias and physical problems as a result of having been raped.

receiving Acquiring possession, control, or title, or lending on the security of, property that has been stolen.

reckless driving Driving with voluntary and wanton disregard for the safety of persons or property.

recklessly Acting in a manner that voluntarily ignores a substantial and unjustified risk that a certain circumstance exists or will result from one's actions.

recognizance A promise to appear in court.

rehabilitative justification A justification for punishment based on the theory that if an offender is reformed, the offender will not commit any more crimes.

resisting arrest Physical efforts to oppose a lawful arrest.

restorative justice A process through which all the parties with a stake in a particular offense come together to resolve collectively how to deal with the aftermath of the offense and its implications for the future.

retributive justification A justification for punishment based on the theory that a wrongdoer deserves punishment for punishment's sake.

RICO *See* Racketeer Influenced and Corrupt Organizations.

riot A tumultuous disturbance of the peace by three or more persons assembling together in the execution of a lawful or unlawful act and committing it in a violent and turbulent manner.

robbery The taking of property by the use of force or fear, where the property is taken either from the person of the victim or in his or her immediate presence.

rout An unlawful assembly that is escalating toward, but does not reach, the level of a riot; an attempted riot.

S

securities fraud A criminal, civil, or administrative offense with the following elements: substantive fraud that is found in the offer, purchase, or sale of a security or in connection therewith; the use of interstate commerce or the mails; and willfulness.

self-defense The justified use of reasonable force by one who is not an aggressor, when the actor reasonably believed it was necessary to defend against what he or she reasonably perceived to be an unlawful and imminent physical attack.

sentencing guidelines A set of standards for sentencing, set by a commission legislatively established for that purpose, that judges in a determinate sentencing system must or may follow.

shakedown When a member of a crime organization uses the threat of violence to get someone to do something for the group.

shopkeeper's rule An exception to false imprisonment laws that gives a shopkeeper the right to restrain a person if the shopkeeper possesses a reasonable belief that the customer has not paid a bill or has shoplifted an item.

shoplifting A crime defined by a specific theft statute to address thefts of merchandise, concealment of merchandise, altering of price tags, and retail theft.

simple burglary The unauthorized entering of any dwelling, vehicle, watercraft, or other structure, movable or immovable, with the intent to commit a felony or any theft therein.

simulated controlled substance A substance representing a controlled substance in its nature, packaging, or appearance, which would lead a reasonable person to believe it to be a controlled substance.

sleep test Whether the dwelling is used regularly as a place to sleep determines whether a dwelling is occupied.

sodomy The unlawful sexual penetration of the anus of one person by the penis of another.

solicitation The act of offering to pay another, or receive payment from another, for sex.

solicitation (incitement) The act of seeking to persuade someone else to commit a crime with the intent that the crime be committed.

specific intent The intention to commit an act for the purpose of doing some additional future act, to achieve some further consequences, or with the awareness of a statutory attendant circumstance.

spousal abuse   Long-term physical abuse by the victim's spouse or partner.

spousal rape   Nonconsensual sex between a woman and her husband, ex-husband, or partner.

statutory law   Law created through state and federal legislatures.

statutory rape   A form of rape involving sexual intercourse between an adult and a child, usually between the ages of 13 and 17.

strict liability   When a person can be convicted of a crime without having any requisite mental state or intention to commit the crime.

subornation of perjury   The crime of procuring another person to make a false oath.

substantial step test   The MPC's test to determine whether the *actus reus* of attempt has occurred, which requires that the suspect must have done or omitted to do something that constitutes "a substantial step" in the commission of the substantive offense.

substantive criminal law   The law defining acts that are criminal.

suppressing evidence   A crime that occurs when a defendant, or a person working on behalf of the defendant, suppresses (hides), destroys, or refuses to produce evidence relevant to a grand jury investigation.

T

tax deficiency   When the proper amount of tax to be paid is greater than the amount shown on a taxpayer's tax return.

tax evasion   The willful attempt to avoid paying legally due taxes; a specific intent crime. Also called *tax fraud*.

terrorism   The deliberate use or threat of violence by groups seeking to achieve political, social, or religious objectives.

theft   A broad category of misconduct against property that includes the crimes of larceny, embezzlement, theft by false pretenses, shoplifting, robbery, and receiving stolen goods.

thief   The original unlawful taker of the property of another person.

three-strikes laws   Laws that impose sentences of 25-years-to-life for those who have been convicted of certain serious offenses three times.

tort   A civil violation; the civil law's equivalent of a crime. A wrongful act that results in injury and leaves the injured party entitled to compensation.

transferred intent   A doctrine that holds a person criminally liable even when the consequence of his or her action is not what the actor actually intended.

true defense   A defense that, if proved, results in the acquittal of a defendant, even though the prosecutor has proved the defendant's guilt beyond a reasonable doubt.

tying arrangement   An agreement that a purchaser must buy additional (or tied) products along with the one product that he or she desires; at the very least, the purchaser must agree to not buy this tied product from any other supplier.

U

under color of authority or office   The requirement for the crime of extortion that the action taken by the perpetrator be in his or her capacity as a public official.

underboss   The second in command of an organized crime family, who is usually the person being groomed to take over for the boss in the event of his death or possible incarceration.

unequivocality test   A test that determines that an attempt has occurred when a person's conduct, standing alone, unambiguously manifests his or her criminal intent.

unlawful assembly   A gathering together of three or more persons with the common intent to achieve a lawful or unlawful purpose in a tumultuous manner.

utilitarian justification   A justification for punishment based on the notion that a social practice is desirable if it promotes the greatest good for the largest number of people.

uttering   Presenting a forged writing and attempting to use it to deceive or cheat.

V

vagrancy   A crime that is vaguely defined as being idle or wandering without visible means of support; no longer a crime in most jurisdictions because of the unconstitutionality of past vagrancy laws.

vehicular manslaughter   A criminal homicide in which the perpetrator caused a death while operating a motor vehicle, either by gross negligence or while under the influence of alcohol or other drugs.

vengeance   The imposition of the punishment in the context of an "eye for an eye" or a "tooth for a tooth"; usually associated with retribution, though the utilitarian may see a benefit in vengeance.

vertical price-fixing   Direct or indirect agreements made between market participants at different levels within a given market, regarding the price at which their product will be resold.

viability   The point at which a fetus can reasonably live outside its mother's womb, with or without artificial support.

voluntary intoxication   A person's self-willed act to introduce substances into the body that a person knows or should know are likely to have intoxicating effects.

voluntary manslaughter   An intentional, unlawful killing of a human being without malice aforethought.

W

white-collar crime   A broad category of nonviolent misconduct involving commercial and financial fraud.

willfulness   The voluntary, intentional nature of a crime (such as arson) or violation of a known legal duty (as in tax evasion).

witness tampering   Illegal conduct with the intent to influence witness testimony, such as by approaching a potential witness with threats or other means to prevent the witness from testifying.

Y

year-and-a-day rule   The causation rule that requires that, in order to classify a killing as a homicide, the victim must die within a year and a day after the act causing death occurred.

Z

zero tolerance   Laws that impose maximum penalties for certain crimes, such as particular sex offenses; also known as one-strike laws.

Photo Credits

Case Index

Subject Index